Literary and visual Ralegh

Manchester University Press

The Manchester Spenser

The Manchester Spenser is a monograph and text series devoted to historical and textual approaches to Edmund Spenser – to his life, times, places, works and contemporaries.

A growing body of work in Spenser and Renaissance studies, fresh with confidence and curiosity and based on solid historical research, is being written in response to a general sense that our ability to interpret texts is becoming limited without the excavation of further knowledge. So the importance of research in nearby disciplines is quickly being recognized, and interest renewed: history, archaeology, religious or theological history, book history, translation, lexicography, commentary and glossary – these require treatment for and by students of Spenser.

The Manchester Spenser, to feed, foster and build on these refreshed attitudes, aims to publish reference tools, critical, historical, biographical and archaeological monographs on or related to Spenser, from several disciplines, and to publish editions of primary sources and classroom texts of a more wide-ranging scope.

The Manchester Spenser consists of work with stamina, high standards of scholarship and research, adroit handling of evidence, rigour of argument, exposition and documentation.

The series will encourage and assist research into, and develop the readership of, one of the richest and most complex writers of the early modern period.

General Editor J. B. Lethbridge
Editorial Board Helen Cooper, Thomas Herron, Carol V. Kaske,
James C. Nohrnberg & Brian Vickers

Also available

*Celebrating Mutabilitie: Essays on
Edmund Spenser's Mutabilitie Cantos*   Jane Grogan (ed.)

Castles and Colonists: An archaeology of Elizabethan Ireland   Eric Klingelhofer

Shakespeare and Spenser: Attractive opposites   J. B. Lethbridge (ed.)

*Renaissance erotic romance: Philhellene Protestantism,
Renaissance translation and English literary politics*   Victor Skretkowicz

Literary and visual Ralegh

Edited by
CHRISTOPHER M. ARMITAGE

Manchester University Press

Copyright © Manchester University Press 2013

While copyright in the volume as a whole is vested in Manchester University Press, copyright in individual chapters belongs to their respective authors, and no chapter may be reproduced wholly or in part without the express permission in writing of both author and publisher.

Published by Manchester University Press
Altrincham Street, Manchester M1 7JA, UK
www.manchesteruniversitypress.co.uk

British Library Cataloguing-in-Publication Data is available

Library of Congress Cataloging-in-Publication Data is available

ISBN 978 1 5261 0695 7 *paperback*

First published by Manchester University Press 2013
This edition first published 2017

The publisher has no responsibility for the persistence or accuracy of URLs for any external or third-party internet websites referred to in this book, and does not guarantee that any content on such websites is, or will remain, accurate or appropriate.

Printed by Lightning Source

Contents

List of illustrations   *page* vii
Acknowledgements   ix
Notes on contributors   xi

Introduction: Of letters and the man: Sir Walter Ralegh   1
Christopher M. Armitage, Thomas Herron and Julian Lethbridge

1 Raleigh in ruins, Raleigh on the rocks: Sir Wa'ter's two Books of Mutabilitie and their subject's allegorical presence in select Spenserean narratives and complaints
  James Nohrnberg   31

2 Spenser and Ralegh: Friendship and Literary Patronage
  Wayne Erickson   89

3 Love's 'emperye': Raleigh's 'Ocean to Scinthia', Spenser's 'Colin Clouts Come Home Againe' and *The Faerie Queene* IV.vii in colonial context
  Thomas Herron   100

4 'Bellphebes course is now observde no more': Ralegh, Spenser, and the literary politics of the Cynthia holograph
  Anna Beer   140

5 Replying to Raleigh's 'The Nymph's Reply': Allusion, anti-pastoral, and four centuries of pastoral invitations
  Hannibal Hamlin   166

6 'Moving on the waters': Metaphor and mental space in Ralegh's *History of the World*
  Michael Booth   200

7 Water Ralegh's liquid narrative: *The Discoverie of Guiana*
   Lowell Duckert 217

8 Ralegh, Harriot, and Anglo-American ethnography
   Alden T. Vaughan 242

9 'Most fond and fruitlesse warre': Ralegh and the call to arms
   Andrew Hiscock 257

10 Ralegh's 'As You Came from the Holy Land' and the rival virgin queens of late sixteenth-century England
   Gary Waller 284

11 Patrilineal Ralegh
   Judith Owens 302

12 Ralegh's image in art
   Vivienne Westbrook 327

13 Where's Walter? The screen incarnations of Sir Walter Ralegh
   Susan Campbell Anderson 348

Sir Walter Ralegh bibliography (1986–2010)
Christopher Mead Armitage 377

Index 390

List of illustrations

7.1 *A map of Guyana, with the courses of the Orinoco and the Marañon, or Amazons; drawn about 1595 by Sir W. Raleigh on vellum*. British Library, Cartographic Items Additional MS. 17,940.a © Trustees of the British Library   *page* 218

12.1 Nicholas Hilliard, Miniature portrait of Sir Walter Ralegh (c. 1581–84). Courtesy of the National Portrait Gallery   328

12.2 Jacobus Houbraken, engraver, Sir Walter Raleigh, 1739, from *Heads of Illustrious Persons of Great Britian*, Knapton, London, 1734–52. © Trustees of the British Museum   345

Acknowledgements

Julian Lethbridge, General Editor of The Manchester Spenser series of which this volume is a part, has provided, from his vast knowledge of Ralegh's era and scholarship about it, invaluable assistance on many matters. Thomas Herron, of the Department of English at East Carolina University, has been full of sustained enthusiasm, suggestions and prompt replies. Christine Shia, Research Associate in the Journalism School at the University of North Carolina at Chapel Hill, has rescued me from numerous electronic entanglements and handled all kinds of tasks with exceptional dedication. Robert Anthony, Curator of the North Carolina Collection, including its outstanding Sir Walter Ralegh Collection, at UNC-Chapel Hill, and Thomas Nixon, Research Librarian at UNC-Chapel Hill, have been invariably helpful. The index has been compiled by Tracy Harvin, English doctoral candidate at UNC-Chapel Hill. Any errors are my responsibility.

Generous financial assistance has been received from a grant by East Carolina University and from an anonymous donor. Special thanks from the General Editor of this series to John Banks at MUP.

Christopher M. Armitage

Notes on contributors

Susan Campbell Anderson is Executive Director of The Cloverleaf School in Atlanta, Georgia

Christopher Armitage is a Professor of English at The University of North Carolina at Chapel Hill

Anna Beer is a Fellow of Kellogg College at the University of Oxford

Michael Booth is an Assistant Professor of English at Oberlin College, Ohio

Lowell Duckert is an Assistant Professor of English at West Virginia University

Wayne Erickson is an Emeritus Professor of Georgia State University

Hannibal Hamlin is an Associate Professor of English at The Ohio State University

Thomas Herron is an Associate Professor of English at East Carolina University

Andrew Hiscock is a Professor of English at Bangor University, Wales

Julian Lethbridge is a Lecturer at the University of Tübingen, Germany

James Nohrnberg is an Emeritus Professor of the University of Virginia

Judith Owens is an Associate Professor of English at the University of Manitoba, Canada

Alden Vaughan is an Affiliate Professor of History at Clark University, Worcester, Mass.

Gary Waller is a Professor of Literature at SUNY Purchase College, New York

Vivienne Westbrook is an Associate Professor of Foreign Languages at the National University of Taiwan

Introduction:
Of letters and the man: Sir Walter Ralegh[1]

*Christopher M. Armitage, Thomas Herron,
and Julian Lethbridge*

In his essay *Of Education*, Milton declared that an ideal education should prepare a man for 'all the offices both public and private of peace and war'. Though Sir Walter Ralegh (1552(?)–1618) left Oriel College, Oxford, and the Middle Temple – one of the Inns of Court – like other men of his time without completing academic requirements, he became prominent in activities both public and private of peace and war.

A teenage soldier on the Continent, he was also a seafarer, explorer, colonizer, historian, poet, and ambitious courtier. His career at court suffered severe reversals from Queen Elizabeth and from King James I, the latter causing him to be imprisoned in the Tower of London in 1603 and executed in 1618. His fame was such that seventy-three variant spellings of his name in English and other languages are recorded in Willard Wallace's 1959 biography. Raleigh and Ralegh, the form he used in the second half of his life, are both used in this volume.

His fame like his actions have caused his identity to become as diversified to modern audiences as the spelling of his name. Rale(i)gh was famously a man of many parts and roles, a man of rich and variable fashion in word and clothes, who went to the chopping block in a shirt stuffed with jewels. A recent biographer begins by proclaiming that he was a 'liar'.[2] Commentators since the seventeenth century have noted his

---

. 1 Our title deliberately echoes that of Jerry Leath Mills, 'Sir Walter Raleigh as a Man of Letters', *Raleigh and Quinn: The Explorer and His Boswell*, ed. H. G. Jones (Chapel Hill: North Caroliniana Society, 1987), 165–79, which copies the title of Frank Wilson Cheney Hersey, 'Sir Walter Ralegh as a Man of Letters', *Proceedings of the State Literary and Historical Association of North Carolina* 25 (1918), 42–54. Of all modern scholars, Mills has done the most to catalogue, analyse and summarize Sir Walter's literary achievements and critical responses to them.
2 Raleigh Trevelyan, *Sir Walter Raleigh* (New York: Henry Holt, 2002), quoting A. L. Rowse. Compare with the opening line of Agnes Latham's 'Introduction' to her edition of Ralegh's poems: 'It is difficult to believe in Sir Walter Ralegh'. Latham (ed.), *The Poems of Sir Walter Ralegh*, 2nd edition (Cambridge, MA: Harvard University Press, 1951), xiii–liii: xiii.

great intellectual ability in scholarly, creative, and pragmatic pursuits.[3] He remains an enigma, a chameleon, but an able and attractive one, and no more so than in his own writings, where he might play the lover, soldier, statesman, merchant-adventurer, sea captain, promoter, and critic of the state all at the same time.

I

Ralegh's literary legacy consists of a highly fragmented oeuvre including many unprinted or pirated poems and works of disputed authorship. After discovery of the *Oceans Love to Scynthia* holographs in the mid-nineteenth century (first printed in 1870)[4] and propelled in part by interest from Spenser scholars, editorial attention in the twentieth century has focused intensely on the shifting sands of his poetry. No collection of Ralegh's poetry produced under his own direction or that of a contemporary, either in print or in manuscript, exists. No more than 'three or four' poems attributed to him were placed together in a book or miscellany at a time. Some if not many poems have surely been lost. As a result, the most up-to-date edition, Michael Rudick's *Poems of Sir Walter Ralegh: A Historical Edition* (1999), sharply reduces the canon once established by Agnes Latham.[5] Many of Ralegh's poems need to be 'recovered, not merely reprinted' and so our understanding of his poetic oeuvre, like our understanding of his career, is beset by a sense of loss and abbreviation.[6] The process of recovering Ralegh's poetry in particular is akin to an archaeological excavation: one must carefully sift through layers of debris to find only traces of what once existed, while those same traces might be in danger of being deconstructed to oblivion with further analysis. Some whole gems shine through the sifting, however: anthologized lyrics like 'Nature That Washed Her Hands in Milk' and 'The Nymph's Reply,' as well as 'The Lie,' called 'perhaps the most famous poem attributed to Ralegh' but not (ironically) without controversy in attribution.[7] As the present

---

3 Michael Rudick, *The Poems of Sir Walter Ralegh: A Historical Edition* (Tempe, AZ: Medieval and Renaissance Texts and Studies, 1998): xvii.
4 J. Hannah, *The Courtly Poets from Raleigh to Montrose* (London: Bell and Daldy, 1870).
5 'quite a large number [of his poems], at least under rigorous standards of evidence and inference, remain in a measure disputable because the reliability of the documented attributions is questionable, coming as they do from non-authorial sources, often chronologically removed from Ralegh's lifetime' (Rudick, *The Poems*, xv). Rudick's edition updates his dissertation, 'The Poems of Sir Walter Ralegh: An Edition' (Ph.D. dissertation, University of Chicago), 1970. See also Latham (ed.), *The Poems*.
6 Rudick, *The Poems*, xvi.
7 Mark Nicholls and Penry Williams, *Sir Walter Raleigh: in life and legend* (London: Continuum, 2011), 147.

collection attests, critical interest in Ralegh's longest and most difficult lyric, *Oceans Love to Scynthia*, remains strong (see the chapters by James Nohrnberg, Anna Beer and Thomas Herron below).

It is a good time to reassess Ralegh's literary output. His letters, like his poems, have recently been re-edited with authority, but not his prose works, which did the most to define his literary reputation prior to the twentieth century.[8] Even if they are written largely by a secretary, letters have the potential to be particularly revealing; many of Ralegh's letters are personal.

Letters are probably the closest we come to the spoken voice of the writer, in particular those that appear to have been written as extensions or substitutes for conversation, or in haste, as opposed to more formal compositions. Even a quick glance at one of the most famous and cited letters, that to Cecil on the death of Cecil's wife in 1596, shows moments of wisdom and experience, and of a tenderness we do not normally associate with Ralegh, but which, on reflection he must have possessed to be such a lover:

> shee hath past the weresume jurney of this darke worlde and hath possession of her inheritance.
> Shee hath left beind her the frute of her love, for whos sakes yow ought to care for your sealf that yow leve them not without a gwyde, and not by greevinge to repine att his will that gave them yow or by sorrowing to dry up your own tymes that ought to establishe them. ...
> The minde of man is that part of God which is in us, which, by how mich it is subject to passion, by so mich it is farther from hyme that gave it us. Sorrows draw not the dead to life, butt the livinge to death … . (Latham and Youings, *Letters*, 155-6)

Of course it also contains what the sceptical might consider, not without all grounds, some posturing, some jostling for place and remembrance.

The History of the World (1614), for all its fullness, rests a massive fragment, ponderous and little read today but too large to be ignored, like the stone feet of Ozymandias, attesting to the hubris of monarchs and the scholarly and political ambitions of its author. The *History* strongly influenced republican sentiment during the English Civil War and was

---

8 Jerry Leath Mills, 'Sir Walter Ralegh,' in *Dictionary of Literary Biography, vol. 173: Sixteenth-Century British Nondramatic Writers*, ed. David A. Richardson (Detroit: Gale Research Books, 1996), 200-16: 212; Mills, 'Sir Walter Raleigh as a Man of Letters' 174-8. For the recent edition of his letters, see Agnes Latham and Joyce Youings (eds), *Letters of Sir Walter Ralegh* (Exeter: University of Exeter Press, 1999).

closely read by Gibbon.[9] In the mid-twentieth century scholars revisited its role in the development of historiography and political science in particular.[10] It is best known today as a mine for gem-like anecdotes, including the famous tribute to Death in its preface:

> O eloquent, just and mighty Death! Whom none could advise, thou hast persuaded; that none hath dared, thou hast done; and whom all the world hath flattered, thou only hath cast out of the world and despised: thou hast drawn together all the far stretched greatness, all the pride, cruelty, and ambition of man, and covered it all over with these two narrow words, *Hic jacet*.

Typical of Ralegh's prose (and some of his verse) is a taut elasticity punctuated by startling revelation.

Two other, more exciting prose works by Ralegh, *A Report of the Truth of the Fight about the Isles of Azores* (1591) and *Discovery of Guiana* (1596), were published in his lifetime and eight more appeared in the

---

9   Nicholls and Williams, *Sir Walter Raleigh*, 335. Gibbon's personal copy of *The History of the World* is now in the Ralegh Collection at UNC-Chapel Hill. Sadly, it contains no notes in Gibbon's hand: Gibbon's diary in the British Library has the following entries: 'August 4, 1761, At length I have fixed on Sir Walter Ralegh for my Hero' but 'July 26, 1762, I am afraid of being reduced to drop my Hero.... The events of his life are interesting : but his character is ambiguous, his actions are obscure, his writings are English, and his fame is confined to the narrow limits of our language and our island. I must embrace a safer and more extensive theme'. The 'safer' makes an all-too appropriate pun on this passage in Ralegh's 'Preface' to the *History*: 'I might have been more pleasing to the Reader, if I had written the Story of mine own Times, having been permitted to draw water as near the Well-head as another. To this I answer, That whosoever in writing a modern History, shall follow Truth too near at heels, it may haply strike out his Teeth. There is no Mistress or Guide that hath led her followers and servants into greater miseries'. D2r, 1677.

10 See, for example, Lily B. Campbell, *Shakespeare's 'Histories': Mirrors of Elizabethan Policy* (San Marino, CA: Huntington Library, 1947), 78–84, 122–3; Leonard F. Dean, 'Tudor Theories of History Writing', *University of Michigan Contributors in Modern Philology* 1 (1947), 1–24; Ernest A. Strathmann, 'Ralegh on the Problems of Chronology'. *Huntington Library Quarterly* 11 (1948), 129–48; Vincent Luciani, 'Ralegh's *Cabinet-Council* and Guicciardini's Aphorisms', *Studies in Philology* 46 (1949), 20–30; Vincent Luciani, 'Ralegh's *Discourses on the Savoyan Matches* and Machiavelli's *Istorie fiorentine*', *Italica* 29 (1952), 103–7; John H. Stibbs, 'Ralegh and Holinshed', *Modern Language Review* 44 (1949), 543–4; Manoochehr Aryanpur-Kashani, 'Sir Walter Ralegh's *Historie of the World* and Persia' (Ph.D. dissertation, University of Colorado, 1958); Christopher Hill, *Intellectual Origins of the English* Revolution (Oxford: Clarendon Press, 1965), 131–224; Herschel Baker, *The Race of Time: Three Lectures on Renaissance Historiography* (Toronto: University of Toronto Press, 1957), 45–41; F. J. Levy, *Tudor Historical Thought* (San Marion, CA: Huntington Library, 1967), 286–94. All of the above are cited and briefly summarized in Jerry Leath Mills, *Sir Walter Ralegh: A Reference Guide* (Boston: G. K. Hall, 1986).

seventeenth century, not counting editions of the same work.[11] Ralegh's prose works have not been edited as a collection since 1829.[12] Scholarly editions of his colonial writings have, however, recently appeared, a clear sign of critical trends.[13]

Ralegh's writings encourage reflection on the multifaceted image he has left behind him for posterity. We continue to fashion Ralegh every bit as much as he fashioned himself. Ralegh's diversified and dramatic life has been the subject of numerous biographies. The latest and perhaps most careful is *Sir Walter Raleigh: In Life and Legend* (2011) by Mark Nicholls and Penry Williams. The book exhausts archival sources and takes advantage of much recent historical and literary work on Ralegh's courtly context, including the above-cited new editions of letters and poems. It is admirably and deeply sensitive to Ralegh's literary remains as relevant to historical analysis. Following the lead of Stephen Greenblatt, the authors acknowledge Ralegh's penchant for 'self-fashioning' in life and art as he blurred (and confused) the two.[14] For Ralegh, all the world was a stage. Yet Nicholls and Williams also emphasize the inescapability of social class in England as a motivating factor in his life. Ralegh's 'essential frailty' resulted from his low birth. This made life

> much harder for the 'expendable' self-made man, and Ralegh, for all his political myopia, understood this well enough... . Ralegh, never forgetting that vulnerability, developed a sarcasm in both his writings and his conversations to cover the weakness. He masks, but never quite conceals it, for sarcasm too easily topples into pessimism and self-pity.[15]

And we may add, there is under all these a marked strain of the melancholy often accompanying genius, an element that can qualify what we call sarcasm or cynicism in Ralegh: the one with weariness, the other

11 See the catalogue of published works in Mills, 'Sir Walter Ralegh', 200–1.
12 William Oldys and Thomas Birch (eds), *The Works of Sir Walter Ralegh, Kt., Now First Collected: To Which Are Prefixed the Lives of the Author*, 8 vols (Oxford: Oxford University Press, 1829).
13 Joyce Lorimer (ed.), *Sir Walter Ralegh's Discoverie of Guiana*. Hakluyt Society 3rd series no. 15 (Aldershot: Ashgate, 2007); Ralegh, *The Discovery of Guiana with Related Documents*, ed. Benjamin Schmidt (New York: Bedford /St. Martin's, 2007); Ralegh, *The Discoverie of the Large, Rich and Bewtiful Empyre of Guiana* (Manchester: Manchester University Press, 1998). See also Joyce Lorimer, 'Ralegh, Walter', in *Encyclopedia of English Renaissance Literature*, ed. Garrett A. Sullivan and Alan Stewart (Wiley-Blackwell 2012), online at www.literatureencyclopedia.com; Alden Vaughan, Chapter 8 below.
14 Nicholls and Williams, *Sir Walter Ralegh*, 341. They agree with Greenblatt's assessment that 'the general concept of life at theatre underlies Ralegh's "dramatic sense of life"' (162). See also Stephen J. Greenblatt, *Sir Walter Ralegh: The Renaissance Man and His Roles* (New Haven: Yale University Press, 1973).
15 Nicholls and Williams, *Sir Walter Ralegh*, 342.

with clear-eyed observancy. Ralegh would repay careful study with the inexhaustible *Saturn und Melancholie* by Klibansky, Panofsky, and Saxl in one hand.¹⁶ Ralegh in this view is a Satan-like figure fixed, despite all his terrestrial and spiritual wanderings, by an unyielding hierarchical order, hence prone to turn inward in despair.¹⁷ This portrait helps to explain the sharp satirical quality to some Ralegh's poetry:

> Say to the Court it glowes,
>   and shines like rotten wood,
> Say to the Church it showes
>   whats good, and doth no good.
> If Church and Court reply,
>   then giue them both the lie.¹⁸

> If all the world and love were young,
> And truth in every Shepherds tongue?
> These pretty pleasures might me move,
> To live with thee, and be thy love
>
> But time drives flocks from field to fold ... .
>
> (Rudick, *The Poems*, 119)¹⁹

The 'If ...', 'might ...', 'But ...' and finally '... no means ...' progression of the latter poem with its melancholy perilously balanced on the edge of self-pity, suggests a guarded engagement with the world amounting to a reluctance to engage or commit, but a reasoned or seasoned reluctance, based on observation, a more honest, if less charming, outlook than in Marlowe's persona; Ralegh's shepherdess has learned that 'Of all which

---

16 Schopenhauer confirms Aristotle in his *Aphorisms* (Kap. II p. 325) (Aristotle, Probl. 30.1), and Cicero gave it the classic latin formulation: '*omnes ingeniosis melancholicos esse*' (*Tusc.* 1.33); the classic modern formulation is German, variously attributed, 'Ohne Melancholie kein Genie'. See also the well-known and fascinating Introduction and the opening chapter of Egon Friedell, *Kultur-Geschichte der Neuzeit* (3 vols, Munich: Beck, 1927–31).
17 Note the attractively titled biography by Margaret Irwin, *That Great Lucifer: A Portrait of Sir Walter Ralegh* (New York: Harcourt, Brace, and World, 1960). For the influence of Ralegh's *History of the World* on Cromwell and Milton, see Nicholls and Williams, *Sir Walter Ralegh*, 332–3; Rodger Martin, 'The Colonization of Paradise: Milton's Pandemonium and Montezuma's Tenochtitlan', *Comparative Literature Studies* 35.4 (1998), 321–55: 328–9. Milton also knew Ralegh's *Discovery of Guiana*: see *A Milton Encyclopedia* (Lewisburg: Bucknell University Press, 1977), s. 'Sir Walter Ralegh'.
18 Ralegh, 'The Lie', in Latham (ed.), *The Poems*, 45–7: 45.
19 We cite Walton's version for the sake of the delicious interrogative after the second line, capturing an appropriate, if not definitive, raised eyebrow – asking not only whether this is to be taken as the assumption made by the question proposed but also whether it is proposed by the suppliant shepherd that such a state of affairs actually obtains.

past, the sorow onely staies',[20] and this persona seems to take Ralegh's advice to Cecil: 'yow should not overshaddo your wisedume with passion butt looke aright into things as the[y] are'.[21]

And yet, some retractions of the satire and cynicism remain:

> What reasons prove, confesse,
> What slaunder sayth, denye
> Lett not untruth with triumphe passe
> Yet never give the lie
> ...
> But when you come againe
> To give the world the lye
> I pray you teach them how to live
> And tell them how to dye.
>
> (Rudick, *The Poems*, 39)

If the desire to climb is quintessentially Romantic, so is this sentimental touch which runs through Ralegh's works. A desire to climb also contributes to an explanation of Ralegh's interest in Edenic New Worlds where he could rule the roost – as Governor of Virginia for instance. His dashing, cutting style advanced himself and the empire; not only was Ralegh influential in setting the terms and attitudes of empire over the next three centuries, but one can see his contribution, as one of the most dramatic and well known of the early colonists, to the attitudes of his spiritual descendants, the individuals creating the British Empire: the drama and swagger of Nelson wearing his regalia in his pride and death aboard the *HMS Victory* are closely related to Ralegh's dangerous swagger and ambitious dress, and to the Richard Grenville Ralegh gives us, in his pride, aboard the *Revenge*, and his death, less romantically, in a Spanish ship, eating wine glasses – Tennyson was not the only Victorian to remember the brave and hopeless fight.[22] Henry David Thoreau stresses Ralegh's swashbuckling character: 'In whatever he is engaged we seem to see a plume waving over his head, and a sword dangling at his side',[23] an important combination to recall in reading the *History*. The swashbuckling side

---

20 Ralegh, *Oceans Love to Scynthia*, in Rudick, *The Poems*, 26–7.
21 Latham and Youings, *Letters*, 155.
22 Tennyson, 'The Revenge: A Ballad of the Fleet'. Undoubtedly idealized, but Ralegh's narrative is the source of the ideal.
23 Thoreau, *Sir Walter Ralegh*, ed. Henry Aiken Metcalf (Boston: Bibliophile Society, 1905): 21. According to Hersey, Ralegh 'did not carve his sentences in alabaster ... he cut them out with his sword'. Hersey, 'Sir Walter Ralegh', 50. Both cited in Mills, 'Sir Walter Raleigh as a Man of Letters' 165, 174. See also description of Ralegh's verse by Seamus Heaney, discussed by Thomas Herron in Chapter 3 below.

of empire easily turns piratical and the scramble for Africa can be seen as a full performance of the rehearsals under Raleigh's direction in the Americas.²⁴ Ralegh never stayed melancholy for long, for activity and melancholy make for bad partners, and the ever-restless Raleigh loved activity: if he lost favour at court in 1593, he got it back in 1597 and was an 'ever-optimistic go-between' until the debacle under King James stuck him in the Tower for fourteen long years.²⁵ But he remained active there, too, siring a child, conducting scientific experiments and writing frenetically; and got parole long enough to undertake the fateful trip to Guiana. Earlier, Ralegh had functioned as an important adviser and favourite²⁶ to the Queen and council. He was able to talk himself out of prison more than once. He always had forward momentum as a man of action who also translated the deed and the thought into words.

All this brilliant drama obscures the hints we have of an unfamiliar inner man, sensitive, unarmed, which breaks the surface from time to time. Of his *History* he excuses himself from concluding ('to confine') with an English history in that he is too old:

> in whom, had there been no other defect (who am all defect) than the time of day, it were enough; the day of a tempestuous life, drawn on to the very evening ere I began. But those inmost and soul-piercing wounds, which are ever aking while uncured, with the desire to satisfie those few friends, which I have tried by the fire of Adversity; the former enforcing, the latter persuading; have caused me to make my thoughts legible, and my self the subject of every Opinion, wise or weak. (*History*, Preface)²⁷

The description of his own life as 'tempestuous', the passing mention of 'inmost and soul-piercing wounds … ever aking', the felt menace of

24 Vivienne Westbrook covers the reception of Ralegh in Chapter 12 below.
25 Nicholls and Williams, *Sir Walter Ralegh*, 125. Before this time, 'Robert Cecil in particular remained happy to take Ralegh's advice on areas in which he could reasonably claim some expertise, and the giving of advice kept a disgraced man in the public eye. Ralegh was determined to make the most of this opportunity, to show that he could still be of use to his sovereign'. (ibid., 85).
26 David Edwards, adjusting Simon Adams's careful work *in Leicester and the Court: Essays on Elizabethan Politics* (Manchester: Manchester University Press, 2002), reassesses who was a genuine favourite at Elizabeth's court and lists only four: Hatton, Leicester, Essex, and Ralegh. (p. 9 of the typescript Dr Edwards very kindly sent us: 'Elizabeth I's Irish Favourite: The Black Earl of Ormond as a Tudor Courtier', forthcoming).
27 See also Cecil's oft-quoted remark on Ralegh at Dartmouth in September 1592 on leave from the Tower to halt the pillage of the *Madre de dios*: 'His heart is broken, for he is extremely pensive, longer than he is busier', and busy he was, for Cecil's next words are the famous 'He can toil terribly', cited by Trevelyan, *Sir Walter Ralegh*, 186, though most biographers accept this, too, as mere role-play and not wholly sincere, but it may be doubted whether Cecil would have been so deceived as to write that Ralegh's heart '*is*' broken.

'Opinion', are such hints which go beyond the merely topological; but it is the fleeting 'few' which opens the glittering, scorchingly proud surface of the meteor and reveals a darker, weaker, more inward, less familiar Ralegh.

What Raleigh thought of himself as a literary artist is a mystery. According to Rudick, 'We are left to infer Ralegh's own notions of an author-function as much from what we do not find as from what the poems we do find have to tell, scattered as they are and, if edited, not by the poet.'[28] Like many poets of his day he fixated on the fickleness of time and fortune, never more than in the prime of his courtly career: 'While the poetry he wrote during this earlier period [in the 1580s and 90s] often promotes his relations with the Queen, it also comments sardonically on the evanescence of the success for which he and other courtiers were striving.'[29] Evanescence and self-awareness: Raleigh was a social climber who wrote about social climbing and a liar who wrote about lying. While in prison in 1593–94 he delved into *contemptus mundi*,[30] but this demonstrates his regular ability to adapt to any environment he was placed into: when forced to be a hermit, he wrote like one.

Another facet of Ralegh's life that may not, perhaps, be stressed enough in studies of his philosophy is the military. This too is changing as critical tides ebb and flow.[31] Life on campaign involved continually shifting locations, temporary and flimsy housing, uncertain pay, lost mail, desertion of colleagues, cynical and syphilitic sex, prolonged exposure to water and weather, political dissolution, plenty of tedium in which to write, and the constant spectre of mortality through combat and ever-present disease. The 'bloody flux' is an apt metaphor for the digestion of bodies, souls, treasure and political allegiances consumed by war. Ralegh first came to official notice serving as a very young man in the horrific French wars and then climbed steeply at court thanks, partly, to the equally brutal Irish wars. At court he occupied the soldierly and extremely important

28 Rudick, *The Poems*, xxi.
29 William Oram, 'Raleigh, the Queen, and Elizabethan Court Poetry', in *Early Modern English Poetry: A Critical Companion*, ed. Patrick Cheney, Andrew Hadfield, and Garrett A. Sullivan, Jr. (Oxford: Oxford University Press, 2007), 113–24: 123.
30 Mills, 'Ralegh as a Man of Letters', 173.
31 See Andrew Hiscock, Chapter 9 below; also Andrew Hiscock, '"Whether the *Macedonian*, or the *Roman*, were the best Warriour": Sir Walter Ralegh and the Conflicts of History', *War in Words: Transformations of War from Antiquity to Clausewitz* (Berlin, Germany: de Gruyter, 2011), 291–306; Vincent Luciani, 'Ralegh's *Discourse of War* and Machiavelli's *Discorsi*', *Modern Philology* 46 (1948), 122–31; Paul A. Jorgensen, 'Theoretical Views of War in Elizabethan England', *Journal of the History of Ideas* 13 (1952), 469–81; Nicholls and Williams, *Sir Walter Ralegh*, 8 and passim; Adam McKeown, *English Mercuries: Soldier Poets in the Age of Shakespeare* (Nashville: Vanderbilt University Press, 2009), 117–18.

post of Captain of the Queen's Guard. He relished piracy, or the armed takeover of ships. He travelled a long way to fight in the Azores and at Cadiz. He travelled even farther and sped his son's and his own demise by attacking the Spanish in the New World. He wrote two tracts with military advice published in 1650.[32] His first published poem commends *The Steele Glass* (1576) by his fellow soldier-poet George Gascoigne. In it, Ralegh focuses on the envy that accompanies achievement. Ralegh later adopted Gascoigne's motto *Tam marti quam mercutio*:[33] he personified the soldier of letters: both Mars and Mercury, earthy strife and intellectual exploration and discovery. Edmund Spenser in a dedicatory sonnet appended to *The Faerie Queene* (1590) notes Ralegh's title as a '*right noble and valorous knight*' and 'lieftenaunt of Cornewaile' and encourages him to 'thonder Martiall stowre, / When so thee list thy lofty Muse to raise'.[34] Spenser allegorizes him in the epic as Timias, who first appears at a siege and thereafter engages in fierce wars and unfaithful loves.[35] 'There are no atheists in foxholes', as the saying goes, but one wonders whether or not the transience of life on military campaign encouraged Ralegh's curious but characteristic blend of scepticism and piety towards God, Queen and country, and his acute interest in time and action in his writings.

Ralegh well understood his worldly actions from a Christian point of view, and he was not insensitive to its demands and consolations, as his conclusion from the scaffold attests:

32 Ralegh, *A Discourse of the Originall and Fundamentall Cause of Naturall, Customary, Arbitrary, Voluntary and Necessary Warre. With the Mistery of Invasive Warre. That Ecclesiasticall Prelates, Have Always Beene Subject to Temporal Princes, And That the Pope Had Never Any Lawfull Power in England, Either in Civill or Ecclesiasticall Businesse, after Such Time, as Brittaine Was Won from the Roman Empire* (London: Printed by T. W. for Humphrey Moseley, 1650); Ralegh, *Excellent Observations and Notes, Concerning the Royall Navy and Sea-service. Written by Sir Walter Rawleigh and by Him Dedicated to the Most Noble and Illustrious Prince Henry of Wales* (London: Printed by T. W. for Humphrey Moseley, 1650).
33 Mills, 'Sir Walter Ralegh', 203.
34 Spenser, '*To the right noble and valorous knight, Sir Walter Raleigh,* Lo. Wardein of the Stanneryes, and lieftenaunt of Cornewaile', *The Faerie Queene*, ed. A. C. Hamilton, revised 2nd edn (Harlow: Pearson, 2007), 733. For Ralegh's role in the dedicatory and commendatory 'back matter' to the epic, see Wayne Erickson (ed.), *The 1590 'Faerie Queene': Paratexts and Publishing. Studies in the Literary Imagination* 38 (2005).
35 Spenser, *The Faerie Queene*, ed. A. C. Hamilton, I.viii.3-5; A. Leigh DeNeef, 'Timias', *The Spenser Encyclopedia*, ed. A. C. Hamilton (Toronto: University of Toronto Press, 1990), 690-1. For more on Ralegh's relationship with Spenser, see chapters by Wayne Erickson, Anna Beer, James Nohrnberg, and Thomas Herron; also Katherine Koller, 'Spenser and Ralegh', *English Literary History* 1 (1934), 37-60. See also Jerry Leath Mills, 'Raleigh, Walter (1554-1618)', in *The Spenser Encyclopedia*, ed. A. C. Hamilton (Toronto: University of Toronto Press, 1990), 584-5; William Oram, 'Spenser's Raleghs', *Studies in Philology* 87 (1990), 341-62.

And now I entreat you all to join with me in prayer, that the great God of
Heaven, whom I have grievously offended, being a man full of all vanity,
and having lived a sinful life, in all sinful callings, having been a soldier, a
captain, a sea captain, and a courtier, which are all places of wickedness
and vice; that God, I say, would forgive me, cast away my sins from me,
and receive me into everlasting life. So I take my leave of you all, making
my peace with God.[36]

Ralegh is a restless man of action, an innovator and a sceptic in a thoroughly Christian context. The subject of mercurial climbing, in status and in thought, is a leitmotif running through his work. But he doesn't lose track of where he stands no matter how pitched the deck. Even his most fragmentary and verbally obscure work, *Oceans Love to Scynthia*, held at its core, literally, a powerful neoplatonized tribute to the central role of the monarchy in the shaping and punishing of his life and career:

> Thos streames seeme standinge puddells which, before,
> Wee saw our bewties in, so weare they cleere.
> Bellphebes course is now obserude no more,
> That faire resemblance weareth out of date.
> Our Ocean seas are but tempestius waves
> And all things base that blessed wear of late[37]

Ralegh would later in life recycle flattering lines to Queen Elizabeth and present them instead to James's wife, Queen Anne. Ralegh knew when and how to manipulate and uphold his society's conservative social order. He did make mistakes. The lands he sold off in a fire sale in Munster helped to turn another unethical upstart, Richard Boyle, into an earl and one of the wealthiest men in Britain.

By sheer force of personality Ralegh halted the plunder of the *Madre di dios*. Cecil, ineffectively on the spot, had called for him to be sent to Dartmouth from the Tower, and was impressed by Ralegh's reception among his own: 'Cecil could not help being impressed by his reception which "I do voice before God is greater than I thought for". Sir John Gilbert wept when he met his half-brother.' And Cecil wrote to Sir Thomas Heneage: 'I assure you, Sir his poor servants, the number of 140 goodly men, and all

---

36 Oldys and Birch (eds), *The Works*, 563. For discussion of the influence of this event in England and abroad, see Andrew Fleck, '"At the time of his death": The Contested Narrative of Sir Walter Ralegh's Beheading', *Heads Will Roll: Decapitation in the Medieval and Early Modern Imagination*, ed. Larissa Tracy and Jeff Massey (Leiden: Brill, 2012), 235–59.

37 'The 11th: and last booke of the Ocean to Scinthia', in Latham (ed.), *The Poems*, 25–43: 34–5; on the numerical centrality of these lines invoking 'Belphoebe' or Queen Elizabeth and ruing her judgement, see Mills, 'Sir Walter Ralegh', 209–11.

the mariners came to him with such shouts of joy as I never saw a man more troubled to quiet them in my life' (Cecil to Thomas Heneage c. 13 September 1992, cited by Trevelyan, *Sir Walter Raleigh*). He remains a still-potent personality.

II

> We digress in the ways of our lives; ...
> the life of Man is nothing else but digression
>
> Ralegh, Preface to the *History*

The phrase 'Ralegh remains' is a verbal proposition indicating continued cultural presence, and this collection is testament to its truth. But it can equally be an adjectivally qualified plural substantive phrase designating a pile of ruins, where 'ruins' means both decayed, and incomplete: fragments.

Ralegh came and went like a meteor – but several times; his life was a series of recursive digressions. One of the most dramatic of the Elizabethans, one of the most popular ever since, one of the most iconic; yet his life was a scattering of fragments, not a meteor but a meteor shower; his legacy likewise: fragmentary remains of a settlement in Virginia, the remains of a career at court, the ruins of a search for El Dorado, the ruining of his family en route, a fragmented military career, the remains of the *Madre di dios* – the Munster plantation, *Oceans Love to Scynthia*, the *History*, his own body and with that his life – all fragmented, unfinished, headless, ruins, remains. A Romantic two centuries before the Romantics perfected the fragment: too restless, too ambitious, too capable of hard work, too meteoric, too dazzling in his too insubstantial, too fiery fire, too much the hare, too much the digressive – what did he finish? – to bring any one project to completion. It all suggests that his contemporaries were amply right to see him as proud as Lucifer, as suffering from hubris: 'Shun to be Raleigh'.[38] The wonder is that the gods left him for so long unpunished.

Substantial and long-lived ruins many of them are, however, for good and ill their stones used as foundations by later, more successful builders: Boyle in Munster, the Pilgrims in the Americas, the Imperialists of later

---

38 William Cecil, Lord Burghley, 'Certain Precepts for the Well Ordering of a Man's Life', in *Advice to a Son: Precepts of Lord Burghley, Sir Walter Raleigh, and Francis Osborne*, ed. Louis B. Wright (Ithaca: Cornell University Press, 1962) for the Folger Library, p. 13. Burghley seems here to be advising Robert not to neglect public opinion. See above p. 8 on Raleigh's remark in the *History*.

centuries; the republican thinkers and actors of the next generation, and through them the Founders of new and lasting empire in the Americas; historians and literary critics of the last century and a half excavating the written remains.

Even his slighter ruins glow and remain: if all he had ever done was to write the 'Nymph's Reply', we should have noted him. Hannibal Hamlin illustrates how deep and how permanent the inner fire of that poem is (see Chapter 5 by Hamlin, below); and the poem may be taken as a symbol of the whole: in whatever Ralegh produced there is a fire as in the heart of an emerald or ruby or diamond.

It is easy to get carried away; and just as easy to turn away in abhorence – nothing has changed in the four centuries since James cut off that proud head. One explanation for the continued fascination is that Ralegh is one of the very few characters whose personality comes through the centuries with an almost tangible presence. One could name Socrates and Caesar from the ancient world; among Ralegh's contemporaries Mary Queen of Scots; among compatriots of later periods perhaps Milton and Winston Churchill; but few others.

But what is that personality? For Ralegh played many parts in his life and all the world was a stage to him. Which of these roles was the real man? What was he to himself in the small of the morning when the heart is most clear-sighted and true to itself?

Ralegh fashioned himself in many ways, words normally taken to mean that the real man is hidden behind these representations. But it is a mistake to think that, because all his appearences are fashioned roles, there lies behind them something that cannot be got at, an essence that is always only represented, perhaps misleadingly or otherwise inadequately. We are misled by a metaphor. It would be better to say that the fashioning, the roles that we see, are expressions of the man; changing the metaphor in this way eliminates the need for something hidden which can only be represented. A representation is always 'of' something; a role is always something other than the player; a fashioning is always made 'out of' something not itself. An expression, on the other hand, may be 'of' something; but it need not be: 'I express myself', or 'I express myself in ...'; so far from hiding, an expression reveals. Each expression of Raleigh, multifarious as they are, is, in this way of looking at it, a genuine part of the man, and the whole man is the sum of all his expressions. There is nothing unique to Ralegh in this, we all express ourselves or fashion expressions of ourselves every day. Ralegh simply does so more variously and copiously than most mortals.

This thought has profound consequences for historical study, including in 'historical study' all forms of literary criticism where one reads works written in the past by men and women not oneself. For it entails that the self, precisely because it is wholly expressed in the roles – which are public for the most part – is in those roles, in principle, accessible. Attention to a role is attention to the person – not behind, but in that role, and the question of Ralegh's greatness is how many roles he played and played convincingly and, for a while at least, successfully.

There are common threads running through the roles of every life, common forms and rhythms and elaborations; Ralegh's ruins are marked by a common, not always obvious, thread, a common presence. The common presence used to be called style. The roles, however different, betray something of the same touch, recognizably similar modes of thought and feeling, of seeing the world and of acting upon it, recognizably similar rhythms and elaborations – the same style. We remark on all this for the reason that Ralegh's is more fragmentary than most, more self-conscious in fashioning roles. For all the strength and apparent vivid immediacy with which his personality comes down to us, he is elusive. The very fragmentation, moreover, provides an opportunity to evade limiting over-precise conceptualization of him, narrowed by exclusions of other possibilities.

In a player of roles there will be continuities and stabilities; for changes – progressions, volte-face, evolutions, discardings, and takings up – do not necessarily occur all at once, suddenly, but in overlapping stages, creating a *process* of family resemblances. Ralegh is not all water and discontinuity; many elements of his thought and modes of feeling and expression will be stable enough to be grasped before they pass away into something related but different, as his youth is stable enough for us to grasp even while it is becoming old age. We do not need absolute permanence of sameness or self-identity in personality, or in any object, to study and describe and begin to know it, only relative stability in the role, stable, that is, relative to our attention span.

But there are many gaps in the personality of Ralegh that are gaps to ourselves because we have not yet fully come to terms with all the ruins, most notably the *History of the World*. We have devoted incredible energies to certain of his roles, in particular the historical study of them in biographical studies, and the fascination with the story and the externals has sometimes diverted energies away from the internals; additionally, times have changed, and, with the shifts in culture, our critical and historical interests have changed with them. There is a feeling, very marked at the two conferences that spawned this book, that not only is there more to do (when is there not?) but that it is high time to do some of it – that our attention has turned to aspects of Ralegh where there are gaps, but that to some extent these gaps are now a hindrance to our interests.

III

In scanning Ralegh studies of recent decades, there is 'an invigorating sense that, despite all the research that has been done in the last five decades, there is still everything to do',[39] and one purpose of this book is to indicate some of the ways forwards in Ralegh studies, in particular the literary studies which form the subject of the book. And in the invigoration of this sense and in the light of the ensuing chapters, we offer some additional suggestions of ways that might be taken.

If we take a look at *The History of the World*, for example, there are some striking lacunae. Lacking a critical edition, we make do with either the selections by C. A. Patrides, with no notes at all, or the ancient and insufficient Oldys–Birch edition, which reaches as far as a note at the bottom of the page from time to time 'citation from Pliny', or Livy with a curt reference to the relevant passage. But the close examination of these citations would repay study.

Some ten editions were published between 1614 (or 1615 probably) and 1678, besides many epitomes, abbreviations, continuations, and such like. It is the first major history written specifically for what we now call the general reader, as a piece of literature – Ralegh is the first of the great English historians, in a line with Hume, Gibbon, Macauley, and Churchill, and until the eighteenth century his book was kept on the shelves of the learned as a standard history. As he helped to domesticate the potato and tobacco, so he domesticated history as literature, an underrated achievement.

The *History* is a wonderful book on several counts, not just because it is Ralegh's. There is first the concept, the structure and design, the organization; these are undoubtedly Ralegh's and if fully studied would tell us a great deal about his mind, the style.[40]

---

39 A remark not about Ralegh, in L. D. Murphy and J. T. Green (eds), *Renaissance Rhetoric: Short-Title Catalogue 1460–1700* (2nd edition, Aldershot: Ashgate, 2006), p. xii.

40 Louise Creighton, writing in the old *Cambridge History of English Literature*, is right to assert that Ralegh is so far master of his material as to handle it with great freedom and apparent ease, he has a 'ready hold' on the 'resources of his vast reading'. (Vol. 4, 60). She reports that it has been computed that 660 authors are cited in the History, and that record exists of his reading for it, containing books not cited. To some extent,

It constitutes a very skilfully told story; organization, or plotting, counts for a great deal and cannot be usefully illustrated in the confines of an Introduction; but localized techniques or effects can at least be pointed to. Two stand out in the seriatim reading. One is the use of the present tense (with good classical precedent in, for instance, Caesar) at moments of drama, which has the effect of seeming to place the reader inside the action, hearing the sorts of remark that could be made only by someone present in the action. Ralegh has an eye for dramatic action and narration – here writes the man of action, as was Caesar:

> Wherefore they appointed one of their Consuls to make war in *Spain*, the other in *Africk*; resting secure of all danger at home, *Titus Sempronius* took his way toward *Africk* with an hundred and sixty *Quinqueremes*, or Gallies of five to an Oar, which preparation may seem to threaten even the City of *Carthage*, to which it shall not come near. (V.3.iii, p. 649)

This is not the only time Ralegh uses the modal 'may' (where we should write 'might'), and the present tense 'seem', the dramatic present (present tense to describe past action); but the next clause is in a future form – so the reader is swung from being present in the action to being all-knowingly above it. Again: '*Scipio*, being both unable to travel by reason of his wound, and withal, finding it expedient to attend the coming of his fellow-Consul; incamps himself strongly upon the banks of *Trebia*' (V.3.iv, p. 651). Shortly thereafter in the same passage, of the Boji who had some Roman commissioners as hostages, 'They had hitherto kept them as pledges, to redeem their own hostages: but now they deliver them up to Hannibal, as tokens and pledges of their affection towards him' (*ibid*).

When some of the Gauls near Trebia fail to deliver the promised necessaries to Hannibal, Hannibal reasons and pleads with them, but: 'Seeing therefore how little they regarded his words, he was bold to be his own Carver; and took from them by force, as much as he needed of that which they had'. Immediately, Ralegh changes tense again: 'Hereupon they fly to the *Romans* for help: and, to make their tale the better, say that this wrong is done them, because they refused to joyn with *Hannibal*'. Falling back into the normal narrative tense, Ralegh writes one of those sentences so

---

as with any vast and learned work, the *History* is partly a team effort. Ralegh was well acquainted with the scholars and antiquarians of his day, and Cotton, Camden, Burhill, and Harriot were all consulted. But however fragmentary the sources, the book gives every appearance of having been written in the final redactions by Ralegh himself. Ben Jonson claims to have written passages of it (not unlikely for Ralegh took Jonson on as tutor to young Carew); but whatever Ralegh used of what others provided him, he adapted it enough so that it became his own.

prophetic of Gibbon: '*Scipio* cared not much for this: he suspected their falsehood, and was assured of their mutability' (V.3.iv, p. 660 [=652]).[41]

Ralegh writes with momentum, and it is sometimes difficult to stop reading. The story is pushed forwards by the narrative style. For example, it is a notable technique that chapters, and sometimes paragraphs, break off with such forwards momentum that one is tempted over the break into the next chapter or paragraph. Where this is not markedly the case, Ralegh provides with great skill a cadence rather than a discord to be resolved by the next chord. For example, Ralegh introduces effective variations among his usually lengthy and often convoluted sentences and here, after a long passage of complicated narrative in correspondingly dense sentences, he concludes the paragraph with a short, direct, and unadorned sentence:

> In the mean while, *Hannibal*, being in great scarcity of victuals, attempted the taking of *Clastidium*, a Town wherein the *Romans* had laid up all their store and munition. But there needed no force; a *Brundusian*, whom the *Romans* had trusted with keeping it, sold it for a little money. (V.3.iv, p. 651)

This variation in the tone and the pregnant but curt phrasing brings only a paragraph to an end; in this case there is little forwards movement; the rhythm of the sentences closes an episode.

The rhetoric is worth close attention. A steady accompaniment to both narrative and discursive passages is the highly patterned sentence or pair of them. Ralegh is not of the Ciceronian school, his prose is drier and more sinuous, nor of the metaphysical school, he is far more straightforward, but the decorative value of the figures of pattern, apart from their intrinsic clarity, was clear to him and he uses such devices frequently. In many of them, as with some of the epithets, it is almost impossible not to hear Gibbon's style, proleptically, *in nuce*: when Scipio dares not give battle to Hannibal, 'the *Gauls*, that hitherto had followed *Scipio* for fear, gathered out of his fear, courage to forsake him' (V.3.iv, p. 651).

Ralegh writes soberly and soldierly, but he is an Elizabethan and does not dispense with the flash of images, any more than Chapman in torturing the equally dry Homer, and the images are largely his own, even

---

41 A particularly striking case of the change of tense serves also to bring an episode to a firm close in mid-section. Of Flaminius's asking about letters from the Senate which might hinder his plan to give battle, Ralegh writes: 'Of this their jealousie, both he and the Senate that did give him cause, are likely to repent' (V.3.v, p. 653) – where again, we have the prophetic narrator both drawing the reader into the immediacy of the action and giving its outcome. It is presumably not accidental that Raleigh writes in his 'Preface', that in a history book we are present at the action.

where he is supposedly following his authorities. Consider for example, the skirmish where Scipio, after seeing his horse defeated by Hannibal's Numdians and himself dangerously wounded, is saved only through being brought off by his son: 'Whilst the *Romans* were busied in helping their Consul; an unexpected storm came driving at their backs' – the Numidian light-horse – the Romans 'all betook them to their speed, and left unto their enemies the honour of the day'. Whereupon, Scipio 'thought it a point of wisdom, having lost so many of his Fleet [soldiers] upon the first puff of the wind, to take Port [retire to camp] with the rest, before the extremest of the tempest overtook him. For he saw by the lowering of the morning what manner of day it was like to prove' (V.3.iv, p. 651). This is an extended image, pursued over a passage of several hundred words. But often the images are more localized, as for instance this, which recalls the image of carvery above: 'Early in the morning he [Hannibal] had sent over *Trebia* some companies of *Numidian* light-horse, to brave the enemy, and to draw him forth to a bad dinner, ere he had broken his fast' (v.3.iv, p. 660 [=652]).

Just after this, in describing that bad dinner, Raleigh produces this breathless sentence for the rout and headlong flight of the Romans. The Romans having foolishly crossed the river, found themselves bested, 'both in number and goodness':

> When therefore the *Roman* horse ranged on the flanks of their foot, were broken by the *Numidians*; when their foot, were charged both in front and flank, by the *Spaniards*, *Gauls* and Elephants; when finally the whole Army was unawares prest in the Rear, by *Mago* and his two thousand, that rose out of their place of ambush; then fell the *Romans*, by heaps, under the enemies swords: and being beaten down, as well fighting in disorder, as flying towards the River, by the Horsemen that pursued them, there escaped no more of six and thirty thousand, than ten thousand of all sorts, Horse and Foot. (V.3.iv., p. 660 [=652])

A rather undignified but vivid image, for example, occurs in the account of Fabius's first arrival and his treatment of the green legions he had brought with him and the broken Roman army surviving from the disastrous battle at Lake Thrasymene: 'He inured his men by little and little, and made them acquainted with dangers by degrees, and he brought them first to look on the Lyon afar off, that in the end he might sit on his tail' (V.3.iv, p. 655). Of great additional interest are Ralegh's interjections, not just for the biographical hints they yield but for the insight they give into his manner of thought: there are interjections on Ireland, and, until they have been collected and studied, we cannot claim to understand Ralegh's attitudes towards Ireland and Irish affairs, not an unimportant part of his life and the experiences which made him what he was, and of his reputation, what others thought of him, and how they represented him. We have, too, scattered about the whole vast book, many comments on warfare and current affairs. When Hannibal invests Spoletum but 'finding it well defended, presently gave it over', Ralegh remarks: 'The malice of a great Army is broken, and the force of it spent in a great seige. This the *Protestant* army found true at *Poictiers*, a little before the battle of *Moncountour*; and their victorious enemies, anon after at *S. Jean d'Angely*' (V.3.vi, p. 653). These interjections are a well-known feature of the *History* but only the labour typical of a critical edition is likely to collect them all. Perhaps even more than the images, they provide some indirect access to what we seek, the man – in his roles as well as in his literary style. It is not too bold a claim that the study of Ralegh will be incomplete until his greatest and by far the most extended literary work is subjected to the kind of detailed study we give to Milton's prose works, or Spenser's shorter poems and prose writings. This in turn entails reading the work, which in turn entails if not a critical edition, at least a reliable reading edition. A diplomatic edition of an early copy of the *History* would be a boon while we await a fully edited and annotated edition.

The first book-length study of the *History* of modern times has appeared while this volume is in preparation. Nicholas Popper argues in *Walter Ralegh's 'History of the World' and the Historical Culture of the Late Renaissance*[42] that Raleigh was self-consciously a participant in the great revival of history in the Renaissance that sought wisdom and guidance there, that sought to bring order to the past and through that to the present, but found eventually that, in developing suitable methods for the study of history, they produced methods for undermining some of the very sources of the original belief in history as a present help, and for challenging, for example, the authority of the Bible in the application of historical method to that book. Ralegh was not a mere dilettante in this business, but, as the library he collected for the purpose and his surviving notebook show, was a competent participant, and thus makes for a good index of the larger movements he was contributing to.

The poetry raises other questions and suggests more work. The task of assigning a canon of securely attributed works needs to continue. The Rudick edition, for all its great value and the thorough work which has gone into it, it not entirely satisfactory. It misplaces the burden of proof,

---

[42] Chicago University Press, 2012. We thank Professor Popper for sending us substantial samples of his MS.

and is unwelcoming as a reading text; the welter of alternative readings makes it difficult to wade through in pursuit of the main. This is part of the difficulty with the transmission of the poetry and is exacerbated by the modern tendency to treat each publication as a separate work with its own identity, a practice well defended by Rudick, and not challenged here. But a companion edition that mediates the welter to the reader in a more manageable form might be very useful – one that has already made some of the decisions a scholar in pursuit of the vanishing style would otherwise need to make. In other words, we need in the light of modern scholarship, and in the wake of Rudick, an edition much closer in its principles to the older practice of best possible earliest text; a critical edition to place beside Rudick's historical edition.

For the letters, we have a new edition, something greatly to be thankful for. These documents can now be studied responsibly without first having to rework the venerable Edwards at each citation. The letters are a goldmine of information, naturally, but even more from the literary point of view are they a mine to dig contentedly and fruitfully after style. Letters reveal, more so than other genre, not just in what they say, but what they imply and entail, and what they do not say, what unguarded moments they betray; and again the attitudes are potentially less deliberate than those of formal writing, though the Renaissance letter was also a formal genre as it rarely is today. In particular the local style of writing will interest literary critics: it would be good to have a full account of their rhetoric, for example, and their imagery. One does not get very far without comparison, and the letters and the *History* make sizeable sources for that purpose. Also, the structures – the manner of unfolding an anecdote, an argument, a plea, a narrative – these, too reveal the man. The letters need to be studied, too, as literature.

Reference tools for Raleigh are not thick on the ground, though we are well served in bibliographies and study-guides (as the editor's bibliography below shows). But some concordances would be useful; so would a list of images, and an index to rhetorical figures. None of these tools – each a great aid in stylistic analyses, it goes without saying – has been generated. But they entail first, digital texts, responsibly edited, reliable, searchable.

On the historical side of affairs, Ralegh's time in France is not well understood. And while it can hardly be said that Ralegh and Ireland, where the evidence is thicker on the ground, has been neglected, one or two areas could usefully be explored. The last detailed study of the Munster plantation was published over twenty years ago, and much of the matter from which the book was compiled was never published.[43] Archaeology in Ireland has accomplished much in the interim and another study would be welcome, especially a detailed analyses of Spenser's and Ralegh's neighbours (new and old) on the Munster plantation. The relation between Ralegh's two plantations, Virginia and Munster, is curious and contentious.[44]

For the scholar, nothing is too small to be interesting, and snippets continue to come to light. A recent study under artificial light of patches on Harriot's Virginian maps has revealed a possible final destination of the Lost Colony.[45] The recent rediscovery of the Burley manuscript has revealed two items not accounted for in the Latham and Youings *Letters*.[46]

Also important is the question of Ralegh's relations with the court while he was in Ireland, and the related question of how far Ireland served as a power base for him – what networks did he have there that provided if not exactly a power base, at least further influence at court in one of its most important epicycles of worry and expense and controversy? Much the same could be said of Raleigh's important support base in the West Country.

Ralegh writes to Robert Cecil about his Irish problems in the same month as he finds himself in prison over the Throckmorton affair, also writing to Cecil in Cynthia-inspired overly florid prose about being

---

43 Michael MacCarthy-Morrogh, *The Munster Plantation: English Migration to Southern Ireland, 1583–1641* (Oxford: Clarendon Press, 1986).
44 On the one hand, as Eric Klingelhofer has argued, there are marked resemblances between them, not least in style of layout. He argues that for Ralegh the two were part of one concept. Paper given at East Carolina University, Conference on Raleigh, 2008. Thanks are due to Professor Klingelhofer for sending us a copy of this paper. Yet there are differences between them: for one thing in Virginia and in the proposals for Guiana there are definite plans for co-operation between the settlers and the local inhabitants who were to be seen, at least in theory, as allies and partners. Ralegh stresses this point, partly as a counterbalance to the very different attitude of the Spanish colonizers, against which he protests. By this time the Spanish policy (or practice) could be seen to have been disastrous. Whether co-operation would have been followed through in practice and whether Ralegh proposed it from humane feelings may well rouse scepticism. But with the Munster plantation, there is no such idea; and this makes for great differences between the two projects, something Ciaran Brady has recently emphasized. (Ciaran Brady, review of Eric Klingelhofer, *Castles and Colonists: An Archaeology of Elizabethan Ireland* (Manchester: Manchester University Press, 2010), *Renaissance Studies* 26, 2 (2012), 310–12).
45 http: / /www.britishmuseum.org /csrmellonpdfs /AR2012-21_u.pdf, accessed 26 May 2012.
46 We have printed these in an Appendix to this Introduction, courtesy of Lincoln Public Record Office and Manchester University Press. Peter Redford provided the transcripts in the course of his work on the Burley MS for the first time. His book on the manuscript is forthcoming in The Manchester Spenser series, Manchester University Press, 2014.

barred from Elizabeth's presence (see Herron, Chapter 3 below). The Cecils are one node of influence and bartering or favour-asking at the London court in Irish affairs as well as local Court affairs.[47] Ralegh's enemies at court as well as in Ireland would pursue their own plans in Ireland and would need or possess influence both at court and locally in Ireland: enemies abounded, but might include Ormond with great influence both sides of the Irish Sea,[48] and perhaps Lord Barry. Traffic between London and Dublin is not always easy to assess, but people such as Florence MacCarthy, one of the greatest of his sept in the 1590s, travel back and forth to London, and so does the Countess of Desmond long after her husband's death. (When Ralegh ends up in the Tower again, MacCarthy is there, too, and we have a letter from MacCarthy saying he is writing his own, Irish history.) Naturally presence at court potentially, and usually in practice, gives increased scope for influencing the powers there and for supporting or back-stabbing, so visits and periods of residence are important to establish.[49] But it is not only the travels and correspondence of the principles that count in networking and conspiring, but those, too, of their servants, whether as letter-bearers or as informal ambassadors with the authority to negotiate and persuade independently.

Familial relations are vital, though there can be no simple equation between blood or marriage and loyal, or consistently loyal alliance. We need a study, even just some diagrams would help, of the networks in which Ralegh was involved, networks of friendship, family and politics, and, importantly, literary networks.

IV

Ralegh's prose writings, from the propagandistic account of the last fight of the *Revenge* to the massive but unfinished *History of the World*, continue to be examined, as does his poetry. The chapters in this book highlight aspects of Ralegh as writer and his visual image that are the subjects of new or renewed scholarly interest. Contributors include literary scholars, a historian and an art historian from three different countries, Canada, Great Britain and the United States, both junior and senior scholars. Seven of the chapters in this volume originated as papers presented at an international conference entitled 'Ralegh and the Atlantic World' held at East Carolina University in Greenville, North Carolina in

---

47 See a recent book by Christopher Maginn, *William Cecil, Ireland, and the Tudor State* (Oxford: Oxford University Press, 2012).
48 Edwards, 'The Irish Favourite'.
49 Edwards, 'The Irish Favourite'.

April 2008, and one emanated from a conference on 'New Explorations into Walter Raleigh: Historiography, Biography, and Canon' held at the Tower of London, January 2009.

Appropriately for a volume in The Manchester Spenser series, four chapters examine the complex, ambiguous relationship between Ralegh and Spenser while they were part of the English settlement in Ireland and afterwards in London. Their interchanges of prefaces and poems referring to the other writer, with Ralegh praising Spenser's *Faerie Queene* and in that poem Spenser apparently representing Ralegh allegorically, are analysed from various perspectives.

In the first of these chapters, Wayne Erickson approaches these authors from the historical context of the meetings between the two authors and concludes that Ralegh played a larger role in Spenser's life than Spenser did in Ralegh's. Anna Beer, Thomas Herron and James Nohrnberg see correspondences between the two authors' poems. Beer links Colin in Spenser's *Colin Clouts Come Home Againe* and Timias in Book III of *The Faerie Queene* with Ralegh as 'Ocean' in *Oceans Love to Scynthia*. She acknowledges the difficulty of determining the genre of that 553-line poem: is it complaint, pastoral, or anti-pastoral satire with political undertones? Thomas Herron also connects the character Ocean with Colin Clout and Timias, while exploring the role of Irish affairs in the relationship of Spenser and Ralegh while they resided in Munster. He argues that colonial motifs in *Oceans Love to Scynthia*, like those in Spenser's poetry, are best understood within an Irish and not only a New World context. James Nohrnberg introduces parallels with classical and later European literature and declares that 'the relative formlessness of Ralegh's confessional poem [*Oceans Love to Scynthia*], paradoxically, is an essential of its form – its water-like changeability'. In these chapters that poem is variously rated from being a potential epic that turns into 'a Petrarchan shambles' to 'one of the most exciting poems of the 1590s'.

The significance of water (as Ralegh's first name was often pronounced) and ocean is also featured in other contexts. Lowell Duckert compares Ralegh's quest for Manoa and its gold, an illusion that recedes in the endlessly merging rivers of Guiana, to the alchemists' quest for gold. Michael Booth notes that Ralegh knew both the freedom of sailing the ocean and long imprisonment in the Tower of London, experiences which are reflected in the metaphors in his *History of the World*. Invoking recent cognitive theory, Booth argues that recognition of personal experience 'can help literary study engage with the texts as the products of individual minds, and not of historical and cultural forces alone'.

Ralegh's military career and his subsequent reflections on it are examined by Andrew Hiscock. Ralegh's teenage experience in the Protestant wars in France and his later combats with the Irish and the Spaniards provided examples of what happens in warfare that he uses in his *History of the World*, in which he has become the 'contrite soldier'. In that magnum opus an 'uneasy dialectic between the material world and apocalyptic history' emerges. Since Ralegh's two journeys to Guiana were basically on reconnaissance – and since he never set foot in the Virginia to which he sent settlers – his 'contribution to empire-building was primarily textual', though he did 'envision England as a great imperial power-in-the-making'. The colonial theme is also a feature of Alden Vaughan's chapter, 'Anglo-American Ethnography'. North American Indians were often regarded as kin to the 'wild' Irish, but Vaughan points out that native interpreters, particularly Manteo, were valuable to both Ralegh and Harriot, and calls Harriot's *Brief and True Report of the New Found Land of Virginia* (1588) 'good amateur anthropology', and Ralegh's *Discovery of Guiana* (1595) 'good amateur geopolitics'.

In addition to the prominence of *Oceans Love to Scynthia* in the above-mentioned chapters, some of Ralegh's shorter poems are featured in other chapters. Hannibal Hamlin analyses the famous exchange between Marlowe's 'Passionate Shepherd to his Love' and Ralegh's 'Nymph's Reply', and the four centuries of variations on that theme. The poem 'As You Came from the Holy Land of Walsingham', often attributed to Ralegh, is revisited by Gary Waller. He postulates that the lingering esteem in Protestant England for the Roman Catholic shrine to the Virgin Mary at Walsingham was analogous to the cult of the Virgin Queen Elizabeth.

Ralegh had three sons, two of whom died in his lifetime. In the riddle poem, 'The Wood, the Weed, and the Wag', Judith Owens detects a growing conflict between the concern of a father for his son and the stern law of the state, ending with the father 'a helpless petitioner for God's intervention'. In Owens's essay on patrilineage in Ralegh's writing, she detects in his *Discovery of Guiana* that despite the flattery of Queen Elizabeth and the covert appeal for her to support imperial expansion, the important role of men such as ships' captains and Indian chiefs, including the willingness to allow a son to be borrowed, is prominent. Reflecting on the famous portrait of Ralegh and his son, Walt, she sees paternal pride but no intimacy.

The last part of the book focuses on visual presentations of Ralegh, a man famous for outward ostentation. The portrait of Ralegh and Walt is one of the numerous varied portraits and statues of Ralegh made from his time to the present that Vivienne Westbrook analyses. Susan Anderson surveys a century of films in which Ralegh is a major or minor character. His versatility and multifaceted career have attracted scriptwriters and directors, whose products reflect the eras – pre-Second World War, wartime, postwar – in which they were made. Her filmography includes BBC spoofs. The volume concludes with a Bibliography of Raleghana from 1986 to 2010, which is meant to complement previous bibliographies compiled by T. N. Brushfield, Jerry Leath Mills and Christopher M. Armitage.[50]

The range of these topics illustrates the latest contributions to the continuing study of one of the most significant figures in the Elizabethan and Jacobean eras.

Appendix

Record Office for Leicestershire, Leicester and Rutlland, Finch, DG7, Lit2 (The Burley Manuscript), f. 92r[51]

Sr Walter Raleighs Apologie for his
last action att Guiana. ~ .

Because I know not whither I shall liue to come before the L.^{ds}
   I haue for his Maties satisfaction sett downe as much as I can
   say either for myne owne defence or against myself as things
   are now construed.
Itt is true that though I acquainted his Matie with myne owne
   intent to land in Guiana yet I never made itt knowne to his
   Matie that the Spaniards had any footing there nether had I
   any authoritie by my patent to remoue the Spaniards from thence
   and therefore his Matie had no interest in the attempt of S^t
   Thome by any foreknowledg thereof in his Matie.
But knowing his Maties tytle to the cuntry to bee the best and most
   christian bycause the naturall lords did most willingly
   acknowledg Q. Eliza: to be theire soueraigne who by mee pro=

---

50 Brushfield, *A Bibliography of Sir Walter Ralegh, Knt.* 2nd edition (Exeter: James G. Commin, 1908); Mills, *Sir Walter Ralegh: A Reference Guide*; Mills, 'Recent Studies in Ralegh'. *English Literary Renaissance* (1986), 225–44; Christopher M. Armitage, *Sir Walter Ralegh, an Annotated Bibliography* (Chapel Hill: University of North Carolina Press, 1987).
51 In the top left margin is a note, probably in Logan Pearsall's hand, reading 'Printed in Edwards II 375'.

mised to defend them from the Spaniards cruelty I made
no doubt but that I might enter the land by force seing the
Spaniards had no other tytle then force (the Popes donation excepted)
considering also that they gott a possession there diuers yeares since
my possession taken for the crowne of England for were not
Guiana his Ma:^(ties) then might I haue as well beene questioned for
a theefe for taking gold out of the kings of Spaines mines as the
Spaniards do now call me a peacebreaker for from any territory
confest to bee the king of Spaines it is no more lawfull to ~~bee~~
take gold then lawfull for the k. of Spaine to take tynne
out of Cornewall.

Now were this possession of theirs al sufficient barr to his Ma.^(ties)
right; the kings of Spaine may as well call them selues Dukes
of Brittaine because they hold Bluet and fortifide there;
and kings of Ireland bycause they possessed Smerick fortified
there and so in other places.

That his Ma.^(tie) was well resolued of his right there I make no kind
of doubt bycause the English both under Mr Charles Leigh and
Mr Harcourt had leaue to plant and inhabite the country.
That Oronoque it self had had long ere this 5000 English in itt I
assure my self had not myne employment at Cales the next yeare after
my returne from Guiana and after yt our iurney to the Ilands
hindred mee for those two yeares after wch Tyrones rebellion

92v

rebellion made her Ma.^(tie) unwilling yt any great number of ships
or men should be taken out of England tyll that rebellion
were ended, and lastly her Ma.^(ties) death and my long imprison=
ment gaue tyme to the Spaniards to sett upp a towne of sticks
couered wth leaues of trees uppon the banks of Oronoque
wch the called St Thome: but they haue neither reconciled
nor conquered any of the Casiques or naturall Lords of the
country, wch Casiques are still in armes agsainst them as by
the ~~Spaniards~~ gouernors letter to the king of Spaine it may
appeare.
That by landing in Guiana there could be any breach of peace I thinke
itt (under favour) impossible for to breake peace where there
is no peace itt cannot bee;
That the Spaniard gives us no peace there itt doth appeare

by the kings letters to his gouernour that they shall put to death
all those Spaniards and Indians that trade *con los Engleses
Enimigos*, with English enemies: yea those very Spaniards
w^(ch) wee encountred att S^t. Thome did of late yeares murder
<u>36.</u> of Mr Halls men of London and myne who landed
without weapon uppon the Spaniards.fayth[52] to trade with them.
Mr Thorne also of Towerstreet in London besyd many other
English was in like sort murdered in Oronoque the yeare
before my deliuery out of the Tower.

Now if this kind of Trade be a peaceable trade there is then a peace
in the Indies betweene us and the ~~Indians~~ Spaniards but if this bee
cruelty, warre and hatred and no peace, the^n shewing no
peace broken by our attempt.

Againe how doth itt stand with the greatness of the K. of Spaine
first to call us enimies when he did hope to cut us in piecies, and
then having fayled to call us peacebreakers for to be an enimy and
a peacebreaker in one and the same action is impossible; but y^e
K. of Spaine in his letters to the Gouen.^r of Guiana dated att
Madrill the [53]29th of March before wee left the Thames call us
Enimicos Engleses.

If itt had pleased ye K of Spaine to haue written to his Matie ^in vj. months
tyme (for wee were so long in preparing) and haue made his Ma.^ie
knowne y^t o^ur landing in Guiana would have drawne after itt
a breach of peace, I presume to thinke his Matie. would haue
stayd o^ur enterprise for ye present. this hee might haue done
wth lesse charg then to leavy [300][54] soldiers and transport 20 pieces
of ordinance from Pueto Rico: wch soldiers added to the garrison of

93r

of S^t. Thome had they arriued before o^ur comming had overthrowne all
o^ur raw companies, and there would haue followed no complaints.
For ~~xxxx~~ the mayne point of landing nere S^t. To. it is true that wee
were of opinion y^t we must have driven the Spaniards out of theire
towne before wee could passe the thick woods uppon the mountayne
of the myne, wch I confesse I did first resolue uppon, but better

---

52 'fayth': the word is smudged by the crossing out of another word, probably 'meaning', and the transcription is not wholly certain.
53 Parkhurst's inscription of the digits «1» and '2' is simply a slighly curved vertical line; here and in the ensuing paragraph I have rendered it as '2', but '19th' or '10' respectively might be correct.
54 The first digit is blotted and unclear.

bethinking myself, I referred the taking of the towne to ye goodnes
of the mine wch if they found to be so rich as it might perswade
the leaving of a garison there to drive away the Spaniards thence
but to haue itt burnt was never myne intent, neither could
they ever giue me reason why they did itt. Uppon there
returne I examined the Seriant Maior and Kemish why they
followed not my last directions for the triall of the myne before
the taking of the towne: They answered me that although
they durst ~~not~~ hardly go to the mine leaving a garrison of
Spaniards betweene them and their boats: yet ^they^ sayd they followed
those later directions and did land betweene the towne and the
mine, and that the Spaniards without any manner of parly sett
uppon them unawares and charged them calling them Petros
Ingleses and by skirmishing wth them drew them into ye very
entrance of the towne befor they knew where they were for as
if any peace had beene in those parts the spaniards
first broake the pece and made the first slaugther, for as the
English could not but land to seek the mine being come thither
to yt end, so being first revyld and chargd by the spaniards
they could do no lesse then repell force by force.
Lastly it is a matter of no small consequence to acknowledg
y^t wee haue offended ye K. of Spaine by landing in Guiana.
For first itt weakens his Maties tytle to the country or quitts itt.
Secondly ther is no king y^t hath ever give the least way to any other
king or state in th traffique of the liues and goods of his
subiects (to witt as in o^{ur} case) that itt shall be lawfull for the
Spaniards to murder us either by force or treason, and nott
lawfull for us to defend o^{ur} selues, and pay them in theire owne
owne coyne, for this proud superiority sand inferiority
wch no absolute monarch ever yelded out or ever will.
Thirdly itt shews the English beares greater respect for the Spaniards
and are more doubtfull of theire forces then either the french or
dutch are who dayly invade all parts of the Indies without being
questioned at theire retourne; yea at my now being in Plymouth
a french gentleman called Florie went thence with 7. sayle
and 300[land. men?] wth comission in the land to burne and sacke
all places in the Indies y^t he could master & yet hath the french
king married a daugther of Spaine.

93v

This is all I can say, other then I haue spent my poore estate, lost
my sonn, and my health, and endured as many sorts of
miseries as ever man did in hope to do his Matie. service; and
haue not to my understanding comitted any hostyle act other then
the entrance uppon a territory belonging to the crowne of
England where the English wee first sett uppon and slayne
by the usurping Spaniards; I returned into England with the
manifest perill of my life with a purpose not to hold my life
by any other art then his Maties. grace, and from wch no man
nor perill could dissuade me: To that grace and goodnesse
and kinglynes I referr myself wch if itt should find that I haue ^not
yet suffred enough it may if itt please add more affliction
to the remaynder of a wretched life. . ~ . ~ .. ~ ..

Record Office for Leicestershire, Leicester and Rutlland, Finch, DG7, Lit2 (The Burley Manuscript), f. 250r[55]

S.r After many great losses and many yeares sorrowes, of both w^ch
I haue cause to feare that I was mistaken in theire ends. It is come
to my knowledg that y^r self whome I know not but by an
honourable fame haue beene perswuaded to giue me and myne
their last fatall blow by obtayning from his Matie the inheri=
tance of my children and Nephews, lost in law for want
of a word, this done there remayneth nothing wth me but
the name of life disployed [dispoyled] of all but the tytle and
sorrowe thereof; his Matie whome I never offended (for I ever
held ^it^ vnnatural and vncomely to hate goodnesse)stayd me
at the graues brinke; not that I hope his Ma:^tie thought me
worthy of many deaths and to behold all myne cast out
of the world wth my self, but as a king who iudging
the poore in truth hath obteyned a promise from God that
his throne shalbe established for ever. And for y^o S.^r seing y^r
faire day is but now in the dawne, and myne drawne
to the evening, y^r owne vertue and the kings grace
assuring you of many good fortunes and much honour I
beseech you not to begin yr first building vppon the

---

55 There is a marginal note at the top right of the page, probably in the hand of Logan Pearsall Smith, reading 'Printed in Edwards II 326'.

ruines of the innocent, and that thire and my sorrowes
attend not y^r first plantation: I haue ever beene bound
to y^r nation ass well for many other graces as for theire true
report of my triall to the kings Ma:^{tie} against whome had
I beene found malignant the hearing of my cause would
not haue chaunged enimies into frends malice into
compassion and the mindes of the greatest number
present into consideration of my estate, it is not in
the nature of fowle treason to begett such fayre
passions neither would it agree wth the duty and loue
of faythfull subiects espetially of y^r owne nation to
bewayle his overthrow that had conspired against theire
most liberall and naturall Lord. I therefore trust S^r.
you will not be the first that shall kill us outright; & whew
downe the tree wth ye fruites and undergoe the curse of the^m y^t enter on
the fields of the fatherlesse, wch if it please you to know the truth are
farr lesse ~~in fame~~ fruitefull in valore then in fame, But y^t so worthy
a Gentlema^n as y^{r}self will rather bind us to y^r service being S.^{r}
gentle not base in birth and allyance wch haue interest therein and my self
wth my uttermost thankfulnesse will ever remayne ready to obey
y^r com~ands. /2[56]

---

[56] The last two lines are written vertically downwards in the left margin.

1

Raleigh in ruins, Raleigh on the rocks
Sir Wa'ter's two Books of Mutabilitie and their subject's allegorical presence in select Spenserean narratives and complaints[1]

James Nohrnberg

All my inward friends abhorred me: and they whom I loved are turned against me.
   Have pity upon me, have pity upon me, O ye my friends;...
   Oh that my words were now written! Oh that they were printed in a book!
                                             (AV Job 19:18-19, 23)

'The end of the bookes ... entreatinge of Sorrow'[2]

... changes and armies *of sorowes* are against me.
                                             (Job 10:17, Geneva Bible)

John Stuart Mill said poetry was not, properly speaking, heard, but rather *over*heard, and, if ever a poem was meant to be overheard, it is the

---

1 The comparison of Raleigh's *Ocean to Cynthia* to Spenser's *Two Cantos of Mutabilitie*, tendered here, is also found in a somewhat different form in Nohrnberg, 'Supplementing Spenser's Supplement, a Masque in Several Scenes: Eight Literary-Critical Meditations on a Renaissance Numen Called *Mutabilitie*', in *Celebrating 'Mutabilitie'*, ed. Jane Grogan (Manchester: Manchester University Press, 2010), 85-135. Both this essay and the author's 'Britomart's Gone Abroad to Brute-land, Colin Clout's Come Courting from the Salvage Ire-land: Exile and the Kingdom in Some of Spenser's Fictions for "Crossing Over"', in *Edmund Spenser: New and Renewed Directions*, ed. J. B. Lethbridge (Teaneck/Madison, NJ: Fairleigh-Dickinson University Press, 2006), 214-91, bruit the triangulation of Molanna/Bregog-Timias-Ocean-Raleigh with Faunus-Colin-Spenser, and Cynthia-Belphoebe-Elizabeth (or her throne-theatre-court). Background information and documentation for the Irish side of Sir Walter's corner can be found in Sir John Pope Hennessy, *Sir Walter Ralegh in Ireland* (1883), ed. Thomas Herron (Dublin: University College Press, 2009).

2 This title is from that of the second book of Raleigh's *The Ocean to Cynthia*; here and throughout I quote Raleigh's poetry from Agnes Latham, ed., *The Poems of Sir Walter Ralegh* (Cambridge, MA: Harvard University Press, 1962); here, 44. Spenser will be quoted from *Poetical Works*, ed. J. C. Smith and E. De Selincourt (Oxford and New York: Oxford University Press, rprnt 1963).

complaint of the distraught Sir Walter Raleigh's *The Ocean to Cynthia*.[3] But we are free to doubt that the 'Cynthia' who was meant to overhear it – Raleigh's sovereign, Queen Elizabeth – would have ever lent it that ear for which it seems so palpably and unavailingly designed. The poem, as we will describe it, with its 'tale that Sorrow bydds thee tell' (*OC* 214), quite eludes Mill's antithesis between *poetry*, oriented on its own consciousness, and *eloquence*, oriented upon another's.[4] Indeed, some part of Raleigh's despairing soliloquy was auditioned by the Queen's poet Spenser, who three times refers to his acquaintance with a major piece by Raleigh featuring 'Cynthia', even if actually hearing some part of that alleged magnum opus may have put Raleigh's protégé to sleep: the *Cynthia* cited in Spenser's proem to Book III of *The Faerie Queene* was apparently a potent soporific. And yet Raleigh himself seems to say the poem we actually have was strong stuff – it was virtually inspired, it being the product of a 'furious madness' that, of itself, '[w]rote what it would' (*OC* 143–6).[5] But such a claim is artful, and must needs dissimulate –

---

[3] John Stuart Mill, 'Thoughts on Poetry and Its Varieties' (1859 version), in *English Critical Essays: Nineteenth Century*, ed. Edmund D. Jones (London: Oxford University Press, 1934 rprnt.), 398–429: 406.

[4] Mill, 'Thoughts on Poetry': 'Poetry and eloquence are both alike the expression or utterance of feeling. But if we may be excused the antithesis, we should say that eloquence is *heard*, poetry is *over*heard. Eloquence supposes an audience; the peculiarity of poetry appears to us to lie in the poet's utter unconsciousness of a listener. Poetry is feeling confessing itself to itself, in moments of solitude and embodying itself in symbols which are the nearest possible representations of the feeling in the exact shape in which it exists in the poet's mind. Eloquence is feeling pouring itself out to other minds, courting their sympathy, or endeavouring to influence their belief or move them to passion or to action.

All poetry is of the nature of soliloquy'. Further, 407: '[W]hen [the poet] turns round and addresses himself to another person; when the act of utterance is not itself the end, but a means to an end, – viz. by the feelings he himself expresses, to work upon the feelings, or upon the belief, or the will, of another, – when the expression of his emotions or of his thoughts tinged by his emotions, is tinged also by that purpose, that desire of making an impression upon another mind, then it ceases to be poetry and becomes eloquence.

Poetry, accordingly, is the natural fruit of solitude and meditation; eloquence, of intercourse with the world.' The kind of court where one spoke covertly, but thus in order to be *over*heard, and where slander and erotic motions were the stuff being communicated this way, is very much the subject of Shakespeare's *Much Ado About Nothing* – or noting.

[5] *FQ* III.proem.4, where Spenser asks what can illuminate his sovereign better than 'that sweet verse, with *Nectar* sprinckled, / In which a gracious seruant pictured / His *Cynthia*, his heauens fairest light? / That with his melting sweetnesse rauished, / And with the wonder of her beames bright, / My senses lulled are in slomber of delight'. (Comparably, Spenser's Belphoebe's foster-mother Diana's uncoiffed hair is 'with sweet *Ambrosia* all besprinkled light' (III.vi.18).) The chronology for – and bibliographic relations between – the 'lamentable lay' referred to in *Colin Clouts Come Home Again* (1595) and the Queen's celebration by Raleigh referred to in *FQ* III's proem (1590), is carefully discussed by Agnes Latham, with the aid of Alexander M. Buchan, in *MLQ* I, 1940, in her edition of *The Poems of Sir Walter Ralegh*: at 'Introduction', xxxvi–xliv.

or else betray – a piece frequently eavesdropping on its own manifestly rhetorical contrivance.

In *The Ocean to Cynthia* the miserable poet's representation of himself in prison and in disgrace – in the soup, so to speak – inevitably shades into his pitiable and pathetic self-advocacy. Mill asks, extending his remarks to music, and in regard to Mozart, 'Who can imagine "Dove sono" *heard*? We imagine it *over*heard':

> Purely pathetic music commonly partakes of soliloquy. The soul is absorbed in its distress, and though there may be bystanders, it is not thinking of them. When the mind is looking within, and not without, its state does not often or rapidly vary; and hence the even, uninterrupted flow, approaching almost to a monotony, which a good reader, or a good singer, will give to words or music of a pensive or melancholy cast. But grief taking the form of a prayer, or of a complaint, becomes oratorical; no longer low, and even, and subdued, it assumes a more emphatic rhythm, a more rapidly returning accent; instead of a few slow equal notes, following one after another at regular intervals, it crowds note upon note, and often assumes a hurry and bustle like joy.[6]

A sincere mind does not revel in grief, but bows speechless beneath it. And although Raleigh's speaker claims it has been a great labour to prevent himself from expressing his passion for the royal vestal, it might appear from his excessive protestation that it was, instead, a great labour to make her believe the lie that he was deeply in love with her.[7] He may well appear to be one of those oratorical 'attitudinizers' Mill discovers, 'almost to a man', among the heads of the largely historical subjects of French painting.[8] But while Raleigh struck his rhetorical pose at court, his desire had cried, give me some food, and, in lieu of Elizabeth Tudor, her attendant Elizabeth Throckmorton had decisively obliged, and answered importunity 'switter swatter'.[9]

---

6 Mill, 'Thoughts on Poetry', 408–9.
7 Similarly: Job's speaking persona, in the Book of Job, might claim it has been a considerable labour to prevent himself from expressing his anger with God, but it might also appear from the excess of his protestations that it would be, instead, a great labour to make anyone believe that he was patiently resigned to his suffering, or utterly incapacitated by it. Job is anything but dumb or genuinely acquiescent.
8 Mill, 'Thoughts on Poetry', 411–12.
9 Elizabeth Throckmorton, after Sir John Aubrey's essayette on Raleigh; found in Henry Purcell's catch *Sweet Sir Walter* (in *Ten Catches*): 'Sir Walter, enjoying his Damsel one night. / He tickl'd and pleas'd her to so great a height, / That she could not contain t'wards the end of the matter, / But in Rapture cry'd out, O sweet sir Walter, / O sweet Sir Walter, O sweet Sir Walter, / O sweet Sir, sweet Sir Walter, O switter swatter, / O switter swatter, O switter swatter, / O switter swatter, O switter swatter.'

Raleigh's poem could warn a reader that there are no True Confessions, only false ones. Former joys, attentions, favours, and deserts are strongly alleged, and form a constant refrain: how could the Queen's subject – and therefore the Queen herself – deny or repudiate them? For just as Raleigh had fondly dreamt Elizabeth's constancy would prolong her devotion to her let's-pretend suitor, so thereafter he vainly hoped her former charities might cover all his sins against propriety: her sense of honour, and his faith, might save him, rather than damn him. But if what Raleigh wants is a suspended sentence, while having no one but himself for an advocate, then the abject suitor has a fool for a lawyer – and a pathetic whine for his chief lobbyist. The rhetoric for the loss of esteem he once so manifestly enjoyed draws a reader into the vicious circle traced by the round-and-round of an aggrieved ego that cannot stop encountering and re-encountering its own offence, the scarcely nameable point of impasse on the broken record where his recital turns into a stutter – one that is as repetitious as it is verbose.

In his Legend of Friendship, Raleigh's friend Spenser supplies the bereft Timias, a counter for Raleigh, with a more effective advocate, a peace-making dove that acts the ambassadorial go-between for whose office Raleigh's poem seems itself to have been quite incompetent.[10] Indeed, confronted by the evidence of Raleigh's unremitting self-advertisement throughout his adventurous life, A. L. Rowse reluctantly concludes 'that underneath the glitter and the excitement, he was a bore about himself'.[11] Moreover, the poet's abjection in his poem likewise suggests that he could be an enterprising operator – but not, to judge by the poem itself, an imperceptible and discreet one.

Among the many scenes offered in Spenser's comparably autobiographical poem, *Colin Clouts Come Home Againe*, is the early one of Raleigh reading from his 'lamentable lay' (164), and among the many other relevant matters in Spenser's piece elsewhere there is the depiction of Raleigh's proficiency as a river-like infiltrator of the taboo territory of the Queen's Ladies in Waiting, along with the compliment to Raleigh as a sea-captain or navigator in the person of Colin's guide and fellow-traveller to the English court – the trans-Atlantic explorer is celebrated as the Shepherd of the Ocean. Raleigh's own poem, with its title referring

---

10 For a full study that proposes that the dove in *Faerie Queene* IV.viii performs a variety of functions, including that of representing a vocation in poetry itself, see Patrick Cheney, *Spenser's Famous Flight: A Renaissance Idea of a Literary Career* (Toronto, Buffalo, and London: University of Toronto Press, 1997).

11 A. L. Rowse, *Sir Walter Ralegh: His Family and Private Life* (New York: Harper, 1962), 186.

to this identity as a mariner, is apparently the piece *alleged as* exchanged with Spenser in advance of the poet's visit with Raleigh to the English court, in order to present his 1590 *Faerie Queene* to her majesty; but Raleigh's poem asks, in so many perplexed words, 'whether the goddess who ruled the waves could ever absolve the privateer who had boarded Elizabeth Throckmorton' – somewhat after (c. 1592).[12]

Raleigh's verses are the abject poetical confession of the distraught courtier's confusion and despair over his – *Sir Wa'ter's* – precipitous descent from royal favour into the muddy mess of political and sexual disgrace: '[F]loods of sorrow and whole seas of woe / The banks of all my hope did overbear, / / And drowned my mind in depths of misery' (*OC* 140–2), complains the speaker-writer. As for the alienated mistress named Cynthia in the title, in the words of Natale Conti, 'Euripides thought that Diana and the Moon were one and the same .... Callimachus therefore claimed that Diana had the skill to inflict very dark catastrophes on anyone she wanted, as these verses testify: "Froward men, on whom thou wilt impress thy grievous wrath... their tilth feeds frost [...] and their wives either are smitten or die in childbirth" (*Dian.* 124–27). For the power to do all of these things was regarded as the special province of the Moon.'[13] In Raleigh's poem the lunar goddess has become one particular mortal's natural disaster.

The theme of Raleigh's poem is a mutability that is *political*: i.e., the precariousness of the ageing courtier's estate, as revealed by his fall from eminence and the loss of his privileged position in court. His good fortune could not endure, nothing like that joy can last, all good things must come to an end. For an experienced person to suppose otherwise is unreasonable, and the memory of the disgraced one's former place in the sun is hardly a consolation. The levée is down, everything in a patron-client relation so carefully built up is destroyed and desolated (*OC* 221–36). But at the same time the mutability in question is also *natural*, and thus one

12 Here I am quoting 'Britomart's Gone Abroad', in Lethbridge, ed., *New and Renewed Directions*, p. 269. The present chapter relies on this previous one for several particulars in reading Raleigh as a recurrent figure in Spenser's canon. It is *Colin Clouts Come Home Againe* that alleges (impossibly) that the two poets auditioned each other's songs about Raleigh's disgrace in 1592 – Spenser/Colin speaking of it allegorically in the Bregog and Mulla story (ll. 92–155), and Raleigh/Ocean more directly with his complaint (ll. 163–75) – both *before* the Shepherd of the Ocean invites the singer Colin to visit Cynthia's (the Queen's) court, in 1589–90, in order to ameliorate his forgotten situation of being 'banisht' to the 'waste' of Ireland (ll. 182–3).

13 *Natale Conti's 'Mythologiae'*, in 2 vols, tr. John Murayan and Steven Brown (Tempe: Arizona Centre for Medieval and Renaissance Studes, 2006), 221–2 (*sub* Book III, Chap. 17: 'On the Moon').

with the material imagery expressing it. Raleigh is thus forced to ask what kind of stuff he's really made of.

Raleigh's allegorical stand-in the narrative of *The Faerie Queene* after Books I and II, where Arthur's squire is not named, is the aforementioned Timias. In Book IV Spenser describes Belphoebe's rustication and mortification of the rejected courtier as penitential: 'No other drinke here did he [Timias] euer tast, / Then running water, tempred with his teares' (*FQ* IV.vii.41). The ascetic is here identifiable with the same exact Sir Walter who poured out his sorrows in *The Ocean to Cynthia*. The mutable element of water, from which came Sir Wa'ter's nickname at court, ruefully appears in all of its forms and variety within his poem, pouring down, welling up, drying out, going vapourously away. Whether actually pirating or merely trading on 'The Admiral of the Ocean Sea', Columbus's inalienable title, in calling himself Ocean Raleigh also burdens this quasi-allegorical nom de plume with reflections like Augustine's on matter itself, in the *Confessions*:

> For myself, Lord, if I am to confess to you with my mouth and my pen everything you have taught me about this question of matter, the truth is that earlier in life I heard the word but did not understand it, and those who spoke to me about it did not understand it either. I used to think of it as having countless and varied shapes, and there I was not thinking about matter at all. My mind envisaged foul and horrible forms nevertheless. I used to use the word formless not for that which lacked form but for that which had a form such that, if it had appeared, my mind would have experienced revulsion from its extraordinary and bizarre shape, and my human weakness would have been plunged into confusion. ... [T]he mutability of changeable things is itself capable of receiving all forms into which mutable things can be changed. But what is this mutabililty? Surely not mind? Surely not body? Surely not the appearances of mind and body? If one could speak of 'a nothing something' or 'a being which is non-being', that is what I would say.[14]

The relative formlessness of Raleigh's confessional poem, paradoxically, is an essential of its form – its water-like, or Walter-like, changeability.

At least once in Raleigh's prolonged yet plotless debate with his fate the aggrieved party seems to say that Elizabeth's or Cynthia's own high noon is also over, and that it is mainly the force of her devotee's imagination and memory that is now keeping her bright (*OC* 104–17). Comparably, the mortal moon of Edmund Spenser's *Two Cantos of Mutabilitie* suffers eclipse in the shadow of the Titaness of Change. In Spenser's subplot Raleigh-as-Molanna, disgraced by the Queen-as-Cynthia, forms a mirror-

---

14 Augustine, *Confessions* XII, vi(6), trans. Henry Chadwick (Oxford World Classics, 1991), 248–9.

like parallel with Spenser-as-Faunus scapegoated by the same unapproachable goddess who is otherwise so much the object of the author of *The Faerie Queene*'s worship and purposes. The Mutabilitie Cantos, we are told, might logically have found their place in a Legend of Constancy. It seems possible that the piece's editorial apparatus was ghost-written by Spenser himself. Elizabeth had made her constancy legendary in her motto *semper eadem*, 'always the same'. The words 'to live with eternitie of her fame' (along with 'and of Virginia' – Raleigh's Virginia) were added to Spenser's Dedication of his magnum opus in 1596, at the front (when the Letter to Raleigh was subtracted, from the back). The word Eternitie appears in the last two, supplemental stanzas to the Two Cantos, thus book-ending the whole 1612 *Works* version of *The Faerie Queene* with both this key word and Elizabeth's own name – as finally encrypted in 'Sabbaoth God'. For Time, that takes survey of all the world, must have a stop – or Sabbath – and so must the Queen's own earthly life.

Raleigh's *Ocean to Cynthia* also works the changes on the conceit of Elizabeth's stedfastness and sempiternity:

> A beauty that can easily deceive
> Th'arrest of years, and creeping age outclimb,
>
> A spring of beauties which time ripeth not,
> Time that but works on frail mortality, ...
>
> A vestal fire that burns but never wasteth,
> The loseth nought by giving light to all,
> That endless shines each where, and endless lasteth, ...
> Blossoms ... that can nor [f]ade nor fall.
>
> (*OC* 183–92)[15]

Ostensibly compliments, these lines might also be read subversively, as a slightly menacing warning about a mere mortal's self-deceiving pretentions to immortality. The moon may prove, so to speak, sublunary. *Things* – given whatsoever they may have been and yet may be – *change*.

The form of *The Ocean to Cynthia* is technically a fraction, if practically a fragment. Its putative enumeration may make it the eleventh

---

15 This passage from *The Ocean to Cynthia* is evidence for the unborn sonnet series hypothesized below, when its burden equated with Raleigh's sonnet-like eighteen-line poem, 'Praisde be Dianas faire and harmles light', where Diana's hymnist says, in his fourth quatrain, 'Time weares hir not, she doth his chariot guide, / Mortalitie below hir orbe is plaste, / By hir the vertue of the starrs downe slide / In hir is vertues perfect image cast' (ll. 13–16): Latham, ed., *Poems*, 11. (With this passage we may compare Jove's attempt to draw the line between temporal change and sempiternal realms untouched by and beyond it, in the Mutabilitie Cantos, at VII.vii.48: 'who is it ... That *Time* himselfe doth moue ... Is not that namely wee / Which poure that vertue from our heauenly cell ...?')

and unfinished twelfth book of an otherwise mainly unwritten poem, as Spenser's Mutabilitie Cantos are the putative sixth and seventh cantos of an otherwise unwritten book of twelve cantos.[16] That underrepresented book would have also been part of a further instalment of a projected twelve book poem. Raleigh says he has wasted twelve years waging war for the Queen (*OC* 120–1), and so it is logical to suppose that each book of his projected poem would have corresponded to one of those glorious years, and that the eleventh book records the poet's eleventh-hour crisis. The twelfth book would have celebrated his and the Queen's reconciliation, just as Spenser's twelfth book would have celebrated the virtual marriage of Arthur and Gloriana.

In both the case of Spenser's poem and Raleigh's we are not talking about the work we have got, of course, yet a work that we nonetheless seem invited to construct, or discern on the receding horizon of the poet's unfulfilled yet plausible intentions. A twelve-book poem would have some claims to being an epic, but the poem we possess is a protracted lyric complaint, of the epyllion kind, featuring a lover alone with his mental image of a remote and impossible she, and compelled by 'Such heat in ice, such fire in frost' (69) as remain in the typical Petrarchan mistress's physical absence. Although the book we have is not a group of such poems, its last fourteen lines are a valedictory readily isolated as a terminal sonnet for a series.

But otherwise the sheer mindless iteration of the waves of the Atlantic seems to have penetrated to Raleigh's rhetoric – the verses are half-written and twice-written all at once: perpetually undoing their burden by ceaselessly redoing its clinches, less a product (like a sonnet) and more a process (like a catalogue), a monotonous litany of woes that are all the same woe, however variously rehearsed. There is much inspired anaphora –

---

[16] Latham discusses the possibility that the numbers may read 21 and 22, and Jerry Leath Mills, in 'Sir Walter Ralegh', in *Concise Dictionary of British Literary Biography, Vol. 1, Writers of the Millde Ages & Renaissance Before 1660*, ed. Matthew J. Druccoli and Richard Layman (Detroit: Gale Research, 1992), 235–50, maintains that 'in 1985 Stacy M. Clanton confirmed in a detailed paleographic study of the manuscript (which is in Ralegh's own hand) the readings '21st' and '22nd'. ... Also to the point is that the '22nd Book' breaks off in the middle of its twenty-second line' (244–5). Mills argues for a 'topomorphic' symmetry of imagery and diction in the '21st Book'. For what it is worth, we note that the first of the two critical appearances of Belphoebe's name occurs midway in the poem's 521½ lines (at *OC* 271; the subsequent instance is at *OC* 327). Latham, *Poems*, 'Introduction', xxxii, cites Buchan's theory that Raleigh planned a great work in twelve books and started with the last two. This leaves out the evidence (in both *FQ* III.proem.4 and the dedicatory sonnet to Raleigh) that such a project was being advanced before the events that were to give rise to the late-numbered books we now have. Both Raleigh–Timias and Spenser–Colin carve Belphoebe–Cynthia on trees (*Colin Clout* 628–47).

> But in my minde so is her love inclosde
> And is thereof not only the beste parte
> But into it the essence is disposde ...
> Oh love (the more my wo) to it thow art
>
> Yeven as the moysture in each plant that growes,
> Yeven as the soonn vnto the frosen grovnd,
> Yeven as the sweetness, to th' incarnate rose,
> Yeven as the Centre in each perfait rovnde,
>
> As water to the fyshe, to men as ayre,
> As heat to fier, as light vnto the soone.
>
> (*OC* 426–35)[17]

– but the result is self-reproducing in a way that can easily seem tedious and automatic. The complainer's self-immersion is so self-destructive that he is virtually drowning himself within himself – or swamping his case within his copious vein of self-pity. Perhaps there is a precedent in the length of Job's complaint – or in its criminal's indictment: 'He is swift as the waters ... Drought and heat consume the snow waters: so doth the grave those which have sinned' (AV 24:18–19).

An ocean never drowns itself, of course. But much churning does not necessarily yield sweet butter – as opposed to a salty froth. Passionately spinning various rhetorical wheels, Raleigh's plaint is not apparently getting anywhere – and has little prospect of doing so beyond its present limits. And yet the poem's canvas of Raleigh's life goes so far as to prescribe (accurately enough) his future retirement package: 'Wee should beginn by such a parting light / To write the story of all ages past / And end the same before th' aprochinge night' (101–2). In prison during most of his life in the reign of James I – for twelve years – Raleigh took at least half his own earlier advice, and wrote the pentateuch of his unfinished *History of the World*, a book immensely popular for many decades after its author's beheading. Fear of hanging may have concentrated his mind in good ways – the book – but also bad: the Guiana project.

But what hidden merits in *The Eleventh Book of the Ocean to Cynthia* caused the Oxford editor Professor Emrys Jones to give nearly the largest single space in his anthology of the period's English verse to the whole text of a piece both so manifestly unfinished and so uncrementally redundant? Jones might invoke the golden opinion of C. S. Lewis that the

---

17 Raleigh's talent for 'Anaphora, or the figvre of report', is recognized by the example in George Puttenham's *Arte of English Poesie*, with its five iterations of 'In vayne': Latham *Poems*, 9.

silver poetry of Raleigh's composition achieves greatness without polish, and that its eloquence of expression transcends the unrelieved drabness of the speaker's subject and his unrelieved fixation on a subject's misery.[18] The poem offers prolific variations on a single morose but virtuoso string, and presumably Professor Jones put in all of its so-called Book Eleven in *The Oxford Book of Sixteenth Century Verse* because it was all or nothing – the anthologist was confronted with a piece quite undifferentiated and unsegmented beyond its quatrains (with a few triads and quinzains). The accumulation of stanzas does not really amount to a torso of a poem, only an invertebrate pile, with water and aridity, deluge and dessication, on every page. Having nowhere to go, the poem keeps starting over, rebeginning its search for a non-existent exit from its maudlin premise: an apparent denial but real conviction that endlessly crying over spilt milk can do the disgraced devotee some kind of good. But 'To taste the sea', it is said, 'all you need is one gulp'.[19]

Over its considerable, prolonged course Raleigh's lament becomes its own gathering of rhetorical relics, a legacy ending up among the Cecil Papers in the Hatfield House archive, where much later times (c. 1868?) discovered the lengthy, pre-Schlegelean poetic 'fragments' that centuries before a tempest-tost Raleigh had shored against his personal ruin. But despite our problems with its form, we can still ask, What kind of literary thing is *Ocean*'s putative eleventh book? A successful determining of its kind and genre might help us cope with the work's formlessness or sprawl, the difficulty of length without appreciable turning-points to articulate it.

Although the poem is a testament and a confession, and offers a kind of witness, especially to Raleigh's regrets, it is preeminently a complaint. In itself, grief is inarticulate, and despite the presence of formal features like metre and rhyme, the Ocean's lament lacks that quasi-episodic, middle-level segmentation that might belong, for example, to a rueful sonnet sequence or series.[20] Although the despairing sentiment and its expression come in waves, or wave-like quatrains, and gatherings of quatrains, there is little anchorage of the utterance in aphoristic or sententious or deductive recapitulation (as in the concluding couplet of a sonnet), and

---

18 C. S. Lewis, *English Literature in the Sixteenth Century Excluding Drama* (London, Oxford, New York: Oxford University Press, 1954; rprnt 1973), 520.
19 From the dialogue in 'Old Swimmers', in Howard Norman's *Kiss in the Hotel Joseph Conrad and Other Stories* (London and Boston: Faber, 1989), 57–78: 77. The story involves a reunion of survivors of a terrible shipwreck ('Why did only one woman tell her story?' Jake said. 'There's a proverb,' Helen said. 'To taste the sea, all you need is one gulp.').
20 See note 15, above.

little of the *da capo* effect of a refrain or recurrence of a repeated formula to resolve lyric utterance upon an assertion of stasis or repletion or formal closure. An example of both missing features is Raleigh's sonnet 'Like truthless dreams', where the refrain of the three quatrains is 'Of which all past, the sorrow only stays', and the conclusive couplet is the viaticum-like 'Whom care forewarns, ere age and winter cold, / To haste me hence to find my fortune's fold'.[21] In other words, 'Provide, provide'. Such an insurance policy Raleigh seems to have intended to create by means of his estates in Ireland, or in his conveyance of Sherborne to his heirs and dependants. But the 'legacy' in *The Ocean to Cynthia*, unlike that of the Mutabilitie Cantos, is radically 'unperfite'.[22] It is a testament that might not hold up very well in a court adjudicating claims to an alienable estate. Does it belong to literature or history? Can it possibly re-secure Ocean's claims to Belphoebe's favours, or must it utterly despair of them?

If Raleigh's *Ocean* is all of an undifferentiated piece, an unsecured and blurted-out confession of regret, or unwilling self-recrimination, does it not differ in some essentials from the subtly variegated variations upon an objectified forlornness and forsakenness as effected by, say, Joachim Du Bellay's *Les Antiquities du Rome*, or his *Les Regrets*? Compare this from the latter sequence:

> Tu n'éprouves, Baïf, d'un maître rigoureux
> Le sévère sourcil: mais la douce rudesse
> D'une belle, courtoiseet gentille maitresse,
> Qui fait languir to coeur doucement langoureaux.
>
> Moi chétif, cependant, loin des yeux de moin prince,
> Je vieilis malhearueux en ètrange province,
> Fuyant le pauvreté: mais las ne fuyant pas

---

21 Quotations of Raleigh's poetry are from *The Poems of Sir Walter Ralegh*, ed. Agnes Latham (Cambridge, MA: Harvard University Press, 1962); 'Like truthless dreams', 12.
22 'Unperfite' is the editorial conclusion regarding the abbreviated canto to which the last two stanzas of Spenser's final piece are proposed to belong. But these two stanzas are in fact as perfect a supplement to the preceding two cantos as those two cantos are to *The Faerie Queene* itself. Given the analogy, those cantos themselves must needs be seen as replicating the greater poem's two instalments. The second of those instalments was published six years after the first (1590, 1596), and the Mutabilitie Cantos were published in 1609, six years after the death of Queen Elizabeth, otherwise the fairy Queen (as in the Letter to Raleigh and the Dedicatory Sonnet to Lord Hunsdon); she died six years after the year in which the Two Cantos may have been written (1597, 1603). Unlike Spenser, who predeceased the Queen by four years (1599), Raleigh still had a long time to live – and his career therefore had future instalments, though apparently he would write little more datable poetry after *The Ocean to Cynthia*, that is, when there was no more Belphoebe.

> Les regrets, les ennuis, le travail et la peiene
> Le tardif repentir d'une espérence vaine,
> E l'importune souci, qui me suit pas à pas.
>
> *(Les Regrets* 24)[23]

> You do not taste, Baif, a master's rigour,
> or that severe look: but the sweet gaze
> of a beautiful, courteous, and gentle mistress,
> who makes one's heart languish in sweet langour.
>
> Myself, ragged, meanwhile, far from the eyes of my prince,
> am grown old, unhappy in an alien location,
> fleeing poverty, but not fleeing
>
> regrets, longeurs, toil, and the pain
> of late repentance of a vain hope,
> and importunate care that follows me step by step.

Or again, with Raleigh-like anaphora,

> Et vu tant de regrets desqquels je me lamente,
> Th t'ébahis souvent commoent chanter je puis.
>
> Je ne chante, Magny, je pleure mes ennuis,
> Or, pour le dire mieux. en pleurant je les chante,
> Si bien qu'en les chantant, souvent je les enchante:
> Violà pourquoi, Magny, je chante jours et nuits.
>
> Ainsi chante l'ouvrier en faisant son ourrage,
> Ainsi le labourerur faistant son labourage,
> Ainsi le pèlerin regrettant sa maison,
>
> Ainsi l'aventureir en songeant à sa dame,
> Ainsi le marinier en tirant à la rame,
> Ainsi le prisonnier maudissant sa prison.
>
> *(Les Regrets* 12)[24]

> And seeing how great the regrets of which I beweep myself,
> You may then wonder even how I sing.
>
> I do not sing, Magny, I weep my melancholy sufferings,
> Or, to put it better, in weeping I sing them,
> If that's singing them well, I sing them often:
> Behold, Magny, how I sing days and nights.

---

23 French text taken from Joachim Du Bellay, *The Regrets: A Bilingual Edition*, tr. David R. Slavitt (Evanston, IL: Northwestern University Press, 2004), 62.
24 Ibid., p. 38.

So sings the worker while doing his work,
So the labourer doing his labour,
So the pilgrim regretting his house,

So the adventurer dreaming on his woman,
So the mariner dragging on his oar,
So the prisoner cursing his prison.

Indeed, when the public ruins of Rome in Du Bellay's *Les Antiquities* are put beside his personal and private regrets, ruination, and 'late repentence' (*Le tardif repentir* (*Regrets* 24)) in his *Regrets*, the former provide the latter with a kind of objective correlative. Somewhat comparably, perhaps, in the volume of Spenser's *Complaints* the author's own grievances and anxieties are contextualized by his translation of the parallel utterance from Du Bellay and Petrarch to which the poet's own woes are tethered (especially those in *The Teares of the Muses*). But in Raleigh's case such a correlative is supplied only by the complementary historical documents and reports and correspondence which are putatively marginalized by, or out of communication with, the discourse of the plaintiff's verse – as if they were inadmissable. The plaintiff would adduce the existence of much evidence in his behalf, and yet he as regularly undercuts it, knowing he lacks a leg to stand on. He is on his knees, and has no friend in court: no Baif or Magny. And no generic guidelines or touchstones, like visions and ruins literature.

Raleigh reflects that 'The Images, and formes of worlds past' are 'All slaues to age, and vassalls vnto tyme / Of which repentance writes the tragedye' (*OC* 174, 179–80). Perhaps as a result, his imagery for a poem ruing his loss of greatness is itself something of a ruin: vague, anamorphic, mercurial, fleeting, unhistoricised, and without the development of much internal context. If he is one of Hardy's 'satires of circumstance', his poem nonetheless suppresses the circumstances themselves as inenarrable. *The Ocean* and *Cynthia* are mainly the counters found in the title and supply only intermittent referents for the text: they are hardly objectively realized entities there, unlike, say, the lover and his mistress in Wyatt's 'They flee from me', or the articulate Titaness in Spenser's Mutabilitie Cantos. Though his discourse is sweeping, Raleigh does not use his occasion to objectify or memorialize or create perspective with different scenes or personae or voices or an evolving dramatic scenario. The drama is all in the intersubjectivity of the abject victim and his alienated political mistress; 'Cynthia', however, has nothing to say herself. In the course of his own stream of mental images for an alternately transcendent and catastrophic relation he almost seems to recognize and repine at his becoming Rouse's compulsive bore, full of a sound and fury that is as meaningless and ineffective as its strutting player's grief is oceanic and unbridled. A dream of a nearly unconditional acceptance keeps foundering on an occasion for a drastic self-scrutiny. Imprisonment has given his pride and his bravado the lie – would he could give it back!

All roads had led the francophilic Du Bellay to a papal Rome he didn't want to be stuck in. The results or remains of his sojourn are a series of published verses, which regularly capture his dark moods in a sonnet form by nature more specific than Raleigh's effluent run of quatrains. Raleigh's relatively infrequent enjambment often takes place not between lines but between quatrains, which therefore can seem themselves as unfinished as the whole poem itself does. Raleigh's outpouring of a boundless grief appears to overflow his poem's formal boundaries in a great stream. Nonetheless, its expression also conforms to a formal and somewhat strict prosodic decorum that regularly end-stops the sense with the line. Raleigh quotes his afore-cited sonnet as prophetic: 'Of all which past the sorrow only stayes. / / So wrate I once, and my mishapp fortolde' (*OC* 123–4), and his quatrains often form neat, fixed and appropriate units, and thus a number of them (seemingly in imitation of Du Bellay's style) also begin each line with the same letter, or part of speech, or the same word, to insist on the four-line parcelling and partitioning of the decasyllabic line-units (where a complete unit of sense is typically contained by a given line). The anaphora, combined with the sense frequently spilling out of any given quatrain, makes for the poem's spate-like profluence, and yet a wave-like regularity: unremitting and steadily recurring undulations of pain, grief, regret, and recrimination. Raleigh has fallen upon the thorns of life, and he is poured out like water. Thus, with the pretence to formal features, and the flouting of their boundaries, Raleigh's poem effectively reveals the raveled sleeve of care at its most unravelled. And like its unpardonable offender, it exhibits sobriety and some larger orderliness or capacity for self-discipline only in ruins.

It is nearly a relief when the poet confesses that age has broken the false hope of his shepherd's staff, and that despair has threatened to throw the poet's pipe into the fire (*OC* 504–7). 'Do then by Diinge' – the potential suicide advises himself – 'what life cannot doo' (*OC* 496). As for life, he expiringly says. 'To God I leue it, who first gave it me, / And I her gave, and she returnd agayne, / As it was herrs' (517–19). Raleigh's stymied persona Timias is similarly self-addressed in Spenser: 'Thy life she gaue, thy life she doth deserue: / Dye rather, dye, then euer from her seruice swerue' (*FQ* III.v.45). Keeping faith with the Queen had meant, in practice, mortifying eros while eroticizing duty, and it left one in the 'malingering, unappeasable desiderium' of a Timias.

II. Spenser's Timias and Marinell as allegories of Raleigh

Lachrymous to a fare-thee-well, Raleigh's maudlin piece is perhaps histrionic in the literary way of the overwrought utterance of dramatis personae inside of fictions and scripts.[25] The coincidence of the histronic with the historic – that is, with the documented historical particulars – suggests not only that the courtier wore his heart on his sleeve but that his histrionic self could often be the real self of a man as performance-possessed as Raleigh apparently was.[26] He threw his whole person into a part that sometimes he showed little desire or capacity to disengage himself from, when the play was over. He would not act a part he did not also live – to the hilt: as if an extreme self-preoccupation had become an inescapable or unwavering delusion as to who he was and /or must be. Raleigh devoted Raleigh to acting a singular role, whether it took a literary form in private or a self-staging form in public. The demonstrable congruence between his poem and contemporary biographical events implies that the histrionic heart of the prisoner in the Tower and the self-dramatizing ego of 'Ocean' are wellnigh indistinguishable. The author writing in the closet and the individual making a spectacle of himself while in custody – these were the same rather extravagant personage controlling – or being controlled by – a very perfervid playbook. He was who he was committed to being: the superior courtier and adventurer, the superior soldier and sailor, the superior mind and the honour-winner, always *par excellence*. A squire, yes, but what a squire! – the only one who was truly company fit for royalty, and who dared promise Elizabeth, in his *Discovery of Guiana*,

---

25 For a late and desperate example of Raleigh as melodramatic actor, feigning madness like David among the Philistines, see Robert Lacey, *Sir Walter Ralegh* (New York: Athenaeum, 1973), 382, and Norman Lloyd Williams, *Sir Walter Raleigh* (Baltimore: Penguin Books, 1962), 258-60, quoting the government's post-execution *Declaration of the Demeanour and Carriage of Sir Walter Raleigh*.

26 The links between Raleigh's long poem, and his performance as reported in the other documents pertaining to his confinement, is impressive. And yet the poem is not so tied to the historical moment or event as to have prevented Raleigh from preserving it long enough to levy, from the two opening stanzas of its fragmentary Book Twelve, lines for his subsequent 'Conjectural First Draft of the Petition to Queen Anne' (Latham, *Poems*, 68-9), the Queen whose royal husband James reigned in England after Raleigh's 'Cynthia' was quite dead. He may have thought he could enter the same river twice, or the same prison, and repeat his luck of deliverance from bonds. But the borrowed stanzas in the draft are dropped from the petition proper, which unsuccessfully urges the same case, but does so less eloquently.

'a better Indies for your majesty than the King of Spain hath'. In terms of Shakespeare's *Midsummer Night's Dream*, only a Raleigh could be the fairy Queen's Indian boy.[27]

Spenserians reading Raleigh's poem will want to know how this unrepentant self-dramatizer *and his poem* got entered into the allegorical romance epic by the notable contemporary who was Sir Walter's literary protégé. For Raleigh's piece inevitably attaches itself to *The Faerie Queene*, with Raleigh as Belphoebe's lover himself appearing in his fellow poet's opus in the very penetrable veil of Arthur's squire Timias: in the Legend of Chastity. Being Spenser's friend, the troubled lover reappears in the Legend of Friendship. He is the servant of Arthur, or the British ideal; the inner-Arthur is the anima-figure Desire-of-Praise – and her hellish counterpart is Philotime, an Aristotelian-Scholastic term for ambitious desire or love of acquiring honours.[28] Besides his knighthood, '[a]mong offices and titles Ralegh held were these: Captain of the Guard, Lord Warden of the Stanneries, Lord Lieutenant of Cornwall, Vice-Admiral of Devon and Cornwall, Ranger of Gillingham Forest, Captain of Portland Castle, and Governor of the Island of Jersey'.[29] Raleigh inscribed on a window 'Fain would I climb, yet fear I to fall', and Elizabeth wrote back, 'If thy heart fail thee, climb not at all'; but she should have written, 'learn to climb by learning to crawl'. For where Timias painfully wallows in Book III, in Book IV he madly grovels: 'the ground he kist' (IV.vii.46). But his titles, emoluments, monopolies, and grants were probably worth it.

The other figure recognizably alluding to Raleigh in Spenser's oeuvre about the time Raleigh wrote his poem is the self-identifying 'shephearde of the Ocean by name' in *Colin Clouts Come Home Againe* (66), where this pastoralist's vexed relations to Cynthia (in place of Belphoebe) are put near the poem's beginning, and where Raleigh also appears, cheek by jowl, as the wantonly amorous Irish river Bregog. But in *The Faerie Queene* itself, the shepherd of the ocean is the sea-god Proteus, and he

---

27 For a discussion of the reading of Shakespeare's play as an Elizabethan allegory of erotic and marital politics, see, inter alia, Nohrnberg, 'Alençon's Dream / Dido's Tomb: Some Shakespearean Music and a Spenserian Muse': *Spenser Studies*, XXII (2007), gen. ed. William A. Oram, Anne Lake Prescott, and Thomas P. Roche, Jr, guest ed. David Galbraith and Theresa M. Krier (New York: AMS Press, 2007), 73–102.
28 Raleigh's 'Giue me my Scallop shell of quiet' imagines a final pilgrimage attaining to 'heauens Bribeles bribeless hall, / Where no corrupted voyces brall; / No Conscience molten into gold; / Nor forg'd accusers bought and sold; / No cause deferd, nor vaine spent Iorney, / For there Christ is the Kings Atturney: / Who pleades for all without degrees, / And he hath Angells, but no fees'. (Ll. 35–42, Latham, *Poems*, 50–1.)
29 This convenient listing is taken from George Garrett, *Death of the Fox* (1971; rprnt New York: Quill / Wm Morrow, no date), 345.

turns out to be a kind of pirate, and so a distant relative of the pirates found in the old Greek prose romances, as well as the Proteus who retains the Homeric Helen and sends her simulacrum to Troy. Although this marine shepherd might seem unrelated to Raleigh, his captive Florimell will become engaged to marry the somewhat unmarriagable bachelor Marinell, who may be a persona for Raleigh in his own right. Marinell controls a no-man's-land between land and sea. Despite the 'will not marry' in his name, Marinell does eventually marry, and so did Raleigh. But he marries only when his bride-to-be has been discovered with Proteus, and freed from the submarine lair where the piratical old lecher has imprisoned her. Raleigh's 'Nature who washt her hands in milk / And had forgot to dry them', might compare with Florimell's departure from the land and the creation of her double while she is at sea: Spenser's Nature chilled her hands in snow, but then remembered to rinse them – in the thaw beginning from the marriage of the Thames and Medway, and culminating in the False Florimell's subsequent dissolution.[30]

In *Colin Clouts Come Home Againe*, the narrator's report of a 'gentle bony lasse' (172) closes the story of Raleigh's marriage (the story of Bregog and Mulla) by asserting the success of the Shepherd of the Ocean's appeal to '*Cynthia* the Ladie of the sea' (166) for forgiveness. This resolution is also found in *Faerie Queene* IV, and likewise in *Colin Clout*:

> His song was all a lamentable lay,
> Of great vnkindesse, and of vsage hard,
> Of *Cynthia* the Ladie of the sea,
> Which from her presence faultlesse him debard.
> And euer and anon with singults rife,
> He cryed out, to make vndersong
> Ah my loues Queene, and goddesse of my life,
> Who shall me pittie, when thou doest me wrong?
> (*CCCHA* 164–71)

The name of the lass confirming the story of the Shepherd of the Ocean's reconciliation with Cynthia is 'Marin', and in this insider we might recognize Mrs Raleigh herself, though she is not actually said to be the inamorata of the Shepherd's, who is otherwise missing from the narrative.

Raleigh's plaintive métier comes up in cantos iv and v of *The Faerie Queene*. Marinell in canto iv and Timias in canto v are potentially two

---

30 The connecting of Raleigh's lyric with the beauties of the two Florimells I owe to a grateful conversation with Prof. David Lee Miller. (The False Florimell is the protégée of a witch, and historically witches are averse to water: L. Frank Baum's Wicked Witch of the West, in *The Wizard of Oz*, is armed with an umbrella; she is annihilated when water is thrown on her.)

aspects of Raleigh, the Elizabethan seaman and arriviste courtier, respectively, because they are metonymically connected, by the contiguity of the two cantos in which they appear, and metaphorically connected, by suffering the malingering and potentially mortal wounds that are wasting them away by the end of each of their respective episodes.[31] And, I shall argue, because of their marital or sexual politics.

In the first case Raleigh as Marinell with his Rich Strond could be, allegorically speaking, the proud mariner and privateer whose prizes brought into British ports were regularly levied for the Crown's cut of the booty from captured Spanish ships.[32] In the second case Raleigh as Timias is the courtier who introduced tobacco, or at least pipe-smoking, from the other side of the Atlantic to the court, along with tobacco's supposedly medicinal properties. (The pipe-smoking Harriot died of cancer of the mouth.)

The Queen's admirer yearned to be of further use to her, after the dangers he had been exposed to in her service in Ireland. As Marinell he is swept off his feet by a type of this queen – the chaste lady-knight Britomart – and he is sorely wounded. Raleigh was eventually shipwrecked, so to speak, on the continence of the Queen, that is, by his own dereliction from maintaining an endless and sterile flirtation with an ageing spinster whose beauty was a kind of extended contrivance of couture, makeup, jewellery, and flattering poetical comparisons. She was twice Raleigh's age when she met him; Puttenham says Raleigh's love-poetry was 'loftie, insolent and passionate', which sounds much like the head-

---

31 'They say that Adonis was killed during the winter, because the growth of plants and many other things comes to a halt during this period. For when the rays of the sun are faint, its strength is weakened, and every process is weakened by the cold' – so Natale Conti, *Mythologiae* IV.13, 'On Venus', Mulryan-Brown trans., 1:330. Here Conti adds: 'One other tale they told was that during his sacrifices the Adonis river used to flow with blood as it made its way down from Mount Libanus'. This bloody river entrails the tapestry of Adonis's demise in the first canto of Spenser's Legend of Chastity, and announces the somewhat venerean debilitation of Marinell and Timias, which is deeded over to them from their ennervate predecessors in the Legend of Temperance: the wasted Mordant, dissolute Cymochles, and slumbrous Verdant.

32 As suggested in Nohrnberg, *The Analogy of 'The Faerie Queene'* (Princeton, NJ: Princeton University Press, 1976), 379, fn 183: 'Britomart admires the booty from the sea, but passes on, 'for all was in her powre' (*FQ* III.iv.180). The Queen, on the contrary, often greeted the ships of her privateers at the docks in person, to exact the Crown's cut on the spot'. For discussion, see Walter S. H. Lim, *The Arts of Empire: The Poetics of Colonialism from Ralegh to Milton* (Newark, NJ: University of Delaware Press, 1998), 154–6. See also *Analogy*, 450, for a more erotic reading of Marinell's spill as the seaman's semen. Perhaps this reading can be supported by equating Marinell, as the sacrificial ox of *FQ* III.iv.17, with the comparable ox depicted in the notorious woodcut for the festival of Priapus in the *Hypnerotomachia*.

strong Raleigh's *personalilty*. But his lament over his dangers abroad sounds like it could belong to Marinell, when he 'writes in the dust, as one that could no more', that he has been 'Alone, forsaken, friendless, on the shore, / With many wounds, with death's cold pangs embraced … Whom love, and time, and fortune, had defaced' (*OC* 91, 89–90). 'On the shore', or on the rocks.

As the Timias who has sustained an almost entirely comparable Adonis-wound, from a boar-spear, Raleigh is ministered to by Elizabeth as his nurse: Belphoebe with weaponry in one hand, and cordials on the other. (For Belphoebe's cult, see Diana's original one in Horace, *Carm.* III.xxii.5–8: 'Thine be the pine that overhangs my dwelling, that gladly through the passing years I may offer to it the blood of a boar practicing its first sidelong thrusts'.)[33] Belphoebe, of course, carries a boar-spear, which is to say, she is the enemy of the lust that wounds the venturesome Timias in the way that the ebony spear of the chaste but maritally inclined Britomart floors the devout bachelor Marinell (whose rich and bestrewn strand in conjunction with his celibacy may convict him of an Onan-like avarice of wasted seed). For Belphoebe was hunting the boar when she came upon the boorish and lecherous coward Braggadocchio, whose advances she warded off with her threatening boar-spear, and Britomart is bent on marriage when she topples Marinell on his treasure-accumulating beach; and Belphoebe is bent on prey when she comes upon Timias.[34]

In Raleigh's poem 'Wrong not, dear Empress of my heart', 'Raleigh's pose was that of the silent lover'.[35] 'I rather choose to want relief / Than venture the revealing; / Where glory recommends the grief, / Despair distrusts the healing.' His *silence was a suitor*. 'He smartest most that hides his smart / And sues for no compassion.'[36] This is exactly the script for Timias's conduct in Spenser's first episode of Timias with Belphoebe. Again, the two poets were in a tale.[37] Indeed, Raleigh's *Ocean* might as well be quoting its author's previous portrait in Spenser's stricken Timias:

---

33 As cited in Conti, *Mythologiae* III.18, 'On Diana', in Mulryan-Brown trans., 1:222.
34 Timias's original's bravado (and thus Raleigh's) may be shadowed by that of Braggadocchio, since the braggart-knight has Trompart for a squire, and Timias, as Arthur's squire, announces his master's approach by sounding the trumpet (at *FQ* I.viii.3–4).
35 Williams, *Sir Walter Raleigh*, 82.
36 'Sir Walter Ralegh to the Queen', in Latham, *Poems*, 18–19.
37 Another poet, Sidney, the same age as Raleigh, died of a thigh-wound sustained in battle, it is said, yet died 'while honourably serving his wife': so Lloyd Williams, *Sir Walter Raleigh* (Baltimore: Penguin Books, 1965), 94. In his elegy for Sidney, Raleigh, with or without irony, calls him 'Petrarch of our time' (line 58); Latham, *Poems*, 'An Epitaph … vpon … Sidney', 5–7: 7.

> ... all liueless, and all healpless bounde
> My fayntinge spirritts sunck, and hart apalde,
> My ioyes and hopes lay bleedinge on the grovnd
>
> (*OC* 161–3)

The vulnerability and the wordplay seem to derive from Spenser on Timias' supposed cure by Belphoebe: e.g., 'O foolish Physick [...] That heales vp one and makes another wound ... as his wound did ... grow hole, / So still his heart woxe sore, and health decayd' (*FQ* III.v.42–3).

The injured Timias, as a bleeding (and emotionally unwholesome) Adonis – but also as a forester (as Raleigh titularly was) – must needs compare with the injured Marinell, a marine Adonis, but also a coastal denizen (as Raleigh was), if only because of the common language Spenser employs for their respective demises. Belphoebe, who cares for Timias, is always found outdoors, in the woodland; Cymoent (or Cymodoce), Marinell's mother, is never found on land, only in the sea. Diana is mainly a forester, like Belphoebe; but, according to Natale Conti, she 'is even supposed to be the patroness of fishermen'.[38] These two identities for the Dianaesque caretakers of the Spenserian Adonis-figures are found in adjacent paragraphs in Conti, where the huntress and the marinized goddess share in the story of Britomartis:

> The ancients offered the following rationale for their belief that Diana controlled hunting. There was once a Nymph named Britomartis (or, as some would have it Bretimartys), who got caught in some nets while she was hunting: she couldn't escape from the nets, especially since a wild animal was about to attack her. So she promised to build a temple to Diana if she escaped unscathed. When she built the temple she dedicated it to Diana Dictynna, named for those hunting nets.
>
> Some say that Diana really cared for Britomartis, ... because the girl was an avid hunter. Thus when Britomartis was running away from the amorous Minos, she threw herself into the sea (into the nets lowered into the sea waters to catch fish), and Diana welcomed her into the company of the gods. (*Mythologiae* III.18, 'On Diana', Mulryan-Brown trans., 1:220)

The piscatorial and predatory motifs Spenser's readers will recognize: from the story of Florimell's escape from a hyena-like monster of lust into her entanglement on the high seas.[39]

---

38 *Mythologiae* III.18, 'On Diana', Mulrayan-Brown trans., 1:221.
39 Florimell is one third of the triadic unfolding of the endangered virtue of chastity as patronized by Britomart and as found in the celibacy of Belphoebe, the beauty of Florimell, and the loveliness of Amoret: see *Analogy*, 461–70.

Florimell's garments are covered with fish-scales from the amorous 'fishers filthy nest', namely his boat, in which this damsel in distress is caught like his prey (III.viii.26, 35). Thus at one end of the story Timias is ambushed and wounded by an arrow shot by the kin of 'that foster fowle' (III.v.13) after pursuing this pursuer of Florimell in hopes of avenging her shame at the hands of this same 'griesly Foster … breathing out beastly lust her to defile' (III.i.16). At the other end of the story Timias wounds the Amoret whom he is attempting to rescue from shameful usage or defilement by Lust. If Timias and then Amoret are vulnerable on the same account, i.e., the 'singults rife' (*Colin Clout* 169) of Sir Walter and Lady Elizabeth Raleigh, then Raleigh-as-Timias keeps turning into his own worst enemy: Lust uses Amoret as his shield, to defend *himself.*

In the aftermath, the allusion to the susceptible Sir Wa'ter is extended in the figure of the exiled and ascetic Timias. An anonymous insider reported the fall of the Queen's favourite from grace. This informant's letter refers to Raleigh's imprisonment in the tower eloquently, Sir Walter 'dwelling, like hermit poor in pensive place, where he may spend his endless days in doubt'. In Book IV the rusticated and quasi-monasticized Timias dwells in a cabin that makes the unwitting Arthur think 'therein some holy Hermit lay'(IV.vii.42). Indeed, these indications are straight out of one of Raleigh's two relevant poems in *The Phoenix Nest* of 1593 ('Like to a Hermite poor'), and they show how encoded poetry was with the careerist and sexual politics of the courtiers who pursued it.[40]

In the first instalment of *The Faerie Queene*, the prelapsarian Timias beheads the third of the lustful foresters at the ford, and 'The carkas with the streame was carried downe, / But th'head fell backeward on the Continent' (III.v.25). The foresters had been pursuing Florimell, who later in her flight from bestial lust loses her cestus, just before she is carried off – Europa-like – to sea. Since no lady can wear the charm, 'Vnlesse that she were continent and chast' (V.iii.28), it's as if Florimell were abandoning continence and the Continent both together. When the overprotective mother of the unmarrying and celibate but nonetheless stricken Marinell incontinently abandons herself to grief, 'She threw her selfe downe on the Continent' (III.iv.34). (Cf. II.vi.1, 'A Harder lesson, to learne Continence / In ioyous pleasure, then in grieuous paine.') The anonymous letter-writer whom we have already quoted reports, by implication, the impregnation of Miss Throckmorton and the disgrace of the discoverer of New Guinea as 'this discovery of the discoverer … not indeed of a new continent, but

---

40 The other poem is 'Like truthles dreames' (Latham, *Poems*, 12: this is the sonnet self-cited in *The Ocean to Cynthia* at line 123).

of a new incontinent'.⁴¹ The same pun seems implicit in the description of the tempestuous psyche of the love-lorn Britomart, who prays at the shore for a gentle gale from Neptune, she invoking him as 'The God of winds, that raignest in the sea, / That raignest also in the Continent' (III. iv.10). Could Spenser want his reader to consider Marinell the discover of new continents/incontinence?

Raleigh of course preferred to know himself as a soldier and a seafarer, a naval captain, but especially as a constant militant against the Continent, meaning against the King of Spain, not against female sexual continence. In his own words in court, defending his innocence of a plot to act with Spain against James I, 'I knew that six times we had repulsed [– the king of Spain's –] forces: thrice in Ireland, thrice at sea – once upon our own coast, twice upon his own. Thrice had I served against him myself at sea, wherein for my country's sake I had expended of my own property forty thousand marks'.⁴² He again refers to this expenditure in his subsequent self-defence, fifteen years later.⁴³ Notwithstanding the 'Rich *strond*' (III.iv.20) and lucrative monopolies (wine, mining, the playing cards tax, a woollen broadcloth export licence, and one to export anything from Munster), all his operations and political reverses eventually left Raleigh the investor close to bankrupt, in the condition of Spenser's 'mariners and merchants' unloading their cargoes to lessen their 'disauenture, or misprize' in 'the quicksand of *Vnthriftyhed*' – or that of Spenser's 'vessels broke / And shiuered ships' on '*The Rock of* vile *Reproche*', prey to the 'birds of rauenous race' (II.xii.19, 7–8) that figure the usurious creditors who devour spendthrifts. Raleigh spent prodigiously, if not altogether ruinously, on his projects of development.

The distress of Marinell equates with that of Timias, if we go by Spenser's conceits for it. Both *pharmakons* fall into the hands of female caregivers armed with magical salves and pharmaceuticals – first nectar, then tobacco.⁴⁴ Found by nymphs, the 'luckless *Marinell*' 'Inglorious ...

---

41 Quoted in Lacey, *Sir Walter Ralegh*, 172.
42 'I knew that six times we had repulsed his forces', etc.: Williams, *Sir Walter Raleigh*, 193–4 with the Attorney General's remonstrance, 196.
43 See Williams, *Sir Walter Raleigh*, 263: Raleigh fifteen years later to James, before his last 'trial', on his harrying of the Spanish (with 'I have spent my poor estate ... I am the first that being free and able to enrich myself, yet hath embraced poverty and peril'). The references are to the friutless personal expense Raleigh incurred in respect of the Virginia Company.
44 Raleigh's identification with tobacco-smoking and its sponsorship was a strong one. For example, a government spy alleged that Marlowe said in Raleigh's company 'the sacraments would have been much better administered with a tobacco pipe': Williams, *Sir Walter Raleigh*, 132. For tobacco's literary-cultural fortunes in Renaissance England, see Jeffrey Knapp, *An Empire Nowhere: England, America, and Literature from 'Utopia' to*

lies in senselesse swond' (III.iv.34, 29), suffering from the '*deadly* wound' predicted by Proteus (28):'all in gore / And cruddy bloud en*wallowed* ... lying in *deadly swound*' (34). Britomart's '*wicked steele*' has skewered his body 'through his *left* side' bearing him 'the length of all her launce, / Till sadly soucing on the sandie shore, / He tumbled on an heape, and *wallowed in his gore*' (16). The diction is nearly identical for the hapless Timias, 'that woefull Squire' found by Belphoebe, when he 'With bloud deformed, lay in *deadly swownd*' (III.v.29): after 'he fell in *deadly swowne* ... he lay *wallowd* all *in his* own *gore*' (26), as a result of 'A cruell shaft, headed with deadly ill', of which the '*wicked steel* stayd not, till it did light / In his *left* thigh' (v.20).

This apparent synonymy makes us think there are ways of reading Marinell not only as Timias-like, but also Raleighesque – like the Raleigh who wrote, in *The Ocean to Cynthia*, 'My ioyes and hopes lay bleedinge on the grovnd' (163), despite 'The many deere achiuements that befell / / In thos pryme years and infancy of love' (168–9) – 'to seeke new worlds, for golde, for prayse, for glory' (61). But if the common element in the two Spenserian characters is their wallowing in their own gory predicament, then Spenser is ahead of the curve, since his first instalment necessarily predates Raleigh's *Ocean to Cynthia* and the reversal of fortune it regretfully commemorates. Nonetheless, canto iv of *Faerie Queene* III is thronged with Spenserian complainers, like Sansjoy at night in the same canto of Book I, 'awake ... in troublous fit' (I.iv.45): there is stormy Britomart in Petrarchan mode at the seashore, addressing her 'Huge sea of sorrow, and tempestuous grief' (III.iv.8); Marinell's mother and her nymphs, 'Lamenting his mishap and heauy plight' (44); and a sleepless Prince Arthur, accusing the felonious Night that has come between him and the pursuit of Florimell: 'disdain / Of his hard hap did vexe his noble breast ... Oft did he wish that Lady faire mote bee / His Faery Queene for whom he did complain: / Or that his Faerie Queene were such as shee: / And euer hastie Night he blamed bitterlie' (54). Arthur's dilemma seems especially Raleighesque, since Raleigh became involved with two women having the same name, but an analogous descrepancy ('y faire' v. 'Faery') was felt by many in Elizabeth's circle, who only found conjugality (or fair ladies) at the expense of the Queen's own favours and attractions.

One of Spenser's six Virgilian half-lines, where we feel invited to supply, though silently, the rest of the line, is the explanatory farewell of Marinell's frustrated mother to her son, when his life seems to have been cut short by the Fates:

'*The Tempest*' (Berkeley: University of California Press, 1988), chapter 4.

> But if the heauens did his dayes enuie,
> And my short blisse maligne, yet mote they well
> Thus much afford me, ere that he did die
> That the dim eyes of my deare *Marinell*
> I mote haue closed, and him bed farewell,
> Sith other offices for mother meet
> They would not graunt.
> Yet maulgre them farewell, my sweetest sweet;
> Farewell my sweetest sonne, sith we no more shall meet.
>
> (*FQ* III.iv.39)

The rhyme words and rhyme scheme ('they well / ... farewell /') might dictate yet another farewell, like the one that follows, 'Yet maulgre them farewell ...', which would then be repeated, and thus express the overall farewell as an even more lingering one. (Another possibility would be: 'Yet graunt [or else *Yet thee*] I bed [= bid] farewell', or 'Tho fates deny farewell'.)

The suppressed half-line of farewell, in Cymoent's virtual complaint, suggests she pauses to silently gather her resolution before daring – by communicating to her son – to resist the heavens' opposition to a fond and bereaved mother's wishes. The passage recalls the lament of Euryalus's mother in *Aeneid* IX, 483–92:

> Nor, when sent on such perilous errand, might thy poor mother bid thee a last farewell [*adfari extremum*]? Thou liest in a strange land, given as prey to the dogs and fowls of Latium! Nor have I, thy mother, led thee – thy corpse [*funera*] – forth to burial, or closed thine eyes, or bathed thy wounds, shrouding thee with the robe which, in haste, night and day, I toiled at for thy sake, beguiling with the loom the sorrows of age. Whither shall I follow? Or what land now holds thy mangled limbs and dismembered body? Is this all, my son, thou bringest back to me of thyself? Is it this I have followed by land and sea?[45]

'Euryali et Nisi' (*Aen.* IX.167: 'of Euryalus and Nisus') is the nearest of Virgil's own half-lines to this passage, the half-line itself fulfilling the poet's personal intentions as stated at IX.446–9: 'Happy pair! If aught my verse avail, no day shall ever blot you from the memory of time, so long as the house of Aeneas shall dwell on the Capitol's unshaken rock, and the Father of Rome hold sovereign sway'. If Marinell is one of the Spenser's legendary or mythopoetic allotropes for Raleigh, then the echo of a unique Virgilian determination to pay tribute to the embodiment of a memorable heroism may make the precedent that much more cogent.

---

45 Rushton Fairclough trans, Loeb *Virgil*, in 2 vols: 2:147.

Marinell's mother among her nymphs would be, in a sense, the Mother Superior that Queen Elizabeth seems to have become among her ladies in waiting and younger male courtiers. Like Marinell's mother, Elizabeth had her prejudice against her darlings' marriages.

III. Reading Spenser's 'Rich *strond*' as bordering on Raleigh's Tempestuous Atlantic and the World's Oceans, with a digression on Marlowe's World-Beater Tamburlaine

The earlier Raleigh was perhaps the single most prominently benefited courtier in Elizabeth's court, and likewise the swain most dependent on the royal favour, and most economically endangered by that favour's loss. Marinell is thus the first character we might point to as 'Raleigh on the rocks', even if Marinell's shipwreck is only potentially that of Raleigh, as his erotic vulnerability to Elizabeth – or her stand-in – is only analogically that of Timias to Belphoebe. For Marinell comes to grief on a continental shore, which does not so much mean Europe – or even the beauty of the Europa-like Florimell – as the unyielding continence of the lady-knight Britomart, a type of the girlhood and celibacy of the Queen, but also of the Queen's dominance on the chessboard of political power.

The Queen in Raleigh's poem has become the Cynthia who controls the seas and the weather, and so we may not be so surprised if her prisoner has also become a fleeting version of Marinell:

> So my forsaken hart, my withered mind,
> Widdow of all the ioyes it once possest,
> My hopes cleane out of sight, with forced wind
> To kyngdomes strange, to lands farr off addrest.
>
> Alone, forsaken, frindless onn the shore
> With many wounds, with deaths cold pangs inebrased
> Write in the dust as onn that could no more
> Whom love, and tyme, and fortune had defaced,
>
> Of things so great, so longe, so manefolde
> With meanes so weake, the sowle yeven then departing
> (*OC* 885–94)

And thus this forlorn soul, in his enfeebled state and in the twilight of his days, is attempting 'to write the story of all ages past […] before th' aprochinge night'. The proposed all-encompassing memoir seems to expand the writing of the poem we've got into a virtual *History of the World*.

'Enriched through the ouerthrow / And wrecks of many wretches', Marinell's holdings are the envy of others, 'which did weepe, / And often wail their wealth, which he from them did keepe' (*FQ* III.vi.22). Comparably, Raleigh monopolized the monopolies. Marinell's riches are the result of the nepotistic favouritism of his grandfather Nereus, whose daughter has persuaded her father 'T'endow her sonne with threasure and rich store', in order 'to aduance his name and glorie more' (III.iv.21). His resulting share of 'The spoyle of all the world', surpassing 'The wealth of th'East, and pompe of *Persian* kings, / Gold, amber, yvorie, perles, owches, rings, / And all that else was pretious and deare' (III.iv.23), sounds like bullion and other cargo from Spanish and Portuguese galleons and carricks, as well as the shadow of Raleigh's gifts from the British throne. It also sounds somewhat like the object of the ventures into Persia of the Muscovy Company. Or the enumeration in William Warner's *Albions England* (XII.70) of the goods travelling with his father (who had sailed with Chancellor) from Brazil and the Cape Verde islands: 'Gold, Ciuit, Muske, Graines, Pepper, Woad, and Iuorie [from] thence he brought'.

If Belphoebe is a goddess like the Artemis of *Iliad* V (445–8) who shelters and heals the wounded Aeneas, when he has been rescued by Apollo and taken to Pergamos ('There Artemis of the showering arrows and Leto within the great and secret chamber healed his wound and cared for him'), and if Timias figures Raleigh, then it seems pretty clear why Timias is medicated with tobacco otherwise from Raleigh's Virginia. But what contemporary reference is found in Marinell's being cured with Nepenthe? Of course Nepenthe is the drink of the gods or the immortals, and Marinell is near-fatally mortal. But how would that touch on Raleigh as a seaman? Why is this particular cure-all *derived* from the ocean? One might suggest that the nectar actually figures ambergris. Here it is in a recent description in *Scientific American*:

> For thousands of years this sea treasure has been highly prized. Middle Easterners historically powdered and ingested it to increase strength and virility, combat heart and brain ailments, or to spice food and drink. The Chinese called it 'dragon's spittle fragrance'. Ancient Egyptians burned it as incense. A British medical treatise from the Middle Ages informs readers that ambergris can banish headaches, colds and epilepsy, among other ailments. And the Portuguese took over the Maldives in the sixteenth century in part to gain access to the island's rich bounty of the redolent stuff.

'Strange but True: Whale Waste Is Extremely Valuable'.[46] Because of its sweet odor, ambergris, a treasured ingredient for perfume, had even seemed effective against the foul-smelling plague. Sir Thomas Elyot's *Castle of Health* cites it among 'comfortatives' for the overheated heart. Of course Nepenthe doesn't sound like ambergris, but its cognate ambrosia, which could also be described as 'good both for earthly med'cine, and heauenly food' (*FQ* III.iv.40), perhaps does. Moreover, the loosened hair of the goddess-like Belphoebe's foster mother Diana is 'with sweet *Ambrosia* all besprinkled light' (III.vi.18).

'Grey amber' might well be found among the salves of the sea gods' 'soueraine leach' Tryphon (III.iv.43). Tryphon cares for Marinell once he has been deposited in a bower resembling the 'hollow bosome' of the 'heaped waves' (III.iv.22) which produced the amber and the ivory bestrewing Marinell's rich strand in the first place. These two natural products are found next to each other in the list of the endowments derived from Nereus. Ambergris was originally just called amber; it was very valuable, and it could not be bred or mined or manufactured by men, and was found only when tossed up by the sea. In other words, Marinell's precious bane may also be a potent balm – like Achilles' lance that could heal the wounds it caused. When Raleigh went among the looters of the *Madre de dios* in the Southwest, he reported to Burghley, 'I could well smell them almost, such hath been the spoils of amber and musk among them'.[47] It was an eighty-pound chunk of ambergris (worth, say, £10 sterling per pound), found on the Bermuda shore, that helped save the British venture in the New World.[48]

'[T]he pretious shore' with Britomart's tempestuous passage 'Along the strond ... bestrowed ... with rich array / Of pearles and pretious stones ... the grauell mixt with golden owre', where she 'would not stay / For gold, or pearles, or pretious stones' (lII.iv.17,18), is an exception, but

---

46 Article by Cynthia Graber, *Scientific American*, 26 April 2007.
47 Rowse, *Sir Walter Ralegh*, 167: citing State Papers 12 /243, 17.
48 See Kieran Doherty, *Sea Venture: Shipwreck, Survival, and the Salvation of the First English Colony in the New World* (London: Macmillan, 2007), 200–2. ('Sea Venture' was the name of the ship that was wrecked on Bermuda while attempting to bring succour to Jamestown.) Perhaps Washington Irving, in his *Knickerbocker Miscellanies*, under the heading 'The Three Kings of Bermuda and Their Treasure of Ambergris', was the first to connect Shakespeare's *Tempest*, and the squabbles of Caliban, Stephano, and Trinculo over supremacy on Prospero's island, with the three men (Carter, Waters, and Chard) who discovered, quarrelled over, and hoped to make off with the ambergris cache (after the shipwreck of Sir George Somers on Bermuda in 1609). The alcoholic and uriniferous stink of Shakespeare's clowns would be in odiferous counterpoint to the rare ingredient of medicines and perfumes found by the sailors.

Marinell's '*Rich strond*' (III.iv, arg.) is otherwise italicised (as at III.iv.20, 'Rich *strond*'), or else one of the two words is further enhanced, either by capitalization (as at III.vi.29, 'that wealthy Strond', or, with a slight pun on 'arrived', when Cymoent's nymphs are 'arrivd vpon the brim / Of the Rich *Strond*', at III.iv.34). That is, the Rich Strand appears as a peculiarly reified entity both known and unknown, a site treated as a proper noun and yet with a comparatively novel or exotic character – like The Barbary Shore, The Gold Coast of western Africa, or The Wild Coast on the Eastern Cape.[49]

And, by extension, the Spanish Main itself. For the 'Rich *strond*' stands for the Gold Coast wherever it is to be found by the international adventurer-profiteer. But if its attachment to Raleigh in the present chapter can be given any credence, then the lucrative shore should also allude to things like the Virginia Company's charter to partake of the riches of the New World. The land in the west was to be the settlers' possession, but the overlordship, like the name, belonged to the Virgin Queen. Raleigh named Virginia after the Queen, at the time of his being knighted for his unsuccessful plan to settle it, which was hatched at his palatial residence at Durham House – just off 'the Strand', in London. But at the same time that the rich strand was Manteo, it was also El Dorado, the golden Peru described by Lopez, the Caribbean occupied by the Spanish, and the generally promising shores of the New World, which could be counted on 'to equalize … Tyrus for colours, Basan for woods, Persia for oils, Arabia for spices, Spain for silks, Narcis for shipping, Netherlands for fish, Pomona for fruit, and by [means of] tillage, Babylon for corn, besides the abundance of mulberries, minerals, rubies, pearls, gems, grapes, deer, fowles, drugs for physic, herbs for food, roots for colours, ashes for soap, timber for building, pastures for feeding, rivers for fishing, and whatsoever commodity England wanteth'.[50] This is taken from a promotional tribute

---

49 Re 'the Eastern Cape': here Port St Johns is situated, at the mouth of the Unzimybu River. A Portuguese ship, the *Sao Joao*, ran aground here in 1552; it is thought to be the present name's origin; its fate appears in epic literature in the curse of Luiz de Camoëns's storm-god Adamastor on the ocean-invading Portuguese navigators and merchant adventurers at *Os Lusiadas*, Canto V, 44–8.

50 Text (frequently quoted by historians) of Rev. Daniel Price, at St Paul's Cross on 28 May 1609, from Charles McLean Andrews and Leonard W. Labaree, *The Colonial Period of American History* in 4 vols (1934–37; reprnt New Haven: Yale University Press, 1964), 1:55. Earlier quoted in Edward D. Neill, *Virginia Vetusta, during the reign of James I* (Albany, NY: Joel Munsell's Sons 1885), 46. For evidence regarding Marinell's possible career, historically speaking, see Kenneth R. Andrews, *Trade, Plunder and Settlement: Maritime Enterprise and the Genesis of the British Empire, 1480–1630* (London: Cambridge University Press, 1984), with the same author's *The Spanish Caribbean: Trade and Plunder, 1530–1630* (New Haven and London: Yale University Press, 1978), and his

in a sermon preached at St Paul's Cross in 1609, and its sentiments about manifest economic destiny are as Raleighesque as they could be: indeed, Raleigh's new ship for the second Guiana voyage (launched in 1616) was named the *Destiny*.

In short, Marinell in real life would be a privateer, buccaneer, and merchant adventurer, under a letter of marque for thievery from Spain, or a royal charter and letters patent for planting a colony or setting up a trading post on distant shores. He is recognizable in the gentleman marauder George Clifford the Earl of Cumberland or Sir John Hawkins or Raleigh's half-brother Sir Humphery Gilbert or Sir Francis Drake, sailing under the English flag but negotiating at the edges of the known world much on their own initiative. During Raleigh's own time, in fact, Drake had touched upon the rich coast of Costa Rica ('rich coast'), and Drake's name attaches to his Pacific landfall there even today.

In Marinell's fall at the hands of Britomart we might also see the demotion of the English outports, by London and the Crown – the London (or Troynouant) which Britomart says will fix its foot on the Thames (*FQ* III.ix.45), and which will expel foreign merchants, and which itself threatened English ports like Bristol and Exeter. But coinciding with the interests of the outports, Parliament would take away the monopolies of London's joint-stock companies – a defeat, as it were, for Marinell, if his original emergence perhaps reflects the formation of the Barbary Company in 1585 or the Guiana Company in 1588. But Marinell's fall may also stand for any untoward event weakening a *foreign* sea-power: in so far as that event stimulated and advantaged English investment in trade and English bids for overseas territory and the ocean traffic that originally belonged to Spain or France, and that was also emerging as Holland's prey as well. The 'Rich *strond*' is thus not only the New World but also the new sphere of trans-oceanic commerce, the burgeoning business of English and European merchants upon the waters extending from their own home shores to the rest of the globe.[51] In 1581 the Queen herself invested some of the profits of Drake's exploit against the Spaniards in the newly formed Turkey Company. A couple of years later came the Venice Company, and thus the beginning of the English incursion upon the sea lanes of the spice trade in the Levant.

Fernand Braudel's observation that in the early modern period commerce moved from trade-fairs to shipping lanes is virtually stated by

---

earlier *Elizabethan Privateering* (London: Cambridge University Press, 1964).
51 This sentence is mostly that of Charles McLean Andrews, *The Colonial Period of American History*, 1:39.

Anthony Jenkinson, of the Muscovy Company, writing on Bukara:

> There is yeerely great resort of Marchants to the Citie of *Boghar*, which trauaile in great *Carauans* from the Countries thereabout adioyning, as *India*, *Persia*, *Bualke*, *Russia*, with diuers others, and in times past from *Cathay*, when there was passage, but this Marchants are so beggarly and poore, and bring so little quantitie of wares, lying two or 3. yeeres to sell the same, that there is no hope of any good trade there to be had worthy the following. ... The *Indians* doe bring fine whites, which the *Tartars* doe roll about their heads ... but golde, silure, pretious stones, and spices they bring none. I enquired and perceiued that all such trade passeth to the Ocean Sea, the vaines where all such things are gotten, are in the subiection of the Portingals.[52]

Raleigh's self-identification as Ocean entails the same perception: traffic in the most precious commodities was now by cargo, not caravan: it was both seaborne and global, and was following in the wakes of Vasco da Gama and the Admiral of the Ocean Sea.

Raleigh's association with the westward thrust across the Atlantic may be compared with Christopher Marlowe's association with a comparable thrust to the East. Thus the third scene of the second part of Marlowe's *Tamburlaine* anachronistically depicts the Tartar conqueror as the master of a sixteenth-century Ottoman Turk, a Spanish conquistador, and a Portuguese navigator. Indeed, a fourth potentate under Tamburlaine's control has defeated Prester John in Abyssinia and virtually reached the source of the Nile. Marlowe's play even refers to the invasion of the unmapped Australia as a future imperial project (Part 2, I.vi.154)! Marlowe's hero predicts, in his way, England's Captain Cook, the Circumnavigator. That is, Marlowe's much less than wholly historic Tamburlaine enjoys an ideal dominion made possible only by the first globalization, upon the flourishing of European sea-power.

---

52 *Early Voyages and Travels to Russia and Persia, by Anthony Jenkinson and other Englishmen with some account of the first intercourse of the English with Russian and Central Asia by way of the Caspian Sea*, ed. E. Delmar Morgan and C. H. Coot, in 2 vols (London: for the Hakluyt Society, 1886), 1:87–8; with Fernand Braudel, *Civilization and Capitalism: 15th-18th Century: Volume 2: The Wheels of Commerce (Les Jeux de l'Echange, 1979)*, trans. Siân Reynolds (New York: Harper & Row, 1982), 26–97, 140–2 ('The return journey'), and 403–8 ('Long-distance trade: the real big business'). See 92: 'After 1622 ... no single fair would ever constitute the obligatory centre of economic life, dominating the rest. For it was now that Amsterdam, which had never really been a city of fairs, began to assert itself, taking over the previous superiority of Antwerp: it was becoming organized as a permanent commercial and financial centre. The fortune of Amsterdam marks the decline if not of the commodity fairs of Europe, at any rate of the great credit fairs. The age of fairs had seen its best days.'

Roma Gill's assertion, in *The Spenser Encyclopedia, sub* Marlowe, that Tamburlaine, when he describes his garb for the conquest of Central Asia remaining to be accomplished, is *quoting* Spenser, rather than plagiarizing him, is quite persuasive;[53] for not only is Marlowe apparently reproducing Book I, he has taken Spenser's passage *introducing* Prince Arthur for the speech comprising Tamburlaine's mightiest claim upon earthly *apotheosis*: at his valedictory expression of his headstrong and triumphal lust for conquest. The idea that Tamburlaine is deluded, in so doing, is suggestive and plausible; but this idea should not exclude the contrary notion that Tamburlaine the world-beater is in fact here being re-embodied as a manifestation of that imperial Arthur met with at the opening of the great compilation of Richard Hakluyt on behalf of English expansionism.[54]

In Spenser's first legend, Arthur serves as the champion of Una in place of the incapacitated Redcrosse Knight. Arthur sails, so to speak, under Redcrosse's flag. We can thus triangulate the heroic endeavour of the knights in *The Faerie Queene* and of the over-reacher in Marlowe's play with the ventures of the English adventurers abroad. Consider, as Michael Murrin has recently urged, Anthony Jenkinson in the East as the agent of the Muscovy Company and thus as a new kind of Crusader. Jenkinson asks us to 'Note that during the time of our nauigation, wee

---

53 *The Spenser Encyclopedia*, ed. A. C. Hamilton (Toronto: University of Toronto Press, 1990), 453: 'Marlowe would not claim these lines as his own: the alexandrine acknowledge Spenser's authorship ... Tamburlaine is *quoting* Spenser – deluding himself that he belongs to the same medieval chivalric tradition as Arthur, and that his approach to Samarcanda is comparable to Arthur's relief of Una'. For the reading of *Tamburlaine*, Parts 1 and 2, in terms of English expansion to the East, see Richard Wilson, 'Visible Bullets: Tamburlaine the Great and Ivan the Terrible,' *English Literary History* 62.1 (1995), 47–68; Wilson, for example, writes trenchantly, 56–7: 'Tamburlaine's subversion of polarity [of West and East], his urge to 'leap from his hemisphere' (*T2*, 1.3.51), shift 'the perpendicular' (*T1*, 4.4.80), 'fix the meridian line' anew (*T1*, 4.2.38), or 'travel to th'antartic pole, / Conquering the people underneath our feet' (*T1*, 5.1.133), belongs, that is to say, precisely to the era of the trading companies, when, as Jean-Christophe Agnew relates, long-distance transactions generated just such triangular relations as Marlowe stages.'

54 Morgan and Coote edn, 1:97. The margin notes: 'The English / flagge in / the Caspian / Sea'. For King Arthur, more or less analogously to Tamburlaine, as in the present paragraph, see Richard Hakluyt, *Principal Navigations* (Glasgow: James MacLehose and Sons, 1903), 1:16: 'Arthur which was sometimes the most renowned king of the Britains, was a mightie, and valiant man, and a famous warriour. This kingdome was too little for him, & his minde was not contented with it. He therefore valiantly subdued all Scantia [Scandinavia] which is now called Norway, and all the Islands beyond Norway, to wit, Island and Greenland, which are appertaining unto Norway, Sweveland, Ireland, Gotland, Denmarke, ... Flanders, ... Lapland, and all the other lands and Islands of the East sea, even unto Russia (in which Lapland he placed the Easterly bonds of his Brittish Empire).'

sette vppe the redde crosse of *S. George*, in our flagges, for honour of the Christians, which I suppose was neuer seen in the *Caspian* sea before'.[55] As Murrin notes in this regard, St. George is a Cappadocian knight whose adversaries are Tartarian Infidels, and Guyon is a voyager who rejects the greed-caused 'troublous stormes, that tosse / The priuate state...: / Who swelling sayles in Caspian sea doth crosse' (II.vii.14). Thus Tamburlaine brags that 'the Christian merchants, that with Russian stems / Plough up huge furrows in the Caspian sea / Shall vail to us as lords of all the lake' (Part I, I.ii.194–6.).

Jenkinson would seem to be the source of Hakluyt's rhetorical question: 'which of the kings of this land [of England] before her majesty [Queen Elizabeth] had their banners ever seen in the Caspian Sea?' And Hakluyt goes on to note that England has circled the globe more than once:

> What English shippes did heretofore ever anker in the mighty river of Plate? passe and repasse the impassable (in former opinion) straight of Magellan, range along the coast of Chili, Peru, and all the backside of Nova Hispania, further than any Christian ever passed, traverse the mighty bredth of the South Seas, land upon the Luzones in despight of the enemy, enter into alliance, amity, and traffike with the princes of the Molluccas and the Isle of Java, double the famous Cape of Bona Speranza, arrive at the Isle of Santa Helena, and last of al returne home most richly laden with the commodities of China, as the subjects of this now flourishing monarchy have done?[56]

This is as full of itself as Tamburlaine with his portfolio of crowns, and as infected with his greedy desire of dominion: and thus also with the ambitions of Raleigh's brand of enthusiastic commercial-imperial braggadocchio. Many saw Raleigh as an ambitious time-server.

Braggadocchio, after all, is virtually a mock-Timias. The scene in which Belphoebe discovers the cowering mock-knight in *Faerie Queene* II.iii anticipates, even while it parodies, the one in which she comes upon the distressed Timias in III.v. When Belphoebe lessons Braggadocchio in the divisions of honourable patriotic endeavour , one of which is service undertaken 'abroad in armes' (II.iii.40), she could be speaking of Raleigh in Ireland, or of Drake on the high seas, those places where honour is

---

55 Michael Murrin, '*Tamburlaine* Part 1, *Faerie Queene* Book I, and the English Search for Asian Silk', paper delivered at Renaissance Comparative Prose Conference, Purdue University, 5 November 2009. See now *Arthuriana* 21.1 (Spring, 2011), 7–19, 'Spenser and the Search for Asian Silk'.

56 Hakluyt, *Principal Navigations, voyages, traffiques & discoveries*, The Epistle Dedicatory to Sir Francis Walsingham, 1:xx. For the extensive collaboration between the Elizabethan adventurers and explorers, and their redoubtable historian-publicist and New World promoter, see Peter C. Mancall, *Hakluyt's Promise: An Elizabethan's Obsession for an English America* (New Haven and London: Yale University Press, 2007).

to be got: 'In woods, in waues, in wars she wonts to dwell, / And will be found with peril and with paine; / Ne can the man, that moulds in idle cell, / Vnto her happie mansion attaine' (41). Among the many referents for the iconic dragon on Arthur's helmet we might well count 'El Draque', as the fearsome English privateer was known to his Hispanic victims. The English naval opportunist had indeed become emblematic, as George Whitney's *Choice of Emblemes* of 1586 can be adduced to show, in an emblem that seems to work a sea-change on the iconography of the control of marine Fortune (see the ships at sea in *In occasionem*, 181). *Auxilio diuino* (203) shows the globe surmounted by the praiseworthy knight's ship, the *Golden Hind*, which is tethered by world-encircling reins in the hand of God, the master-mariner's guide: 'By pirates, theeues, and cruell foes, that long'd to spill his blood. / That wonder greate to scape: but, God was on his side, / And throughe them all, in spite of all, his shaken shippe did guide. / And, to requite his paines: By helpe of power deuine. / His happe, at lengthe did aunswere hope, to finde the gouldenmine'. Whitney's advisory conclusion – 'you, that liue at home, and can not brooke the flood, / Geue praise to them, that passe the waues, to doe their countrie good' – gives the palm to Drake.[57] Belphoebe would surely concur and approve. Raleigh's name Ocean, and Spenser's Shepherd of the Ocean, refer to the great globe as a whole: as the proper theatre for English ventures and operations.

There is a Spenserian and /or Elizabethan strand, then, involving Marinell at one end, and, at the other, the Shepherd of the Ocean in the Irish Sea in *Colin Clouts Come Home Againe*: that is, if Marinell is a double for Timias as Raleigh, and if that other shepherd of the ocean, namely Proteus, is also a type of Raleigh, in yet another guise. For while Marinell in effect cedes or forfeits his riches to Britomart on the shore, with his downfall fulfilling a fatal prediction of Proteus, Proteus finds a celebrated beauty at sea – Florimell – and takes her captive as his prize. As Book VI of *The Faerie Queene* can be read to show, beauty is potentially another word for booty, and the beautiful Florimell – raised on that hierophanic site of congregated beauty, Mt Acidale (*FQ* IV.v.5) – is also the spoil of the seas. Marinell has lost not only riches, but also Florimell; Proteus, as a kind of grizzled privateer or sea dog, has appropriated Florimell not only as a treasured beauty but also as marine booty – when he deprives the lustful Fisher of his prey and prize – 'streight did he hayle / The greedie villein from his hoped pray' (III.viii.31). Thereupon Proteus gave his

---

57 *A Choice of Emblemes by Geffrey Whitney*, ed. Henry Green (New York: Benjamin Blom, 1967).

predecessor a good thrashing with his shepherd's staff – Raleigh and his kind did rather the same thing to Spanish and Portuguese treasure ships coming back from their respective new worlds, loaded with spoils from the West and the East. Marinell gets Florimell back from these rival buccaneers only upon a decision by Neptune, or the Secretary of the Navy. The legalities surrounding this property's restoration suggest an award made by a high court: a legal grant, not so unlike Raleigh's title to Sherborne.

Raleigh ('Marinell'), or his lawyer ('Cymoent'), did not successfully sue to have some part of Raleigh's estate or emoulements awarded or restored to him as compensation for damages or costs. Neither was Mrs Raleigh ever accepted back into the Queen's court after being sent to the Tower, but certainly Raleigh was a great beneficiary, in Ireland, of the largesse of the Crown, and Raleigh's interests in the Southwest, and among the Cornish sailors there, made this part of the country, from his point of view, practically a 'farm' or monopoly in its own right, and thus itself somewhat like Marinell's 'Rich *strond*'. Indeed, even amidst the pregnancy scandal, Raleigh was being given his estate at Sherborne. More pertinently, Marinell may lose real title to his rich strand in Book III, but he does acquire a wife in Book V. Florimell is loyal to her love for Marinell, throughout the period of his galling incapacitation. It is news of his demise that is said to have caused her flight from court in the first place (III.v.9).[58]

The domestic marital politics of Elizabeth's court, exemplified by Raleigh, can be read into the courtships of both Amoret (abducted from among Venus's ladies in waiting), and Florimell (released from imprisonment – and a wintry celibacy – at the suite of Marinell to his mother). Florimell's loyalty to Marinell sounds somewhat like Bess Throckmorton's lifelong attachment to Raleigh, even if it can only apply specifically to her history after the fact of Spenser's poem. Cymoent thought it 'vaine … to complaine' to any meaner personage than 'Maiestie', namely 'the seas sole Soueraine' – who says 'of double wrong ye plain' and thereupon favours her suit in behalf of Marinell's otherwise deleterious love for the abducted and unattainable 'waift' Florimell (*FQ* IV.xii.29–31). Much might rest on the identity of 'Marin', the 'gentle bonny lasse' in *Colin Clout* (172–3), who says Raleigh 'did plaine' 'Right well … That could great Cynthiaes sore displeasure breake, / And moue to take him to her grace againe' (174–5). If Bess was the bonny lass, she cannot have been referring to anything other than the purposes of Raleigh's woeful plaint, backed up by her father's notable contribution from his family's private rich strand.

---

58 For a psychological explanation for the anachronic precipitation of Florimell's departure from court, after she is already in flight past Britomart, yet before Britomart has toppled Marinell, see Nohrnberg, *Analogy*, 437–8.

IV. Reading Sir Wa'ter's political/Petrarchan mistress through Spenser's Belphoebe

As Britomart, the British virgin Queen and 'martiall Mayd' (*FQ* III.ii.9) lords it over Marinell and his prizes in Book III, and, as Belphoebe, she repudiates Timias's bad faith in Book IV (viii.36). This same Belphoebe is virtually the sole named personage in Raleigh's *Ocean to Cynthia*, where there are scarcely any other gods and goddesses, personifications are vestigial, and no supporting cast is named or engaged, unless we count the fates and fortune and a sole Phoebus (see *FQ* III.v.27: '*Belphoebe* was her name, as faire as *Phoebus* sunne'). That is, Belphoebe stands in for all of them, including the otherwise once named Cynthia of the poem's title.

Because in Raleigh's poem one misses the kind of internal turning-points and arguments that give sequences like *Astrophil and Stella* their compelling drama and dramatic interest, one seizes upon the main utterance in Raleigh's poem that reaches out to an extratextual anchorage with the invocation of literary company, namely Spenser's published dramatization and invocation of Raleigh as the devotee of the goddess-like Belphoebe, with whose invention (as Cynthia) Spenser credits Raleigh in his letter to him published with the first instalment of his epic romance.

The first instance of Belphoebe by name in Raleigh's 'eleventh book' comes exactly midway, at the lament over the loss of a clear if narcissistic representation of himself in the effluent stream of royal favour:

> The streames seeme standinge puddells which, before,
> Wee saw our bewties in, so were they cleere.
> Belphebes course is now obserude no more,
>
> That faire resemblance weareth out of date.
> Our Ocean seas are but tempestius waves
> And all things base that blessed wear of late.
>
> (*OC* 269–74)

Raleigh no longer sees *himself* in his 'Ocean seas': 'That faire resemblance' *also* 'weareth out of date'. The same change in Belphoebe towards Raleigh is recorded in Spenser: 'Is this the faith, she said, and said no more, / But turnd her face, and fled away for euermore' (*FQ* IV.vii.36). In the canto following this contretemps, beauty is said to have been made 'to represent / The great Creatours owne resemblance bright' (IV.viii.32), that is, *before* it was degraded by the abuses of lust of the eyes and lust of the flesh, as represented in two of the three foul foresters attacking Timias in Book III, and before beauty was successfully counterfeited, in the case of the False Florimell, by a Luciferan spright originally possessed of a 'fayre resemblance above all the rest' (III.viii.8) – the rest of the demons at the witch's dispose in the same canto of Book III, where that operator's demonic arts create the fake. We can chart the progress of the degradation of beauty in Spenser's first instalment, from the place in Book II where the narrator first hymned Belphoebe's brilliant countenance:

> In her faire eyes two liuing lampes did flame
> Kindled aboue at th'heavenly makers light.
> And darted fyrie beames out of the same
>
> (II.iii.23)

In the eighth canto Book III the true Florimell ventures on the 'tempestius waves' of those 'Ocean seas' in Raleigh (*OC* 273),[59] while the witch contrives equivalent peepers for her false and chilly simulachrum:

> In stead of eyes two burning lampes she set
> In siluer sockets, shyning like the skyes,
> And a quicke mouving Spirit did arret
> To stirre and roll them, like a womans eyes:
>
> (*FQ* III.viii.7)

So, we might moralize, the image-making power that once created a Belphoebe eventually re-figures her as a haunted or moribund Petrarchanism: as Raleigh says, a 'faire resemblance' yet one perhaps destined to '[wear] out of date' (*OC* 272).

The Queen's disenchantment with Raleigh, his loss of election in the presence of a stern, jealous and potentially merciless judge, curtails his facility in celebrating her as the fair, kindly and charitable Belphoebe:

> A Queen shee was to mee, no more Belphoebe,
> A Lion then, no more a milke white Dove;
> A prissoner in her brest I could not bee,
> Shee did vntye the gentell chaynes of love.
>
> Love was no more the love of hydinge
> All trespase, and mischance, for her own glorye.
> It had bynn such, it was still for th'ellect,
> But I must bee th'exampell in loves storye
>
> (*OC* 327–34)

For Elizabeth, here and in Spenser's Book IV, and unlike Belphoebe in his Book III, had not rescued or redeemed Raleigh/Timias – th'exampell in

---

59 For the diction, compare Spenser's 'storms of fortune and tempestuous fate' (in *FQ* VI.ix.31), and Raleigh's 'moyste teares' allegedly wept by marble before the 'tempestious tymes' of an oncoming storm (*OC* 126–7).

loves storye' – from the kin of the lecherous foul forester of Timas's first encounter, but rather had treated the knight himself as a disreputable or even despicable reincarnation of the 'greedie lust' who is Amoret's 'rapist' (see *FQ* IV.viii.proem).

With Job the client might complain against his deity, 'If I be wicked, woe unto me; and if I be righteous, yet will I not lift up my head. *I am full of confusion; therefore see thou mine affliction; For it increaseth. Thou huntest me as a fierce lion: and again thou shewest thyself marvellous upon me. Thou renewest thy witnesses against me, and increaseth thine indignation upon me; changes and war are against me*' (AV Job 10:15b–18; Geneva Bible: '... returne and shewe thy self maruelous vpon me ... armies *of sorowes* are against me').

There are mythological precedents for the woodland goddess's double character. In the text of Homer (*Iliad* XXI.483) Artemis is specifically 'a lion towards women', though one translator has softened this into a less vindictive or cruel and more heroic character, 'a lion *among* women'. But originally she was a spiteful, threatening goddess, an arrow-like huntress and archer; and she was also the patroness of creatures inherently feral, the wolf that brings down the deer. Thus she is also 'given [...] leave to kill any [women] at [her] pleasure' (*Iliad* XXI.484), though 'better [she should] hunt down the ravening beasts in the mountains and deer of the wilds' (*Iliad* XXI.485). Maternity itself can be a slayer of women, as the Amoret of Spenser's Book IV might remind us, since Amoret is bloodied by Timias as if she too were polluted by sexual relations – or by the birth of Raleigh's child.

In some places the cult and epithets of the rather unforgiving or else plainly vindictive Artemis (or Artemis Adrasteia) are found shared with those of Nemesis or retribution – (see Nonnus, *Dionysica* 48.37ff. for late, literary evidence; and also Commodianus, *Instructiones*, 1.18); this syncrasy would seem conformable to the twin aspects of Raleigh's Belphoebe. Spenser's comparable Queen sounds like the Artemis 'who sits on her throne of Glory' (Sophocles, *Oed. Tyr.* 161 – see Pausanius, IX.17.1) in that her two aspects, Belphoebe and Gloriana, respectively reign in the woods and the capital called Cleopolis ('glory city').[60] But has Raleigh's beloved dove turned into a more particular lion? One wonders,

---

60 The forest retreat resembling a 'stately Theatre' (*FQ* III.v.39) – into which Belphoebe introduces Timias – may be understood as a rustic counterpart of the capital, like the present-day Camp David in relation to The White House. In (re-)connecting Belphoebe to Gloriana, I have had the advantage of a lecture by classicist Ivana Petrovic, 'Artemis in Cult and Literature: "Goddess of the Peripheries" or City-Goddess' (University of Virginia, Dept. of Classics, 1 April 2008).

for a Swiss tourist shown around the Tower of London by one of Raleigh's Yeoman of the Guard writes that lions were caged there, and remembers that one of the beasts was actually named Elizabeth.[61]

The Queen, when gentle and forgiving, could be Raleigh's 'milke white Dove', and just such a pacific and Venus-like reminder of that part of Belphoebe's nature inveigles itself into her attention in Spenser's Legend of Friendship, acting the go-between on Raleigh's or Timias's behalf. The jewel this dove brings to Belphoebe, or back to her, hung as it were on 'the gentell chaynes of love' (*OC* 323), will later appear snaked in a Saxon-like interlacement on the Queen's sleeve in the highly emblematic Rainbow Portrait.[62] The dove consoles Timias by cooing, probably, Raleigh's first name, 'Wa'er, Wa'er'. The rainbow, like the dove, can be read as a symbol for a Noachic grant of amnesty. And thus Raleigh got his freedom, in exchange for recapturing for the Crown £80,000 from the largest galleon – *the Madre di dios* – the English had ever taken, captured in the Azores and brought into port at Dartmouth.

The 'cult of Elizabeth' is obviously inculcated by paintings like the Rainbow Portrait, but the embroidery in this example also subtly records the *cultivation* of Elizabeth, by means of Raleigh's – or rather his brother-in-law Arthur Throckmorton's – gift of a fat ruby to make his family's peace with the throne after the disgrace of Arthur's sister. The Queen's costume positively announces her being thrown this kind of sop by her wearing of the favour on her sleeve. Here is Throckmorton's own statement to Cecil of his plan to intercept his sovereign with the prize gem during an entertainment:

> If I may mind to come in a masque brought in by the Nine Muses, whose music, I hope, shall so mollify the easy softened mind of her Majesty as both I and mine may find mercy. The song, the substance I herewith sent to you – myself, whilst the singing, to lie prostrate at her Majesty's feet till she says she will save me. Upon my resurrection the song shall be delivered by one of the Muses, with a ring made for a wedding ring set round with diamonds and with a ruby like a heart placed in a coronet, with this inscription, *Elizabetha potest*. ... I desire to come in before the other masque, for I am sorrowful and solemn, and my story shall not be long.[63]

---

61 Williams, *Sir Walter Raleigh*, 125–6.
62 The Rainbow Portrait is now found on the cover of the Penguin paperback *Faerie Queene*. A copy of this iconic painting presently hangs over the desk in Raleigh's house in Youghal, where Spenser is alleged to have worked on his verse as a guest – perhaps composing *Colin Clout* in particular.
63 Taken from Rowse, *Sir Walter Ralegh*, 193, quoting Arthur Throckmorton to Robert Cecil, *Salisbury MSS*. V. 99.

For in prison Raleigh writes that his account is indeed down: 'Our dearest treasures and our heart's true joys, / The tokens hung on breast and kindly worn, / Are now elsewhere disposed or held for toys, / / And those which then our jealousy removed, / And others for our sakes then valued dear / The one forgot, the rest are dear beloved, / When all of ours doth strange or vild appear' (*OC* 262–68). This probably refers back to incidents like the one involving Sir Christopher Hatton, nicknamed Mutton by the Queen, and his jealousy of Raleigh, with Elizabeth being sent from Hatton a token of a bucket and a bodkin to signify his despair over the advancement of Sir Wa'ter and the favouring of *his* tokens.[64]

Thinking of the ruby jewellery in connection with Arthur Throckmorton's purchase of the Queen's favour for the scapegrace Raleighs, one also thinks of the lines Shakespeare wrote for the fairy whom Puck encounters at his introduction on to the stage in *A Midsummer Night's Dream*:

> I do wander everywhere
> Swifter than the moon's sphere;
> And I serve the Fairy Queen,
> To dew her orbs upon the green.
> *The cowslips tall her pensioners be.*
> *In their gold coats spots you see:*
> *Those be rubies, fairy favours;*
> *In those freckles live their savors.*
> I must go seek some dewdrops here,
> And hang a pearl in every cowslip's ear.
>
> (II.i.6–15)

The fashionable Raleigh wore a pearl in his ear, in honour of the Queen's own favourite adornment. But if the Queen's most avid servant and luckiest pensioner is also a pecculating pirate, as well as an official and nocturnal 'Esquire of the [Queen's] Body Extraordinary' (and Captain of the Queen's Guard), we might also quote Braggadocchio's Shakespearean counterpart Sir John Falstaff on Raleigh's type of forester, gentleman, and lunar lover:

---

64 Hatton was recognized as a sheep (nicknamed 'Mutton'), Elizabeth claiming to care for him as his shepherdess, and he as her bell-wether. He was also appeased by Elizabeth's symbolical message of a rainbow and a dove, to say that there should be no more destruction by Wa'ter. In Spenser's Legend of Friendship these devices are suggested by Timias's dove and ruby, and are set in balance in the Rainbow Portrait, where the Queen holds a rainbow in her right hand, and wears the Throckmorton jewel on her left sleeve. For the rivalry between Raleigh and Hatton and the devices expressing it, see Lacey, *Sir Walter Ralegh*, 38–9, and Williams, *Sir Walter Raleigh*, 63–4 (where we learn that Hatton also sent, by the same ambassador – Sir Thomas Henneage – as brought book, bodkin, and bucket, a small 'fish-prison': to suggest Raleigh be straitly confined).

Let not us that are squires of the night's body be called thieves of the day's beauty. Let us be 'Diana's foresters', 'gentlemen of the shade', 'minions of the moon', and let men say we be men of good government, being governed, as the sea is, by our noble and chaste mistress the moon, under whose countenance we steal' (*1 Henry IV* II.ii.24–9).

In real life, this recalls the actions of the privateers, and things like Raleigh's complaint about the division of the spoils of the *Madre di dios*:

> My ship first boarded her and only stayed with her; and brought her into harbour, or else she had also perished upon Scilly. ... I was the cause that all this came to the Queen, and that the King of Spain spent £300,000 the last year ... I that adventured all my estate, lose of my principal and they have double.[65]

But of course the mariner who boarded the good ship Bess Throckmorton had no letter of marque permitting his depredations; and he had stolen, or hijacked, a bit too much for himself – too much of the day's booty under the night's shade.

V. 'A Man Distract': Reading Raleigh's pre-depiction in the *Romanzi*

> Sera toujours Roland par amour furieux?
>
> DuBellay[66]

The Ocean to Cynthia continually bruits and answers the question of what Raleigh's beloved Belphoebe had been like, before she ceased to be so likeable. Yet wasn't she always, as Braggadocchio found at the outset, in her first appearance in Book II of Spenser's *Faerie Queene*, a dangerous object for a courtier's desires? Like a woman, the sea is mutable and untrustworthy, and vice versa: 'Yet will shee bee a wooman for a fashion,' Raleigh's Ocean says mock-forgivingly, in trying to explain Cynthia's conduct towards her spurned devotee: perfection supplemented her mind with 'a change of fantasy, / And left her the affections of her kind, / Yet free from every evil but cruelty' (210–12). By the mutable sex or kind we are to understand the topos in Petrarch, 'Woman by nature is a changeable thing: so that I know a loving mood lasts only a little time in a lady's heart,' this echoing Virgil on Dido, at *Aeneid* IV.569, *Varium et*

---

65 Raleigh, writing ruefully to Burghley about his share in the capture of the *Madre di dios*, as compared to that of others more fortunate: E. Edwards, *Life of Sir Walter Ralegh*, II:76–8, as cited by Rowse, *Sir Walter Ralegh*, 168.
66 'Will it always be Roland for furious love?': Joaquim Du Bellay, *Les Regrets* 23, on the subject of literary models for Ronsard's *Franciad*.

mutabile semper femina, 'woman is always variable and mutable'.[67]
The changeable woman who is a kind of double for the goddess Fortuna is a feature of the *romanzi*. When the fixation of Boiardo's title character Orlando on the elusive Angelica seems threatened by a rival in the person of Ranaldo, the Paladin plunges into a self-pitying complaint against the mutability and brevity of human enjoyments, which are always mingled with *sventura* – Orlando had thought that, as a result of Angelica's favour, he would never know sadness, but now he knows that losing what you've gained is more agonizing than not gaining it at all. Fortune has only given him one day of joy (*OI* I.xxv.52-4) – namely the one Angelica's departure has taken away.[68] What's worse, Angelica has only been using him – even if he does not know this. In a later episode, Orlando takes on some ferocious man-eaters at great risk to his life, but having saved the fair one from these villains, he is contented with his *aventura* (II.xix.50), and thereafter he tells King Norandino, 'I lost everything at war / Except my arms and this damsell, / Which Fortune kindly left to me' (II.xix.59).[69] Later still, Ranaldo despairs of possessing this same maiden, whom he thinks Charlemagne will award to Orlando for the King's rescue. But the messenger says Orlando may be delayed: Ranaldo's horse is fast, so he 'ought to try [*provar*] his *ventura*' (II.xxiv.29). In other words, whenever Angelica comes up, so does the subject of good or bad luck: fortune or misfortune. Elizabeth is thus cast as Raleigh's Angelica naturally enough, both by Spenser, and Raleigh himself.

Raleigh's poem 'As you went to Walsingham' gives us both the adorable or grateful Elizabeth, and the hostile or alienated one. Another contemporary poem begins: 'In the wracks of Walsingham / Whom should I choose / But the Queen of Walsingham / To be guide to my muse'.[70] This

---

67 *Donna es mobile*. Cp. Boccaccio, *Il Filostrato*, viii, 30: 'Giovane donna è mobile'. For Elizabeth as Dido, see, inter alia, Nohrnberg, 'Alençon's Dream / Dido's Tomb', with citations (73-102). Elizabeth's changeability in the argument and design of the Two Cantos, alluded to in *Analogy* 739-40, 747, 769, is treated with reference to her marital politics in 'Supplementing Spenser's Supplement'. Cf., also, *FQ* I.vii.34: 'As when siluer *Cynthia* wexed pale and faint, / As when her face is stayned with magicke arts constraint'.
68 This and several of the following sentences are taken more or less directly from Nohrnberg, 'Orlando's Opportunity: Chance, Luck, Fortune, Occasion, Boats and Blows in's *Orlando Innamorato*', in *Fortune and Romance: Boiardo in America*, ed. Jo Ann Cavallo and Charles Ross (Medieval and Renaissance Text Society: Arizona State University Press, 1998), 31-75: 49.
69 Translations are taken from Charles Ross, tr., Matteo Maria Boiardo, *Orlando Innamorato* (Berkeley: University of California Press, 1989).
70 See <www.walsinghamanglicanarchives.org.uk/walsinghamballads.htm> for this information; and 'A Lament for Our Lady's Shrine at Walsingham', in *Recusant Poets: With*

may well mean that in Norfolk the idolized Virgin Queen had taken over from the previously idolized Queen of Heaven. Queen Elizabeth had made a royal progress through Norfolk in 1578, and her royal father had visited the shrine there three times, the last time twenty years before it was destroyed by the Reformers. A member of Elizabeth's entourage, Philip Howard, Earl of Arundel, may possibly have written the poem ('In the wracks of Walsingham'), somewhat in Raleigh's own vein of an alienable adoration or devotion. The wreck ('wracks') in question makes Walsingham a subject for ruins poetry, a potential complaint genre that is eminently Spenserian. Compare the 'golden glittering tops' that 'pierced once to the sky' with the come-down:

> Owls do skrike where the sweetest hymns
>   Lately were sung,
> Toads and serpents hold their dens
>   Where the palmers did throng.

How like the fate of the 'High towers, faire temples, goodly theatres' (*RT* 92) of the little Rome of Spenser's Verulam in her complaint in *The Rvines of Time*:

> Where my high steeples whilom vsde to stand,
> On which the lordly Faulcon wont to towre,
> There now is but an heap of lyme and sand,
> For Schriche-owle to build her balefull bowre:
> And where the Nightingale wont forth to powre
> Her restles plaints to comfort wakefull Louers,
> There now haunt yelling Mewes and whining Plouers.
>
> (127–33)[71]

Raleigh's possibly comparable Walsingham poem is a dialogue that seems intended as 'verses for his Queen-goddess-sweetheart',[72] for the first speaker in the poem asks if a pilgrim returning from Walsingham has met his – Raleigh's – 'true love'. The pilgrim in turn asks how one might recognize her. The Raleigh-figure answers:

---

    a Selection from Their Work, [Series] I, *Thomas More to Ben Jonson*, ed. Loiuse Imogen Guiney (New York: Sheed & Ward, 1939), 355–6, for the text.

71 For the connection of this imagery with Scripture (Isaiah 13 and 34, Jeremiah 50, Zephaniiah 2, and Revelation 18) see *Analogy*, 236–8. For the Walsingham poem in these lights see Philip Schwyzer, *Archaeologies of English Renaissance Literature* (Oxford and New York: Oxford University Press, 2007), 84–107.

72 So Williams, *Sir Walter Raleigh*, 108.

> 'She is neither white nor brown
> But as the heavens fair.
> There is none hath a form so divine,
> In the earth or the air'.
>
> 'Such an one did I meet, good sir, [the pilgrim answers]
> Such an angelic face,
> Who like a Queen, like a nymph, did appear
> By her gait, by her grace'.
> 'She hath left me here all alone, [the first speaker now reveals,
>   in accents of Sir Thomas Wyatt]
> All alone as unknown,
> Who sometime did me lead with herself
> And me loved as her own'.[73]

How the Queen walks, 'by her gait, by her grace', is the means to know her. 'Her angelick face, / Like *Phoebe* fayre', introduced this same goddess into Spenser's *Shepheardes Calender*,[74] where the Virgilian gait in question was implicitly invoked by Thenot's emblem referring to 'Elisa' as Virgil's Venus in the disguise of a nymph of Diana, and Hobinall's emblem 'O dea certe', as the goddess or grace who may be a *dea quarta* – an English Diana surpassing the classical Minerva, Juno, and Venus. But here the worshipper has *himself* become the Walsingham ruin, deserted by the object of his devotion.

Raleigh's first speaker, the abandoned courtier forsaken by the fickle, faithless woman dissimulated by his supposed deity, despairs of his wasted commitment:

> She hath lefte me here all alone
> All allone as vnknowne,
> Who somtymed did me lead with her selfe,
> And me loude as her owne.   (17–20)
> [...]
> I haue loude her all my youth,
> Butt now ould, as you see,
> Loue lykes not the fallyng frute
> From the wythered tree.
>   (25–28)[75]

---

73 'As yov came from the holy land', ll. 9–20, in Latham, *Poems*, 22–3.
74 'Aprill', ll. 64–5. Cynthia being advanced as a Fourth Grace, Colin's poem on Eliza uses 'grace' or 'graces' four times (and he uses 'disgrace', which he fears, once).
75 To quote another of the poets' poets, whose aspiring subject appears to be aspiring towards the moon: 'Bestarred is the Daughter of Heaven's house, and cold, / He has seen her often, she sat all night on the hill, / Unseemly the pale youth clambered toward her,

In the longer and less economical *Ocean to Cynthia*, Raleigh says nearly the same thing, where his terminated service is bewept as a total loss:

> Twelue years intire I wasted in this warr,
> Twelue yeares of my most happy younger days,
> But I in them, and they now wasted ar,
> Of all which past the sorrow only stayes.
>
> So wrate I once, and my mishapp fortolde
>
> (*OC* 120–4)

He despairs of a return to his mistress's favour, yet maintains his love, which has become his faith, or his personal Walsingham, with Elizabeth as the unreliable object of a displaced but stedfast Marian devotion:

> The wrongs recevde, the scornes perswade in vane....
>
> And thoughe these medcines worke desire to ende
> And ar in others the trew cure of likinge,
> The salves that heale loves wovnds and do amend
> Consvminge woe, and slake our harty sythinge [sighing],
>
> They worke not so, in thy minds long deseas.
>
> (*OC* 416–21)

Time, the wounded heel tries to tell himself, must in time heal all wounds, and yet his poem seems to confess that he is a ruin past repair.

VI. Cynthia observed by the poets / the poets crazed by Cynthia

> The Homeric hymnographer, who wrote a hymn to the Moon [...] even said that she washed herself in the ocean waters before she put on her clothing, as these verses indicate: 'Whensoever bright Selene, having bathed her lovely body in the waters of Ocean'.
>
> Natale Conti, *Mythologiae*, III.17, 'On the Moon'[76]

Raleigh's letter to Sir Robert Cecil from the Tower rehearses much the same array of comparisons as the Walsingham poem does: 'My heart was never broken till this day, that I hear the Queen goes away so far off – *whom I followed so many years with so great love and desire, in so many journeys, and am now left behind her, in a dark prison all alone ... I that was wont to behold her riding like Alexander, hunting like Diana, walking*

---

till / Untimely the peacock screamed, and he wakened old.' So John Crowe Ransom, in a poem called 'Blackberry Winter', on a disappointed cultivator of the Muse awakening from his life-long courtship and Endymion-like dream of a career in poetry, in the service of what Robert Graves called the White Goddess.

76 Mulryan-Brown trans., 1:210.

like Venus, the gentle wind blowing her fair hair about her pure cheeks, like a nymph; sometime sitting in the shade like a goddess, sometime singing like an angel, sometime playing like Orpheus'.[77] There seems little doubt that this string of compliments was intended for either the eyes or the ears of the Queen herself. It also seems likely, as we said at the outset, that she never saw or heard these fine words, in so far as they are the substance of *The Ocean to Cynthia*.

During the house-arrest of Raleigh (in his own quarters), the poet Arthur Gorges intervened between the prisoner and his gaoler – Sir George Carew – when the latter tried to prevent Sir Walter from breaking out of his rooms overlooking the Thames, and from approaching, in disguise and by boat, the silent sovereign abroad on the river, 'to ease his mind but with a sight of the Queen; or else, he protested, his heart would break'. Inteferring in the struggle to keep Raleigh confined, Gorges's hand was bloodied for his trouble – but this succeeded in ending the attempted prison-break. Gorges then reported to Robert Cecil that 'Sir. W. Ralegh will shortly grow to be Orlando Furioso if the bright Angelica persevere against him a little [= much] longer'. And an attached but removable note slyly suggested that Cecil might want to let the Queen herself see this report of the encounter. Instead, she put both Raleighs in the Tower.

The Ocean to Cynthia reports its agonies as if they were the same events as those just sketched concerning 'Raleigh Furioso':

> And as a man distract, with trebell might
> Bound in stronge chaynes douth strive, and rage in vayne,
> Till tyrde and breathless, he is forst to rest,
> Fyndes by contention but increas of payne,
>
> And fiery heat inflamde in swollen breast,
> So did my minde in change of passion
> From wo to wrath, from wrath returne to wo,
> Struglinge in vayne from loves subiection.
>
> (*OC* 153–60)

We may doubt that Cecil facilitated the motion in the note, to pass on Gorges's report to the Queen; but in any case, it's our first notice, *avant*

---

77 As quoted in Rowse, *Sir Walter Raleigh*, 163, and Lacey, *Sir Walter Ralegh*, 172. Italics mine. Both authors find factiousness, insincerity, and a lack of self-reproach in Raleigh's devices and effusions here, including the poet's numbering himself among those 'vassals vnto tyme / Of which repentance writes the tragedye' (*OC* 179–80). For 'Raleigh Furioso' in the context of Elizabethan court culture, see Miranda Johnson-Haddad, 'Englishing Ariosto: *Orlando Furioso* at the Court of Elizabeth I', *Comparative Literature Studies* 31:4 (1994), 325–50.

le lettre, of the extending of the comparison of Elizabeth to Ariosto's Angelica towards Spenser's Book IV in his second instalment of 1596. Angelica was the celebrated beauty who ministered to the wounded foot-soldier Medoro as Belphoebe had ministered to Timias in Book III in 1590. But Raleigh himself is now generating or regenerating the conceit of himself as an Orlando driven insane by his love for Angelica, as Orlando was crazed by the knowledge of Angelica's affair with Medoro. Orlando went mad with jealousy when he discovered the legend of the two lovers' amour carved on the trees in the forest of Ardennes. But Spenser will make Arthur into the discoverer of the love recorded on trees, namely Timias's devotion to the offended Belphoebe – and Arthur, in spite of his infatuation with her public counterpart Gloriana, is in no great danger of going out of his mind. Thus Spenser makes Timias into a Medoro, but an insane one, 'a man distract' like Orlando. Timias, like Medoro, will carve his beloved's name on the trees, but at the same time he as good as forgets his own.[78] Timias's idolatry is paralleled in *Colin Clout*; Colin resolves to celebrate Cynthia on his return home: 'Her name in euery tree I will endosse' (632). It is thus the jealous deity of the Two Cantos first appears in Ireland, as in the poet's *Epithalamion* (374).

'He who is not jealous cannot love,' according to the second of the thirty-one rules of love near the end of Andreas Capellanus's *Art* (Bk II, ch. viii). The theme of the jealous lover who suspects the truth of the beloved and suffers the 'wound of jealous worm' (*FQ* II.iv.28), 'That canckerworme, that monster, *Gelosie*' (*Hymn to Love*, 267), runs from Boccaccio, Chaucer, and Ariosto, and thereafter through much of *The Faerie Queene*: in Redcrosse's doubting of Una's truth in Book I ('he burnt with gealous fire' (I.ii.5)); in Phedon's suspecting Claribell's fidelity in Book II (where once the pair was 'without gealous feares, / Or faultie thoughts' (II.iv.18)); in Malbecco's fearing for Hellenore's honesty in Book III (she joyed 'to be free from hard restraint and gealous feares' (III.ix.4)); and in Scudamour's sojourn at the House of Care in Book IV, where he is disheartened by Amoret's apparent disloyalty (he departs as one 'dismayed with gealous dread' (IV.v.45, while at IV.vi.28 he rejoices 'That all his gealous feare he false had found')). But the theme comes home to its Ariostan roost in Timias's Orlando-like distress, later in this same fourth legend of friendship, at Belphoebe's reproof of her devotee's infidelity: 'Is this the faith, she said, and said no more' (IV.vii.36).

---

78 For these intertextual relations, within the context of *Faerie Queene* IV, see *Spenser Encyclopedia* 274, col. 3, and 279, cols 3–4. See also Nohrnberg, 'Britomart's Gone Abroad', 214–19 and 278.

Love is himself a jealous God and vengeance is his – or rather hers, when Belphoebe becomes angry and well nigh vindictive, and trains her arrows on the disgraced squire as once she did on Braggadocchio, and somewhat as Florio/Filocolo's thwarter Diana did, in Boccaccio's *Filocolo* (III.xxiv), when she also enlisted aid in afflicting the lover's heart from the house of her half-sister Jealousy. Raleigh's Ocean says his Cynthia was 'Devin in wordes, angellical in voyce', and that the 'cordiall sweetness' of her 'comforts ... cannot dye'. This recalls Belphoebe ministering to Timias in Book III of *The Faerie Queene*. But Raleigh's poem does not so much derive from Spenser's first instalment, as re-inscribe itself in his second. For Timias' carving of Belphoebe's name on trees (at the end of canto viii of Book IV) may well refer to the writing of Raleigh's poem to Cynthia, the product 'of a wasted minde, / The blossumes fallen, the sapp gon from the tree, / The broken monuments of [his] great desires,' in Raleigh's own, maudlin words (*OC* 12–14). Timias's care-ridden condition, with its likeness to that of the Care afflicting Scudamour with jealous suspicion, also jibes with this self-despairing description. And the words Timias inscribes on the trees likewise accord with those mute utterances that unfortunates incarcerated in the Tower of London carved on their prison's unforgiving walls.

'Alone, forsaken, frindless onn the shore / With many wounds, with deaths cold pangs inebrased' (*OC* 88–90) – that does indeed sound like the fallen Marinell – and 'fludds of sorrow and whole seas of wo / The bancks of all my hope did overbeare' (140–1) sounds like his mother Cymoent. But Raleigh's Queen has become not only the goddess controlling the seas and the weather – 'What storms so great but Cynthias beames appeased [?]', as Raleigh's poem asks rhetorically (*OC* 118) – but also the Cynthia met in John Lyly and the Belphoebe met in *Faerie Queene* IV: the lunar goddess, not herself so easily appeased, who drives men mad and causes their degradation into wretches. Thus, Raleigh says, sorrow 'drowned my mind in depths of misery' (*OC* 142): 'Sometime I died, sometime I was distract, / My soul the state of fancy's tragedy; / Then furious madness, where true reason lacked, / / Wrote what it would, and scourged mine own conceit' (143–6).

The original of this scourge was a fit of jealousy, namely the 'furious madness' as found in that Orlando who was *furioso*, being provoked by Angelica's jilting of Ariosto's supremely illustrious paladin for a quite unremarkable infantryman. But in the English knight's case, i.e., Raleigh's case as Spenser's Timias, the betrayer is a male squire, and the jealous guardian of a lady's honour – veritably the traditional figure of Daunger

– is a quasi-divine female. Thus it is Belphoebe herself who suffers a jealousy like that which Raleigh had formerly so much aroused in his rivals at court. Such a sexual inversion is immortalized in the relation of the unfaithful Dante to that pilgrim's stern reprover Beatrice, though Belphoebe is at least as much like the Diana who employs Jealousy to plague the heart of Bianciflore's lover Florio in Boccaccio's *Filocolo*; we may compare the 'iealouse feare' of the Goddesse Venus in *Muipotomus* (129), regarding Cupid's rumoured patronage of her attendant maiden Astery – a potential Cupid-Psyche affair that the jealous deity would gladly thwart.

For the *relation* of Belphoebe and Ocean/Timias is indeed a jealous one. As Andreas Capellanus's Seventh Dialogue had once laid it down, jealousy is 'a true emotion whereby we greatly fear that the substance of our love may be weakened by some defect in serving the desire of our beloved,' since 'jealousy between lovers is commended by every man who is experienced in love' (Parry, 102). Paired with *Doubt* in Spenser's Masque of Cupid in the last canto of *Faerie Queene* III, *Daunger* is characterized as imperilment, but is eyed warily by Feare, or dread of rejection; *Daunger* is paired with *Doubt*, who also has a kind of soul-mate in the subsequent masquer named *Suspect* – and who is as unhappily paired with *Dissemblance*. And yet, despite Spenser's dangerous and suspicious version of Belphoebe in *Faerie Queene* IV, she could also be understood as participating in that quasi-godly kind of jealous care and concern over the endangered virtue and reputation of the dissemblance-prone beloved, and that same guardianship's and sponsorship's zealous support of the endangered party's reputation for integrity.[79]

The Nebuchadnezzar-like condition into which the rejected Timias falls in Spenser's Book IV is perhaps not the only example of the courtier's infused yet self-inflicted lunacy in *The Faerie Queene*: there is also, as previously mentioned, the Faunus whom Cynthia seems to have made a little crazy in the Mutabilitie Cantos (whether by turning the goatish pan into a voyeur, or, thereafter, into a panic-stricken scapegoat). Here the poet again intertwines his narrative with the story of Raleigh's marital caper – for the sixth and last time in the poet's canon, though it is represented here twice: that is, if the pregnant Mrs Raleigh is not only Molla-

---

[79] For jealousy as love's hallmark in Andreas Capellanus, see at some length, Bk I, chapter vi, 'Seventh Dialogue,' in *The Art of Courtly Love*, tr. John Jay Parry (New York: Columbia University Press, 1941), 91–107. Our quote here is from 102. For rich and pertinent citation, especially patristic, on vulgar and godly jealousy in medieval and Renaissance counterpoint, see Charles R. Smith, 'Jealousy: Chaucer's Miller and the Tradition,' *Chaucer Review* 43.1 (2008), 16–47.

na's lover Fanchin in drag, but also Diana's unchaste nymph Callisto in disgrace. Yet another model for Raleigh–Timias's hermit-like mortifications are those of Amadis de Gaul, whose penitential rustication (for an imagined offence to his mistress Oriana) Spenser assigns to the squire, upon his offence to the virginal and celibate Belphoebe.[80]

Is it possible that the conversion of the trees to the uses of Timias's

80 After Nohrnberg, *Analogy*, 45. For Spenser's repeated allegorizing of Raleigh's marriage via the vehicles of topopoesis, and chivalric and pastoral romance, see 'Britomart's Gone Abroad', 256–7, 269–71. For Faunus as undone by curiously seeking into 'the secrets of princes', see 'Britomart's Gone Abroad', 273–4. For those who 'against [a prince's] will have a knowledge of his secrets, being aware that they are singled out, and all opportunities watched against them, they lead the life of a stag, full of fears and suspicions' – this being, according to Bacon (*Wisdom of the Ancients*, X), following Natale Conti, *Mythologiae* VI.24, the implications of the fable of Actaeon. Compare Conti, VI.24: 'The ancients also used this story to keep us from getting too curious about things that are none of our business. In fact the private affairs of others can prove to be very damaging to a lot of people when they come out. I refer to the business of a country's chief citizens, her most important men, and particularly of the gods, who won't hesitate to destroy someone who knows their secrets, even when their suspicion is based on slimmest of evidence', and also Bk X, *sub* Actaeon 'The ancient writers also made it clear that we shouldn't get too curious about anything or pursue a line of inquiry that's none of our business. For a lot of people have been destroyed after they found out about a leader's confidential deliberations'. (Mulryan-Brown tr., 2:564, 2:916). Likewise Abraham Fraunce, *The Third parte of the Countesse of Pembrokes Iuychurch* (London: for Thomas Woodcocke, 1592), 43r: 'we ought not to be ouer curious and inquisitive in spying and prying into those matters, which be aboue our reache, least we be rewarded as *Actaeon* was. Ouid. 2 de tristib. "Inscius Actaeon vidit sine veste dianam: / Praeda fuit canibus non minus ille suis. / Scilicet in superis, etiam fortuna luenda est, / Nec veniam laeso numine casus habet". Or lastly, thus, a wiseman ought to refrain his eyes, from beholding sensible and corporall bewty, figured by *Diana*: least, as *Actaeon* was deuoured of his owne dogs, so he be distracted and torne in peeces with his owne affections, and perturbations.' Fraunce's citation from Ovid comes from a passage lamenting the exiled poet's offence to Augustus: 'Why did I see what I saw? Why render my eyes guilty? / Why unwillingly take cognizance of a crime? / Actaeon never intended to see Diana naked, / but still was torn to bits by his own hounds. / Among the high gods even accidents call for atonement: / when deity's outraged, mischance is no excuse' (*Tristia* II, 103–8, tr. Peter Green, *Ovid: The Poems of Exile* (Harmondsworth: Penguin Books, 1994), 27). The Roman poet's self-condemnation might be pronounced by either Raleigh as Ocean, or Spenser as Faunus. Allegorically understood (or seen as Conti's and Fraunce's Actaeon), the offending satyr is guilty of some kind of *un*lawful espial: as in spying into *arcana imperii* (state secrets), violating the royal discretion, lifting the veil on the Queen's conscience, or encroaching upon her right to keep her own counsel – if we read the episode in the light of Lowell Gallagher, *Medusa's Gaze: Casuistry and Conscience in the Renaissance* (Stanford, CA: Stanford University Press, 1991): e.g., 37–58, 96–7, 169–262 ('The Trial of Duessa'). Gallagher (245–6) notes the Spenserian narrator's revelation of Mercilla's judicial reticence and indecision at *FQ* V.ix.50, at the end of the trial episode, which begins with the royal censure of Mercilla's critic Malfont – lately a would-be satirical poet – for *lèse-majesté* and treasonously slandering 'that Queene for forged guile' (V.ix.25). With the example of Malfont, the satirical author of *Mother Hubberds Tale* might be obliquely warning himself.

idolatry was partly suggested by the report that Miss Throckmorton's 'sweet Sir Walter' had impregnated her, despite her famous protests, up against a tree? Faunus's own offence comes from daring, with Raleigh–Molanna's contrivance, to look on beauty bare, then laughing aloud on viewing the forfended place, namely Cynthia's nearly nameless 'somewhat': which is my 'old sweet etcetera' by another name, an object hardly worth trying to specify further without indecency or redundancy.[81] The vaguely derogatory periphrasis occupies the place in the *Two Cantos* of the Virgilian missing half-line that ought to have rimed with 'about', at *Faerie Queene* II.iii.25: I'd lamely suggest 'breechclout', for the missing clothing that should appear above Belphoebe's ham, to cover her virgin knot – or whatnot – below her chemise.[82]

If Raleigh can be translated into (and moralized as) Spenser's Molanna, with the sceptophilic Faunus read as Spenser himself, then the somewhat Rabelaisian 'some-what' shows the poet acknowledging that the celebration of Raleigh's Cynthia as his own Belphoebe, with 'The prayse of her fresh flowring Maidenhead' (*FQ* III.v.54), was *risqué*, potentially risible,

81 The word 'some-what' is a variant on a traditional usage of 'what-not' for the female's private parts, euphemistically a woman's *comment le nomme-t-on*, 'how does one do the name', or *comment a nom* – 'how to name' – as in Rabelais, *Gargantua and Pantagruel*, II.15, III.8, and IV.47.
82 David Scott Wilson-Okamura, 'Belphoebe and Gloriana', in *English Literary Renaissance*, 39.1 (Spring, 2009), 47–73, points out that the six 'Virgilian' half-lines in *The Faerie Queene* are all inspired by episodes asking to be read in conjunction with specific scenes and texts in the *Aeneid*, and that here we should be comparing Virgil's Dianaesque Venus, and his Virgilian Camilla, and the Renaissance/Homeric Penthesilea. But what about Loius Montrose's idea that the half-line for the anatomical blazon of Belphoebe's clothes alludes to Elizabeth's missing crotch, rather than just the Virgilian encounter of mortal hero with goddess-in-huntress-guise? 'I am cloven,' the monarch said, regarding the supposed deficiency of her sex; but Wilson-Okamura argues that 'Queen Elizabeth did not classify cleavage as a mystery of state'. Such a reference would be in bad taste, he declares, *Elizabeth's petticoat is not showing here*; the 'groin' should be read not so much anatomically as architecturally, it being like the pillars of Camilla's tomb in the *Roman d'Eneas* or the lady's castle-keep in *The Romance of the Rose*. The edifice would be a priestly one, indicating an ideal sacerdotal celibacy appropriate for the husband-like head of the Church (as Innocent III argued regarding his own papal office). Artemis is, so to speak, a temple to Artemis, of which only the iconic pillars – Belphoebe's legs – remain. Even if Belphoebe's light chemise may not really be a priest's surplice, the surplus suggestion can hardly be faulted for ingenuity. Though Belphoebe may be a species of – or aspect of – a 'virgin mother', it is still not quite right to say that Spenser omits unmentionables from voyeuristic consideration altogether. Not, at least, in the Bower of Bliss, where one of the provocative bathing beauties shrouds her breasts yet may well expose much more than those. So one might continue to read Belpohebe's hemistich or half-line as her hiked-up hem-line, given that Guyon's responsiveness (as it were to the Girls Gone Wild at Acrasia's Playboy Mansion) is anticipated by the aroused Braggaocchio's reaction to Belphoebe in her slightly fetishized hunting outfit (a getup, as it were, from Abercrombie and Bitch).

and fraught with taboo from the start – just as was Raleigh's celebration of Elizabeth as Cynthia, and his two subsequent references to her as Spenser's Belphoebe.[83] The poets had been playing with icy fire, and skating on thin ice, whether writing satirical verse at a clerkish desk among the wild Irish, or hazarding life in ships that ventured on the high seas and risked shipwreck on foreign shores. Yet they were doing Belphoebe's own bidding, and the Queen's own work, since she is the one who implicitly berates carpet champions like Braggadocchio for avoiding the honourable toil ordained by Sweat, Blood and Tears – 'to seeke new worlds, for gold, for prays, for glory' (*OC* 61), 'Abroad in armes, at home in studious kind [...] In woods, in waues, in warres' (*FQ* II.iii.40–1) – but also in *words*, in the homely study or the lonely prison cell, where these two literary collaborators both attempted brave things in prose or rhyme.

VII. Coda: Cynthia after Belphoebe, in 1602 and 1609

> The tyme, that passeth nyght and day,
> And resteles travayleth ay,
> And steleth from us so prively
> That to us seemeth sykerly
> But goth so faste, and passeth ay,
> That ther nys man that thynke may
> What tyme that now present is ...
> The tyme, that may not sojourne,
> But goth, and may never retourne,
> As water that doun renneth ay,
> But never drope retourne may;
> There may nothing as tyme endure,
> Metall or erthely creature,
> For alle thing it fret and shall;
> The tyme eke, that chaungith all,
> And all doth waxe and fostred be,
> And alle thing distroieth he;
> The tyme, that eldith our auncessours,
> And eldith kynges and emperours,
> And that us alle shal over comen,
> Er that deth us shal have nomen;
>   Chaucer, *The Romaunt of the Rose*, ll. 369–77, 381–94[84]

---

83 See 'Britomart's Gone Abroad', 255–60, 266–7, 269–75.
84 Text from *The Works of Geoffrey Chaucer*, 2nd edition, ed. F. N. Robinson (Boston: Houghton Mifflin, 1957), 569.

> Hast thou not dragged Diana from her car …?
> Edgar Allan Poe, 'Sonnet – To Science'

An anonymous poem published in 1602 provides the critical link between our two poets' Belphoebe/Cynthia of the 1590s, and the literary Cynthia that Elizabeth has survived as, after Spenser's death, and after the Queen's mortal body was committed to the ground, 'earth to earth'. Raleigh presumably did not write this poem, yet surely he could have inspired it:

Ode of Cynthia[85]
The ancient readers of heaven's book
Which with curious eye did look
   Into Nature's story
All things under Cynthia took
   To be transitory.

This the learnéd only knew,
But now all men find it true;
   Cynthia is descended,
With bright beams, and heavenly hue,
   And lesser stars attended.

Lands and seas she rules below,
Where things change, and ebb, and flow,
   Spring, wax old, and perish;
Only Time, which all doth mow,
   Her alone doth cherish.

Time's young Hours attend her still
And her eyes and cheeks do fill
   With fresh youth and beauty
All her lovers old do grow,
But their hearts; they do not so,
   In their love and duty.

Celestial or no, Elizabeth was a lady whom Time would famously surprise: and that in the very next year (1603).

The Raleighesque devotion of the ode's courtly lovers must surely thereupon end, or redirect itself to James I. That is, with the probable exception of Sir Walter, who outlived his political mistress by so many

---

85 Text from Francis Davison, ed., *A poetical rhapsody containing diuerse sonnetes, odes…* (London: John Baily: 1602), as reprinted in *Elizabeth I and Her Age*, ed. Donald Stump and Susan M. Felch (New York: Norton, 2009), 514–15. Somewhat similarly, in 1595, Richard Barnfield's *Cynthia* (1595) concludes by saying that the moon 'monthly changeth', while the poet tells the Queen 'thou dost ne'er decline' (l. 175) (text in Stump and Felch, 592).

years, and who so disastrously pursued that trans-Atlantic colonial project he first conceived in her reign. But as Aeneas Silvius pontificates on the subject of fortune, *Caduca omnia sub luna: quanto altius extollimur, tanto periculosius cadimus* (all things are perishable beneath the moon, and the higher we are raised up, so much the more dangerously are we exposed): Raleigh proved this true *in excelsus*.[86] Nonetheless, advanced minds (his perhaps among them) had concluded that the alleged difference between the celestial and mundane worlds had no basis in physical reality. It was simply untrue – in the words of Sylvester's translation of a notable passage in DuBartas – that 'Death's lawes alone / Reach but the Bodies unto *Cynthia's* Throne'.[87] The learnéd now knew there was no quintessence, the universe was alterable and perhaps extinguishable. Enter Spenser's Mutability, who in 1609 claims the planetary deities are subject to mutation no less than bodies on earth. A year later Galileo became a Copernican: the Moon's phases had shown up on Venus. And this has suggested one further reading of Molanna. The Galilean recognition of the phases of Venus and the telescopic observation of the Moon are also credited to Sir Thomas Harriot. If spying on Cynthia is made to

---

86 Aeneas Sylvius Piccolimini, *Opera*, Epist. Lib. I, 188 (and variant *sub* 'Gnomologia ex omnibus Sylvii operibus collecta') (Basil: Henricpetrina, 1551; repr. Frankfurt: Minerva, 1967), 761 and appendix, gamma 2.

87 Sallust DuBartas, *The First Week*, trans. in *Complete Works of Joshua Sylvester*, ed. A. B. Grosart, in 2 vols (New York: AMS Press, 1967, rprnt), 1:22. The quote is from *Du Bartas His Divine Weekes: 'The First Day of The First Week'*, ll. 374ff. French text: *The Works of Guillaume De Salluste Sieur Du Bartas*, in 3 vols, ed. Urban Tigner Holmes, Jr, John Coriden Lyons, and Robert White Linker (Chapel Hill: University of North Carolina Press, 1938), *La Premier Sepmaine*, 'Le Premier Jour'; see ll. 344ff., in Holmes, Jr, ed., 2:206–7 (from l. 344, 'Et que tout va ça bas a change d'heure en heure'); the lines Sylvester translates are ll. 349f. ('L'astre argenté' (in Holmes, 2: 207) = 'Cynthia's throne'). In 'L'Envoy' to his version of Du Bellay's *Antiquities*, the *Rvines of Rome*, Spenser salutes the rise of '*Bartas*' after Du Bellay. For the astronomic learning of the School of Night, and the connection of Harriot to Molanna in Spenser's Two Cantos, see Frederick Turner, *Natural Classicism: Essays on Literature and Science* (New York: Paragon House Publishers, 1986), 111–49, and especially 125–6. See also Erik Klingelhofer and James Lyttleton, 'Molana Abbey and Its New World Master,' *Archaeology Ireland* (Winter, 2010), 32–5. And for the treatment of astronomic discourse in biblical texts, especially in one Didacus à Stunicá's *Commentary on Job* (1584) at Job 9:6 (*Qui commovet terram de loco suo et columnae eius concutiuntur*), see Jules Speller, *Galileo's Inquisition Trial Revisited* (Frankfurt: Peter Lang, 2008), 80–5; Pierre Gassendi, with notes by Oliver Thill, *The Life of Copernicus: 1473–1543* (Fairfax, VA: Xulon Press, 2002), 271–5; and Jerzy Dobrzycik, ed., *The Reception of Copernicus' Heliocentric Theory* (Warsaw: Polish Academy, 1972), especially Juan Vernet, 'Copernicus in Spain', 271–92. Stunicá writes (edn. of 1591, 41): 'No place is given in holy writ that says as openly that the earth does not move than this which says that move it does' – from the Latin quoted in James Spedding et al., ed., *The Works of Francis Bacon, Vol III: Philosophical Works* (London, 1887), in *Descriptio Globi Intellectualis et Thema Coeli*, at 741, n. 1.

stand for the actual observation of the Moon by an astronomer equipped with a telescope, then it seems significant that Raleigh's brilliant colleague had actually lived at the abbey, after his return from the New World (and before entering the service of the Earl of Northumberland in London in 1593); Harriot had been given the Molanna holding in return for his management of Raleigh's Irish properties. Presumably Harriot could have provided not only Raleigh but also associates like Spenser with the latest intelligence about matters natural and mathematical, the moon's appearance – when scientifically scrutinized – included. Moreover Spenser's Nature, 'Still moouing, yet unmoued from her sted' (*MC* vii.13), could well be the earth itself, as found in Job 9:6, 'He who moves the Earth from its place, and its pillars are shaken', with which a Copernican heliocentrist would respond to the traditional, Ptolemaic counter-text of Ecclesiastes 1:4, 'But the earth remains forever'. – *Eppur si muove.*

The noteworthy conceit of the anonymous 'Ode of Cynthia' is at the heart of Spenser's doubly posthumous Two Cantos, though inversely: the conceit of a Cynthia pursuing the chase in her rebellious territories in the Irish woodlands on earth, while threatened in the heavens with a lunar eclipse – at the same boundary between the celestial and sublunary worlds transcended by the anonymous poet's licence in the above-quoted tribute of 1602.[88] Raleigh outlived his Tudor sovereign, and the publication history of *The Faerie Queene* outlived its royal subject (given the fact that the last part of the poem saw print only six years after her death); that history outlived its mortal author as well (Spenser had died a decade earlier). But while Raleigh's *Ocean to Cynthia* hardly conceives of itself as surviving its danger-fraught occasion and the courtier-author's present emergency, Spenser's *Two Cantos of Mutabilitie* hardly conceives of itself as doing anything else.

Both poems are a courtier's complaint, but only Spenser's makes it to a higher court and secures a goddess's transcendental judgement – even if the poet penultimately demurs from it, reusing the parting language of all his earlier complaints.[89] For example,

---

88 See *The Cosmographia of Bernardus Silvestris*, tr. Winthrop Wetherbee (New York and London: Columbia University Press, 1973), 105, for the nodal point. For the lunar frontier generally, see C. S. Lewis, *The Discarded Image* (Cambridge: Cambridge University Press, 1964), 3–4, 32, 41, 95–101, 108–9, and the traditional authorities: Aristotle, *De Caelo* II.iv, *Meteorologica* I.iii, *De Gen. et Cor.* II.iv, Pseudo-Aristotle, *De Mundo* v–vi, and Cicero in Macrobius, *Commentary on the Dream of Scipio*, at 'Scipio's Dream', chapter 4 [3].

89 Particularly instructive attention has been drawn to this inheritance by Prof. Mark Rasmussen, in 'Mutabilitie and Complaint', a paper he gave at the conference 'Eterne in Mutabilitie' at Kilkenny and Carrick on Sur, 9–11 May 2009.

> Alas, on earth so nothing doth endure,
> But bitter griefe and sorrowfull annoy:
>> Which make this life wretched and miserable,
>> Tossed with stormes of fortune variable.
>
> When I behold this tickle trustles state
> Of vaine worlds glorie, flitting too and fro,
> And mortall men tossed by troublous fate
> In restles seas of wretchedness and woe
>> I wish I might this wearie life forgoe,
>> And shortly turne vnto my happie rest, …
>>> And ye faire Ladie…
> When ye these rhymes doo read,
> Loath this base world and think of heauens bliss:
>   (*Visions of Petrarch*, 6–7)

Other Spenserian examples of this rhetoric abound, but all of the following are taken from *Complaints*, the 'few parcels' Spenser's printer has gathered together as 'grave and profitable', 'complaints and meditations of the worlds vanitie', in the wake of the success of his publication of *The Faerie Queene*: '[H]e that of himselfe is most secure, / Shall finde his state most fickle and vnsure' (*Visions of the Worlds Vanitie*, 12); 'O vaine worlds glorie, and vnstedfast state / Of all that liues' (*Rvines of Time* 43–4); 'all things do change that vnder heauen abide' (*RT* 206); 'Ye faire Ladie … loath this drosse of sinful worlds desire' (*RT*, 'L'Envoy'). Nature concedes to Mutabilitie 'that all things stedfastnes doe hate / And changed be' (vii.58), and the poet, thinking on Mutabilitie's case and yet deeming her 'vnworthy … Of the Heav'ns Rule', is thus also moved to 'Loath this state of life so tickle, / And loue of things so vaine to cast away; / Whose flowring pride, so fading and so fickle, / Short *Time* shall soon cut down' (viii.1), even while he also thinks hopefully on what Nature has said implying the triumph of eternity.

If Cecil chose not to forward Raleigh's histrionic letter to the Queen, this might help explain why Raleigh's comparable poem on the letter's subject ended up lost among the Cecil papers. No such explanation can be proposed for the conservation and belated publication of the 'parcell' containing Spenser's *Two Cantoes*. By the time of their posthumous printing not only was their Cynthia deceased, but so also were almost all of the dedicatees of the sonnets attached to the poem celebrating 'that Emperesse … that Faerie Queene' ('To … Hunsdon') themselves. If there were a single remaining Elizabethan who could have been expected to understand the meaning and the value of conserving Spenser's great and last complaint, it would not have been a deviously artful and self-protecting secretary of state like Cecil, but an unrepentant survivor and loyalist like Sir Walter.

Cynthia herself, as referred to by that specific, mythological name, drops out of the second canto of *The Faerie Queene*'s great pendant, except for the stanza where the planetary goddess's cognomen is derived from the earthly 'Cynthus hill' (VII.vii.50). But the poetical etymology of Elizabeth's own name survives in the poet's last published line, as if perpetuating itself with that 'eternity of her fame' bespoken by the poet at his poem's outset. As the urn-shaped dedication's eternizing prediction hopefully anchors the commitment of *The Faerie Queene*'s author to the Queen forever, so the covert repetition of Elizabeth, as found in the supplement's allusive last line ('Sabbaoth God' read as '*Eli* Sabbaoth [or *Sabbath*]'), assertively brackets the poem's whole oeuvre with the Tudor sovereign's Christian cognomen. Curiously, the women Spenser and Raleigh married had both also been christened with that 'gracious name' Elizabeth. Each of the married men had expressed his regret for his amorous truancy in regard to the Virgin Queen (see *FQ* VI.x.28), but surely both the poets had been faithful in their fashion.

Of course the perpetual youth of the Elizabeth in the 'Ode of Cynthia' merely shadows the eternity of the deity. God alone is genuinely eternal, from everlasting to everlasting. Against the Raleighesque expression of the 'Ode' we must set not only the reinstated Eli-Sabbaoth instatiated by the end of the Mutabilitie Cantos, but also the contemplations of Florio's Montaigne at the end of the *Apology of Raymond Sebond*:

> Seeing all things are subject to pass from one change to another, reason, which therein seeketh a real subsistence, finds herself deceived, as unable to apprehend anything subsistent and permanent; forsomuch as each thing either cometh to a being and is not yet altogether, or beginneth to die before it be born. ... Homer made the Ocean father and Thetis mother of the gods thereby to show that all things are in continual motion, change, and variation.[90]

Montaigne quotes Lucretius on the universality of change in the world, 'No one thing like itself remains; all things do pass; Nature doth change and drive to change each thing that was' (*De Rerum Naturae* V.828–9).[91] And as he regards this flux, Montaigne recapitulates: 'there is no constant existence, neither of our being nor of the objects. And we ... and all mortal

---

90 *Selected Essays of Montaigne*, ed. Walter Kaiser (Boston: Houghton Mifflin, 1964), 84–247: 244.
91 Ibid., 245.

things else do incessantly roll, turn, and pass away. Thus can nothing be certainly established, ... both he judging and judged being in continual alteration and motion'. For '[w]e have no communication with being,' because 'nothing remaineth or ever continueth in one state'.[92] These last are nearly Nature's own words in Spenser, 'all things stedfastnes doe hate / And changed be' (*MC* vii.58), agreeing with Mutability's 'nothing here long standeth in one stay' (*MC* vii.47): even if Nature goes on to argue that things in the world, when rightly considered, 'are not changed from their first estate' (*MC* vii.58), that is, when seen under the aspect of the saeculum and their generic-ness.

Montaigne, on the other hand, refuses to credit that subsistence of the Creation – like Adonis 'eterne in mutability' (*FQ* III.vi.48) – for which Spenser's Nature ultimately tries to argue:

> But then what is it that is indeed? That which is eternal: that is to say, that which never had birth ... and to which no time can bring change or cause alteration. ... For time is a fleeting thing, and which appeareth as in a shadow, with the matter ever gliding, always fluent, without ever being stable or permanent. ... As much happeneth unto nature, which is measured according unto time which measureth her; for no more is there anything in her that remaineth or is subsistent; ... it were a sin to say of God, who is the only that, that he was or shall be; for these words are declinations, passages, or vicissitudes of that which cannot last nor continue in being. Wherefore we must conclude that only God *is*, not according to any measure of time, but according to an immovable and immutable eternity, not measured by time, nor subject to any declination, before whom nothing is nor nothing shall be after, nor more new or more recent, but one really being, which by one only *now* or *present* filleth the *ever*; and there is nothing that truly is but he alone [...].[93]

Montaigne's sentiment is anticipated in Marguerite de Navarre's chant on the dominion of time – 'très variable / Et muable' – over all things, with the poem's commendation at its final stop 'A Celluy qui est sans temps'.[94] Behind this poem lies the *Romance of the Rose*'s own reflection on Time, 'who has it in his power to age all mankind' (*RR* 387–8).[95] Montaigne's language could have inspired Spenser's turn towards God at the very

---

92 Ibid., 244, 245.
93 Ibid., 246.
94 Text in *Nine Centuries of French Women Poets: The Distaff and the Pen*, ed. and tr. Norman R. Shapiro (Baltimore: Johns Hopkins University Press, 2008), 112–15.
95 Guillaume de Lorris and Jean de Meun, *The Romance of the Rose*, tr. Charles Dahlberg (Princeton: Princeton University Press, 1971), 36.

end of the Mutabilitie Cantos,[96] and it surprises the epicurean atomism of Montaigne's proceeding discourse – which has been radically sceptical about our knowing virtually anything. But would it have altogether surprised the equally sceptical Raleigh, even if he himself – unlike Job, or Spenser, or Montaigne – may have hardly had any Eternal God to turn to, or merely to overhear him?

Perhaps not. For in the same place we have been quoting from, Montaigne had described the growth and decline of human life from the seed in the womb in its first phase to an 'aged decrepit man' in its seventh and last phase, that is, 'in the end'.[97] The *Romance of the Rose* (after the translated verses quoted at the head of this section) reflects on the figure of Time who has aged Old Age, whom the narrator reckons ruefully 'Was fair sumtyme, and fresh to se, / Whan she was in hir rightful age; / But she was past al that passage, / And was a doted thing bicomen' (ll. 404–8). Raleigh has a prose passage in *The History of the World*, somewhat similar to Montaigne's, on the seven ages of man as constituting a planetary week: 'Our infancie is compared to the Moon, in which we seem only to live and grow, as plants [do]', and so on to the last and seventh day, which is comparable to Saturn, 'wherein our days are sad and overcast, and in which we find by dear and lamentable experience, and by the loss which can never be repaired, that of all our vain passions and affections past, the sorrow only abideth' (*History*, I.ii.5).[98] Whether or not this summation contemplates the passage in Montaigne, it is clearly written in language that has gone to school with *The Ocean to Cynthia*: 'Of all which past the sorrow only stayes' (*OC* 123). 'So wrate I once,' the author adds – but as appears now, also more than once.

---

96 As argued by Ayesha Ramachandran, 'Mutabilitie's Lucretian Metaphysics: Scepticism and Cosmic Process in Spenser's *Cantos*', in *Celebrating Mutabilitie*, ed. Jane Grogan (Manchester: Manchester University Press, 2010), 220–45.
97 Montaigne, *Selected Essays*, 245
98 As quoted at more length in *Analogy*, 737, *sub* 'The Triumph of Time'. Compare the ending of the third sonnet of *The Rvines of Rome*, referring to the time-like Tiber remaining a constant running through ancient Rome's eroding remnants: 'O worlds inconstancy! / That which is firm, doth flit and fall away, / And that is flitting, doth abide and stay.' The imagery for the stability of change within the mutability of things in the aggregate has ancient analogues: e.g., Ecclesiastes 1:7–8, 'All the rivers go into the sea, yet the sea is not ful; for the rivers go unto the place, whence their return, and go. All things are ful of labour' (Geneva Bible: Heb. *all of things are wearisome ones*; Vulgate, 'everything is *difficile*').

2

Spenser and Ralegh
Friendship and Literary Patronage[1]

Wayne Erickson

> all accounts agree in giving him a commanding presence.
> Sir John Pope Hennessy, discussing portraits of Ralegh, 1883[2]

Like many Spenserians and, I suppose, many Ralegheans, I have wanted to call Spenser and Ralegh friends,[3] at least in the guarded manner adopted by Jerry Mills in his article on Ralegh in the *Spenser Encyclopedia*. He writes that, '[f]or Spenser, Ralegh was more than a patron', that in the Letter to Ralegh and in Spenser's dedications to Ralegh, 'there are suggestions of strong ties approaching a close personal friendship' (584).[4] That may be a fairly accurate statement of the relationship between Spenser and Ralegh, but it requires qualification: Ralegh was more important to Spenser's life than Spenser was to Ralegh's, just as Spenser scholars need Ralegh more than Ralegh scholars need Spenser. In the context of Ralegh's large, varied, and turbulent life, Spenser must be accorded a very small place, as any historian's assessment or any biography of Ralegh

---

1 I thank Steve May for advice about a few details of my argument, Jean Brink for helpful comments on an earlier draft, and Bill Oram for many years of discussion and debate about Spenser's and Ralegh's relationship.
2 *Sir Walter Ralegh in Ireland* (London: Kegan Paul, Trench, 1883), 144.
3 This chapter is informed by and includes scattered material from a series of articles in which I explore Spenser's and Ralegh's relationship as depicted in the texts in which their personae interact with one another. See Wayne Erickson, 'Spenser's Letter to Ralegh and the Literary Politics of *The Faerie Queene*'s 1590 Publication', *Spenser Studies* X (1992), 139–74; 'Spenser and His Friends Stage a Publishing Event: Praise, Play, and Warning in the Commendatory Verses to the 1590 *Faerie Queene*', *Renaissance Papers* (1997), 13–22; and 'Spenser Reads Ralegh's Poetry in(to) the 1590 *Faerie Queene*'. *Spenser Studies* XV (2001), 175–84. See also Kathrine Koller's seminal article, 'Spenser and Ralegh', *ELH* 1 (1934), 37–60, and the indispensible series of articles by William A. Oram, including 'Elizabethan Fact and Spenserian Fiction', *Spenser Studies* 4 (1983), 33–47; 'Spenser's Raleghs', *Studies in Philology* 87 (1990), 341–62; and 'What Did Spenser Really Think of Sir Walter Ralegh When He Published the First Instalment of *The Faerie Queene*?' *Spenser Studies* XV (2001), 165–74.
4 Jerry Leath Mills, 'Walter Raleigh', in *The Spenser Encyclopedia*, ed. A. C. Hamilton, et al. (Toronto: University of Toronto Press, 1990), 584.

attests. The same kind of contextual adjustment should apply to Ralegh's patronage of Spenser, which looms large in accounts of Spenser's literary career. Ralegh apparently took care of his friends and relatives,[5] and he certainly read and supported all kinds of literature, but his patronage of writers, including Spenser, played a very small part in his vast life. The scant record of Ralegh's patronage of writers consists primarily of seventeen dedications of books to Ralegh (two by Spenser), most of them brief epistles that acknowledge favours, plead for protection, and implicitly claim by their presence Ralegh's endorsement of the publications.[6] Of more significance as a sign of friendship, perhaps, are the commendatory verses Ralegh wrote at three distinct periods of his career: an eighteen-line poem for George Gascoigne's *The Steele Glas* in 1576, two sonnets for Spenser's 1590 *Faerie Queene*, and a sonnet for Arthur Gorges's translation of Lucan's *Pharsalia* in 1614. The commendations do put Spenser in a fairly elite group, but they provide neither sufficient evidence of intimate friendship nor a clear indication of the kind and degree of Ralegh's patronage of Spenser, even when coupled with Spenser's letter and dedicatory sonnet to Ralegh, printed with Ralegh's commendatory sonnets among the texts appended to the 1590 *Faerie Queene*.

What does, however, provide most Spenserians and Ralegheans with sufficient proof of a close relationship between Spenser and Ralegh is *Colin Clouts Come Home Againe*, which includes not only a playful dedicatory epistle to Ralegh[7] but also a pastoral account of a meeting between Colin Clout and the Shepherd of the Ocean and their trip together to Cynthia's court. Biographers and literary critics alike tend to read Spenser literally when he tells Ralegh in the dedication that the poem 'agree[s]

---

5 Ralegh's letters contain evidence of his treatment of both his friends and relatives and his enemies and opponents; see Agnes Latham and Joyce Youings, ed., *The Letters of Sir Walter Ralegh* (Exeter: University of Exeter Press, 1999). Also revealing is an extant early (1597) will made by Ralegh; see A. M. C. Latham, 'Sir Walter Ralegh's Will', *The Review of English Studies* 22 (1971), 129–36.

6 See Franklin B. Williams, *Index of Dedications and Commendatory Verses in English Books before 1641* (London: The Bibliographical Society, 1962), 154. The wide range of books dedicated to Ralegh, close to a book a year from 1583 to 1603, provides a fairly accurate measure of his broad interests: four on voyages of discovery, three on geography, three of contemporary poetry, two each on history and religion, and one each on medicine, music, and horticulture.

7 Compare Andrew Zurcher, 'Getting It Back to Front in 1590: Spenser's Dedications, Nashe's Insinuations, and Ralegh's Equivocations', in *The 1590 'Faerie Queene': Paratexts and Publishing*, ed. Wayne Erickson, *Studies in the Literary Imagination* 38 (2005), 173–98. Zurcher reads Spenser's dedication to Ralegh as 'remarkably terse, even backhanded' (184), and constructs a plausible narrative of literary and political events that proposes a break between Spenser and Ralegh some time before Spenser writes his dedication in late 1591.

with the truth in circumstance and matter'.[8] With that apparent endorsement from Spenser, scholars apply whatever formula they prefer for decoding the historical allegory. Even those biographers of Ralegh and Spenser who otherwise most scrupulously seek documentary evidence for their accounts, lacking anything more concrete in this instance, usually read Spenser's pastoral quite literally, as a factual record of events and proof of relatively intimate friendship between Spenser and Ralegh.[9] Among Spenserians, debates concerning appropriate methodologies for interpreting Spenser's historical allegory have a long and contentious history,[10] but, with few exceptions, critics find it irresistibly convenient to treat the relationship between Colin Clout and the Shepherd of the Ocean as an accurate portrayal of biographical and historical events and of Spenser's and Ralegh's friendship.

Even in some of the best biographies, old and new, and in some of the most solidly convincing readings of the poem, scholars sometimes get carried away. Robert Lacey, for instance, in his solid popular biography of Ralegh, describes *Colin Clouts Come Home Againe* as 'a rare

---

8 Edmund Spenser, *The Yale Edition of the Shorter Poems of Edmund Spenser*, ed. William A. Oram et al. (New Haven: Yale University Press, 1989), 525. Spenser's dedication to Ralegh of *Colin Clouts Come Home Againe* is dated 27 December, 1591, though the poem was not published until 1595, and some revisions were made in the interim; see Sam Meyer, *An Interpretation of Edmund Spenser's 'Colin Clout'* (Notre Dame, IN: University of Notre Dame Press, 1969), 150–1. No one knows why the poem was not published until 1595.

9 Spenser's few biographers have not yet substantially questioned the blanket assumptions implied by the summary assessment of Alexander C. Judson: 'With the arrival of Raleigh at Kilcolman [in 1589], we enter upon a well-documented period of Spenser's life, for this visit, and the subsequent journey of the two men to England, are faithfully portrayed in *Colin Clouts Come Home Againe*' (*The Life of Edmund Spenser* (Baltimore: The Johns Hopkins University Press, 1945), 136). All of Ralegh's many biographers, popular and scholarly alike, use *Colin Clouts Come Home Againe* as more or less documentary evidence of events in Ralegh's life during the late summer and autumn of 1589; see Edward Edwards, *The Life of Sir Walter Ralegh, Together with His Letters*, 2 vols (London: Macmillan, 1868), I:120–9, and the appropriate sections from every biography that follows this early and definitive one, especially, among the best, William Stebbing, *Sir Walter Ralegh: A Biography* (Oxford: Clarendon Press, 1899), 71–2; Edward Thompson, *Sir Walter Ralegh: Last of the Elizabethans* (New Haven: Yale University Press, 1936), 69–71; and Willard M. Wallace, *Sir Walter Raleigh* (Princeton: Princeton University Press, 1959), 68–71. For an especially circumspect account of Ralegh's meeting with Spenser in 1589, see David B. Quinn, *Ralegh and the British Empire* (New York: Macmillan, 1949), 146–7.

10 See especially Edwin A. Greenlaw, *Studies in Spenser's Historical Allegory* (Baltimore: The Johns Hopkins University Press, 1932), and Michael O'Connell, *Mirror and Veil: The Historical Dimension of Spenser's 'Faerie Queene'* (Chapell Hill: University of North Carolina Press, 1977). For a brief but insightful comment on Spenser's fictional depictions of Ralegh, see Oram, 'Elizabethan Fact and Spenserian Fiction'.

piece of journalism'.[11] According to Lacey, the poem recounts a scene during which 'Walter obviously flattered Spenser'; 'But Walter had not travelled up the Blackwater simply to sit at Spenser's feet and listen to extracts from *The Faerie Queene*. He had verses of his own that he wanted expert opinion on'. Ralegh's apparent candidness in sharing his poetry with Spenser, his willingness 'to speak his mind straight out', convinces Lacey that 'Spenser had obviously struck a sympathetic chord in him'.[12] And the story continues in that vein, relatively restrained compared to descriptions of the scene in some other popular biographies. From a more scholarly context, Lin Kelsey's fine article about Spenser and Ralegh includes a moment that may over-read the fiction. Writing of Colin Clout and the Shepherd of the Ocean, Kelsey remarks that 'the delight the shepherds take in each other's song reflects the pleasure of two poets who discover that they speak the same language', noting as well that she has not come upon another instance in European pastoral of two shepherds sharing a pipe in a single singing match.[13] Although the thought of Spenser and Ralegh sharing a pipe is hard to resist, readers should certainly be wary of collapsing fiction into biography. As Sam Meyer argued long ago, *Colin Clout* is a poem, not a diary, and 'blurr[ing]' the distinction 'between Colin Clout as a *persona* and Edmund Spenser as a person' distorts both the history and the fiction.[14] At the very least, any biographical evidence from the poetry should be lightly qualified, as Jerry Mills does in his summary statement: 'In *Colin Clout*, we get a picture of an unusually close relationship between poet and patron' – *picture* being the operative word.[15]

So how well might Spenser and Ralegh have been acquainted? The documentary evidence is slim. Spenser and Ralegh can be placed in proximity two or perhaps three times during Spenser's life. During 1580 and 1581, Ralegh served as captain under Lord Grey in Ireland when Spenser was Grey's secretary, and strong evidence places both Spenser and Ralegh at the siege and massacre at Smerwick in early November 1580. They may have met then, near the beginning of their careers when, as William A. Oram argues, their social status was closer to equal than it would soon

---

11 *Sir Walter Ralegh* (New York: Atheneum, 1974), 142.
12 Ibid., 141, 142, 142. Compare J. H. Adamson and H. F. Folland, *The Shepherd of the Ocean: An Account of Sir Walter Ralegh and His Times* (Boston: Gambit, 1969), 184–8, a similar account in another satisfactory popular biography.
13 'Spenser, Ralegh, and the Language of Allegory', *Spenser Studies* XVII (2003), 185.
14 Meyer, *An Interpretation*, 142.
15 Mills, 'Walter Raleigh', 584.

become,¹⁶ though it is very difficult to gauge, here at the beginning or later, the degree to which social status determined the nature of their relationship. Indeed, the relationship between Spenser and Ralegh offers an especially complex instance of an issue of irresolvable contention among early modern scholars – how to read rank, class, and status. Whatever the answer, Ralegh's rise in power and prestige at court was imminent. Recent research by Steven W. May proves beyond reasonable doubt that Ralegh travelled to England by mid-December 1580 carrying 'secret matters of intelligence', which he presented to the Privy Council in a 'grand slam performance' that cemented relationships with Burghley and Walsingham and moved the Queen to reward Ralegh with 'his elevation to esquire extraordinary'.¹⁷ If Spenser saw Ralegh again between the time Ralegh returned to Ireland in early 1581 and went back to England near the end of that year, Spenser would have encountered a man well on his way up and, as it turned out, one step away from becoming Elizabeth's favourite.

The next time that most biographers of Spenser and Ralegh put the two together is late summer and autumn 1589, when Ralegh supposedly visited Spenser at Kilcolman and, in late autumn, took him to England – the story relayed in *Colin Clouts Come Home Againe*. Though no documentary evidence substantiates Ralegh's visit to Kilcolman, Ralegh certainly was in Munster, maybe as early as May, and there is no good reason to doubt that the two may have visited one another; even David B. Quinn surmises that Ralegh 'saw something of Edmund Spenser' during 1589, though he quickly adds that Ralegh was 'more preoccupied with lawsuits than with poetry'.¹⁸ But this may not have been the first time Spenser and Ralegh had seen each other since 1580 or 1581. Strong though partially circumstantial evidence suggests that Spenser and Ralegh encountered each other the year before, either between April and June or between mid-September and November 1588, times during which Ralegh could conceivably have been in Ireland,¹⁹ where most of his biographers put him during some of this time, looking to the affairs of the vast lands he had recently acquired and serving as mayor of Youghal.²⁰ Spenser, as Clerk of the Council of Munster and secretary to Sir Thomas

16 'What Did Spenser Really Think of Ralegh', 166.
17 'How Ralegh Became a Courtier', *John Donne Journal* 27 (2008), 136, 137, 137.
18 *Ralegh and the British Empire*, 146, 146–7.
19 I thank Steven W. May for checking his extensive notes to determine Ralegh's potential whereabouts during 1588.
20 See, for instance, Edwards, *Life*, I.96, 111; Stebbing, *Sir Walter Ralegh*, 65; Wallace, *Sir Walter Raleigh*, 63; and Quinn, *Raleigh*, 145–6, who cites S. Hayman, *Notes of the Ancient Religious Foundations at Youghal* (Youghal, 1855), 58–9, on Ralegh's mayoralty of Youghal for 1588–89.

Norris, President of Munster, was probably in Cork and Youghal during some of this time, though he travelled extensively with Norris throughout the year.[21] Sometime in 1588, Norris leased and took up residence in the College of Youghal, where Ralegh also had a house, which inspires Raymond Jenkins to imagine Ralegh and Spenser meeting 'frequently' during 1588 at Ralegh's house, where their 'friendship ... ripened'.[22] Even if Jenkins exaggerates a bit in his rehearsal of these supposed meetings, the possibility that Spenser and Ralegh met in 1588 provides a potential answer to a question that has puzzled me ever since I first read Jean R. Brink's 1994 article on the dating of Spenser's Letter to Ralegh.[23]

According to the Letter, appended to the 1590 *Faerie Queene*, Ralegh 'commanded' Spenser to defend and explain his poem.[24] But when? Spenserians who consider the question at all almost unanimously assume that Ralegh must have issued the command during 1589, when Spenser and Ralegh were supposedly together in Ireland and England. Since the letter is dated 23 January 1589, which most assume to be Old Style, that is, 1590, several months before the publication of *The Faerie Queene*, Spenserians have usually imagined Spenser's writing his little treatise while in England with Ralegh. Jean Brink's evidence, however, for New Style dating of the Letter – 1589 rather than 1590 – is so compelling as to seem nearly incontrovertible to me. Surveying earlier bibliographical studies, Brink finds proof that, quoting W. W. Greg, '"almost all books"' printed in London between 1550 and 1650, excepting some early law books, were dated '"according to the calendar year"', a practice that William Ponsonby, Spenser's publisher, employs without apparent exception.[25] Furthermore, concerning Spenser's books, Brink points out that the Letter to Ralegh is 'the only instance in which a date internal to a Spenserian dedication is modernized'.[26] This bibliographical evidence, coupled with the remainder of Brink's argument, which is equally convincing, suggests strongly that

---

21 See Raymond Jenkins, 'Spenser: The Uncertain Years 1584–1589', *PMLA* 53 (1938), 353–5. See also Judson, *Life*, 110–27, and Willy Maley, *A Spenser Chronology* (Lanham, MD: Barnes and Noble, 1994), 46–7.
22 Jenkins, 'Uncertain Years', 356, n55, who cites S. Hayman, *The Handbook of Youghal* (Youghal, 1852), 53.
23 'Dating Spenser's Letter to Ralegh', *The Library*, 6th series 16 (1994), 219–24.
24 Edmund Spenser, *The Faerie Queene*, 2nd edition, ed. A. C. Hamilton, text ed. Hiroshi Yamashita and Toshiyuki Suzuki (Harlow: Pearson Education, 2001), 714. All references to the Letter to Ralegh, the Commendatory Verses, the Dedicatory Sonnets, and *The Faerie Queene* are to this edition and will be cited in the text.
25 Ibid., 221. Brink quotes Greg, *Some Aspects and Problems of London Publishing between 1550 and 1650* (Oxford: The Clarendon Press, 1956), 83.
26 Ibid., 220.

Spenserians should revise their assumption about the date of the Letter. Thus, Spenser received Ralegh's command to explain himself either, most likely, somewhere in Munster – perhaps Cork, Youghal, or, indeed, Kilcolman[27] – during 1588 or by some other means than face-to-face contact; furthermore, if the former, more convincing, scenario is the case, Brink's dating of the Letter comes close to documentary evidence that Spenser and Ralegh met before 1589.

During these relatively brief periods of contact, Spenser and Ralegh certainly became acquainted and may have become friends, attracted to each other by their similar political views and their mutual interest in poetry, though Steven May remarks that Ralegh wrote 'most of his ambitious poetry ... when he was out of favour', that he 'used his pen [only] when other means of action were denied him'.[28] Perhaps Ralegh was mildly fascinated by someone who was devoting a good deal of time and energy to poetry; Spenser was definitely fascinated by Ralegh. But the nature of the relationship remains rather obscure, and the documented relationship does not appear to explain sufficiently the enigmatical qualities of tone adopted by Spenser and Ralegh in their written interactions with each other, especially in the material appended to the 1590 *Faerie Queene*.

Some critics, however, find the tone and meaning of these dedicatory and commendatory texts relatively straightforward. Much of that critical commentary concerns supposed differences of opinion between Spenser and Ralegh about the kind and value of the poetry they write, though issues of competition and class-consciousness creep into these discussions of poetic value. According to Patrick Cheney, when Spenser writes about Ralegh's poetry, he aims to suggest that 'Ralegh's verse inverts the *honourable* end of [Spenser's] own civic verse'.[29] Jeffrey Morris goes even further: 'Spenser has seized upon the gaps and weaknesses in his patron's poetic efforts and has used them to forward his own identity as the right poet for the English nation.'[30] William A. Oram sees Spenser in his dedicatory sonnet to Ralegh both instructing Ralegh and mildly intimidated by him: Ralegh 'has settled for amateur status, and the decision is a mistake', but Spenser does not reprimand Ralegh 'directly' because 'Ralegh is a great man and his patron, and to stress the criticism would risk that necessary

---

27 See Ray Heffner, 'Spenser's Acquisition of Kilcolman', *Modern Language Notes* 46 (1931), 493–8.
28 *Sir Walter Ralegh* (Boston: Twayne, 1989), 133. See also Wallace, *Sir Walter Raleigh*, 69.
29 *Spenser's Famous Flight: A Renaissance Idea of a Literary Career* (Toronto: University of Toronto Press, 1993), 134 (emphasis in original).
30 'Poetic Counsels: The Poet–Patron Relationship of Spenser and Ralegh' (Diss. Pennsylvania State University, 1993), 283.

support'.³¹ Apparently, Ralegh does not notice Spenser's disapproval. James P. Bednarz, interpreting Ralegh's Petrarchan spin on Spenser's epic in 'A Vision vpon this conceipt of the *Faery Queene*', sets up Spenser, 'an outsider, a low-level colonial administrator', as the passive foil of Ralegh's assertion of originative power: 'Ralegh usurps Arthur's central position in the epic', apparently without Spenser's knowledge or complicity.³² In my written responses to these critics, I have often suggested a little less dead seriousness and a little more fun between Spenser and Ralegh, noting variations on a playfully ironic tone in Ralegh's commendatory poems and in Spenser's letter and dedicatory sonnet and imagining that Spenser and Ralegh could be writing about each other's poetry as friends, collaborators, and intellectual equals.³³ Among commentators on these commendatory and dedicatory texts, Edward Thompson, in his essential 1936 biography of Ralegh, comes closest to characterizing the tone of intimate play and self-conscious wit that I discern in them. Thompson avers that the texts 'carry the sincerity of unselfish affection' while simultaneously displaying a 'charming hyperbole' that emerges as a sophisticated 'interchange of Chinese compliments': Spenser and Ralegh enact a friendly yet teasing literary engagement while 'delighting in their own grace and turns of phrase and emphasis'.³⁴ Thompson's brief but subtle analysis feels very satisfying to me.

Nonetheless, as a means of analysing anew the complexly enigmatic tone of the texts in which Spenser and Ralegh interact, I want to look at a brief parenthetical participial phrase from that packed, expansive, eloquent, and sly first sentence of the Letter to Ralegh. With so much going on, the phrase – '(being so by you commanded)' – is easy to read over without a thought, but here it is in context:

> SIR knowing how doubtfully all Allegories may be construed, and this booke of mine, which I haue entituled the Faery Queene, being a continued Allegory, or darke conceit, I haue thought good aswell for auoyding of gealous opinions and misconstructions, as also for your better light in reading therof (being so by you commanded,) to discouer vnto you the general intention and meaning, which in the whole course therof I haue fashioned, without expressing of any particular purposes or by-accidents therein occasioned. (714)

---

31 'Spenser's Raleghs', 346. Oram has, over the years, subtly qualified his stance without substantially changing it; see 'What Did Spenser Really Think of Ralegh'.
32 'The Collaborator as Thief: Ralegh's (Re)Vision of *The Faerie Queene*', *ELH* 63 (1996), 285, 283.
33 See Erickson, 'Spenser's Letter to Ralegh', 139–47, 153–61; 'Spenser and His Friends', 13–19; and 'Spenser Reads Ralegh's Poetry', 175–84.
34 *Sir Walter Ralegh*, 70, 71, 71, 71.

Of course, in the next sentence – 'The general end therefore of all the booke is to fashion a gentleman or noble person in virtuous and gentle discipline' (714) – Spenser obeys Ralegh's command. Or, sort of, because this short and well-known sentence is another mouthful: Spenser fashions nobles as characters who, if the nobles read them rightly, will teach the nobles how they ought to behave. But that's not the point here: it's the command itself, why it's there, and how the possibilities of its tone expose the relationship between Spenser and Ralegh, producing some combination of tense and intimate interaction.

Command is a strong word, with immediate martial associations; it's what commanders do: give orders to inferiors, to those under their command. In which case, Ralegh behaves like a superior and Spenser registers obedience born of rank anxiety. But it's not even quite clear what exactly Ralegh commands Spenser to do; that is, he may tell Spenser to defend himself against attack by the proverbial Momuses by exposing his poem's upright and innocent didacticism, or, as the syntax seems to imply, he may simply want Spenser to provide some 'better light' for reading the 'dark conceit'. If Ralegh seeks merely some illumination, the mildly ironic overstatement mitigates the force of the command. If, on the other hand, Ralegh has found something in the poem that might stir up trouble, he demands from Spenser some assistance in performing one of the primary duties of a patron: to implicitly defend the work by being associated with it through a dedication – to vouchsafe the work, to vouch for it and to protect it. In other words, Ralegh registers his scepticism about what might be going on behind all the veiling, shadowing, clouding, and colouring that Spenser discloses and declares as his allegorical method.

Either way, and they both know it, Ralegh's request or demand for an explanation and Spenser's apparent inclination to do so anyway derives from a source that, so far, has been invisible in plain sight, an elephant in the living room of this poem: Elizabeth, the Faery Queen, and, especially, Cynthia and Belphoebe. Ralegh, in fact, makes an even more radical demand of Spenser in his second commendatory verse: 'If Chastitie want ought, or Temperaunce her dew, / Behold her Princely mind aright, and write thy Queene anew' (721). If Elizabeth doesn't like your poem, I can't do anything for you; you must rewrite your already published poem, or at least produce the damage control that the Letter supposedly entails. Instead, Spenser wades in deeper, dragging Ralegh along with him. When he explains the 'particular' 'intention' of 'that Faery Queene', 'conceive[d]' by him as 'our soueraine the Queene, and her kingdome in Faery land', Spenser lets Ralegh know that the part of her that he 'expresse[s] in Belphoebe' has been 'fashion[ed] ... according to your owne excellent conceipt of Cynthia' (716). In other words, as James Nohrnberg has recently pointed out, Spenser 'credits [Ralegh] with virtually inventing Belphoebe'.[35] At this point, Ralegh may be regretting that he ever commanded the wily poet Spenser to explain himself, for Spenser has enlisted him as a co-conspirator; or Ralegh may be a witting and active collaborator.

Things get even more sticky in the proem to Book 3, for there, after Spenser spends three stanzas convincing himself and his readers that no 'liuing art' can 'figure plaine' the 'glorious portraict' of his 'dred Soueraine', he recommends that if Elizabeth 'couet[s]' to see herself 'pictured' in 'liuing colours, and right hew', she should study the 'sweet verse, with *Nectar* sprinckeled' of her 'gracious seruant' Ralegh, whose depiction of 'his heauens fairest light' sends Spenser over the edge: 'That with his melting sweetnesse ravished, / And with the wonder of her beames bright, / My senses lulled are in slomber of delight' (3-4). This ecstatically sensuous description of Ralegh's poetry makes it nearly impossible for readers who have just turned the page from the liquid pleasures of the Bower of Bliss not to see Ralegh, and Spenser with him, slumbering vicariously in the arms of Cynthia as Acrasia. But Spenser isn't done. Since the 'delitious Poet' Ralegh can 'picture' Cynthia 'more liuely' and 'more trew' than he can, Spenser allows Ralegh to sexualize the Queen's mortal body while Spenser's 'rusticke Muse' innocently 'sing[s]' Ralegh's 'mistresse['s] prayse'. Furthermore, 'If ought amis [Cynthia's] liking may abuse', 'let [Ralegh] mend' it (5), Spenser commands, which is either a provocation to which Ralegh responds in his second commendatory verse, where he tells Spenser to do the mending himself, or Spenser's revision of the proem in response to Ralegh's poem. Who's commanding whom, and when? With versions of commands and counter-commands being hurled back and forth, and with Spenser and Ralegh implicating each other and themselves in their various poetic re-creations of the Queen, as Ralegh especially does in his 'Vision vpon this conceipt of the *Faery Queene*', it becomes rather difficult to take Ralegh's initial command very seriously.

Whether or not Spenser and Ralegh were intimate friends, they were, for a time, literary collaborators, and, whether or not Ralegh ever got Spenser into the court to read to the Queen, Ralegh was, for a time,

---

35 James Nohrnberg, 'Britomart's Gone Abroad to Brute-land, Colin Clout's Come Courting from the Salvage Ire-land: Exile and the Kingdom in Some of Spenser's Fictions for "Crossing Over"', in *Edmund Spenser: New and Renewed Directions*, ed. J. B. Lethbridge (Teaneck, NJ: Fairleigh Dickinson University Press, 2006), 276.

something more than a patron: he was, to a small degree and from one perspective, a contributor to *The Faerie Queene*, inventor of the conceit that Spenser associates with Belphoebe and a fictionalized character in Spenser's poetry. Spenser was a small part of Ralegh's huge life; in contrast, Ralegh became a large part of Spenser's, a commanding presence, in which the connotation of *command* resides somewhere between an authoritarian order and a reaction to something impressive – it demands attention and already has it. Ralegh's impressive presence, like an object of desire, commands Spenser's attention, in both senses of the word. Maybe that helps to explain why Spenser was especially obsessed with Ralegh's love life, marriage, and disgrace, as allegorized in the stories of Timeas, Belphoebe, and Amoret in *The Faerie Queene*; Bregog, Mulla, and Mole in *Colin Clouts Come Home Againe*; and Molanna, Faunus, and Cynthia in the Mutabilitie Cantos.[36] Or perhaps Spenser really did attempt to protect and defend his patron and, in doing so, tried to understand and illuminate the workings of court intrigue, though it is also worth remembering what F. J. Levy has been implicitly arguing for years and repeats in his essay for the 1996 volume *Spenser's Life and the Subject of Biography*: 'Spenser never understood the political system at court well enough to manipulate it.'[37] Still, as Oram argues after quoting this same passage from Levy, Spenser's 'refusal ... to abandon his former patron' when Ralegh was out of favour 'may have been a matter of temperament rather than one of understanding', a stubborn 'refusal to abandon a position he feels is right', which Oram calls 'one of Spenser's most enduring characteristics'.[38] That kind of independence of mind would certainly have been attractive to Walter Ralegh. On the other hand, maybe, after his brief youthful stabs at preferment at court, which led to his position as Grey's secretary, Spenser never really desired to manipulate court politics. Whatever the truth of any of these speculations, Ralegh's momentous and tumultuous career, in which Spenser played a minor role, did indeed captivate the great poet and dutiful civil servant.

---

36 These identifications, among others, are staples of Spenser criticism, but see, most recently, Nohrnberg, 'Britomart's Gone Abroad', 267–82. Compare J. B. Lethbridge, 'Raleigh in Books III and IV of *The Faerie Queene*: The Primacy of Moral Allegory', *Neophilologica* 64 (1992), 55–66, who cautions against unmediated readings of Timias as Ralegh. Similarly, as noted above (note 11), Meyer, in *An Interpretation*, cautions against literal readings of the historical allegory of *Colin Clouts Come Home Againe*.
37 'Spenser and Court Humanism', in *Spenser's Life and the Subject of Biography*, ed. Judith H. Anderson, Donald Cheney, and David Richardson (Amherst: University of Massachusetts Press), 75.
38 Oram, 'What Did Spenser Really Think of Ralegh', 173.

3

Love's 'emperye'

Raleigh's 'Ocean to Scinthia', Spenser's 'Colin Clouts Come Home Againe' and *The Faerie Queene* IV.vii in colonial context

Thomas Herron

> Ralegh always wrote with immediate purpose, with persuasion as his goal.
> Leath Mills[1]

Literary critics Jerry Leath Mills, Mary C. Fuller, Walter S. Lim, and Richard Frohock have demonstrated the bold rhetorical strategies, complicated ethnographic discourse and anxiety-fraught motivations behind English New World promotional tracts, such as Raleigh's *Discovery of the Large, Rich and Bewtiful Empire of Guiana, with a relation of the great and Golden Citie of Manoa (which the spanyards call Ell Dorado)* (1596). Desire for 'the great and Golden' in this case fuels artistic creation and authorial posturing. Lim analyses its blatant self-promotion, ethnographic typecasting, and utopian dreams.[2] Mills admires the *Discovery*'s finely tuned

---

1 Mills, 'Sir Walter Ralegh', in *Dictionary of Literary Biography*, Vol. 172: *Sixteenth Century British Nondramatic Writers*, ed. D. A. Richardson (Detroit: Gale Research Books, 1996), 200–16: 212. For a politicized reading of 'Ocean to Scinthia' that influences Mills's own, see Leonard Tennenhouse, 'Sir Walter Ralegh and the Literature of Clientage', in *Patronage in the Renaissance*, ed. Guy Fitch Lytle and Stephen Orgel (Princeton, NJ: Princeton University Press, 1981), 235–58. See also Steven May, *The Elizabethan Courtier Poets: The Poems and Their Contexts* (Columbia: University of Missouri Press, 1991), 126–32 (in a chapter entitled 'Utilitarian Poetics: Gorges, Ralegh, and Essex'). I would like to thank Dr Mills for his advice on an early draft of this chapter, as well as Christopher Armitage, Darryl Gless, Julian Lethbridge, Sean Aube, and anonymous readers for the press for their comments. The chapter was first presented on 25 February 2006 as 'Sir Walter Raleigh's Poetry and the Munster Plantation' for the conference, *Plantation Ireland: settlement and material culture, c.1550–c.1700*, sponsored by the Irish Post-Medieval Archaeology Group and the Society for Irish Historical Settlement, Cork, Ireland. Select proceedings from that conference and additional papers (some referenced here) are found in James Lyttleton and Colin Rynne, eds, *Plantation Ireland: Settlement and Material Culture, c.1550–c.1700* (Dublin: Four Courts Press, 2009).

2 'The primary aim of *The Discoverie of Guiana* is to convince Elizabeth I of the trials experienced and undergone by the courtier in the service of his Queen, as well as to give ample proof that the Eden of Guiana does in fact exist'. Walter S. Lim, *The Arts of Empire* (Cranbury, NJ: Associated University Presses, 1998), 44.

Aristotelian rhetoric and declares that the tract 'succeeded more as a literary work than as an immediate incentive to investors or statesmen', and Frohock goes so far as to proclaim Raleigh's forceful narrator in the *Discovery*... the model 'British Imperial Protagonist', a valuable trend-setter for later literary 'Planter-Heroes'.[3] Greater critical scrutiny, in other words, has highlighted the significant literary and cultural achievement of Raleigh's colonial prose.

We should therefore be able to turn the tables and look for colonial motifs and motivation in Raleigh's poetry as well. To do so is to broaden standard readings of his poetry that identify courtly political strategies and *realpolitik* typical of Elizabethan Petrarchan lyrics,[4] so as to include colonial, imperial readings as well. Raleigh is a perfect test-case for this sort of analytical amalgamation of New Historicist-style readings of Petrarchan love-complaint.

A second reason for doing so is to emphasize the epic strain in Raleigh's most ambitious poem, 'Ocean to Scinthia', which contains a highly confused blend of genres: not only is it a Petrarchan love lyric shaking with courtly ambition and psychological duress but it is also a highly politicized pastoral complaint with a strongly elegiac and self-pitying tone, wherein Raleigh imagines 'my ioys interred' and 'buried' when he loses the Queen's favour ('Ocean' 21.1, 411):[5] the deeply frustrated Raleigh sings at the funeral of his own desires. Despite its length, the poem is lyric, not narrative.[6] Yet it has an energetic, seagoing drive. This drive, as well as the poem's multi-book structure, helps identify 'Ocean to Scinthia' as an epic fragment. The speaker beseeches the Queen's aid to continue his effort 'to seeke new worlds' (21.61) and new heroic heights on behalf of art and colonial empire.

In this regard, the poem shadows Edmund Spenser's 'Colin Clouts Come Home Againe' as in many other particulars, including identical

---

3 Mills, 'Sir Walter', 213; Richard Frohock, *Heroes of Empire: The British Imperial Protagonist in America, 1596-1764* (Newark, NJ: University of Delaware Press, 2004), 24–9, 167–80, passim. See also Mary C. Fuller, 'Ralegh's Fugitive Gold: Reference and Deferral in *The Discoverie of Guiana*', *Representations*, 33 (1991), 42–64.

4 See Tennenhouse, 'Sir Walter Ralegh'; Stephen Greenblatt, *Sir Walter Ralegh: The Renaissance Man and His Roles* (New Haven, CT: Yale University Press, 1973).

5 All references to 'Ocean to Scinthia' and other Raleigh poems, unless otherwise indicated, are taken from Agnes Latham ed., *The Poems of Sir Walter Ralegh* (Cambridge: Harvard University Press, 1962). I do not follow her numbering of the two Books of 'Ocean to Scinthia' as 11 and 12; instead I follow the numbering, 21 and 22, given by most scholars, including Mills, 'Sir Walter', and Stacy M. Clanton, 'The 'Number' of Sir Walter Ralegh's *Booke of the Ocean to Scinthia*', *Studies in Philology* 83 (1985), 200–11.

6 Steven May, *Sir Walter Ralegh*. Twayne's English Authors Series 469 (Boston: G. K. Hall, 1989), 45.

metre and rhyme scheme, generic conflation, numerological significance, pastoral imagery, Irish subject matter, emphasis on streams and seafaring, as well as despairing laments coupled with neoplatonized praise of the Queen and her imperial /colonial purpose.[7] Like Spenser's shepherd-avatar Colin Clout, but to a more melancholy extent, Raleigh's poetic voice indicates deep frustration at the fickleness of worldly fortune and simultaneously justifies Raleigh's own worth by highlighting his past epic 'labours' on behalf of the Queen. Raleigh evokes the treasures that his future actions might again acquire. The poem does not rest entirely in despair, therefore, but alternates that despondency with a positive (but always short-lived) emphasis on possible, future action should the Queen take him back into favour.

With the vernal resurrection of Raleigh's spirit comes the hope of expanding England's empire: this promise is repeated in overt and subtle ways throughout the poem. Raleigh was not only a 'courtier, soldier, explorer and travel writer', as Ruth Padel summarizes his achievements in the opening sentence to her recent edition of his poems,[8] he was also a planter. It is therefore vital to note here that the Queen's imperial-colonial outlook in the late 1580s and early 1590s, the likely date of composition of 'Ocean to Scinthia', included Raleigh's Irish prospects every bit as much as his New World ones. The poem was likely written at the same time that Raleigh wrote to Robert Cecil promoting his Irish concerns (Part II, below). Discovering a more prominent Irish component to Raleigh's poem, so far neglected, is therefore another, third, important reason for assessing its colonial context(s).

Key to understanding the Irish subtext of 'Ocean to Scinthia', furthermore, is to understand the poem's acknowledged relation to the work of Edmund Spenser. The first we hear of (what is probably) 'Ocean' is reference to it in the Proem to Book III of Spenser's *The Faerie Queene* (1590)

---

7 Spenser registers great pessimism and anxiety about his Irish situation in parts of his poetry, including *The Faerie Queene* VII.vi.55 ('The Mutabilitie Cantos') and 'Colin Clouts Come Home Againe' 312–19, but he does not lose hope (see discussion, below). For analysis of 'Colin Clouts' as a mixed-genre pastoral poem in transition towards epic, see Patrick Cheney, 'Spenser's Pastorals: *The Shepheardes Calender* and *Colin Clouts Come Home Againe*', in *The Cambridge Companion to Spenser*, ed. Andrew Hadfield (Cambridge: Cambridge University Press, 2001), 79–105: 83, 98. That epic strain (I argue here) corresponds with a similar sense of potential colonial purpose in 'Ocean'. Cheney perceptively connects the authors' mutual interests in Ireland with their shared literary ambitions: 'Colin begins his song to Cynthia with 'The shepheard of the Ocean' (66) because Spenser's Irish pastoral friendship with Raleigh led to the epic voyage to their English sovereign's court' (Cheney 99).

8 Padel, 'Introduction', in Ruth Padel, ed., *Sir Walter Ralegh: Poems Selected by Ruth Padel* (London: Faber and Faber, 2010), ix–xvii: ix.

and in 'Colin Clouts Come Home Againe' (c.1591; published 1595). In the latter poem, Spenser describes Raleigh sharing verses on 'Cynthia' with him (in his guise as Colin Clout) at Kilcolman Castle, County Cork, presumably in 1589. Colin responds to the poetry enthusiastically with his own 'piping' verse ('Colin Clouts Come Home Againe' 60–79).[9] Both were New English planters in Munster and so here is one colonial 'shepherd' piping to another. Spenser quite literally situates Raleigh's poem in an Irish context. Raleigh's view of colonial endeavour in 'Ocean to Scinthia' is not a positive one, although he does stress *potential* colonial success, as does Spenser. This chapter considers the possibility that 'Ocean' developed not only in reaction to Raleigh's courtly woes, including the Throckmorton disgrace of 1592, but also as a result, or reflection, of his colonial progress in the New World and Ireland in the 1580s and 1590s.

Hence, while Pauline Croft argues for a division between various types of Raleigh's writing, poetry and history on the one hand versus swashbuckling colonial propaganda on the other,[10] further examination reveals that such a dichotomy is simply not possible and should not be judged in such absolute terms. Far from his image as a carefree buccaneer, Raleigh was more profoundly involved in Ireland than many people are aware of, and his in-depth involvement there fuelled his creative art and that of critical colleagues such as Spenser.

I. Raleigh's Love to Ireland and Modern Poets and Critics

It is certainly strange that, given Raleigh's active and articulated New and Old World colonialism in the 1590s and our current climate of politically hypersensitive literary criticism, including postcolonial theory and extensive attention to Spenser's Irish subject matter, no mainstream critic has stressed the specifically colonial purpose and subject matter of Raleigh's *poetry* in particular. There is one exception, the poet Seamus Heaney. In recently published interviews, Heaney frankly and forthrightly acknowledges the skill of both Spenser and Raleigh while situating their work as products of an aggressive, Protestant, colonial-planter mentality, one still very much in evidence in his home country of Northern Ireland today.

> I have this fancy about the quality of decisiveness, the clean beheading stroke you get in Walter Ralegh's poetry, that it's related to the professional English

---

9   Spenser, 'Colin Clouts Come Home Againe', in *The Yale Shorter Poems of Edmund Spenser*, ed. William A. Oram et al. (New Haven, CT: Yale University Press, 1989), 525–62. All references to the poem in this chapter are taken from this edition.
10 Pauline Croft, review of Robert Lacey, *Sir Walter Ralegh* (London: Weidenfeld and Nicolson, 1973), in *English Historical Review* 90 (October 1975), 894.

captain [i.e., Raleigh himself] who cut the heads off Spanish soldiers at the Smerwick massacre in Ireland. That renaissance *sprezzatura* gives you style in the line, but it also gives you a ruthlessness with the sword. Raleigh is a soldier-poet in the full sense – it's not the 'pity of war' but the exultation of his swordsmanship that you feel in his work.[11]

Heaney is off the mark if referring to the highly allusive, ambiguous, darkly brooding, erratically punctuated and syntactically tortured 'Ocean to Scinthia' as somehow 'decisive' and 'clean'-stroked. Other poems better suit the description.[12] Raleigh does, however, call his verse in 'Ocean' 'simpell wordes' at the outset (21.2), and it is not the vocabulary of the poem but the subject, object, and syntax that mostly confound, sometimes over the course of a stanza or two or three. The poem needs clearer punctuation and conjunctions for the sake of comprehension (e.g., 'And will not know while hee knows his own passion / The often and vniust perseverance / In deeds of love', 21.315–17).

Heaney, moreover, is complimenting his 'style': Raleigh does demonstrate *sprezzatura* when writing gracefully and inventively in the poem ('Thy lines ar now a murmeringe to her eares / Like to a fallinge streame which passinge sloe / Is wount to nurrishe sleap, and quietness', 21.362–4), and by compacting deeply allusive meaning into his 'simpell' wordes, including some astonishing images buzzing about his 'sadd heart' like 'sorrow suckinge bees' (21.413–15). A courtier's 'swordsmanship' might resemble fencing, after all: dazzling, feinting, deliberately confusing and deadly quick.

Regardless of style, more relevant to our discussion here is Heaney's apt reading of 'Ocean' as invested in Irish colonial politics. Heaney offers a politicized reading of 'Ocean to Scinthia' elsewhere, for he wrote a poem, 'Oceans Love to Ireland', that riffs on Raleigh's title and that carries a similar message as his interview comment. In the poem, Raleigh, a.k.a. 'Ocean', forcibly seduces a woman against a tree and 'ruins' her

---

11 Seamus Heaney, quoted in Dennis O'Driscoll, *Stepping Stones: Interviews with Seamus Heaney* (New York: Farrar, Straus, and Giroux, 2008), 455. Heaney also compares Hrothgar's Danes in their 'bawn' at Heorot to Spenser and Raleigh at Kilcolman, threatened by Irish grendels: Heaney, 'Introduction', *Beowulf: A New Verse Translation*, ed. and tr. Seamus Heaney (New York: W. W. Norton 2000), ix–xxx: xxx. For analysis of Spenser's influence on Heaney, see Jane Grogan, 'After the Mutabilitie Cantos: Yeats and Heaney reading Spenser', in *Celebrating Mutabilitie: Essays on Edmund Spenser's 'Mutabilitie Cantos'*, ed. Jane Grogan (Manchester: Manchester University Press, 2010), 295–314.

12 For example, Raleigh's well-known and forthright 'Nimphs reply to the Sheepheard', a response to Marlowe's 'Come Live With Me and Be My Love'. Certainly Raleigh's *sprezzatura* can be found in this deft, playful, graceful, imitative, and witty retort built on a foundation of monosyllabic diction and tone of command.

(an episode taken from the famous 'swisser-swatter' episode described by John Aubrey),[13] just as England violently conquers and impregnates Ireland and its native language with its foreign 'iambic drums / Of English'. Perceptively, Heaney sees Raleigh's poeticized desire for 'Cynthia', or the English Queen, as figuratively analogous to (and /or aiding and abetting) Raleigh's desire for Irish land.[14]

A contemporary audience, like Edmund Spenser or Robert Cecil, is likely to have appreciated the poem's colonial significance as well. Raleigh was greatly concerned with Irish affairs much of his adult life. Appropriation of Munster land and its exploitation was something he had aimed for in his first 'swashbuckling years' of 1579-81, when he rose to fame as a soldier fighting for the New English during the Desmond rebellion (1579-83). At that time, he had unsuccessfully tried to take Barry's Island, Co. Cork, from Lord Barry and his son, and he kept his hand in Irish affairs after returning to London. He was on hand at court to benefit from the ensuing plantation and both visited and directed ambitious industry in the province of Munster in the late 1580s and early 1590s. Unlike others he tried hard to fill the quotas for imported settlers set by the Crown.

In this context, the speaker's lament of being in a 'Twelue yeares... warr', having spent 'Twelue yeares of my most happy younger dayes' ('Ocean' 120-1) aptly describes Raleigh's hard work in the queen's service, including both fighting the Irish and later creating the Munster plantation (and other important projects) in occasionally hostile circumstances. It also dates the poem to c. 1592, or twelve years after 1580.[15]

Raleigh's heroic actions while a soldier in Ireland also inspired allegorized episodes in Spenser's romance-epic *The Faerie Queene*, which is dedicated in part to Raleigh. Spenser allegorizes Raleigh's tumultuous love life in that work through the character, Timias. Spenser sharply criticizes Raleigh's behaviour in the latter regard, including (it is suggested here) its impact on Irish plantation politics (Part III, below). Plantation politics also appears to have inspired Raleigh's own poetry (Parts IV and V, below). Through 'Ocean to Scinthia' we gain valuable insight into the colonial *mentalité* of one of the Munster Plantation's prime movers

---

13 Aubrey, *Brief Lives*, ed. Andrew Clark, 2 vols (Oxford: Oxford University Press, 1898), 179. Cited in Lacey, *Sir Walter Ralegh*, 40.
14 'Yet his superb crest inclines to Cynthia / Even while it runs its bent / In the rivers of Lee and Blackwater': Heaney, 'Ocean's Love to Ireland', in *North* (1975) (Reading: Faber and Faber, 1989), 46-7. For a close reading of the poem with a feminist bent, see Karen M. Moloney, 'Heaney's Love to Ireland', *Twentieth Century Literature* 37.3 (Autumn 1991), 273-88.
15 Latham, ed., *Poems*, 16-17, 18-19; May, *Sir Walter Ralegh*, 46.

and shakers and its largest landowner, Raleigh, a fellow writer-planter of the greater writer but lesser planter, Spenser. Not only does Raleigh's portrayal of himself get echoed in Spenser's poems, based in Ireland, but Raleigh, like Spenser, simultaneously advertises Ireland's (and the New World's) plantation wealth as a topos of desire and as a spur to literary, epic achievement. Raleigh's achievement was frustrated by the Queen's punitive actions and purse strings, as the softer and sometimes benevolent moon-like Cynthia turned into the blazing sun of royal jealousy and harsh Justice during the Throckmorton scandal in particular. Should the Queen only love and patronize him again, beseeches Raleigh, then he will return her investment with loving tribute of his own: more imperial and colonial wealth and poetry as well.

This chapter is therefore meant to qualify recent judgements of 'Ocean' that stress its subject matter and fragmentary and rough nature as overwhelming evidence of anxiety, pessimism, and despair: Pierre LeFranc, for example, finds that its scattered style expresses a torn soul ('âme dechirée'); Greenblatt sees in it 'an abandoned lover's gesture of despair' of inward, cosmic proportions: '*Ocean to Cynthia* is not only about the death of love but about the death of a whole imaginative world sustained by that love'. Robert Stillman finds disillusionment with the 'cult' of Queen Elizabeth and hence 'the exhaustion of a whole order of symbolism upon whose existence [Raleigh's] status at court, his identity and the coherence of his world depended'. More recently, Miri Tashma-Baum supports these readings and stresses the poem's transcendent despair that 'bespeaks an inwardness whose break with society ... is radical'.[16]

There is good reason for thinking along these lines. The conclusion to the primary, twenty-first Book, for example, describes how 'Dispaire' encourages the speaker to burn his 'pipe' that sings the praises of his Cynthia, while

16 Pierre LeFranc, *Sir Walter Ralegh, Écrivain: l'oeuvre et les idées* (Paris: Librairie Armand Colin, 1968), 134; Greenblatt, *Sir Walter Ralegh*, 86, 76, 82; Stillman, '"Words cannot knytt": Language and Desire in Ralegh's "The Ocean to Cynthia"', *Studies in English Literature* 27 (1987), 35–51: 36. These three opinions are sympathetically cited in Miri Tashma-Baum, 'A Shroud for the Mind: Ralegh's Poetic Rewriting of the Self', *Early Modern Literary Studies* 10.1 (May 2004), paragraph 33 and endnote 19 (http: / /purl.oclc.org /emls /10–1 /tashrale.htm, accessed 25 January 2010). Tashma-Baum stresses the poem's transcendent despair that 'bespeaks an inwardness whose break with society ... is radical' (paragraph 33). Jerome S. Dees, 'Colin Clout and the Shepherd of the Ocean', in *Spenser Studies: A Renaissance Poetry Annual* (New York: AMS Press, Inc.), 15 (2001), 185–96 (189, 193) supports Greenblatt's reading of Raleigh's poetry. Greenblatt (76) relies on the assumption, despite contrary evidence in Spenser, that the poem has its *origins* in the 1592 Tower crisis: 'It was in this crisis, in the shock and frustration and anguish of imprisonment that *Ocean to Cynthia* was born'.

> Constraynt me guides as old age drawes a stonn
> Agaynst a hill, which over wayghty lyes
>
> For feebell armes, or wasted strenght to move.
> My steapps are backwarde, gasinge on my loss,
> My minds affection, and my sowles sole love,
> Not mixte with fancies chafe, or fortunes dross.
>
> To God I leve it, who first gave it me,
> And I her gave, and she returned agayne,
> As it was herrs. So lett his mercies bee,
> Of my last comforts, the essentiall meane.
>   Be it so, or not, th'effects, ar past.
>   Her love hath end; my woe must ever last.
>
>   (21.507–22)

Raleigh imagines himself as Sisyphus, rolling a stone eternally up the steep hill of courtly favour (and time). Her love has fled; his hellish 'woe must ever last', a powerfully pessimistic conclusion to the fragmentary poem's main Book.

This despondency nonetheless has hope built into it if read with Christian symbolism in mind (whether or not Raleigh was himself an atheist). Raleigh alludes to the wealthy disciple Joseph of Arimathea entombing his God-given Lord and 'spirit', or the image of the Queen (his 'sowles sole love', which is the likely pronoun referent for 'it' in lines 517–19).[17] Raleigh takes 'backwarde' steps from the 'stonn' as if in *congé* to his divine mistress. If we pursue the latter, Christian significance to the reading, then the despair of the image is qualified by hope of resurrection, even if the poet doesn't openly say so: 'she', like his poetry, might 'return agayne',[18] just as she once 'returned agayne' his love: 'So lett his mercies bee. ... Be it so, or not, th'effects, ar past. / Her love hath end; My woe must ever last'. Be it so ... *or not*.

The twenty-first Book therefore ends on an ambivalent note of despair leavened with hope, while the twenty-second Book begins on a qualified

---

17 'So Ioseph toke the bodie, and wrapped it in a cleane linnen cloth, / And put it in his newe tombe, which he had hewen out in a rocke, & rolled a great stone to the doore of the sepulchre, and departed'. Matthew 27:59–60 in Lloyd E. Berry, *The Geneva Bible: A Facsimile of the 1560 Edition* (Madison, WI: University of Wisconsin Press, 1969).

18 The poem's future included re-turning for another Queen, Anne, in 1618: Raleigh, once more in the Tower, considered petitioning her with a short poem that included fragments from 'Ocean to Scinthia'. The first two stanzas of that draft are the first two stanzas of Book 22 from the original MS. Raleigh was a shameless recycler of *billets doux* to the high and mighty. See Raleigh, 'Conjectvral First Draft of the Petition to Qveen Anne' and 'S.W. Raghlies Petition to the Qveene 1618' in Latham, ed., *Poems*, 68–71. See also LeFranc, *Sir Walter Ralegh*, 523; Greenblatt, *Sir Walter Ralegh*, 13.

note of rebirth and 'creation' in nature: images of 'dayes delights ... springetyme ioyes fordvnn ... dawne' when the 'risinge soonn of youth / Had their creation, and weare first begun', are soon followed, again, by 'winter sadd' ('Ocean' 22.1–4). Raleigh's poem veers sharply between optimism and (mostly) despair but includes strong glimpses of the former. To be in the Queen's favour again would be to recreate the 'springtime' of his own younger days, presumably in the early to mid-1580s when he was a 'rising soonn' at court 'created' by her God-like majesty. He demonstrates a similar troubled optimism in his correspondence to Elizabeth's closest counsellors, including letters focused on his Irish concerns written at the same time as the likely date of 'Scinthia'.

II. The Cecils of Hatfield House

We don't know who read or heard 'Ocean to Scinthia', other than Spenser, who may have known only parts of what we now have. The poem complains powerfully about the speaker's desertion by the Queen and his forced inactivity. But was Raleigh's audience primarily Elizabeth I?[19] Other than Elizabeth, suggested recipients include first and foremost the powerful Cecil, Lord Burghley family. Raleigh's poem was first published in 1870, soon after its discovery in Hatfield House, which location indicates that it may have been sent directly to the Cecils as original audience. Commonly noted also is a letter from Raleigh strikingly similar in maudlin tone and mythological subject matter to 'Ocean to Scinthia'. Raleigh sent it while in the Tower to Robert, a privy councilor and son of the Treasurer William Cecil, Lord Burghley, in July, 1592:

> the Queen goes away so far of, – whom I have followed so many years with so great love and desire, in so many journeys, and am now left behind her, in a dark prison all alone ... even now my heart is cast into the depth of all misery. I that was want to behold her riding like Alexander, hunting like Diana, walking like Venus, the gentle wind blowing her fair hair about her pure cheeks, like a nymph ... Behold the sorrow of this world![20]

Young Cecil must have shared the same poetical sap as Raleigh (or so Raleigh judged his tastes).[21] The letter encourages dating the poem to

---

19 Greenblatt doesn't think so, arguing that the poem's portrait of Elizabeth was highly critical and was 'probably never shown to the Queen'. Greenblatt, *Sir Walter Ralegh*, 79. See also May, *The Elizabethan Courtier Poets*, 131–2.
20 Edwards, *The Life of Sir Walter Ralegh*, 2 vols (London: Macmillan, 1968), 2.51–2.
21 Robert Cecil 'was Ralegh's friend, a poet, and a collector of verse. He was the likeliest person of Ralegh's acquaintance not only to appreciate the "Cynthia" poems but to share them with the Queen'. May, *Sir Walter Ralegh*, 47.

Raleigh's period of imprisonment in the Tower, and, like others from that time, demonstrates Raleigh's supposed mental anguish and 'sense of exaggerated, unjust punishment'.[22]

What are not commonly noted are two other surviving letters sent by Raleigh to Robert Cecil that same month, both of which focus exclusively on Ireland. Both of them allude to political storms (called a 'tempest' in one) brewing among Irish rebels, especially in Ulster (where the Nine Years' War was to originate in 1594). Raleigh's immediate aim seems to be his release from prison so that he can go to Ireland and combat this threat ('I will, at three days' warninge, rayse her a better bande, and arme it better tenfold ...'). He indicates his desire to sail off and plays on his 'Water' or 'Ocean' identity when he closes the second letter with a simile of himself 'like a fish cast on dry land, gasping for breath, with lame leggs and lamer loonges'.[23] Put Ocean back on the sea and he'll fight for the Queen: he will do so first in Ireland.

The other main message in both letters concerns the difficulties his disgrace has caused with the 'dotinge' Lord Deputy of Ireland, William Fitzwilliam, labelled the 'cousen' of Cecil (see also Part III, below). These difficulties concern his Irish properties and Raleigh argues that the livelihood of his tenants on the plantation is greatly threatened because of the Lord Deputy's exactions, they being 'in a strang country newly sett downe to builde and plant'. Alarmingly, the defence 'of all Munster' is at stake, since one of Raleigh's castles (hence also the 'Queen's') had been seized and leased out to a 'cussen of a rebel' who was 'planted ... in the place of Inglishe men'. Here we see Raleigh equating his colonial territory with the Queen's, as well as the common equation of New English colonial progress in Munster with the security of the country.[24] Raleigh in each letter indicates that he has written to Robert's father directly about these matters, for he fears that Fitzwilliam has slandered him.[25] Raleigh in turn

---

22 Greenblatt, *Sir Walter Ralegh*, 78.
23 Christopher Hatton, a rival of Raleigh, gave Elizabeth 'a small bucket so there would be "less of Wa'ter Raleigh", and a small fishtank to signify that "water creatures should be constrained"'. Carolyn J. Bishop, 'Raleigh Satirized by Harington and Davies', *Review of English Studies* 89 (February 1972), 52–6: 54, citing Norman L. Williams, *Sir Walter Raleigh* (London: Eyre and Spottiswoode, 1962), 49. Hatton was also Raleigh's main neighbouring landowner along the Blackwater river in Munster.
24 Edwards, *Life*, 2.48–51.
25 Compare with Spenser's dedication to Raleigh affixed to 'Colin Clouts Come Home Againe' and signed from Kilcolman ('the 27. of December. 1591'), which asks Raleigh to protect him from 'evill mouthes, which are always wide open to carpe at and misconstrue my simple meaning'. Spenser, 'To the right worthy and noble Knight *Sir Walter Raleigh ...*' in Oram, ed., *Yale Shorter Poems*, 525–6: 526.

asks the Cecils to protect him in his own counter-propaganda campaign in letters.

In another letter to Robert Cecil, written from Sherborne a year later, 10 May 1593, Raleigh employs figurative watery language when he declares himself 'lost in the River of Burdens' and regrets that the 'French warrs' have distracted the Crown from the 'defens next the hart', i.e., the subjection and proper economic exploitation of Ireland:

> If Her Majestye conseder it aright, she shall fynde it no small dishonour to be vexed with so beggarly a nacion, that have neather armes nor fortificasion; but that acursed kingdome hath always bynn but as a trafique, for which Her Majestye hath paid both fraight and custome, and others receved the marchandize; and other then such shall it never be.[26]

Raleigh's pessimism does not prevent him from suggesting that a better and more 'honour'-able way exists to conquer that 'beggarly' nacion, if only the Queen should follow good advice ('If Her Mejestye conseder it aright'). Others are wasting her 'marchandize', not he.

It is suggested here that 'Ocean to Scinthia' echoes this correspondence with the Cecils: Raleigh's allusions to military and colonial matters in the poem are meant to remind readers that he continues as a necessary player for empire. If he is locked up or cut down, then he can't cut down, lock up or plant the Irish. If we are to believe Spenser, Raleigh began some version of the poem before his period of imprisonment in 1592, and this ur-'Scinthia' found ready welcome and inspired Spenser at Kilcolman to sing his own pro-colonial epic-pastoral paean to the Queen. Or Spenser wrote the same after reading Raleigh's finished product as we have it. What is likely is that the 1592 crisis forced Raleigh's hand into going more public with the poem, at least as far as Elizabeth and /or her main counsellors. William Cecil was one of the key architects of Ireland's plantation schemes and, if he bothered to read the poem, would have understood colonial references therein. Both he and his son were well aware of Raleigh's Irish dilemma and desires. Raleigh would later, in 1594, petition both Cecils in favour of the suit of the Old Englishman Patrick Condon concerning Munster lands (Raleigh had worked out a timber deal with Condon).[27] Raleigh's 'hunting like Diana, walking like Venus' letter to Robert Cecil in 1592 does not mention Ireland, but the other letters to him in the same month do. Coincidentally, 'Ocean to Scinthia' declares, in language designed to appeal to Robert Cecil, at least, that Raleigh's love and agonies

---

26 Edwards, *Life*, 2.79.
27 Cf. note 44, below.

on behalf of Queen and empire and specifically in Ireland must not be forgotten, and colonial progress there should not be neglected.

III. Spenser

The purpose here is not to re-examine fully the relationship between Spenser and Raleigh (which has been hashed over and constantly reassessed, but not usually with their colonial relationship in mind),[28] only to highlight how 'Ocean to Scinthia' inhabits a shared imperial or colonial context involving Ireland as does Spenser's own poetry. Much recent work among historians and literary critics (present author included) has stressed the fundamental importance of Ireland, and the Munster rebellion and plantation in particular, in forming the political and aesthetic basis of Spenser's arcane and lengthy allegories, indeed his entire epic purpose (which has an imperial resonance that of course goes beyond Ireland).[29] Spenser stood to gain from attaching himself to and encouraging Raleigh's continued industry on their plantation and in their mutual art. As Wayne Erickson writes in Chapter 2 above, Spenser needed Raleigh's support far more than the other way around.[30]

Both Raleigh and Spenser are historians in verse. Spenser in his 'Letter to Raleigh' appended to *The Faerie Queene* (1590) describes himself as a 'poet historical', and when Ralegh comments upon his art in *The Ocean to Cynthia*, he compares his labours, significantly enough, to those of a historian ... 'To write the story of all ages past / And end the same before

---

[28] The most important assessment remains Katherine Koller, 'Spenser and Ralegh', *English Literary History* 1 (1934), 37–60. See also Jerry Leath Mills, 'Raleigh, Walter (1554–1618)', in *The Spenser Encyclopedia*, ed. A. C. Hamilton (Toronto: University of Toronto Press, 1990), 584–5; William Oram, 'Elizabethan Fact and Spenserian Fiction'. *Spenser Studies* IV (1983), 33–47; William Oram, 'Spenser's Raleghs', *Studies in Philology* 87 (1990), 341–62; Lin Kelsey, 'Spenser, Ralegh, and the Language of Allegory', *Spenser Studies* XVII (2003), 183–213; and the debate, 'Spenser and Ralegh: Four Papers in Exchange', *Spenser Studies* XV (2001), William Oram, 'What Did Spenser Really Think of Sir Walter Ralegh When He Published the First Instalment of *The Faerie Queene*?', 165–74; Wayne Erickson, 'Spenser Reads Ralegh's Poetry in(to) the 1590 *Faerie Queene*', 175–84; Dees, 'Colin Clout and the Shepherd of the Ocean'; Michael Rudick, 'Three Views on Ralegh and Spenser: A Comment', 197–204. See also Erickson's reassessment in Chapter 2 above and other studies, cited below.

[29] The most comprehensive of these is Richard McCabe, *Spenser's Monstrous Regiment: Elizabethan Ireland and the Poetics of Difference* (Oxford: Oxford University Press, 2002). See also Willy Maley, *Salvaging Spenser: Colonialism, Culture And Identity* (New York: St. Martin's Press, 1997); Andrew Hadfield, *Edmund Spenser's Irish Experience: Wilde Fruit and Salvage Soyl* (Oxford: Clarendon Press, 1997); Thomas Herron, *Spenser's Irish Work: Poetry, Plantation, and Colonial Reformation* (Aldershot: Ashgate, 2007).

[30] Erickson, p. 89 above.

the'aprochinge night' (97, 102-3).[31] Both authors knew that poetry had a worldly relevance and ethical imperative as suited renaissance historiography.

That Spenser and Raleigh may have composed, or at least shared, verses together on the Munster plantation, including direct reference by Spenser to what is probably 'Ocean to Scinthia' in some form, is known from Spenser's account of their 'piping' or 'singing' contests at Spenser's Kilcolman estate, as related in his poem, 'Colin Clouts Come Home Againe' (lines 56–79, 160–75), dedicated to Raleigh, published in 1595 but dated to 1591 and presumably describing Raleigh's visit to Ireland in 1589:

> His [Raleigh's] song was all a lamentable lay,
> Of great unkindnesse, and of usage hard,
> Of *Cynthia* the Ladie of the sea,
> Which from her presence faultlesse him debard.
>
> (164–7)

This would appear to make clear Spenser's knowledge of Raleigh's 'Ocean to Scinthia' (or some version of it) in 1595, if not earlier.[32] Spenser also famously praises and advertises Raleigh's colonial ambitions in the New World when he mentions the ongoing exploration of Peru, the Amazon and 'fruitfullest *Virginia*' in Book II of *The Faerie Queene* (II.proem.2), published in 1590. In the Proem to Book III, published in the same volume, Spenser describes a poem Raleigh wrote about his '*Cynthia*' as 'sweete verse, with *Nectar* sprinkled' whose praise of the Queen he will complement with his own poem (i.e., *The Faerie Queene*) that celebrates her political and personal virtues:

> Ne let his [Raleigh's] fairest *Cynthia* refuse,
> In mirrours more then one her selfe to see,
> But either *Gloriana* let her chuse,
> Or in *Belphoebe* fashioned to bee:
> In th'one her rule, in th'other her rare chastitee.
>
> (III.proem.5.5–9).

Elizabeth will see herself bifurcated allegorically in the 'mirror' of Spenser's verse (between Gloriana and Belphoebe), which is inspired by the mirroring techniques of Raleigh's poetry to 'Cynthia', as both portray Elizabeth I in similar mythological fashion; Spenser also mirrors his own image and that of Raleigh as they mirror each other, 'piping' back and

---

31 Stillman, '"Words cannot knytt"', 37.
32 For a sceptical analysis of the shepherd exchange, see Sam Meyer, *An Interpretation of Edmund Spenser's 'Colin Clout'* (Cork: Cork University Press, 1969), 142–71.

forth in 'Colin Clouts Come Home Againe'. Spenser also creates an allegorical representation of Raleigh in the narrative portion of Book III of *The Faerie Queene*: Spenser dramatizes a military scuffle in Ireland involving Sir Walter, who is allegorized as the heroic Timias (cf. below). Furthermore, 'Colin Clouts Come Home Againe' echoes the verse form (iambic pentametre quatrains rhyming ABAB, with some variation) and pastoral 'piping' of 'Ocean to Scinthia'. Spenser wants his poetic and political identity to be linked to Raleigh's in this literary hall of mirrors. Raleigh, in turn, patronized and heavily favoured Spenser's political ambitions and admired (was even jealous of) his poetry: Raleigh famously introduced Spenser and his epic poem to court, in 1589–90, compares him (in the first commendatory sonnet to the 1590 *Faerie Queene*) to Petrarch and Homer, and, in his second commendatory sonnet to *The Faerie Queene*, again employs the mirror conceit: 'Behold her Princely mind aright, and write thy Queene anew. / Meane while she shall perceiue, how far her virtues sore / Aboue the reach of all that liue, or such as wrote of yore'.[33] Raleigh understood that Spenser was both imitating and outdoing his own poetic flattery.[34]

Raleigh functioned as a real or virtual patron and hero for Spenser. *The Faerie Queene* 1590 edition is dedicated in part to Raleigh and appended to it is an expository letter to him, which Spenser says that Raleigh 'commanded' him to write so as to better explain the poem's allegory.[35] In Book III, Spenser portrays Raleigh allegorically as Prince Arthur's heroic and unfortunate squire Timias. When these events involving Timias are read against John Hooker's account (published in 1586 in Holinshed's *Chronicles*) of Raleigh's deeds fighting at a ford in Munster in 1581, during the Desmond rebellion, it becomes apparent that Timias is a chivalric conqueror of the Irish.[36] Timias is miraculously cured of his wounds by a merciful Belphoebe, a.k.a. Queen Elizabeth. Then, in Book IV (first published in 1596) of *The Faerie Queene*, following the Throck-

---

33 Raleigh, 'Another of the same', in Edmund Spenser, *The Faerie Queene*, ed. A. C. Hamilton, Hiroshi Yamashita, and Toshiyuki Suzuki, 2nd edition (Edinburgh: Pearson Education, 2001), 721.
34 Compare with Spenser's insistence in 'Colin Clouts' (line 78) that he and Raleigh do not envy one another's skill in song.
35 Spenser, *The Faerie Queene*, 714: Erickson in Chapter 2 above discusses the uses here of 'commanded'.
36 James Bednarz, 'Ralegh in Spenser's Historical Allegory', *Spenser Studies* IV (1983), 49–70: 52–8. The three villains who ambush Timias allegorize an attack organized by the Old English lord David, Lord Barry. They would also loosely correspond with the three Fitzgeralds of Desmond who formed the core leaders of the rebellion: the earl (Gerald), his brother (John), and their cousin (James Fitzmaurice Fitzgerald).

morton scandal, Raleigh-as-Timias reappears as a melancholy, dejected but beseeching and finally redeemed lover of Belphoebe (IV.vii.38–46 and viii.2–18). Raleigh was indeed gradually restored to favour at court, but not until 1597.[37]

William Oram has rightly stressed the courtly politics of *The Faerie Queene* Books IV-VI and Raleigh's role therein, including reference to 'Colin Clouts', etc., in order to argue that Spenser was criticizing Raleigh in the hope that Raleigh would write more about 'epic' deeds (to 'thunder martial stowre', in Spenser's own words)[38] instead of wallowing in effete, Petrarchan self-pity in courtly fashion. But Oram pulls shy of suggesting that Spenser wants Raleigh to step up his political involvement in Ireland specifically, so as to support the New English enterprise there; instead, Oram separates Raleigh's ambitions at court from his (and Spenser's) efforts in Munster: 'Ralegh appears as an ambiguous figure in the poetry [of Spenser] precisely because he embodies what Spenser had for good or ill given up in moving to Ireland'.[39] One should emphasize instead that

---

37 Walter Oakeshott, *The Queen and the Poet* (London: Faber and Faber, 1960), 93–9; Jean Brink, 'The Masque of the Nine Muses: Sir John Davies's Unpublished 'Epithalamion' and the 'Belphoebe–Ruby' Episode in *The Faerie Queene*', *Review of English Studies* 23 (1972), 445–7.

38 Words used in Spenser's dedicatory sonnet to Raleigh, '*To the right noble and valorous knight, Sir Walter Raleigh,* Lo. Wardein of the Stannereyes, and lieftenaunt of Cornewaile', in Spenser, *The Faerie Queene,* 733.

39 Oram, 'Spenser's Raleghs', 342. See also Oram, 'What Did Spenser' and Oram, 'Elizabethan Fact'. For a rebuttal that stresses instead a pro-colonial portrait of Raleigh in 'Colin Clouts', see J. Christopher Warner, 'Poetry and Praise in *Colin Clouts Come Home Againe* (1595)', *Studies in Philology* 94.3 (1997), 368–81: 381. On the portrayal of Raleigh in Spenser's dedicatory sonnet in the context of Ireland and empire, see also Thomas Herron, 'Ralegh's Gold: Placing Spenser's Dedicatory Sonnets', in *The 1590* Faerie Queene: *Paratexts and Publishing*, ed. Wayne Erickson, *Studies in the Literary Imagination* 38.2 (Autumn 2005), 133–47: 136–9. For more on Raleigh's personal failings in Ireland and Spenser's criticism of the same, in his posthumously published 'Mutabilitie Cantos' (the fragment of Book VII of *The Faerie Queene*), see Judith Owens, 'Professing Ireland in the Woods of Spenser's Mutabilitie', *Explorations in Renaissance Culture* 29.1 (Summer 2003), 1–22; James Nohrnberg, 'Britomart's Gone Abroad from Brute-land, Colin Clout's Come Courting from the Salvage Ire-land: Exile and the Kingdom in Two of Spenser's Fictions of "Crossing Over"', in *Edmund Spenser: New and Renewed Directions*, ed. Julian Lethbridge (Madison, NJ: Fairleigh-Dickinson Press, 2006), 214–85: 269–75; Thomas Herron, 'Native Irish Property and Propriety in the Faunus Episode and *Colin Clouts Come Home Againe*', in *Celebrating Mutabilitie*, 136–77: 164–8. For a critique of Bednarz's New Historicist readings of Spenser's depictions of Raleigh, but again without discussion of their colonial relationship, see Wayne Erickson, 'Spenser and His Friends Stage a Publishing Event: Praise, Play, and Warning in the Commendatory Verses to the 1590 *Faerie Queene*', *Renaissance Papers* (1997), 13–22: 15–17. For a reading of Raleigh as multiple heroes in Book VI of *The Faerie Queene*, see Jeffrey B. Morris, 'To (Re)Fashion a Gentleman: Ralegh's Disgrace in Spenser's Legend of Courtesy', *Studies in Philology* 94 (Winter 1997), 38–58. For a valuable reminder that Spenser

the route to successful land grants and tenure in Munster ran in large part through the London court and law courts, including by sanction of the Queen, whose great 'grace ... and bounty most rewardfull' Colin will seek in person thanks to the Shepherd of the Ocean, a.k.a. Raleigh (Spenser, 'Colin Clouts' 187). Spenser needed Raleigh's connections and any sympathy at court he could muster.[40] 'Colin Clouts' certainly disdains the vanities and corruption of the court, especially flatterers, crooked social-climbers and bad love poets (i.e., shades of Raleigh's own behaviour), but it does so only after extended praise of its many luminaries. These include English noblewomen who married into powerful Irish nobility, i.e., Frances Howard, the Countess of Kildare and Elizabeth Sheffield, the Countess of Ormond.[41] Among writers, Spenser praises most loudly the poet William Alabaster, who had written a fragment of a Latin epic celebrating Queen Elizabeth and whose immediate family became deeply involved in the Munster plantation, probably as tenants on Raleigh's lands, in 1595.[42] Is there a connection between Spenser's poem and the Alabaster family activity in Munster? Who knows? Spenser would, nonetheless, logically temper criticism of Raleigh's courtly woes with encouragement of his pro-imperial and heroic persona and connections at court and in Ireland, as the storm clouds of the Nine Years' War gathered over Munster in the mid-1590s. What Spenser and we get from Raleigh in return, 'Ocean to Scinthia', is limp-wristed but still focused on the power of the Queen to enlarge her empire, if she so wished.

Spenser's decision to publish 'Colin Clouts Come Home Againe' in 1595 (a year before he is thought to have written *A View of the Present State of Irelande*), together with 'Astrophel', Spenser's lament for the military hero

---

is interested in teaching more than historical lessons in the Timias episode, see Julian Lethbridge, 'Raleigh in Books III and IV of *The Faerie Queene*: The Primacy of Moral Allegory', *Studia Neuphilologica* 64 (1992), 55–66.

40 Similarly, Steven May argues that 'Pastoralism in the 'Ocean to Cynthia' emphasizes not only the poet's humble status, it specifically acknowledges the court as the centre of bounty'. May, *The Elizabethan Courtier Poets*, 130.

41 Herron, 'Native Irish', 159–61.

42 Alabaster's entire family, his father, mother, three brothers and two sisters (but not William) all left for the Munster plantation in 1595 (the same year as publication of *Colin Clouts*). William's elder brother, George, soon died there, and the family returned to Colchester in 1596. The Alabasters probably worked as tenants on Raleigh's lands because they had followed their relatives by marriage, the Winthrops (later of Massachusetts fame), to Ireland, and the Winthrops were tenants of Raleigh. See Eleanor Coutts, 'The Life and Work of William Alabaster, 1568–1640' (Doctoral Thesis, University of Wisconsin-Madison, 1956), 52–4, 98; Michael MacCarthy-Morrogh, *The Munster Plantation: English Migration to Southern Ireland, 1583–1641* (Oxford: Clarendon Press, 1986), 199.

Sir Philip Sidney, which is followed by a reprinting of Raleigh's elegy to the same, alongside elegies by the Irish colonist Lodowick Bryskett and others, may be explained in these terms: Spenser, former muster master of Kilcullen, Co. Kildare, wanted to martial the New English troops in print, so as to offer consolation and solidarity to the New English planters while reminding the London audience of their hard-working existence fighting and planting for Protestantism on the fringe of the burgeoning English empire.

As I have argued elsewhere, Book VI of *The Faerie Queene* also promotes Raleigh's territorial claims in Munster against his nemesis, David, Lord Barry. The Blatant Beast who hounds Spenser's heroes there represents in part the verbal attacks and slander of Old English lords (Roche and Barry in particular) against their New English neighbours, such as Raleigh and Spenser (Spenser had his own legal hassles with his and Barry's neighbour, Lord Roche; Raleigh himself had harassed and arrested Lord Roche in Munster in 1581, as narrated by Hooker). The Beast is temporarily 'chained' by the hero Calidore and his voice 'murd up' (VI.xii.34.4), a possible allusion to the temporary imprisonment, for six days in 1588, of Lord Roche: to humiliate and muzzle the Blatant Beast, even temporarily, represents a victory over native Irish and Old English local power and courtly influence.[43] Ethnic allegiances could be tricky or disregarded, however. In 1594, Raleigh joined legal forces with the Old English lord Patrick Condon, a mortal enemy of Roche, against Spenser's New English neighbour Arthur Hyde.[44] By linking his plight with Raleigh's, Spenser promotes his own interests while shoring up or creating planter solidarity against native Irish and /or Old English threats in Munster. But Spenser might also disapprove of some of Raleigh's alliances.

One can't avoid overt signals linking Raleigh to the Irish scene in *The Faerie Queene*. Before the Blatant Beast fights Calidore, and before Raleigh-as-Timias is restored to Belphoebe's favour in Book IV, Timias appears changed, or rather degenerated from his former heroic self. Thanks to his ill-fated amatory adventures he has become a 'despair[ing]' (IV.vii.43.2) wood-dweller, with 'heary glib deform'd and meiger face, / Like a ghost late risen from his graue agryz'd' (IV.viii.12.6–7), the very image, complete with Irish 'glib' (a low-hanging forelock), of a dejected

---

43 Herron, *Spenser's Irish Work*, Chapter 10 passim and 220.
44 Herron, 'Native Irish', 167; MacCarthy-Morrogh, *The Munster Plantation*, 103–4; Lefranc, *Sir Walter Ralegh*, 580; Raleigh's two letters, dated 15 June 1594, from his estate at Sherborne to William and Robert Cecil and concerning Condon, are reprinted in Agnes Latham and Joyce Youings, eds, *The Letters of Sir Walter Ralegh* (Exeter: University of Exeter Press, 1999), 111–13.

refugee of the Irish woods. Such refugees included native soldiers known as 'woodkern', and sad Timias resembles also the beaten arch-rebel Rory Og O'More in the eleventh woodcut of John Derricke's pro-Henry Sidney and pro-New English propaganda piece, *The Image of Irelande* (1581). The name *Timias*, furthermore, understood to be based primarily on Greek *time*, or 'honour', may have relevant Irish etymological roots that point towards this tension between his Petrarchan and martial aspects: *tim*, 'soft, yielding, pliant, feeble', was used in the context of late medieval and early modern love poetry, as well as *timne*, the 'act of commanding'.[45]

Timias also resembles a mad exile in the wilderness, or *geilt* in Irish, like the mythological northern Irish king Sweeney, whose various transgressions transfigure him into a tree-hopping, bird-like creature spouting poetry.[46] Spenser uses the word in this context: we spy Timias in disgrace immediately after we read of Amoret (an allegorized Elizabeth Throckmorton) running frantically through the woods like a 'Gelt' (IV.vii.21.3) from a nasty, long-haired, phallus-like creature who personifies lust. Lust apparently reflects Raleigh's own destructive desires,[47] and the monster is shot at the door of his cave-dwelling by Cynthia's (i.e., Queen Elizabeth's) arrow, thus punishing him (and Raleigh) and rescuing Amoret in her 'Gelt'-like state. But in a weird psycho-sexual moment, Amoret is transfixed by the image of Lust's body and blood spilling into the cave (IV.vii.31-2). Amoret, we can surmise, has lost her innocence. Her gelt remains her guilt, and Raleigh, in the figure of Timias, remains reduced to the same wild state, a sulking, cave-dwelling, uncivilized victim of the same scandal. Both Raleigh and Throckmorton would be exiled from Elizabeth's court. Like rapacious Lust, or a mad Irish king, Raleigh (and his wife) remains outside the pale of good repute.

---

45 *Dictionary of the Irish Language: Based Mainly on Old and Middle Irish Materials* (Dublin: Royal Irish Academy, 1990), *s.v.* 'tim'. On the etymology of his name, see also note 90, below.

46 Roland Smith, 'King Lear and the Merlin Tradition', *Modern Language Quarterly* 7 (1946), 153-74 (for specific reference to Spenser's use of the term in *FQ* IV, see pp. 168-9n); Conor McCarthy, *Seamus Heaney and Medieval Poetry* (Cambridge: D. S. Brewer, 2008), 20-30. For Spenser's 'Gelt' glossed as the Irish word by A. C. Hamilton, following *OED*, see Spenser, *The Faerie Queene*, 461n.

47 Mills, 'Raleigh, Walter', 584. As noted by McCarthy (*Seamus Heaney*, 20-3), the word *geilt* may have a cognate in English *guilt*. Given the painful fate of Lust, Spenser is also likely punning on the verb *to geld*, or castrate, and perhaps *gilt* as in *gold* (cf. German 'Gelt'). As noted in his will, Raleigh had an illegitimate child in Ireland, Alice Gould, presumably from a liaison there. Her mother may have been the daughter of the Attorney General of Munster, James Gould, in which case Alice was conceived during Raleigh's visit in 1588-89: Raleigh Trevelyan, *Sir Walter Raleigh* (New York: Henry Holt, 2002), 146-7; Latham and Youings, eds, *Letters*, 379-80. Alice may have been a bastard from his earlier soldier days, however. See Herron, 'Ralegh's Gold', 138.

As I argue elsewhere, Spenser's eerie description of Timias echoes his earlier episode of the long-haired and rail-thin character Despair, in Book I of the 1590 *Faerie Queene*, who almost convinces the hero, Red Crosse Knight, to kill himself. This passage, in turn, echoes the infamous famine description in Spenser's *View*, to which Despair has been linked based on his ghostly description and close verbal echoes between the two works.[48] Spenser therefore turns Timias into another version of the despairing, starving woodkern, or a potentially treasonous (because rebellious and lustful) and certainly 'savage' representation of a man, Raleigh, normally obsessed with his proud and rich appearance at court: not a flattering portrait.

Why? What links a disgraced Raleigh during the Throckmorton affair to Irish and especially Munster politics? Clearly Spenser finds the figure of Irish-tinged famine and despair a fitting psychological analogy for Raleigh's miserable state, cast out of the Queen's favour and barred from her nourishing riches. Timias's Irish disguise makes further sense in so far as it conveys Spenser's concurrent despair at Raleigh's sudden weakness in England *and* in Ireland, and the danger – including great fiscal loss to Raleigh – that the Throckmorton chain of events might entail in Munster especially. After the Throckmorton scandal broke in 1592 and the Queen finally recognized in public that Raleigh had impregnated and married one of her maids of honour, she clapped him in the Tower. According to his own letter written to Robert Cecil in 1592 (above), Raleigh's improper behaviour in London opened him to further accusation and legal prosecution in Munster by his rival and enemy, Lord Deputy William Fitzwilliam. He states that his 'disgraces' have 'past the seas' and caused the Lord Deputy to punish him, including a 'dispeopled' plantation.[49] As D. B. Quinn relates, in 1592 Raleigh's lucrative timber and mill industry in Munster – another subject promoted in *The Faerie Queene*[50] – was suspended for a year and a half as the Lord Deputy pressed him on treason charges, eventually dropped, for selling naval timber (and not only barrel staves, as permitted) to the Spanish and for channelling infor-

---

48 Herron, *Spenser's Irish Work*, 195–6; M. M. Gray, 'The Influence of Spenser's Irish Experiences on *The Faerie Queene*', *Review of English Studies* 6 (1930), 413–28. See the related argument in Owens, *Enabling*, 133–42.
49 See also II of this chapter. Transcripts of the correspondence are found in Sir John Pope Hennessy, *Sir Walter Ralegh in Ireland* (1883), ed. Thomas Herron (Dublin: University College Dublin Press, 2009), 89–91; Latham and Youings, eds, *Letters*, 68–9, 71–2; Edwards, *Life*, vol. 2.48–51.
50 Christopher Burlinson, *Allegory, Space and the Material World in the Writings of Edmund Spenser* (Cambridge: D. S. Brewer, 2006), chapter 8 ('Deforestation and the Spenserian Wood'); Herron, *Spenser's Irish Work*, 122–7.

mation to Catholic recusants from the Continent. Raleigh and his agent Henry Pyne were excused and their timber industry eventually restored, and they pressed forward with their dark, forest-devouring mills, but not before Raleigh and Pyne had a good sulk in the murky woods of political disrepute and financial ruin.[51]

In Book IV of *The Faerie Queene*, Timias's amatory peccadilloes endanger his service to Prince Arthur, or the New English cause, in the allegory. The central virtue of Book IV is friendship, and so one could extrapolate from this episode that Raleigh isolated himself not only on a moral and spiritual level as a lecherous potential traitor to the Queen, or Belphoebe (a.k.a., Cynthia), but also by jeopardizing his status as a nearby economic engine, friend, and literary patron to the New English of the Munster Plantation, and Spenser in particular. Spenser's beglibbed Timias, yet another version of the starving Irish portrayed in the *View*, rots in a forest like a threatening and threatened woodkern precisely because Raleigh and the Munster planters could no longer cut down those very trees with a free hand. If they could, they would further the plantation goals by expelling the kern from his treacherous hiding places, including forest clearance, cultivate the land and thus fend off the 'despair' of famine, while giving a lucrative return on the Queen's loving investment in the plantation. (This return includes the artistic produce of Spenser's poetry, such as *The Faerie Queene*, the 'wilde fruit, which saluage soyl hath bred', as he himself calls it in his dedicatory sonnet to the earl of Ormond.)[52] Moreover, when Raleigh did cut down these woods, he either got himself involved in potentially treasonous trade with the Spanish, or he did so in co-operation with former Old English enemies like Roche, who was Spenser's constant antagonist, and to the detriment of fellow New English planters like Condon. Raleigh compromised New English solidarity for the sake of making money, which should surprise no one.

Raleigh's exclusion from the Queen's court in 1588–89 is likely alluded to in 'Colin Clouts Come Home Againe', when Spenser describes the piping of Raleigh's 'song'. In the poem, the Queen 'is the genius of her nation's expansionist ambitions':[53]

---

51 David Beers Quinn, *Raleigh and the British Empire*, 2nd edition (London: English Universities Press, 1962), 149–51, 153–5; Lacey, *Sir Walter Ralegh*, 169–70.
52 Spenser, 'To the right Honourable the Earle of *Ormond and Ossory*', in Spenser, *The Faerie Queene*, 730. Note also Spenser's description in 'Colin Clouts' (288–9) of himself (and Raleigh) disembarking into England to present himself and his poetry at court: 'There did our ship her fruitful wombe unlade, / And put us all ashore on *Cynthias* land'.
53 Lim, *The Arts of Empire*, 52. Lim (32–4) discusses 'Ocean to Scinthia' at further length, albeit without colonial specificity.

> Those be the shepheards which my *Cynthia* serue,
> At sea, beside a thousand moe at land:
> For land and sea my *Cynthia* doth deserue
> To haue in her commandement at hand
>
> ('Colin Clouts' 260–3)

Yet Raleigh is 'debard' from his Queen '*Cynthia* the Ladie of the sea':

> His song was all a lamentable lay,
> Of great unkindnesse, and of usage hard,
> Of *Cynthia* the Ladie of the sea,
> Which from her presence faultlesse him debard.
>
> (164–7)

Cynthia, or Elizabeth, controls the seas. Since Raleigh's alias in the poem is 'The shepheard of the Ocean' (66), which corresponds with Raleigh's self-identity as 'Ocean' in 'Ocean to Scinthia', Spenser in 'Colin Clouts' emphasizes Raleigh's imperial potential while serving her on the ocean. Yet Spenser ambiguously notes that the 'sea' (a potential object of the pronoun 'which') is what also literally keeps Raleigh from his Queen. Raleigh is across the Irish Sea from her but not completely out of her favour, as he made clear in his own letter to his cousin Sir George Carew in 1589, around the time he visited Kilcolman: whatever the scandal over his tiff with the Second Earl of Essex, he came to Munster to secure his 'prize' lands there.[54] In Spenser's poem, Raleigh's goddess, the Queen, will not accrue wealth if 'Ocean's' labour is frustrated for long, 'debarred' from her presence and not permitted to return. In Raleigh's own poem, without the Queen's support, when 'Bellphebes course is now obserude no more', then 'Our Ocean seas are but tempestius waves / And all things base that blessed wear of late' ('Ocean' 21.271–4). Transatlantic riches are *debased* when the Lady of the Sea confounds the labour of her 'Ocean'.

As a Cork planter, Spenser would have been highly aware of trade routes in and out of Munster to Wales, England and elsewhere, not only to export timber and hides but also for the lucrative wool market centred in Cork City (where Spenser perhaps sets his wedding poem, 'Epithalamion': it spotlights the 'merchants daughters' celebrating the festivities (167)).[55] Raleigh received a licence to export woollens in 1584, and Spenser himself probably participated in the wool export market from

---

54 Raleigh to Carew, 27 December 1589, transcribed in Edwards, *Life*, 2.41–3. On the Irish relevance of his 'prize', see also Kelsey, 'Spencer, Ralegh', 207 n.5.
55 Spenser, 'Epithalamion', in *Yale Edition*, 662–79: 668 (line 167).

his home at Kilcolman.[56] '[W]ith the arrival of the English planters in the later half of the sixteenth century, pastoral activity greatly increased across Munster', and once Raleigh cut down all the trees, he would be expected to farm and raise sheep and cattle in their stead.[57] Naming Raleigh 'the shepheard of the Ocean' emphasizes the value (real and potential) of this Irish market whose product would be shipped across the Irish sea to England, the Netherlands and places beyond. Placing Raleigh alongside himself in a world of shepherds in a pastoral poem such as 'Colin Clouts Come Home Againe' has the same effect: Spenser's choice of genre alone advertises the artistic and economic potential of Raleigh, himself and his planter brethren merrily piping away while the wolves prowled nearby.

Economics and imperial concerns bind Raleigh and Spenser in a symbiotic relationship as closely as their poetry does. The Queen is needed to fend off the Irish wolves (i.e., thieves, rebels and perhaps priests)[58] with her armies and money and to regulate the terms of trade and favour her servants. She is in consequence the glorious inspiration and implored subject of their poems. She must be wooed through hard work and loving words. In 'Colin Clouts Come Home Againe', Spenser describes his journey to visit her at court, brought there by Raleigh:

> The shepheard of the Ocean, quoth he [i.e., Colin],
> Unto that Goddesse grace me first enhanced,
> And to mine oaten pipe enclined her eare,
> That she thenceforth therein gan take delight,
> And it desired at timely houres to heare,
> All were my notes but rude and roughly dight.
>
> (358–63)

Elizabeth is the prime (if not exclusive) referent for the 'One' repeatedly invoked, chant-like, in the numerical centre of the poem, a prime position that, according to neoplatonic principles, indicates her spiritual radiance and inspiration throughout:[59]

---

56 Tennenhouse, 'Sir Walter Ralegh', 236; Eric Klingelhofer, 'Edmund Spenser at Kilcolman Castle: The Archaeological Evidence', *Post-Medieval Archaeology* 39.1 (2005), 133–54: 149.
57 Colin Breen, *An Archaeology of Southwest Ireland, 1570–1670* (Dublin: Four Courts Press, 2007), 171; Nicholas Canny, 'Raleigh's Ireland', in *Raleigh and Quinn: The Explorer and His Boswell*, ed. H. G. Jones (Chapel Hill: North Caroliniana Society, 1987), 87–101: 95.
58 Compare with the image of dangerous wolves and thieves threatening Kilcolman in Spenser, *The Faerie Queene* VII.vi.55.
59 David W. Burchmore, 'The Image of the Centre in *Colin Clouts Come Home Againe*', *Review of English Studies* 28 (1977), 393–406. For a counter-argument that the 'One' here refers to Colin's local love Rosalind, not Cynthia /Elizabeth and /or Spenser's bride

> To her my life I wholly sacrifice
> My thought, my heart, my love, my life is shee,
> And I hers ever onely, ever one:
> [Centre of poem]
> One ever I all vowed hers to bee,
> One ever I, and others never none.
>
> ('Colin Clouts' 475–9)

Colin (a name close to 'colonial')[60] will transfer this inspiration directly into deeds on the landscape: Orpheus turns graffiti artist as, enthused by Cynthia, he promises to 'record', 'endosse', and 'engrosse' (all legal terms) the name of '*Cynthia*' 'for ever' in the Irish landscape of trees, stones, and 'murmuring waters', as 'witnesse of her bountie here alive' (631–47).[61]

Rejected and dejected kern-like Timias in *The Fairie Queene* also engraves his '*Belphebe*' on 'euery tree' (IV.vii.46) and will find succour from his goddess in the following canto. Timias, i.e., Raleigh, and Colin, i.e., Spenser, both write *on*, literally and figuratively, the Irish land, as a means of making the Queen's imperial claim there (and their labours on her behalf) more explicit.

Raleigh opens 'Ocean to Scinthia' by invoking his own dead and buried spirit, now that he has lost the Queen's favour: the poem begins, 'Sufficeth it to yow my ioyes interred' ('Ocean' 21.1): the 'you' here is unspecified: does he mean the general reader, his (presumed) royal audience and / or his own 'ioyes', called 'Ioyes vnder dust that never live agayne' (21.4)? Near the end of the poem he is weary, not enthused: 'Thus home I draw, as deaths longe night drawes onn' (21.509), an image closely evocative of the concluding gloom in Virgil's first eclogue and in 'Colin Clouts' 952–5: Colin is 'loath to part' despite the darkening skies.[62] Book 21 of 'Ocean' thus ends and begins on a dark note, and the set of verses at its exact centre (counting a total of 544 lines in both Books) is also depressing. They are missing at least one line at their centre, since, unusually, they consist of two stanzas of only three lines apiece (instead of the usual four) with two of the lines rhyming in each (the first and third lines in 21.269–71 and

---

Elizabeth Boyle, see Warner, 'Poetry amd Praise', 378–9. For discussion of world-weary Raleigh in 'Ocean' as critiquing Spenser's neoplatonism in 'Colin Clouts', and Spenser's 'reaffirmative' response to Raleigh's poem, see Dees, 'Colin Clout and the Shepherd of the Ocean', passim.

60 Maley, 'Salvaging Spenser', 32–3.
61 For analysis of Spenser's legalisms, including in regard to Ireland (but not this episode specifically), see Andrew Zurcher, *Spenser's Legal Language: Law and Poetry in Early Modern England* (Cambridge: D. S. Brewer, 2007).
62 LeFranc (*Sir Walter Ralegh*, 520–1) theorizes that Raleigh borrows from Spenser the habit of using long and diphthonged vowels, which often indicate a melancholy mood.

272–4).⁶³ They therefore imitate the three-line stanzas used consistently in the fragmentary '22 Boock, entreatinge of Sorrow'. Four other sets of three-line stanzas appear in the poem (lines 21.101–3, 150–2,⁶⁴ 158–60, and 478–80), two of these end with an image of tearing or breaking (a torn, rent and pierced heart in line 152 and breaking bands in line 480) and one with an image of approaching night that stops the process of writing: 'We should begin by such a parting light / To write the story of all ages past / And end the same before the approaching night' (101–3). The highly self-aware Raleigh highlights his writing process as a race against time as well as an anguished one: here and elsewhere, form follows function as the stanza exaggerates its subject by truncating it through violent tearing or loss of vision /light.⁶⁵ Raleigh returns to the hobbling three-line stanza in the second, i.e., 22nd, fragmentary Book of the poem, which abruptly concludes after seven stanzas of the same with another image of a failed harvest, its last line cut in two like a young shoot: 'For tender stalkes – ' (22.22).

That the 'love', or favour, of the Queen *could* be the 'Centre' (21.433) of Raleigh's own reciprocating love and inspiration, hence of his imperial actions on her behalf, is described elsewhere in the poem in metaphysical, neoplatonic terms reminiscent of Spenser.⁶⁶ Elizabeth's love is 'all in

---

63 I am grateful to Jerry Leath Mills for indicating this centre point in the poem. As caveat, there are other three-line stanzas in the 21st Book, but the coincidence here of the central placement of these two stanzas and mention of Belphoebe 'observed no more' indicate a witty and deliberate effort at numerical ordering on Raleigh's part. In his discussion of the poem, Mills ('Sir Walter') focuses on various numerological patterns (including the coincidence of a 22nd Book that ends midway through the 22nd line) and discusses the burning sun imagery of lines 275–8, so close to the centre, as themselves significant because indicating the central importance of the Queen's punishing justice (the monarch, in standard mythopoeic fashion, being figured as the sun). In this case, the absent-presence of the Queen from the landscape in the very centre lines is followed by her harshness only: Raleigh's lament once again.
64 These three lines are followed by a five-line stanza (lines 153–7) and so both could be part of an irregularly rhymed pair of stanzas (150–53 and 154–7).
65 Joyce Horner *implies* as much when she states that lines 101–3 'stand out' as an 'unfinished' quatrain, wherein 'the poet has gone beyond the sailor standing on the shore to the brevity of life, the erasing, effacing power of time, the vanity of human effort'. Horner, 'The Large Landscape: A Study of Certain Images in Ralegh', *Essays in Criticism* 5.3 (July, 1955), 197–213: 201. Other irregular stanzas based on number of lines in Book 21 are lines 132–3 (two unrhymed lines); 153–7 (five lines, but see above note); 331–5 and 400–4 (five lines each); 521–2 (the concluding rhymed couplet).
66 Compare with the opinion of Kelsey ('Spenser, Ralegh', 194; 210, n. 27) that Raleigh, unlike Spenser, does not aim at metaphysical meanings with his poetry: his poetry does not attain 'sacred philosophical and moral realms' but remains essentially pragmatic in focus. See also Dees for discussion of "Raleigh 'tortured scrutiny'" of Spenser's neoplatonism in *Colin Clouts* (Dees, 'Colin Clout and the Shepherd of the Ocean', 188).

oon' to him (21.43–4) and her beauty could be 'loves ground, his essence, and his emperye' (21.178) if not wasted by time and fortune; her beauty carries 'th'effects of pourfull emperye' (200). It is 'powerful' when it 'pours' into him and expands its 'emperye' over and through him, not when, by contrast, it makes him (and her) poor.[67]

The central stanzas to Book 21 make a similar cruel and metaphysical witticism as the conclusion to Book 22. They refer to Belphoebe, the ocean and a pastoral landscape feature ('streames') and are soon followed by reference to a 'plowmans' 'fielde' (21.275–6), all attacked by drought, fire and storms:

> Thos streames seeme standinge puddells which, before,
> Wee saw our bewties in, so weare they cleere,
> Bellphebes course is now obserude no more,
> [*Centre of Poem*]
> That faire resemblance weareth out of date.
> Our Ocean seas are but tempestius waves
> And all things base that blessed wear of late
>
> And as a fielde wherin the stubbell stands
> Of harvest past, the plowmans eye offends,
> Hee tills agayne or teares them vp with hands,
> And throwes to fire as foylde and frutless ends.
>
> (21.269–78)

Raleigh's message, when juxtaposed with Spenser's, is telling: in the absence of the Queen, explicitly invoked here as 'Bellphebe', also Cynthia, a.k.a. the moon (or is it the sun?),[68] which is 'out of date' (calendrically) and 'obserude no more', disaster ensues. As a result, nature is defaced (like the poem, missing at least one line from its centre, and another line soon after that) and plunged into a wintery state: it lacks not only the pulsing life of the spring season and its watery floods (re-energizing 'Wa'ter' himself) but the harmonizing power of the pastoral, Orphic artist labouring on its, his, and the Queen's behalf: the farmer and his produce are 'foyld' and 'fruitless', and 'Ocean' lacks the moon (or the sun) both to illuminate and to govern its waters: all are thrown into anguished and unprofitable ('base') torment.

Writing fails its master while paradoxically calling attention to its powerful ability to connote failure. In so far as Raleigh patterns his poem's

---

67 Compare with an earlier pun on the 'poure remayninge' of the sun's rays (21.79).
68 'The moon is not mentioned at all in the five hundred and odd lines [of 'Ocean to Scinthia']. Cynthia is the sun not the moon and the sun has set'. (Horner, 'The Large Landscape', 199). But Cynthia may be figured obliquely here as the moon 'out of date' (21.272).

numerological conceit in co-ordination with 'Colin Clouts Come Home Againe', as he seems to co-ordinate so much else (including versification and subject matter), then 'Ocean to Scinthia' offers a sour alternative to Spenser's poem. Spenser loudly complains of vanities at court ('Colin Clouts' 688–730, 775–90) and 'wayling … wretchednesse … bloodie issues … grisly famine… nightly bodrags… hue and cries' and lack of 'safety' in Munster (312–16), but is (literally) an optimist at heart. Despite the abuses of court and in Ireland, proclaims Colin, 'we poore shepheards whether rightly so … Do make religion how we rashly go, / To serve that God, that is so greatly dread' (795–8). His companion Cuddy is witness to his divine vision:

> 'Shepheard it seemes that some celestiall rage /
> Of love… is breath'd into thy brest,
> That powreth forth these oracles so sage,
> Of that high powre'
>
> (823–6)

By contrast, the centre of Raleigh's inspiration, the Queen, is 'out of date' and the shadow of her absence blankets her overseas territories as well as her court.

IV. Ocean's 'Scinthia'

It is this dilemma of the beseeching colonial imperative, reflected in Spenser's and Raleigh's contemporary verse, and not only Raleigh's loss of personal and political favour at the English court, that I would suggest influences Raleigh's lengthiest and most complex poem, the unpublished 'The 21st: and last booke of the Ocean to Scinthia', followed by the fragment 'The end of the bookes, of the Oceans love to Scinthia, and the beginninge of the 22 Boock, entreatinge of Sorrow'. Ascertaining the number, attribution, and dating of various scattered poems attributed to Raleigh is a critical mare's nest, but 'Ocean', at least, is in his hand and critical consensus (though not unanimous) dates it to around 1592–93, that is, in the immediate wake of the Throckmorton scandal, when the imprisoned Raleigh would have had time and motive to pen it and other, minor gems such as 'My boddy in the walls captived' (included in the same MS as 'Ocean'). The primary reason for dating the poem to this time, moreover, is its content: as an extended Petrarchan love lyric lamenting his 'fortune's', overthrow thanks to the cruel beauty of his love, Cynthia, while simultaneously praising her divine personal and political virtues, critics have traditionally read the poem as a clearly apologetic appeal from the

'Ocean', or Raleigh himself, to the Queen in courtly fashion to reinstate him in her favour. Elizabeth is figured as the fickle yet merciful moon-goddess who (in line with the allegory) attracts the ocean waters, but more explicitly she is the sun that 'Just'ly (21.298) punishes malefactors such as Raleigh: she threatens to dry up and burn her unprotected Walter, or 'Water', as he was known.

This reading makes perfect sense, but what has been underemphasized or ignored by critics are the explicitly imperial and colonial dimensions of the poem. The sun, of course, is also a standard metaphor for the ruler who guides, inspires, and nourishes her subjects.[69] This takes an agricultural turn in that Raleigh is fixated on the power of the sun's beams to warm the earth and inspire 'labour' in her subjects. In 'Ocean', the 'perfection' of Elizabeth's 'mind' and 'immortal pour' are like 'fiery soon beames that on yearth do beate' (21.205-7); yet when she, like 'Phebus' is 'dessended', so is 'every toyle and labour ended' (21.97-9), including the 'labour' of his mind (21.104). When abandoned by her favour, Raleigh is

> as the yearth yeven in cold winter dayes
> Left for a tyme by her life gevinge soonn,
> [Which] Douth by the poure remayninge of his rayes
> Produce some green, though not as it hath dunn
>
> (21.77-80)

'Some green' remains, of course, as the poem woefully attests. The sun that burns Raleigh and plunges him into darkness might also nourish new plantation and reinvigorate his own 'rising soonn of youth' (22.2), if it would only lessen its harshness.

The poem's confused genre also points it in an imperial direction. Most critics agree that it was deliberately written as an epic fragment, since it consists of the completed twenty-first and partial twenty-second Books of what was or was intended or pretended to be a much longer work: 'for what really mattered was the vague impression of epic scope and grandeur'.[70] The numbering may recall Homer's *Odyssey*, another work of errant ocean-born desire that focuses on a military veteran whose

---

69 Herron, *Spenser's Irish*, 102-13. For comparison, Virgil portrays Augustus as the sun in the opening of the *Georgics*, as does Spenser Elizabeth I in the Proem to *The Faerie Queene*. Horner, 'The Large Landscape', 199 notes the odd fact that Raleigh, in this poem nominally to 'Cynthia', uses sun imagery for Elizabeth rather than moon imagery; but this is not entirely true (cf. note 68, above). Like the moon, it is implied, she will always pull 'Wa'ter' to and fro. See also Raleigh's poem, 'Praised be Dianas faire and harmles light': 'Praisd be hir beams, the glorie of the night, / Praisd be hir power ... Praisd be that force, by which she moues the floods', Latham, ed., 10-11.
70 Greenblatt, *Sir Walter Ralegh*, 62.

adventures span twenty-four books. Odysseus finally conquers the suitors and claims his home in Book 22, prompting the re-wooing of Penelope in Book 23. It is not easy to read any continuous narrative into 'Ocean to Scinthia', but the speaker also 'draw[s]' 'home' at the conclusion of Book 21 (509).[71] He does not go so far as the re-conquest of Elizabeth's affections, however. That can only be hoped for and (as we have seen) Raleigh's material and artistic growth in the conclusion of Book 21 is doubtful, and Book 22 a mere fragment: his future is imperiled.

Raleigh hints in the beginning of the poem at his desire to write a 'hygher kynd' (21.10) of poetic endeavour that is replaced by this Petrarchan shambles instead. Instead of 'thinges' written 'so great, so longe, so manefolde' (21.93), what we get is a sort of love-stunted epic, 'Of longe arections such the suddayne fall' (21.228–30). Amid the languid pool of laments, however, a bold and sometimes angry pulse occasionally surfaces, an epic thrust. The poem constantly alludes to the movement of water, both rivers and seas, which flow away from and towards the Queen. The poet's figurative imagination in the opening stanzas traces 'high flowinge streames' that travel down to 'brinish sand' and 'ocean' (21.17, 24, 33), an image of escape from land but also voyage and tribute to the sea and (hence) the Queen (Raleigh's being the tributary stream of verse).[72] Life on a sailboat is viscous, a prolonged marginal state of interrupted sleep, sickness, half-dry clothes, veering motion and spray on face and skin, but with adventure and a port in mind. The sailor is saturated, 'groggy', like Tennyson's Ulysses, who yearns to sail anew, to 'drink / Life to the lees'.[73] As Lin Kelsey eloquently notes,

> The witty expansion of Elizabeth's nickname 'Water' into 'Ocean' [in the poem] suited both Ralegh's ambitions, which were known to be boundless (the sea of Ecclesiastes, after all, is never 'full'), and his style, which was both haughty and 'salt' in the Renaissance sense of stinging and pungent.[74]

Elizabeth's ocean is also Raleigh's ocean, in and around him and permeating his work, driving him on, stinging others and threatening to drown him.

---

71 In *History of the World*, however, 'Ulysses gets dismissed in one sentence' (Horner, 'The Large Landscape', 208).
72 For examination of the Walter-as-tributary-water trope in his own poetry and in Spenser's, including rich use of the Alpheus myth, see Kelsey, 'Spenser, Ralegh', 188 passim. See also chapters by Beer, Booth, and Nohrnberg in this book.
73 Alfred, Lord Tennyson, 'Ulysses' (1833; 1842), in *The Norton Anthology of English Literature*, ed. M. H. Abrams. 2 vols, 5th edition (New York: W. W. Norton, 1986), 2.1108–10 (ll. 6–7).
74 Kelsey, 'Spenser, Ralegh', 191.

Nor is Raleigh's Petrarchism[75] necessarily the opposite of epic endeavour. As Roland Greene has argued at length, Petrarchism could itself have strong colonial resonances and rhetorical uses in its figuration of the conventional 'cruel fair', the lovely yet treacherous lady, turned metaphorically into a land to be loved, pursued, and conquered: the lady is both the sovereign power inspiring the adventurer and the territory to be won (the land both prefigures and becomes part of the sovereign nation). According to Greene, a central source-poem utilized in this way 'innumerable' times in early modern literature is Petrarch's *Canzoniere* 189, commonly known (in English) as 'My ship laden with oblivion'. According to the poem's explicit maritime conceit, the speaker is tossed by the elements of fortune and /or fate and is both guided and led astray by his cruel love at the helm. This made the poem a natural choice for frustrated and frequently lost lovers, sailors, and discoverers from Columbus on: as noted by Greene, Raleigh even uses its motifs in his *Discovery ... of Guiana*.[76] 'Ocean to Scinthia' in its content and arguably its very title alludes to Petrarch's poem. The light of the night-time heavens having extinguished itself, the forlorn speaker of the poem rests 'alone, forsaken, frindless on the shore' (21.89) and he tries to find his 'hoped port' amid turbulent 'stormes' (21.485, 489; cf. also 61–4).

Because of this colonial tradition of the Petrarchan lyric and the epic genre, which need not be at cross-purposes, we can begin to read the poem's unobtainable loved one, or Cynthia, not only as Queen Elizabeth but also as a somatic metaphor for home and colony, or the empire writ large: a territorial trope for the 'home' (21.509) or 'port' (21.485) that Raleigh has adventured his whole life to achieve, both in England *and* abroad, in Guiana, in the aptly named Virginia, and in Ireland. Another poem in Raleigh's hand makes this metaphor explicit: Queen Elizabeth, or 'Cynthia', is

> as the valley of perue
> whose summer ever lastethe
> tyme conqueringe all she mastreth
> By beinge allwaye new.[77]

---

75 The poem contains hallmarks of conventional 'Petrarchan' love poetry, including standard images of self-destructive and painful desire (e.g., the chased and wounded 'hart', 21.455–7), idolization of the 'cruel fair' mistress and fits of passion expressed in clichéd paradoxes (e.g., 'Such heat in Ize, such fier in frost remaynde, / Such trust in doubt, such cumfort in dispaire' 21.69–70).

76 Greene, *Unrequited Conquests: Love and Empire in the Colonial Americas* (Chicago: University of Chicago Press, 1999), 14–15, 141–3.

77 Rudick, ed., *The Poems*, 46; LeFranc, *Sir Walter Ralegh*, 522–3; Horner, 'The Large Landscape', 212.

Elizabeth imagined as 'Peru' in a state of eternal 'summer' (whether or not she conquers time, or time conquers her, or time conquers itself by conquering what she herself 'mastreth') demonstrates how Raleigh conflates the body of the Queen with a desired colonial territory, while simultaneously using the common colonial trope of paradise to describe that country.[78] The image also recalls Spenser's mention of 'Peru' in his fillip to Raleigh's colonial exploits on behalf of the Queen in the Proem to Book III of *The Faerie Queene*. Raleigh writes 'Ocean to Scinthia' within the same paradigm, evoking worlds old and new that remain to be 'conquered' and 'mastered' not only by time but by him and the Queen.

His desires, paradoxically, while calling him home to England, by their very nature propel him to the same 'kyngdomes strange, to lands farr off addrest' (21.88) that have become his place of exile. On behalf of Queen, empire, personal glory and enrichment he tries 'To seeke new worlds, for golde, for prayse, for glory, / To try desire, to try loue seuered farr' (21.61-2), and yet this 'soyle farr off' (21.486) becomes wretched when it and the Queen cuts off her 'love' for (and from) him.[79] As a result,

> From frutfull trees I gather withred leues
> And glean the broken eares with misers hands,
> Who sumetyme did inioy the weighty sheves
> I seeke faire floures amid the brinish sand
>
> (21.21-4)

The ocean with its margin of 'brinish sand' promises opportunity, yet the speaker fruitlessly seeks these 'faire flours' in a place of figurative exile, where flowers presumably *cannot* flourish because saturated with salt water (catching the flavour, in turn, of his own tears).[80] In these places

---

78 As Horner, 'The Large Landscape', notes (210–11), a lengthy passage in Raleigh's *History of the World* describes the 'microcosm' (210) of man's body as like a landscape. For further analysis of the somatic metaphor of the female sovereign body put to colonial (including Irish) use in Spenser's poetry, see Benjamin Meyers, 'Pro-War and Prothalamion: Queen, Colony and Somatic Metaphor among Spenser's Knights of the Maidenhead', *English Literary Renaissance* 37 (2007), 215–49. For discussion of the colonial 'weight' of Peru in this poem, see Padel, *Selected Poems*, xv–xvi.

79 Because this 'soyle farr off' is then compared to 'Sestus shore, Leanders late resorte' along the Hellespont, Edmund Gosse conjectures that Raleigh here alludes to the narrow channel of the Irish sea: referenced in Latham, ed., *Poems*, xlii.

80 An exception would be the flowering mangrove trees found proliferating near the Orinoco Delta of Venezuela, i.e., Raleigh's 'Guiana'. In South America, mangroves are especially notable in the region stretching from the Delta to the Gulf of Paria: www.eoearth.org /article /Coastal_Venezuelan_mangroves (accessed 28 December 2010). Raleigh mentions succulent oysters (if not flowers) growing plentifully on mangrove trees on the island of Trinidad and also many such trees in 'Guiana', in both his *Discovery*

the colonial trope of the poem is made explicit: he has been abandoned in a place that might, instead, become a flowering paradise if her love is *not* severed from him as a result, partly, of his own behaviour.

Joyce Horner's sensitive and eloquent reading of the poem's landscapes notes that 'Throughout the poem ... the dominant imagery is of the earth and not the sea. Much of it is conventional landscape of the pastoral, a winter pastoral'.[81] Raleigh's function as Ocean is to bring us to land, including Spenser's, and not abandon us at sea. As a consequence of the Queen's anger, however, the pastoral landscape is no longer pleasurable nor profitable for the speaker. Raleigh despairs at the conclusion of Book 21:

> Unfolde thy flockes, and leue them to the fields
> To feed on hylls, or dales, wher likes them best ...
> Thy hart, which was thir folde, now in decay
> By often stormes, and winters many blasts
> All torne and rent, becomes misfortunes pray,
> Falce hope, my shepherds staff, now age hath brast.
>
> (21.497–504)

The speaker has given up on the sheepfolds and pastoral worlds of the kind nurtured by Colin Clout. Raleigh's negative emphasis on earth and soil, however frigid or scorched, nonetheless brings territory and cultivation to mind (as well as the bounty of the London court),[82] although the speaker's anxiety is heightened by his exile from the loved one's affections to 'kyngdomes strange', or places such as the New World[83] or Ireland.

Why Ireland? The speaker of Raleigh's sonnet 'Farewell to the court', published in *The Phoenix Nest* (1593) and usually dated post-1589, describes himself 'in vnknowne waies' and 'As in a countrey strange', most appropriately Ireland;[84] the poem may directly reflect Raleigh's hurt feelings after a tiff with the Second Earl of Essex, who (according to one

---

... *of Guiana* and his *History of the World*. See Robert Hermann Schomburgk, ed., *Discovery of the Large, Rich and Beautiful Empire of Guiana*, by Walter Raleigh (London: Hakluyt Society, 1848), 3–4n.

81 Horner, 'The Large Landscape', 201; see also 212: 'Perhaps the sea repelled him by its sterility. Nine-tenths of him, after all, is practical, active, dominant. He wished to see the world mapped and planted, if possible by Englishmen'.

82 May, *The Elizabethan Courtier Poets*, 130.

83 Horner, 'The Large Landscape', 200–1.

84 'Farewell to the court', in Latham, ed., *Poems*, 12. 'Les côtes qui ont disparu derrière l'horizon sont celles de l'Angleterre et l'expression 'country strange' désigne l'Irlande' (LeFranc, 'Sir Walter Ralegh', 80n); A. L. Rowse, *Ralegh and the Throckmortons* (London: Macmillan, 1962), 157.

contemporary) 'chased M. Raleigh from the Court, and hath confined him into Ireland', at which point Raleigh visited Spenser.[85] Raleigh describes Ireland as a 'strang country' for colonists in one of his letters to Robert Cecil, dated July 1592 (see above).[86] In 'Ocean to Scinthia', the world and his own thoughts become 'strange and vilde' (21.268) when the speaker feels rejected. Raleigh may again allude to Ireland here, as a daunting and 'strange' wilderness akin to his bewildered state of mind. But like Petrarch's dejected lover in *Rime* 189, the central paradox that Raleigh wishes to promote for the sake of sympathy is that Cynthia's disdain has exiled him to this wilderness,[87] and yet his loving service on behalf of Cynthia, especially his colonial endeavours to Virginia and Ireland, are what led him to such great personal, financial, and logistical hardship in the first place: the Queen both inspired his adventure and is the ultimate shareholder in it, and therefore is partly to blame for what he did and failed to do for love of her and the sake of empire.

Having promoted his project in the wilderness (literally and /or in his mind), Cynthia is doubly cruel to abandon him there. Despair from losing her love makes him feel yet further lost in the dangerous wilds, which are, nonetheless, desired and have the *potential* for reform should his art – which is painfully nourished in the same place and /or in the Tower – succeed in taming his surroundings and thus placating his Queen. Berowne[88] in Shakespeare's *Love's Labours Lost* (c. 1594–95) declares that the love poet's lines 'would ravish savage ears, / And plant in tyrants mild humility' (4.3.322–3). Instead the Queen's 'pourfull emperye' punishes the tortured Raleigh like 'most violent infections, / Thes be the Tirants that in fetters tye / Their wounded vassals, yet nor kill nor cure' ('Ocean to Scinthia' 21.200, 195–7).

Should she not patronize him, or deliberately ruin him or literally imprison him at 'home', she will pull him back from further worldly glory on her and his behalf: for 'Whom Loue defends, what fortune overthrowes? / [...] /When shee did well, what did ther elce amiss?' – words that Spenser would have approved of – and yet, 'When shee did

---

85 Kelsey, 'Spenser, Ralegh', 184; quoted at 207 n.5. Raleigh's proud response (to his cousin Sir George Carew, dated 27 December 1589) concerning the argument with Essex was that he, Raleigh, went to Ireland to look after his "prize" or lands there. Kelsey ibid.; Edwards, *Life*, 2.41–3.
86 Edwards, *Life*, 2.49.
87 One fancies a subtle link between 'Scinthia' and *Scythia*.
88 Identified as a possible parodic figure for Raleigh's supposed 'school' of neoplatonic philosophizing, in Frances Yates, *The Occult Philosophy in the Elizabethan Age* (1979) (London: Routledge, 2001), 177; Yates, *A Study of* Love's Labour's Lost (Cambridge: Cambridge University Press, 1936), 120–6.

ill what empires would have pleased?' (21.52–4) To paraphrase the third line, 'who can please an angry Queen?' but also, 'when the Queen is ill-disposed, why should I create an empire for her?' The imperial context of the poem is made explicit. A few lines later Raleigh continues his vexed self-examination of how best to express his 'Love' for the Queen through the 'consayte' (i.e., conceit) of both his poetry and her imperial-colonial guidance. It is *in* that poetry, indeed, a reflective image of Cynthia, or the Queen, that he tries to find this guidance:

> The honour of her loue, Loue still devisinge,
> Woundinge my mind with contrary consayte,
> Transferde it sealf sumetyme to her aspiringe
> Sumetyme the trumpett of her thoughts retrayt;
>
> To seeke new worlds, for golde, for prayse, for glory,
> To try desire, to try loue seuered farr,
> When I was gonn shee sent her memory
> More stronge then weare tenn thowsand shipps of warr,
>
> To call mee back, to leue great honours thought,
> To leue my frinds, my fortune, my attempte,
> To leue the purpose I so longe had sought
> And holde both cares, and cumforts in contempt.
>
> (21.57–68)

The poetry is knotty with caesuras and shifts of thought (adding to its sense of torment), highly ambiguous and, as often with Raleigh, acutely aware of its own creative intelligence. The first stanza tells us that Raleigh's poetry, which his own 'Loue' is 'still devisinge', is motivated by the Queen's 'honour' *and* the 'honour' he has in serving her. The second line tells us that writing poetry inspired by and in her 'honour' 'wounds' him, as it would hurt any rejected but not utterly dejected lover wounded at heart, and so he expresses his love-pangs in paradoxes or Petrarchan 'contrary consayte[s]'. As he is her servant, his poetry operates on behalf of her ambitions ('her aspiring'), but also sounds a 'trumpett' in 'retrayt' when those ambitions (like his own) 'Sumetyme' change or fail. Hence her and his 'trumpet' is his poem, which (employing military terminology) declares or trumpets her (and his own) aspiring honour in verse: by 'her thoughts retrayt', Raleigh refers to the fact that his poem captures in verse and 'trumpett[s]' these thoughts, while also acknowledging that the battle is not always won on his or her behalf.

His poetry, he also confidently implies, is privy to the innermost 'retreats' of the Queen's mind. This implication of intimate (including sexual)[89] familiarity with the Queen is a constant strategy in the poem and is enforced by such ambiguous syntax: what signifies the person or mind of Raleigh and what signifies the Queen in the poem is sometimes impossible to separate: Raleigh thus drives home the question, 'Since I am already so entwined with your thoughts and desires, how can you possibly do without me?' In line with these eroticized mind-games played with the Queen (at least in his own imagination), Raleigh stresses his ready status as a colonial military adventurer in her service. To 'try desire' or love her is to constantly 'seeke new worlds, for golde, for prayse, for glory'. And yet her loving call also 'seuers' him from this honourable exploit by calling him home. His trumpet sounds his aspiring advance and his retreat.

Reading Raleigh against Spenser once again emphasizes the imperial significance of the former: the close association of *honour* and *trumpet* with Raleigh is explicitly made by Spenser in *The Faerie Queene* I.viii.3–5 and II.ix.11, wherein the allegorical stand-in for Raleigh, the character Timias, has a name based on the Greek word for 'honoured', *timios*. Timias, moreover, successfully blows his trumpet in battle on behalf of Prince Arthur, when they fight the monster Orgoglio, emblematic of puffed-up Catholic and Spanish power and pride.[90] Spenser dedicates his epic primarily to Queen Elizabeth, and Books I–III (1590) especially celebrate Raleigh's heroism as Timias: some of Timias's heroic acts in Book III, as James Bednarz has shown, are based loosely on Raleigh's early military adventures in Ireland.[91] Spenser also flatters Raleigh's naval expertise when he compares him to the sea-god Triton 'blowing loud his wreathed horn' and commanding the seas in 'Colin Clouts Come Home Againe' (245–6). The trumpeting Raleigh, in 'Ocean to Scinthia', in turn reminds the Queen of his military service on her behalf, including in Ireland.

In deliberately ambiguous syntax in the next stanza, Raleigh may allude to Christopher Marlowe's Helen of Troy ('the face that launched a thousand ships' in *Dr Faustus*) and hence (yet again) epic, imperial subject matter when he compares his 'memory' of Elizabeth (and the Queen's memory of him) to 'ten thowsand shipps of warr', or military means placed at his disposal, that spur him on 'To seeke new worlds, for golde, for prayse, for glory / To try desire, to try loue seuerred farr'; simultaneously, however, these ships reverse direction when her /his memory

---

89 Innuendo abounds; for example, the aching poet is compared to a lamb which 'Playes with the dug though finds no cumfort ther' (21.72; see also 21.322–3).
90 For the etymology of Timias and analysis of his character, see A. Leigh DeNeeff, 'Timias', in *The Spenser Encyclopedia*, 690–1, and discussion of Irish *tim*, above.
91 Cf. note 36, above

'call[s] mee back, to leue great honours thought / To leue my frinds, my fortune, my attempte' (61–8). Raleigh may refer to what must have been the painful decision by the government, in 1588, to divert Raleigh's ships from returning to his 'frinds' and 'fortune' at Roanoke Island and use them instead to fight the Armada with the fleet: instead of seeking 'new worlds', they now are 'shipps of warr' for the defence of the homeland. The colonists had disappeared by the time Raleigh's ships did reach Roanoke the following year.[92]

Hence, ironically, when Elizabeth recruited Raleigh's ships as war ships, she saved the homeland but paradoxically did what King Philip of Spain's ships had intended (in part) to do all along: to vanquish England and its nascent colonial power in the New World. Raleigh is damned if he does, damned if he doesn't contribute his ships. Raleigh understands, of course, that, without patriotically defeating the Armada, Roanoke would have perished in any case: Raleigh is absolved of fault, if not guilt, in leaving the Roanoke colonists high and dry. Yet, now that the Armada had been vanquished, he could fruitfully call the Queen's attention to his ongoing colonial ambitions and past sacrifice on her behalf.

Where would he concentrate his colonial endeavours in 1587–96? Munster, mainly, where a rich prize claimed much of his attention, representing far more than simply a poor hermit's wilderness into which he was exiled.[93] In 1587, Raleigh was given a figurative goldmine in Munster: 42,000 acres, the largest allotment by far of any of the Munster planters and among the best land offered, lying in the fertile and readily exploitable Blackwater river valley. Raleigh eventually sold his holdings in a fire sale in 1602 to Richard Boyle, who made himself Earl of Cork with them.[94] After 1596, Raleigh might be described as an absentee landlord in Ireland without 'much conviction', as Pauline Croft terms him, but not before.[95] In

---

92 Steven May prefers a reference to Raleigh's abortive Panama voyage of 1592. May, *Sir Walter Ralegh*, 46–7.
93 See his poem, 'Like to a Hermit Poore' (Latham, ed., *Poems*, 11–12) also included in *The Phoenix Nest* (1593) and commonly dated to the time around his Irish exile in 1589. Raleigh's plantation seat at Lismore had been a famous centre of learning and Benedictine monastery in the early and later Middle Ages: not unsuitable for a 'hermit'.
94 Canny, 'Raleigh's', 97; Canny, *The Upstart Earl: A Study of the Social and Mental World of Richard Boyle, First Earl of Cork, 1566–1643* (Cambridge: Cambridge University Press, 1982), 6.
95 Pauline Croft, review of Robert Lacey, *Sir Walter Ralegh* (London: Weidenfeld and Nicolson, 1973), in *English Historical Review* 90 (October 1975), 894. D. B. Quinn, *Raleigh*, states that 'Certainly, throughout 1587 and 1588, men, women and children were moving into Raleigh's Irish estates' (139). As late as 1595 Raleigh licenced iron-mills there (155). There was a failed effort in 1596 to transfer iron operations from Sussex Weald to Raleigh's estates in east Cork (Colin Rynne, 'The Social Archaeology of

'Ocean to Scinthia', 'strange' colonial Ireland, like the poem's 'new worlds', does not function merely as an anecdotal backdrop but rather as a fundamental part of its imperial, Petrarchan conceit: like the Queen herself, the country fuels the driving erotic energy of Raleigh's despairing art.

V. Love, war and riches

Of the imperial conceits in 'Ocean', some refer explicitly to 'new worlds' and colonial opportunity there. But in line 120, Raleigh refers to his relationship with Elizabeth as a 'warr' lasting 'twelve yeares', about the time between his initial service as a soldier in Ireland, from the end of 1579, and the suggested date of composition of the poem, 1592–93.[96] The 'war' is a spiritual (including amatory) struggle on behalf of the Queen but also a real one. Raleigh's Irish warfare (narrated at length in Hooker) helped to destroy the Earl of Desmond and thus create the Munster Plantation from his attainted lands. Raleigh himself describes the Desmond rebellion in his *Report of the Fight about the Iles of the Açores* (1591), in the part where he confronts arch-rebel John of Desmond's son, who tried to lure the English sailors and soldiers to the Spanish cause during the Azores skirmish.[97] Ergo, Raleigh's war in Munster was still being played out in his own mind nearly twelve years later during his sea-going campaigns, i.e., around the time he was composing 'Ocean'. 'The more one reads the poem, the more one is struck by its violence, which comes in gusts and then dies down'.[98] Raleigh in 'Ocean' aligns his military service with his prolonged wooing of the Queen, a painful and protracted effort, or labour, that parallels, in turn, Raleigh's attendant interest in Irish land, as we have seen. In the repeated violence of the poem, Raleigh keeps this agony in service of the Queen continually in mind.

Raleigh does not use the words 'Ireland' or 'Munster' anywhere in the poem. He does employ telling and repeated images deriving from industry in nature, however, including a georgic emphasis on tillage and empire. He alludes to terrestrial empire in the poem's effort to turn 'waste' and 'sorrow' (21.122–3) into 'Loves ground, his essence, and his emperye'

Plantation-Period Ironworks in Ireland: Immigrant Industrial Communities and Technology Transfer, c.1560–1640', in *Plantation Ireland*, 248–64: 258). Raleigh may have withdrawn his interests but not his tenants in the later 1590s: an elaborate map of his Mogeely estate dates from 1598 (Canny, 'Raleigh's', 95–6). See also Conclusion below.

96 LeFranc, *Sir Walter Ralegh*, 103; Quinn, *Raleigh*, xvi; Oakeshott, *The Queen*, 21 and passim.
97 Bednarz, 'Ralegh in Spenser's', 56–8.
98 Horner, 'The Large Landscape', 203.

(21.178). He celebrates the power of 'Love', implying the Queen's favour, 'who from high heaven douth on their feilds dissend / Fillinge their barns with grayne, and towres with treasure' (21.310–11). Elizabeth here resembles Jove raining water and gold alike to bless the earth and her people: the potential for colonial fruition is there, although Raleigh's fields, like his heart, have become 'frutless' of late, full of 'stubbell ... Of harvest past'.[99] He hasn't given up entirely: like the ploughman at the centre of the poem, he 'takes delight another seed to sow' (21.275–9) – he writes another verse – while again lamenting his outcast state.

'Ocean to Scinthia' highlights forestry, which again returns us to the poem's occasional fixation on the New World and on Munster.[100] Raleigh equates 'frutfull trees' (21.21) with the rewards of the Queen's favour, but lack of love instead 'wither[s]' these leaves in the same line (cf. also 21.470). The leaves are akin to 'ears' of corn, or agricultural plenty (21.22). Consistent with weather metaphors elsewhere, the clouding of the cruel-fair's divine countenance causes 'The firme and sollide tree' to become 'both rent and rotten' (21.256), or worthless for sale.[101] Anyone who understood Raleigh's industry in Ireland would immediately think of his prospects there. Turning forests into timber and fuel (or charcoal) for iron mills was his main pursuit in Munster.[102] Exploitation of Irish woods developed rapidly thanks to the burgeoning trans-Atlantic economy in wood staves especially, thus linking Raleigh's Irish prospects into an ocean of opportunity.[103] No trees, or rotten trees, and no profit followed. Raleigh juxtaposes an image of withered trees with the useless 'Cynders of extinguisht fiers' at the beginning of his poem (13–16). Raleigh then describes himself as 'All in the shade ... Vnder thos healthless trees I sytt alone' (21.25–6), a passage that closely echoes Spenser's portrayal of the despairing, Irish-like Timias in the forest in *The Faerie Queene* Book IV. Once again we're asked to equate the Queen's ill favour with an evil landscape of trees so densely set they let in little light upon the isolated

---

99 Raleigh later uses a standard pastoral trope of dejection, while referring to sheep and labour, when he wishes to 'Vnfolde thy flockes, and leue them to the feilds' ('Ocean to Scinthia' 21.497) now that all 'my labours weare desayte' (i.e., 'deceit', 465).
100 See for example Thomas Harriot's catalogue of trees and their uses in his *Brief and True Report of the New Found Land of Virginia* (1588).
101 For comparison, Dees remarks on the 'heavily commercial vocabulary' in lines 21. 465–9 ('My love was falce: ... A fraude bought att the prize of many woes ...') as evidence of the speaker's despair. Dees, 'Colin Clout', 193–4.
102 Quinn, *Raleigh*, 155; on Raleigh's Irish smelting industry, see Canny, 'Raleigh's', 95.
103 Kenneth Nicholls, 'Woodland Cover in Pre-Modern Ireland', in *Gaelic Ireland: Land, Lordship and Settlement c.1250–c.1650*, ed. Patrick J. Duffy, David Edwards, and Elizabeth Fitzpatrick (Dublin: Four Courts Press, 2001), 181–206: 199.

speaker. Summer *otium* turns forest of Error redolent of his colonial situation in Spenser's poetry.[104]

A second material fixation of the poem is terrestrial and mineral, as one might expect from the committed mineralogist Raleigh.[105] Raleigh refers to 'gold' and mineral wealth (21.61) as he does in the *Discovery … of Guiana*. He focuses on underground passages, such as the 'deip caves' (21.450) of his heart, rocked by the gusty earthquake of his passion for the Queen. In this same passage he describes the Queen's piercing of his 'hart', a common pun on the human heart and the male deer (Cynthia is a huntress, and the hart was in the crest of Raleigh's coat of arms, c.1585, when he was made a knight and Governor of Virginia):[106]

> So in the Centre of my cloven hart,
> My hart, to whom her bewties wear such wovnder,
> Lyes the sharpe poysoned heade of that loves dart
>
> (21.455–7)

We then hear of the 'fretting rust' of Cupid's arrow as it mixes with his blood (21.457–60), a direct echo of his earlier reference to his poisonous condition whereby 'The hardest steele' of constant 'affection' is 'eaten with softest ruste' (21.255) of neglect and scorn. Here, cheek by jowl to his complaint of 'rotten' trees (21.256), we have an explicit reference to wasting iron weapons, another potential echo of plantation industry. Iron ore had been imported and refined in Ireland earlier, but the first recorded use of the blast furnace and 'indirect' method of iron manufacture in Ireland was established by Sir Thomas Norris, near Raleigh's estate at Mogeely, in County Cork, in 1593. The workers may have lived in Raleigh's village there.[107] In 'Ocean to Scinthia', Raleigh may be alluding to this manufacture in Ireland left to rust and rot.[108] Raleigh takes a conventional image,

---

104 Compare also with the lonely Colin Clout under a winter-blasted tree in the 'January' and 'December' eclogues of Spenser, *The Shepheardes Calender* (1579).
105 On Raleigh's iron and mining industry in Ireland, see Quinn, *Raleigh*, 255; Rynne, 'Social Archaeology', passim; as involving Raleigh in Spenser's *Faerie Queene* Book II, see McCabe, *Spenser's Monstrous Regiment*, 124–5. In regard to tin mines (stannaries) in his native Devonshire, see Joyce Youings, 'Raleigh's Devon', in *Raleigh and Quinn*, 69–85: by the late sixteenth century the industry had 'passed its peak' and Raleigh persuaded 'many' of the miners 'to go to Ireland' (81).
106 Oakeshott, *The Queen*, 12–13, 22 and plate 2.
107 Rynne, 'Social Archaeology', 258. For more on Mogeely in its plantation context, see Eric Klingelhofer, *Castles and Colonists: An Archaeology of Elizabethan Ireland* (Manchester: Manchester University Press, 2010), 73–8. See also map of Raleigh's estates on p. 67.
108 Note also how the guardian nymphs near Kilcolman wield 'steele darts' to protect their herd of deer from 'wylde wolues which seeke them to devoure' in Spenser's 'Epithalamion' (70). Such nymphs generally are followers of Diana in Spenser's poetry: Charles Grosvenor Osgood and Henry Gibbons Lotspeich, eds, *The Minor Poems: Part Two* by

Cupid's dart, which doubles as Cynthia's, or Diana's hunting arrow, and lodges it despairingly in his own bosom, or the 'Ocean', whose salt tears logically cause it to rust.

The image of wasted resources in his 'hart' is reinforced forty lines later when he compares that organ to a sheepfold 'now in decay, / By often stormes... All torne and rent' and 'pray' to 'misfortunes'. 'Dispaire' thereafter threatens to burn his 'pipe' that sang Scinthia's praises (21.502-7). The violent image pictures his anxiety at abandonment by the Queen, which would mean the end to a comfortable pastoral world, worldly fortune and poetic inspiration as well. By analogy, the colonial means by which Raleigh nourished himself and the empire are now painfully wasted in his possession or turned against him, as he and his poetry are the victims of this sad 'fortune'. Should Raleigh's poem fail to convince the Queen, and /or Burghley, then all of his protracted military, colonial, and artistic labours will be reduced (as he himself concludes in adjacent agricultural and mineral metaphors) to 'fancies chafe, or fortunes dross' (21.516).

VI. Conclusion

Despite its often pessimistic tone and emphasis on the speaker's sorrowful and 'vilde' state, Raleigh's poem makes a similar appeal to English colonial sensibilities and crude desire for material wealth as does the *Discovery ... of Guiana* and Spenser's *The Faerie Queene*. It is far more than a prospector's map or an imperial rapist's spreadsheet, however. 'Ocean to Scinthia' portrays psychological distress in compelling and ingenious fashion. Like 'Colin Clouts Come Home Againe', to which it bears strong affinities in style and content, it is a literary feast, deploying a mixture of epic, pastoral, Petrarchan and neoplatonic motifs, including numerological symbolism and somatic metaphors, that reflect courtly clichés and colonial desires in the New World and (especially) Ireland.

This reading of the poem does not aim to flatten its meaning or its many psychological insights, paradoxes, and contradictions by running it through a New-Historicist wringer. It does, however, redirect the poem's political emphasis (long acknowledged) from the court to Raleigh's other fields of action *as well*. This reorientation takes advantage of a generation's worth of new scholarship on Spenser's Irish situation and subject matter (including Raleigh), and it situates the poem in a 'discourse community'

Edmund Spenser, *The Works of Edmund Spenser: A Variorum Edition*, 11 vols (Baltimore: Johns Hopkins Press, 1947), VIII, 465.

focused on Spenser, the Munster plantation, and power-players at the London court. It also helps to modify a reading that stresses only the poem's inwardness, exhaustion, and /or despair at his courtly failures. The Munster plantation grew out of the ashes of the Desmond earldom and Raleigh writes a meandering, violent, fragmentary series of elliptical and echoing complaints (a romance-epic in miniature, as it were) that nurtures seeds of hope and resurrection amid the ashes of his own 'cloven' sheepfold 'hart'. His release from the Tower in late 1592 was occasioned by the looting of colonial spoil from a captured Spanish carrack. Raleigh the sower of verse 'takes delight another seed to sow' and he certainly kept on writing, planting, mining and plundering long afterwards.

Nor does this chapter contradict Nicholas Canny's argument that Raleigh's interest in the Munster plantation was already waning by 1594, since the 'pessimistic' Raleigh had rented the entire estate out by that date for £200 per annum and even considered selling his lands in 1596.[109] In the immediate aftermath of the Throckmorton disgrace, Raleigh's attention was still very much fixed on his Munster holdings, from which he and his tenants, including those described as 'merchants',[110] made a handsome profit selling timber especially. Raleigh, like his lesser neighbour Spenser, understood how fragile a bulwark this plantation was against enemies within and without the empire. Raleigh certainly knew that without the Queen's love and the Cecils' approval, all of his work in Ireland and the New World, on the ground and on the page, would become an 'Idell labour, and a tale / Tolde out of tyme that dulls the heerers eares; / A marchandise whereof ther is no sale' ('Ocean' 21.357–9).

---

109 Canny, 'Raleigh's Ireland', 97.
110 Ibid., 94.

4

'Bellphebes course is now observde no more'
Ralegh, Spenser and the literary politics of the Cynthia holograph

Anna Beer

There exist four poems in Sir Walter Ralegh's own hand which were discovered amongst the Cecil papers at Hatfield House in the mid-nineteenth century. Michael Rudick, the most recent editor of Ralegh's poetry, points out that these four poems 'as far as can be known, were not published in any form and most probably never circulated beyond Ralegh's most immediate acquaintances'. For Rudick, this means that 'we can at best speculate about what state of authorial finish the holograph copies represent', but the poems nevertheless represent a remarkable addition to our understanding of both Ralegh's poetry and, I will argue, one of his immediate acquaintances, Edmund Spenser.[1] Through formal analysis and informed consideration of the historical moment, I hope to elucidate the literary politics of the four poems at the time of their production. In moving between historicist and loosely deconstructive readings, I am influenced by the work of scholars such as David Lee Miller who argued over twenty years ago for 'historical criticism to acknowledge the textual force and value specific to poetry, both as verse and as fiction'.[2]

The contents of the Hatfield manuscript poems are not as well known as they might be, and therefore what follows is a brief introduction to the four poems. The opening septet ('If Synthia be a Queene, a princes, and supreame'), apparently offers the succeeding poems to the Queen, but in a riddling form. Then follows a sonnet which begins 'My boddy in the walls captive', and goes on to demonstrate that its author speaks 'to dead walls'. The third poem is by far the longest of the four, being an extended and sometimes disjointed lament of 522 lines, which ends in dejection ('her

---

1 *The Poems of Sir Walter Ralegh: A Historical Edition*, ed. Michael Rudick (Tempe, AZ: MRTS for RETS, 1999), xiv–xv.
2 David Lee Miller, *The Poem's Two Bodies: The Poetics of the 1590 Faerie Queene* (Princeton, NJ: Princeton University Press, 1988), 3.

love hath end, my woe must ever last'). This long poem is entitled 'The 21th and last booke of the Ocean to Scinthia', indicating Ralegh's name for himself and for his Queen. The final poem, a series of tercets, continues to bemoan Ralegh's 'unrepayred loss' (l. 21) and breaks off completely in mid-line at the start of the eighth stanza: it is entitled 'The end of the boockes, of the Oceans love to Scinthia, and the beginninge of the 22 boock, entreatinge of Sorrow'.

It is usually assumed that the poems are a response to a very real loss of power. As a result first of his clumsy efforts to conceal from Queen Elizabeth I his marriage to Elizabeth Throckmorton, and his subsequent lack of tact in the presentation of their baby son, Damerei, Ralegh was put under house arrest in the summer of 1592, and then imprisoned for some weeks in the Tower of London.[3] Sir Walter would never regain the kinds of power, wealth, and influence that he had achieved prior to this period. It seems likely that Ralegh sent his four poems to Sir Robert Cecil at some point during this summer of political crisis. Ralegh believed at the time that Cecil was an ally, and may have hoped that he would pass the poems on to the Queen. Their survival in the Cecil papers suggests that they did not reach their intended reader. Whether Cecil retained them in an attempt to marginalize his rival further, or whether they were retained in order to protect Ralegh from the potentially problematic impact of his own words, remains unclear.[4]

These four poems (here designated the Cynthia holograph, following Michael Rudick's heading in his edition of the poems) continue to court critical controversy. One of the few points of agreement is that they defy easy generic categorization.[5] The poems have an affinity with some of the most fashionable genres of the early 1590s, offering echoes of sonnet

---

3 For the most recent account of the events of the summer of 1592, see Anna Beer, *Bess: The Life of Lady Ralegh, Wife to Sir Walter* (London: Constable, 2004).

4 It is also possible, as Jerry Leath Mills argues, that the poems we have are a draft, annotated by Ralegh for future revision, *Concise Dictionary of British Literary Biography* (London: Gale Research, 1991), 1:245.

5 The very title of the longest poem in the series is disputed: is it the 21th or the 11th 'and last booke of the Ocean to Scinthia'? The case for 21th has been made in recent years, but that still leaves readers to speculate about the existence or whereabouts of the other twenty books, the meaning of the riddling opening septet, or the significance of Ralegh's occasional emphases and ellipses. Most late twentieth-century critics deem the apparent complexity of *The 21th booke* a symptom of breakdown, whether of the author or of language itself. This tradition was started by Stephen Greenblatt, *Sir Walter Ralegh: The Renaissance Man and His Roles* (New Haven: Yale University Press, 1973) and has been continued by New Historicist, feminist, and post-structuralist critics. The critical consensus remains that the poem is not only unfinished but unfinishable: Robert E. Stillman, '"Words Cannot Knytt": Language and Desire in Ralegh's The Ocean to Cynthia', *Studies in English Literature* 27 (1987), 35–52.

sequences, presaging the epyllion, and working with the conventions of complaint. Nevertheless, the longest of the four poems, *The 21th booke*, foregrounds one genre above others: pastoral. The generic cues include Ralegh's opening insistence on 'simpell words' (l. 2) and the closing references to his shepherd's pipe (l. 505). The generic modulations present within the poem are, paradoxically, themselves indicative of the pastoral mode, as are the repeated gestures towards the failure of the genre and its values, since pastoral is notoriously critical of its own practices.[6] It is the nature of those gestures that is my initial focus here, and their significance both for the understanding of Ralegh as poet, and his relationship with Edmund Spenser. Whilst it is obvious that Ralegh and Spenser repeatedly and anxiously represented Queen Elizabeth I in their writing, I will be arguing that the Cynthia holograph probes the identity not only of the Queen but also that of its author. Self (Ocean) and other (Scinthia) are conflated in a poetic world in which the one cannot be separated from the other. In the second part of my analysis, I will argue that Ralegh's explorations of identity become a critique of Edmund Spenser's allegorical fictions.

The Cynthia holograph engages in complex ways with idealistic pastoral, a genre predicated upon the pursuit of *otium* (a longing for the ideal and an escape from the actual). There is debate as to whether, in its original classical context, the concept involved more an optimistic embrace of an alternative to public duty, but, by Ralegh's time, writers were fascinated by the precariousness of any pastoral retreat into *otium*, whether practically or existentially.[7] *The 21th booke* can be read as an extended meditation on the topic, moving towards *otium*, even attempting to sustain it, but invariably suffering a poetic malfunction. This is perhaps not surprising, since

---

6 Harry Berger Jr, for example, notes, writing about the *Shepherd's Calendar*, that pastoral narrative is self-consciously critical of its own commitment to the genre, in *Revisionary Play: Studies in the Spenserian Dynamics* (Berkeley: University of California Press, 1988), 320, whilst Robert Stillman comments that 'generic [re]definition is the characteristic activity of Renaissance pastoralism' pointing to Sidney's *Old* and *New Arcadias* in *Sidney's Poetic Justice* (Lewisburg: Bucknell University Press, 1986), 64. Michael Everton offers a fine analysis of the debate about the vexed line between pastoral and anti-pastoral in 'Critical Thumbprints in Arcadia: Renaissance Pastoral and the Process of Critique'. *Style* 35 (2001), 1–17.

7 Thomas G Rosenmeyer, *The Green Cabinet: Theocritus and the European Pastoral Lyric* (Berkeley: University of California Press, 1969) offers a detailed discussion of *otium*, both in its classical representations and in the later Elizabethan period. Whilst challenging Poggioli's understanding of *otium* as a pessimistic impulse (68), Rosenmeyer acknowledges that writers such as Lodge, Spenser, Drayton, and Shakespeare offer a vision of *otium* 'not quite the one featured in Theocritus' (69–71, 90).

Ralegh in his own century was perceived as a particularly trenchant critic of the illusion of *otium*, ascribed as author of the response to the poem 'Come live with me and be my love', which was itself ascribed to Christopher Marlowe. The response to 'Come live with me', whether entitled 'Loves answer', 'Loves response' or the 'Answer of the Milk maids mother', begins and ends by acknowledging the attractions of *otium*, but reveals those attractions as empty fictions, supplied by the 'shepperds tongue'.

> But could youth last and love still breed,
> Had joys no date nor age no need
> Then those delights my mind might move
> To live with thee, and be thy love.[8]

If the pursuit of *otium* can be described as the attempt to eternize a single moment, then the Nymph's reply offers a reminder of the power of time and death to ensure the failure of that attempt. A related trope is found in the clumsily eloquent retelling of the Hero and Leander story that precedes the final attempt at pastoral in *The 21th booke*. Christopher Marlowe, possibly at around this time, transformed the tale (which originally ended with Neptune orchestrating the death of Leander by drowning) into a witty celebration of the erotic, leaving his lovers in bed as the poem breaks off. In contrast, Ralegh's retelling of the young lovers' story not only begins abruptly but ends in incoherence and paradox: 'Shee sleaps thy death' (l. 490), 'Shee is gonn, Shee is lost, shee is found, she is ever faire' (l. 493). There is no sea-god at work here, lascivious or otherwise, merely a feminine nemesis. The moral, such as it is, is fatalistic rather than regenerative: 'Do then by diing what life cannot doo' (l. 496). The Hero and Leander episode demonstrates both the inability of *The 21th booke* to sustain a genre, as this brief foray into something akin to epyllion collapses, and the movement of the erotic into stasis and death. What seems clear is that *The 21th booke* is conducting the reader on a journey to the dark side of *otium*, whether understood as inertia, disillusion, or death.[9]

These apparently troubling moments in the Cynthia holograph, whether considering form or content, are, however, rooted in another aspect of pastoral, its capacity for profound satire. Alongside the passages of panegyric and critique, Ralegh utilizes what has been described as the genre's ability to 'describe the dependency of patronage relations

---

8 Izaak Walton's version, printed in 1653, see *Poems of Ralegh*, ed. Rudick, 119–20.
9 Rosenmeyer, *Green Cabinet*, 71, argues, following Schiller, that the pastoral mode is about the 'reaching of equilibrium not paralysis'. Ideally, of course, that is the case but the point being made here is that Ralegh's poem works to deconstruct the ideals of pastoral.

and the paradoxical freedom of exile.[10] The dependency produced by patronage relations was complemented by a further, related, form of dependency, since Ralegh and his contemporaries operated in a court culture of exchange, which relied on a high degree of verbal mimicry.[11] These related dependencies, upon patrons and poetic exchange, are both written into the Cynthia holograph. Ralegh, typically, complicates the dynamic with his profound self-reflexivity. The septet which opens the Cynthia holograph is merely one of a series of gestures that run like a seam through the manuscript, drawing attention to Ralegh's own writings in the past ('So wrate I once', l. 124). In a related move, Ralegh draws attention to the materiality of his work, and the place of any particular poem in his oeuvre. When he writes 'keipe thes amonge the rest' (l. 2 of the opening poem), he alludes both to the very papers in the reader's hands, and 'the rest' of the writer's oeuvre. Indeed, these kinds of allusions could be deemed Ralegh's signature, indicative of a preoccupation with readers, interpretation, repetition and imitation, which continued right to the end of his life.

Ralegh enacts these various dependencies, political and textual, in the Cynthia holograph, but he also invokes the freedom of exile, if only partially. That Ralegh's vision of the poet as exile is not sustained throughout *The 21th booke* may be symptomatic of a wider issue, described by Michael Everton in his sophisticated analysis of Sidney's use of pastoral. Everton argues that, in order to function as a criticism of the status quo, pastoral needed to offer either nostalgia for the past or hope for a golden age in the future, with both nostalgia and hope articulated from a position of necessary exclusion. He goes on, however, to suggest that in Sidney's fictions, 'the boundaries that are forever necessary to mark the separation of the pastoral landscape from corrupted civilization and its cities are compromised'. Thus the critical function of the text itself founders, since there 'are no more havens from which to launch disguised critiques of courts or the corrupted reason of man'.[12] Similarly to Sidney, Ralegh cannot sustain the fiction of the truth-telling outsider, in part because of the intrusion of political reality. The unfinished, fractured poetry of the Cynthia holograph, which can sustain neither its critique

---

10 Michelle O'Callaghan, 'Pastoral', in *A Companion to English Literature Renaissance and Culture*, ed. Michael Hattaway (Oxford: Blackwell, 2002), 308.
11 See James P. Bednarz, 'The Collaborator as Thief: Ralegh's (Re)Vision of *The Faerie Queene*', *English Literary History* 63.2 (1996), 281. Bednarz offers a useful analysis of the ways in which Ralegh and Spenser produce poetry that is both interlocked and autonomous.
12 Everton, 'Critical Thumbprints', 7–8.

of the court nor its celebration of the perception of the exile combine, in fact serves to underline one of the messages of dark pastoral, that the very genre is failed, has failed, will fail.

The point is made early in *The 21th booke*: if the writer were not dead, then he would witness his mishap in 'hygher kind' (l. 10), indicating epic. Two related readings of the poem as a response to epic are plausible. On the one hand, to articulate the failure or inadequacy of the pastoral mode could, in an echo of Virgil, signify a readiness for epic. Alternatively, following Theocritus, the work may operate as a lament for a lost heroic past. As Judith Haber demonstrates, writing specifically of Theocritus but mindful of pastoral as a whole, at the heart of the *Idylls* lie questions about the relevance of the epic style, questions that are complicated by the textual presence of absent heroes, or contemplation of heroism past.[13] This uneasy interplay between bucolic and epic is present in Ralegh's poetry, which recreates, to follow Haber's phrasing, in diminished, textual forms the heroism that their author has left behind ('To seeke new worlds, for golde, for prayse, for glory' l. 61, or 'leve great honours thought', l. 65). This tension between the public world of honour and achievement, and the private, erotic world of advancement is redolent of sonnet sequences, not least *Astrophil and Stella*, which also toys with visions of heroic action, past and future. With the impossibility of 'hygher kind' (l. 10) the possibility of epic, the life of heroism, has been lost: 'the hardest steele eaten with softest ruste' (l. 255). At these moments, the lament for Ralegh's lost heroism comes close to a wider critique of a world gone soft, shifting the Cynthia holograph away from *otium* towards ideologically driven pastoral satire, *negotium*, yet never quite sustaining its polemic.

Instead, throughout the Cynthia holograph, Ralegh appears more consistently engaged with something akin to pastoral elegy. This is a fitting genre with which to explore an impossible love, or an irrevocable loss.[14] As both Milton and Tennyson recognized, following Theocritus' *Lament for Daphnis*, pastoral elegy offered the opportunity to hint at the homoerotic within the hyperbolic framework of mourning.[15] Ralegh, in contrast, uses the genre's hyperbole to explore the irreparable breach between subject and monarch. By the end of *The 21th booke*, the speaker

---

13 Judith Haber, *Pastoral and the Poetics of Self-Contradiction* (Cambridge: Cambridge University Press, 1994), 12 and 15.
14 See Stephen Guy-Bray, *Homoerotic Space: The Poetics of Loss in Renaissance Literature* (Toronto: University of Toronto Press, 2002).
15 Ibid. 4 and 18. See also Matthew Curr, *The Consolation of Otherness: The Male Love Elegy in Milton, Gray and Tennyson* (Jefferson, NC: McFarland & Company, 2002) for compelling readings within this tradition.

is a man apart, writing from a position of isolation or alienation. The seriousness of his predicament is heightened, however, by the speaker's refusal to allow any consolation from the pastoral world. Later, Spenser's presence in the Cynthia holograph will be explored more fully, but here it is enough to note that Ralegh refuses the kinds of consolations articulated by Spenser in *Colin Clout's Come Home Again*, or, less conclusively, in *The Faerie Queene*. In Spenser's work, Colin and the 'straunge' Shepherd of the Ocean share a pipe:

> he tooke in hond
> My pipe before that aemuled of many,
> And plaid theron [...]
> So piped we, untill we both were weary.
>
> (ll. 72–9)

In this homosocial world of courtier/poets sharing pipes, similarity links Colin and the Shepherd of the Ocean, Spenser and Ralegh. A similar dynamic is apparent in *The Faerie Queene*. After many travails, many of them involving female, courtly figures, Timias is reunited with Arthur. The reunion of squire and knight is described by the Longman edition as strongly erotic (p. 655) and the text allows an older, wiser, but weaker Timias to return, for a moment at least, to his first incarnation, the lovely boy in the service of Arthur.[16]

In contrast, *The 21th booke* demonstrates an almost aggressive exclusion of the homosocial, let alone the homoerotic. This is the more strange, since recent studies of early-modern cultural practice suggest that friendship or love between men was often easier to comprehend than friendship or love (rather than lust) between men and women.[17] Male/male relationships were given more value than those between men and women, and valued precisely because such a relationship could be one of equality and likeness. This principle of likeness (upheld by nature) was used to legitimize relations between members of one sex, and yet Ralegh disdains to turn to the consolations of men in his poems.

Instead the speaker enters a state of radical isolation in which pastoral itself is insufficient. *The 21th booke* ends with a farewell to his flocks: 'Unfolde thy flockes and leve them to the fields' (l. 497); 'falce hope, my

---

16 Edmund Spenser, *The Faerie Queene*, ed. A. C. Hamilton (Harlow: Pearson Longman, 2nd edition, 2007), 665 referring to VI.viii.27.

17 Alexandra Shepard, *The Meanings of Manhood* (Oxford: Oxford University Press, 1993), especially 119–20; Anna Bryson, *From Courtesy to Civility: Changing Codes of Conduct in Early Modern England* (Oxford: Clarendon Press, 1998); and Laurie Shannon, 'Nature's Bias: Renaissance Homonormativity and Elizabethan Comic Likeness', *Modern Philology* 98 (2000), especially 185.

shepherds staff, now age hath brast' (l. 504); his pipe, given by love's own hand, may be thrown to the fire. Ralegh, the pastoral elegist, is by definition experiencing loss and is denied the consolations of pastoral community (so vividly represented by Spenser) from start to end of his poem: 'I sytt a lone' (l. 26), 'no sheapherds cumpanye' (l. 29).

There were, however, other potential consolations available to Ralegh within the tradition of pastoral elegy. Most pertinent, there was the possibility of the social, literary or political success, indeed preferably all three at once, to be derived from the eloquent articulation of loss. Ovid's account of the birth of pastoral elegy offers a paradigm. In *Metamorphoses*, Apollo accidentally kills his beloved Spartan boy, Hyacinth. As consolation, he transforms him into a flower and offers a lament: 'the beloved of the lover is, paradoxically, killed by him – and, in dying, yields him his new genre'.[18]

I would argue that this is precisely what occurs in the Cynthia holograph, which anatomizes the textual relationship between Ralegh and Queen Elizabeth.[19] The prefatory sonnet is a powerfully sustained metaphor of imprisonment, in which the speaker demonstrates that his mind is trapped not just *by* the memory of Cynthia but actually *in* her memory: 'fast fettered in her auntient memory' (l. 4). This prison of memory was originally 'delightfull' (l. 9), but now both his 'keeper' and his 'fare' have changed. He is his own keeper, since 'Dyspaire bolts up my dores' (l. 13). His despair leaves his consciousness trapped within Cynthia's mind, where, as will be articulated in *The 21th booke*, he is 'slayne with sealf thoughts, amased in fearfull dreames' (l. 19). As Jerome Dees argues, comparing Ralegh's work with Spenser's *Colin Clout's Come Home Again*,

---

18 Micaela Jacan, *Ramus* 17 (1988), 121–2 quoted in Guy-Bray, *Homoerotic Space*, 18.
19 Tashma-Baum reads Ralegh's earlier poem, 'Prais'd be Diana's fair and harmless light' (which is headed, in manuscript collections, 'Sheepherd to QE') in a similar way, arguing that the poem 'represents the Elizabethan court as a timeless, serene, perfect world, complete and self-enclosed. ... Elizabeth is the creator, the mover and the aesthetic and moral centre of this world, and the poem uses the specular language of 'light' 'beams' and 'perfect image' (l. 16) to describe what is a fantasy of full imaginary identification, achieved through poetry, of the courtier with her'. As Tashma-Baum points out, the closing line of the poem (as so often with Ralegh) offers a twist to the apparent praise. When Ralegh writes 'With *Circes* let them dwell, that thinke not so', the possibility of thinking 'not so' is injected into the poem. Miri Tashma-Baum, 'A Shroud for the Mind: Ralegh's Poetic Rewriting of the Self', *Early Modern Literary Studies* 10.1 (1 May 2004). For my earlier understanding of the textual relationship between Ralegh and his Queen, see Anna Beer, "Knowinge shee can renew': Sir Walter Ralegh in Praise of the Virgin Queen', *Criticism* 34 (1992), 497–515, which argues that the Cynthia holograph operates as 'sophisticated political address, a courtier's attempt to show his fitness for service through the medium of poetry', 511–12.

'Cynthia is *in* Ralegh's mind in a way that is radically different from the way she may be said to be *in* Colin's mind'.[20]

This psychic imprisonment is played out in a further metaphor. Ralegh had at times represented himself as water in his earlier courtier poetry (for example, 'Our Passions are most like to Floods and streams') and he was known as 'Water', in part because of his own pronunciation of his given name. In *the 21th Book*, however, the Queen is also figured in terms of water, most notably in the passage starting at l. 221. Now, in stark negation of the speaker's titular identity as Ocean, he is identified with the riverbank, overwhelmed with snow melt.[21] He is no longer Shepherd *of* the Ocean, master of himself, he is being destroyed *by* the ocean, and within the metaphoric framework of the poem that ocean is both his self and the Queen. Images of drowning ('dround my minde in deapts of misery', l. 142) and dissolution punctuate the poem. Worse still, the speaker might be dissolved by water, but neither a sign of his dissolution nor its source remains: 'nor any shew or signe of weet douth byde' (l. 240). At the same time, the speaker continues as water, but neither stream nor ocean. He is marble that weeps (l. 127), or an icicle that cries 'secreat teares', reduced to his element in 'wastinge dropps' (ll. 134–5). 'Water' Ralegh is now merely a producer of tears, and those do not even leave a mark. What remains fascinatingly uncertain is who is doing what to whom, all part of the dazzling working out in metaphor of the psychological imprisonment and symbiosis described in the prefatory sonnet.[22]

What is explicitly expressed in *The 21th booke* is that its author has previously created 'Th' Idea remayninge of thos golden ages' (l. 348).[23]

---

20 Jerome Dees, 'Colin Clout and the Shepherd of the Ocean', in *Spenser Studies: A Renaissance Poetry Annual* (New York: AMS Press, Inc.), XV (2001), 189.
21 Laurie Shannon argues that Ralegh is responding to Elizabeth's apparent or threatened reversion to a *natural* state (the stream will, if left to its own devices, 'runn att large in th'auncient channels'). This natural state exists in tension with the patriarchal, heteronormative controls that Ralegh, and his fellow male courtiers, seek to impose upon the unmarried Queen. Elizabeth, however, refuses to 'be constrained within the logics of a heterosexually mixed paradigm'. Shannon, 'Nature's Bias', 194.
22 Lin Kelsey argues that Ralegh's mind's 'long deseas' is a slow de-seaing, and thus involves a process of desertification: 'Spenser, Ralegh, and the Language of Allegory' in *Spenser Studies: A Renaissance Poetry Annual* (New York: AMS Press, Inc.) XVII (2003), 190–1. The drying up of water appears, however, less threatening than its plenitude.
23 The Renaissance understanding of Plato's concept of the Idea (an eternally existing pattern or archetype of any class of things, of which the individual things in that class are imperfect copies, and from which they derive their existence) is epitomized by the following quotation from Philemon Holland, *Plutarch's Philosophie, commonlie called, the Morals* tr. 1603 (1657), 813: 'Socrates and Plato suppose, that these Ideæ bee substances separate and distinct from Matter, howbeit, subsisting in the thoughts and imaginations of God - that is to say, of Minde and Understanding'.

That 'Idea' no longer has currency, and, in narrowly socio-political terms, the outcome emerges equally plainly. Ralegh's writings are 'now ann Idell labour and a tale / tolde out of tyme' (ll. 357–8). In conceptual terms, there is a certain logic at work. Symbiosis now works to destroy identity. Both Ralegh and Elizabeth are represented in terms of the element of water, and the result, played out in the poem, is that 'water' destroys 'Ocean'. Simultaneously, bearing in mind that creation of the 'Idea' was predicated upon symbiosis with the created, the dissolution of the maker's mind (of 'Ocean') means that the 'Idea' will die too.

> Bellphebes course is now observde no more
> that faire resemblance weareth out of date
> our Ocean seas are but tempestius waves
> and all things bass that blessed wear of late
>
> (ll. 271–4)

Having delineated the nature and implications of this symbolic symbiosis (and annihilation), *The 21th booke* goes on to play with the possibility of release by invoking two cognitive modes. Both centre on the word 'fancy', but I would argue that Ralegh deploys two understandings of the term: as desirous imagination ('when first my fancy erred', l. 3) and as a cognitive expression, closely related to *phantasia* ('my fancy in the hearse', l. 11). The latter usage draws on scholastic psychology, in which fancy was understood to be synonymous with fantasy, with both terms referring to the mental apprehension of an object of perception or the faculty by which this is performed, and, more specifically, the representations of things not present to the senses. Medieval and then Renaissance philosophers of mind were building upon the confusing body of work on the imagination produced by Aristotle, most notably *De Anima*. In that work, Aristotle argued that *phantasia* is 'that in virtue of which we say that an image occurs to us, and we are not using the word in some metaphorical sense' (*De Anima*, chapter three, 428a 1–4). Later, he wrote of 'the soul's never thinking without a mental image' but here he uses the rare term *aisthema* (431a 15–20).[24] In Aristotle's thinking, the term *phantasia* does

---

24 Aristotle, *De Anima (On the Soul)*, ed. Hugh Lawson-Tancred (London: Penguin Books, 1986). See Malcolm Schofield, 'Aristotle on the Imagination', in *Aristotle's De Anima*, ed. Martha C. Nussbaum and Amelie Oksenberg Rorty, *Essays on Aristotle's De Anima* (Oxford: Clarendon Press, 1992), 249–53, for the debate as to whether imagination is an appropriate translation of Aristotle's term *phantasia*. It is contested, for example, whether Aristotle actually argued that 'while judgement is fallible, direct intuition – the apprehension of the essence of a single object – is not': see William David Ross and John L. Ackrill, *Aristotle* (London: Routledge, 1995), 93, and the critique by Schofield, 'Aristotle', 263.

triple duty since it 'designates the capacity, the activity or process, and the product or result', and has thus produced confusion in subsequent commentators. Dorothea Frede has, however, helpfully summarized the significance of the active, cognitive function of imagination in Aristotle's thinking. Perception and reason are necessary for cognition, but given that there can be a wide gap between the two, at least one of the functions of imagination is to bridge that gap.[25]

The 21th booke foregrounds this interpretive tradition when it considers 'fancy in the hearse'. Here, the death of fancy is represented not as the death of sexual desire, but as the death of cognition, the death of the 'eyes of my minde' (l. 108). Without cognitive power, the speaker is 'defaced' (l. 92), a word which encompasses not merely the marring of appearance, the obliteration of the written word, and defamation, but also, importantly, the blotting out of existence, memory, and thought.

When considering the term 'fancy', it is, however, almost impossible to exclude the later, more familiar understanding of the term as desirous imagination, if only because the two understandings have been confused within the Western intellectual tradition. Indeed, Aristotle himself connected *phantasia* with desire. He argued that

> our desire for (and, thus, pursuit of) anything not actually present to the senses must be mediated by an image of the desired object. Aristotle's treatment is morally neutral, but his notion of desirous imagination may later have become conflated with the Hebraic concept of *yetser*, the willful (but also semi-divine) faculty in humanity that led to Adam's (and, indeed, all subsequent) sin. At any rate, in the Judaeo-Christian intellectual tradition (from ancient to relatively recent times) imagination, although recognized as indispensable to cognition, was usually profoundly distrusted. Unless strictly disciplined by reason it would soon lead us into concupiscence and sin.[26]

This is an understanding of fancy embedded in the literature of Ralegh's time, and can be related to contemporary debates, couched in the language of neoplatonism, about the soul, reason, and the body. The

---

25 See Dorothea Frede, 'The Cognitive Role of *Phantasia* in Aristotle', in *Essays*, ed. Nussbaum and Rorty, 282. Spenser uses the verb 'imagine' four times in *The Faerie Queene* in the sense of 'to represent to the mind something not present to the senses'. As the entry on imagination in the *Spenser Encyclopaedia*, ed. A. C. Hamilton (London: Routledge, 1990, 392) points out, he designates the faculty of imagination by fantasy or, more frequently by its contraction fancy and is alert to the close contemporary association of fancy with poetry, fiction, falsehood, lust, and even heresy.

26 Nigel, J T. Thomas (2004), 'Imagination', in *Dictionary of Philosophy of Mind*, ed. C. Eliasmith, http: / /philosophy.uwaterloo.ca /MindDict /imagination.html, accessed 21 April 2009.

fifteenth-century neoplatonist Ficino opened the door to the view that the body might have a role in the elevation of the soul. Ficino argued that, while the soul might be satisfied with the idea of the beloved, 'the eye and spirit require the presence of the body, and the soul, which is usually dominated by them, is forced to desire the same thing'.[27] English poets, as Catherine Gimelli Martin demonstrates in her subtle analysis of the poetry of this period, responded to this aspect of Ficino's work, turning away from the 'high' neoplatonism of France and Italy. Poets, including Spenser, were 'more willing to imagine a place for the body in the quest for the One, whilst still decrying Lust'. In Spenser's case, this entailed condoning the sexual act within marriage. In so doing 'he converts platonism from the mere worldly game and pretence played by the *trattatisli* and courtiers' into 'a self-contained, self-complete experience'.[28] Spenser's serious neoplatonism is predicated on what the *Spenser Encyclopedia* summarizes as 'the Platonic myth of the soul's gradual descent into the fleshly body and its ability to reascend to the realm of Being [which] for Spenser was an equivocal analogue of Christian doctrine'.[29] Spenser, as David Lee Miller makes clear, works comfortably within these 'low' neoplatonic tropes in order to praise his queen.

> Taking his cue from the Queen's political transformation of chivalric and Petrarchan rhetorics, Spenser draws on the resources of Neoplatonism to infuse the monarch's body politic with an erotically compelling visionary glory: the transcendental beauty that the Platonic lover beholds in the personal soul of his Beatrice or Laura is assimilated to Elizabeth's political power in the vision of a 'lover' who seeks her favour as ardently as Arthur seeks Gloriana, and whose historical gestalt is as profoundly constituted by the fiction and figure of royal sovereignty as Fairyland itself is.[30]

Ralegh's stance, at least in the Cynthia holograph, is different. Earlier, in passing, a couple of divergences between Spenser and Ralegh were noted, such as their different approaches to homosociality as consolation, or to desirous fancy. Perhaps the most important divergence between the two writers is, however, related to this discussion of fancy and neoplatonism. David Lee Miller argues forcefully for Spenser's position. He may criticize his Queen, but he does not 'break the frame of his foreconceit, which is both a powerful ideological synthesis and a deeply interested

---

27 Marsilio Ficino, *Commentary on Plato's 'Symposium' on Love*, trans. Sears Jayne (Woodstock, CT: Spring Publications, 1985), 115.
28 Catherine Gimelli Martin, 'The Erotology of Donne's Extasie and the Secret History of Voluptuous Rationalism', *Studies in English Literature 1500-1900* 44 (2004), 121-47.
29 *Spenser Encyclopedia*, 665-6.
30 Lee Miller, *The Poem's Two Bodies*, 20.

mystification'.[31] Ralegh, I would argue, does precisely what Spenser does not: he breaks the frame of his foreconceit. The Idea is exposed as a mere metaphor. In *The 21th booke* the power of the Queen herself is now simply an 'outworne concayte' (l. 295) whereon the speaker built. The 'concayte' is revealed as generated by (desirous) fancy, and is now challenged by the speaker's 'strong reason' which knows that 'formes externall' cannot last, that beauty does not last (l. 173, l. 176). A list of the beauties and perfections that *seemed* to last forever is countered by the reality:

> Thes weare thos marvellous perfections,
> the parents of my sorrow and my envy
> Most deathfull and most violent infections
> Thes be the Tirants that in fetters tye
> their wounded vassals, yet nor kill nor cure,
> but glory in their lastinge misery
>
> (ll. 193–8)

'Thes seeminge bewties' (l. 177) are fictions, fantasies, images, and conceits that produce 'pourfull emperye ...' (l. 200, Ralegh's ellipsis). Fantasy here is delusion, and must be countered by rational knowledge of the physical reality: that Cynthia is a woman and 'so douth shee pleas her vertues to deface' (l. 204, turning the tables neatly on the speaker's earlier defacement). It seems only fitting that Cynthia's most significant feminine characteristic is 'a change of fantasye' (l. 210). Therefore, if Spenser reinvigorates the empty platitudes of courtly neoplatonism with a serious consideration of earthly love and marriage, Ralegh rejects both the court and its neoplatonism. What he puts in their place is revealing.

In the closing passages of *The 21th booke* there is a return to the appreciation of fancy as cognition, rather than (feminised) delusion.[32]

> in thy minds long diseas
> externall fancy tyme alone recurethe,
> all whose effects do weare away with ease
> love of delight while such delight indureth
> stayes by the pleasure, but no longer stayes ...
> But in my minde so is her love inclosde
> And is therof not only the best parte,
> but into it the essence is disposde ...
> ...

---

31 Ibid.
32 The relationship between the beginning and end of *The 21th booke* may well indicate what Mills (*Concise Dictionary of British Literary Biography*, 244) describes as the 'topomorphic composition of the poem, since beginnings and ends of poems are frequently linked in this way'.

> Oh love it is but vayne, to say thow weare
> ages, and tymes, cannot thou poure outrunn ...
>
> Thow art the sowle of that unhappy minde
> which beinge by nature made an Idell thought
> began yeven then to take immortall kynde
> when first her vertues in thy spirrights wrought, ...
> from thee therefore that mover cannot move
> because it is becume thy cause of beinge
>
> (ll. 421–43)

This as an assertion that the mind, when not diseased (Ralegh's spelling 'diseas' allows for both lack of ease, and physical illness), *can* perceive essence even if it cannot articulate it, with the ellipses here indicating, graphically, the difficulty of utterance.

By the end of *The 21th booke*, with the exiled speaker turning towards (but not reaching) home, the avowed aim is to return the cognitive part of himself that was given to him by God, to God. The poem argues that he has given that part of himself to Elizabeth, and she has returned it to him. It is thus God, not Elizabeth, who will provide the means for Ralegh's 'last cumforts' (l. 520). Ralegh is left with the possibility of true cognition (not external fancy), imbued with and dedicated to, God. Perhaps surprisingly, the consolation, such as it is, exists here. It involves a re-dedication of the poet to his maker, and a renunciation of his own role as poet-maker.

This movement between understandings of 'fancy' has significance beyond the philosophical or religious. It exemplifies Ralegh's changing relationship with Edmund Spenser in the early 1590s.[33] Once alerted to Ralegh's engagement with Spenser, other passages of the *Cynthia* holograph become illuminating. The lines quoted earlier, which announce that Belphoebe is no more, are, for example, preceded by a perverse rewriting of an aspect of Spenser's project in *The Faerie Queene*. Spenser had offered his Queen 'mirrours more than one' (III.Proem.v.6) fulfilling the role of the poet as the provider of mirror(s) to the magistrate. Bart van Es argues that the image of the mirror, which appears in each of the first three instalment's Proems, demonstrates that 'Spenser was profoundly self-conscious about the interactive dynamic that sustained his fiction. Historical collections such as the Tudor *Mirror for Magistrates* were 'mirrors' precisely because the message they bore changed in relation to their reader'.[34] In *The 21th booke* Ralegh too deploys an image

---

33 For an example of the debate, see *Spenser Studies: A Renaissance Poetry Annual* (New York: AMS Press, Inc.), XV (2001).
34 Bart van Es, *Spenser's Forms of History* (Oxford: Oxford University Press, 2002), 145.

of reflection. His mirror is, however, a standing puddle, that was once a stream. As elsewhere in the poem, Ralegh and his queen are merged, and it remains unclear who holds the mirror, and whose reflection is being seen, a confusion compounded by the rare presence of the first-person plural pronoun.

> Thos streames seeme standinge puddells which before,
> Wee saw our bewties in, so weare the[y] cleere
>
> (ll. 269–70)

Ralegh's 'standinge puddells' and Spenser's 'mirrours more than one' may be a small example, but it is indicative, I believe, of a broader dynamic of dialectic.[35] Jerome Dees is right, for example, to argue that both *Colin Clout* and the Cynthia holograph ask the same question: 'How do I write about Cynthia?' Spenser, according to Dees, gives a neoplatonic answer, which is then critiqued by Ralegh who subjects Spenser's easy solution to 'a sceptical, at times tortured, scrutiny'.[36] That scrutiny is visible even in the riddling septet that prefaces, along with a sonnet, *The 21th booke*. The septet begins with a conditional clause, which whilst considering what Cynthia is (a Queen, a princess and supreme) also begs the question as to what she really is.

---

35 Something similar might be visible in both poets' concern with arithmetology, and in particular the number 22. Although there is much debate about the significance of Book II, ix, stanza 22 (known as the arithmelogical stanza) it is agreed that Platonic concepts are being invoked, and, more particularly, the number 22 is viewed as the number of the soul. Fowler argues that the stanza is meaningful in terms of Pythagorean and Platonic arithmology, and that the stanza shows 'the *incommensurateness* of mind (circle) and body (triangle), and the difficulty of establishing proportion between them: a fact with painfully real psychological and moral consequence'. See Alastair Fowler, *Spenser and the Numbers of Time* (London: Routledge & Kegan Paul, 1964), 265–7. See also J. Leath Mills, 'Spenser's Castle of Alma and the Number 22: A note on Symbolic Stanza Placement', *Notes and Queries*, 14:12 (1967), 456–7. In a later study, Jerry Leath Mills (*Concise Dictionary of British Literary Biography*, 245) changed his perspective slightly: 'the number twenty-two, in Spenser's works, usually symbolizes chastity, virginity and self-denial', but there is no mention of the soul. Is it a coincidence that, in the Cynthia holograph, the final poem is entitled 'The end of the boockes, of the Oceans love to Scinthia, and the beginninge of the 22 boock, entreating of Sorrow', (Ralegh's punctuation), and that this '22 boock' breaks off in the middle of line 22? If Ralegh is responding to Spenser with his own theory of the soul, it is hard to fathom what that theory might be, although, in the light of the argument that follows, it could signal a form of rebirth for the soul after the crisis explored in *The 21th booke*. The point is not to establish which of the two poets is the better philosopher (although Spenser is certainly the more explicit philosopher), but to recognize the grounds of the debate, whether conscious or not between the two writers.
36 Dees, 'Colin Clout', 188.

> If Synthia be a Queene, a princes, and supreame,
> keipe thes amonge the rest, or say it was a dreame,
> for thos that like, expound, and those that louth, express,
> meanings accordinge as their mindes, ar moved more or less,
> for writing what thow art, or showing what thow weare,
> adds to the on dysdayne, to th'other butt dyspaire,
> Thy minde of neather needs, in both seinge it exceeds.

If the Cynthia holograph asks the question 'how do I write about Cynthia' then it must also ask the question 'how do I write about myself?', since self and other have been conflated in a poetic world in which Ocean cannot be separated from Cynthia.

Ralegh's answer to this question, I suggest, becomes his most significant critique of Spenser's fictions, and, more specifically, Spenser's fictions of Ralegh. In the 1590 edition of *The Faerie Queene* Spenser represented 'the Right noble, and Valorous, Sir Walter Raleigh knight' as his most prominent patron, the recipient of 'A Letter of the Authors expounding his whole intention in the course of this worke'. Ralegh also appears as a friendly rival poet, the Shepherd of the Ocean, most notably in the Proem to Book III. Here he is the author of 'that sweet verse, with Nectar sprinckeled, that with his melting sweetness ravished', leaving *The Faerie Queene*'s narrator in a 'slomber of delight' (III.Proem.4). Ralegh, the 'delitious poet' (III.Proem.5.1), also receives a Dedicatory Sonnet ('To thee that art the sommers Nightingale') in which Spenser describes his patron's rhymes as 'streames, that like a golden showre / Flow from thy fruitfull head'. There is no question that on one level Spenser acknowledges and celebrates Ralegh's political and literary identities. What is interesting is the ways in which those identities are constructed by Spenser, and, I would argue, sexualized and effeminized by Spenser. Perhaps it is no coincidence that Spenser placed passionate Ralegh on the border between the men and the women in the dedicatory sonnets to *The Faerie Queene*.

It was, however, not just Spenser who expressed awareness of and ambivalence about the conjunction of Ralegh's literary, political and sexual powers, as is evident in the attribution of the poem 'Would I wer chaungde, into that goulden Shower' to Ralegh.[37] Puttenham spoke for

---

37 This chimes with a poem attributed to Ralegh in manuscript, which carries a similar erotic charge. It opens: 'Would I wer chaungde, into that goulden Shower, / That so divinely stremed from the Skyes, / To fall in droppes upon the dainty Flower, / Wher in her bed, she solitary lyes' (ll. 1–4). The poem indulges in a fantasy of erotic immersion, whereby Narcissus falls into the fountain, is drenched, dies, but succeeds in ending his life in that he 'loved best' (ll. 17–18).

his generation when he described Ralegh as 'lofty, insolent, passionate'.[38] The last term can refer both to the poet and to the effect of his poetry. It suggests anger and excess, a person who is easily swayed by emotions, perhaps even effeminate.[39] But it also posits that Ralegh is a passionate poet, that is, his poetry is able to arouse the passions, one of the special duties of the poet. As Katherine Craik has demonstrated, Ralegh's contemporaries understood poetry to work on the body: satires bite and sting, elegies soothe and heal, and tragedies stir up and then purge.[40] For Ralegh to be deemed a 'passionate' poet is therefore to place him at the nexus of two related but antithetical traditions of poetic production, which see creativity and the creation of emotion in the reader as both cathartic and dangerous.

Spenser's view was not unique, therefore, but his fictions of Ralegh have been influential. It is in the figure of Timias that readings of Spenser's understanding of Ralegh's political, literary, and sexual powers converge. This is not to argue for a simple identification of Timias with Ralegh. In Colin Burrow's words, *The Faerie Queene* is a 'bewildering amalgam of topicality and timelessness'.[41] The reader is rarely allowed to settle into a one-dimensional historical allegorical reading, but this has not stopped generations of critics from asserting such readings.[42] The fact that the

38 Puttenham's adjectives can refer both to the man and to the poetry. He is 'lofty' (high, but also haughty, insolent, proud, exalted in rank, directed to high objects) and his poetry is also 'lofty': 'elevated in style or sentiment; sublime, grandiose', and (perhaps relevant to Sir '*Water*' Ralegh's name) it is a term occasionally used of the sea or the wind. The *Oxford English Dictionary* is determined to give another of Puttenham's descriptions of Ralegh, 'insolent', a positive interpretation, whilst acknowledging that the word is invariably pejorative, signifying that the individual is 'proud, disdainful, haughty, arrogant, overbearing; offensively contemptuous of the rights or feelings of others', not to mention 'extravagant, immoderate, going beyond the bounds of propriety', and used about 'the powerful, rich, or successful, their actions'. None of these conventional meanings applies to Ralegh however, the *OED* announces, since Puttenham according to the *OED* meant 'swelling, exulting: in good sense. *Rare*'. The usage is so rare indeed, that it only applies to Puttenham's analysis of Ralegh!
39 See J. Fletcher, *Wit without Money* (London, 1639), II, sig. D2, 'Thou art passionate, hast thou beene brought up with girles'.
40 Antonio Posio wrote in 1562: the 'poet must arouse anger, fear, hope, and the other passions'. See Katharine Craik, *Reading Sensations* (Houndmills: Palgrave, 2007), 1–5 who sets out early-modern understandings of 'passionate cognition' with reference to literature.
41 Colin Burrow, *Epic Romance: Homer to Milton* (Oxford: Clarendon Press, 1993), 100.
42 Many of these readings are based on the continued circulation of inaccurate versions of the events that surrounded the crisis of 1592. Particularly pervasive is the idea that Ralegh eloped with Bess Throckmorton (he did not); that she was one of Elizabeth's Maids (she was a Gentlewoman of the Privy Chamber); that Ralegh called Bess Serena (speculation based on two posthumously circulated poems); and that the Queen was motivated by sexual jealousy (she was far more angry at Ralegh's bare-faced lies).

squire Timias hardly appears in Books I and II of *The Faerie Queene*, and when he does he is defined more by his 'heben launce' rather than any individual qualities, often goes unmentioned. The primary epithet used to describe him in these early books is 'gentle', but he is also 'courageous' in the service of his master, Arthur, and an instrument of grace. Moreover, although the episodes between Belphoebe and Timias have inspired the most critical ink, Spenser actually begins and ends his representation of Timias by focusing on his relationship with Arthur. Each man saves the other at regular intervals (Timias saves Arthur twice in the space of a canto, II.xi) and the final reconciliation of Arthur and his dearly loved squire is one of the most emotionally charged of the work.

Historical allegory is much easier to locate in Book III, and lies at the heart of identifications of Ralegh as Timias, yet even here Spenser's representation of the relationship between Belphoebe and Timias is riven with 'sharp ambivalence'.[43] The bare bones of the narrative are as follows. Unlike the knights Arthur and Guyon, Timias does not pursue Florimell, the 'fairest Dame', but goes after the 'foule foster' who has threatened her. If, as Berger points out, his companions' chivalric motive is not entirely free of sexual desire then Timias is, at this stage of the proceedings at least, detached from the erotic. He is repeatedly called a lovely *boy* (my italics) subservient to his lord Arthur, and his actions fit with his name, which echoes 'honour' in Greek. All is changed after Timias's honourable battle with the three Fosters. Spenser notes that 'They three be dead with shame, the Squire lives with renowne' (III.v.25.9) but the squire has been wounded in the thigh by the Foster who represents lust of the flesh. The injection of lust is thus a violation of Timias's previous nature. What is worse is that the lust is directed towards Belphoebe, the fair virgin committed to 'spotlesse fame of chastity' (III.v.54.1–4). Timias strives to suppress his futile desire: 'Long while he strove in his corageous brest, / With reason dew the passion to subdew' (III.v.44.1–2) but in doing so, 'his hart woxe sore, and health decayd' (III.v.43.2).

Some of the finest criticism in recent years sees the roots of the ambiguities and ambivalence in the representation of Timias and Belphoebe in Spenser's attitude to his literary sources as much as to his human contemporaries. As is well known, the Belphoebe /Timias episode in Book III is borrowed from Ariosto's *Orlando Furioso*, but adapted in significant

---

See for example, M. Lindsay Kaplan, *The Culture of Slander in Early modern England* (Cambridge: Cambridge University Press, 1997), 43, who recycles these narratives in an otherwise exemplary account of early-modern slander and *The Faerie Queene*.
43 Lee Miller, *The Poem's Two Bodies*, 225.

ways. In Ariosto, Angelica pities, rescues, revives, loves and then marries Medoro. In Spenser, Belphoebe pities (briefly), rescues and revives Timias, but it is Timias who then falls in love with Belphoebe, but with no possibility of sex and /or marriage. For Colin Burrow, Spenser's frustrated desire to 'correct' his literary source, *Orlando Furioso*, creates the numerous tensions within the text.[44] In *The Faerie Queene*, the moment in which Belphoebe first sees the wounded Timias 'draws massive erotic dynamism from its original, which Spenser struggles to contain'. Burrow sees the tension in this stanza derived from the displacement of desire onto Timias from Belphoebe, a necessity because of Belphoebe's chastity. This leads to 'great pressure on the syntax of this stanza', which, in turn, leaves the reader in doubt as to whose eyes are melting.[45]

For Burrow, that desire to 'correct' Ariosto is generated by the political conditions of Spenser's own time: 'the pressure of the contemporary once again transfigures Ariosto: courtly devotion to the Queen is used to put a stop to his unstoppable eroticism'.[46] For David Lee Miller, the political conditions, and the ideology of the Queen's two bodies underpinning those conditions, create further serious faultlines in the allegory of Timias and Belphoebe: 'the "masculine" perseity of Elizabeth's *political* body depends on the "feminine" fertility of the natural body in which it breeds, while the virgin self-enclosure of that lesser body in turn calls the reproduction of the body politic into crisis'. The result is Timias's 'anguished experience of his insufficiency (his symbolic castration)'.[47]

Spenser's gendered transpositions from *Orlando Furioso* are another aspect of this process. The transfer of lines which originally referred to Ariosto's Angelica on to Timias serve, not so much to castrate Timias, as to feminise and eroticise him. Timias is 'wasted' by his 'service' to (or the lack of opportunity to service, if one adopts Ariostan ribaldry) Belphoebe. The poor poetry he produces when corrupted by lust is a similar signal of emasculation and impotent desire. The passage in which Timias laments his state in poetry is one of those that seems to encourage a historical allegorical reading, since Timias's poetry is rather like a poor imitation of Ralegh's, but riddled with erotic puns on dying: 'Dye rather, dye, then ever so faire love forsake' (III.v.45.9, then repeated in variant form in 46.9 and 47.9).[48] Overall, Spenser's reworking of this literary sources, allied to

---

44 Burrow, *Epic Romance*, 110.
45 Ibid., 111.
46 Ibid., 113.
47 Lee Miller, *The Poem's Two Bodies*, 234–5
48 As Burrow argues, Timias's monologue on restraint insistently exploits the sexual potential of 'dye' (*Epic Romance*, 113).

his overriding need to portray Belphoebe's power, results in the portrayal of a weakened and emasculated Timias /Ralegh.

By the time Timias returns in Book IV, it is much harder to locate a consistent historical allegory. What remains present, however, is the linking of Timias with lust of the flesh. A grotesque and explicit representation of Lust dominates the canto within which Timias (still 'that lovely boy', IV.vii.23.6) is reintroduced. Timias saves Belphoebe's twin, Amoret, from Lust, but in so doing injures her.

> There she him found by that new lovely mate,
> Who lay the whiles in swoune, full sadly set,
> From her faire eyes wiping the dewy wet,
> Which softly stild, and kissing them atweene,
> And handling soft the hurts, which she did get.
> For of that Carle she sorely bruz'd had beene,
> Als of his owne rash hand one wound was to be seene.
>
> (IV.vii.35)

Spenser use of language here is suggestive rather than explicit, but nevertheless has drawn erotic readings of 'wound'. Certainly, this is Belphoebe's interpretation of the moment. In a superbly terse put down she exclaims 'Is this the faith' and leaves (IV.vii.36.8).

The outcome is that honourable Timias becomes associated with 'fowle dishonour'. This is Belphoebe's assessment, and may well be Spenser's, and Timias' response merely exacerbates the problem. He renounces his warlike weapons, vows never to speak to women, sets himself apart, and spends his time in complaint, striving 'his hard mishap in dolor to deplore' (IV.vii.39). Lust has achieved its victory. Timias lets his hair grow in a sign that he is consumed by desire, similar to the wild and salvage man who violates Amoret (IV.vii.8). The lovely boy, the courageous squire, is erased: mute and dumb, 'out of all mens knowledge he was worne at last' (IV.vii.41.9).

There are two aspects in this representation that are significant to my argument here. The first concerns the stability, or otherwise, of the Timias /Ralegh identification. Julian Lethbridge has demonstrated that the putative historical allegory is not entirely convincing in Book IV. The most pressing problem is Amoret: who is she? But the Timias /Ralegh identification is also tenuous. All that links the two, according to Lethbridge, is the practice of standard melancholia: 'Timias does nothing but mourn; by the time Ralegh was restored to favour, he had explored Guiana, published an account of his journey, mounted an invasion of Cadiz with

Essex, and rebuilt and landscaped Sherborne'.[49] To Lethbridge's list could be added the fact that Ralegh had become the father of a son, Walter, in 1593. Lethbridge's argument is correct but I draw a different conclusion from it. Timias is strikingly *unlike* Ralegh the man of action, naval military leader, explorer, colonizer, fluent propagandist, West Country landowner, parliamentary fixer, and patriarch of the family that is seen in the historical records of the period 1589–95. By the end of Book III, Timias, once a lovely boy, is rather like the abject, self-dramatizing, emasculated courtier Ralegh of the summer of 1592. And so Timias remains for most of the rest of *The Faerie Queene*, unable to free himself entirely from an identity created, in Book III, by the foul foster (lust of the flesh) and then sealed by the encounter with Lust in Book IV.

It is possible to interpret the brief narrative of reconciliation that occurs between Belphoebe and Timias in Book IV as embodying Spenser's hopes for his erstwhile patron.[50] It has already been suggested that to make the historical allegory work, allusions need to be strained to breaking point, but, more importantly, Timias is *not* freed from his subjection to Lust.[51] It is this that makes him unrecognizable, both to Belphoebe and later to Arthur. Belphoebe sees the unhappy boy, singing a lamentable lay, with his 'glib' (a thick mass of matted hair on the forehead and over the eyes), but she knew him not. The best that can be said is that he had 'beene some man of place' before 'misfortune did his hew deface' (IV.viii.14).

49 J. B. Lethbridge, 'Raleigh in Books III and IV of *The Faerie Queene*: The Primacy of Moral Allegory', *Studia Neophilologica* 64 (1992), 57.
50 1 See Bednarz, 'Collaborator as Thief', 65, who argues that the reconciliation places blame on the Queen and absolves Ralegh, and, more recently, Kaplan, who argues that Belphoebe is at fault: 'by misinterpreting love as lust, Belphoebe condemns honourable behaviour as dishonourable, and thus becomes a source and not a silencer of slander' (*Culture of Slander*, 44). Owens, *Enabling Engagements*, 139–40, offers an interesting alternative view of these passages, which allies Arthur with Spenser, rather than his patron. For Owens, Arthur's reading of Timias's inscriptions invites the reader to distinguish between Timias's writing of Belphoebe and Spenser's, and to compare, finally, Ralegh's *Book of the Ocean to Cynthia* and Spenser's *The Faerie Queene*. Thus Arthur remains baffled by Timias's 'BELPHEBE' and Timias's Belphoebe consequently remains inert, unable to exert any explicatory or reformative force. In contrast, Spenser's Belphoebe produces effects on both plot and reader. Owens goes on to argue that the Cynthia holograph records the collapsing of mythology – of intelligible history – into mere flux, and locates this failure in the solipsism of Ralegh's conceit of Elizabeth. Therefore, for Owens, Ralegh's poetry is an auto-critique, rather than a critique of Spenser.
51 The cooing of the dove could apparently sound like 'water': 'that name pronounced with a burr may sound to a demented mind like a dove's cooing' (*Faerie Queene*, ed. Hamilton, 466). For an attempt to fix the historical allegory of this moment, see J. R. Brink, 'The Masque of the Nine Muses: Sir John Davies in The Faerie Queene', *The Review of English Studies* 92 (1972), 445–7.

A somewhat intemperate gloss on the reconciliation in the Longman Spenser is revealing here. Timias, in refusing to acknowledge his errors, is behaving in a 'typically male fashion' (*sic*), blaming God and Belphoebe, but never himself.[52] The Longman editors are being led by Spenser here, in that the reader is seeing Timias through Belphoebe's critical eyes by this stage of the narrative, and Timias is dumb, in both senses of the word. Timias may suggest that Belphoebe should 'deeme aright' (IV.viii.17.4), but there is no indication that she does change her mind about her erstwhile lover. Her 'inburning wrath' begins to abate, and Timias is allowed a 'happie life with grace and good accord' (IV.viii,.18.2). In the service of Belphoebe, he never recovers his previous identity, that of the lovely, courageous, honourable boy squire to Arthur.

By the time Timias reappears in Book VI, he is a weakened figure. He is able to withstand Despetto, Decetto, and Defetto, but becomes one of the many victims of the Blatant Beast, saved only by the intervention of Arthur. Left by Arthur, Timias remains with Serena to recover: 'Their hearts were sicke, their sides were sore, their feet were lame' (VI.v.40.9).[53] Crucially, Timias's wounds are 'corrupt and cureless', and 'festered privily' (VI.vi.2.5 and 5.2). This is not a reformed figure, but a man who still needs to be kept away from the snares of lust, as the Hermit explains. He must learn the 'outward sences to refraine / From things that stirre up fraile affection' (VI.vi.7.6–7), and 'Abstain from pleasure, and restraine your will / Subdue desire, and bridle loose delight' (VI.vi.14.5–6).

Therefore, once reconciled to Belphoebe, Timias becomes even more insignificant to the narrative even though 'he himself so well and wisely bore' (VI.v.12.8). He is brought back into Book VI to enact, again, a pattern of (unlucky) victimhood, and salvation at the hands of one stronger than him, Arthur, not once but twice. The moral allegory is hammered home as Timias is lectured about 'outward sences' and 'will, desire and loose delight'. He is allowed a final reconciliation not with Belphoebe but with Arthur. The homosocial, if not the homoerotic, once again proves to be Spenser's sign of closure.

If there is a historical allegory at work, it only works consistently in Book III of *The Faerie Queene*, when a minor character, Timias, is given

---

52 *Faerie Queene*, ed. Hamilton, 468.
53 It is unlikely that this passage refers to Ralegh's secret marriage to Elizabeth Throckmorton. It relies on an identification of Serena as Throckmorton, on the basis that Ralegh may have written two poems to Serena. It is unfortunate for this argument that these two delightful poems ('Nature that washt her hands in milke' and 'now Serena, bee not coy') were attributed to Ralegh posthumously, and that the former does not mention Serena in the body of the poem.

a particular allegorical burden. This allegorical burden could not have been inspired by the events of 1592, since it predates them, but it did create a figure that then could carry the weight of subsequent events. Even though the text itself makes any historical allegory at best elusive, at worst illogical, it is all too tempting to try to map, in general terms, the figure of melancholic Timias, injured and contaminated by lust, on to the fallen Sir Walter Ralegh. Even if it is accepted that the historical allegory is sustained throughout, then the message for Ralegh is not a hopeful one. Elizabeth /Belphoebe has spurned him, and Ralegh /Timias is gone from men's knowledge. Irredeemably infected by lust, he remains corrupt and cureless. Quite where, to quote Lethbridge, 'historical allegory gives way to moral allegory' (p. 55) will be determined by individual readers, but what is certain is that Spenser's *moral* allegory is sustained, and explores a character injured by, and then subsumed by Lust.

The legacy of Spenser's representation of Ralegh, whether as delicious, ravishing poet or as Timias through the palimpsest of allegory, is that even now we understand him through Spenser's lens. Bednarz writes for example, of Ralegh's relationship with Queen Elizabeth, that 'he alone dared to proclaim a specifically sexual attraction, based on compelling physical desire' whilst Philippa Berry argues that Ralegh wrote poetry to 'affirm his own fantasised self-image as an explorer and charter of hitherto unknown territories' and that his capacity to control the Queen had depended on 'his erotic appeal to her as a woman, through the constantly deferred promise of sexual gratification'.[54] In a less direct way, this assumption permeates otherwise insightful analyses, such as that of Judith Owens. She argues that Spenser's description of Timias derives from Ralegh's own poem 'Like to a Hermit Poore', which she asserts was written in response to his 1592 fall from favour, and was then published in *The Phoenix Nest*, in 1593. *The Faerie Queene*, according to Owens, thus draws on Ralegh's self-representation: 'Timias is transformed, that is, into an image previously fashioned by Ralegh'.[55] Michael Rudick's edition, however, shows that 'Like to a Hermit Poore' was attributed posthumously to Ralegh, and was, in its transmission history, as much connected with his execution in 1618 as with his fall from power in 1592.[56] Then and now, therefore, Ralegh is being understood through the lens of Spenser's

---

54 Bednarz, 'The Collaborator as Thief', 287, and Philippa Berry, *Of Chastity and Power: Elizabethan Literature and the Unmarried Queen* (London: Routledge, 1989), 148 and 151.
55 Judith Owens, *Enabling Engagements: Edmund Spenser and the Poetics of Patronage* (Montreal and Kingston: McGill-Queen's University Press, 2002), 139.
56 Rudick, *The Poems*, 135–6.

representation. The Cynthia holograph can be read as an attempt on the part of Ralegh to free himself from Spenser.

It was not easy to do. Spenser echoes through the Cynthia holograph, evident in, for example, Ralegh's occasional moves into the georgic mode, complete with Spenserian alliteration: a ploughman tears up the stubble in his field, 'and throwes to fire as foylde and frutles ends / and takes delight another seed to sow' (ll. 278–9). Ralegh continues: 'So douth the minde root up all wounted thought / and scornes the care of our remayninge woes' (ll. 280–1). These nods towards the English vernacular tradition, in which the shepherd had become a ploughman, echo the 1590 ending of *The Faerie Queene* which uses the georgic conceit of the poet-ploughman at rest, and either presage or honour the fascination with home in *Colin Clout*.[57]

Despite, or because, of these elements, I would argue that after years of collusion and symbiosis, years of metaphorically sharing a pipe, the Cynthia holograph suggests that Ralegh had at last recognized that Spenser had been more critical than he had hitherto realized. The date of composition of *Colin Clout* may be relevant here. Although it is impossible to be certain, it is likely that the Cynthia holograph was written in the summer of 1592, whilst *Colin Clout* is ostensibly dated (on its print publication in 1595) to winter 1591. If that is not a disingenuous dating, it is probable that Ralegh would have seen Spenser's work in manuscript. Whether he did see *Colin Clout* or not (and it would have lacked the Bregog episode, presumably), is, in fact, unimportant: there was enough Spenser material available for Ralegh to gain a clear sense of his erstwhile protégé's writing of his patron. Nevertheless, *Colin Clout's Come Home Again* continues the process of sexualization that I would argue Ralegh is trying to counter. Ralegh as Shepherd of the Ocean is said to 'empierce a Princes mightie heart' (l. 431), whilst Ralegh as courtier 'secretly did his love enjoy'(l. 145).[58] It is possible to go further. One answer to Patrick Cheney's bemused question with regard to *Colin Clout* (why would Spenser return to pastoral since it is the form from which he

---

57 I am grateful to Andrew Hadfield for discussion of this point.
58 There is debate about the allegorical significance of the Bregog episode, in which the 'wanton' River Bregog, deceives his love's father, is discovered, and 'did lose his name: so deare his love he bought' (l. 155). Kelsey reads the episode as referring allegorically to Spenser/Colin (Bregog is Colin's river), in 'Spenser, Ralegh', 185–7. The majority of other critics who choose to read the episode allegorically see a narrative of Ralegh's fall from political favour through his secret marriage to Bess Throckmorton. Patrick Cheney summarizes the possible interpretations: 'Spenser's Pastorals: *The Shepheardes Calender* and *Colin Clouts Come Home Againe*', in *The Cambridge Companion to Spenser*, ed. Andrew Hadfield (Cambridge: Cambridge University Press, 2001), 99.

longs to escape?) is that pastoral offered a literary space in which Spenser could continue to place Ralegh within a myth of dependency, as both poet and courtier.[59] In *Colin Clout*, the deceitful, wily, 'wanton Bregog' may enjoy his love, but ultimately exposed, and 'scattred all to nought'. By implication Ralegh too is reduced to nothing, and for the familiar reason of his sexual indiscipline. The somewhat edgy dedication of *Colin Clout* to Ralegh in 1595, described by Andrew Zurcher as remarkably terse, even backhanded, coupled with the newly minted Bregog passage and neoplatonic philosophy, suggests that the post-1592 reality was that Spenser and Ralegh were no longer sharing a pipe.[60] It is perhaps suggestive that David Lee Miller's analysis of one of the apparently laudatory passages in the 1590 *Faerie Queene* prefigures this process. He offers a close reading of the stanza 'let that same delitious Poet lend ...' (III. Proem.5) pointing to the two 'let' clauses: let the poet of melting sweetness lend a little leave to Spenser's rustic muse, and let Elizabeth be content to see herself in mirrors more than one. He goes on to argue that 'if the parallelism were sustained, the two mirrors would turn out to be Ralegh's verse and Spenser's, but as the stanza moves to its close Ralegh drops out of the picture'. In this apparently casual transition, Ralegh, the poetry of melting sweetness and the royal body natural have all disappeared together 'to be replaced by focus on Elizabeth's private virtue'.[61] When the expanded edition of *The Faerie Queene* appeared soon after *Colin Clout*, Ralegh had been more explicitly erased with the removal of the Raleghan back matter. Ralegh, as poet, patron and courtier, has been defaced, but Spenser's previous representation of him endured.

The Cynthia holograph marks the end, I would argue, of sympathetic collusion between Spenser and Ralegh, at least on Ralegh's side. The competing definitions of fancy, with Spenserian desirous imaginings displaced by true cognitive understanding, are one aspect of Ralegh's critique. Most importantly, however, when Ralegh writes that Queen Elizabeth is no longer Belphoebe he is invoking not *his* myth but that of Spenser. If pastoral elegy is understood as a genre in which the loved one is killed by the author, but the death yields the consolation of a new genre, then it is possible to see that, within the literary world of the Cynthia

---

59 Cheney, 'Spenser's Pastorals', 82–3.
60 See Andrew Zurcher, 'Getting It Back to Front in 1590: Spenser's Dedications, Nashe's Insinuations, and Ralegh's Equivocations', *Studies in the Literary Imagination* 38.2 (2005), 173–99, which offers support for my argument. Zurcher is right to be intrigued by the dating of 27 December 1591, and its potential link to the Throckmorton affair. See Beer, *Bess*, for a narrative of this period, although more work remains to be done.
61 Lee Miller, *The Poem's Two Bodies*, 153

holograph, Walter Ralegh kills both Belphoebe/Cynthia and himself as Shepherd and Ocean. In so doing, he gets close to creating a radical new genre: the Cynthia holograph contains one of the most exciting poems of the 1590s. The social and political crisis that precipitated the Cynthia holograph in the first place would ensure that Ralegh's journey to the dark side of pastoral, not to mention his challenge to Spenser, would remain hidden from the vast majority of his contemporaries. It also signalled the end, with a few notable exceptions, of Ralegh's career as a poet.[62] As so often with Sir Walter Ralegh, one is left wondering what would have emerged if he had had the opportunity or inclination to complete what he had begun.[63]

---

62 There is much debate about the dating of Ralegh's poetry, and it is possible that some of Ralegh's shorter poems were written in the later 1590s, most notably 'The Lie'. But Michael Rudick has demonstrated that only a handful of poems were *attributed* to Ralegh in the period 1603–18: see *Poems*, 67–80. One was in print, a dedicatory sonnet to Arthur Gorges's translation of Lucan's *Pharsalia*. Two which circulated in manuscript were reworkings of earlier poems, including the final poem in the Cynthia holograph which was extended for a new audience, Queen Anne of Denmark. Ralegh's most famous poem was a revision of the last stanza of 'Nature that washt her hands'. Beginning 'Even such is time which takes in trust', this was the poem that Ralegh wrote into the flyleaf of his Bible the night before he was executed.
63 My closing comment reflects an aspect of Ralegh studies over the past three centuries. Michael Rudick (*Poems*, xvi and xvii) describes it as a 'reckoning with loss that still obligates, and sometimes motivates, scholars when they deal with the Ralegh canon'. This sense of loss originates, Rudick speculates, in a 'desire to narrow the distance between Ralegh's ostensibly meagre poetic canon and his major distinction as a national hero'.

5

Replying to Raleigh's 'The Nymph's Reply':
Allusion, anti-pastoral, and four centuries of pastoral invitations

Hannibal Hamlin

In 1653 Christopher Marlowe's 'Passionate Shepherd to his Love' and Sir Walter Raleigh's 'Nymph's Reply to the Shepherd' were printed, certainly not for the first time, but in what have become their standard versions – six stanzas of four lines in iambic tetrametre couplets – in Izaak Walton's *The Compleat Angler*.[1] This was the first time 'The Nymph's Reply' was attributed to Raleigh, an attribution which has been generally accepted ever since.[2] Although the poems had been paired together since at least 1599, Walton's pastoral scene incorporating the two poems (or 'songs') is important because it helps demonstrate why Raleigh's poem, more than Marlowe's, was responsible for the long tradition of imitative, adaptive,

---

1 In Walton's 1655 edition, he added a stanza to each of the poems; his source for these is unknown. Nevertheless, it is the six-stanza versions that have become standard, as in Christopher Marlowe, *The Complete Poems and Translations*, ed. Stephen Orgel (Harmondsworth: Penguin Books, 1971), 211–12. Citations from these poems will be from this edition. For some alternative versions, see Samuel A. Tannenbaum, 'Unfamiliar Versions of Some Elizabethan Poems', *PMLA* 45.3 (1930), 809–21.

2 Michael Rudick, in *The Poems of Sir Walter Raleigh: A Historical Edition* (Tempe, AZ: Arizona Centre for Medieval and Renaissance Studies, 1999), cites and agrees with the conclusion of John Hannah (*Poems by Sir Henry Wotton, Sir Walter Raleigh, and Others*, 1845), 'I should be sorry to believe that Walton was mistaken' (lxv). But Walton still remains the principal authority for this attribution, even though there is a copy of *England's Helicon* in the John Rylands University Library of Manchester with 'alias Sr Walt Ralegh' penned in a contemporary hand at 'The Nimphs Reply'. See Bevan's commentary in Izaak Walton, *The Compleat Angler 1653–1676*, ed. Jonquil Bevan (Oxford: Clarendon Press, 1983), 390–1. For further details about the transmission of the poems in manuscript, and about matters of attribution, see Rudick, lxv; Hyder Rollins, ed., *England's Helicon*, 2:186–90; Suzanne Woods, '"The Passionate Shepherd" and "The Nimphs Reply": A Study of Transmission', *The Huntington Library Quarterly* 34.1 (1970), 25–33. Woods is certainly right that since the Marlowe-Raleigh poems were songs, they were partly transmitted orally, but that this was the primary means of transmission is surely an overstatement, since they were also continuously and easily available in print (see below).

and parodic pastoral poems of invitation and reply that has persisted for over four hundred years.

On the third day of Walton's piscatorial adventure, the experienced angler Piscator is instructing the ignorant Viator on the fine techniques of angling. Piscator first catches a 'gallant *Trout*', but then, disappointingly, only a 'great loggerheaded *Chub*'. At this point, as they turn back to their inn, Piscator remembers that he has come this way before. He tells his companion that 'under that broad *Beech tree* I sate down when I was last this way a fishing'.[3]

This phrase signals the beginning of a formal pastoral episode, since Walton self-consciously alludes to the famous, seminal opening of Virgil's first eclogue:

> Thou Tytire lying at thine ease, under the broade beeche shade,
> A countrey song dost tune right wel, in pipe of oate straw made,
> Our countrey borders we doo leave, and Medowes sweete forsake,
> Our countrey soyle we shunne, but thou in shade thine ease dost take,
> Teaching the woodes of Amaryll most fayre, a sound to make.[4]

With this intertextual relationship in mind, it comes as no surprise that when Piscator was formerly sitting under this beech tree, 'the birds in the adjoining Grove seemed to have a friendly contention with an Echo, whose dead voice seemed to live in a hollow cave, near to the brow of that Primrose hill'.[5] Echoing song is a convention of Virgilian pastoral in two senses: Tityrus teaches the woods to echo his lover's name, Amaryllis, but pastoral poetry has also been conventionally echoic, or allusive, at least since Virgil's *Eclogues* echoed Theocritus's *Idylls*. But here Walton also evokes the Ovidian myth of Echo, the nymph whose fruitless love for Narcissus causes her to wither away into a mere voice that haunts woods and caves. It also comes as no surprise that Piscator's memory includes pastoral song, and an exchange of song at that, since another convention of classical pastoral is the singing contest. In Piscator's memory the song 'contest' was between a milkmaid and her mother:

> As I left this place, and entered into the next field, a second pleasure entertained me; 'twas a handsome Milk-maid, that had cast away all care, and sung like a *Nightingale*; her voice was good, and the Ditty fitted for it; 'twas that smooth song which was made by *Kit Marlow*, now at least fifty years

---

[3] Walton, *Compleat Angler*, 88.
[4] Virgil, *Eclogues* I, lines 1–5, in *The Bucolics of Publius Virgilius Maro*, tr. Abraham Fleming (1575), sig. C.i.
[5] Walton, *Compleat Angler*, 88.

ago; and the Milkmaids mother sung an answer to it, which was made by Sir *Walter Raleigh* in his yonger dayes.[6]

As if to prove that time does not pass in the pastoral world, Piscator and Viator then come upon exactly the same milkmaid and her mother, in exactly the same place, and they ask them, in exchange for the chub, to sing the same songs by Marlowe and Raleigh, which they happily do.[7] Marlowe's 'Passionate Shepherd' poem is a pastoral lyric, but only when Raleigh's 'Nymph's Reply' is added to it does the pair provide the model for Walton's fully developed scene; Raleigh converts a lyric into a dialogue, a single song into a pastoral singing contest.

If the form of Raleigh's reply, or rather the joint-form it created in combination with Marlowe's invitation, was critical to subsequent literature, the nature of Raleigh's response, his sceptical critique of pastoral idealism, proved equally influential. That many of Raleigh's poems express a similar scepticism, emphasizing mutability, decay, and the passage of time, seems also to support Walton's attribution to Raleigh of 'The Nymph's Reply'. This attitude is evident, for instance, in 'Nature that washt her hands in milke', in which Raleigh describes the corrosive effects of time on nature and humanity:

> But time (that nature doth despise,
>   and rudelie gives her lawes the lie)
> makes mirth a foole and sorrowe wise,
>   his hands doe neither washe or drie
> But being made of steele and rust,
>   Turnes snowe, and silke, and milke to dust.[8]

A similar emphasis on the inability of humanity or nature to resist time appears in a verse of 'The Lie', one of the most popular poems generally attributed to Raleigh:

> Tell age it dayly wastethe
> tell honour how it alters

---

6 Walton, *Compleat Angler*, 89.
7 The *otium* of Theocritus is, as Thomas G. Rosenmeyer puts it, 'the vital experience of a moment which it's known will be brief, but which is so fully entertained that the future and the past are largely shut out' (*The Green Cabinet: Theocritus and the European Pastoral Lyric* (Berkeley and Los Angeles: University of California Press, 1969), 86). The stasis in which Piscator's milkmaid and her mother seem suspended is a delightful, gentle parody of Theocritean *otium*, which has a particular poignancy, given that Walton is writing, as Virgil was, in the aftermath of civil war. Tityrus and Piscator may be able to recline under a shady tree, but many of their contemporaries were homeless or dead.
8 *Poems of Sir Walter Raleigh*, 112. Except for 'The Nymph's Reply', subsequent quotations from Raleigh poems will be from this edition.

> tell bewtye that she boastethe
> tell favour that she flatter
> and if they shall replye
> gyve every one the lye.
>
> (31-2)

Finally, the opening of Raleigh's longest poem, 'The 21th and last booke of the Ocean to Scinthia', not only resembles the 'Nymph's' worldview but also uses similar language to her 'Reply'. The Ocean laments 'the blossumes fallen, the sapp gon from the tree', just as the nymph sings, 'The flowers do fade, and wanton fields / To wayward winter reckoning yields'. The Ocean's 'high flowinge streames' filled with 'mudd' and 'brinish sand' correspond to the nymph's observation that 'The rivers rage and rocks grow cold'. Even similar birds and animals appear in the longer poem:

> all in the shade yeven in the faire soon dayes
> under thos healthless trees I sytt a lone
> wher joyfull byrdds singe neather lovely layes
> noe phillomen recounts her direfull mone,
> No feedinge flockes, no shepherds companye
> that might renew my dollorus consayte.
>
> (48-9)

(While the singing birds, Philomel, the shepherds and their flocks mentioned in 'The 'Nymph's Reply' are pointedly not present in 'The Ocean to Scinthia', the description of their absence has the ironic effect of making them seem present in the poem.) The source of Raleigh's anti-pastoral worldview is impossible to determine. However, it is interesting to note that Raleigh's experience of the real world may have been conducive to a rather less idealized view of the pastoral world than Marlowe's. Marlowe was always a city dweller, but Raleigh was born in Devon, a long way from London, and, by the time the Shepherd-Nymph poems were written, likely in the late 1580s, he had also spent time in the wilds of Ireland (wild for the English, at any rate) where daily life involved few pastoral idylls, but rather a great deal of suffering, labouring, fighting, and dying.

Of course, Marlowe was capable of plenty of scepticism himself. This may have been one reason he and Raleigh were drawn to each other's work. (Their actual connection remains murky. The claims of M. C. Bradbrook and others for Marlowe's and Raleigh's membership in a like-minded 'School of Night' have been largely rejected. There remain some tantalizing contemporary comments, however, linking the two men as sceptics and free-thinkers.)⁹ Marlowe's scepticism is more cynical, though, and his poem, unlike some of its imitators or antecedents, is not really a naive rustic love poem but a self-consciously artificial seduction poem. Marlowe's shepherd is no real shepherd, after all, since he is able to provide not just flowers but fine embroidered clothing, slippers with 'buckles of the purest gold', and a belt that, though it is 'of straw and ivy-buds', has also 'coral clasps and amber studs'. By contrast, Raleigh's worldly-wise nymph not only recognizes the shepherd's sexual motive but challenges the very pastoral principles on which his argument is based. Time is the key. Marlowe's poem describes delights that seem outside of time and reality, envisioning a sort of country-life theme-park or a pastoral playground like the one constructed at Versailles for Marie Antoinette. His narrator, playing at 'Passionate Shepherd', invites his love to observe real shepherds, but not to do any practical shepherding. And he promises his love that the shepherds will 'dance and sing / For thy delight each May morning'; whether the shepherds themselves may have had more pressing tasks than performing for the lovers seems not in consideration. On the other hand, Raleigh's nymph presents the pastoral world as if in time-lapse photography, where all nature withers, dies, and grows cold:

> If all the world and love were young,
> And truth in every shepherd's tongue,
> These pretty pleasures might me move
> To live with thee and be thy love.
>
> But Time drives flocks from field to fold,
> When rivers rage and rocks grow cold,
> And Philomel becometh dumb;
> The rest complains of cares to come.[10]

Raleigh's harshest comment on idealized love is also evident in this passage, in his specific identification of the unnamed birds that in Marlowe's poem chirp madrigals. 'Philomel becometh dumb' not only because birds don't sing all the time in the real world, nor because the nocturnal nightingale ceases with the dawn, but because, in Ovid, Philomel is raped by her brother-in-law, has her tongue cut out, and is transformed into a nightingale. In Ovid, there is a fine line between seduction and rape, and Raleigh's

---

9 See 'Sir Walter Raleigh', by Mark Nicholls and Penry Williams, *Oxford Dictionary of National Biography*; Edward Thompson, *Sir Walter Raleigh: Last of the Elizabethans* (London: Macmillan and Co., 1935); David Riggs, *The World of Christopher Marlowe* (London: Faber & Faber, 2004); M. C. Bradbrook, *The School of Night: A Study in the Relationships of Sir Walter Raleigh* (Cambridge: Cambridge University Press, 1936).
10 In Orgel, ed., Marlowe, *Complete Poems*, 212.

nymph seems well aware that what philosophers of the *carpe diem* school generally have in mind for their pupils may not always be in those pupils' best interests.[11] Walton was aware of Raleigh's manipulation of Ovidian myth, since his milkmaid sings 'like a Nightingale'. (In Walton's gentler vision, Philomel is not dumb but sings, and such music does not come at the price of rape, mutilation, and animal metamorphosis.)

Raleigh's reply poem creates what Paul Alpers, borrowing a concept from Kenneth Burke, calls a 'representative anecdote'. As Alpers explains this, such an 'anecdote is representative in that (1) it is a typical instance of an aspect of reality and (2) by being typical, it serves to generate specific depictions, or representations, of that reality'.[12] Essentially, the anecdote generates a genre by establishing a conventional setting, character(s), and basic plot. For Alpers, the general representative anecdote of pastoral is herdsmen and their lives, but there are more specific anecdotes that have generated their own imitative traditions within the broad genre of pastoral. Marlowe's 'The Passionate Shepherd to his Love', for instance, is a *pastoral invitation* based on roughly similar invitations in Theocritus, Virgil, and Ovid. The representative anecdote of this subgenre is thus the shepherd inviting his beloved to live with him. Tellingly, however, these classical invitations all remain unanswered. In Theocritus, the Cyclops Polyphemus offers a range of rustic delights, but only notionally, since he is speaking to himself, and Galatea never hears his invitation:

> And pleasant milke I drinke, which from the strouting bags is pressed.
> Nor want I cheese in summer, nor in Autumne of the best,
> Nor yet in winter time, my cheese-rackes ever laden are,
> And better can I pipe, than anie Cyclops maie compare.
> O Apple sweet, of thee, and of my selfe, I use to sing,
> And that at midnight oft, for thee, aleavne fawnes up I bring,
> All great with young, and foure beares whelps, I nourish up for thee.[13]

But Polyphemus knows that Galatea is repelled by his 'one onlie brow, with bristles strong / From one eare to the other eare', his 'one eie' and his

---

11 Patrick Cheney also sees the insertion of Philomel as Raleigh's 'self-reflexively identifying Spenser's influence upon himself', since in the November eclogue of *The Shepheardes Calender* Spenser identified Colin Clout, his poet-persona, as 'The Nightingale ... sovereigne of song' ('Career Rivalry and the Writing of Counter-Nationhood: Ovid, Spenser, and Philomela in Marlowe's "The Passionate Shepherd to His Love"', *ELH* 65.3 (1998), 523–55.
12 Paul Alpers, *What Is Pastoral?* (Chicago and London: University of Chicago Press, 1996), 13–14.
13 *Sixe Idillia, that is, Six Small, or Petty Poems, or Æglogues, chosen out of the right famous Sicilian Poet Theocritus* (Oxford, 1588), sig. A4.

'hugie nose'. He fantasizes about Galatea accepting his invitation, but he knows it is fantasy:

> O Cyclops, Cyclops, whither is thy wit and reason flowne?
> If thou wouldst baskets make, and cut downe browsing from the tree,
> And bring it to thy Lambes, a great deale wiser thou shouldst be?[14]

In Ovid's version, unlike Theocritus's, Galatea does overhear Polyphemus, while lying on the lap of her lover Acis, though the Cyclops doesn't know it. Ovid's Polyphemus has a better self-image than Theocritus's, taking pride in his bigness, his shagginess, and his single eye, which he likens to the sun: 'Why, / Views not the sun all things from heaven? Yet but only one eye / Hath he'.[15] Nevertheless, though the Cyclops can't fathom why Galatea loves 'dwarf Acis' instead of him, he recognizes that she does; thus his passion turns from love to vengeance, marking a generic shift from comedy to tragedy in Ovid's retelling of the myth. In Virgil's second eclogue, the shepherd Corydon – a less monstrous version of the pastoral lover than the Cyclops – pines for the fair boy Alexis. (The gender shift may have interested Marlowe; according to the *OED*, Marlowe's 'kirtle' was primarily a man's garment, and it's worth noting that in Walton the poem is sung by a girl – presumably as if to a male lover – without changing a word. As David Riggs puts it, Marlowe's 'poem does not ask and does not tell' whether his lover is male or female.)[16] Corydon's invitation, like the Cyclops's, is a soliloquy, and he similarly closes by calling himself a rustic fool. By writing a reply to Marlowe's shepherd, Raleigh turned the shepherd's unanswered plea into a dialogue, transforming the representative anecdote and creating a new pastoral subgenre.[17] It is the exchange or contest of Marlowe's shepherd and Raleigh's nymph that seems to have fascinated poets ever since.

Even before the first printed version of Raleigh's reply in 1599, Marlowe's poem had had an immediate influence, and must have circulated quickly

---

14 *Idillia*, sigs. A4–A4v. On the reception of Theocritus's Idyll, see H. M. Richmond, 'Polyphemus in England: A Study in Comparative Literature', *Comparative Literature* 12.3 (1960), 229–42. Richmond's discussion of 'conventional situations' anticipates in some ways Alpers's use of the 'representative anecdote'.
15 *Ovid's Metamorphoses, Translated by Arthur Golding* [1567], ed. Madeleine Forey (Harmondsworth: Penguin, 2002), Book 13, lines 1001–3.
16 Riggs, *The World*, 108.
17 No genre is ever truly new, of course, and the pastoral invitation and response genre initiated by Marlowe–Raleigh is a variation on the ancient pastoral singing contests in Theocritus and Virgil. That Marlowe's and Raleigh's lyrics are regularly referred to as songs is a sign of this.

in manuscript.[18] Marlowe himself seems to have been fixated on it, since he alludes to it in most of his own plays. For example, Tamburlaine (who starts life as a shepherd) says in Part 1, 'Disdains Zenocrate to live with me?' (I.ii.82).[19] Later, speaking not of Zenocrate but the general Theridamas, whom he has invited to join him, Tamburlaine concludes, paraphrasing Marlowe's Shepherd,

> If thou wilt stay with me, renowned man, ...
> Then shalt thou be competitor with me,
> And sit with Tamburlaine in all his majesty.
>
> (I.ii.188, 208–9)

In *The Jew of Malta*, Ithimore begs the courtesan Bellamira to come with him to Greece:

> Thou in those Groves, by Dis, above,
> Shalt live with me and be my love.
>
> (IV.ii.115–16)

In *Edward II*, Gaveston poses himself the question,

> What greater blisse can hap to Gaveston,
> Then live and be the favourit of a king?
>
> (I.i..104–5)

Finally, in *Dido, Queen of Carthage*, Ganymede asks Jupiter for presents, to which the god responds, 'And shall have Ganimed, if thou wilt be my love' (I.i.49). These key lines from 'The Passionate Shepherd' seem to have become for Marlowe almost a signature.

Allusions to Marlowe's lyric by other writers occur as early as 1590, in Thomas Lodge's *Scillaes Metamorphosis*, and in Shakespeare's *Merry Wives of Windsor*, which dates from perhaps 1597. Lodge's poem is, ironically,

---

18 The earliest extant MS of both (Marlowe's) 'Come live with me' and (Raleigh's) 'If all the world' is the Lilliat miscellany in the Bodleian (Rawlinson Poetry 148), dating from the 1590s. Neither poem is attributed. Like anyone writing on the reception of the Marlowe–Raleigh dialogue poems, I am indebted to R. S. Forsythe's 'The Passionate Shepherd; And English Poetry', *PMLA* 40.3 (1925), 692–742. Forsythe's survey is relatively unsophisticated in distinguishing echoes, allusions, imitations, and accidental resemblances, and some of the works he sees under the influence of Marlowe–Raleigh are not convincingly so. There are also many more poems that respond to Marlowe–Raleigh than he lists. But the breadth of his study seems all the more impressive for having been done without the aid of the computer. From Forsythe on, scholars and editors have added to the list of works in the Marlowe–Raleigh tradition. I am indebted to many of these, but to cite for each work the first critic to note its allusions or indebtedness would make my notes cumbersome and provide information of little use.
19 All citations of Marlowe's plays taken from Christopher Marlowe, *The Complete Plays*, ed. J. B. Steane (Harmondsworth: Penguin Books, 1969).

in praise of solitary life – his speaker possibly making a virtue of necessity in a way Polyphemus and Corydon could not – and it is not his lover but his Muse whom he asks to 'dwell with me' in a landscape that he imagines peopled by nymphs, 'Washing their ivorie in those murmuring springs, / At whose kinde fall the birds with pleasure sings'.[20] Lodge's inclusion of a cave in his pastoral landscape, 'By Natures hand enforst in marble vaines', evokes the figure of Echo, who, since Ovid's account, inhabits such caves ('Her bones, they say, were turned to stones'),[21] and who represents both lovelorn solitude and, as John Hollander points out, poetic allusion itself.[22] In Shakespeare's play, Marlowe's poem is quoted directly, or rather sung from memory, by Parson Evans. This suggests that, as in Walton's *Compleat Angler*, the poem was actually known by some as a song. At least one possible melody for it has been discovered in William Corkine's *The Second Booke of Ayres* (1612).[23]

It was likely due to the inclusion of these lines in *Merry Wives* that the first appearance of the poem 'Come live with me and be my love' in print was under the name of William Shakespeare in the pirated 1599 anthology, *The Passionate Pilgrim*. (In this instance the first line actually reads just 'Live with me.') It was also in this little volume that the poem was first paired with 'The Nymph's Reply'. (It was here entitled 'Love's answere', and only the first stanza was printed.) Like the poem it answers, it too was attributed to Shakespeare. The next year, in 1600, both poems were included in a much more important anthology, *England's Helicon*. For the first time, the invitation poem was attributed to Marlowe and given its now-familiar title, 'The passionate shepherd to his love'. It was expanded to six stanzas, from the four in *The Passionate Pilgrim*. The response was now entitled 'The Nimphs reply to the Sheepheard', also expanded to six stanzas, and ascribed to 'Ignoto' ('unknown'). Following the reply appeared another poem by 'Ignoto', given the perfunctory title, 'Another of the same nature, made since'. The poem is actually another invitation, not another reply, and it adds little of substance to Marlowe's original, simply adding more tempting pastoral delights, including

---

20 Thomas Lodge, 'In commendation of a solitarie life', *Scillaes Metamorphosis* (London, 1590), sigs E–E2.
21 *Metamorphoses*, line 497. This is one of Golding's better lines, capturing the nature of Echo in the echoing rhyme and the open, hollow vowels of 'bones' and 'stones'.
22 John Hollander, *The Figure of Echo: A Mode of Allusion in Milton and After* (Berkeley, Los Angeles, and London: University of California Press, 1981).
23 Frederick W. Sternfeld and Mary Joiner Chan, 'Come Live with Me and be My Love', *Comparative Literature* 22.2 (1970), 173–87; Woods, '"The Passionate Shepherd"'. Since Raleigh's poem is formally identical to Marlowe's, it could have been sung to the same tune, as indeed could most of the other tetrametre imitations.

'nimble Fairies' dancing and singing 'melodious sounds' and no fewer than 'Ten thousand Glow-wormes':

> If these may serve for to entice,
> Your presence to Loves Paradice,
> Then come with me, and be my Deare:
> And we will straite begin the yeare.
>
> (41-4)[24]

If the Nymph was sceptical even about Marlowe's invitation, she could probably have resisted this anonymous one too. 'Another of the same' is not really an adaptation, let alone an example of sophisticated allusion, but an imitation of the most basic kind.[25]

From *England's Helicon* to the present, Marlowe's and Raleigh's poems have been paired as standard inclusions in anthologies. They appeared together in Thomas Percy's *Reliques of Ancient English Poetry* (1765), Thomas Young Crowell's *Red-letter Poems by English Men and Women* (1885), Arthur Quiller-Couch's *Oxford Anthology of English Poetry* (1900), John Matthews Manly's *English Poetry 1170–1892* (1907), and Ephraim Chambers' *Cyclopaedia of English Literature* (1920), to name only a few of the best-known earlier anthologies.[26] Because they were printed in the spuriously Shakespearean *Passionate Pilgrim*, the poems were also included in many editions of Shakespeare. Readers would have found the lyrics in John Benson's edition of Shakespeare's *Poems* (1640), and the complete works edited by Nicholas Rowe (1709–10), Alexander Pope (1723–25), Pope and William Warburton (1747), Samuel Johnson (1765), John Bell (1774), Johnson and George Steevens (1778), among others. Since they were also included in the nearly four hundred editions

---

24 In Marlowe, *Complete Poems*, 213–14.
25 On Renaissance imitation, see Thomas M. Greene, *The Light in Troy: Imitation and Discovery in Renaissance Poetry* (New Haven and London: Yale University Press, 1982). The practice of imitation ranges from schoolboy exercises in mimicking the classics to sophisticated reappropriations of the sort Greene calls 'heuristic imitation', as in Wyatt's adaptations of Petrarch's sonnets, or Spenser's and Milton's complex reconfiguration of Virgilian (and Ariostan) epic. The status of 'Another of the same' is best expressed by its title.
26 Anthologies containing the poems proliferated in the eighteenth century, especially collections of songs (though often printed without music), for instance, *The Historical and Poetical Medley: or Muses Library; Being a Choice and Faithful Collection of the Best Antient English Poetry* (London, 1738); *The Bull-Finch: Being a Choice Collection of the Newest and Most Favourite English Songs* (London, 1746; many times reprinted); *The Choice Spirit's Chaplet; or, a Poetry from Parnassus* (London, 1771); *The Bird: Containing a Choice Collection of the Most Admired Love, Hunting, and Bacchanalian Songs* (London, 1780); *The Banquet of Thalia, of the Fashionable Songster Pocket Memorial* (London, 1788); *The British Songster* (London, 1788).

of *The Compleat Angler*,[27] there has probably been no time since their first publication when the Marlowe–Raleigh poems were not easily and widely available in print and subject to imitation and allusion.

After the anonymous poet included in *England's Helicon*, the next imitator of Marlowe and Raleigh was a Scot, or rather, as he termed himself, a 'Scoto-Britane', Alexander Craig, who seems to have followed James VI and I to London in 1603. There he published his *Amorose Songes, Sonets, and Elegies*, in which appeared his 'Alexis to Lesbia', a close imitation of Marlowe, though Craig's names harken back to Marlowe's original classical sources. Craig's fourteen stanzas pack in even more pleasures than the eleven of the second Ignoto poem in *England's Helicon*, and the landscape shifts toward the seaside, depicting dolphins and ocean billows as well as mermaids singing on the rocks. Craig makes some clever variations on Marlowe's original. For example, Marlowe's passionate shepherd offers a richly decorated 'belt of straw and ivy-buds', whereas Craig's Alexis promises 'My Arms shalbe a Belt to thee'.[28] Craig was also clearly writing about poetry as much as love, since Lesbia's cap will be the shepherd /poet's 'Lawrell Crowne: / Which drest of Daphne's haire shall shine'. In other words, Lesbia will be to Alexis what Daphne was to Apollo: his muse and his crown. In addition, Lesbia will listen to Echoes not from caves but from Alexis's breast. This complex allusion stands as a figure for poetic allusion itself, the echoes of Marlowe (and behind him Virgil, Ovid, Theocritus) resounding in Craig's 'Sonnets shrill'. The metaphor is unfortunate, however, since it also seems to suggest that Alexis's breast is hollow (and, like Echo herself, unable to make original statements). Furthermore, both Daphne and Echo are figures of unrequited love, the former fleeing her would-be lover, and the latter chasing the self-involved Narcissus. But perhaps Craig is aware of these ironies, since the whole point of these myths of Echo and Narcissus and Apollo and Daphne seems to be that poetry originates in thwarted desire. Craig develops the Marlowe–Raleigh pastoral exchange into a sequence, adding not only 'Lesbia her answer to Alexis', which imitates Raleigh's 'The Nimphs reply', but 'A new perswasion to Lesbia', 'A Letter to LESBIA, shewing his discontents', a 'Sonet to Lesbia', and finally 'Lesbia her answer'. Lesbia ultimately relents, but given her changes of mind and the number of invitations it takes to woo her, it wouldn't be surprising if she needed a few more 'perswasions' after all.

As the seventeenth century progressed, poets added to the number

27 Bevan's tally. See Walton, *Compleat Angler*, v.
28 Alexander Craig, *The Amorose Songes, Sonets and Elegies* (London, 1606), sigs. K4–K8v.

of pastoral invitations and replies, sometimes in the stanzas of four octosyllabic lines that Marlowe and Raleigh made canonical, sometimes in looser adaptations. Metres and stanza forms are among the conventions that define a literary genre, but a metre can also constitute an allusion, if not on its own then certainly in conjunction with other allusive markers.[29] Robert Herrick's 'To Phillis to love, and live with him', for instance, abandoned Marlowe's and Raleigh's four-line stanzas, but his lines are still written in the tell-tale iambic tetrametre. Herrick's catalogue of pastoral delights is especially lovely, but the argument is essentially identical to Marlowe's. Herrick's invitation seems more honest and genuine than Marlowe's, however, reflecting the influence of the anti-idealism in Raleigh's reply. This is partly since the speaker stresses that what moves 'Others to Lust' moves him to 'Love'. But what he offers also reflects a more realistic set of rural pleasures, rather than the artificial fantasies of courtly pastoral. His Phillis is enticed with a 'Gowne / Made of the Fleeces purest Downe', and 'Chaines and Carkanets / Of Primroses and Violets', and with 'Possets, Wassails fine, / Not made of Ale, but spiced Wine'. Even the 'Ribbands, Roses, Rings, Gloves, Garters, Stockings, Shooes, and Strings / Of winning Colours' seem less like Marlowe's gold buckles and 'fair-lined slippers' than the sort of stuff the pedlar Autolycus hawked to the country fairgoers in *The Winter's Tale*.[30]

Broader adaptations include Michael Drayton's 'Second Nimphall' from *The Muses Elizium* (1630) and, perhaps most famously, Milton's companion poems, 'L'Allegro' and 'Il Penseroso', first printed in his 1645 *Poems*. Drayton's poem begins in common or ballad metre, what Shakespeare's Bottom calls 'eight and six', but it shifts into iambic tetrametre, and the debt to Marlowe–Raleigh is clear in the inclusion of his recognizable invitation formula (the most familiar allusive 'trigger' in this literary tradition):[31] the shepherd Lalus offers the lass Lirope a lamb, and

---

29 See William Irwin, 'What Is an Allusion?' *The Journal of Aesthetics and Art Criticism* 59.3 (2001), 287–97. Irwin cites and disagrees with Michael Leddy ('The Limits of Allusion', *The British Journal of Aesthetics* 32 (1992)), who rules out 'the possibility of forms and styles alluding' (289). In many of the poems in the Marlowe–Raleigh tradition, the rhyming tetrametres are one of the signals that mark the poem as yet another pastoral invitation or reply. Such formal allusions are not always complex, but they are allusions.
30 *The Poems of Robert Herrick*, ed. L. C. Martin (London, New York, and Toronto: Oxford University Press, 1965), lines 54, 9–10, 19–20, 47–8, 51–3.
31 'Trigger' is the term used by Richard Garner (*From Homer to Tragedy: The Art of Allusion in Greek Poetry*) to refer to the word or phrase or other signal in a poem that announces an allusion and points the reader to the earlier work. Cited in Gregory Machacek, 'Allusion', *PMLA* 122.2 (2007), 522–36. Machacek rejects 'trigger', as well as other terms like 'signal', 'marker', or 'activation', and proposes instead 'reprise'. His concern is not to relegate the alluding work to a secondary status, but 'reprise' inadequately reflects

closes his wooing with the lines, 'This Lirope I have for thee, / So thou alone wilt live with me'. The 'Second Nimphall' actually features a singing contest, with two competing country lovers offering invitations to 'Lirope the bright'. Like Drayton's work, Milton's poems also begin in a different metre but then shift to octosyllabic couplets. L'Allegro invites the goddess Mirth to come join him, and then asks if he can join her and her nymph-follower, Liberty:

> And if I give thee honour due,
> Mirth, admit me of thy crue
> To live with her, and live with thee,
> In unreproved pleasures free ...
>
> (37–40)[32]

He concludes, 'These delights, if thou canst give, / Mirth with thee, I mean to live'. Il Penseroso, by contrast, offers his invitation to Melancholy, calling, 'Com pensive Nun, devout and pure', closing with the same formula: 'These pleasures *Melancholy* give, / And I with thee will choose to live' (31, 175–6). Milton's poems are densely allusive, essentially a practical demonstration of poetry's dependence upon the trope of allusion.[33] The presence of Philomel ('Il Penseroso', 56), while it also recalls Raleigh's 'Nymph's Reply' and Ovid's seminal account of the myth, also includes Spenser in its range of echoes. (As Patrick Cheney points out, 'in *The Shepheardes Calender* Spenser had selected the Philomela myth as his arch-myth of pastoral poetry'.)[34] Furthermore, Shakespeare, apart from being invoked by name, is alluded to in Milton's stories of '*Faery Mab*' ('L'Allegro', 102) and in numerous details of L'Allegro's landscape: the Lark (41), which in *Cymbeline* 'at heaven's gate sings' (II.iii.19) and which 'sings hymns at heaven's gate' in Sonnet 29; the 'Beds of Violets blew' (21) like Oberon's 'bank where the wild thyme grows, / Where oxlips and the nodding violet grows' (*Midsummer Night's Dream* II.i.249–50); and the 'Sweet-Briar' and 'twisted Eglantine' (47–8) also growing on Oberon's

---

the function of the 'trigger' in both alerting the reader to the presence of an allusion and in directing the reader to the prior work.

32 Roy Flannagan, ed., *The Riverside Milton* (Boston and New York: Houghton Mifflin Company, 1998), 65–77.

33 It is no surprise, then, that two of the most prominent theorists of allusion and intertextual relationships in English and American poetry see Milton as the first allusive poet in the modern sense. See Harold Bloom, *The Anxiety of Influence: A Theory of Poetry* (New York: Oxford University Press, 1973), and John Hollander, *The Figure of Echo: A Mode of Allusion in Milton and After* (Berkeley: University of California Press, 1981). Of course, though Milton was a master of complex allusion, he hardly originated the practice, nor indeed did poetic 'anxiety' begin with him.

34 Cheney, 'Career Rivalry', 532.

bank ('with sweet musk roses and with eglantine', II.i.252).[35] Milton's pastoral is also peopled with characters from Virgil (Corydon, Thyrsis, Phillis) and Theocritus (Thestylis). Roy Flannagan notes further allusions to Shakespeare, Spenser, Marston, Drayton, and others.[36] In keeping with, and in imitation of, the Marlowe–Raleigh exchange to which they allude, Milton's companion poems are themselves in dialogue, so that the two poems are in conversation with each other as well as with the long pastoral tradition.[37]

Like the broader pastoral genre of which it is a part, the Marlowe–Raleigh tradition of invitations and replies is thickly and incestuously allusive, with chains of allusions stretching back to the classical originals of Theocritus and Virgil and incorporating many of the major subsequent examples of the genre, which themselves allude to each other.[38] This sometimes seems like a palimpsest or cacophany, in which there are so many layers of allusions to allusions, so many reverberating echoes of echoes, that distinguishing specific poetic relationships is both impossible and pointless.[39] Yet

---

35 The Arden Shakespeare: *Cymbeline*, ed. J. M. Nosworthy (London and New York: Routledge, 1969); *Sonnets*, ed. Katherine Duncan-Jones (London: Thomas Nelson, 1997); *A Midsummer Night's Dream*, ed. Harold F. Brooks, Arden Shakespeare (London and New York: Routledge, 1979). Bloom argues that Milton was free of the anxiety of influence himself though he was a principal cause that it was in other poets, but this is an exaggeration. For the young Milton, Shakespeare was evidently a source of considerable anxiety; the allusions to Shakespeare in 'L'Allegro' represent the poet 'warbling his native woodnotes wild', relegating him to the status of an unconsciously productive poet of nature, not a serious intellectual or craftsman. In 'On Shakespeare', Milton's sonnet included in the Shakespeare Second Folio (1632), Shakespeare is represented as a potential basilisk, looking on whose works may turn other poets to (mute) stone.
36 *Riverside Milton*, passim.
37 Milton seems to have had the Marlowe–Raleigh exchange in his ear again when writing *Arcades*; the singer of the third song sings, 'Nymphs and shepherds, dance no more / ... / Bring your Flocks, and live with us' (*Riverside Milton*, 93). I owe this reference to James Nohrnberg.
38 Allusion functions backwards in time and tradition, of course, the later works alluding to earlier ones. Although for a much later reader, it sometimes seems as if allusions point to the future as well as the past, an earlier work 'recalling' to the reader works chronologically more recent, which in fact, if not in appearance, allude back to the earlier work themselves. Thus a reader of Walton might only subsequently come to read the Marlowe–Raleigh poems as well as the classical poems from which they derive. The temporal phenomenology of allusion is complex and sometimes counter-intuitive.
39 Such dense and manifold intertextual echoing, seemingly beyond any conscious authorial control, comes close to the different kind of intertextuality described by Mikhael Bakhtin and Julia Kristeva, referring to the interwoven cultural and linguistic fields out of which texts are woven. See Bakhtin, *The Dialogic Imagination: Four Essays*, ed. Michael Holquist, and tr. Caryl Emerson and Michael Holquist (Austin: University of Texas Press, 1981); Kristeva, *Desire in Language: A Semiotic Approach to Literature and Art*, ed. Leon S. Roudiez, tr. Thomas Gora, Alice Jardine and Leon S. Roudiez (New York: Columbia University Press, 1981).

for so learned and self-conscious a poet as Milton, the individual links in the allusive chain come to be more clearly articulated, and it is important for the reader to recognize that his participation in the Marlowe–Raleigh conversation includes the voices of Theocritus and Virgil, Shakespeare and Spenser as well as his own.[40]

The most famous lines from Marlowe and Raleigh also crop up as fragmentary allusions within prose works and plays; as the original poems, as well as the practice of alluding to them, become more familiar, poets can invoke the shepherd and nymph with increasingly subtle triggers. In Robert Greene's *Menaphon* (1589), for instance, the eponymous shepherd wooes his love Samela, offering her garlands of 'the cowslip, the primrose, and the violet', milk, wool, and mountain walks, concluding, 'As much as Menaphon owes shall be at Samela's command if she like to live with Menaphon'.[41] Another example is the anonymous *Choice, Chance and Change: or, Conceits in their Colours* (1606), which begins with 'A Dialogue, after a friendlie greeting, upon a sodaine meeting betweene *Arnolfo* and *Tidero*: as they travailed upon the way, betwixt Mount Jerkin, and the great City at the foot of the wood, in the long valley'. Early in this dialogue, Arnolfo asks Tidero, 'I pray thee, let us be merry, and let us live together'. Tidero responds, 'Why how now? Doe you take me for a woman, that you come upon mee with a ballad, of Come live with me and be my Love?'[42] (This more conservative attitude to gender and sexuality must be partly tongue-in-cheek, since homosexual love was a prominent theme of not only Marlovian but classical pastoral.) Turning to drama, the third act of Mary Pix's play *Ibrahim, the Thirteenth Emperor of the Turks* (1696, premiered at Drury Lane) includes 'A Dialogue Song. Suppos'd to be between a Eunuch Boy and a Virgin', written by Thomas D'Urfey and

---

40 My use of 'conversation' here, as well as maintaining the sense of pastoral dialogue, is also another way of expressing T. S. Eliot's 'tradition', the body of literature inherited and contributed to (and therefore constituted) by every poet. See 'Tradition and the Individual Talent', *Selected Essays*, new edition (New York: Harcourt, Brace & World, Inc., 1960; first edition 1932), 3–11. Allusion is one means by which writers demonstrate an awareness of tradition and participate in it, invoking but at the same time interpreting and shaping to their own purposes (making them new, in Ezra Pound's famous phrase) the works of their predecessors. On the relationship between tradition and allusion in Eliot's essay, see Joseph Pucci, *The Full-Knowing Reader: Allusion and the Power of the Reader in the Western Literary Tradition* (New Haven and London: Yale University Press, 1998), 8, n. 13.

41 Robert Greene, *Menaphon*, ed., Brenda Cantar (Ottawa: Dovehouse Editions, 1996), 112–13.

42 Alexander B. Grosart, ed., *Choice, Chance and Change (1606) or Glimpses of Merry England in the Olden Time*, in *Occasional Issues of Unique or Very Rare Books*, 17 (by subscription, 1881), 3.

set to music by Daniel Purcell (younger brother of Henry). In the familiar tetrametre couplets, 'She' resists the wooing of 'He', arguing that, among other things, the linnets sing better than he does:

> For they Lifes happy pleasures prove,
> As they can Sing, so they can Love.[43]

In William Taverner's *The Artful Husband* (1717, performed at Lincoln's Inn Fields), a comedy of manners spiced with a little cross-dressing, the happy ending is punctuated with an allusion to Marlowe–Raleigh:

> Sir Harry Freelove: *We only here a Taste of Pleasure prove,*
> Mr Winwife: *But what augments the Happiness of Life,*
> *Is to preserve a Friend, and to reclaim a Wife.*[44]

At this point in the tradition, even a word or two – 'pleasures prove', or 'be my love'[45] – from the Marlowe–Raleigh dialogue is enough to invoke the poems and their context: the pleasures of love offered and resisted. In *Ibrahim*, 'She' follows Raleigh's model and rejects the male seducer (though what exactly 'He' has in mind is unclear, since he is a 'Eunuch Boy'); in *The Artful Husband*, Sir Harry Freelove feebly channels Marlowe's lustful shepherd, but the last word is given to Winwife, who pronounces the superiority of wedded love to any pastoral dalliance.

The long tradition spawned by Marlowe–Raleigh demonstrates that for most readers it was Raleigh who won the debate. While there are some sunny imitations of Marlowe by Herrick and others (including William Herbert, Earl of Pembroke, who invites his lover to 'live within this Park, / A Court of joy and pleasures Ark'),[46] many of the post-sixteenth-century invitation poems incorporated the anti-pastoral perspective of Raleigh's reply, even when no reply is literally attached. In *The Compleat Angler*, for instance, Walton features John Donne's 'The Bait', a poem which adapts the pastoral invitation, appropriately for Walton's purposes, to the conventions of the piscatorial eclogue. Donne's poem is invitation rather than reply, but the 'golden sands' and 'crystal brooks' quickly turn into slime and mud, freezing and cutting reeds and shells. And even though angling might seem an appropriate metaphor for seduction, it turns out to be the poet himself who is hooked:

---

43 Mary Pix, *Ibrahim, The Thirteenth Emperor of the Turks: A Tragedy* (London, 1696), 16–17.
44 William Taverner, *The Artful Husband: A Comedy* (London, 1717), 69.
45 These phrases are particularly resonant, easy to recognize, because of the strong rhymes 'prove' and 'love'.
46 William Herbert, Earl of Pembroke, 'A Sonnet', *Poems* (London, 1660), 38–9.

> For thee, thou needst no such deceit,
> For thou thy self art thine own bait;
> That fish that is not catch'd thereby,
> Is wiser far, alas, than I.[47]

Another anti-pastoral invitation poem is J. Paulin's 'Love's Contentment', which borrows the trope of the loverss's ashes contained in a 'well-wrought urn' from Donne's 'The Canonization'. Paulin invites his Clarinda to 'love according to our state', a state which, in this poem written during the Civil War, seems able to exist only in the lovers' minds, or perhaps only in death:

> In this content we live and love,
> And in this love resolve to die:
>
> That when our souls together fled,
> One urn shall our mixed dust enshrine,
> In golden letters may be read,
> Here lie Content's late King and Queen.[48]

In Paulin's poem, the lover is as aware as his beloved of the pressures of Time. Another famous, if looser, imitation, Andrew Marvell's 'To his Coy Mistress', incorporates Raleigh's anti-pastoral even more ingeniously. (The influence of the Marlowe–Raleigh poems on Marvell's is less obvious than in other poems in the tradition, yet Marvell writes in the familiar tetrametre couplets, and the poem is clearly an invitation. There are also specific similarities in content, like the riverside location and the presence of hasty Time.) Marvell's invitation is now phrased in the conditional tense, the pastoral delights available only 'Had we but world enough and time'. But his lover, like Paulin's, hears 'Time's winged chariot hurrying near' and knows his 'echoing song' will not be heard in the grave. Unlike Paulin's lover who resigns himself to love in death, however, Marvell's conversely urges, 'Now let us sport us while we may'. As he puts it, *contra* both Donne and Paulin,

> The grave's a fine and private place,
> But none I think do there embrace.[49]

---

47 John Donne, 'The Bait', in Walton, *Compleat Angler*, 138.
48 In Marlowe, *Complete Poems*. Nothing is known about Paulin, whose poem survives only in manuscript (Harley 6918).
49 Andrew Marvell, 'To His Coy Mistress', lines 1, 22, 27, 37, 31–2, in *The Penguin Book of Renaissance Verse 1509–1659*, ed. H. R. Woudhuysen (Harmondsworth: Penguin Books, 1992), 372–3.

Thus, anti-pastoral becomes an argument for *carpe diem*. Marvell found in the arguments of Raleigh's nymph a stronger argument for the real (sexual) invitation of Marlowe's passionate shepherd, in that the transience of life argues for the immediate enjoyment of earthly pleasures. The fact that 'joys have date' urges not abstinence but speedy consummation. Raleigh transformed Marlowe's 'melodious birds' into the mournful Philomel; in Marvell the lovers become 'am'rous birds of prey' who devour Time.

From this point, the pastoral invitation tradition developed in a variety of ways. One anonymous Restoration poet took Raleigh's scepticism to its extreme in 'Come live with me and be my Whore', which is nasty yet original:

> And when we both shall have the Pox,
> We then shall want both Shirts and Smocks,
> To shift each others mangy hide,
> That is with Itch so pockifi'd;
> We'll take some clean ones from a hedge,
> And leave our old ones for a pledge.[50]

Some poets absorbed Raleigh's negative perspective on pastoral into darker invitation poems that represent the possibilities for love as hopeless. In William Wordsworth's 'The Mad Mother', published first in the 1798 *Lyrical Ballads*, a grief-stricken woman addresses her dead baby:

> And if from me thou wilt not go,
> But still be true till I am dead,
> My pretty thing! then thou shalt sing
> As merry as the birds in spring.

But there is only silence from the child, despite the woman's further pleading:

> But thou wilt live with me in love, ...
> Now laugh and be gay, to the woods away!
> And there, my babe, we'll live for aye.[51]

Wordsworth's poem radically revises the invitation tradition in multiple ways. First, the speaker is a woman and a mother, and she is addressing her

---

50 *Westminster Drollery. Or, A Choice Collection of the Newest Songs & Poems Both at Court and Theatres. By a Person of Quality.* (London, 1671), 16–17. Given the nature of this poem, one might reasonably doubt the collector's 'quality'.
51 *The Poetical Works of William Wordsworth*, ed. Thomas Hutchinson, rev. Ernest de Selincourt (London: Oxford University Press, 1936, rpr. 1965), 115, lines 56–60, 67, 99–100. The poem in this edition is retitled 'Her Eyes Are Wild'.

child, not a lover, so the love expressed is maternal not erotic. But the child is already dead, which is the clearest sign of the mother's madness. Lost in her grief-stricken imaginings, her irrational pleadings are emotionally far beyond the comical desire of Theocritus's Polyphemus or even the scepticism about time and love of Raleigh's nymph. Like Raleigh's Philomel, though, the baby is dumb. A full appreciation of Wordsworth's 'The Mad Mother' depends on the reader's perception of his deeply ironic troping of earlier poems in the Marlowe–Raleigh tradition. This is imitation of the most heuristic kind (in Thomas Greene's terms) or what John Hollander calls transumptive or metaleptic echo;[52] far from 'Another of the same', Wordsworth's poem alludes to Marlowe's pastoral invitation only to revise it towards a natural realism even more stark than Raleigh's.

Few variations on Raleigh's theme are as bleak as Wordsworth's, but a number of poems in the tradition also abandon any hope of love and embrace solitude instead, following, consciously or not, the early model of Lodge in *Scillaes Metamorphosis* noted above. William Henry Ireland labels his 'Begone; I'll hear no more of love' a parody, but it might be better termed an imitation:

> Away, straw belts and ivy buds;
> Away with clasps and amber studs;
> Nor these, nor thou, again shalt move
> My stubborn heart to melt with love.[53]

Despite its absolute rejection of the terms of Marlowe's invitation, Ireland's poem is quite plausible as the bitter response of the lover rejected once too often.

Solitude was not only the result of rejection, however, but sometimes it was a conscious choice, especially by Romantic poets in search of the natural sublime. The reformer John Thelwall's 'Stanzas written in 1790' is an invitation not to a nymph or a lover but to Simplicity:

> O! sweet Simplicity! dear, rustic fair!
> Hence shall my song thy worth, o'er all, approve!
> Come – live with me; my pure affections share,
> With native Honour, and with artless Love.

---

52 For Greene, see above n. 25. John Hollander, *The Figure of Echo*, 113–32. Carmella Peri interprets Hollander's category of echo or allusion in psychoanalytic terms as a poetic 'separation-individuation'. 'Knowing and Playing: The Literary Text and the Trope Allusion', *American Imago* 41.2 (1984), 117–28, 124.

53 W. H. Ireland, *Rhapsodies* (London, 1803), 139–40. Ireland was also a forger of documents and manuscripts by Shakespeare and others. See James Shapiro, *Contested Will: Who Wrote Shakespeare?* (New York: Simon & Schuster, 2010), 32–6.

This poet has tired of pursuing fame through 'rural metaphor' (having perhaps learned, like Raleigh in 'The Lie', that 'honour ... alters'), but he now hopes that 'With plain Simplicity my heart shall dwell'. The poem closes with a repetition of the invitation formula:

> Come live with me, my fix'd affections share
> With native Honour and with artless Love.[54]

The slightly later, but still pre-Wordsworthian, 'Poetical Effusion: Written after a journey into North Wales, February, 1794', by Charles Lloyd, invites no one to join the poet on his journey.[55] 'Nature, alone canst boast the power / To reillume the melancholy eye', Lloyd writes. Even while advocating solitude, however, the poet addresses an imaginary audience – the many lovesick shepherds in the pastoral tradition:

> If thou, perchance, hast ever felt the smart
> Of unrequited friendship, go and soothe,
> In independence wild, thy wearied heart! –
> The charm of solitary pleasures prove,
> Ye who the world's cold scorn may sometimes move
> To curse mankind! – and ye that doubt and fear,
> Oh! see how Nature shall instruct you there,
> All rapture to the heart, all music to the ear.[56]

Lloyd invites others to embrace the pleasures of solitude, so long as they don't impinge on his own. This is an invitation Raleigh's nymph might have accepted.

A subtler Romantic response to Marlowe–Raleigh is John Keats's poem 'Fancy', published in *Lamia, Isabella, The Eve of St. Agnes, and Other Poems* (1820). An allusion to Marlowe's 'kirtle' signals Keats's engagement with the invitation poem in his apostrophe to Pleasure:[57]

> Let, then, winged Fancy find
> Thee a mistress to thy mind [...]
> With a waist and with a side
> White as Hebe's, when her zone
> Slipt its golden clasp, and down
> Fell her kirtle to her feet,

---

54 John Thelwall, *Poems Chiefly Written in Retirement* (Hereford, 1801), 108–10.
55 After writing this poem, Lloyd met Coleridge and was so impressed by him that he gave him an annual stipend so long as he could remain in his company.
56 Charles Lloyd, *Nugae Canorae* (London, 1819), 1–4.
57 On the peculiar archaism of Marlowe's 'kirtle', see S.K. Heninger, Jr, 'The Passionate Shepherd and the Philosophical Nymph', *Renaissance Papers 1962*, 63–70.

> While she held the goblet sweet,
> And Jove grew languid.[58]

Keats inverts the conventional invitation by urging that his 'lover', Fancy (analogous to Simplicity, Solitude, the Muse, and other earlier allegorical transformations of the nymph), should not be invited anywhere, but allowed to roam free:

> Let the winged Fancy roam,
> Pleasure never is at home.
>
> (94–5)

And yet, when allowed to roam, Fancy will nevertheless return to the poet and bring *him* gifts:

> All the heaped autumn's wealth,
> With a still, mysterious stealth:
> She will mix these pleasures up
> Like three fit wines in a cup,
> And thou shalt quaff it: – thou shalt hear
> Distant harvest-carols clear;
> Rustle of the reaped corn;
> Sweet birds antheming the morn:
> And, in the same moment – hark!
> 'Tis the early April lark.
>
> (35–44)

In Keats's poem, Marlowe's madrigals become anthems, sung by a morning lark (not a nightingale) out of Shakespeare by way of Milton.[59] Marlowe's straw and buds are here too, but they are the real thing, not transmuted into coral and amber. Keats is aware of Raleigh's reply too, with its reminders of the passing of Time; this is not a poem of May mornings like Marlowe's, but an autumn poem by the master of the 'season of mists and mellow fruitfulness'. He knows, as he writes, that cheeks fade, maidens age, eyes grow weary, faces and voices tire with familiarity, and 'Every thing is spoilt by use'.[60] But this is why Keats tells

---

58 John Keats, *Complete Poems*, ed. Jack Stillinger (Cambridge, MA, and London: Belknap Press of Harvard University Press, 1978), 223–5, lines 79–80, 84–9.
59 See above, p. 178. The Marlowe–Raleigh tradition has grown over the centuries since Milton, Keats adding further links to the allusive chain.
60 It is tempting to think of Keats coming to this position not only through Raleigh but through his own illness, which ended his life at the age of twenty-six, but this poem was written in 1818 when he was not yet sick. Even then, however, he was familiar with sickness and death: his father died in an accident in 1804, his mother, of tuberculosis, in 1810, and his brother Tom, of the same disease in 1818 (and was presumably sick from earlier in the year).

the reader to make Fancy 'mistress to thy mind', where she can roam free and stay young forever. (Perhaps happily, he ignored his own advice, falling in love with Fanny Browne in the same year 'Fancy' was written; he died three years later.)

Bryan William Procter's 'A Phantasy' follows Keats in turning the beloved into a figure of the imagination. 'Thou wilt live with me', the poet writes, because 'Time may alter: Youth be dead; / And the Spring may hide her head / ... But *Thou* ever wilt remain'.[61] Like Marlowe's, Procter's is an invitation poem, but, like Keats, he shares Raleigh's awareness of time and mutability. The only means by which he can attain the object of his desire is by turning it into a fiction; the object will remain his, free of time, but only because it isn't physically real. Another strategy along these lines is expressed in Thomas Campbell's 'On Getting Home the Portrait of a Female Child, Six Years Old, Painted by Eugenio Latilla'. The poet calls out to the child's image, 'Type of the Cherubim above, / Come, live with me, and be my love!'[62] Unlike real girls, however, this painted one will never age or die, and the poet can be certain of the acceptance of his invitation, because he has purchased the painting (now at the University of Dundee) and put it on his wall.

Among other nineteenth-century poems alluding to Marlowe–Raleigh, those by John Clare and Alfred Tennyson stand out. Clare wrote a number of poems alluding to Marlowe–Raleigh.[63] One written late in his life incorporates the realism of Raleigh's reply without its scepticism. It represents the invitation of a realistically depicted country lover to a city girl:

> I ask thee from thy bustling life
> Where nought can pleasing prove
> From city noise & care & strife
> O come & be my love.[64]

Clare offers his love essential pastoral elements: 'echod melody', thrushes (not nightingales) that 'chant their madrigals', and fiddles that play for dancing. The poet's love, Mary, is invited to be a participant, not just a

---

61 Barry Cornwall [Bryan William Procter], 'A Phantasy', *English Songs* (1851), 37–8.
62 *The Poetical Works of Thomas Campbell*, ed. W. Alfred Hill (London: George Bell and Sons, 1891), 253–4. Campbell died in 1844. He edited *Specimens of the British Poets* (7 vols, 1819), which included the Marlowe and Raleigh poems.
63 The pastoral invitation was a mode that seemed to appeal to Clare. See, for instance, 'An Invite to Eternity' and 'The Invitation' in *'I Am': The Selected Poetry of John Clare*, ed. Jonathan Bate (New York: Farrar, Straus and Giroux, 2003), 276–7, 280–1.
64 John Clare, *The Later Poems*, ed. Eric Robertson (Oxford: Clarendon Press, 1984).

spectator.⁶⁵ Clare's pastoral world is also full of mirth – Mary's 'mirth', the 'harmless mirth' of the country, and the combination of 'music mirth & all' – which suggests he had in mind Milton's 'L'Allegro' as well, with its invitation to 'heart-easing Mirth'. By contrast, Tennyson's engagement with the tradition is as different from Clare's as can be. In *In Memoriam*, Tennyson's extended elegy for his friend Arthur Hallam, the poet cries, 'O Sorrow, wilt thou live with me / No casual mistress, but a wife'. Like Wordsworth's, this is an invitation that shares Raleigh's view of the passage of Time, but from the deeper perspective of one who has already lost his love; the beloved is dead, and all the lover has left is, like Keats or Procter, a mental image or state, in this case a state of grief.⁶⁶ Tennyson's tone is complex, and far from simply melancholic. He proposes marriage to Sorrow, whom he imagines 'sometimes lovely like a bride'. He also envisions having 'leave at times to play / As with the creature of my love'.⁶⁷ This is a poem not about a period of mourning but about a life permanently changed by loss.

Poets of the United States were among the most radical in their variations on the tradition. The New Yorker Philip Freneau, one of the most important eighteenth-century American poets, wrote 'To an Alien, Who After a Series of Persecutions Emigrated to the Southwestern Country. – 1799 –':

> Where you are gone the soil is free
> And freedom sings from every tree,
> 'Come quit the crowd and live with me!'⁶⁸

Although the American Revolution was still fresh in memory, Freneau was an ardent opponent of the policies of George Washington, which he saw as a return to tyranny. The invitation he imagines (and would like himself to receive) is not to love but to freedom, located in the territories not yet part of the Union. In another American invitation poem, William

---

65 Mary was a delusion, a girl from Clare's childhood to whom, in his madness, he thought he was married, in addition to his real wife. See Jonathan Bate, *John Clare: A Biography* (New York: Farrar, Straus and Giroux, 2003), 435–6.
66 There has been much written about the homoeroticism of *In Memoriam*, and Tennyson's decision to include in the elegy an imitation of Marlowe 'The Passionate Shepherd' may be revealing about his feelings toward Hallam. The darkness of the invitation is derived from Raleigh's nymph, but Tennyson may have noted that Marlowe's shepherd could be in love with another shepherd as well as a nymph.
67 *In Memoriam A.H.H.*, section LVIII, in *Poems of Tennyson 1830–1870*, ed. T. Herbert Warren (London: Geoffrey Cumberlege, Oxford University Press, 1912, rpr. 1946), 394–5.
68 Philip M. Freneau, *A Collection of Poems, on American Affairs and a Variety of Other Subjects* (New York, 1815), 1:100–2.

Gilmore Simms turned the shepherd into an Indian Hunter, who calls,

> Indian maiden, Indian maiden, wilt thou fly
> With me to the valley and the grove,
> Where sunshine shall light for ever the sky,
> And watch the young buffalo rove –
> And be my love and trim for me,
> The yellow buckskin moccasin.[69]

Marlowe's shepherd offered 'amber studs'; Simms's hunter has moccasins with 'rich variety of beads', but all he offers the maiden is the opportunity to trim them.

As more poems around the English-speaking world were added to the invitation tradition and allusions to Marlowe–Raleigh became increasingly familiar, some allusions became more self-conscious. In 'The Pursuit of Patronage', for instance, by the Irish poet Thomas Dermody, not only is Marlowe's familiar opening included as an actual quotation, rather than an allusion (most theorists of allusion agree that it must be at least to some degree covert),[70] but Marlowe is referred to by name:

> Who, led by sweet Simplicity aside
> From pageants that we gaze at to deride,
> Has not, while wilder'd in the bow'ry grove,
> Oft sigh'd: 'Come, live with me, and be my love'?
> Yet, oh! be love transform'd to deadly hate,
> As freezes memory at Marlow's fate.[71]

Dermody laments Marlowe's murder, as well as the inability of poetry to prevent it. The American poet Alice Cary, who played variations on the invitation in several poems ('Proposal', 'Autumn', 'A Wintry Waste') also cites its first author in 'The Lover's Interdict':

> When you have ceased to watch the airy spring
>   Of her white feet, a fallen beech hard by,
> The yellow earth about the gnarled roots dry,

---

69 W. G. Simms, 'Indian Hunter's Song', *Lyrical and Other Poems* (Charleston, 1827), 167–8.
70 See the discussion in Pucci, *The Full-Knowing Reader*, 6, 38–40. Pucci usefully suggests that allusion is covert only in form, not function, since otherwise the reader could hardly recognize it. Formally, however, there is a distinction between overt quotation, signalled with quotation marks, and allusion, which, no matter how obvious, depends upon the recognition of the reader. Hollander's use of the term 'echo', rather than 'allusion', allows him to play with the metaphor of volume, suggesting that some echoes are louder or softer than others, but the shift in terms also suppresses both author and reader, since 'echo' implies an acoustic phenomenon independent of both.
71 Thomas Dermody, *The Harp of Erin* (London: Phillips, 1807), 49–50.

> And if you hide thee, you will hear her sing
> That song Kit Marlowe made so long ago –
> 'Come live with me, and be my love', you know.[72]

In 'So fine-ear, stooping with a stedfast will', Thomas Westwood (an English poet in the circle of Charles Lamb) hears a 'thrill of music' like the one Cary promises, singing *'Come live with me and be my love'*.[73] And in his weird and marvellous 'The Vision of Cathkin Braes', the late Scottish poet Edwin Morgan has a vision of a famous femme fatale:

> Who has not heard of LAUREN BACALL'S grace?
> But I have looked upon her face to face.
> Most fervently she sang: 'Come live with me
> And be my love, and make my morning tea,
> And we may all the silken pleasures prove
> Of bearskin rugs, bear-hugs, and bunny-love'.
> So sang that mouth which like a red red rose
> Swayed in the dusk; and passed – where no man knows.[74]

The so-familiar allusion comes, by its easy familiarity, to stand for allusion itself, so that the poet who uses the allusion is openly admitting to an engagement with the poetic tradition, conceived as a diachronic version of the original (at least notionally) synchronic conversation between shepherd and nymph. With his parody of Marlowe's invitation, sung by Lauren Bacall, Morgan signals to his reader that his is an allusive mode, and the reader should also then recognize the allusions to 1 Corinthians 13 ('face to face') and Robert Burns ('My love is like a red, red rose').

Cary's and Westwood's poems indicate one material explanation for the long popularity of the Marlowe–Raleigh poems. Cary's reference to 'That song Kit Marlowe made so long ago' is of course a close copy of Walton's Piscator, who describes 'that smooth Song which was made by *Kit Marlow*, now at least fifty years ago'. Westwood is certainly thinking of Walton, since the song he quotes is preceded by a 'quaint discourse – Piscator's homily, / The voice we honour – Auceps grave reply – / Venator's jest'. (The title of his poem, 'Bi-Centenary', refers to the two hundred years since Walton's death.)[75] Indeed, a subsubgenre of fishing poems developed, which alludes to the Marlowe–Raleigh poems in the specific context of Walton's fishing book. Another example is Martin Farquhar Tupper's

---

72 *The Poetical Works of Alice and Phoebe Cary* (Boston, 1880), 213–14. Cary died in 1871.
73 'The Bi-Centenary', II, *Twelve Sonnets and an Epilogue* (Cambridge, 1884), n.p.
74 *Collected Poems* (Manchester: Carcanet, 1996), 43–9.
75 Westwood was also the author of *The Chronicle of 'The Compleat Angler' of Izaak Walton and Charles Cotton* (London, 1864), a historical bibliography of editions of the book.

'Fly-Fishing', in which the poet delights in a personification of his trout stream, with 'her pale-green kirtle flashing fleet' and 'her tinkling silver feet, / That ripple melodies'.[76] (Farquhar also takes 'golden sands' from Donne's 'The Bait'.) 'Fly-Fishing' is not an invitation poem, eschewing the essential 'Come live with me', but the other allusions to Marlowe–Raleigh–Donne, via Walton, are quite distinct. Walton's *Compleat Angler* has been one of the most persistently popular books in English literary history, constantly reprinted throughout the eighteenth and nineteenth centuries. As a result, 'The Passionate Shepherd' and 'The Nymph's Reply' were common culture for literate (armchair?) anglers throughout this period. (As were, incidentally, Donne's 'The Bait' and 'An Invitation to Phillis', the invitation poem Charles Cotton included in his continuation of *The Compleat Angler*, published in 1676.)

Parody was the preferred mode of response for some poets, parody being in this case an imitation that is formally close but comical. This may reflect a fatigue with the over-familiarity of the subgenre. An early Victorian example of this parodic mode (represented even earlier by the Restoration 'drollery' cited above) is Thomas Moore's 'A Blue Love-Song', in which the shepherd and nymph are transformed into Victorian bookworms (a lover and his blue-stocking):

> Come wed with me, and we will write,
> My Blue of Blues, from morn till night.

The poet hopes they will

> show the world how two Blue lovers
> Can coalesce, like two book-covers,
> (Sheep-skin, or calf, or such wise leather,)
> Letters at back, and stitch'd together,
> Fondly as first the binder fix'd 'em,
> With nought but – literature betwixt 'em.[77]

This clever parody plays with Donne's Elegy 19, in which Donne compares human bodies and 'books' gay coverings' and asks, with a coy pun, why his lover needs 'more covering than a man?'[78] Samuel Hoffenstein's 'Invocation' calls for his lover to abandon the traditional haunts – 'leafy hill' and 'crystal spring' – of classical pastoral:

---

76 *Three Hundred Sonnets* (London, 1860).
77 *Poetical Works* (1840–41).
78 John Donne, Elegy 19 'To His Mistress Going to Bed', *The Complete English Poems*, ed. A. J. Smith (Harmondsworth: Penguin Books, 1971, repr. 1996), 124–5.

> Come live with and be my love
> In statutory Christian sin,
> And we shall all the pleasures prove
> Of two-room flats and moral gin.[79]

Ogden Nash's 'Love under the Republicans (or Democrats)' features his characteristically playful rhymes:

> Come live with me and be my love
> And we will all the pleasures prove
> Of a marriage conducted with economy
> In the Twentieth Century Anno Domony.[80]

Cecil Day-Lewis, in an early poem, presented a relatively straightforward parody of Marlowe's invitation. But it takes on the darker perspective of Raleigh's reply in suggesting, for instance, that 'At evening by the sour canals / We'll hope to hear some madrigals'. The lover offers a kind of 'peace and plenty', but really only 'bed and board' and 'chance employment'.[81] These are non-courtly, working-class pleasures, modest at best. Parodies along these lines become increasingly tired, though there are occasional revitalizations of this strain in the tradition, like Kate Benedict's 'Atlantic City Idyll':[82]

> Come bet with me and be my luck
> and bring me gimlets tart with lime.
> We'll chase the wily holy buck
> and toss the dice and sneer at time.[83]

The poem has not just topical cleverness but some literary self-consciousness: the 'holy buck' transforms into cash the kind of deer

---

79 Samuel Hoffenstein, *A Treasury of Humorous Verse* (New York: Liveright, 1946), 12–15.
80 *The New Yorker*, 8 October 1930, 28.
81 'Two Songs' from *A Time to Dance* (1935). Day-Lewis returned to the Marlowe–Raleigh tradition in a later, more complex poem, 'Ideal Home', in *The Gate and Other Poems* (1962).
82 More ordinary parodies (amusing but not especially interesting) include Jacob Henrici's 'A Microscopic Serenade', published in *Scribners* in 1879, inviting his love into the world of microbiology, where 'protophytes shall homage pay, / And protozoa hail thee queen'. Henry Austin Dobson wrote 'The Passionate Printer to his Love', apparently commissioned by a printers' journal in 1906, Franklin Pierce Adams, columnist for the *New York Tribune*, wrote 'The Passionate Householder to his Love' ('Come, live with us and be our cook'), and *The Saturday Evening Post* featured Corinne Rockwell Swain's 'The Passionate Paleontologist' (26 Jan. 1924) and Norman R. Jaffray's 'The Passionate Leopard to his Love' (23 Mar. 1929). There are also 'The Passionate Profiteer to His Love' by Olga Katzin Miller (1942), and 'The Passionate Congressman to His Constituents' by Michael Silverstein, a.k.a. the 'Wall Street Poet'.
83 Kate Benedict, 'Atlantic City Idyll', online at *Cosmoetica: The Best in Poetica* www.cosmoetica.com /VM.htm (accessed 17 May 2009).

hunted by love poets like Sir Thomas Wyatt, in 'Whoso list to hunt' (the more familiar pun for Wyatt and his contemporaries was on the 'hart' and 'heart'). The poem closes with a grotesque transformation of the last line of Shakespeare's *Love's Labour's Lost*: 'And Armless Annie tongues her lyre' (versus Shakespeare's 'While greasy Joan doth keel the pot'). John Updike's 'To an Usherette' is just another light variation on the old theme, but Babette Deutsch's 'Dispassionate Shepherdess' adds something new. For one thing her poem shifts the balance of power from the traditional male wooer to a woman who wants love only on her own terms:

> Do not live with me, do not be my love.
> And yet I think we may some pleasures prove
> That who enjoy each other, in the haste
> Of their most inward kissing, seldom taste.[84]

One wonders whether Marlowe's shepherd, for all his posies, could have handled such a shepherdess, who has all of the scepticism of Raleigh's nymph but is still up for proving some pleasures, the more fleeting the better.

A more serious line of responses to Marlowe–Raleigh is less wedded to the strict form of the tetrametre lyrics and their specific vocabulary. Robert Frost's poem 'A Line-Storm Song' from *A Boy's Will* (1915), for example, is not immediately recognizable as a pastoral invitation, until the lover finally calls 'Come over the hills and far with me / And be my love in the rain', a refrain repeated with small variations at the end of stanzas two and four.[85] Frost's addition of the rain is enough to indicate the influence of Raleigh's more sober, realistic perspective on love and nature. Much more complex is the 'August' section of Robert Bridges's retelling of Apuleius's *Eros and Psyche*. In her wanderings, Psyche encounters the God Pan, and it is in Pan's voice that we hear the pastoral invitation:

> ... O I know a drink
> For care, that makes sweet music in the throat.
> Come live with me, my love; I'll cure thy chance:
> For I can laugh and quaff, and pipe and dance,
> Swim like a fish, and caper like a goat.[86]

Though he borrows Marlowe's line, Bridges' Pan also seems to know Donne's 'The Bait' (swimming like a fish) and Theocritus (in the Greek

---

84 *Coming of Age: New and Selected Poems* (Bloomington: Indiana University Press, 1959), 56.
85 Robert Frost, *A Boy's Will* (New York: Henry Holt and Company, 1915), 56–7.
86 *Eros and Psyche: A Poem in Twelve Books* (London: George Bell and Sons, 1894), 78.

too, since 'caper' comes from *capra* or goat). Since Pan sings this song 'his pipe laid by', Spenser is also present: in *The Shepheardes Calender* the rejected Colin Clout 'broke his oaten pype' in frustration, even though he knows it pleases 'rude *Pan*'.[87] Thus, by means of allusion, Bridges gathered the long pastoral invitation tradition into his poem, renewing it once again.

Williams Carlos Williams announces his position on the pastoral debate up front in 'Raleigh Was Right'. His poem argues that 'the country will bring us no peace' and that love is 'itself a flower / with roots in a parched ground'. It presents an argument about pastoral poetry in general, rather than about the possibilities of happiness in love, on which the Marlowe–Raleigh exchange was more focused. Even so, Williams's position is more ambiguous than his title suggests, since the exquisite, delicate beauty of the poet's question about violets somewhat belies its own implications:

> What can the small violets tell us
> that grow on furry stems in
> the long grass among lance shaped leaves?[88]

Perhaps they can't tell us anything specific (Williams was an Imagist after all), but their beauty communicates something. The direct engagement of Williams's title was bound to generate further arguments, and, sure enough, the Irish-American poet Greg Delanty, in 'Williams Was Wrong', argues pointedly that 'I find peace in everything around me'. Delanty's celebration of a seascape is not an invitation, however, and has little to do with the larger Marlowe–Raleigh tradition. The tradition clearly did interest Williams himself, though, as evidenced in another short lyric, 'The Observer':

> What a scurvy mind
> whose constant breath
> still stimulates
> the forms of death –
> unable or unwilling
> to own the common
> things which we must
> do to live again
> and be in love and

---

87 Edmund Spenser, *The Shepheardes Calender*, 'January', lines 72, 67, in *Edmund Spenser: The Shorter Poems*, ed. Richard A. McCabe (Harmondsworth: Penguin, 1999), 37.
88 *The Collected Poems of William Carlos Williams*, vol. 2: 1939–1962, ed. Christopher McGowan (New York: New Directions, 1988), 88.

> all its quickening
> pleasure prove – [89]

Whatever his views on country life, it is clear that in this poem Williams, favouring Marlowe over Raleigh, would have us embrace the opportunities for love, as love is essential to life.

Unlike Williams, however, most modern poets favour Raleigh's side of the debate, or, like many of their predecessors, incorporate his scepticism into their own invitation poems. Allen Ginsberg, in his early 'A Further Proposal' (1947), described the kind of poetic invitation offered by Marlowe's shepherd and his followers as a 'costly courtesy, or curse'. He offers a different kind of invitation, apparently (according to Ginsberg's own note) addressed to Neal Cassidy, to whom the young Ginsberg was passionately attracted. The poem is full of Raleigh's scepticism, but also more open about the sexual implications that are only implicit in Marlowe, to whom Ginsberg may have been drawn because of his reputed homosexuality. Though the poet is 'of sceptic mind' he will find in his lover 'A Resurrection of a kind', yet this kind of 'resurrection' sounds more like an erection, developing the peculiar 'wisdom' promised in an earlier stanza:

> For your share and recompense,
> You will be taught another sense:
> The wisdom of the subtle worm
> Will turn more perfect in your form.[90]

In one sense, the 'subtle worm' may be mankind, echoing the biblical expression of humility and corruption, 'I am a worm and no man' (Ps. 22:6). But it also suggests the serpent of Genesis, 'more subtle than any beast of the field' (Gen. 3:1). Of course, given the apparently sexual nature of Ginsberg's invitation, this 'worm' is also probably a penis. These allusive contexts come together in Ginsberg's seduction poem: sexual knowledge and transgression, sexual organ, sexual intercourse. Raleigh's and Marlowe's poems also come together in Ginsberg's: if Ginsberg (author of the Beat Jeremiad *Howl*) is as anti-idealist as Raleigh's nymph, he is as keen on sexual pleasure as Marlowe's shepherd, and more explicitly with men.

---

89 Ibid., 66. Both 'The Observer' and 'Raleigh Was Right' were published in *The Wedge* (1944), though an earlier version of the latter was written for the long poem *Paterson* (even though it wasn't published until later). See ibid., 17–18.
90 *Collected Poems 1947–1980* (New York: Harper and Row, 1984). Ginsberg notes that this early poem, a 'college imitation', was dedicated to Neal Cassidy in the first years of their friendship, which was a sexual one.

Another sceptical modern poet, Louis MacNeice, wove allusions to Marlowe–Raleigh into his 'Suite for Recorders' (1950–51), beginning with a variation on 'The Nymph's Reply':

> If shepherd to nymph were the whole story
> Dying in holocausts of blossom,
> No midwife and no middleman
> Would contravene the upright sun.
> If Raleigh to Marlowe on the other
> Hand were an uncontested audit,
> Then Thames need only flow to mock
> A death in tavern or on block.[91]

While both poets are dead – Marlowe stabbed in a Deptford tavern, Raleigh beheaded in the Tower – the perspective on time and art here is Raleigh's. 'Though Time drives ships from sail to steam', the modern poet argues, death comes to all poets as well as to all they love. The invocation of the flowing Thames draws in Spenser's refrain from *Prothalamion*, 'Sweete *Themmes* runne softly, til I end my Song', as well as T. S. Eliot's appropriation of it in *The Waste Land*, a poem pre-eminently about allusion and intertextuality.[92] Spenser asks the Thames to run softly so he can sing his song, whereas MacNeice sees the continuous flowing of the river, an image of time, as mocking the poets whose songs were too soon cut short. There may be some small consolation in that kings die too: 'Tamburlaine / Found no more in his earthly crown / Than was allowed to Corydon'. The final section of MacNeice's poem is an invitation, but a muted and self-consciously tentative one. 'Come, my sheep, my goats', he writes, but he is really thinking, and singing, not of his flocks but of an unnamed woman 'Who passed but once this way'. 'Dare I expect a reply / To the song I sung to her once?' he asks. The poet turns back to his pastoral tasks, and yet, though he may get no reply, and has no audience, he sings anyway:

> Come, this pipe is only on loan, I only a hireling,
> Yet, though my hire be due
> And always unpaid, and my songs, heard by you only,
> Must needs be always unheard,
> Come, my flocks, where this twilit wall still holds the noon-heat;
> Now I will sing of Her.

---

91 *Ten Burnt Offerings* (New York: Oxford University Press, 1953), 13–20.
92 Edmund Spenser, *Prothalamion*, line 18 (and thereafter, as refrain), *Shorter Poems*, 492. T. S. Eliot, *The Waste Land*, lines 183–4, *Collected Poems* (London: Faber & Faber, 1963), 70.

MacNeice's poem responds vividly to the long pastoral tradition preceding it. Incorporating a scepticism darker even than Raleigh's (European Jews in the postwar 1950s had experienced more than 'holocausts of blossoms'), the poem nevertheless closes with a pastoral invitation. MacNeice reaches even further back to Marlowe's originals for his model: like Theocritus's Polyphemus and Virgil's Corydon, this shepherd sings only to himself.[93] Thus he sings not only of his memory of the earlier song he sang to Her but also of those who have similarly sung before him.

Poets show no signs of losing interest in the Marlowe–Raleigh tradition. At the height of Haight-Ashbury's 1960s love-in, Lawrence Ferlinghetti wrote a lovely imitation, 'Come lie with me and be my love', expressing all of Marlowe's desire but purged of its implicit sexual aggression. The poem closes, 'And let our two selves speak / All night under the cypress tree / Without making love'.[94] The chasteness insisted on here is all the more surprising for having been written in the age of free love. W. D. Snodgrass joined the tradition of parodies, but with more originality than most:

> Come couch with me mit Freud und Lust
> As every evening's last connection;
> Talk to me; prove the day like Proust;
> Let what comes next rise to inspection.[95]

'Freud' puns on the name of the psychoanalyst and the German word for 'joy', just as the couch is a place both for analysis and for the sex that analysis is usually obsessed with. Proving 'the day like Proust' might involve dwelling on every sensual pleasure, like the famous eating of the madeleine in *Swann's Way*, though the following line has a strongly sexual suggestion, especially after 'Freud und Lust' (though Snodgrass is also likely playing against the phrase's use to refer to religious joy and desire, as in Buxtehude's cantata, *Jesu, meine Freud und Lust*). One of the best parodies, perhaps because it is also one of the most twisted, is Peter de Vries's 'Bacchanal':

> 'Come live with me and be my love',
> He said, in substance. 'There's no vine
> We will not pluck the clusters of,
> Or grape we will not turn to wine'.

---

93 MacNeice was a student of Classics, and 'Suite for Recorders', despite its very English topical references, was written during a stay in Greece.
94 *Starting from San Francisco* (New York: New Directions, 1967), 36.
95 'Invitation', *Not for Specialists: New and Selected Poems* (Rochester, NY: BOA Editions, 1996), 243. The poem was apparently written with his wife, Kathy, in mind. See Lynn Levin, 'On Corresponding with W. D. Snodgrass', *Contemporary Poetry Review* (online) www.cprw.com /Misc /snodgrass.htm, accessed 11 May 2009.

> It's autumn of their second year.
> Now he, in seasonal pursuit,
> With rich and modulated cheer,
> Brings home the festive purple fruit;
> And she, by passion once demented,
>
> – That woman out of Botticelli –
> She brews and bottles, unfermented,
> The stupid and abiding jelly.[96]

De Vries not only quotes Marlowe's opening line, making it more citation than allusion, but he further distances us from it with the qualifier 'in substance'. In other words, he didn't actually say *this*, but something like it, just as de Vries's poem is not Marlowe's but only something like it.[97] In fact, it isn't much like Marlowe's, not even 'in substance'. The invitation is only reported, and the remaining two stanzas narrate a decline that confirms the worst predictions of Raleigh's nymph: it's no longer spring or summer but autumn, and the passion seems to be gone. She, the woman out of Botticelli – Venus? Primavera? Flora? – was 'once demented' by it, but no longer. The 'stupid' (dulled? deadened?) jelly abides unfermented, bottled in jars like Welch's, but it hardly excites. This is a bacchanal domesticated and diminished.

Marlowe's 'The Passionate Shepherd to his Love' has been one of the most popular Elizabethan lyrics for centuries. After all, how many Renaissance poems have been included in the *Annual Report of the Ohio State Board of Agriculture*, as Marlowe's was in 1905?[98] Yet for most of the four centuries of its history, Marlowe's poem has appeared only with Raleigh's 'The Nymph's Reply' beside it. And it is Raleigh's reply that generated a dialogue among poets that has continued for most of those four centuries, producing alternative replies, replies to replies, parodies, imitations, and allusions of all sorts. This diachronic poetic dialogue is as appropriate to pastoral as the (notionally) synchronic exchange between shepherd and nymph with which it began. Singing contests are, after all, one of the

---

96 *The New Yorker*, 4 November 1950, 126.
97 Other poems alluding to, imitating, or adapting Marlowe–Raleigh include Hervey Allen's 'Summer' (*Wampum and Old Gold*, 1971), Sandra Gilbert's 'On the Train' (*Blood Pressure*, 1988), Selima Hill's 'Green Glass Arms' (*Violet*, 1997), Derek Mahon's 'Penshurst Place' (*In Their Element*, 1977), Douglas Crase's 'Covenant' (*Conversation Pieces*, ed. Kurt Brown and Harold Schechter (New York, London, and Toronto: Everyman's Library, 2007), 33), and Chard deNiord, 'After Marlowe', *Literary Imagination* 10.3 (2008), 295.
98 *Annual Report for the Ohio State Board of Agriculture for 1905* (Springfield, OH: State Publishers, 1906). On page 387 Marlowe's poem is cited in full in the midst of a report on sheep.

most familiar conventions of pastoral from Theocritus to the present.[99] Alpers points out that the word 'convention' – derived from the Latin *convenire*, to come together – can mean both a literary 'usage', such as a pastoral invitation beginning 'Come live with me', and a 'convening', like a meeting of scholars or the convening of so many poets over time with Marlowe and Raleigh.[100] 'Conventions', like those that happen in convention centres and hotels, are about people coming together. In poetry, allusion represents a similar kind of convening of poets, in Christopher Ricks's words 'a way of escaping solitude' and 'companionship of a kind'.[101] Allusion allows poets to communicate with their predecessors and brings old poems to new life. The allusive poet connects to the poems of the past but simultaneously needs, as Ezra Pound urged, to 'make it new'. As Ricks writes, 'allusion is itself a way of looking before and after, a retrospect that opens up a new prospect'.[102] Thus, even though the nymph rejected the shepherd's invitation, her reply – Raleigh's reply – transformed a soliloquy, or a solipsistic dialogue of one, into an ongoing poetic conversation.

---

99 As one can see, for instance, in the 'Duelling Banjos' sequence in John Boorman's film of James Dickey's brutal anti-pastoral novel, *Deliverance* (1972).
100 Alpers, *What Is Pastoral?*, 80–1.
101 Christopher Ricks, *Allusion to the Poets* (Oxford: Oxford University Press), 92.
102 Ibid., 86.

6

'Moving on the waters'
Metaphor and mental space in Ralegh's *History of the World*

Michael Booth

The week after Sir Walter Ralegh's execution, John Chamberlain reported in a letter that 'The people were much affected at the sight, insomuch that one was heard to say that we had not such another head to cut off'.[1] Ralegh's readers four hundred years later may be inclined to grant that his head *was* rather exceptional; in addressing ourselves to the literary Ralegh we are, perhaps, exhibiting an interest in the question of just what went on in his head. One thing that certainly did go on there was metaphor, which I will discuss in this chapter in relation to its purposes and contexts, as is not unusual in literary criticism; less conventionally though, with Chamberlain's remark as warrant if one is needed, I will also consider metaphor as a matter of cognition – not to argue that Ralegh's head differed fundamentally from others, but because his strong impulse for metaphor illuminates for us what every head can do. Illumination of this kind is, I think, one of the fundamental purposes of literary study, and I consider Ralegh here as I am inclined to consider writers and literary figures generally: not as exceptional beings in respect of their mental faculties but as exemplary or consummate users of those faculties, who reward reading because they stimulate the same in us.

A picture of the mind that has lately come to prominence on the cognitive side of the discipline of linguistics conceives of metaphor as fundamental to all, or nearly all, linguistic meaning, and as involving the interaction of 'mental spaces'. I think that literary studies can learn something to its benefit from this new field for several reasons: First, because any substantive insight into the nature of metaphor will be useful to those who study literature and the literary. Second, because these cognitive findings usefully contextualize the rhetoric of spatiality that is a common denominator in literary criticism; critics frequently resort to a spatial vocabulary as their ultimate grounds of argument, speaking of

---

1 Augustine Birrell, *More Obiter Dicta* (London: William Heinemann Ltd, 1921), 118.

connections, gaps, centres, margins, sites, boundaries, parallels, intersections, of opening up a space for one matter or another, of situating a problem or themselves. And third, with regard to my present subject, because Ralegh as a historical individual had a notably rich relationship to physical space, in ways shaped by his time and milieux; he knew a dizzying surplus of space in the lands and rivers of Amazonia and on the ocean that brought him there, and he knew a dreadful privation of it in his long imprisonment, during which the wide open spaces through which he'd voyaged may well have remained with him as 'mental spaces' informing his thought.

Ralegh's rhetorical purposes in *The History of the World* were clearly overdetermined. The text, written during his dozen years in the Tower, reflects both his desire for a commutation of sentence from King James and his despair of that possibility. It shows his eloquence in self-justification as well as his disdain for the indignity of pleading. Combating a reputation for impiety and atheism, Ralegh put on display a knowledge of scripture and an apparent reverence for its moral teaching and its mystery. His very enthusiasm for interpreting it, though, indeed his assumption of a right to interpret it, overshadowed in the short term his claims to orthodoxy, and served more to reinforce than to dispel the popular and royal prejudices against him.

In its historical sweep *The History of the World* intimates the freedom of the mind, and its habitual recourse to aquatic metaphors keeps in view the sources of its authority – the author's personal history as an oceanic voyager, and that history's inextricable link with his former status as close counsellor to the Queen who had nicknamed him 'Water'. Appreciating the literary Ralegh, I think, occasions some reflection on metaphor, allusion, implication, and overdetermination, all of which can be described in terms of mental spaces and their combination or 'blending'; moreover, as I will hope to demonstrate, Ralegh's remarks on the interpretation of figurative language emphasize certain semantic considerations – those of *image*, *similitude*, and *man-as-microcosm* – in a way that strikingly anticipates some of the insights of current cognitive linguistics. This chapter does not aim at a comprehensive exegesis of *The History of the World*, but at exploring how cognitive approaches can help literary study engage with texts as, in part, the productions of individual minds, and not of historical and cultural forces alone.

I will briefly recapitulate here some of the premises of conceptual-blending theory. It maintains (a) that thought is an epiphenomenon of embodied, physical experience; (b) that even before we articulate thoughts in language,² we think in scenarios, and indeed in brief nonverbal stories, scenarios set in motion; (c) that we constantly, without noticing it, assimilate new information into human-scale scenarios – an impulse reflected in our tendency towards personification in thought and our preference for the vivid and visceral; (d) that we may have active in our minds at any moment several distinct scenarios which, notwithstanding their logical incongruity in some respects, we are able to combine experimentally on the basis of their perceived congruity in other respects; we reason our way to new understandings through a process that is at once perfectly logical and radically illogical. One might ask, 'how can anything be both logical and illogical?' Blend theory is useful, in part, precisely because it explains why we can make rational use of contradictions, why we can unpack them into alternative possible perspectives.

Aristotle says both that '*all people* carry on their conversations with metaphors' and that metaphor is 'the hallmark of genius'.³ If these statements seem a bit contradictory, one way of reconciling them is suggested by the work of the literary critic Owen Barfield; according to Barfield, the mind is equipped with both an analytical, discriminating function and a 'poetic' or assimilating function, and poets are those who prefer the latter, 'enabling them to intuit relationships which their fellows have forgotten, relationships which they must now express as metaphor'.⁴ Sir Walter Ralegh was a poet in the sense of a maker of verses, but he was also a poet in Barfield's sense – a poetic writer of prose, a vivid writer, achieving concise expression through apt figuration. Poetic expression, as Barfield notes, is generally characterized not only by aptness but also by strangeness; it offers a convincing glimpse of the way things are, but at a cost in cognitive dissonance, as normally incompatible frames of reference are forced into momentary co-operation.

In his *History of the World*, at one point, Ralegh shrugs off a hostile public, remarking '[A]s we see it in experience, that dogs doe always barke at those they know not; and that it is in their nature to accompany one another in those clamors; so it is with the inconsiderate multitude'.⁵

---

2 This is not to deny that thought can arise in response to speech and writing, or that in the moment of articulation it accommodates itself to language and is 'subdued to what it works in, like the dyer's hand', to borrow a phrase from Shakespeare's Sonnet 111.
3 As Gilles Fauconnier and Mark Turner note in *The Way We Think* (New York: Basic Books, 2002), 17.
4 Barfield, *Poetic Diction: A Study in Meaning* (Middletown, CT: Wesleyan University Press, 1973), 87–8.
5 Ralegh, *The History of the World*, ed. C. A. Patrides (Philadelphia: Temple University Press, 1971), 45–6.

The comparison proposes an experiential unity between being criticized and being barked at. Anyone might intuitively recognize such unities, but the poetic writer is the person moved to articulate them, in momentary rebellion against the common-sense, analytical rationality that insists upon distinguishing a person from a dog. The rebelliousness of metaphor is closely tied to the aforementioned 'genius' of it. When a given metaphor joins the idiom where 'all people carry on their conversations', the rebellion in it is embraced, attenuated through diffusion, and eventually forgotten. The rich texture of metaphor in Ralegh's writing matches the rebellious streak, noted by his contemporaries, that eventually provoked King James to imprison and execute him. John Aubrey describes Ralegh as 'damnable proud', and notes that in his military service he was 'perpetually differing' with his commander, Lord Deputy Gray;[6] so did Ralegh perpetually differ with the grey authority of the prosaic in verbal expression.

The defiantly counter-rational or paradoxical quality of metaphor is central to the phenomenon that cognitive linguists Gilles Fauconnier and Mark Turner have dubbed 'conceptual blending' in their book *The Way We Think*.

Frames, emergent meaning

As I have said, 'blending', in its cognitive-linguistic sense, does not mean confounding or confusion, but rather a temporary collocation of disparate conceptions, whose properties and elements are experimentally combined. This process involves the simultaneous apprehension of two domains – in the case of Ralegh's metaphor above, those of writing a book and facing down a pack of dogs – and the projection of some elements from each domain into a mental space where hybrid conceptions (such as critic-dogs) can emerge and be tailored, quickly and unconsciously, for relevance and usefulness. Some elements in each domain have an analogue in the other. In both domains of Ralegh's metaphor, there is a person whose presence elicits antagonism from others – in one case it is a writer and in the other a pedestrian; in the blended conception, they are fused. As is apparent from the context in which he proposes the metaphor, Ralegh's purpose is to explain away the antagonism towards him. He offers a blended conception in which antagonism toward the writer is fused with that toward the pedestrian. The latter antagonism is assumed to have causes including the intrinsic belligerence of the antagonists, the fact that they do not know their victim, and the fact that they do not think

---

6 John Aubrey, *Brief Lives*, ed. Anthony Powell (London: The Cresset Press, 1949), 322–3.

independently of one another. The blend attaches these stipulations to the antagonism faced by the writer. Note that in the writerly reality, we have been offered no real evidence that Ralegh's critics are belligerent or do not know him, or do not think independently. Note also that in the dog scenario where those factors exist, they are accepted attributes of dogs and are not discreditable to them. In the blend, however, the blind aggression of Ralegh's critics takes on a new significance; because the critics are humans in polite society, these qualities appear in them as faults or vices. As Ralegh says, the critics are an 'inconsiderate' multitude. The imputation of distasteful behaviour and character springs from the conceptual blend.

The two mental spaces involved are each structured by a familiar scenario or conceptual frame. The blended conception recruits from Ralegh's actual situation the general roles of writer and critic, and the particular instances of Ralegh and his unnamed antagonists to fill those roles; meanwhile, the blend recruits from his heuristically privileged 'dog' scenario the attributes of mindless conformity, malice, menace – and probably also the qualities of filth, servility, etc. that are culturally available as associations with 'dog', and that redound insultingly upon those equated with dogs; the blend's alchemy thus produces something else, an insult, which highlights for us the creative aspect of blending, its ability to generate *emergent meaning*.

Each conceptual frame carries with it a certain minimal structure of human roles bearing some relation to each other. We tend to think in terms of people, and of people's roles in scenarios, which are among the things that we can superimpose and combine. Dogs are not people, which is part of Ralegh's insult, but the reason they are traditionally called 'Man's best friend' is precisely that they are familiar actors in easily comprehensible human scenarios. One of the insights of conceptual blending theory is that blending is governed by various constraints, including a sort of conservation of commonplace experience; it makes a great deal of sense to characterize one's literary detractors as dogs, but it would be much more unusual to characterize actual dogs as literary detractors; doing so could be wittily apropos, but only in very specific contexts – for instance if one were conversing with someone else who already knew one to have faced such detraction. Ralegh is introducing that fact about himself, and using the more broadly familiar scenario of the dogs to do so. Any mental spaces and their blended space comprise a *network*, of which there are various kinds. Ralegh's dogs exemplify a 'single-scope' network in which one of the domains is distinctly weighted to impart its richer semantic content to the blend – 'richer' because the more visceral or familiar the imagined scenario is (confronting dogs), the more easily it will give rise to inferences that can be transferred onto a more abstract domain (addressing criticism).

Remarking how drinking vessels, which were then often made of wood or leather, 'will ever retaine a savour of their first liquor', Ralegh notes that it is 'equally difficult either to cleanse the mind once corrupted, or to extinguish the sweet savour of virtue first received when the mind was yet tender, open and easily seasoned'.[7] Given the two scenarios of drinking from a cup and moral education, the impulse towards heuristic single-scope blends makes the former more generally useful for describing the latter than vice versa; it works very well to say 'this youth has been seasoned like a cup', but it would be a much more extravagant act of figuration to make the comparison the other way around, and to say 'this cup has been morally educated', if one meant only to say that it retained a scent. That word 'extravagant' is perhaps just the right one here, with its Latin meaning of 'wandering outside'. Outside of what? Outside the immediate, sensory frame of reference that structures so much of our thinking. As a rule, our comprehension demands that phenomena move into, not out of, this frame of reference. Acts of explanation tend to pull in the direction of the body and the senses.

Another type of conceptual integration network is the 'double scope' network, where blending occurs between scenarios which are not markedly asymmetrical in their visceral accessibility, and where the domains or frames are equally weighted, causing productive inferences to flow equally in both directions from the blend.

Images, similitudes, Man-as-microcosm

Ralegh was not only a user of metaphors; he was also a conscious student of them, finding it notable, for instance that 'Zoroaster...took the word *fire* to express God by'.[8] Working with scriptural and classical materials in preparing his *History of the World*, he was at pains to model what we now call the close-reading of such material:

> By the lively image of other creatures did those Ancients represent the variable passions and affections of mortal men; as by Serpents were signified deceivers; by lions, oppressors and cruel men; by swine, men given over to lust and sensuality; by wolves, ravening and greedy men; which also St Matthew resembleth to false Prophets, *which come to you in sheep's clothing*

7 Ralegh, *The History of the World*, 109.
8 Ibid., 87.

but inwardly they are ravening wolves; by the image of stones and stocks, foolish and ignorant men; by Vipers, ungrateful men.[9]

The serpents that signify deceivers and the lions that signify oppressors and cruel men are examples of single-scope blends, in that the point of these metaphors is a lesson not in zoology but in ethics and culture. The animals lend their visceral impact to somewhat more diffuse kinds of human interaction-scenarios. A lurking snake is like a human deceiver, only more so; the snake scenario is more compact in time and space, and more condensed in causality (the snake strikes and you are harmed). The analogy amplifies the urgency of avoiding human deceivers who are likely to harm the unwary.

St Matthew's warning against false prophets '*which come to you in sheep's clothing but inwardly they are ravening wolves*' is a blend of blends. The unrighteous man is a wolf; the righteous man is a sheep. These two intuitive blends are then projected together into a human frame of disguise – itself a perfectly reasonable shorthand for the imposture of a false prophet. Perfectly reasonable, but utterly at odds with all we know about wolves and sheep, neither of which wears clothing, let alone employs it for deceptions. We also have the seeming paradox of something that is inwardly ravening; the verb can mean either throwing a fit (compare 'rave') or taking by force (compare 'rapine'), but neither of these actions can properly be done inwardly. The passage offers what we might justly condemn as a mixed metaphor[10] and yet it has become a commonplace of Western civilization. Why? Because conceptual blending is governed by several competing constraints; in some circumstances, one principle prevails, and in other circumstances, another. In the present case, the perceived value or relevance of the warning, with its vivid elements (sheep and wolves, disguises) and indeed with the memorably paradoxical compounding of those elements, has been felt to be useful in a way that outweighs the cognitive cost of coping with an impossible, incoherent scenario.

I will here resume my list of blending-principles with a focus on several of the constraints, or competing imperatives of cognition, which variously lead our minds to… (e) preserve, within a blend, as much order or structure as possible from each of the original or 'input' domains;

---

9   Ibid., 130. Ralegh's italics.
10 An anonymous reader of this chapter has rightly pointed out that Ralegh himself might not have had any objection to mixed metaphors, since that concern, in a broader cultural sense, seems to become prominent in the later seventeenth century. Still, people in Ralegh's time were certainly capable of desiring and requesting clarification of figurative expressions, as for instance Shakespeare's Sir Andrew Aguecheek: 'Wherefore, sweetheart? What's your metaphor?' *Twelfth Night*, I.iii.71–2.

(f) achieve smooth integration or coherence in the combining of them; (g) use existing patterns – e.g. conventional tropes or symbols (sheep, wolves) – for efficient bundling of semantic information; (h) strengthen the 'vital relations' in a given conceptual scenario, such as time, space, part/whole, cause/effect, intentionality – a strengthening that often entails a certain *compression*, as with the snake example above; (i) establish durable links among mental spaces, so the network will not vanish from the domain of working memory where it is unconsciously operating; (j) make a blend that can easily undo itself, can present its original, distinct domains clearly to rational analyis; (k) maximize the relevance of each element taken into the blend.

In St Matthew's admonition, the integration principle (f) gives way, as does the relevance principle (k); what is the relevance of clothing to wolves? Clothing has been preserved, in the blend, as a piece of conceptual structure belonging to the frame shared by the righteous and the unrighteous man, who wear it but cannot be distinguished by it. The irrelevance of clothing to any real wolf's behaviour toward a sheep violates the relevance principle, but this loss is the gain of the 'unpacking' principle (j), as it presents an incongruity which demands to be accounted for. As this issue of unpacking suggests, the operation of conceptual integration networks is somewhat like that of a machine which can be run forward or backward. Run it forward to create blends, following the integration principle, and you have Owen Barfield's 'poetic' mind observing resemblances between things in order to understand intuitively what they are; run it backward, following the unpacking principle, and you have Barfield's analytic mind that splits single meanings into separate and isolated concepts. Like systole and diastole in the heart, blending and unblending are reciprocally necessary to the life of the mind.

Ralegh quotes St Matthew with interest and approval, because Matthew is propounding a useful conceptual blend, bringing mental spaces together effectively. Ralegh's alertness to metaphor, though, has a sceptical or critical dimension as well, and his very proficiency makes him equally apt to unpack blends into separate mental spaces, to exercise Barfield's analytic principle as incisively as he does the poetic principle. 'For shall we say', he asks, 'that it is out of *affection* to the earth, that heavy things fall towards it? Shall we call it *Reason*, which doth conduct every River into the salt Sea? Shall we tearme it *knowledge* in fire, that makes it to consume combustible matter?'[11] In asking these questions he is advancing

---

11 Ralegh, *The History of the World*, 76.

the cause of science rather than poetry, subjecting received notions to analytical scrutiny.

Ralegh says that the ancients employed 'the lively image' of various creatures, and that St Matthew 'resembleth' wolves to false prophets. These wolves, like the figurative chorus of detracting dogs, involve an image and a resembling. When Ralegh says that *'God made man, in respect of the intellect, after his own image and similitude',*[12] he likewise underlines a nexus between intellect, image, and similitude. As regards the creation of man, the important point for Ralegh is that *'Man was made after the image of God, in minde, or in that he had a mind'.*[13] If Raleigh anticipates conceptual-blending theory in his focus on the relation between similitude and image, and their centrality to the working of minds, he does so again when he says that

> [I]n the little frame of man's body there is a representation of the universall, and (by allusion) a kind of participation of all the parts thereof, therefore was man called *Microcosmos*, or the little world ... [h]is breath may be resembled to the aire; his naturall heate to the inclosed warmth, which the Earth hath in it selfe ... the haires of mans body, which adornes or ouershadows it, to the grasse ... our generatiue power to Nature, which produceth all things; our determinations, to the light, wandring, and vnstable clouds ... the thoughts of our minde, to the motion of Angels; and our pure understanding ... to those intellectual natures, which are always present with God [14]

On the one hand Ralegh is simply recapitulating the widespread early modern premise, adopted from Protagoras, that 'Man is the measure of all things'. On the other hand, from a modern and secular rather than a Renaissance Christian-humanist perspective, he seems also to ratify cognitive-theoretical postulates. The 'little frame of man's body' offers 'representation of the universal' inasmuch as it gives access to the universe and whatever universals can be made intelligible to us. As Fauconnier and Turner write, 'Human beings are evolved and culturally supported to deal with reality at human scale – that is, through direct action and perception inside familiar frames, typically involving few participants and direct intentionality.... It seems that the construction of the network with a blend at human scale and the appropriate connections to a complex array of mental spaces is what generates the impression of global insight'.[15]

---

12 Ibid., 122.
13 Ibid.
14 Ibid., 126–7.
15 Fauconnier and Turner, *The Way We Think*, 322.

When Ralegh says that 'Man, thus compounded and formed by God, [is] an abstract or modell, or brief Storie of the Vniuersal',[16] it is particularly interesting that he should resort to the terms 'abstract' and 'brief story', since, as the same theorists have written, 'A scenario at [human] scale typically involves a simple story'.[17] Our mental models are not static, but in some sense unfold *as stories* to generate the inferences that we rely on. As his erudite references to diverse biblical, classical, and philosophical writings make clear, one thing that was going on in Ralegh's head was what we now call intertextuality. The stories that he used for interpreting the world and making judgements and decisions were clearly present to him as distinct conceptual frames that could give rise, as needed, to networks of conceptual integration. Metaphor and intertextuality are central considerations in contemporary literary criticism; part of the value of blend-theory is the opportunity it offers for seeing these terms as naming two facets of a single phenomenon, rather than as separate and irreducible mysteries in themselves. Another benefit is the strong vindication that blend-theory might offer, to our broader intellectual culture, for the conviction long and strenuously espoused by literary academics that stories or narratives of all kinds are of great importance.

Sir *Water* Ralegh

Aubrey reports that Ralegh 'studied most in his sea-voyages, where he carried always a trunk of books along with him, and had nothing to divert him'.[18] Not surprisingly, Ralegh's metaphors were often aquatic, regardless of what subject he happened to be considering: 'Shall we call it *Reason*, which doth conduct every River into the salt Sea?' Ever conscious of mortality – being already, indeed, legally dead – Ralegh muses that '[T]his tide of man's life, after it once turneth and declineth, ever runneth with a perpetual ebb and falling stream, but never floweth again'[19]; '[W]hen wee once come in sight of the port of death, to which all winds drive us; and when by letting fall that fatal Anchor, which can never be weighed again, the Navigation of this life takes an end'.[20] Ever mindful of the libel of atheism against him, Ralegh says that those who grant nature 'any first or sole power, have therein no other understanding than such a one

---

16 Ralegh, *The History of the World*, 126.
17 Fauconnier and Turner, *The Way We Think*, 323.
18 Aubrey, *Brief Lives*, 324.
19 Ralegh, *The History of the World*, 128.
20 Ibid., 66.

hath, who looking into the stern of a shippe, and finding it guided by the helme and rudder, doth ascribe some absolute virtue to the piece of wood, without all consideration of the hand, that guides it, or of the iudgment, which also directeth and commandeth that hand'.[21] Ever meditative on the limits of human understanding, he writes that

> [A]s all the Rivers in the world, though they have diverse risings, and diverse runnings; though they then some-times hide themselves for a while under ground, and seem to be lost in Sea-like Lakes; doe at last find, and fall into the great Ocean: so after all the searches that humaine capacity hath; and after all Philosophicall contemplation and curiositie; in the necessitie of this infinite power, all the reason of man ends and dissolues it selfe.[22]

With regard to smaller nations absorbed by the ancient empires discussed in his *History*, he says, '[H]erein I have followed the best Geographers: who seldome give names to those small brookes, whereof many, ioyned together, make great Rivers; til such time as they become united, and runne in a main streame to the Ocean Sea'.[23]

Ralegh also waxes nautical when touching on the sore subject at the heart of his book, the fickleness of kings and the fate of their courtiers in disfavour. Glancing bitterly at the figure of the unprincipled yet thriving courtier, he says 'Neither is it sufficient to be wise with a wise Prince, valiant with a valiant, and just with him that is just ... but he must also ... sail with the tide of time, and alter form and condition, as the state or the state's master changes'.[24] He says that a virtuous man is well advised to avoid politics, where his fate will be that of a sailor who can't adjust his sail: 'for as he that first devised to add sails to rowing vessels, did either so proportion them, as being fastened aloft and towards the head of his mast, he might abide all winds and storms, or else he sometime or other perished by his own invention: so that man which prizeth virtue for it selfe, and cannot endure to hoise [*sic*] and strike his sails, as the diverse natures of calmes and stormes require, must cut his sails, and his cloth, of mean length and breadth, and content himself with a slow and sure navigation (to wit) a meane and free estate'. Here then is a compendium of ways that the world's waters mirror the life of Man, according to Ralegh: life is navigation; death is adumbrated in the ebb of tides, the dropping of the anchor, and the arrival in port; nature is a rudder, not a helmsman; reason runs its winding course into the unfathomable; all

21 Ibid., 103.
22 Ibid., 74.
23 Ibid., 79.
24 Ibid., 117.

particular and local histories flow into one grand one; the good man is probably a bad sailor on the waves of fortune, and the bad man a good one. Imaginative movement upstream or downstream seems to carry with it, to Ralegh's mind, different conceptual structure for the framing of meaningful comparisons. And for all the fatalism of his finding death in the ebb tide and the return to port – a fatalism which is the dominant note of his poetry of all periods as well – we can sense a keen yearning in the figure of the anchor 'which can never be weighed again', and an ardor for what he calls 'the Navigation of this life'.

What part do the governing principles of blending play in these nautical metaphors? His figuration of death as an ebb tide pointedly violates the topology principle (e) – the imperative to preserve conceptual structure – because actual tides are notably cyclical; Ralegh's phrase 'perpetual ebb' intimates a paradox, which is then made quite explicit: unlike ordinary tides, this is one that 'never floweth again'. The remark draws part of its poetic force from this paradox or frame-clash, but paradox is not the whole point. Topology (e) is being violated here for a gain in human-scale immediacy. Everyone from Shakespeare to Otis Redding has found the ebb tide a fit symbol for failure, ennui, and mortality, but this is possible only because the conventional trope refers us to our smallest-scale experience of tides – in the range of minutes or hours, but not days; the metaphor succeeds imaginatively through a dramatic compression (h) of the vital relation of time, from a human lifespan to an hour at the shore.[25]

The topology principle (e) is similarly compromised in his characterization of death as the 'port to which all winds drive us' – which would make this port radically unlike any real port; the dramatic compression here is of number, from innumerable winds and bearings in an actual sailing life to only one in the blend. The integration principle (f) is perhaps only weakly at work in this allegorical scene, as the port, the winds and the anchor seem to be all equally imbued with the imminence of death, but not because of any particular maritime logic; this independence seems characteristic of allegory in general, and it may be that 'allegory' is what we call a blend where the impulse toward story-making

---

25 The human-scale scenario of trying to catch a particular boat animates Shakespeare's famous figure 'There is a tide in the affairs of men. / Which, taken at the flood, leads on to fortune; / Omitted, all the voyage of their life / Is bound in shallows and in miseries'. *Julius Caesar*, IV.iii.218–21. The boat departing at high tide will get you clear of the shoals. Here too, there is a compression of time to the small scale of one tidal cycle. What differs is the mapping of roles in the tidal scenario. In Ralegh's figure, the ebbing tide is one's life itself, one's failing energy. In Shakespeare's, the tide is a moving target, a passing opportunity that one must move energetically to exploit.

(b) overwhelms the integration principle that would otherwise strive for internal coherence.

It is the relevance principle (k) that underlies Ralegh's argument for construing the scriptural word *Eden* as a proper name rather than simply as the Hebrew noun for 'pleasure'. 'For,' he says, 'what sense hath this translation ... *he planted a garden in pleasure*, or that *a River went out of pleasure to water the garden*?'[26] Ralegh questions the respective relevances of river and garden to a conceptual blend of man's first abode with 'pleasure'. Allowing *Eden* to be both an adjective and a proper noun, he unpacks its meaning into two separate mental spaces, citing a precedent in his experience: '*Eden* ... signifieth in the Hebrew, pleasantnesse or delicacie, as the Spaniards call the country opposite the *Isle of Cuba, Florida*: ... as *Florida* was a countrie, so called for the flourishing beautie thereof, so was *Eden* a region called pleasure, or delicacie ... and as *Florida* signifieth flourishing: so *Eden* signifieth pleasure, and yet both are the proper names of countries'.[27]

The intensification of vital relations (h) is apparent in most of Ralegh's metaphors. The fixed sail in foul weather, for instance, is a nicely vivid figure for the more diffuse and intangible virtue that sinks good men at court; the space and time in which the sail's logic plays out are compressed, and involve fewer agents. The vital relation of intentionality is also heightened in the blend that Ralegh is challenging when he asks 'Shall we call it *Reason,* which doth conduct every River into the salt Sea?'; that is, whoever may have spoken of the 'reason' that guides rivers was imputing more intentionality to them than Ralegh is willing to accept, and he accordingly calls for an unpacking of the blend. A heightened if still modest intentionality is also apparent in 'letting fall the fatal anchor' as a metaphor for death, and of course in Ralegh's equating life with navigation. A heightening of intentionality is the point of his picture of God as navigator of the world, and also his invocation of 'the hand, that guides it, [and] the iudgment, which ... directeth and commandeth that hand'.

It is not entirely surprising that an early modern *History of the World* should begin with a discussion of Genesis, nor that the author of this one, having titled one section *How it is to be understood that the Spirit of God moued upon the waters, and that this is not to be searched curiously* – should then search it curiously for many pages. Since 'moved on the waters' is an English translation, Ralegh looks into each language in the chain of transmission for connotations that may have been added or lost along the way:

26 Ralegh, *The History of the World*, 132.
27 Ibid.

After the creation of Heauen and Earth, then voide and without forme, the Spirit of God moued upon the waters. The *Seuenty Interpreters* vse the word *super-ferebatur*, moued vpon or ouer: *incubat*, or *fouebat* ... which words *incubare* or *fouere* importing warmth, hatching, or quickening, haue a speciall liking ... *The word is taken of birds hatching their yong, not corporally, but in a spiritual and unexpressible manner.* Some of the Hebrewes conuert it to this effect ... *The Spirit of God did flutter* ... Arias Montanus [uses] these wordes ... *The Spirit of God effectually and often mouing, keeping warme, quickning and stirring upon the face of this double liquor.*[28]

As for 'double liquor' as an alternative translation for 'the waters', Ralegh explains that

The word which the Hebrews call *Maim*, is not to be understood according to the Latin translation simply, and as specificall water; but the same more properly signifieth liquor. For (according to Montanus) ... *Maim* ... *is a double liquor* (that is, of divers natures) *and this name or word the Latines wanting a word to express it, call it in the plural Aquas, Waters.*[29]

Ralegh's scholarly investigation leads him from the abstract English verb 'move' to a vivid scenario of birds hatching their young, with connotations of warmth, quickening and fluttering. Unpacking the cultural construct of 'God's word' into the diverse representations made by different languages, he is defying any literalist theology that would elide that difference, that would suppress the 'unpacking' principle and halt inquisitive reading. Ralegh has also discovered, at the core of this passage, a Hebrew word signifying 'a liquor of diverse natures'. In Ralegh's hands, or rather in his head, the reason of man perseveres in unpacking blends, revealing the diverse natures of things that time and chance and ignorance otherwise confound. The Spirit of God, in Ralegh's understanding of Genesis is *a certaine diuine power, or strength euery where, actiue and extending, and stretching through all, finishing and filling all things*'; that is, something not unlike the creative human imagination that engenders and animates a conceptual blend.[30]

The *Maim*, or liquor of diverse natures over which this spirit moves, is *materies ad omnem rem conficiendam habilis, matter apt to become everything*, not unlike the physical sensorium that supplies the frames, scenarios and basic metaphors that give rise to our thoughts. Minding

28 Ibid., 92.
29 Ibid., 91.
30 The divine 'finishing and filling' he speaks of has a close analogue in the process of 'composition, completion and elaboration' by which mental spaces become blended. See *The Way We Think*, 48.

his reputation, Ralegh is careful to furnish his inquiry with a disclaimer, metaphoric and aquatic as usual: '[T]o be ouer-curious in searching how the all-powerful Word of God wrought in the creation of the world, or his all-piercing and operative spirit distinguishing, gaue form to the matter of the Vniuresall, is a labour and search like vnto his, who not contented with a knowne and safe ford, will presume to passe ouer the greatest Riuer in all parts, where hee is ignorant of their depths'.[31]

'Saucy in censuring'

A strain of metaphor particularly convergent with the premise of embodied cognition is the trope of personification (see c), as when Ralegh apologizes for the weakness of his conceits, saying the weakness 'shows their legitimation and true *parent*', as if they were his human progeny.[32] He alludes elsewhere to those monarchs who have 'made their own fancies both their Treasurers and Hangmen'. He laments that ignorance 'is now become so powerful a Tyrant, as it hath set true Philosophie, Phisik and Divinity in a Pillory',[33] and he remarks also that the law is 'in his own nature ... no other than a deaf Tyrant'.[34] All this talk of tyrants, pillories, and hangmen might make one wonder whether Ralegh had something he was trying to say on this score, and of course he did. As Stephen Greenblatt has observed, Ralegh's *History* is, above all, 2,700 pages of 'unending examples of God's just punishment of wicked kings'.[35]

The last sentence of Ralegh's appended preface, and therefore quite possibly his last word of the project, is a characteristic combination of stoicism and bravado, scorning to 'beg [the] good opinion' of his readers, on the grounds that it does not matter what anyone thinks of him now: 'For conclusion, all the hope I haue lies in this, That I haue already found more ungentle and uncourteous Readers of my Loue towards them, than euer I shall do again. For had it beene otherwise, I should hardly haue had this leisure, to haue made myself a foole in print'.[36] Yet Raleigh's hauteur is not uniform. 'But seeing', he says, 'that Princes (who ought to imitate God in all they can) do sometimes for causes to themselves known, and by mediation, pardon offences both against others and themselves, it were

---

31 Ralegh, *The History of the World*, 94.
32 Ibid., 79.
33 Ibid., 72.
34 Ibid., 109.
35 Greenblatt, *Sir Walter Ralegh: The Renaissance Man and His Roles* (New Haven: Yale University Press, 1973), 133.
36 Ralegh, *The History of the World*, 81.

then impious to take that power and libertie from God himself which his substitutes enjoy. God being mercy, goodness and charitie himself'.[37] King James did not take the hint from this ostensibly theological musing, and ordered Ralegh's *History* suppressed as 'too saucy in censuring the acts of kings'.[38]

We will never know whether Ralegh might have awakened goodness, mercy, and charity in King James if he had been able to restrain himself from writing things like 'whoever shall tell any great man or Magistrates, that he is not just, the Generall of an army, that he is not valiant, and great Ladies that they are not fair, shall never be made a Counsellor, or a Captaine, or a Courtier',[39] and 'every fool is wonne with his own pride and others' flattering applause'.[40] It might also have helped if he had refrained from reflecting that nations are 'sometimes governed by kings, sometimes by magistrates, [and] sometimes by the people themselves',[41] thus evoking the same interest in republican government that, according to John Aubrey, first earned him the King's intense and hostile suspicion.[42] It might have helped if he had not so insistently underscored the point that kings in their power retain the image of God *provided that* 'they exercise the office or magistracy to which they are called, and sincerely walk in the ways of God, which in the Scriptures is called walking with God'.[43] Here is an interesting conceptual integration: by virtue of an anthropomorphic figuration of divinity (see c) and a conceptual frame of companionable walking (see b) which imports the mutual acceptability of the companions, Ralegh is able to make 'walking with God' signify behaviour from the king, which the context is enough to link with the possibility of the King's pardoning him; Ralegh may be too proud to beg, but he's also too stubborn to give up, and he has sufficient cognitive fluidity to embed his implicit entreaties and also his bitter criticism in the conceptual structure attached to his nominal subject matter. Sadly, King James as a reader was far too meticulous in the relevance principle to let slide any remark that could bear a seditious construction, and he was infinitely more disposed to integrate any general observations on politics or religion with the conceptual frame of an insolent subject than with that of a repentant king.

In the end, Aubrey says '[Ralegh's] head was cut off. At which time

37 Ibid., 109.
38 Isidore Abramowitz, *The Great Prisoners* (New York: Dutton & Co., 1946), 189.
39 Ralegh, *The History of the World*, 117.
40 Ibid., 117.
41 Ibid., 160.
42 Aubrey, *Brief Lives*, 327.
43 Ralegh, *The History of the World,*, 124.

such abundance of blood issued from his veins that showed he had stock of nature enough left to have continued him many yeares in life, though now above 3-score years old, if it had not been taken away by the hand of violence'. Anyone on hand who had read the *History* with attention to its reflections on Man might have then recalled Ralegh's observation that 'His blood, which disperseth itself by the branches of the veins through all the body, may be resembled to those waters, which are carried by brookes and rivers over all the earth'.[44] Aubrey says of Ralegh that 'he was no slug; without doubt, [he] had a wonderful waking spirit, and great judgement to guide it'.[45] We might say, invoking that primal figure of consciousness and creation, that Ralegh's was a spirit that moved on the waters – in real transoceanic voyages while engrossed in his books, in voyages of the mind from his prison in the Tower, and on a deep river of images and similitudes in the intellectual life that he took to be the essential manifestation of divinity in humankind.

---

44 Ibid., 127.
45 Aubrey, *Brief Lives*, 324.

7

Water Ralegh's liquid narrative
The Discoverie of Guiana[1]

Lowell Duckert

Readers of Walter Ralegh's *Discoverie of the Large, Rich, and Bewtiful Empyre of Guiana* (1596) expected solid gold, as did Ralegh himself during his voyage the previous year. Remarkably, the journey to El Dorado came up with *liquid* instead; one of the treasures the expedition actually produced was a chart of Guiana's waterways 'not yet finished' (Fig. 7.1).[2] Indeed, water permeates everything in the narrative. Ralegh laments that 'being al driuen to lie in the raine' and 'with the weete clothes of so many men thrust together' his situation was more unsavoury than any prison in England (16). Saturated by the Guianan aquascape, Ralegh recognizes the power that water has over his expedition, and, consequently, his narrative. Rivers both propel and thwart his progress, and the explorer frequently becomes lost even with the aid of native pilots. In a particularly harrowing moment, an Arwacan promises to bring Ralegh to the great Orenoque River, but he has been away too long to remember any of it. Ralegh recounts his close call:

> [A]nd if God had not sent vs another helpe, we might haue wandred a whole yeere in that laborinth of riuers, ere we had found any way, either out or in, especiallie after we were past the ebbing and flowing, which was in fower daies: for I know all the earth doth not yeeld the like confluence of streames and branches, the one crossing the other so many times, and all so faire and large, and so like one to another, as no man can tell which to take: and if we went by the Sun or compasse hoping thereby to go directly one way or other, yet that waie we were also caried in a circle amongst multitudes of Ilands, and euery Iland so bordered with high trees, as no man could see any further than the bredth of the riuer, or length of the breach. (36)

1 Several currents have moved this project along, for which I am thankful: the audience of the Southeastern Medieval Association conference in St Louis; friends and faculty at George Washington University, especially Jeffrey Jerome Cohen, Jonathan Gil Harris, and Jonathan Hsy; and the stream closest to me, Rock Creek.
2 *The Discoverie of the Large and Bewtiful Empire of Guiana*, ed. V. T. Harlow (London: Argonaut Press, 1928), 25. All quotes hereafter refer to the Harlow edition.

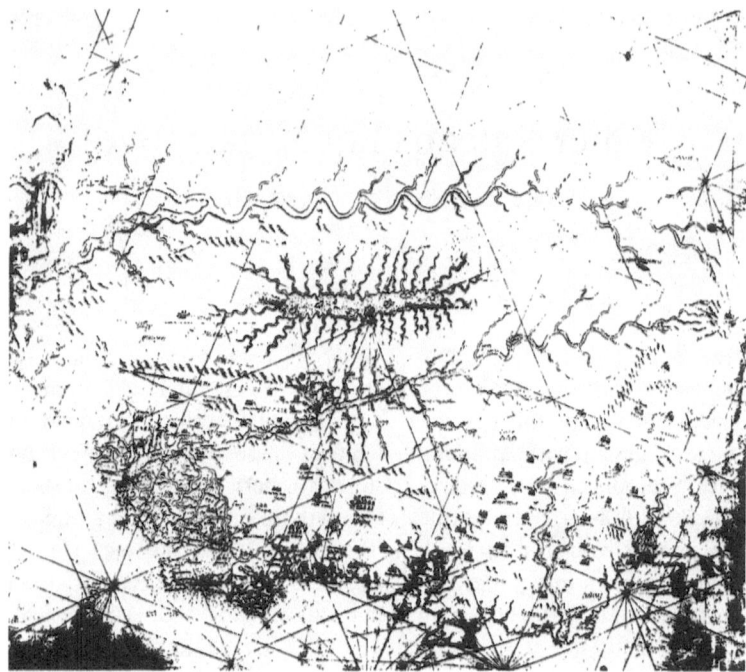

Figure 7.1 *A Map of Guyana, with the courses of the Orinoco and the Marañon, or Amazons; drawn about 1595 by Sir Walter Raleigh*, on vellum. British Library.

Ralegh here loses the reader in the labyrinthine prose of the *Discoverie*. Endless intersections – turbulent connections between 'confluences' and 'crossings' – disorient him; they beg a direction to take, although being so near one another no man can tell which direction or position to move. Instruments are ineffective, sight is limited, and the traveller endlessly circulates around self-repeating island 'multitudes'. This hapless spot of multiplicity would not seem ideal for an assuring English explorer like Ralegh who promises repeatedly to lead his readers and country to the promised gold of El Dorado. It seems that there is only fruitless labour in this labyrinth. Ralegh is Theseus without Ariadne, aimless and anti-heroic, utterly and hopelessly lost. Carried away by his effusive language, bested by the environment, he and his voyage fail.

Ralegh cannot afford to get lost at this juncture. His discomposure on the delta problematically exists within his narrative that guarantees, but never delivers, a navigable route to El Dorado. For Ralegh, the early 1590s were the nadir of a career that had blossomed the decade before.

He and his investors staked much in his discovery: the foray into Guiana was at once an effort to challenge Spanish interests, fill England's coffers, and regain the infinite favours of Elizabeth I that had ceased in 1592 after Ralegh secretly married one of her ladies-in-waiting, Elizabeth Throckmorton. Understandably, Ralegh's courtly detractors and (later) critics pointed out the discrepancy between a popular and engaging text on the one hand and, on the other, a serious investment in England's geopolitical interests that came up short. After all, this is the poet-explorer who not only describes bewildering jungle labyrinths and vast riches just beyond the horizon, but also 'verifies' the headless men of Mandeville's *Travels* (c. 1356), drinks from a poisonous pond that turns salubrious at midday, adds to the fable of the Amazons, and reiterates the stupendous accounts of his Spanish predecessors and native allies. In short, Ralegh's failed conquest and the *Discoverie*'s incredible anecdotes cost him dearly, muddying his reputation during and after his lifetime. David Hume's *History of England* (1754–63) provides the most caustic example: '[F]ull of the grossest and most palpable lies that were ever attempted to be imposed on the credulity of mankind'.[3] Ralegh's navigational blunder underscores what Hume regards as the author's chronic problem of credulity, then, and ultimately boils down to a simple exposure of Ralegh's 'extravagant' claims as lies (564). Despite Hume's huffing, several contemporaries like George Chapman redeemed Ralegh's overall failure in proto-imperialistic terms;[4] for the twentieth-century historian D. B. Quinn, Ralegh's enduring legacy is that he helped establish England's first territories in the New World.[5] What is more, for some critics Ralegh is less a father of colonialism

---

3 *The History of England*, 4 (New York: Harper and Brothers, 1864), 289, 564.
4 Composed shortly after Ralegh's voyage, *De Guiana, Carmen Epicum* (1596) anticipates England's grand course: '*Riches*, and *Conquest*, and *Renowme* I sing'. Chapman's commentary poem compares Ralegh to Jason. The '*Argolian* Fleet' should be sent forth by Elizabeth upon the '*Guianian Orenoque*': 'Then most admired Soueraigne, let your breath / Goe forth vpon the waters, and create / A golden worlde in this our yron age' (lines 14, 159, 161, 30–2). *The Poems of George Chapman*, ed. Phyllis Brooks Bartlett (New York: Modern Language Association of America, 1941), 353–7. Also see IV.xi of Edmund Spenser's *The Faerie Queene* (1590) in which the noble *Thame* and his train surpass the rivers of the world. The Amazon River is fit for taking: 'And shame on you, o men, which boast your strong / Annd valiant hearts, in thoughts lesse hard and bold, / Yet quaile in conquest of that land of gold' (IV.xi.22.3–5). *The Faerie Queene*, ed. Thomas P. Roche, Jr (London: Penguin, 1978).
5 *Raleigh and the British Empire* (New York: The Macmillan Company, 1949) is the standard account of 'tropical imperialism' (271). I generally avoid teleological and /or colonial readings in this chapter; the narrative's fluctuations and multiplicities, rather, are my focus. For a more straightforward historical approach, see Richard Schomburgk's edition (London: The Hakluyt Society, 1848). Benjamin Schmidt nicely balances historical readings and literary criticism in the introduction to his edition (Boston: Bedford /St. Martin's, 2008).

than a performer on a global stage, a new-historical paradigm of self-fashioning.[6] All this is to say that there are too few ways out of the slippery labyrinth that is the *Discoverie*: one reading demands that we view Ralegh as a self-conscious poet unjustly punished for his imaginations without material proof (the title page in fact tells of feats 'performed'); the other that we plot him in a neat teleology, one bend in the mighty river of history that culminates in the British Empire. Critical interpretation, like Ralegh himself, slips away like water held in a hand.

What are we to make of Ralegh's fluvial text, its numberless disorientations, the fluidic stage it creates? Rather than recuperate the *Discoverie* against failure, or somehow prove his extraordinary claims, or even *exit* the labyrinth, I want to pose a new question here: What happens if we stay *in* the labyrinth? How might disorientations actually prove useful to Ralegh? Realistically, we know that Ralegh needs, first, to explain away a lacklustre expedition and, second, to recruit potential Guianan investors. He never acquires the unlimited gold he promises. As a result, he embarks upon a flowing medium that keeps a crucial gap open between truth and fiction, subject and (golden) object, words and things – the rivers themselves. In other words, Ralegh incorporates the disorientating effects of the Guianan aquascape in order to maintain the unverifiability of *his own* account and thereby keep it current. Rather than present a stable trajectory from point to point, rivers always lead the explorer *elsewhere* off the map: just a little farther around the bend, Ralegh claims, is the gold of El Dorado. In turn, these aleatory water-routes without end grant the *Discoverie* its own multiplicity. Water floods the text, dispersing meaning(s) rather than foreclosing them. Ink and water do the same work; Ralegh depends on it. We should recall here that Ralegh was also known as 'Water' Ralegh; an aquatic avatar represented by an empty bucket sent to Elizabeth by a rival courtier, Christopher Hatton;[7] a moniker derived from his broad Devonshire vowels; and his Queen's personal term of endearment. Ralegh was akin to water, even obsessed with it, and in the *Discoverie* he flows like and with his text.[8] To be clear:

---

6 One of the most notable studies of Ralegh's 'selves' is by Stephen Greenblatt, *Walter Ralegh: The Renaissance Man and His Roles* (New Haven: Yale University Press, 1973). Greenblatt calls the first Guiana voyage 'theatricalism in action', a 'calculated performance' of propaganda that displays Ralegh's powers of self-fashioning and self-dramatization (99).

7 Simon Schama, *Landscape and Memory* (New York: Vintage Books, 1995), 307.

8 My current project expands on the ontological implications of (non)humans flowing together. Putting ecocriticism in conversation with actor-network modes of inquiry –

reconceiving 'Water' Ralegh and his text as liquid entities is not a way out of the text's difficulties, but rather a rediscovery of water's influence upon Ralegh's strategic process of deferral. Once we explore these fluvial traces, we learn that 'Water' is not just a nickname, but in fact a methodology.

Now let us re-enter that labyrinth with Ralegh's strategic liquidity in mind. The scene of endless connections between island chains and jungle streams transforms into something of narrative possibility rather than helplessness. 'Water' Ralegh's streamy recollections, and the *Discoverie* in general, orientate the reader in the direction of disorientation, just in time for Ralegh to extend his hand and guide the reader to the destination of his choice – just short of the riches of Manoa, just short of an *Ewaipanoma* village inhabited by headless men (as we will see). Ralegh loses his readers in order to bring them back out and follow him on successive enterprises. Failure, deferral – and here, disorientation – are advantageous 'directions' to take. In fact, Ralegh foresees his readers' responses. He treats his crew essentially like the readers of his narrative. None will continue to El Dorado, physically or in the imagination, 'had we not perswaded all the companie that it was but onlie one daies worke more to attaine the lande where we should be releeued of all we wanted, and if we returned that we were sure to starue by the way, and the world would laugh vs to scorne' (40). Ralegh pushes his crew, and his readers, to persevere with only one day's more effort (albeit repeatedly), against the scorn of the unbelieving world. To the crewman who cannot see any farther across the breadth of one river in the labyrinth of rivers, Ralegh offers his leadership. To the reader who cannot breach the similar gulf of scepticism in the narrative, he offers fellowship via his credible report of Guianan gold. Both offers operate on the clause of an indefinitely deferred gold – a contract written in water. 'Guiana' derives from the Indian word for 'water' (*guiana*);[9] like Ralegh's stream-like prose, its waters carry us to golden hordes that can be sought but never attained.

An objection might be made here: Why does not Ralegh simply close the critical distance rather than layer the *Discoverie* with ambiguities, missteps, and deferrals? Did he *want* to fail? In a poem written before

---

from the likes of Gilles Deleuze and Félix Guattari, Bruno Latour, and Michel Serres – I argue for *living* water, one actant within a burgeoning meshwork of subject-object alliances. 'Water' Ralegh is a metaphor for textual multiplicity; at the same time, he is a positive example of embodied becomings that are constantly in flow. The aquascape touches him, enters him, and moves him to new material connections that vibrate desire.

9 Schmidt, *Discovery*, 20.

1602, 'A Poesie to Prove Affection Is Not Love', Ralegh equates the goal of desire with the death of desire:

> Desire himselfe runnes out of breath,
> And getting, doth but gaine his death:
> Desire, nor reason hath, nor rest,
> And blinde doth sildome chuse the best,
> Desire attain'd is not desire,
> But as the sinders of the fire.[10]

Although the exact date of the poem is unknown, it is tempting to consider Ralegh composing the 'Poesie' after (or even during) the Guianan expedition of 1595. According to Ralegh, desire remains desire as long as it is constantly deferred. Similarly, Ralegh's desire for gold in the *Discoverie* is constituted, and given life, by deferral; to actually attain his golden object of El Dorado would put out the 'fire' – the death of the desires that animate his entire narrative. But knowing the mission *might* fail and *wishing* it to fail are not quite the same. Of course, Ralegh could finally reverse his fortunes by achieving (in his mind) the real gold. Surprisingly, he finds himself not at the mercy of a *lack* that he must sustain, but in the embrace of a desire that he must not allow to run out of breath. Thus Ralegh's perambulations do not prove his desire to fail as much as they point up the aquascape itself as a 'geography of desire' – a liquid place that keeps 'Water' Ralegh and his text *flowing* without rest.[11] Desire as movement, movement as desire: Ralegh searches the aquascape and discovers what Gilles Deleuze and Félix Guattari call the material process of connection.[12] True, his mission historically was a failure; he calls-in a liquid strategy of deferral to gloss over his deficiencies; and his hope for personal gain and reinstatement at court quickly dissolves. Yet the *Discoverie* is also a powerful example of connection at work: water, author, reader, and text are all embedded in desires that defer their completion. Avoiding the getting, these desires prefer to spill over and create new connections, and new meanings, instead. Ralegh might have wished for solid gold, but, in doing so, he demonstrates the pleasures of liquidity as well.

---

10 *The Poems of Sir Walter Ralegh*, ed. Agnes M. C. Latham (Boston: Houghton Mifflin, 1929), 41–2, lines 19–24.
11 See Alfred K. Siewers, *Strange Beauty: Ecocritical Approaches to Early Medieval Landscape* (New York: Palgrave Macmillan, 2009), 5. This chapter extends Siewers's groundbreaking study into early modern territory.
12 See Mark Bonta and John Protevi, *Deleuze and Geophilosophy, A Guide and Glossary* (Edinburgh: Edinburgh University Press, 2004), 76.

This chapter departs from its own slippery shoreline. Nevertheless, there are a few essential points of departure. (1) The aquascape of Guiana infuses the *Discoverie*, combining linguistic and fluvial forms of liquidity. As we saw above, the rivers animate Ralegh's rhetorical strategy; I call this process *liquid narrativity*. Ralegh's circulated story at court and his eventual publication known as the *Discoverie* reflect a double deferral: he widens the discursive gap between language and truth just as he widens the physical gap between himself and the Guianan gold. Yet rivers grant the narrative those meaning-flows that resist solidification. As pathways of desire without end, they also prevent Ralegh's (and his readers') desires from being extinguished. Hence liquidity is at once a literary trope (a metaphor for the multiplicity of language that keeps his narrative going) and a material manifestation (the physical touch of water). The liquid 'laborinth' is only one example. (2) Like an authorial riverbed of sorts, the *Discoverie* contains a series of fluctuating topographical layers. Liquid narrativity applies to the multitude of intertextual narratives Ralegh uses: a remarkable array of texts, voices, and multiple-hand accounts. Ranging from an Amerindian boy to Spanish histories, these other *liquid* narratives valuably sustain desire, for they allow the imagination to flow as Ralegh himself flows through the aquascape.[13] (3) Finally, in his attempts to create a credible narrative, Ralegh's discourse approaches a kind of authorial alchemy; just as alchemical knowledge depends upon ambiguity for its perpetuation, so too does the *Discoverie*. Ralegh as textual alchemist puts stories in motion. To consider the narrative as an alchemical text, to grant it that aspect of mysterious inventiveness and *liquid* knowledge, fittingly aligns it with the creative and prolific potential of the 'laborinth' with which we began. Far more than just a poetic exercise, financial cover-up, or colonial failure, 'Water' Ralegh's liquid narrative is an example of ecopoesis in action: the positive desires shared between, and inherent in, text and watery world. We cannot help being swept away by the *Discoverie*'s affirmative flows.

Our entrance entails a shift from solid to liquid. To be sure, Ralegh's investors demanded fiscal profits in addition to whatever imaginative

13 This is to depart slightly from Mary B. Campbell's influential reading of narrative in the *Discoverie* as that which establishes Ralegh as a protagonist and hence a powerful symbol of subjectivity. Ralegh's creation of new words in new worlds – the problem of writing experience – is a significant one. Here I focus on the words already available to Ralegh. If we travel with Ralegh, as Campbell argues, I argue that we also travel with many others, even nonhuman (watery) ones. *The Witness and the Other World: Exotic European Travel Writing, 400–1600* (Ithaca: Cornell University Press, 1988), 211–54, esp. 233–6.

ones he might provide. Unlike his Spanish competitor, Antonio de Berrío, the conquistador of Guiana, Ralegh only has the words of the *Discoverie*. Berrío 'dispatched his Campmaster for Spaine with all that he had gathered, therewith to leuy soldiers, and by the shew thereof to draw others to the loue of the enterprize' (33). The previous explorers of Guiana brought back numerous material goods. On his deathbed, Johannes Martines (Juan Martin de Albujar) donated to the Church the beads of gold from El Dorado, the sole pieces of the city's elusive treasure that he managed to protect from thieves. Domingo de Vera, taking possession of Guiana on Berrío's behalf, brought back 'diuers rarities which he carried to the *Spanish* king' and which were displayed in Seville to public amazement (24). Yet Ralegh brings hardly anything back. He tested a small quantity of Guianan ore, publicly believed to be fool's gold, which he assured his readers to be real in the *Discoverie*'s preface. This might be the same ore he sent to his patrons Sir Robert Cecil and Charles, Lord Howard again promising that 'wee tried them to be no *Marquesite*, and therefore such as the Spaniards call *El Madre del oro*, which is an vndoubted assurance of the generall abundance; and my selfe saw the outside of many mines of the white sparre, which I know to be the same that all couet in this worlde, and of those, more then I will speake of' (63–4). With only promises of a general abundance, how might Ralegh expect, like Berrío, to 'draw others to the loue of the enterprize'? How does Ralegh persuade his readers to become capital investors in multiple expeditions without material proof?

Interpellating his audience as fellow questers of the imagination for El Dorado, Ralegh treats them as potential capital investors who, like him, want to reach, and profit from, the promised golden end of his unfinished story – a task easier narrated than done. Ralegh can only imagine the gold as a future rather than present satisfaction. Repeatedly in the *Discoverie* the natives guarantee him a larger prize farther ahead: '[I]f wee entred the lande over the mountaines of *Curaa*, wee should satisfie our selues with golde and all other good things' (53). But this satisfaction remains endlessly deferred to an indefinite future: it is a promise that can never be realized. Eventually his desire for gold causes him to hallucinate about his surroundings: '[E]uery stone that we stooped to take vp, promised eyther golde or siluer by his complexion' (55). The mountains resemble nuggets of golden ore: '[W]e sawe al the hils with stones of the cullor of Gold and siluer' (63), Ralegh observes, but these gold and silver mountains remain on a distant horizon that he never reaches. Everywhere the Guianan landscape is a golden signifier of a perpetually deferred or distanced gold. When a Spaniard convinces him that one such stone promising gold or silver indicates an abundant mine underground ('*El Madre del oro*'), Ralegh moves on. Digging the mine would be the obvious choice in an effort to authenticate his report; Ralegh, however, utters promises instead:

> But it shall bee found a weak pollicie in mee, eyhter to betray my selfe, or my Countrey with imaginations ... were I not assured that the sunne couereth not so much riches in any part of the earth. (55)

Imaginations do not produce riches – but neither does Ralegh. Rather than attempting to close the ambiguous gap of language in his narrative between words (his report) and things (the gold), he keeps it open. When he finally locates mines he finds excuses to prevent digging: he claims that the mines are too well protected by hard stone; the rivers suddenly surge higher; or he lacks the necessary tools and men. Ralegh always aims for the metaphorical mother lode, El Dorado, rather than small profit. Indeed, he assures his readers that he could have brought back plentiful, but not extraordinary stores of gold 'if I had not shot at another marke, than present profit' (44).

Ralegh's solution in the *Discoverie*, here and elsewhere, is the liquidity of language. Liquid language distances signifiers from their signifieds and leads signifiers to other signifiers instead. Words, not just explorers, labour in the 'laborinth'. Mary Fuller, perhaps the sharpest reader of deferral in the narrative, considers El Dorado as the anchoring yet perpetually deferred referent in Ralegh's economic and linguistic fantasies. His expedition, she argues, is the search for a golden referent of language. When words might be tried against things he turns away from the aims of his discovery – to create a true report of Guiana – and gestures instead towards language itself: '[W]hat appears to be a turn away from language into "the concrete and everlasting world" dissolves into a multiple references back into the order of language'.[14] Fuller usefully illustrates how Ralegh's language actively militates against closing the gap between signs and their referents. These gaps are precisely the impediments writers faced when writing America, but in Ralegh's hands they are to be inhabited, exploited, and augmented. He inundates his readers with promises from the very first line of the dedication: 'For your Honours many Honourable and friendlie parts, I have hitherto onely returned promises'. Ralegh is astutely aware of the predicament facing him, therefore it is interesting that he concludes his narrative by extended his promise once more to

---

14 'Ralegh's Fugitive Gold: Reference and Deferral in *The Discovery of Guiana*', in *New World Encounters*, ed. Stephen Greenblatt (Berkeley: University of California Press, 1993), 218–40, here 223.

his readership: 'For the rest, which my selfe haue seene I will promise these things that follow and knowe to be true' (71). Ralegh heaps promises upon more promises. In fact, his repetition of 'more' bespeaks his supplementary intent, conspicuously rhyming with the absent 'ore' of his obsession. Whoever accepts Ralegh's offer and then journeys to Guiana will find there 'more rich and bewtifull cities, more temples adorned with golden Images, more sepulchers filled with treasure, then wither *Cortez* found in *Mexico*, or *Pazzarro* in *Peru*' (71).

Thus the 'weak pollicie' Ralegh argues against actually disguises his interest in imaginations as a useful policy. It is now clear that we should examine *how* Ralegh employs the multiple dissolutions of language, not whether he could actually tender his promises. Despite the persuasiveness of new economic critics like Fuller, however, I do not wish to explore the *Discoverie*'s historical-economic threads.[15] Instead, I seize upon the broader semiotic breakdown of language these critics observe in the *Discoverie* in order to magnify Ralegh's strategy of liquid narrativity – the waterways of words and ancillary narratives that propel his text. The *Discoverie*'s intertextuality is seldom addressed for any work it performs; what is more, the aquascape's active role goes unnoticed. Benjamin Schmidt's bibliographic study describes Ralegh's genres as active, meaning that they invite different processes of reading: 'It is not simply that the *Discovery of Guiana* streams its words along in a forceful rush of prose – the result, no doubt, of Ralegh's kinetic literary style and his imperative call (in this case) to colonial action. It is, further, the very bibliographic design of the volume' (472). Even with the thrust of Ralegh's prose which 'convey[s] the audience headlong' into subsequent passages, Schmidt focuses on the broader interplay between content and

15 As the (m)ore conflation might suggest, Ralegh weaves the economic and the linguistic together in order to suspend his deferred promises indefinitely. New economic theorists have explored the homologous relationship between gold and language. Jean-Joseph Goux views gold-language as the stable economy of signs, where each word is anchored by a real referent just as money's value is guaranteed by a gold standard. According to Goux, this model is superseded in the modern era by the system of token-language, more aptly described as the endless fungibility of signs: 'Gold money becomes a metaphor for the failure of the realist or representational system of language ... the linguistic order based on the gold value of language is headed for bankruptcy' (13). *The Coiners of Language*, trans. Jennifer Curtiss Gage (Norman, OK: University of Oklahoma Press, 1994). Similar-minded critics of the *Discoverie* point out Ralegh's linguistic economies. William West, for example, describes the credit Ralegh seeks as analogous to the early modern shift from gold as an autonomous signifier of value (a bullionist perspective) to gold as a representation of value, an absent elsewhere (a financial form of credit). See 'Gold on Credit: Martin Frobisher's and Walter Ralegh's Economies of Evidence', *Criticism* 39 (1997), 315–36.

form (473).[16] How the flowing content involved may guide the flow of form escapes his analysis. Shannon Miller's study of Ralegh's influential circle addresses the *Discoverie*'s stream-like composition. Miller argues that we reconsider Ralegh's patrons as a system of production. Effectively decentring Ralegh, she intriguingly returns to the literal meaning of 'influence' (*influere*: 'to flow in') to show how '[t]he 'flow-in' of other streams builds an ever-changing, ever-shifting inundation, allowing for the multiple influxes that necessarily comprise the artistic or intellectual project'.[17] Miller's study importantly describes a liquid process of narrative influence; this process touches not only Ralegh's personal circle but also the intertextual accounts that comprise his intellectual project.[18] Consequently, influence not only decentres Ralegh and the typical sites of power relations (like the new historical approaches to which Miller responds) but also disperses any investment in core meaning. Truth is equally unmoored by 'flows-in' and 'flows-out' of influence, and Ralegh was highly aware of the liquidity of language in this regard. Better yet, the energetic flows of the aquascape unmoor these relations in a physical sense. Sending Ralegh headlong, water 'streams [his] words'.

So far, our movement away from solid ground has introduced liquidity in the *Discoverie* as the integral, and influential, part of Ralegh's rhetorical strategy of deferral – a strategy that keeps the ambiguous gap open between language and truth and allows his and his readers' imaginations to profit creatively and (he hopes) financially. We may now gain a better starting point for Ralegh's watery words in and of the *Discoverie*. Where do the liquid narratives take him? Where do they take us? Ralegh truly loves stories; he begins in Trinidad surrounded by them. Although ostensibly

---

16 'Reading Ralegh's America: Texts, Books, and Readers in the Early Modern Atlantic World' in *The Atlantic World and Virginia, 1550–1624*, ed. Peter C. Mancall (Chapel Hill, NC: University of North Carolina Press, 2007), 454–88.
17 *Invested with Meaning: The Raleigh Circle in the New World* (Philadelphia: University of Pennsylvania Press, 1998), 2.
18 Joyce Lorimer's recent Hakluyt Society edition allows the reader to compare the discovered manuscript edition to the printed version of 1596. Her conclusion likewise distributes authorial agency: 'The [1596] version ... was not an unmediated account of his experiences in Guiana but rather a carefully edited version of them. The comparison ... demonstrates that the final product was not what Ralegh had wanted, but rather what already engaged investors ... felt it was advisable to publish' (xcv). I would consider Ralegh's questionable collaboration another instance of his narrative's liquidity. See Joyce Lorimer, ed., *Sir Walter Ralegh's* Discoverie of Guiana (London: The Hakluyt Society, 2006), esp. xxi–ii. She speaks specifically about editing and gold mines in *Untruth and Consequences: Ralegh's* Discoverie of Guiana *and the 'Salting' of the Gold Mine* (London: The Hakluyt Society, 2007).

at war with Spain, he invites several Spaniards on board to gather information. The same evening a small canoe of two Indians arrives, 'the one of them being a Casique or Lord of people called Cantyman', known to the English scout and Ralegh's predecessor Captain Whiddon (13). 'By this Cantyman wee vnderstood what strength the Spaniardes had, how farre it was to their Citie, and of Don Anthonio de Berreo the gouernour, who was said to be slain in his second attempt of Guiana, but was not' (13). Although this exchange might be read as Ralegh's compulsive disingenuousness and dissembling – he does, for example, disguise the reasons why he is in Guiana – it also indicates Ralegh's inexhaustible curiosity. He invites not just people but stories on board. Berrío later becomes a major voice in the *Discoverie*, saturating Ralegh's story with a vocality that is not wholly his own: for almost a third of the narrative Ralegh restates Berrío's failed attempts at penetrating the Guianan interior. And it is through Berrío that Ralegh reads Martines – supposedly the first European to see Manoa and responsible for the moniker 'El Dorado' – since Berrío conveniently has a copy of Martines's narrative (19). Indeed, the *Discoverie* is full of others' reports. However, the inclusion of these narratives is accompanied by a marked scepticism about their veracity. Ralegh, after all, double-checks Berrío's warnings about the unnavigable rivers he embarks upon.

In the midst of this scepticism is Ralegh's own search for El Dorado and the promise of its illimitable gold. The immediate problem facing him is that he must situate his narrative authority amidst these other, popular, Spanish stories. It may come as no surprise that Ralegh attempts to showcase his narrative superiority by downplaying his Spanish predecessors' accounts. Although Berrío's proceedings past and purposed are helpful (34), Ralegh carefully couches his authority in particularly nationalistic terms. In doing so, he might avoid (only momentarily) the accusations of dubiousness that beleaguer his report. Ralegh believes that whichever ruler conquers the Guianan empire will become the most prosperous in the world. At the same time, this ruler will eclipse the famed voyages of the conquistadores, even the King of Spain:

> I shall willingly spend my life therein, and if any else shalbe enabled thereunto, and conquer the same, I assure him thus much, he shall performe more than euer was done in *Mexico* by *Cortez*, or in *Peru* by *Pacaro*, whereof the one conquered the Empire of *Mutezuma*, the other of *Guascar*, and *Atabalipa*, and whatsoeuer Prince shall possesse it, that Prince shalbe Lorde of more gold, and of a more beautifull Empire, and of more Cities and people, then eyther the king of Spayne, or the great Turke. (16)

Ralegh reiterates this claim at the end of the *Discoverie* (we will see) in a final effort to gain Elizabeth's involvement and stymie the flow of Spanish specie. His passionate entreaty does not hesitate to speak about the profits of Guiana for the English body politic. Indeed, infinite riches await the conqueror. Here the quest for gold becomes a mission that serves the national interest. The discovery and acquisition of gold raises England to the ranks of her greatest rivals (with Ralegh assuredly skimming some benefits himself). His quest has a startling urgency:

> [I]f wee consider the many millions which are daily brought out of *Peru* into Spaine, wee may easely beleeue the same, for wee finde that by the abundant treasure of that countrey, the Spanish King vexeth all the Princes of Europe, and is become in a fewe yeares from a poore king of *Castile* the greatest monarke of this part of the worlde, and likelie euery day to increase, if other Princes forsloe the good occasions offered, and suffer him to adde this Empire to the rest, which by farre exceedeth all the rest: if his golde now indaunger vs, hee will then be vnresistable. (18–19)

Ralegh teaches a simple equation: increase England's store of gold and England increases its empire and dominion over others. Following Ralegh's logic, conquering Guiana and possessing its gold would then allow England to thwart, if not surpass, its European rivals. The *Discoverie* would undergo multiple translations in a short time. For his English audience, this last point sought to strike nationalistic chords in Ralegh's most powerful bureaucratic investors: his dedicatees Cecil and Lord Howard.

England's supersession of the Spanish King mirrors Ralegh's appropriation of Spanish narratives in the *Discoverie*. Ralegh admits that he possesses the correct knowledge of his surroundings. He is quick to predict the almost seamless transfer of territorial control from Spain to England: '[A]nd it seemeth to me that this Empire is reserued for her Maiestie and the *English* nation, by reason of the hard successe which all these and other *Spaniards* found in attempting the same, whereof I will speake brieflie, though impertinent in some sort to my purpose' (22). Ralegh might find it 'impertinent' to his purpose in the narrative, but his lengthy digressions of Spanish failures – the 'ends' and 'tragedies' of '*Oreliano, Ordace, Osua, Martynes,* and *Agiri*' (23), to name a few – are useful not only in projecting English superiority but also in illustrating his narrative as the rightful conveyor of that inheritance. When Ralegh describes how Berrío's unsuspecting company fell ill after drinking the reddish water of Amapaia, for instance, he simply asks the natives for assistance: '[T]hey told me that after the *Sun* was neere the middle of the skie, they vsed to fill their pots and pitchers with that water, but either before that time, or towards the setting of the *Sun* it was dangerous to drinke of, and in the night strong poison' (28). Berrío's company is decimated. Ralegh uses the Spaniards' drinking problem to shore up his gainful advantage as a narrator, learning 'diuers other riuers of that nature among them which were also ... verie safe to drink' and then pressing on (28).

Reiterating Berrío's narrative in the *Discoverie* gives Ralegh an excellent chance to one-up his rival. Like a sardonic commentator, Ralegh humiliatingly portrays Berrío as an amateur explorer completely disorientated: 'But [Berrío] knew not the names of any of these, but *Caroli* only, neither from what nations they descended, neither to what Prouinces they led, for he had no meanes to discourse with the inhabitants at any time: neither was he curious in these things, being vtterlie vnlearned, and not knowing the east from the west. But of al these I got som knowledge, and of manie more, partly by mine own trauel, and the rest by conference' (29).[19] Ralegh, of course, can emphasize his singular knowledge (the 'I') even while his knowledge is dependent upon his Indian interpreters: the old, the travelled, and the powerful chieftains of provinces and towns.[20] Berrío tries to dissuade Ralegh from this enterprise – natives will fly from Europeans, the rivers are impassable – but Ralegh enters anyway. He tests Berrío's 'unlearned' admonishments for himself. 'Many and the most of these I found to be true, but yet I resoluing to make trial of all whatsoeuer hapned' (34). It is clear that the 'I' of Ralegh is the end point of 'proceedings past and purposed'. Ralegh forges ahead, using the narrative pitfalls of others to establish the *Discoverie* as the authoritative report of the golden Guianan empire.

Here would be a suitable place to end our intertextual journey with 'Water' Ralegh: he uses Spanish accounts to his advantage, detailing their failed enterprises in order to gain support for his own expedition, shore up nationalistic sentiment (and even skirt the Black Legend), all

---

19 Ralegh's interest in local poison is also to this point: 'But I was more beholding to the *Guianians* than any other, for *Anthonio de Berreo* told me that he could neuer attaine to the knowledge thereof, and yet they taught me the best way of healing as wel thereof, as of al other poisons' (49).

20 For more on the role of the interpreters, see Alden T. Vaughan, 'Sir Walter Ralegh's Indian Interpreters, 1584–1618', *The William and Mary Quarterly* 59 (2002), 341–76. Vaughan considers Ralegh a figure of transculturation, 'the principal link ... between native interpreters and English overseas ventures'(375). Vaughan's intriguing essay describes Thomas Harriot's and Ralegh's successful attempts in language education, both in England and in the 'language lab' of the New World (375). Several natives stayed with Ralegh in his Thames-side mansion and two or more visited him in the Tower. The native boy, Cayowaroco, Topiawari's son, was one out of the approximately twenty natives attributed to Ralegh explorations.

the while providing a highly entertaining account. The greatest challenge to this satisfying conclusion is that, ultimately, Ralegh's expedition fails. He adds to the list of tragedies. The Spanish intertextuality, however, is a useful part of Ralegh's liquid narrativity. By correcting others' mistakes, disproving facts, and translating foreign texts, Ralegh establishes himself as an El Dorado encyclopaedia. Yet this knowledge must necessarily be incomplete if he is to keep flowing through the Guianan geography of desire. Always (un)certain of the gold's whereabouts, he travels just far enough to surpass his predecessors (save Martines), but just close enough to his goal without actually reaching it. Uncertainty ensures that he is never at a lack for movement; his material connections keep coming as a result: he leaves his readers with a partial discovery that thereby demands more enterprise, more imagination, more desire. The episode at Amapaia in fact underscores the relationship between deferred knowledge and intertextuality. Apprehending the brackish waters' daily transformation seems to solidify the *Discoverie*'s authority. But by ingesting these waters, 'Water' Ralegh goes with the flows that move his liquid narrative along endless paths and across newer horizons. Ralegh's immersion in the very stuff of his narrative could not be clearer.

Like the potable waters of Guiana, the hydrographical chart not yet finished confirms Ralegh's preference for liquid meaning over hardened forms of knowledge (Fig. 7.1).[21] Ralegh promises a map of Guiana, one to be viewed only under strictest secrecy after its completion: '[Y]our Lordship shall receiue in a large Chart or Map, which I haue not yet finished, and which I shall most humbly pray your Lordship to secret, and not to suffer it to passe your own hands' (25). Rivers are important in Guiana, but none so much as the Caroni regarded as the entrance to El Dorado. Significantly, the Caroni is the only river not mentioned on the map. Far from betraying Ralegh's reconnaissance anxieties, the absence of the Caroni on the map serves yet again to signal the gap between words and things Ralegh exploits – or in this cartological example, lines and things – since the Caroni's absence stands in for something which is supposedly there in the Guianan jungle, but only on the condition that the reader credits Ralegh with its route. He cannot fully draw the route to El Dorado for the primary reason that he could not realistically reach the city; nor could he possibly visit all the innumerable waterways of Guiana during his brief mission. Instead, his chart's 'not yet finished' areas are the terra

---

21 Harlow speculates that a chart circulated amongst friends and supporters of Ralegh after he returned to England, probably drawn by Harriot. Henry Percy received a map like the one described (25n).

incognita of the imagination. The chart keeps these imaginative routes flowing. Ralegh urges his readers to go along with him and visualize '[h]ow all these riuers crosse and encounter, how the countrie lieth and is bordred, the passage of *Cemenes*, and of *Berreo*, mine owne discouerie, and the way that I entred, with all the rest of the nations and riuers' (25). If there is room for error in Ralegh's authoritative chart, then, it is infinite space to be explored, inhabited, desired.

Although told years after the Guianan expedition, one final map scene from Ralegh's *History of the World* (1614) accentuates the *Discoverie*'s liquid narrativity. He remembers 'a pretty jest' told to him by a Spanish gentleman:

> The fictions (or let them be called conjectures) painted in maps do serve only to mislead such discoverers as rashly believe them, drawing upon the publishers either some angry curses or well deserved scorn; but to keep their own credit, they cannot serve always. To which purpose I remember a pretty jest of Don Pedro de Sarmiento, a worthy Spanish gentleman, who had been employed by his king in planting a colony upon the straits of Magellan: for when I asked him, being then my prisoner, some questions about an island in those straits, which methought might have done either benefit or displeasure to his enterprise, he told me merrily, that it was to be called the Painter's Wife's Island: saying, that whilst the fellow drew that map, his wife sitting by desired him to put in one country for her; that she, in imagination, might have an island of her own.[22]

To have an island of one's own undoubtedly evokes possession. Roland Greene describes the homology of fictions and islands in early accounts of imperial conquest that 'constitute[s] an especially prevalent ideologeme of the intersection between humanism and imperialism' and hence reads the wife's island as an example of 'a marker left by the powerful discourses at work in early modern writing' (8). Although Fredric Jameson's ideologeme is suitable for Greene's larger study of Petrarchan imperialism, Ralegh's fictions-islands are markers of a more humanistic fictitiousness, islands that are certainly not unrelated to discourses of imperialization but also islands that need not be inextricably moored to these historical delineations, either. As Ralegh suggests, to have an island of one's own is also to paint, to draw upon, to create.[23] Ralegh uses the anecdote to

---

22 Quoted in Roland Greene, *Unrequited Conquests: Love and Empire in the Colonial Americas* (Chicago: University of Chicago Press, 1999), 8.
23 In this regard, Ralegh uncannily prefigures Gonzalo in *The Tempest* (1611). Antonio and Sebastian chastise Gonzalo for his foolish imagination. What will he *not* think of? '*Sebastian*: I think he will carry this island home in his pocket, and give it his son for an apple. / *Antonio*: And sowing the kernels of it in the sea, bring forth more islands!'

address the question between fiction and truth that haunts his *History*;[24] and yet he describes conjectures in a tolerant, even amused tone. It is this play between fictions and truths that aligns the mapmaker with the Ralegh of the *Discoverie*. Even if islands-fictions cannot serve always they may still keep their 'credit' – a telling word relative to Ralegh's search for credibility in his narrative. This is not to say that fictions do not serve at all, but that Ralegh is best at putting questionable fictions into the service of his own deferral: his map of Guiana that must remain *unfinished* and *unknown*; the *unnamed* mapmaker and wife; and the second-hand report of the painter's story from, yet again, a Spanish source. Reading the islands of the *Discoverie* through the islands of the *History* demonstrates how Ralegh moves (us) around a Guiana populated by islands-fictions, an aquascape soaked with liquid language and narratives. Ralegh acts as both the painter and the painter's wife, proliferating and inhabiting islands of his own via that other telling phrase of the *Discoverie*: 'in imagination'.

Envisioning Ralegh as a kind of island-inventor grants him an impressive authorial agency, but it also ensures that this creativity is shared with the teeming waters around him. The multiplicity of language and the *Discoverie*'s 'multitudes of Ilands' flow together. Water rises higher and flows fiercer in the narrative, constantly washing the gold just beyond Ralegh's reach: 'And to say the truth all the branches and small riuers which fell into *Orenoque* were raised with such speed, as if wee waded them ouer the shooes in the morning outward, we were couered to the shoulders homewarde the very same daie' (43–4). Guiana's aqueous network blocks Ralegh's progress and yet transports him to new narrative possibilities as well. It is meaningful that Ralegh, immediately after describing his fluctuations in the 'laborinth', is taken to the tools of the *alchemical* trade. Like the mapmaker's canvas of creativity we noticed earlier, the aquascape now becomes a laboratory of language. Giving chase to four canoes coming downriver, Ralegh runs two of them ashore. One of the canoes is loaded with bread for trade. The other contains three Spaniards, 'who hauing heard of the defeat of their gouernour in *Trinedado*, and that we purposed

---

(II.i.89–92) Gonzalo's seeds engender islands and ideas in a liquid form (the sea) symbolic of the most fluidic medium of all – the imagination. Here, the infinite opportunity to sprinkle apple-seed islands in the mind and 'bring forth more islands' echoes the infinite possibilities and trajectories similar to Ralegh's rivers. Quotation is from *The Norton Shakespeare*, ed. Stephen Greenblatt et al., 2nd edition (New York: W. W. Norton, 2007).

24 For an introduction to the early modern period's gradual separation (if we may call it so) between fiction and truth, see William Nelson, *Fact or Fiction: The Dilemma of the Renaissance Storyteller* (Cambridge, MA: Harvard University Press, 1973).

to enter *Guiana*, came away in those *Canoas*: one of them was a *Cauallero*, as the Captaine of the *Arwacas* after told vs, another a soldier, and the third a refiner' (42). Creeping around the bushes by the abandoned canoes, Ralegh makes a fascinating discovery: 'I saw an Indian basket hidden, which was the refiners basket, for I found in it, his quicksiluer, saltpeter, and diuerse things for the triall of mettals, and also the dust of such ore as he had refined, but in those *Canoas* which escaped there was a good quantity of ore and gold' (43).

Ralegh inexplicably knows the contents of the lost canoe but chooses not to pursue. Fuller notes that the canoe chase typifies the scene of discovery in the narrative – another example of the simultaneous search for the referent and the desire for distance between words and things.[25] But the other metals discovered by Ralegh should not be overlooked, especially since alchemy was an intimate subject to him. Elizabeth was known for sponsoring alchemical experimentation and mineral works in the latter part of her reign. It was during this time that Ralegh developed a reputation as a 'chymist' – his library contained seventeen works on chemistry and medicine – and according to the seventeenth-century biographer John Aubrey he 'studied most in his sea voyages, where he carried always a trunk of books along with him'. John Hester dedicated a book of medicines to him under the pseudonym, no less, of the Renaissance polymath Paracelsus. His close circle included alchemical dabblers: Henry Percy 'the wizard Earl', Thomas Harriot, and even his faithful Captain Keymis. After his return, Ralegh brewed a Balsam of Guiana with famous powers (he allegedly cured Queen Anne's fever) and continued to brew alchemical concoctions in the Tower of London during his imprisonment there.[26]

It is amusing to imagine Ralegh brushing up on his alchemy during the long voyage of 1595, but his chemical background proves more

25 Mary C. Fuller, *Voyages in Print: English Travel to America, 1576-1624* (Cambridge: Cambridge University Press, 1995), 66.
26 See Katherine Eggert, 'The Alchemist and Science', in *Early Modern English Drama: A Critical Companion* (Oxford: Oxford University Press, 2006), 208. Her contribution to the volume is a notable introduction to alchemy in the period (200-12). Ralegh built his own chemical still and left behind a collection of chemical and medical recipes. Charles Nicholl's chapter on the balsam provides a quick overview. *The Creature in the Map: A Journey to El Dorado* (New York: William Morrow, 1995), 278-87. Walter Oakeshott catalogues Ralegh's impressive library, including his alchemical works, in 'Sir Walter Ralegh's Library', *Library* 23 (1968), 285-327, see 288. Deborah Harkness's recent work on 'Big Science' in Elizabethan England traces the connections between mining, alchemy, and royal patronage, implicating the emergent adventures to the New World and those close to Ralegh: Robert Dudley, Humphrey Gilbert, and William Cecil. See *The Jewel House: Elizabethan London and the Scientific Revolution* (New Haven: Yale University Press, 2007), 169-80.

consequential when we take into account the *Discoverie*'s composition. The discarded bit of refiner's quicksilver unites his arcane interests with his rhetorical strategy in the narrative, thereby transforming him into a kind of alchemical author. Alchemy depends on obscurity and deferred knowledge passed down from master to apprentice. Lee Patterson's work on alchemy in Chaucer's *Canon's Yeoman's Tale* defines this knowledge as a negative knowledge, or 'the logic of the supplement'.[27] In short, instead of closing the gap between word and thing, language and truth, alchemy operates on multiplication, substitution, and excess; as a result, meaning is always in motion: 'the disclosure of an original meaning becomes the multiplication of meanings; as each signified is revealed to be only another signifier, the act of revelation becomes itself a concealment' (35). To speak the truth of alchemy would deprive it of its efficacy. Hence, the truth becomes unsayable. Moreover, alchemical writers often promise to clarify the obscurities or failures of other alchemists (40). Lastly, alchemy markedly affects concepts of self-representation since it pushes the practitioner to near-theatrical heights. As a result, the endlessly multiplied revelations (concealments, really) turn into acts of *self*-revelation. The Yeoman's self is left equally in motion, unmoored, 'his language multiplying itself – proliferating uncontrollably – yet never finally grasping the essence it seeks. The more he talks about the self that so fascinates him, the more dispersed it becomes, leaving him a cipher, an absence, a desire – a being who seeks rather than an object sought' (39).

Ralegh's *Discoverie* is a striking analogue to the Chaucerian example: to reach El Dorado would effectively immobilize his narrative. The truth of the matter must be unknowable. Ralegh's derision of previous explorers and his pronouncements of superior knowledge recall the competitive nature of alchemists. And quicksilver, the alchemical 'translator' par excellence, importantly adds translation and mediation into the narrative mix. Ralegh remarkably copies, and translates, a large section of Francisco Lopez de Gomara's 'generall historie of the Indies'.[28] Thus the 'triall of metals' in the riverside brush symbolizes the transmutation of his narrative into the narrative gold of El Dorado and the approval of the reading public. Just as the Yeoman, Ralegh's trademark performativity and desire for gold certainly categorize him as a being who seeks across the Guianan landscape. Perhaps unlike the Yeoman, though, Ralegh revels in this self-mobility, using it to his advantage as he pursues

---

27 Lee Patterson, 'Perpetual Motion: Alchemy and the Technology of the Self', *Studies in the Age of Chaucer* 15 (1993), 35.
28 Author of *Cronica de Indias* and *Historia de la Conquista de Neuva-España* (1552–53).

an 'object [infinitely] sought'. Understanding Ralegh's watery language as an alchemical discourse in the *Discoverie* – with its inherent multiplicities, translations, supplements, and ambiguous gaps – reveals Ralegh-as-Hermes's intent to layer language upon language, promise upon promise, in the hope of attracting future investors to his Guianan enterprise. Like the coiling confluences of the Guianan rivers, mercury and its diverse things symbolize the narrative's boundless diversities and multiplications of meaning. Alchemy's liquid knowledge parallels his narrative's liquid language – truth keeps on slipping.

I have traced the pathways of liquid narrativity as far as possible (for now): the liquidity of language, as it relates to intertextuality and Ralegh's rhetorical strategy of deferral; the liquid aquascape, as much as it emanates desire and thus perpetuates his movement; and liquid knowledge, as much as the narrative, like an alchemical text, prefers (un)certainty, dispersion, and multiplicity over the stultifications of truth. As a kind of open-ended closure, and thus taking a cue from Ralegh, I turn to perhaps one of the most imaginative digressions of the *Discoverie*. Ralegh departs from his golden observations late in the text – shortly after his meditation on 'weak pollicie' – and tells a story about Guiana's headless men, the *Ewaipanoma*, who are straight from the pages of Mandeville: an 'ugly folk ... who have eyes in each shoulder; their mouths are round, like a horse-shoe, in the middle of their chest'.[29] He never encounters them; instead, a native boy informs Ralegh about them on the journey back to England:

> [B]ut it was not my chaunce to heare of them til I was come away, and if I had but spoken one word of it while I was there, I might haue brought one of them with me to put the matter out of doubt. Such a nation was written of by *Maundeuile*, whose reportes were held for fables many yeares, and yet since the East *Indies* were discouered, wee finde his relations true of such thinges as heeretofore were held incredible. (56–7)

Unfortunately, the notice comes too late. Mandeville's *Travels* (c. 1356) provided author-explorers with not only a useful epistemological frame-

29 *The Travels of Sir John Mandeville*, trans. C. W. R. D. Moseley (1983; rpt, London: Penguin, 2005), 137. Mandeville resurfaces as '[o]ur great traveller' in the *History*, 'who died in the year 1372, and had seen so much of the world, and of the East India, we accounted the greatest fabler of the world; yet had he another reputation among other nations, as well able to judge as we. Witness the monument made of him in the convent of the friars Guillimins in Liege, where the religious of that place keep some things of his, *comme pour honourable mémoire de son excellence*, "for an honourable memory of his excellency", saith Guichardine'. *The Works of Sir Walter Ralegh, Kt.*, 5 (Oxford: Oxford University Press, 1829), 373.

work for planning their voyages but also a means to verify their own extraordinary descriptions. Ralegh certainly read Mandeville; his library demonstrates his avid reading, and he famously toted books with him on his numerous adventures.[30] There were sceptics, too, of course. By the early modern period, the *Travels* could just as easily be viewed as spurious popular fiction rather than unequivocal fact.

Ralegh characteristically prefers to keep the matter of the *Ewaipanoma* doubtful, leaving conspicuously unanswered the question of whether or not the monstrous nation exists. It is here that we arrive at the *Discoverie*'s supreme moment of intertextuality, for his reference to 'Maundeuile' draws on all three branches of liquid narrativity that I have been tracing in this chapter. By ushering in the *Travels*, Ralegh demonstrates his larger endeavour in the *Discoverie* to blur the boundaries between fiction and fact. The fluvial aspects of Mandeville's narrative – its unattainable realms, vast riches, strange creatures, and fluid pathways – grant the *Travels* an infinite capaciousness that is useful to a liquid writer like 'Water' Ralegh who seeks the same limitlessness for his own narrative. Ralegh alludes to this capacity immediately after his chance to capture an *Ewaipanoma*. Although both accounts – the native boy's and Mandeville's – would seem to corroborate the existence of the headless men, Ralegh notes his inability to resolve the matter once and for all:

> [W]hether it be true or no the matter is not great, neither can there be any profit in the imagination, for mine owne part I saw them not, but I am resolued that so many people did not all combine, or forethinke to make the report. (57)

It is not worth trying to pinpoint the existence of the headless men (how could I?) with anthropological guesswork.[31] There is much more to gain by Ralegh's confession. The profit in the imagination he alludes to emphasizes the profits in the imagination Ralegh and his narrative acquire by incorporating the narratives of others. His imagination profits ('progresses')

---

30 Ralegh owned a 1485 edition of Mandeville. See Oakeshott, 'Sir Walter Ralegh's Libary', 320.
31 For an extensive anthropological discussion of the *Discoverie*'s various ethnographies and ethnologies, see Neil Whitehead's edition (Norman, OK: University of Oklahoma Press, 1997). His 'positive anthropological re-evaluation' speaks the longest about the headless men, acknowledging Ralegh's reference as an important example of 'collected cultural meaning' between natives and Europeans (94, 13). Whitehead concludes by claiming, 'Paradoxically then, it is Ralegh's overt, comparative ethnographic allusion to Mandeville's account of the *Acephali* that distorts rather than clarifies his implicit ethnographic observation of a native trope of "acephalism"' (93). I illuminate this paradox by focusing on the usefulness of this 'distortion' to the narrative.

endlessly down the rivers that drive him and his desire for Guianan gold (*OED*).[32] Like the fabled gold of El Dorado, the acephali are to be taken at Ralegh's watery word;[33] they represent an absence Ralegh pushes his readers to imagine and believe. The *Travels* generate the biggest profit for the *Discoverie*: they ensure that Ralegh's unauthenticated liquid text ceaselessly progresses, thereby carrying his and his readers' imaginations and desires to possibilities untold. Whether the headless men be 'true or no' is not the issue for an explorer who revels in the splashy middle space between these two choices. To be fair, liquid narrativity up to this point has always involved Ralegh's profiting-progressions. Yet Mandeville offers Ralegh the most forceful direction to take: an undertow of imagination that leads in multiple directions at once.

Although nearly all of Ralegh's intertextual moments in the *Discoverie* come at strategic moments, the position of Mandeville's 'matter' in the narrative is particularly meaningful. Told about them on the way home, Ralegh's failure to bring back an *Ewaipanoma* calls to mind his larger failure to bring back the promised gold. And still Ralegh continues to speak; he does not end his descriptions of the *Ewaipanoma* at this expected point. Instead, he adds yet another story. Ralegh describes his story-swapping with a Spaniard in Trinidad:

> When I came to *Cumana* in the west *Indies* afterwards, by chaunce I spake with a spanyard dwelling not farre from thence, a man of great trauell, and after he knew that I had ben in *Guiana*, and so farre directlie west as *Caroli*, the first question he asked me was whether I had seene anie of the *Ewaipanoma*, which are those without heades: who being esteemed a most honest man of his word, and in all thinges else, told me that he had seen manie of them: I may not name him because it may be for his disaduantage, but he is well known to *Monsier Mucherons* sonne of London, and to *Peter Mucheron* marchant of the *Flemish* shipp that was there in trade, who also heard what he auowed to be true of those people. (57)

---

32 I treat 'profit' as a multivalent term, as it would have been to Ralegh as he composed the *Discoverie*. See senses 1, 3, 4, and 5 in the *OED*: a favourable circumstance or condition; a material benefit; progress, advancement; a financial gain.

33 Ralegh briefly mentions another strange nation from Mandeville, the Amazons, during his conversation with Berrío. Unlike the headless men, however, Ralegh tries harder to keep the matter of the Amazons *out of* doubt: '[B]icause of some it is beleeued, of others not: And though I digresse from my purpose, yet I will set downe what hath been deliuered me for truth of those women' (26). All previous accounts match up except for the Amazons' fabled mastectomy: this ritual, according to Ralegh, 'I do not finde to be true' (27). Although Ralegh is more authoritative regarding the 'truth' of the Amazons (and hence less effective, I think), both nations serve the same strategic purpose.

This anecdote is another example of Ralegh's characteristic turning away from the chance to confirm reports. He has the opportunity to seek the parties involved, but Peter, like Mandeville and Ralegh, is a man of travel, and presumably the Flemish ship has set sail, making that merchant's story impossible to verify. Ultimately, Ralegh's liquid narrative is never wholly his. These stories of the headless men are always in the process of (re)telling – one may hear about them, but never verify their existence. More importantly, they are transnational, carried to far-off places (by merchant vessels) and spoken in different tongues (Spanish, Flemish). These liquid stories are narrative slipstreams that purposefully defer the truth of the *Discoverie*. Almost expectedly, Ralegh *moves on* after he mentions the Flemish ship. His next topic is rivers, no less: geographical musings about the river west of Caroli, the Casnero, and the numerous points of interest beyond it. As with the relentless promises of gold yet to be found, Ralegh speaks of stories left behind and stories left untold, gesturing towards those 'profit[s] in the imagination' waiting to be told. And it is this mobility and emphasis on motion that ultimately aligns his text with the process of alchemy. Ralegh's *Discoverie* is about putting stories in motion, of supplementing stories with stories, like the endless motion of a traveler drifting down (un)navigable rivers towards an infinitely deferred goal.

Ralegh's alchemical motion continues until the end of the *Discoverie* when he finally turns to Elizabeth, his most important reader. Ralegh compares his offering of Guiana to Columbus's offering of the Indies to Elizabeth's grandfather, Henry VII:

> The west Indies were first offered her Maiesties Grandfather by *Columbus* a straunger, in whome there might be doubt of deceipt, and besides it was then thought incredible that there were such and so many lands and regions neuer written of before. This Empire is made knowen to her Maiesty by her own vassal, and by him that oweth to her more duty then an ordinary subiect, so that it shall ill sort with the many graces and benefites which I have receaued to abuse her highnes, either with fables or imaginations. (74–5)

Intriguingly, Ralegh's blandishment echoes his earlier reference to Mandeville: '[W]ee finde his relations true of such thinges as heeretofore were held incredible' rings similar to 'and besides it was then thought incredible that there were such and so many lands and regions neuer written of before'. By way of association, Ralegh likens himself not only to Columbus, as they both offer gifts to English sovereigns, but also to Mandeville since both Mandeville and Columbus told tales of incredible lands and regions hitherto unknown in writing. Ralegh's promise, one of his last, is noteworthy more for its astonishing transmutations of narrative than it is for its personal poignancy. Fuller, for instance, ultimately posits Ralegh's deferral as a reaction to his tumultuous relationship with Elizabeth. The profit of deferral, Fuller argues, is the deferral of sexual violence: Guiana maintains its 'maidenhead'.[34] I wish to expand on Fuller's point, for I find the profit in the imagination crucially evoked in this scene, just as Mandeville's spirit, like Columbus's, is similarly invoked. Mandeville returns one last time. Ralegh attempts to re-establish credit with Elizabeth by stressing his duty as her own vassal who thereby lacks all cause for deceit. Once more Ralegh seemingly equates 'imaginations' with a betrayal to self and country, an abrogation of duty and an inconceivable abuse of his Queen. Yet his narrative, operating as it does on deferral and an endless desire that can never be closed, requires these same imaginations to endure. Ralegh requires the stories he plants in his readers' minds to profit and increase, enlisting them as potential investors in his next adventure. Incorporating Mandeville, in the end, amplifies those profits in the imagination Ralegh truly desired for his liquid narrative – nonabusive, prolific, credible – indeed, pleasurable.

It is this same simultaneous disavowal and employment of the imagination that exposes Ralegh's hope for the *Discoverie* to profit in the imaginations of others. At the same time, Ralegh's task of inventiveness configures him as a type of alchemical writer, a liquid narrator who willingly takes up the *Travels*' potentiality. Unfortunately for Ralegh, he continually struggled to find the type of credit he sought, finally executed by James I on a trumped-up treason charge after returning empty-handed from his second voyage to Guiana in 1617. The *Discoverie* was stupendously popular, however, undergoing numerous publications and translations shortly after its 1596 publication.[35] Fittingly, water energizes its afterlives. One of the *Discoverie*'s first editors, Robert Schomburgk, wistfully describes the oozy relationship between aquascape and imagination in his preface to the 1848 Hakluyt Society edition: 'Every page, nay almost every sentence, awakened past recollections, and I felt in imagination transported once more into the midst of the stupendous scenery of the Tropics. As Her Majesty's Commissioner to survey the boundaries of British Guiana, I explored in 1841 that wondrous delta of the Orinoco' (vii). Visiting Ralegh's text prompts Schomburgk's revisitation to Guiana

---

34 *Voyages*, 235.
35 For more on the *Discoverie*'s textual afterlives, see Schmidt, 'Reading', 454–509.

in his imagination. This image of a poetic journey jars against the image of a man of science and geography sent to explore a region during the height of the British Empire, an empire he recalls Ralegh also helped build. (He amuses himself by thinking about the inchoate empire of the early seventeenth century.) Schomburgk discovers that the wondrous delta that invigorated Ralegh also enlivens his own personal narrative – both explorers are caught in its deluge of desires that liquid narrativity affirms.

Where do we, like 'Water' Ralegh, flow from here? During his stay in the Tower from 1603 to 1616, Ralegh could not stop thinking about water. He even wrote about his aquatic other self in the *History*, comparing humankind to a watery network: the 'blood which disperth itself by the branches or veins through all the body, may be resembled to these waters which are carried by brooks and rivers overall the earth'.[36] And he surely thought about Guiana as he described the great rivers of antiquity in the same work, maybe pausing now and then to remember the river garden he planted around his home at Sherborne Castle on the Yeo River. Ralegh had an intimate relationship with aquascapes closer to home. A fastidious gardener at Sherborne, Ralegh owned approximately fourteen thousand acres of land. Dotting the landscape were red cedars supposedly grown from seeds brought back from Virginia. He cleared and planted Black Marsh, for instance, spending much time and money, according to Sir John Harington, 'drawing the river through rocks into his garden'.[37] Admittedly, the Tower is an unlikely stop along our aquatic journey; its rigidity seems only to dam possibilities, not permit them. Ralegh had learned in 1595, though, that the road to El Dorado is not a solid road of conquest but a convergence of fluvial pathways, liquid trajectories of imagination and desire. And he held on to this lesson. Listed among his last possessions in the Tower are a 'stob' of gold, possibly a gift from the sage Guianan leader Topiawari, and a description of the River Orenoque.[38] It is fascinating, at last, to consider the investment Ralegh placed in his own imagination during his last days, clasping the solidity of a golden object, but flowing, nevertheless, with the Orenoque.

---

36 *The Works of Sir Walter Ralegh, Kt.*, 2 (Oxford: Oxford University Press, 1829), 59.
37 Quoted in Nicholl, *The Creature*, 45–6.
38 In a letter written from Thomas Naunton, Secretary of State, to Thomas Wilson is an 'inventory of such things as were found on the body of Sir Walter Rawleigh, Knight, the 15th day of August, 1618'. The inventory was compiled shortly after Ralegh's failed escape attempt from the Tower. See Schomburgk's edition, 228.

8

Ralegh, Harriot, and Anglo-American ethnography

Alden T. Vaughan

If Sir Walter Ralegh can legitimately be called 'the father of the British Empire', he is with comparable accuracy 'the father of Anglo-American Ethnography'. ('Ethnography' here means extensive, informed descriptions of a people and their culture; 'Anglo-American' encompasses English writings about America, whether composed on the scene or in Europe.) A case can be made that Thomas Harriot was the first major English ethnographer because his *Briefe and True Report of the New Found Land of Virginia* appeared eight years before Ralegh's *Discoverie of the Large, Rich and Bewtiful Empire of Guiana* and is in most respects a better ethnographic work,[1] but without Ralegh's intercession, I contend, Harriot almost certainly would never have written his book. It was Ralegh, whose royal patent of 1584 led to the first English venture in Virginia (a label that applied, at the time, to the whole North Atlantic seaboard between Florida and Canada), and who appointed the accomplished scientist and 'servant' in Ralegh's household, Thomas Harriot, to study the region's natives, natural resources, and geography. It was Ralegh who also, implicitly if not explicitly, directed Harriot to compile the *Briefe and True Report* to counteract criticism of England's first settlement on the southern Virginia coast. And the most widely disseminated version of Harriot's *Report* – the illustrated edition published in 1590 by the Flemish engraver Theodor de Bry – was dedicated by de Bry to Sir Walter in a

1   Thomas Har[r]iot, *A Briefe and True Report of the New Found Land of Virginia* (London: [Printed by Robert Robinson,] 1588). In this chapter I use the second edition, published at Frankfort, 1590, because of its wider circulation and, most important, its inclusion of the John White illustrations and Harriot's captions, as reprinted in facsimile by Dover Publications, 1972. Similarly, rather than the original edition of Walter Ralegh, *The Discoverie of the Large, Rich and Bewtiful Empyre of Guiana ... Performed in the Yeere 1595. By Sir W. Ralegh Knight* (London: Printed by Robert Robinson, 1596), I use the most recent, most thoroughly annotated, and most accurately transcribed edition: *Sir Walter Ralegh's Discoverie of Guiana*, ed. Joyce Lorimer (London: Ashgate, for the Hakluyt Society, 2006).

lavish frontispiece, featuring Ralegh's coat of arms, in recognition that *'this little Booke'* is *'a thinge which by reigtte dooth allreadey apparteyne unto you'*.[2]

Six years after the publication of that edition (i.e., in 1596), Ralegh made his own contribution to an emergent English-language ethnography in the *Discoverie of Guiana*. Neither that book nor Harriot's *Briefe and True Report* was primarily a descriptive account of the natives in their respective areas of culture contact, but both authors devoted far more attention to Indian bodies, customs, and beliefs than had their countrymen before them. Several Spanish writers, to be sure, had written extensively about the peoples they encountered in areas of Spanish conquest, and a few early French efforts at ethnography survive.[3] But until Harriot described the Indians of Roanoke Island and vicinity, Englishmen had written very sparsely about the natives of the so-called 'New World'.

Captain George Best's account of Sir Martin Frobisher's three voyages to Baffin Island in the 1570s is partly an exception to, and partly an example of, early modern England's sparse interest in ethnography. Best's *True Discourse of the Late Voyages of Discoverie for the Finding of a Passage to Cathaya* was published in 1578; in 1600 Richard Hakluyt reprinted it with minor variations in *Principal Navigations ... and Discoveries of the English Nation*.[4] Although Best addressed a wide variety of topics as he described Frobisher's experiences in northeastern Canada, by and large he limited his remarks about the indigenous populations to incidents in which they could not be ignored – for example, exchanges of goods, skirmishes, kidnappings (of natives by Englishmen or Englishmen by

2 The quotation is from Harriot, *Briefe and True Report*, 3–4. In this and other quotations in this chapter I have retained the spelling of the original except for i /j and u /v, which are changed to modern usage. Harriot's career is recounted in several biographies, most notably John W. Shirley, ed., *Thomas Harriot: Renaissance Scientist* (Oxford: Clarendon Press, 1974), especially the chapters by Shirley on 'Sir Walter Ralegh and Thomas Harriot' (16–35) and by David B. Quinn on 'Thomas Harriot and the New World' (36–53); and John W. Shirley, *Thomas Harriot: A Biography* (Oxford: Clarendon Press, 1983).

3 For Spanish ethnography, see, for example, Francisco López de Gómara, *Historia General de las Indias* (Saragossa: Guillermo de Mills, 1552); French discussions include André Thevet, *Les Singularities de la France Antarctique* (Paris: Christophe Plantin, 1558). And see more generally Anthony Pagden, *The Fall of Natural Man: The American Indian and the Origins of Comparative Ethnology*, rev. ed. (Cambridge: Cambridge University Press, 1986).

4 George Best, *A True Discourse of the Late Voyages of Discoverie, for the Finding of a Passage to Cathaya* (London: Printed by Henry Bynnyman, 1578); reprinted in Richard Hakluyt, *The Principal Navigations Voyages Traffiques & Discoveries of the English Nation*, 3 vols (London: Printed by George Bishop, Ralph Newberie, and Robert Barker, 1598–1600), 3:47–96.

natives) – where Best's ethnographic comments are brief and utilitarian. Only at the end of his book, as an apparent afterthought, does Best give his readers 'a generall and briefe Description of the Countrey, and the condition of the people'. In the 1578 edition of the *True Discourse*, the ethnographic epilogue occupies only six quarto pages in a tract of nearly 175.[5] Several other English authors who chronicled the Frobisher expeditions less extensively than did Best also contributed little to England's understanding of Baffin Island's natives and their culture,[6] although one can glean a sense of English ambivalence toward cultural strangers from these early efforts.

A more concise example of England's seeming indifference to New World ethnography is Sir George Peckham's *True Report of ... the Newfound Landes* (1583), which mentions the natives' cannibalism, human sacrifice, and 'continuall warres' as justifications for English domination but makes no effort to describe the various native societies and cultures. Rather, Peckham wants his readers to understand that Indians as well as Englishmen will benefit – commercially, politically, and spiritually – from the expansion of Christian Europe. Native culture need not be described, Peckham implied, because it was inferior to the Europeans' and would soon be extinguished.[7] Five years later, Harriot would present a different standard of ethnography based on different assumptions.

Because Ralegh's and Harriot's first task in the English colonization of America was to promote investment in the Roanoke Island outpost and, more broadly, to kindle English enthusiasm for overseas settlement, the *Briefe and True Report* does not begin with ethnography. Rather, the whole first section presents information for investors in search of quick profits, principally the 'merchantable commodities' of the Roanoke region of the Atlantic Coast that could readily be harvested or extracted and shipped to England or Continental Europe: silk grass, flax, hemp, turpentine, timber,

---

5 The three parts of Best's *True Discourse*, each devoted to one of Frobisher's voyages, are separately paginated. The section on the natives of '*Meta Incognita*' appears on 60–6 (third pagination); on the book's final three pages Best describes fauna and meteorological matters.

6 See Dionyse Settle, *A True Reporte of the Laste Voyage* [i.e., the second] *into the West and Northwest Regions ... by Capteine Frobisher* (London: Henrie Middleton, 1577); Thomas Churchyard, *A Prayse and Reporte of Maister Martyne Forboishers Voyage to Meta Incognita* (London: Andrew Maunsell, 1578); Thomas Ellis, *A True Report of the Third and Last Voyage into Meta Incognita* (London: Thomas Dawson, 1578).

7 George Peckham, *A True Reporte, of the Late Discoveries and Possession, Taken in the Right of the Crowne of Englande, of the Newfound Landes: by that Valiaunt and Worthye Gentleman, Sir Humphrey Gilbert Knight* (London: Printed by I. C. for John Hinde, 1583), especially sigs C3v–C4, F2v–F3.

animal skins, and the era's cure-all, sassafras – to name but a few of the enticing possibilities. Yet even in this section of the *Briefe and True Report* Harriot reveals some details of native life, such as the Indians' application of dyes made from roots and bark (potentially useful to the English cloth industry) to their hair and faces, and the absence from coastal Virginia of copper and silver ore but the Indians' acquisition of ornaments made of those metals from hundreds of miles inland.[8] Such information told readers something about the Indians while hinting at economic possibilities at Roanoke and farther west.

Potential colonists were another crucial audience for Harriot's tract. Without a substantial population of English workers, export crops would not be grown or not be harvested in profitable quantities. (Harriot did not see the Indians as a major source of labour, in tacit rejection of the Spanish colonial model that had brought wholesale misery and resistance in Latin America. The English edition (1583) of Bartolomé de las Casas's indictment of his countrymen had recently and graphically provided the evidence.)[9] The second section of *Briefe and True Report* describes the natural products of the Roanoke region that would sustain English families and contains more information about the natives than did the first section. They lived comfortable and healthy lives, Harriot contended, by growing maize, beans, peas, pumpkins, and other indigenous crops. Englishmen would live even more comfortably, Harriot predicted, by adding European plants and employing European farming techniques, for the Indians neither tilled the soil nor systematically used manure of any kind – animal dung, fish, or wood ashes.[10] Although Harriot's several paragraphs on Indian agricultural practices are humdrum to modern eyes, they must have fascinated the agrarian-minded Elizabethans. Imagine: no manure, yet Indian harvests, sometimes twice a year from the same fields, are far better than in England!

What especially catches the modern eye in the second section of *Briefe and True Report* is Harriot's discussion of tobacco. To propitiate their gods, the Indians cast powdered tobacco into fires; to quell storms they tossed some into the air, as they did after surviving great danger, accompanied by 'strange gestures, stamping, somtime dauncing, clapping of hands, holding up of hands, & staring up into the heavens, uttering therewithal and chattering strange words & noises'. To promote good

---

8 Harriot, *Briefe and True Report*, 7–12.
9 Bartolomé de las Casas, *The Spanish Colonie, or Briefe Chronicle of the Acts and Gestes of the Spaniards in the West Indies* (London: Thomas Dawson for William Brome, 1583).
10 Harriot, *Briefe and True Report*, 13–21, especially 14–15.

health, the Indians sucked tobacco smoke through clay pipes 'into their stomacke and heade; from whence it purgeth superfluous fleame & other grosse humors, openeth all the pores & passages of the body: ... wherby their bodies are notably preserved in health, & know not many greevous diseases [with which] wee in England are oftentimes afflicted'. Like many of his countrymen, Harriot subscribed to the Indians' assumption that tobacco was beneficial. He would die in 1621 of cancer in his nose.[11]

The third and final section of *Briefe and True Report* is, in the context of this chapter, the most interesting and important. 'Of the nature and manners of the people' was, for its time, a brief but innovative example of cultural anthropology. Harriot accounts at the outset for this section's brevity. It is limited to 'a word or two' about the Indians, he admitted, because he had left the 'large discourse thereof until time more convenient hereafter'; and Harriot tantalizes his readers several more times with hints of the greater coverage of many topics to be found in a separate discourse.[12] Near the end of his *Briefe and True Report*, Harriot finally explains that 'this is all the fruites of our labours, that I have thought necessary to advertise you of at this present: what els concerneth the nature and manners of the inhabitants of *Virginia* ... I have ready in a discourse by it self in maner of a Chronicle ... [which] when time shall bee thought convenient shall be also published'.[13] In sum, the *Briefe and True Report* is a précis of the much longer Chronicle, which Harriot intended to publish but never did. Although Harriot says more in his published text than any Englishman before him about American natives, the lost manuscript, should it ever be found, would surely enhance his credentials as England's foremost ethnographer of the sixteenth century.

To what extent Harriot's published and unpublished texts depended on Indian assistance is difficult to measure, but it was, I propose, substantial. During Harriot's year on the Carolina coast (mid-1585 to mid-1586), he visited Indian villages, entered Indian houses, and spoke with Indian leaders – putting to good use the skill in coastal Algonquian

---

11 Harriot, *Briefe and True Report*, 16; Shirley, *Harriot: A Biography*, 425–6. See also David B. Quinn, ed., *The Roanoke Voyages, 1584–1590: Documents to Illustrate the English Voyages to North American under the Patent Granted to Walter Ralegh in 1584*, 2 vols (London: Hakluyt Society, 1955), 1:344–6.
12 Quinn (*Roanoke Voyages*, 1:368 n.5) thinks that Harriot's 'Leaving large discourse thereof until time more convenient hereafter' refers to the captions he will write for White's drawings, but I think it far more likely that the 'large discourse' is his Chronicle, which he had apparently drafted but not completed and, alas, never published.
13 Harriot, *Briefe and True Report*, 24, 32–3. The Chronicle, Harriot makes clear, did not concern the Indians alone but also narrated the history of exploration and colonization at Roanoke.

he had acquired the previous year from two men who had been brought to England in 1584 by the first scouting expedition to America under Ralegh's aegis: Manteo, from the island of Croatan, south of Roanoke, and Wanchese from Roanoke Island. Those two indigenous Americans lived in England from mid-September 1584 until early April 1585, almost certainly at Durham House, Ralegh's London mansion on the north bank of the Thames, where the Indians learned to speak some English and Harriot studied their language.[14] After six and a half months of linguistic and cultural sharing, Manteo and Wanchese accompanied the scientist Thomas Harriot, the artist John White, and more than one hundred English settlers back to Roanoke Island. For reasons unknown, Wanchese thereafter shunned the colonists, but Manteo lived with and aided them so thoroughly that in 1587 he would become the first recorded convert to Anglican Christianity and be dubbed by the colonists 'a most faithfull Englishman'.[15]

Despite Harriot's keen interest in Algonquian linguistics, he could not have conversed unaided with every Indian he met in 1585–86. 'The language of every government is different from any other', he noted, 'and the farther they are distant the greater is the difference'.[16] Even with Indians near the English outpost, Harriot's ability to communicate was limited. He tried to describe to his readers the Indians' religious beliefs and customs, on the basis of his conversations with 'some of their priestes', but admitted that for 'want of perfect utterance in their language' his explanations were incomplete. But Manteo was usually at hand, it seems, and surely he spoke many of the regional dialects as well as the English he had learned from Harriot and others during his two-month voyage to England in 1584, his six-plus months in London, and nearly four-month voyage from London to Roanoke in 1585 – in sum, twelve months of intensive exposure to the English language, as well as the daily practice of living among the colonists in the Roanoke Colony in 1585–86. Manteo seems to have been an apt pupil, and Harriot, it is reasonable to speculate, was deeply indebted to his assistance for information about coastal Virginia geography and

---

14 The language lessons undoubtedly began informally on the voyage to England in 1584, whether or not Harriot was on board. No list of passengers survives, but the likelihood is strong that Ralegh assigned Harriot to the scouting expedition under Captains Philip Amadas and Arthur Barlowe. See Shirley, *Harriot: A Biography*, 104–7. For Harriot's innovative work with languages, see Vivian Salmon, 'Thomas Harriot (1560–1621) and Algonkian Linguistics', in Salmon, *Language and Society in Early Modern England: Selected Essays, 1981–1994*, selected and ed. Konrad Koerner (Amsterdam and Philadelphia: J. Benjamins, 1996), 143–72.
15 'The fourth voyage made to Virginia', in Hakluyt, *Principal Navigations*, 3:284.
16 Harriot, *Briefe and True Report*, 25, 27.

culture – information that formed the basis of the *Briefe and True Report*. In the second section of the book, for example, Harriot concludes his description of a dozen kinds of indigenous trees with a lamentation that 'there are many other strange trees whose names I knowe not but in the *Virginian* language, of which I am not nowe able ... to trouble you with particular relation'. Harriot probably got the Indian labels from Manteo but did not have an opportunity to find English equivalents.[17]

Harriot, I further contend, must have relied heavily on Manteo in England as well as in America as he drafted and revised the *Briefe and True Report* and the more detailed Chronicle. The high marks that historians and anthropologists have long given Harriot for the accuracy of his little book strongly suggest the collaboration of a genuine expert on Roanoke culture. Not coincidentally, I believe, Manteo's second London sojourn – this time for about nine months – coincided almost exactly with the probable dates of the *Briefe and True Report*'s composition. Manteo and another native of the area, Towaye, had accompanied the whole Roanoke contingent when it departed in early June 1586 after a year of declining stability and inadequate support from home.[18] During the hasty, stormy exit from the island on Sir Francis Drake's homeward-bound fleet, much of Harriot's ethnographic evidence – notes, artefacts, some of John White's drawings – was lost, making Harriot even more dependent on his Indian informants.[19]

In London, Manteo and Towaye surely lived in Durham House with Harriot and Ralegh, as had Manteo and Wanchese two years before, until early May 1587, when a new contingent of English settlers (destined to become the famous 'Lost Colony') departed for Roanoke and then, according to their instructions, on to Chesapeake Bay to found a City of Ralegh.[20] Before his second departure for America, Manteo had lived in an English-language environment – on shipboard, in England, and

---

17 Ibid., 23.
18 Nothing is known about Towaye except that he went to England, probably in the summer of 1586, and returned to Roanoke the following spring. Presumably his contact with Englishmen was of much shorter duration than Manteo's and therefore his command of English far inferior to Manteo's. That does not preclude some contribution by Towaye to Harriot's descriptions of the Roanoke region.
19 Glimpses of Manteo's contributions to the English outpost in 1585–86, the hasty departure from Roanoke Island, and the loss of writings and probably drawings is documented in Ralfe Lane, 'An Account of the ... Englishmen Left in Virginia by Sir Richard Greenevill ...', in Richard Hakluyt, *The Principall Navigations, Vioages and Discoveries of the English Nation* (London: George Bishop and Ralph Newberie, 1589), 737–47, especially the final page.
20 Hakluyt, *Principall Navigations*, 764, 770–1.

at Roanoke – for nearly three years and would have been fluent in the foreigners' language and knowledgeable about their culture. It is hard to imagine that Manteo would not have been at Harriot's elbow through most of the second sojourn in London.

Precisely when Harriot wrote the *Briefe and True Report* and the longer Chronicle has never been determined, but he probably had completed at least a draft of the former by early 1587. Harriot began the report, undoubtedly on Ralegh's orders, to silence the slanders about the first Roanoke Colony's short, dismal career, a task that Ralegh would have assigned to Harriot soon after the latter's arrival in England with Drake in late July 1586. The last date by which Harriot could have completed his book is October 1587, when Richard Hakluyt mentioned in a dedication to Ralegh that the Roanoke area's commodities 'are faithfully and with great judgement committed to writing ... by one of your followers [undoubtedly Harriot], which remayned there a full twelvemonth ... in the diligent serch of the secretes of those countries'. David B. Quinn, the outstanding authority on the Roanoke Colony, suggested the likelihood of completion by May 1587 – nine months after Harriot presumably received the assignment from Ralegh.[21] Assuming that Harriot wrote either the longer or the shorter description of the Roanoke region and its inhabitants by that date, Manteo was on hand to assist with the whole project; if the later date is used, he could have assisted with the preliminary draft. Although Harriot never explained, in print at least, what role Manteo played in the composition of the *Briefe and True Report* or the Chronicle, it probably was substantial. I suggest that the first significant English-language ethnographic treatise resulted from a unique partnership of Ralegh (as initiator and underwriter), Harriot (as principal author), and Manteo (as technical consultant), each of them essential to the final product.

If a picture is worth a thousand words, John White must be added to the list of coauthors because the edition of 1590 contained more than a score of his artistic impressions: two maps of eastern Virginia (one a close-up of Roanoke) and twenty-one drawings of local Indians – or, rather, Theodor de Bry's copper etchings of White's water-colour paintings – which added immeasurable visual specificity to Harriot's verbal descriptions. The de Bry edition, published in Latin, German, French, and English, became

---

21 René Laudonnière, *A Notable Historie Containing Foure Voyages Made by Certayne French Captaynes unto Florida*, trans. Richard Hakluyt (London: Printed by Thomas Dawson, 1587), epistle (precedes sig. A); Quinn, *Roanoke Voyages*, 1:387 n.4. Harriot closes the 1588 edition of *Briefe and True Report*: 'I take my leave of you, this moneth of February.1588' (new style) and appends a list of errata ('Faults escaped'), which suggests that the book had been typeset prior to that date.

a bestseller and allowed the Harriot–Manteo–White–de Bry portrayal of native culture to reach illiterate as well as literate 'readers' throughout Europe.[22]

The introductory page to the portfolio of illustrations announces that these 'True Pictures and Fashions of the People in that Parte of America now Called Virginia' are by John White, whom Sir Walter Ralegh 'sent thither speciallye' to make a pictorial record. Harriot wrote the captions in Latin, which de Bry induced Hakluyt to translate into English for the English edition. (Harriot's Latin version appears in the Latin edition of 1590.) Ranging from about one hundred words to nearly four hundred each, the captions tell much about eastern Algonquian stature and physiognomies (both male and female, young and old), as well as the Indians' habits of clothing, hair styles, body paint, and ornaments. On a more communal level, the captions describe Indian fishing, boat-making, cooking, praying, dancing, and other activities. Of special interest – judging from the frequency of reproductions – are White's schematic representations of 'The towne of Pomeiooc', a small pallisaded village, and, even more popular, 'The Towne of Secota', a larger and more varied community. Both towns appear orderly and clean, the people active and happy, in support of Harriot's conclusion that 'This people ... lyve cherfullye and att their harts ease'.[23]

Such a bucolic view of Virginia's indigenous population was part of Ralegh and Harriot's promotional agenda. It was not enough to persuade potential investors and immigrants that Virginia was bountiful; it must also be safe. At the outset of his section of the *Briefe and True Report* on the inhabitants' 'nature and manners', Harriot assured his readers that they 'are not to be feared'; rather, the natives 'shall have cause both to feare and to love us, that shall inhabite with them'. But if warfare between colonists and Indians did occur, Harriot added comfortingly, the latter's weapons were mere bows, arrows, and clubs, and their simple tactics would be ineffective against English military discipline and up-to-date weaponry. The Indians' 'best defence', Harriot recalled from the skir-

---

22 On White's drawings see Paul Hulton and David B. Quinn, *The American Drawings of John White*, 2 vols (London and Chapel Hill: The British Museum and the University of North Carolina Press, 1964); Paul Hulton, *America 1585: The Complete Drawings of John White* (Chapel Hill: University of North Carolina Press and the British Museum, 1984), and more generally, Bernadette Bucher, *Icon and Conquest: A Structural Analysis of the Illustrations of de Bry's Great Voyages*, trans. Basia Miller Gulati (Chicago: University of Chicago Press, 1981, orig. publ. Paris 1977).

23 Harriot, *Briefe and True Report*, [66]–[69]. Cf. White's less stylized versions in Hulton, *America 1585*, 62, 66.

mishes in 1585–86, was 'running away'. White's drawings reinforce the notion of Indian passivity. Although several of the men in the illustrations portfolio carry bows and arrows, none is depicted in a threatening posture. The only reference to war in the twenty-three captions observes that 'When they go to battel they paynt their bodyes in the most terible manner that thei can devise'.[24]

Contrasting sharply with the Harriot–White–de Bry benign portrayal of coastal Virginians are the likenesses of three Picts and two of their neighbours that White had copied, de Bry explained, from 'a oolld English cronicle'. The reason for appending these striking full-page, full-length pictures of largely naked, extensively tattooed, and heavily armed men and women was 'to showe how that the Inhabitants of the great Bretannie have bin in times past as sauvage as those of Virginia'. Readers of the *Briefe and True Report* would, presumably, absorb a hopeful lesson: that the Indians, like the ancient Britons, would soon become as civilized as the English, and – implicit in the drawings but explicit elsewhere in *Briefe and True Report* – that they would also embrace Christianity. As Harriot argued earlier in the book, if the colonists apply 'good government' toward the natives in English America, 'they may in short time be brought to civilitie, and the imbracing of true religion'.[25] Harriot's message, reinforced by White's drawings, used ethnography to promote empire.

Sir Walter Ralegh's *Discoverie of Guiana* of 1596 is far longer than Harriot's *Briefe and True Report* and its author, of course, is more prominent, but Ralegh's book has earned far less praise as history and literature. Like Harriot's book, its broad primary purpose was propaganda in the service of empire, yet Ralegh's immediate goal was to promote his plan to extract immense riches for the Queen and glory for himself from a new sphere of English interest. Accordingly, the structure of his book is wholly different from Harriot's. There are no separate sections on export commodities, or life-sustaining crops, or descriptions of the people. Rather, Ralegh weaves together his search for gold and silver, his conflict with Spaniards on the island of Trinidad and elsewhere, his exploration of Guiana, especially its innumerable rivers, his negotiations with native caciques, and his random insights into native culture. The resulting narrative is less ethnographic than Harriot's; none of Ralegh's contemporaries would have carried it to

24 Harriot, *Briefe and True Report*, 24–5, 46.
25 Ibid., 25, [75]–[85]. On the intellectual significance of the five ancient Britons, see Alden T. Vaughan, 'English Paradigms for New World Natives', in Vaughan, *Roots of American Racism: Essays on the Colonial Experience* (New York: Oxford University Press, 1995), 34–54, especially 44–9.

Guiana as a handbook of native culture as one could have taken Harriot's to Roanoke. Yet Ralegh's book was tremendously valuable as a guide to Guiana's political and geographic divisions and subdivisions. If Harriot's *Briefe and True Report* was good amateur anthropology, Ralegh's *Discoverie of Guiana* was good amateur geopolitics.

There is, of course, the embarrassing matter of Ralegh's gullibility – as critics have long insisted. He described Amazons, those 'warlike women' who (at least those near Guiana) 'do accompanie with men but once a yeer, and for the time of one moneth, which I gather by their relation to be in Aprill. At that time all the Kings of the borders assemble, and the Queenes of the *Amazones,* and after the Queens have chosen, the rest cast lots for their *Valentines*. This one moneth, they feast, daunce, & drinke of their wines in abundance; & the Moone being done, they all depart to their owne Provinces. If they conceive, and be delivered of a sonne, they returne him to the father, if of a daughter they nourish it, and reteine it'.[26] And so forth. But Ralegh prefaced all this with the warning that he was only repeating what he had been told by a cacique and that, while some people believe it, others do not. He is reporting rumour, not ethnography.

Less defensible is Ralegh's account of 'a nation of people, whose heades appeare not above their shoulders'. This too he attributes not to what he has seen but to what he has been told. He admits it 'may be thought a meere fable, yet for mine owne part I am resolved it is true, because every child in the provinces of *Arromaia* and *Canuri* affirme the same'. And not only children. The cacique's eighteen- to twenty-year-old son who accompanied Ralegh back to England confirmed the story and seems to have enlarged on it in response to Ralegh's scepticism. Ralegh remained doubtful, but he was reluctant to deny the evidence he had heard. '[F]or mine owne part I saw them not, but I am resolved that so many people did not all combine, or forethinke to make the report'.[27]

Like Harriot's book, the authenticity of Ralegh's ethnography depended to a large extent on native interpreters during the gathering of information – however fanciful at times – in Guiana and, very likely, during the actual writing in London. Early in the *Discoverie of Guiana,* Ralegh refers to 'my Indian interpreter, which I caried out of England'. This man must have gone to England in 1594 with the scouting expedition under Captain Jacob Whiddon that closely paralleled the Roanoke expedition of exactly a decade earlier which took Manteo and Wanchese to London. Because Ralegh continued to acknowledge an interpreter's help in Guiana

26 Ralegh, *Discoverie of Guiana*, ed. Lorimer, 63.
27 Ibid., 155, 157.

but fails to give him a name, it is possible, but unlikely, that there was more than one. Ralegh described his interpreter as 'an Indian that spake many languages, & that of *Guiana* naturally'[28] and told briefly how 'our interpreter' assured a group of Indians that Ralegh's party came in peace. Elsewhere in his narrative, Ralegh explained the he 'caused my Indian interpreter at every place when we departed, to know of the losse or wrong done' so that the English could made amends or restitution.[29]

In any case, Ralegh almost certainly took back to England the Indian interpreter he had brought to Guiana in 1595 and several more natives of northeastern South America. His principal interpreter in 1595, apparently the man subsequently identified in English documents as John Provost, was originally from Trinidad but had lived in Guiana and could speak a variety of dialects. He was also adept in English, probably as early as 1596, for by then he had been with the English for two years. (He would hone his language skills for several years after 1596 in the household of Sir John Gilbert, a veteran of the 1595 expedition and related to Ralegh. Later, back in Guiana, Provost was known among English explorers as an Indian who 'could speake our language well'.) Early in 1596 Provost accompanied Lawrence Keymis back to Guiana as the principal interpreter in 'the second voyage to Guiana' – Ralegh's of 1595 was the first; Whiddon's of 1594 was only a reconnaissance – but this skilled linguist had already been available to assist Sir Walter in the drafting of the *Discoverie of Guiana* on shipboard during the long voyage home in the summer of 1595, and, after their arrival in September, at Durham House. The book manuscript was not entered into the Stationers' Register until the following March, after a preliminary draft, completed in early November, had been reviewed by Sir Robert Cecil and others, but John Provost was unlikely to have been consulted at that late stage.[30] His input would have occurred early in the process, when Ralegh was recording native names, places, and relationships.

Other natives of Guiana may also have helped in the preliminary stage. Ralegh unquestionably took to England in 1595 the cacique Topiawari's eighteen-year-old son, Cayowaroco, who remained in England for nearly

---

28 Ibid., 31, 73.
29 Ibid., 121, 125.
30 Lawrence Keymis, *A Relation of the Second Voyage to Guiana, Performed and Written in the Yeare 1596* (London: Printed by Thomas Dawson, 1596), title page; Alden T. Vaughan, *Transatlantic Encounters: American Indians in Britain, 1500–1776* (New York: Cambridge University Press, 2006), 30–6; Ralegh, *Discoverie of Guiana*, ed. Lorimer, xxi, xxiv–xxvi; *A Transcript of the Registers of the Company of Stationers of London*, 3, ed. Edward Arber (London: Privately printed, 1876), 9 (entry for 15 March).

a year, and three or four unnamed inhabitants of the Orinoco region.[31] (Both Cayowaroco and Ralegh's interpreter should be in de Bry's famous etching of Ralegh and Topiawari in a tent, because Ralegh's text puts them at the scene. De Bry omitted them, probably to highlight Ralegh's role.) Without one or more interpreters, I submit, Ralegh could not have written the book he did. Even a superficial reading of *Discoverie of Guiana* reveals a profusion of Indian place names and personal names that would defy a stranger's ability to record from memory. Smart as Ralegh was, and even with the aid of his field notes (assuming that he took notes along the way), he could scarcely have remembered all those Indian words, all those geographic details, all those ethnic relationships, all those diplomatic complexities, without the aid of natives of the area as he was composing his narrative. The *Discoverie of Guiana*, almost as much as Harriot's book, I believe, was a team effort.

The practice of bicultural composition launched by Harriot and Ralegh persisted for several decades in English ethnographic writings about America. Bilingual natives assisted writers in early Virginia and, a bit later, in early New England as they gathered information about indigenous cultures for the edification and entertainment of English readers. The likelihood of Indian contributions to the actual writing of ethnographic accounts after 1600 is, however, harder to document, although it remains plausible. Two chroniclers of early Virginia – Captain John Smith and William Strachey – illustrate the ongoing assistance of bilingual Indians to the gathering of information, but Smith and Strachey also reveal the difficulty of pinpointing Indian roles in the composition of books and pamphlets, even though both writers drew inspiration from Harriot and Ralegh, as evidenced by their frequent citation of those worthy predecessors, often in ways that reflect close reading of the *Briefe and True Report* and the *Discoverie of Guiana*.

Smith, whose many writings feature ethnographic descriptions of a pretty high order, included several pages of Harriot's book nearly verbatim (with proper credit) in his *Generall Historie of Virginia, New-England, and the Summer Isles* (1624), and Smith's autobiographical *True Travels, Adventures, and Observations* (1630) summarizes in one paragraph Ralegh's whole book on Guiana.[32] Strachey, like Smith, cribbed some of his infor-

31 On the additional Indians on Ralegh's return from Guiana, see Vaughan, *Transatlantic Encounters*, 30–3; Cayarowaro's return to Guiana is documented in Lady Ralegh to Sir Robert Cecil, July 1596, in Ralegh, *Discoverie of Guiana*, ed. Lorimer, 287.
32 John Smith, *The Generall Historie of Virginia, New-England, and the Summer Isles: with the Names of the Adventurers, Planters, and Governours from their First Beginning. An:*

mation from Harriot and referred occasionally to Ralegh in his *Historie of Travell into Virginia Britania*, completed in 1612 and known to exist in at least three manuscript copies by 1616, although none was published until 1849. The Harriot–Ralegh legacy flourished in the writings of the two most comprehensive historians of the early Virginia Colony.

Harriot's influence was nearly inevitable, one might argue, given the *Briefe and True Report*'s remarkable dissemination. The first edition of 1588 was reprinted almost immediately in Richard Hakluyt's *Principal Navigations* of 1589; the de Bry illustrated edition appeared the next year in four languages, and Hakluyt included the English version again in his expanded *Principal Navigations* in 1600. And while Ralegh's *Discoverie of Guiana* did not enjoy such wide distribution in its day as did Harriot's book, popular demand led to three editions, each completely reset, in 1596, and much of it appeared again in 1599, with seven illustrations, in volume 8 of de Bry's *Great Voyages*.[33] In the four-plus centuries since their first publication, both books have had numerous editions, popular and scholarly, right to the present. The English version of the 1590 edition of *Briefe and True Report* has long been available in good facsimile editions, and in 2007 the University of Virginia Press issued a lavish reprint of the Latin version, with exquisite coloured plates and informative essays by Peter Stallybrass and Karen Ordahl Kupperman. The Hakluyt Society in 2006 published a new scholarly edition of Ralegh's book – replacing, in effect, the edition it had sponsored in 1848.[34]

The Harriot–Ralegh legacy was manifest not only in the quantity and quality of ethnographic reporting by Smith and Strachey but also in those authors' reliance on Indian informants. Strachey credited 'Kempes an Indian, who died the last yeare of the Scurvye at James towne' and 'who could speake a pretty good deale of English', with providing important information about native society. Similarly, Strachey acknowledged aid from 'the Indian Machumps, who was sometyme in England, and comes to and fro amongst us,'[35] though Strachey stops short of saying

---

1584. to this Present 1624 (London: Printed for Michael Sparkes, 1624), 9–12; Smith, *The True Travels, Adventures, and Observations of Captaine John Smith, in Europe, Asia, Affrica, and America, from Anno Domini 1593. to 1629* (London: Printed for Thomas Slater, 1630), 48–9.

33 The best discussions of Ralegh's ethnography are the introduction and notes to *Discoverie of Guiana*, ed. Neil L. Whitehead (Norman: University of Oklahoma Press, 1997). On the illustrations, see 101–4.

34 *The Discovery of the Large, Rich, and Beautiful Empire of Guiana ... by Sir W. Ralegh*, ed. Robert H. Schomburgk (London: Hakluyt Society, 1848).

35 William Strachey, *The Historie of Travell into Virginia Britania*, ed. Louis B. Wright and Virginia Freund (London: Hakluyt Society, 1953), 34, 61–2, 98.

that either Kemps or Machumps helped him write his book. John Smith also named various Indians – including Pocahontas and Powhatan – as sources of information, sometimes ostensibly verbatim, in several of his publications.[36] And although providing information is not the same as co-authoring, English writers of that day rarely credited anyone for anything except the patronage of high-ranking persons.

One could extend the list of early English writers in America who followed the Harriot–Ralegh model of drawing on native assistance somewhat beyond the 1620s and well beyond the Virginia Colony. It is probably a truism that advice from Indians, direct or indirect, was essential to any accurate description of native society, but as long as the actual writing took place in England, as it did until permanent colonists began to produce their own ethnographic accounts, the door was open to collaboration from bilingual Indians in England. By the third decade of the seventeenth century, however, such Indians became scarce, primarily because the former English outposts had become permanent colonies. At that point, Indians who opted to learn the newcomers' language did it on the western side of the Atlantic and never set foot in England.

If today's custom had prevailed in the sixteenth and early seventeenth centuries of authors beginning or ending their books with several pages of acknowledgements – to colleagues, librarians, spouses, children, even the family pets – we would have a better idea of just who helped Harriot, Ralegh, and the other early American writers compose their ethnographic descriptions. I have no doubt that such acknowledgements, if honestly expressed, would have included many Indian names, and that some of those names, especially Manteo's and John Provost's, would have had places of honour – even, perhaps, on the title page.

---

36 John Smith, *A True Relation of Such Occurrences and Accidents of Noate as Hath Hapned in Virginia* ... (London: Printed for John Tappe, 1608), sigs C1v–C2v, D1v; Smith, *The Proceedings of the English Colonie in Virginia* ... (Oxford: Printed by Joseph Barnes, 1612), 44–6, 60–5; Smith, *Generall Historie*, 74–7. Smith's earliest and most direct description of native Virginians does not cite his sources, but in addition to his own observations he has clearly drawn on conversations with Powhatan and other Indians. See Smith, *A Map of Virginia. With a Description of the Countrey* ... (Oxford: Printed by Joseph Barnes, 1612), 19–38.

9

'Most fond and fruitlesse warre'
Ralegh and the call to arms

Andrew Hiscock

I saw in the third civill warre of France, certaine Caves in Languedoc, which had but one entrance, and that very narrow, cut out in the mid-way of high Rockes, which we knew not how to enter by any ladder or engine, till at last, by certaine bundles of straw, let down by an yron chaine, & a waighty stone in the middest, those [Catholics] that defended it, were so smothered, as they rendred themselves, with their plate, mony, and other goods therein hidden.[1]

This interjection, taken from Ralegh's magnum opus *The History of the World* (begun c. 1608, first published 1614), is squeezed into a much larger narrative devoted to Alexander the Great's encounters with the Persians. The disarming manner in which the rigours of military engagement are recounted here and elsewhere in the huge chronicle is far from unrepresentative for an age well accustomed to the savagery of European warfare.[2] However, in many ways, the arresting examples of Ralegh's interventions in the international politics of the Atlantic world and the Elizabethan Plantation of Ireland have served to obscure the fact that his first experiences of the battlefield were as an adolescent supporting the Huguenot cause in the French Wars of Religion. To a great extent, this state of affairs has been shaped by the surviving correspondence and

---

1 Sir Walter Ralegh, *The History of the World* (London: Walter Burre, 1634 [1614]), 4.2.16.165. All references to the *History* hereafter are to: Book; Chapter; Section; Page. In this particular context, see also: 'I remember it well, that when the Prince of *Condé* was slain after the Battell of *Jarnac* (which Prince, together with the Admiral *Chastillan*, had the conduct of the *Protestant* Armie)' (5.2.3.332).
2 In this context, see for example the following extract from Sir Walter Ralegh, *The Discoverie of the Large, Rich, and Bewtiful Empire of Guiana* (1596), 'and therefore taking a time of most aduantage, I set upon the *Corp duguard* in the euening, and haueing put them to the sword, sent Captaine *Calfield* onwards with 60. soldiers, & my selfe followed with 40. more & so toke their new city which they called *S. Ioseph*, by breake of day: they abode not any fight after a few shot, & al being dismissed but only *Berreo* & his companion, I brought them with me abord, and at the instance of the Indians, I set their now City of *S. Iosephs* on fire'. (6–7).

publications of Ralegh himself which repeatedly focus attention upon his commitment to the *translatio imperii* for England in a westerly direction – although, as we shall see, Ralegh remained mindful of 'thes French warrs, which ar endless'.[3] Indeed, this discussion explores the manner in which war became such a consuming source of interest and enquiry for Ralegh that it penetrated every aspect of his enormously diverse textual output, shaping his thoughts on political integrity, cultural heroism, and human epistemology.

Ralegh and 'thes French warrs'

J. H. Elliott argued that 'those who fought in the Protestant ranks [of the French wars] all subscribed, even if only through the fact of comradeship in arms, to a common vision of the world. It was a world in which the Christian was engaged in ceaseless struggle against the power of Satan'.[4] Nonetheless, whatever the truth of the matter in terms of individual commitment, David J. B. Trim remains persuasive in his more general contention that the Elizabethan regime's 'allowing [of] companies of volunteers to serve on the Continent, [of corsairs to] use English ports as bases, and sending [of] occasional sums of money or shipments of arms ... may seem more suggestive of an approach governed by *realpolitik*, rather than religious fervour'.[5] It remains unsurprising that generations of Elizabethan gentry and aristocrats, reared on the literatures and practices of chivalric conduct, sought to distinguish themselves in the heroism of combat beyond England's shores. And it was at the age of sixteen or seventeen that Ralegh was introduced to this theatre of war, as Thomas Churchyard recalled in *A generall rehearsall of warres, called Churchyardes choise* (1579):

> M. Henry Champernowne of Deuonshire ... serued in the cause of the Protestantes of Fraunce, of his own proper charges in the second Ciuile warres, with xij. gentlemen or more. And in the thirde Ciuile warres after the battaile of Iarnag [Jarnac], he serued with an hundred men of his owne proper costes. Likewise accompanied and followed ... [by, amongst others,] Walter Rawley ... maister Henry Champernowne, as one desirous of renowme, and greedie of glorie gotten by seruice, remained till his death ... and many of those gentlemen that he brought with hym, augmented so

---

3 See note 46.
4 J. H. Elliott, *Europe Divided 1550–1598* (London: Fontana /Collins, 1974), 108.
5 David J. B. Trim, 'Seeking a Protestant Alliance and Liberty of Conscience on the Continent, 1558–85', in *Tudor England and its Neighbours*, ed. Susan Doran and Glenn Richardson (Houndmills: Palgrave, 2005), 153–4.

muche his fame, that to this daie his deedes and theirs, are moste noblie spoken of, greatly to the honour of all our Englishe Nation.[6]

Ralegh was related to the Champernownes through maternal ties of kinship. By the late 1560s the Huguenot cause was again faring badly, and in 1569 he joined the contingent led by his relative, Henry, to cross the Channel and to join the ranks of their beleaguered co-religionists. The rallying call on the flag of Champernowne's company was distinctly chivalric in tenor: *Det mihi virtus finem*. If Rory Rapple has underlined that 'The urge to praise soldiers has proved strong in most cultures', it remains equally apparent that this appetite was very far from being sated at Elizabeth's accession when, as Rapple adds, 'England's martial reputation was at its lowest point since the reign of Henry VI'.[7] The Crown acquiesced in ventures such as Henry Champernowne's as *un mal nécessaire*. For, as Sir Thomas Smith pointed out in *De republica anglorum*, 'when [men of war] haue no externe seruice wherewith to occupie their buisie heads & handes accustomed to fight and quarell, [they] must needes seeke quarels and contentions amongest themselues'.[8] By 1570 Henry was dead and buried in France, but some indication of the growing rapprochement between the family and the Huguenot party in the years which followed may be given by the fact that Henry's uncle, Sir Arthur Champernowne, vice-admiral for the county of Devon, contracted a marriage between his son, Gawine, and the third daughter (Roberde) of the Huguenot military commander Gabriel de Lorges, Comte de Montgommery. Indeed, Sir Arthur would later dine with Admiral Coligny in Paris in 1572, two months before the St. Bartholomew's Day Massacre.

Benjamin Schmidt has recently promoted the battlefields of France in the second half of the sixteenth century as a military 'finishing school' for English gentlemen: if that were the case, it must certainly have been a horrific initiation into the butchery of war.[9] At the battle of Moncontour

6 Thomas Churchyard, *A generall rehearsall of warres, called Churchyardes choise* (1579), sig. K2v.
7 Rory Rapple, *Martial Power and Elizabethan Political Culture* (Cambridge: Cambridge University Press, 2009), 1, 48. Rapple also justly draws attention to the paucity of opportunities for social mobility for the aspiring 'gentleman' in the second half of the sixteenth century: 'Whereas great opportunities to make fortunes in spite of the sequence of one's birth had arisen in the heyday of the dissolution of the monasteries, under Mary and Elizabeth that sort of bonanza would not repeat itself' (ibid., 57).
8 Sir Thomas Smith, *De republica Anglorum The maner of gouernement or policie of the realme of England* (1583), 95.
9 Benjamin Schmidt, 'Reading Ralegh's America: Texts, Books and Readers in the Early Modern Atlantic World', in *The Atlantic World and Virginia 1550–1624*, ed. Peter C. Mancall (Chapel Hill: University of North Carolina Press, 2007), 458.

(1569) in Vienne, for example, the Huguenot dead numbered at least six thousand, and perhaps as many as ten thousand. In the ensuing rout, the Protestant forces were in complete disarray, as Ralegh himself acknowledged decades later in his *History*:

> yet did that worthy Gentleman, *Count Lodowick of Nassau*, brother to the late famous *Prince of Orange*, make the retrait at *Moncontour* with so great resolution, as hee saued the one halfe of the *Protestant* Armie, then broken and disbanded, of which my selfe was an eye-witnesse; and was one of them that had cause to thanke him for it.[10]

If scholarly narratives of Elizabethan political intervention are inevitably dominated by accounts of conflict with the imperial forces of Philip II or the colonization of Ireland, there is every evidence in the intellectual and artistic life of the period that the French wars were not eclipsed in the public mind as a consequence of these other, ongoing hostilities. John Foxe's evocations of the Duc de Guise ('the great Archenemy of God')[11] in the *Acts and Monuments* were echoed in a number of ways in Anne Dowriche's *The French historie* (1589) and Marlowe's *Massacre at Paris* (1592), for example – and in all likelihood in Webster's lost tragedy *The Guise* (1615?).[12] Moreover, in recent decades, critical insights have encouraged readers to view Sir Terwin and Sir Treuisan in Book One of *The Faerie Queene* as intimations of the destruction of Protestant Terwin (Thérouanne) by Catholic forces in 1553, and the expulsion of their fellows from Trevisan (Treves) in the early 1560s.[13] Much has been justly made in literary and cultural histories of Philippe de Mornay's close relations with the Sidneys, the advances of the Duc d'Anjou to the Virgin Queen, Francis Bacon's sojourn at the English Embassy at Paris, and the participation of Robert Devereux, Earl of Essex, in Henri IV's Normandy campaign of 1591. Nonetheless, this conflict was kept more generally in the eyes of the Elizabethan reading public with the regular publication of pamphlet literature, such as *An edict set forth by the French king, for appeasing of troubles in his kingdome* (1570), *A mervaylous discourse vpon the lyfe, deedes, and behaviours of Katherine de Medicis Queene mother* (1575), *A Catholicke apologie against the libels, declarations, aduices, and consultations made,*

---

10 *History*, 5.2.8.419.
11 John Foxe, *Actes and monuments*, II (1583), 2112.
12 For further discussion here, see Charles R. Forker, *Skull Beneath the Skin. The Achievement of John Webster* (Carbondale: Southern Illinois University Press, 1986), 134ff.
13 See: Russell J. Meyer, 'From Thérouanne to Terwin?', *Spenser Newsletter*, 6 (1975), 18–19; John J. O'Connor, 'Terwin, Trevisan, and Spenser's Historical Allegory', *Spenser Studies* 87 (1990), 328–40.

written, and published by those of the League, perturbers of the quiet estate of the realme of France (1585), *The contre-Guyse* (1589) and *The mutable and wauering estate of France* (1597). Ralegh would remain in France for at least two years, but by 1572 he had proceeded up to Oriel College, Oxford, from where he would eventually move on to the Inns of Chancery. Yet his youthful recollections excerpted at the beginning of this discussion segue effortlessly in his *History* (composed years later in the Tower) into a forthright appreciation of the military lessons to be learned from such experiences:

> I remember these things, but to give caution to those that shall in times to come invade any part of those Countries, that they alwayes, before they passe into the Land, burne down the grasse and sedge to the East of them; they may otherwise, without any other enemy than a handfull of straw set on fire, dye the death of hony-Bees, burnt out of the Hive.[14]

The schooling of the soldier

The seemingly irrepressible reflex to revisit and to draw wisdom from the theatres of war, both past and present, was to shape much of Ralegh's career as a published writer. Indeed, conflict in all its guises seems to have dogged him. The Elizabethan diplomat Dudley Carleton is attributed with the infamously barbed tribute to Ralegh that 'Never was a man so hated and so popular in so short a time'; and the violence of this response was echoed throughout his adult life on the public stage – whether as the *parvenu* favourite at Elizabeth's court, or the victim of what appears to have been an almost pathological enmity on the part of James VI /I on his accession to the English throne.[15] Quite apart from his recurring roles in court lobbying and factionalism in the late Elizabethan and Jacobean periods, Ralegh's own textual meditations were drawn inexorably to the business of military intervention. And such is the overriding nature of this attraction that in Book One of *The History* (when he is endeavouring to scrutinize the *doings* of 'the men of renown before the Floud. ... From the birth of Enoch the sonne of Seth, to the time of Henoch the sonne of Jared'), it is revealing that he clearly finds himself in some difficulties: he discovers that 'there is nothing remembered by Moses' of this period apart from genealogical details, and thus confesses dejectedly

---

14 *History*, 4.2.16.165.
15 Cited in Thomas Birch (compiler), *The Court and Times of James the First*, ed. Robert Folkestone Williams (London: Henry Colburn, 1849), I:20.

of the warre, peace, government, and policy of those strong and mighty men, so able both in body and wit, there is no memory remaining: whose stories if they had bin preserved, and what else was then performed in that newnesse of the World, there could nothing of more delight have been left to posterity.[16]

Ralegh's unfinished *History* closes at the point of the Second Macedonian War (146 BC), yet even in its present state it extends to nearly fifteen hundred folio pages. In the *History*'s multifarious discussions, the ongoing drama of whole empires locked into vast military campaigns and the labours of conflict resolution quickly emerges as amongst the most decisive and spectacular arenas of human experience. Like so many of his contemporaries, Ralegh remained convinced throughout his life that such internecine struggles warranted the attention of anyone seeking to participate in the development of the commonweal; and he quickly found nourishment for this deep-seated belief in the wealth of secular and sacred literatures which had survived from antiquity into his own time. Indeed, the editions of Latin literatures circulating widely in the vernacular amongst the *literati* of Tudor England rendered it difficult to avoid such conclusions. Sir Alexander Barclay's translation of Sallust's *Famous cronycle of the warre, which the romayns had against Iugurth vsurper of the kyngdome of Numidy* appeared as early as 1522, and was followed in 1544, for example, by Sir Anthony Cope's *Historie of two noble capitaines of the worlde, Anniball and Scipio of theyr dyuers battailes and victories … out of Titus Liuius*. Despite the fact that Sir Arthur Golding remains most famous in more recent literary histories for his translation of Ovid's *Metamorphoses*, it should be noted that his *Eyght bookes of Caius Iulius Caesar conteyning his martiall exploytes in the realm of Gallia* (1565)[17] was equally of import for his early Elizabethan readership, accompanied in 1579 by Sir Thomas North's *Liues of the noble Grecians and Romanes by that graue learned philosopher and historiographer Plutarke*. By 1591 Sir Henry Savile had published translations of the *Histories* and the *Life of Agricola* by Tacitus as well as 'A View of Certain Military Matters, or Commentaries concerning Roman Warfare' (c. 1598, published in Latin in 1601) which drew attention to the schemes of transport and military building undertaken by the Romans. And at the beginning of the

16 *History*, 1.5.7.67, 1.5.7.69.
17 In this context, it is interesting to note an earlier Henrician publication striking an explicitly patriotic note in its rendering of Caesar's writing for an English audience: *Iulius Caesars commentaryes, newly translatyd owte of laten in to englysshe, as much as concernyth thys realm of England sumtyme callyd Brytayne: whych is the eld'yst hystoryer of all other that can be found, that euer of thys realme of England* (1530).

seventeenth century, Sir Clement Edmondes, 'remembrancer of the Citie of London', published *Obseruations vpon the fiue first bookes of Caesars commentaries setting fourth the practise of the art military ... for the better direction of our moderne warres* (1601).

Such publications in the vernacular existed quite independently of the Latin editions of writers such as Caesar and Tacitus which were being read throughout Europe in authoritative versions in the gentleman's library as well as for consumption in the classroom. Attending to the latter in *The Education of Children* (1588), William Kempe emphasized that the class's attention should not only be devoted to the likes of Virgil, Horace, Terence, and Ovid: there should also be a privileged position reserved for political history in the curriculum, which is to say, the extensive accounts of Roman empire-building in campaigns waged against resisting peoples, described in the works of Livy, Sallust, Plutarch, Tacitus, and '*Iulius Caesar* the first and greatest Emperour that euer liued'.[18] Interestingly, when in the 1570s Ralegh's half-brother, Sir Humphrey Gilbert, pondered reform of the educational system, he urged that the classroom was no place for philosophy and dismissed the likes of Strabo and Cicero from the syllabus. Instead, he urged that geometry lessons should be devoted to 'Embattlings, fortifications and matters of war, with the practice of artillery'.[19]

The counsel of war

During his long years of imprisonment (1603–17), with his own powers of cultural intervention thus severely circumscribed, Ralegh's meditations upon military conflict found expression in a variety of textual genres: the essay, confessional, chronicle, conduct book and his correspondence. More than thirty years after his execution in 1618, the publication *Judicious and Select Essayes and Observations By that Renowned Knight Sir Walter Raleigh* (1650) made its first appearance on the London bookstalls, and it pondered anew and at great length for its Interregnum readership the rationale and logistics of war-making.[20] The *Judicious and Select*

---

18 William Kempe, *The Education of Children* (1588), sig. D1r. This contention might be compared with that of Ralegh himself: 'it is well knowne, that *Rome* (or perhaps all the world besides) had never nay so brave a Commander in war as *Julius Caesar*: and that no *Roman* armie was comparable unto that which served under the same *Caesar*.' See *History*, 5.1.1.263.
19 I am indebted for these references to Rapple, *Martial Heroism*, 80–1.
20 For an age which had been profoundly (and violently) exercised by a prolonged interrogation of Early Stuart sovereignty, an indication of Ralegh's cultural capital at this time may be sufficiently signalled with reference to the printer's prefatory matter to the collection: here, the reader is alerted to the fact that '*Raleighs* very Name is Proclamation

Essayes contained a number of prose pieces which had been completed during the later, Jacobean period of his life, such as 'Excellent Observations and Notes, concerning the Royall Navy and Sea-service', and 'Apologie for his voyage to Guiana', relating to the final, doomed expedition of 1617. However, the collection also included a vigorous discussion entitled 'A Discovrse of the Originall and Fundamentall Cause of Naturall, Customary, Arbitrary, Voluntary and Necessary Warre. With the Mysery of Invasive Warre'. The latter incorporated a good measure of characteristically forthright political comment and is thought to be the last prose work (c. 1616) that Ralegh composed during his long period of enforced residence in the Tower. Given the vicissitudes of his own life and the dominant emphases of his long career in the public eye, it is perhaps unsurprising that Ralegh began his discussion in the following manner:

> The ordinary Theme and Argument of History is War, which may be defined the exercise of violence under Soveraigne Command, against withstanders force ... as for Armes, Discipline, and whatsoever else belongeth to the making of War prosperous, they are only considerably in degree of perfection, since naked savages fighting disorderly with stones, by appointment of their Commanders, may truly and absolutely be said to War.[21]

From this perspective, warfare had remained the inevitable consequence of any growth in political society since what the Ancients termed the collapse of the Golden Age or what the Faithful remembered as the Fall from Eden. Nonetheless, the call to arms represented an action freely available to even the most primitive of peoples who had at their disposal only a stunted vocabulary of savage violence. Given this painful state of affairs, how could the business of war be fashioned into an elevated vocation for a sinning world? This desire to secure a *dignitas* for the soldier spurred Ralegh on at various points in his career to weigh in the balance the relative merits of heroic causes, effective leadership, rigorously disciplined troops, and the expert use of available technology.

In this context, the great Carthaginian general Hannibal was a figure who constituted a focus of consuming interest for Ralegh in his *History*; and it is surely significant that two of the most impressive engravings from this volume are devoted to his decisive victory over the Romans

---

enough for the *Stationers* advantage'. See Sir Walter Ralegh, *Judicious and select essayes and observations* (1650), sig. A4r. (Indeed, even by 1628, the posthumous publication in Europe of *The Prerogative of Parliaments in England* hailed the author on its titlepage as 'the worthy (much lacked and lamented) Sir Walter Raleigh Knight'. See *The Prerogative of Parliaments in England* (1628). For further discussion, see Andrew Hiscock, 'Ralegh and the Arts of Memory', *Literature Compass* 4 (2007), 1–28.)

21 'A Discovrse of ... Warre', in *Judicious and Select Essayes*, 1–2.

at the battle of Cannae in 216 BC during the Second Punic War. This campaign is linked by Ralegh directly to Amilcar's binding of his son Hannibal to an oath of hatred against Rome – and his readers are left in no doubt as to the implications of Amilcar's legacy of malice to his son, most especially for those Jacobeans thinking of enemies closer to home on the Iberian peninsula: 'it is inhumane, to bequeath hatred in this sort, as it were by Legacy, it cannot be denied. Yet for mine owne part, I doe not much doubt, but that some of those Kings, with whom we are now in peace, have received the like charge from their Predecessors, that as soone as their coffers shall be full, they shall declare themselves enemies to the people of England'.[22] Rather than practising the providentialist hermeneutic which is so often attributed to him as chronicler, in this particular instance Ralegh turns to the pressing need of the island nation to respond to the emergency of self-defence in times of conflict. He urges his readers to focus upon the arguments for war by adopting narrative modes learned from the works of Machiavelli and Guicciardini, foregrounding questions of human motivation, leadership skills, the processes of cause and effect, and the whims of *Fortuna*.

Many of his discussions composed in the same years as the *History* (but published much later in the *Judicious and Select Essayes*) concentrate upon the shrewd management required to exploit fully the resources at the disposal of the early modern age: 'the sword, the Arrow, the Gun, with many terrible Engines of death'. If Ralegh laments in characteristically plangent tones that butchery must express itself in human society because 'there hath no meanes been found of holding all mankind at peace within it self', he devotes time and energy in the 'Discovrse of ... Warre' to a consideration of the legitimacy of natural war. This is a subject which would most famously preoccupy his Dutch contemporary Hugo Grotius in the latter's substantial publication *De Jure Belli ac Pacis* (1625).[23] However, Ralegh begins his own rather briefer enquiries by reflecting upon the ways in which war is frequently articulated in terms of a collective strategy for survival – thus, nations levy armies when they find themselves in need of greater space and sustenance:

> the *Gaules*, who falling upon Italy under their Captaine *Brennus*, told the Roman Ambassadours plainly that prevalent arms were as good as any title, and that valiant men might account to be their owne as much as they could get; That they wanting Land therewith to susteine their people, and the

---

22 *History*, 5.3.1.362. For further contexts for these sentiments, see Lawrence Kemys, *A Relation of the Second Voyage to Guiana* (1596), sig. F1r.
23 'A Discovrse of ... Warre', in *Judicious and Select Essayes*, 2–4.

Tuscanes having more then enough, It was their meaning to take what they needed by strong hand, if it were no: yielded quietly. Now if it were well affirmed by Lawyers, that there is no taking of possession more just, then *In vacuum venire*, to enter upon Land uninhabited, As our Countrymen have lately done in the Summer Islands: Then may it be inferred, that this demand of the *Gaules*, held more of reason then could be discerned at first view.[24]

This summary rehearsal of now familiar arguments concerning *de facto* authority and the colonization of hitherto 'uninhabited' land (in this case, that of the English in the Bermudas) leads on to a more varied, but not necessarily more nuanced, examination of less 'natural' causes for war, such as ambition, greed, threatened danger, revenge, political revolution, religion and 'of old time ... Women have been the common Argument of these tragedies'.[25] When Ralegh sought to establish a portrait of unharnessed belligerence in barbaric societies, he returned to the thematic emphases of nomadism, lawlessness, violence, political anarchy and occult practices described in antiquity, most readily identifiable in Herodotus's *Histories*, Pliny's *Natural History*, and Strabo's Geography; and such discursive strategies for cultural polarization are also widely in evidence in the work of Ralegh's contemporaries.[26] In *Of the Russe commonwealth* (1591), for example, Giles Fletcher described to his dedicatee, Elizabeth I, the 'true and strange face of a *Tyrannical state* (most vnlike to your own)', and subsequently conjured up the disturbing vision of a population in which the 'number of their vagrant and begging poore is almost infinite: that are so pinched with famine and extreame neede, as that they begge after a violent and desperate manner, with *giue mee and cut mee, giue mee and kill mee,* and such like phrases'.[27] Significantly, this is a note which had also been struck on an earlier occasion by the Hungarian humanist scholar Stephen Parmenius, who accompanied Ralegh's half-brother, Sir Humphrey Gilbert, on his final, fateful 1583 voyage to Newfoundland

---

24 Ibid, 5.
25 Ibid., sig. E4r.
26 For further discussion here, see Andrew Hiscock, 'Barking Dogs and Christian Men: Ralegh and Barbarism' in *Writing the Other. Tudor Humanism / Barbarism*, ed. Zsolt Almasi and Michael Pincombe (Cambridge: Cambridge Scholars, 2008), 168–82. Interestingly, Robert P. Kraynak has highlighted how Hobbes would later associate barbarism particularly with Native Americans, Eskimos, Germanic tribes, and the period prior to the founding of the Greek city-states. However, Hobbes also concentrated upon the ways in which 'civilized' society might produce barbaric social systems. See Robert P. Kraynak, 'Hobbes on Barbarism and Civilization', *The Journal of Politics* 45:1 (February 1983), 90, 93–4.
27 Giles Fletcher, *Of the Russe Common Wealth* (1591), sig. A3v, and 116–17.

in which both men lost their lives. In Parmenius's poem *De Navigatione* (1582), we learn that 'ardere in bella necesque / Sarmaticas gentes'.²⁸

War and regression

Even when Ralegh focused in his *History* upon antique civilizations deeply revered in his own society (such as Ancient Greece), he was compelled to bear witness to arresting scenes of violent hostilities allied to a more general narrative of social collapse. In a discussion preliminary to an account of the Theban wars, for example, he concedes that

> It is true that in these times Greece was very salvage, the inhabitants being often chaced from place to place, by the Captaines of greater Tribes: and no man thinking the ground whereon he dwelt his owne longer than he could hold it by strong hand ... briefly, Greece was then in her infancie.²⁹

As the *History* progresses, the chronicler is seen to invest in this way in paradigms of cultural maturation with increasing frequency: pondering in brief the failure of more recent English medieval kings to consolidate their military triumphs on the European continent with a grand scheme of empire-building, Ralegh concludes that in those earlier centuries the monarchs were still 'more warlike than politique'.³⁰ Nonetheless, more generally in his writings, Ralegh clearly does not (and cannot) advocate a paradigm of political maturation which unfolded in a uniform manner across the globe. If, in the 'Discovrse of ... Warre', he seeks for once to elide the contrary political ambitions of the Western nations in the promotion of a shared experience of 'civilized' political structures, he does so to the detriment of strife-ridden continents elsewhere:

> Our Westerne parts of Europe indeed have cause to rejoyce, and give praise to God, for that we have been free about 600 years, from such Inundations, As were those of the Gothes, Hunnes, and Vandalls, yea from such as were those of our owne Ancestors, the Saxons, Danes, and Normans, But howsoever we have together with the feeling, lost the very memory of such wretchednesse, as our Fore-fathers endured by those Wars, of all other the most cruell. Yet are there few Kingdomes in all Asia that have not been ruined by such overflowing multitudes within the same space of these last six hundred yeares.³¹

---

28 'Russia also has a burning thirst /For war and slaughter'. See David B. Quinn and Neil M. Cheshire, eds, *The New Found Land of Stephen Parmenius* (Toronto: University of Toronto Press, 1972), 88–9.
29 *History*, 2.13.7.368.
30 *History*, 5.1.1.265.
31 'A Discovrse of ... Warre', in *Judicious and Select Essayes*, sigs D2v–D3r.

This construction of an integrated political economy and identity for Western Europe is not at all representative of an author who was much more attracted to questions of cultural division and religious schism. Thus, like many of his contemporaries, he is most likely to reflect upon the great discrepancies and volatility that existed in the course and speed of political and spiritual development amongst the variety of nations that people the earth. Indeed, as Rapple has stressed more generally, cultural expectations of regression are frequently seen to characterize the Elizabethan engagement with Ireland, for example: 'the way in which factionalism and theft stalked the land [of Ireland] was obviously retrograde, a throwback to an English *status quo ante*, the horrors of the Wars of the Roses'.[32] And, as Alden T. Vaughan demonstrates in his discussion in Chapter 8 above, this theme was pursued at length in a famous publication dedicated to Ralegh and penned by a member of his circle, the mathematician Thomas Harriot's *briefe and true report of the new found land of Virginia* (1590 ed., first published 1588). Here, at several reprises, the reader is asked to revert to a meditation of 'tymes past [when] the Pictes ... wear sauages, and ... neuer felle to carye a we [away] their [enemies'] heads with them'.[33] The collective experience of bloodthirsty conflict and violent tribal struggle may be assigned to accounts of societies distant in time and place; but, as the account of early Greece above demonstrates, Ralegh and his contemporaries often subscribed to the centuries-old belief that all communities had to endure a brutish 'infancie' and, indeed, might frequently re-encounter it in times of war. In 1598 an English translation was published of *Aristotles politiques, or Discourses of gouernment. Translated out of Greeke into French* ['by Loys Le Roy, called Regius'], *with expositions taken out of the best authours, specially out of Aristotle himselfe, and out of Plato*.[34] Here, the late Elizabethan reader was treated to yet another perspective upon perplexingly degenerative nature of military conflict:

> Plato in *Menexenus* writeth, that in Greece they called all other people Barbarous, that had no communion of liuing or language with the Grecians,

---

32 Rapple, *Martial Heroism*, 304. Equally importantly, however, Rapple insists upon the range of Elizabethan moral and political responses, observing that 'the Irish were not thought to be necessarily untrustworthy, and indeed in many respects, the intimacy of Irish politics at both the local and national level made systematic ethnic discrimination unworkable' (ibid., 219–20). This is underlined in quotations from the accounts of Nicholas Malby in the 1570s (ibid., 223).
33 Thomas Harriot, *A briefe and true report of the new found land of Virginia* (1590), sig. E2r.
34 Rapple stresses that 'Whereas Aristotle had explicitly made riches a precondition of true nobility, Cicero had stated unequivocally that virtue was true nobility and that this virtue had to be expressed in deeds done for the commonwealth' (Rapple, *Martial Power*, 26).

and that they accounted them for slaues ... The Barbarians not rightly obseruing the order and prouidence of nature, employ their wiues as much in all respects as their slaues, laying as great burdens vpon them as vpon their seruants. As in these dayes the Lanquenets going a warfare, cause their wiues to carrie their necessaries with them.[35]

It is revealing that when Ralegh himself pursues a similar line of enquiry crossing the wide expanses of time and space in the final book of his *History*, he acknowledges that '*Caesar* himelfe doth witnesse, that the *Gaules* complained of their own ignoraunce in the Art of War ... What greater wonder is it, that such a people was beaten by the *Romans*, than that the *Caribes*, a naked people, but valiant, as any under the skie, are commonly put to the worse by small numbers of Spaniards?'[36] At such moments, his readers are not asked to focus upon the oppositional politics of warfare simply in terms of degrees of cultural (im)maturity, we are also being asked to acknowledge gendered and /or racialized contradistinctions in the formulation of a barbaric Other. These were distinctions which had preoccupied writers since the time of Aristotle and Herodotus, and were frequently exploited in early modern publications.[37] Amongst Ralegh's own contemporaries, the future Archbishop of Canterbury, George Abbot, gave particular stress in one of his sermons to the impoverished faith of primitive peoples, invoking 'Those Ethnickes who knew little or nothing of true pietie ... People ruder then the Greekes and more barbarous then the Romanes ... I meane the Westerne Indians, the dull people of America, who thought that thunder and lightning & tempest were sent by the Sunne'.[38] And most famously in his *Apologie for Poesie*, Philip Sidney moved immediately from a consideration of 'our neighbour country Ireland, where truly learning goeth very bare' to the 'most barbarous and simple Indians'.[39]

Given the limitations of time and space in this discussion, it cannot be possible to give a full account of Ralegh's own experiences of brutal

---

35 Aristotle, *Aristotles politiques, or Discourses of gouernment* (1598), Bk I, ch. I, 7.
36 *History*, 5.1.1.264.
37 In this context, see *History*, 2.14.2.382: 'Thucydides, a writer of unquestionable sincerity, maketh it plaine, that the name of Barbarians was not used at all in Homers time, which was long after the warre of Troy ... I thinke that Paris had no regard either to the rape of Europa, Medea, or Hesione, but was merely incited by Venus, that is, by his lust, to doe that which in those dayes was very common. For not onely Greeks from Barbarians, and Barbarians from Greeks, as Herodotus discourseth; but all people were accustomed to steale women and cattell, if they could by strong hand or power get them: and having stolen them, either to sell them away in some farre Countrie, or keep them to their owne use.'
38 George Abbot, *An exposition vpon the prophet Ionah* (1600), the III lecture, 46.
39 See Sir Philip Sidney, *A Defence of Poetry*, ed. J. A. Van Dorsten (Oxford: Oxford University Press, 1966), 'Narration', 20.

military engagement and slaughter in the Plantation of Ireland which are discussed at length elsewhere in this book. Nevertheless, from the Elizabethan period onward, it is clear that there was a widespread cultural association in early modern print culture between the colonial projects across the Irish Sea and those further afield in the Americas.[40] In a dedicatory letter of 1587 to Ralegh, Richard Hakluyt stressed that 'it is not to bee denied, but that one hundred men will doe more nowe among the naked and vnarmed people in *Virginea*, then one thousande were able then to doe in Irelande against that armed and warrelike nation'.[41] And this axis of comparison would retain its currency throughout the early modern period. William Morrell's *New-England* (1625), for example, described the deviousness of the warlike Indian chiefs which resembled the 'deepe wyle' with which 'the *Irish* long withstood / The *English* power', whereas William Wood's *New Englands prospect* (1634) found that the 'deepe groane' of the grieving native American resembled '*Irish*-like howlings'.[42]

Ralegh served in Ireland in the years 1580 and 1581 and, under Lord Grey's command, his forces (amongst other activities) slaughtered the disarmed Catholic contingent sent by Gregory XIII to assist the Fitzgerald rebellion. Elizabeth had been excommunicated by the Pope in 1570 and thereafter, as Rapple emphasizes, 'throughout Europe Elizabeth was widely viewed as an illegitimate, lewd excommunicate'.[43] Under the command of Colonel Sebastiano di San Guiseppi, the Spanish and Italian troops found themselves besieged at Smerwick in County Kerry in September 1580. Hemmed in on the Dingle peninsula between English ships and Grey's army, the garrison capitulated. Once it was confirmed that that all arms had been surrendered, the company of some five to six hundred men was

---

40 For wider critical discussion here, see for example: K. R. Andrews, Nicholas P. Canny, and P. E. H. Hair, eds, *The Westward Enterprise: English activities in Ireland, the Atlantic and America 1480–1650* (Liverpool: Liverpool University Press, 1978); David J. Baker and Willy Maley, eds, *British Identities and English Renaissance Literature* (Cambridge: Cambridge University Press, 2002); Nicholas P. Canny, *Kingdom and Colony: Ireland in the Atlantic World 1560–1800* (Baltimore: Johns Hopkins University, 1988); Andrew Hadfield, *Literature, Travel and Colonial Writing in the English Renaissance 1545–1625* (Oxford: Oxford University Press, 1998); Andrew Hadfield, *Shakespeare, Spenser and the Matter of Britain* (Houndmills, Basingstoke: Macmillan /Palgrave, 2004); Shannon Miller, *Invested with Meaning: The Raleigh Circle in the New World* (Philadelphia: University of Pennsylvania Press, 1998).
41 See Richard Hakluyt, 'To the Right Worthie and Honourable Gentleman, Sir Walter Ralegh … R[ichard] H[akluyt] wisheth true felicitie', in René Goulaine de Laudonnière, *A notable historie containing foure voyages made by certayne French captaynes vnto Florida* (1587), n.s.
42 See respectively: William Morrell, *New-England* (1625), 20; William Wood, *New Englands prospect* (1634), chapter XIX 'Of their deaths, burials, and mourning', 93.
43 Rapple, *Martial Heroism*, 88.

cut down by the besiegers in an assault led by their captains. Grey himself wrote back to London, 'There were 600 slayne; munition & vittaile great store, though much wasted through the disorder of ye souldier, wch in y^t furie could not bee helped'.[44] Indeed, recollecting this event over a decade later, John Hooker reported that 'capteine Raleigh together with capteine macworth ... entered into the castell & made a great slaughter, manie or the most of them being put to the sword'.[45]

The significance of Ralegh's later engagement with military politics of Ireland and the extensive grant to him of 42,000 acres in the Munster plantation in 1587 is analysed in Thomas Herron's discussion in Chapter 3 above. However, on 10 May 1593 in response to the latest 'Irish combination', Ralegh wrote from his Dorset home to Robert Cecil, conjuring up (as was his wont on so many occasions) the vision of an imperial England beset by foes and consumed in remorseless conflict:

> Therbe ... others in Irland that lye in waite not suspected, which I most feare ... Wee ar so busyed and dandled in thes French warrs, which ar endless, as wee forgett the defens next the hart. Her Majesty hath good cause to remember that a million hath been spent in Irland not many yeares since. A better kingdome would have bynn purchased att a less prize and that same defended with as many pence if good order had bynn taken ... If Her Majestye conseder it aright shee shall fynde it no small dishonour to be vexed with so beggarly a nation, that have neather armes nor fortification ... and other then such shall it never bee.[46]

Ireland did not offer the lure of gold for settlers, but in English eyes it remained dangerously receptive to the influence of the Catholic powers in Europe and thus had to be secured militarily – whilst always keeping a watchful eye on the necessity of thrift. As has been witnessed above, early modern print culture relating to the Plantation widely invested in the promotion of Irish barbarism: indeed, the avenging Francisco in Webster's *The White Devil* (1612) confides, 'Like the wild Irish I'll ne'er think thee dead / Till I can play at football with thy head' (IV.i.136–7). It is manifestly apparent that the Elizabethan regime expressed no queasiness whatsoever about the brutal repression of Irish resistance. Remorseless

---

44 Cited in Vincent P. Carey, 'Grey, Spenser and the slaughter at Smerwick', in *Age of Atrocity. Violence and Political Conflict in Early Modern Ireland*, ed. Clodagh Tait, David Edwards and Pádraig Lenihan (Dublin: Four Courts Press, 2007), 90.
45 John Hooker, 'The Svpplie of the Irish Chronicles extended to this present yeare of our Lord 1586, and the 28 of the reigne of *queene Elisabeth*', in Raphael Holinshed, *The Second volume of Chronicles* (1586), 171.
46 Letter 60: 'To Sir Robert Cecil from Sherborne, 10 May 1595'. See Sir Walter Ralegh, *The Letters of Sir Walter Ralegh*, ed. Agnes Latham and Joyce Youings (Exeter: University of Exeter Press, 1999), 93–4.

violence was deployed both as a military strategy and as a deterrent by the occupying armies. Recalling his kinsman Humphrey Gilbert's 1569 campaign in Munster in a letter to Walsingham in 1581, Ralegh submitted that he had 'never heard nor read of any man more feared then [Gilbert] is among the Irish nation'.[47] The atrocities of the Munster campaign and the siege of Smerwick were very far from being isolated events in the account of Elizabethan dealings with Ireland. Just within the ten-year span following the slaughter at Smerwick, there were massacres performed by the troops of Sir John Norris and Francis Drake at Rathlin Island (1575), and two years later at Mullaghmast by Elizabethan troops. As Clodagh Tait, David Edwards and Pádraig Lenihan have highlighted, one of the governing stimuli for such conduct may indeed have been that the members of the English military forces were often

> recent arrivals in Ireland, with few ties to the local areas in which they operated or to the people whom they fought: their own loved ones were in little danger of immediate revenge attacks ... As well as getting rid of troublesome enemies, the use of massacre, murder and martial law communicated messages of strength and intent.[48]

The lessons of antiquity

Decades later, imprisoned within the confines of the Tower, Ralegh demonstrated a much keener interest in his prose narratives in the *protocol* of warfare. This is certainly the case in his account of the mercenary campaigns against the Carthaginian empire, for example. The decision of the Gaulish leader, Autarius, to put his prisoners 'to horrible death, by torments', together with the stonings of the resisting forces and the forcible amputation of hands of Carthaginian captives, is judged sternly by the presiding historian: 'Of this cruelty I need say no more, than that it was execrable severitie'.[49] With even greater solemnity in the final book of his *History*, Ralegh concludes:

---

47 Cited in Rapple, *Martial Heroism*, 238.
48 Clodagh Tait, David Edwards, and Pádraig Lenihan, 'Early Modern Ireland: A History of Violence', in *Age of Atrocity*, ed. Tait et al., 24. However, David Edwards underlines that 'endemic though warfare undoubtedly was [in early modern Ireland] there is little evidence to support the suggestion by reform-centred scholars that it produced an especially high level of bloodshed'. See Edwards, 'The escalation of violence in sixteenth-century Ireland': 'Ultimately, however, the fact that during wartime Irish armies chose not to slaughter the peasantry was more a matter of economics than ethics. People were a precious resource in early sixteenth-century Ireland' (ibid., 46).
49 *History*, 5.2.3.330.

there is no Profession more unprosperous than that of men of Warre, and great Captaines, being no Kings. For besides the envie and jealousie of men, the spoyles, rapes, famine, slaughter of the innocent, [de]vastation, and burnings, with a world of miseries laid on the labouring man, are so hatefull to God, as with good reason did *Monluc* the Marshall of *France* confesse, That *were not the mercies of God infinite, and without restriction, it were in vaine for those of his profession to hope for any portion of them: seeing the cruelties, by them permitted and committed, were also infinite*.[50]

We may find ourselves unexpectedly in the company of the contrite Soldier rather than the Historian at such moments, but it becomes increasingly apparent that such *personae* are not granted autonomous narrative identities. They compete for our attention in the authorial interventions throughout the chronicle, variously exciting responses of pathos and despair. In the complex textual environments of the *History*, Ralegh's reading subject is thus located within a dialectic, a very uneasy negotiation, between the material world of early modern politics and the symbolic world of apocalyptic history – and his *History* never fully resolves this unremitting conflict for the reader.

More generally, it had become a commonplace in Reformist thinking to regard the very business of human existence in terms of warfare. In one of his sermons preached during the reign of Edward VI, for example, Hugh Latimer affirmed the familiar tenet that '*Militia est vita hominis super terram*, The life of a man or woman is nothing ells but a warfare, it is nothing but a continuall battailyng & warring'.[51] And Ralegh's own historical writing is particularly influenced by such thinking. He observes, for example, in the *History* that, 'It is also a token of worldly wise man, not to warre or contend in vaine against the nature of times wherein he liveth: for such a one is often the author of his own misery'.[52] Most notable in an age given over to religious schism and polemic was the widespread appetite to theologize cultural alterity; and for English Reformists this discourse quickly formulated itself in terms of the monstrous ignorance, moral vacancy and spiritual decay of the Catholic Church. In John Foxe's magnum opus, the *Actes and Monuments*, Ralegh's notable predecessor in the business of chronicling barked, 'what is there almost in the pope's church, but either it is mingled, or depraved, or altered, or corrupted, either by some additions interlaced, or by some diminution mangled and

50 *History*, 5.6.2.617.
51 Hugh Latimer, *27 sermons preached by the ryght Reuerende father in God and constant matir [sic] of Iesus Christe* (1562), sig. 77v.
52 *History*, 1.1.15.17.

mutilated, or by some gloss adulterate, or with manifest lies contaminate?'[53] Pursuing an analogous line of enquiry in the 'Discovrse of ... Warre', Ralegh picks the bones of centuries-old narratives in order to unveil, in all its enormity, the present state of political emergency:

> It was the Rule of our Blessed *Sauiour, By their works you shall know them*, what the works of those that occupied the *Papacie*, have been since the dayes of *Pepin* and *Charlemaine* who first enabled them with Temporall donation, The *Italian* writers have have testified at large. Yet were it needlesse to cite *Machiavell*, who hath recorded their doings, and is therefore the more hatefull, or *Guicciardine*, whose works they have gelded, as not enduring to heare all that he hath written, though he spake enough in that which remains. What History shall we Read (excepting the *Annales* of *Caesar Baronius*, And some books of *Fryars*, or *Fryarly Parasites*) which mentioning their Acts doe not leave witnesse of their ungodly dealing in all quarters.[54]

It is in such evocations of insuperable cultural division that Ralegh, like Foxe, affirms the urgency of the commitment to national defence against an inveterate foe. This kind of adversarial cognitive mapping can be witnessed throughout *The History of the World*, as in following comparison of the Persians resisting Alexander the Great's advances and those of the Celts in North Wales resisting those of the Romans under the command of Julius Agricola: 'Yet Britaines were men stout enough, the Persians were very dastards'.[55] Indeed, even as his readers progressively navigate through the tangled narratives of the trials and tribulations of antique peoples in the final book of the unfinished *History*, this patriotic metanarrative is never left open to speculation:

> If therefore it be demanded, whether the *Macedonian*, or the *Roman*, were the best Warriour? I will answer: The *Englishmen*. For it will soone appeare, to any that shall examine the noble acts of our Nation in warre, that they were performed by no advantage of weapon; against no savage or vnmanly people; the enemy being farre superiour vnto us in number, and all needfull prouisions, yea as well trained as we, or commonly better, in the exercise of warre.[56]

---

53 Foxe, *Actes and Monuments* (1583), 584.
54 'A Discovrse of ... War', in *Judicious and Select Essayes*, sigs E7r–E7v.
55 *History*, 4.2.3.144. This may be compared with the following contention in the *History*: 'In *Caesar's* time *France* was inhabited by the *Gaules*, a stout people, but inferiour to the *French*, by whom they were subdued; even when the Romans gave them assistance' (ibid., 5.1.1.263).
56 *History*, 5.1.1.262. See also: 'That the militarie vertue of the English, prevailing against all maner of difficulties, ought to be preferred before that of the Romans, which was assisted with all advantage that could be desired' (ibid., 5.1.1.265).

Tudor England and the management of hostilities

One of the most famous examples from Ralegh's corpus of writing in which he indulges in the remorseless demonization of the warlike nation is the pamphlet *A report of the truth of the fight about the Isles of Açores, this last summer,*[57] *betwixt the Revenge, one of her Majesty's Ships, and an Armada of the King of Spain* (1591) – a text which often became required reading in the classroom for generations of schoolchildren from the Victorian period onward. In this account, attempting to occlude the loss of a valuable vessel from Her Majesty's fleet and a singular display of military incompetence, Ralegh endeavours to scotch the rumours which 'are diversely spread ... [by] the Spaniards according to their usual manner'. Thus, England's great enemies are found once again to be deviously circulating any number of 'false & slanderous Pamphlets, advisoes and letters, to cover their own loss', just as they had in the aftermath of the Armada when it was apparent to everyone that their invincible navy was on that occasion defeated 'by thirty of her Majesty's own ships of war, and a few of our own merchants ... beaten and shuffled together'.[58] Here, Ralegh's narrator is as exercised by the need to create a model of heroic resistance to the ever encroaching powers of Philip II's empire as he is to vilify the seemingly innumerable forces of Continental Catholicism. It is notable that in this instance even the base men of war on the Spanish galleons are compelled to bear witness to the peerless fortitude of Sir Richard Grenville on the *Revenge*.

However, the celebrated example of the *Report* numbers but one endeavour in Ralegh's writing career designed to excite vigorous reader engagement by exploiting prejudices concerning cultural difference. Perhaps with just such a figure as Ralegh in mind, Churchyard contended that 'sometymes through the greatnesse of their myndes, [those] that galloppes after glorie, are carried awaie to seeke out newe kyngdomes'.[59] Ralegh travelled on the first occasion to Guiana (modern-day Venezuela) in 1595, and *The discouerie of the large, rich, and bewtiful empire of Guiana* (1596), like all his textual accounts of England's imperial project, is deeply penetrated with the political insecurities of the Elizabethan ruling elite and the rapacity of the growing community of speculators ever alert to the riches continually drawn across the Atlantic by the gold fleets of Philip II. In such discussions Ralegh is eager to legitimize the Elizabethans' claims

---

57 Referring to August 1591.
58 *A report of the truth of the fight about the Isles of Açores* (1591), sigs A3v–A4r.
59 Churchyard, *A generall rehearsall of warres*, sig. M3r.

to colonies overseas by calling to mind their dealings with this Atlantic world in the past. He notes, for example, that native English adventurers competed with their Iberian rivals to survey the coast of the new lands during the reign of Henry VII: 'The west Indies were first offered Her Maiesties Grandfather by Columbus, a straunger, in whome there might be doubt of deceipt'.[60] The *impresa* of the Spanish royal house was *Non sufficit orbis* (The world does not suffice), and Ralegh's *Discoverie* offers the opportunity to his fellow countrymen to redress what he perceives as the gross economic and political advantages which England's enemy has enjoyed as a consequence of its American possessions:

> It is his Indian Golde that indaungereth and disturbeth all the nations of Europe, it purchaseth intelligence, creepeth into Councels, and setteth bound loyalty at libertie, in the greatest Monarchies of Europe. If the spanish king can keepe vs from forraine enterprizes, and from the impeachment of his trades, eyther by offer of inuasion, or by beseiging vs in Britayne, Ireland, or else where, he hath then brought the worke of our perill in greate forwardnes.[61]

One of Ralegh's officers on this voyage, Lawrence Keymis, shadowed the steps of his master in performing a repeat journey to Guiana in 1596, and in publishing an account of his travels. In his own *Relation of the Second Voyage to Guiana* Keymis affirmed, with a vehemence equal to that of Ralegh himself, that the 'Castilians ... [in South America] preached nought els but auarice, rapine, blood, death, and destruction to those naked, sheeplike creatures of God'.[62] However, in this context, Ralegh's reader might be tempted to enjoy the irony that, in an aside from the fourth book of the *History*, the author dispenses with the suasive tones of his wonted textual *personae* and disarmingly submits:

> We finde it in daily experience, that all discourse of magnanimity, of Nationall Vertue, of Religion, of Liberty, and whatsoever else hath bin wont to move and incourage virtuous men, hath no force at all with the common-Souldier, in comparison of spoile and riches ... *Car où il n'y a rien a gaigner que des coups, volontiers il n'y va pas.* No man makes haste to the market, where there is nothing to be bought but blowes.[63]

---

60 *Discouerie*, sig. O2r.
61 *Discouerie*, sig. 3v.
62 Lawrence Keymis, *A Relation of the Second Voyage to Guiana*, sig. F2v. In equally belligerent terms, Ralegh asserted in his 1618 'Apology' (which attempted to justify his past conduct) that 'True it is, that the Spaniards cannot endure that the English Nation should looke upon any part of America, being above a fourth part of the whole knowne world; and the hundredth part neither possessed by the Spaniards nor to them known'. See 'Sir Walter Rawleigh His Apologie for his Voyage to Guiana', in *Judicious and Select Essayes*, 51.
63 *History*, 4.2.4.148.

Yet if Ralegh is regularly inscribed in modern critical narratives of early modern colonization, it must be acknowledged that his contribution to empire-building in this period was principally textual in nature. His journeys to Guiana in 1595 and 1617 resulted largely in reconnaissance missions. Ralegh himself never set foot in the New World of Virginia, but he did fund five expeditions during his lifetime to the colony and clearly continued to envisage his native land as a great imperial power in-the-making, if it would only seize its destiny. Even in the final months before his downfall and arrest in 1602 he wrote in prophetic mode, 'I shall yet see it [Virginia] an English nation'.[64]

War and the mythologies of empire

When Ralegh draws his reader across to the New World, he is often found (like so many colonial publicists in this period) to be at great pains to mystify the ordeals and miseries which have now come to be associated with European settlement in the Americas: 'All the most of the kings of the borders are already become her Maiesties vassals: & seeme to desire nothing more then her Maiesties protection, and the returne of the English nation'.[65] As has been widely appreciated in recent scholarship, European publications which treated the New World invested deeply in this gendered discourse of seduction and submission, both in terms of narrative development and the reproduction of images.[66] More generally, given the profoundly volatile environment of attritional politics in which England found itself in the final decades of the sixteenth century, it was perhaps unsurprising that Elizabethan writers continued to be preoccupied with the salvific prospect of a *Venus Armata*. Indeed, in his ill-fated publication opposing the Alençon match, *The discouerie of a gaping gulf whereinto England is like to be swallowed by another French mariage* (1579), John Stubbe celebrated Elizabeth in explicitly military terms as 'our Queene, the chiefe officer in England, our most precious rych treasure, our Elizabeth IONAH and ship of good speede, the royall ship of our ayde, the hyghest tower, the strongest hold, and castle in the land' – and had his right hand cut off by Her Majesty's servants for his

---

64 Cited in Edward Thompson, *Sir Walter Ralegh: The Last of the Elizabethans* (London: Macmillan, 1935), 51.
65 *Discouerie*, sig. A4r.
66 And, of course, nowhere is this more apparent than in the second edition (1590) of Harriot's *Briefe and true report* which was published with Theodore de Bry's engraved plates.

trouble.[67] If Ralegh acknowledges in the course of his own discussion that an imperial future for the English nation may warrant the intervention of men of war, it is made abundantly clear that the inevitable rewards for such hostilities will far outweigh any initial experience of hardship in this land of plenty:

> The common soldier shal here fight for gold, and pay himselfe in steede of pence, with plates of halfe a foote brode, wheras he breaketh his bones in other warres for prouant and penury ... There is no countrey which yeeldeth more pleasure to the Inhabitants, either for these common delights of hunting, hawking, fishing, fowling, and the rest, then *Guiana* doth ... It hath a kinde of beast called *Cama*, or *Anta*, as bigge as an English beefe, and in greate plenty.[68]

Such Golden Age geographies were made available in the *Discouerie* and would continue to figure in English colonial publications for generations because Elizabeth and her successors were unwilling to bankroll in a sustained manner any initiatives regarding the founding of an Atlantic empire.[69] Moreover, butchery and slaughter were recurring features of the Elizabethan participation in European politics, whether it was in Ireland, in the Low Countries, or in the Atlantic World. In the *Discouerie* Ralegh is determined to expose the polluting influence of Hispanic domination and the heavy price of England's political inertia in such a situation, but this should not dull our own senses to the constructedness of the imperial future he unveils for the English. Mary B. Campbell affirms with notable vigour that 'Ralegh's intentions were no better than those of Cortés ... like Cortés, Ralegh pays close attention to "internal" dissensions among the indigenous people, aware that he cannot conquer without native allies ... My point is that Ralegh's political ethics were about as low as those of any other Renaissance man of action'.[70] Indeed, in this context, Vincent

---

67 John Stubbe, *The discouerie of a gaping gulf whereinto England is like to be swallowed by another French mariage* (1579), sig. C2r. Jonson may have had such tributes in mind when he has his own Queen of Faery hailed in *The Alchemist* as 'our castle, our Cinque Port, / Our Dover pier, our what thou wilt' (III.iii.18–19).

68 *Discouerie*, 94. In this context, Pierre Lefranc underlines the following: 'même quand elles sont plus longues, les descriptions de Ralegh sont fréquemment cernées de considerations pratiques ... lorsque le regard de Ralegh s'attarde sur certains détails du paysage, décrits avec precision, c'est souvent avec l'intention d'indiquer au lecteur que le relief et la végétation se prêtent à la pénétration, où au contraire s'y opposent: le coup d'œil reste militaire'. See Pierre Lefranc, *Sir Walter Ralegh Écrivain* (Paris: Librairie Armand Colin, 1968), 551.

69 See respectively: John Donne, *The Sermons of John Donne in Ten Volumes*, edited by George R. Potter and Evelyn M. Simpson (Berkeley and Los Angeles: University of California Press, 1959), IV:266; Ralegh, *History*, sig. C2v.

70 See Mary B. Campbell, *The Witness and the Other World: Exotic European Travel Writing*,

P. Carey remains timely in his reminder that 'in the Kerry Gaeltacht as late as the end of the nineteenth century, parents are reported to have substituted the traditional phrase of admonishment to children for bad behaviour "cughat an pucha" with the warning "cughat an Rawley", or watch out for the Ralegh!'[71]

Ralegh the strategist: logistics and lines of command

If in publications such as the *Discouerie* Ralegh fails to proffer even the most basic pragmatic analysis and advice to willing colonists that would have been made available (in admittedly foreshortened form) in a work such as Francis Bacon's essay 'Of Plantations', when he turns his attentions to theatres of war in Europe, the case is altered. In the essay entitled 'Excellent Observations and Notes concerning the Royall Navy and Sea-Service' (published 1650, evidence of composition in the periods 1597–98, c. 1608, and after 1612), Ralegh proves himself much more systematic and focused in his thinking about England's urgent need to assert itself politically and to expand its influence across the globe than is the case in his less critically neglected exploration narratives. Here, adopting the narrative persona of experienced military strategist, he pursues a theme familiar throughout his publications and correspondence – that the nation's well-being is intimately bound up with the vigilant maintenance of her military forces. Indeed, he shows himself at pains to set out the requisite topics for discussion concerning the ordering of suitable casks for sea journeys, the activities of press-gangs, the organization of 'cook-rooms', and the transportation of munitions:

> your lowest Tyre of Ordnance must lye foure foot clere above water when all loading is in, or else those your best pieces will be of small use at the Sea in any growne weather that makes the Billoe to rise, for then you shall be enforced to take in all your lower Ports, or else hazard the Ship. As befell to the *Mary Rose* (a goodly vessell) which in the days of King *Hen.* 8 being before the Isle of *Wight*, with the rest of the Royall Navy, to encounter the French Fleet, with a suddain puff of wind stooped her side, and tooke in water at her Ports in such abundance, as that she instantly sunk downeright and many gallant men in her.[72]

400–1600 (Ithaca and London: Cornell University Press, 1988), 240, 241.
71 Vincent P. Carey, 'Grey, Spenser and the Slaughter at Smerwick', in *Age of Atrocity*, ed. Tait et al., 87.
72 'Excellent Observations and Notes concerning the Royall Navy and Sea-Service', in *Judicious and Select Essayes*, 11–12.

Throughout the *Judicious and Select Essayes*, in order to reverse his nation's recurring political experience of marginalization and displacement in European affairs, Ralegh gravitates again and again to the strategic importance of military strength. His reader is reminded forcefully in 'A Discourse of the invention of Ships, Anchors, Compasse &c. The first Naturall Warre, the seuerall, use, defects, and supplies of Shipping, the strength and defects of the Sea forces of England, France, Spaine, and Venice, Together with the five manifest causes of the suddaine appearing of the Hollanders' (composed 1608–10?) that 'whosoever commands the Sea, Commands the Trade: whosoever Commands the Trade of the world: Commands the Riches of the world and consequently the world it selfe'.[73] Furthermore, we are left in no doubt that England has been far from politically prudent hitherto in looking to its own interests:

> But there is no state growne in hast, but that of the united provinces, and especially in their Sea forces, and by a contrary way to that of *France*, or *Spaine*, the latter by Invasion, the former by oppression; For I my self may remember when one ship of her Majesties, would have made forty *Hollanders* strike sayle, and to come to Anchor. They did not then dispute *De mari libero*, but readily acknowledg'd the English to be *Domini maris Brittanici*: That we are lesse powerfull then we were, I doe hardly believe it, For although we have not at this time 135 ships, belonging to the subjects, of 500 tuns each ship, as it is said we had in the 24. yeare of Queen *Elizabeth*, at which time, also upoon a generall view and muster, there were found in *England* of all men, fit to beare armes, eleaven hundred and seaventy two thousand, yet are our Merchants ships, now farre more warlike and better appointed then they were, and the Navy Royall double as strong as then it was ... I say then if a *Vanguard* be ordeined of these *hoyes*, who will easily recover the wind of any other ships, with a Battaile of 400 other warlike ships, and a Reare of thirty of his Majesties ships to sustaine, relieve and countenance the rest (if God beat them not) I know not what strength can be gathered in all *Europe* to beat them.[74]

In reviewing his whole career as an author and political adventurer, it soon becomes apparent that this 'Theme and Argument ... of War' which Ralegh described at the opening of his 'Discovrse of ... Warre' not only dominates his historical writings, but haunts every aspect of his prose writing. Whether in his essays, his exploration narratives of the New

---

73 'A Discourse of the invention of Ships, Anchors, Compasse &c. The first Naturall Warre, the seuerall, use, defects, and supplies of Shipping, the strength and defects of the Sea forces of England, France, Spaine, and Venice, Together with the five manifest causes of the suddaine appearing of the Hollanders', in *Judicious and Select Essayes*, 20.
74 Ibid., 27–30.

World, his correspondence, or his great folio *The History of the World*, Ralegh turns repeatedly to the question of war as a cognitive building block with which to establish his social and political vision.

Final phase: the unheeded adviser

At the close of this discussion, it is timely to recall that Ralegh does not fail in his compendious *History* to draw attention at several reprises to the failing fortunes of those who serve as men of war.

> It were an endlesse and a needlesse worke to tell how many hundreds, or rather thousands, hoping of Captaines to make themselves kings, have by Gods justice miserably perished in the attempt. The ordinary, and perhaps, the best way of thriving by the practice of Armes, is to take what may be gotten by the spoyle of Enemies, and the liberality of those Princes and Cities, in whose service one hath well deserved. But scarce one of a thousand have prospered by this course.[75]

Yet whatever the irrepressible nature of Ralegh's melancholia in evidence throughout much of the *History*, his *Instructions to his sonne and to posteritie* (1632) and his verse, for example, this ageing Prisoner in the Tower was forced to assume a more sanguine disposition towards his last royal master (and gaoler), 'his Majestie hath already paid the greatest part of that debt. For besides the relieving by Pensions all the poorer sort, hee hath honoured more Martial men than all the Kings of *England* have done for this hundred yeers'.[76] In 1607, the world-weary Ralegh had petitioned James I's consort, Anne of Denmark, from the Tower to be allowed to join the Jamestown settlement. In the event, only his nephew, Ralph Gilbert, was permitted to represent the family on the voyage to America. Since his trial in 1603 Ralegh had been pronounced legally dead. He was eventually permitted to serve his irascible King with a last voyage to Guiana in 1617 in search of gold – however, the Stuart monarch had already forewarned the Spanish of his itinerary and the venture was thus doomed to fail.

Despite his various experiences of disempowerment, Ralegh never forsook his identities of published writer and courtly correspondent. He remained eager to respond to the ever-present threat of war and invasion

---

75 *History*, 5.6.2.618. See also: 'the number of those that have purchased absolute greatnesse by the greatnesse of their warlike vertue; is farre more in seeming than in deed … [in] my late Soveraignes time … her Majesty had no lesse cause to vse the seruice of Marshal [martial] men … yet, according to the destiny of that profession, I do not remember that any of hers, the Lord Admirall excepted … were either enriched, or otherwise honoured, for any service by them performed' (*History*, 5.6.2.618).
76 *History*, 5.6.2.619.

through the business of writing itself – and to memorialize himself into the bargain. Indeed, even as the most famous inmate of the Tower of London Ralegh knew how to attract a sympathetic audience in times of adversity with a highly varied repertoire of self-dramas: 'drawing after me the chaines and Fetters whereunto I have been thirteen yeares tyed in the Tower, being unpardoned and in disgrace with my Soveraigne Lord'.[77] With his customary passion, Ralegh insisted that in a letter to his cousin and Privy Councillor, George, Lord Carew, in the summer of 1618 that

> the Spaniards give us no peace there [in the Americas], it doth appear by the king's letter to his governor that they shall put to death all those Spaniards and Indians that trade *con los Engleses enimigos* – with English enemies. Yea, those very Spaniards which we encountered at St Thome did of late years murder thirty-six of Mr Hall's men of London, and mine, who landed without weapon, upon the Spanish faith to trade with them. Mr Thorne also, of Tower Street in London, besides many other English, was in like sort murdered, the year before my delivery out of the Tower.[78]

One of Ralegh's earliest lyrics had been a dedicatory poem 'in commendation of the Steele Glasse' (1576) by George Gascoigne, and the belief continues that the young Devon man liked Gascoigne's motto so much (*Tam Marti quam Mercurio* – 'dedicated to Mars as to Mercury') that he adopted it as his own. In both life and in death Ralegh also became a focus for the martial ambitions of competing European powers. Indeed, his execution in 1618 seems to have served to raise his international profile even further – exactly as his enemies had feared. Spain's agent in London wrote back to his master in code that '[t]he death of this man has produced a great commotion and fear here, and it is looked upon as a matter of the highest importance, owing to his being a person of great parts and experience, subtle, crafty, ingenious, and brave enough for anything'.[79]

A few years before his execution, the imprisoned Ralegh endeavoured (as earlier generations of humanist scholars had advised) to endear himself as a political servant and adviser with a new manuscript presented to his implacable sovereign in 1615. In the event, this new production would do little to assuage the unfailing enmity of his master. It was entitled *A Dialogue between a Counsellor of State and a Justice of the Peace on the*

---

77 'Apologie', in *Judicious and Select Essayes*, 1.
78 Letter to George, Lord Carew, summer 1618, in Ralegh, *The Letters of Sir Walter Ralegh*, 249.
79 Cited in Anna Beer, *Sir Walter Ralegh and His Readers in the Seventeenth Century* (London: Macmillan, 1997), 96.

subject of the King's prerogative, and the wide-ranging discussion returned attention on a number of occasions to the previous adult male who had sat upon the English throne: 'Now for King Henry the eight: if all the pictures and patternes of a mercilesse Prince were lost in the World, they might all againe be painted to the life, out of the story of this King'.[80] If, on his own accession to the throne in 1603, James sought to establish an Empire of Great Britain with its own flag, coinage, and imperial leader, Ralegh remained deeply disappointed by the administration's foreign policy of rapprochement with Spain. Indeed, in his captivity and final voyage to Guiana in 1617, he stood as an abiding victim of it. In the 1615 *Dialogue*, an excursus on English parliamentary history, Ralegh turned back to the theme which began this discussion – England's involvement in French wars. As we have seen, he had despaired in the *Discouerie* of the failure of the early Tudors to enlist the services of pioneers like Columbus to build a mighty future for the nation: thus, Henry VII had squandered the prospect of an Atlantic Empire; and in comparison with this lost opportunity, Henry VIII's vain attempts at French campaigns of conquest inevitably appeared contemptible in Ralegh's eyes. Indeed, in the 1615 *Dialogue*, he distilled some of his final thoughts on these doomed military endeavours, and has his Justice of the Peace ponder the grave implications of failed leadership in times of peace and war:

> And for King Henry the eight, although he was left in a most plentifull estate yet hee wonderfully prest his people with great payments; for in the beginning of his time it was infinite that he spent in Masking and Tilting, Banquetting and other vanities, before he was entred into the most consuming expence of the most fond and fruitlesse warre that euer King vndertooke.[81]

---

80 Sir Walter Ralegh, *The Prerogative of Parliaments in England* (Middelburg, 1628). Facsimile (Amsterdam: Walter J. Johnson /Theatrum Orbis Terrarum Ltd, 1974), sig. A4v.
81 *Prerogative of Parliaments* (1974), 53.

10

Ralegh's 'As You Came from the Holy Land' and the rival virgin queens of late sixteenth-century England

Gary Waller

The remarkable poem traditionally attributed to Sir Walter Ralegh, 'As You Came from the Holy Land', deserves special attention, both for its remarkable poetical resonance and as an indication of broader cultural shifts in late Elizabethan England. There is, as with so many poems ascribed to Ralegh, some question concerning the poem's authorship. As Steven W. May notes, Ralegh's poetry 'presents one of the most difficult editorial problems of the English Renaissance'. MS Rawlinson poet 85 attributes it to him, and both Agnes Latham and Katherine Duncan-Jones agree. Michael Rudick, however, excludes the poem from his carefully limited list of poems definitely attributable to Ralegh. To adapt Susanne Woods's wise conclusion of her discussion of the authorship of 'The Passionate Man's Pilgrimage', 'I do not insist', she says, that Ralegh wrote it, 'but I am confident he could have, and I tend to think he did. Neither content nor style eliminates him, while the weight of manuscript attributions combined with the concluding tone of the poem appear to me to keep him firmly in the running'.[1] The hypnotic beauty of the lyric amply justifies its presence in anthologies and many lists of best poems, and it has become widely accepted as part of the central canon of English short poems.

For the purposes of my argument, I assume Ralegh's authorship, not least (as Duncan-Jones and Woods argue) because so many of its details fit both his public and his literary lives. My focus here is on both the poem

---

1 Steven W. May, *The Elizabethan Courtier Poets: The Poems and Their Contexts* (Columbia: University of Missouri Press, 1991), 362; Agnes M. C. Latham, ed., *The Poems of Sir Walter Ralegh* (London: Routledge, 1951), 120–2; Katherine Duncan-Jones, 'Raleigh's "Walsingham": A Faux-Naif Ballad', *Critical Survey* 4 (1969), 90–2; Michael Rudick, *Poems of Sir Walter Ralegh: A Historical Edition* (Ithaca: Cornell University Press, 2000), 85–6; Susanne Woods, '"The Passionate Man's Pilgrimage": Ralegh Is Still in the Running', *Modern Language Studies* 8. 3 (Autumn 1978), 12–19.

itself and the associated tune and related poems that lie behind it. Both melody and words combine to provide much of that hypnotic power, its brilliance resting on the incantatory rhythms, the slow, almost ritualistic, way it builds its repetitive spell. I will also explore the poem's association with the 'holy land' of the opening line, since it is one of a number of poems from the late sixteenth century that articulate a nostalgia for the long-ruined shrine of the Virgin Mary at Little Walsingham in Norfolk. Ralegh's Walsingham poem is all the more interesting since it was written in the heart of Elizabeth's Protestant court at a time when Catholics were (or were presented as) menacing to both England's state religion and its nationhood.

Few non-Catholic English people late in the century would have recognized Our Lady of Walsingham and her shrine, except in memory, as one of the hundreds of ruins scattered across the English landscape caused by the devastation of the Dissolution of the monasteries in 1538. Yet Walsingham had once been home to a shrine that drew many thousands of pilgrims; it had been centred on what the reformers and iconoclasts saw as an idolatrous statue of the Virgin Mary and relics like a vial of her milk taken, Erasmus (tongue-in-cheek) assured his readers, directly from her breasts.[2] Even twenty years after the shrine's destruction, the Elizabethan Church's homilies could warn against Our Lady of Walsingham as an idol, and the Homilies' primary author, Bishop John Jewel, spoke of the blasphemy of regarding Mary as 'our lady and goddess'.[3] By late in the century, the shrine was partly in ruins, partly transformed into the home of a minor member of the Sidney family, who had been rewarded for supporting the Crown during the Dissolution. By then, however, at least in court circles, the name 'Walsingham' would be primarily recognized as that of Elizabeth's powerful and somewhat sinister minister, the spymaster Sir Francis Walsingham, who died in 1590. But the name had also come to refer to the subject and title of a popular folk ballad, both the words and a tune. References to it are sufficient in number to suggest that it was a well-known part of Elizabethan popular culture. In his celebrated collection of traditional ballads and songs, the eighteenth-century bishop Thomas Percy noted that 'the scene of this beautiful old ballad is laid near Walsingham, in Norfolk, where was anciently an image of the Virgin Mary, famous all over Europe for the numerous pilgrimages made

---

2 Desiderius Erasmus, *The Pilgrimage of Pure Devotion* (London, 1536), in *Tudor Translations of the Colloquies of Erasmus (1536–1584)*, facsimile repr., introd. Dickie A. Spurgeon (Delmar: Scholars' Facsimiles and Reprints, 1972), 53.
3 *Certain Sermons Or Homilies Appointed to be Read in Churches in the Time of Queen Elizabeth* (London, 1855), 158.

to it, and the great riches it possessed'.[4] It is from that later period of antiquarian and somewhat nostalgic medievalism that it becomes known as the 'Walsingham Ballad'.

It was once thought that Ralegh's version was the original. But as Alison Chapman has shown in a careful survey of references to different versions of the ballad, just as the Walsingham tune occurs in many variations, Ralegh's is just one of a number of variations of the words. Indeed, though we conventionally speak of 'it', the Walsingham ballad is really a family of words and music. Ralegh's poem is the most celebrated literary member of this family, just as William Byrd's Walsingham Variations is the most famous musical member. But neither is the original. Both words and music in fact merge in Ralegh's ballad, and, to appreciate the significance of his piece, we need to look at both music and words.[5]

First, to the Walsingham tune. It was one of the most popular tunes of the period. There are over thirty extant musical variants of 'Walsingham' from the period by over twenty composers, found in many published and unpublished collections, including the century's premier collection of keyboard songs, the Fitzwilliam Virginal Book. Byrd's composition has been universally praised for the extraordinary technical virtuosity of its twenty-two variations. John Bull's versions, also in the Fitzwilliam Book and likely written to compete with Byrd's, is also one of the greatest (and longest, at nineteen minutes) keyboard pieces of the time. Both composers clearly take over a melody that had evidently become part of Elizabethan folklore and elaborately and lovingly enhance it. There are also lute settings of 'Walsingham' by, among others, Francis Cutting, John Dowland, Edward Collard, and John Marchant.[6]

Byrd's most likely dates from the 1580s. He was the premier Elizabethan keyboard composer, and, despite his unwavering Catholicism, was employed in Elizabeth's own chapel. Jeremy Smith terms him the Shostakovich of his age, in that he conformed to the regime but directed much of his work to opposing it, at least in sentiment. As Master of the Queen's music, he dutifully composed for the Anglican liturgy and (like Ralegh himself) celebrated the Queen in anthems, including 'O Lord, make thy

---

4 Thomas Percy, *Reliques of Old English Poetry: Consisting of Old Heroic Ballads, Songs etc* (New York: F. Warne & Sons, 1887), 183.

5 Alison A. Chapman, 'Met I with an old bald Mare': Lust, Misogyny, and the Early Modern Walsingham Ballads', in *Walsingham in Literature and Culture from the Middle Ages to Modernity*, ed. Dominic Janes and Gary Waller (Farnham: Ashgate, 2010), 217–31.

6 For a detailed discussion of Byrd's variations, see Bradley Brookshire, 'Bare Ruin'd Quiers, Where Late the Sweet Birds Sang': Covert Speech in William Byrd's Walsingham Variations', in Janes and Waller, *Walsingham*, 199–216.

servant Elizabeth our Queen', and madrigals like 'This sweet and merry month of May', in which 'Eliza' is described as 'the Queen of second Troy'. But most of Byrd's music shows affinities with, if not outright allegiance to, those recusant forces that were actively trying to undermine the Elizabethan settlement and bring about England's return to Rome. His music is overwhelmingly preoccupied with what Joseph Kerman terms 'guilt-ridden prayers for mercy or at least expressions of personal penitence, laments for Jerusalem, the destroyed city, or the Babylonian captivity', all themes that are easily interpreted in terms of the religious situation in which Byrd and his fellow recusants found themselves. Kerman argues that 'Byrd's impressive, deeply felt motets of the 1580s should be viewed as covert protests, prayers and exhortations voiced on behalf of the beleaguered Catholic minority'.[7]

Bradley Brookshire describes Byrd's Walsingham variations as his *roman à clef*. Placing the composition in the context of Elizabethan religious tensions, he argues, reveals how Byrd's stylistic features made clear his religious allegiances. Byrd opens as if he were writing a choral work: a single cantoral voice gives the first two bars; a tutti of four to five voices responds and then rises to a complex cadence, a pattern that is repeated throughout, and which mirrors the characteristic pattern not of his secular ballads but of his motets.[8] The persecuted English Catholics with whom Byrd was closely associated would have immediately made the connection between the tune and their own plight. The result is a composition in which nostalgia for Walsingham interrogates the Reformation and the consequent spiritual impoverishment of England. Bull's variations likewise go far beyond what a setting of a ballad would demand. By choosing the Walsingham tune, both composers are affirming their commitment to Catholicism and the memory of the Virgin's shrine at Walsingham. The tune becomes a passionate expression of loss and defiance, no doubt all the more easily articulated because, as music, it would escape the verbal scrutiny or censure that a poem might attract. For Catholics, the tune's continuing presence and popularity in late Elizabethan and Jacobean England constituted both a memory of what Walsingham had once represented and an affirmation of an alternative to the hegemony of the Reformation.[9]

---

7 Joseph Kerman, 'Byrd's Settings of the Ordinary of the Mass', *Journal of the American Musicological Society* 32.3 (1979), 408.
8 Brookshire, 'Bare Ruin'd Quiers', 202.
9 Wilfrid Mellers, 'John Bull and English Keyboard Music – II', *The Musical Quarterly* 40 (1954), 561, 571. For the Bull version, see also Peter J. Seng, *The Vocal Songs in the Plays of Shakespeare* (Cambridge, MA: Harvard University Press, 1967), 131–42; F. W. Sternfeld, 'Ophelia's Version of the Walsingham Song', *Music and Letters* 45 (April 1964), 108–13.

Now to the words of Walsingham Ballad, which from the start seem to have been associated with the basic tune with which the musical composers worked, though in fact they eventually have a very different history. The words also reflect the typical folk origins of the ballad form, with a communal rather than an individual author. The ballad, says Mary Ellen Brown, is a fluid, dynamic practice: simple in diction, direct in narrative, focused in emotion, communally based rather than individual. The Walsingham ballad incorporates elements found in ballad collections from Bishop Percy in the eighteenth-century ballad revival onwards – the magical and marvellous; the romantic and tragic; and the semi-historical.[10] As with other ballads, which emerge in print out of a folk rather than a literary culture, can we deduce there was some kind of Walsingham Ur-Ballad? Did the words get adapted to an existing tune? Or was the tune written for the Ur-version of the Ballad's words? It is impossible to say. Ballads grow from desires and needs that may be ideologically as well as stylistically marginal in changing societies. Thus they are often redolent with nostalgia for a past world, not merely for an individual loss or lack, serving to bring from the margins of a culture feelings, desires, and a class or subgroup's aspirations or losses. Typically the nostalgia is transferred from its original object to a new set of associations, as certainly seems to be the case with Ralegh's version.

The poem's basic situation is of a question-and-answer dialogue between an abandoned lover and a pilgrim on a road – presumably, since it is somewhere on a road to Walsingham, what medieval pilgrims to the Shrine knew as the 'Walsingham Way' – the pilgrim who is returning from the Shrine. Opening lines vary slightly, as is common in a folk lyric: 'As I went to Walsingham', 'Have at you to Walsingham', and 'As you came from [the holy land of] Walsingham'. In some versions some explicit connections to ongoing activities at the Shrine of the Virgin are made: 'As I went to Walsingham to the shrine with speed / Met I with a jolly palmer in a pilgrim's weed' – though that may be a construct of nostalgia, not a clue to the date of composition. The bereft speaker then bewails that his lover has also gone on pilgrimage but has not returned. The key question is whether the pilgrim has seen her. Asked how she would be recognized, he attempts to describe her. That seems, at least, to be the general starting point for most versions: what follows may vary somewhat. Bishop Percy's eighteenth-century collection of ballads includes another quite distinct narrative, a dialogue between a pilgrim and a herdsman. The pilgrim,

---

10 Mary Ellen Brown, 'Placed, Replaced, or Misplaced?: The Ballads' Progress', *Eighteenth Century* 47 (2006), 123.

who turns out to be a woman, is wanting to learn the way to Walsingham so she may repent and die – she has treated her lover so cruelly that he has died and she wishes to join him. Having the speaker be a woman, of course, is a characteristic shared with Shakespeare's version which I will discuss briefly later.

Ralegh's version may be the high point of the Walsingham ballad, but the evolution of the words and their connotations takes a very different path in the seventeenth century. With the music, the connotations remain sympathetic to the Catholic sense of loss and nostalgia; the words, however, become associated with idolatry and sexual scurrility. Walsingham is evoked in a number of poems and plays and in incidental references, but it becomes a place not merely for contrition, punishment, and death but a symbol of sexual depravity, an expression of the idolatrous sexualization of the Virgin that the Reformers saw in the medieval Church's over-valuation of the Virgin Mary. Chapman discusses allusions to Walsingham in works by Thomas Deloney, George Attowell, in Beaumont and Fletcher's *The Knight of the Burning Pestle*, in Francis Quarles's *The Virgin Widow*, and in a number of anonymous plays and poems. Walsingham, she argues, becomes 'associated in the popular imagination with sexual immorality, even long after its relationship to a specific shrine in Norfolk had been half-forgotten'. References to the Walsingham Ballad become a kind of code phrase for corrupt sexual practices, to the point that, in *The Virgin Widow*, simply whistling the Walsingham tune might be seen as sexual insult.[11] This development of the poem-ballad reflects the Protestant view of Walsingham just as surely as the tradition of musical variations, starting with Byrd, reflects the Catholic.

Ralegh's version was probably written in the early 1590s: in 1596 Nashe mentions the Ballad in *Have with You to Saffron Walden* as if everyone would understand the reference. If Brookshire's argument on the date of the Byrd variations of the tune is correct, some version of both the words and music would have been common knowledge a decade before at least. But its transformation, as Ralegh's poem vividly illustrates, demonstrates how Walsingham had by the 1590s become at least in part detached from its Catholic origins, and was becoming a broader though no less rich symbol of human loss, tragedy, and nostalgia. It is not coincidental that these signs emerge in the last decade or two in the century, in the restless post-Armada decade, when a number of poets and dramatists were

---

11 Alison Chapman, 'Met I with an old bald Mare', 226. I am especially indebted to Professor Chapman for her penetrating analyses of the poetical tradition of the Walsingham ballad.

stating to sidle up to the forbidden trappings of Catholicism. Walsingham clearly has become, and not just for Catholics, a mysterious place of loss and nostalgia, contrition, punishment, and even death; the religious significance of Walsingham may have faded but its liminal suggestiveness has remained.

It is curious then why Ralegh, determined to assert himself in the ultra-Protestant court of Elizabeth through poetry as well as courtiership, soldiery, exploration, and general opportunism, fastened on to the ballad. Was he aware of its Catholic associations? Did he, simply, just like the tune? Or did his opening lines come to him from some greater awareness of the existing words of the ballad? Or – most intriguing of all speculations – was he aware that for his six weeks' confinement in the Tower of London in 1591 for offending the Queen by his secret marriage there was another prisoner, Philip Howard, the Catholic Earl of Arundel, who knew the Walsingham ballad and who evidently had strong feelings for it, and who had likely written a poem on the loss of Walsingham himself? They would have had little else in common than their coincidental imprisonment: Howard was imprisoned for his religious faith, for outright rejecting the Elizabethan regime; Ralegh was imprisoned for, in effect, pursuing the court's demands too desperately. We know Howard had been a favourite of Elizabeth in the late 1570s just as Ralegh was a decade later. But in 1583, Howard was arrested for allegedly associating with Mary Stuart and openly avoiding Protestant religious services. In 1584 he openly announced his conversion to Catholicism, and spent seven years under sentence of death in the Tower, dying of dysentery there in 1595. His Walsingham poem, along with other devotional poetry and translations, may be earlier. But it may have been written while he was in the Tower. It is very explicitly a 'Catholic text' not merely a 'religious one', to use Alison Shell's useful distinction.[12] In one of Howard's other poems, entitled a 'Fourfold Meditation', there are some stanzas on the Virgin Mary, omitted from the 1606 published edition, in which he 'developed a telling contrast with that earthly virgin, Queen Elizabeth, whom he had formerly adored' and the figure who was at the centre of Walsingham, sentiments which are exactly echoed in his Walsingham poem. For him, as for increasing numbers of Catholics, the usurping earthly queen who now ruled England had proved to be a false queen, betraying her people and their traditional faith. The final note of the poem is not nostalgia but outright indignation: 'Weep, weep O Walsingham, / Whose dayes

---

12 Alison Shell, *Oral Culture and Catholicism in Early Modern England* (Cambridge: Cambridge University Press, 2007), 17.

are nightes, / Blessings turned to blasphemies, / Holy deedes to dispites' cries the indignant poet who ends with a denunciatory couplet: 'Sinne is where our Ladye sate, / Heaven turned is to helle; / Sathan sittes where our Lord did swaye, / Walsingham, oh, farewell!'[13]

Clearly, the Howard poem (like Ralegh's, it is beset with authorship issues) could have been written only by someone with strong, outspoken Catholic sympathies. What, then, even without possible connections between the two men, do we make of the place of Walsingham in Ralegh's haunting poem?

Ralegh's Walsingham poem follows the common outline – an abandoned lover asking a pilgrim if he has been to the 'holy land' of Walsingham and whether he has seen his lover who has abandoned him. After setting out the initial situation, however, his version takes a very distinctive turn. The initial dialogue between the sympathetic but puzzled pilgrim and the abandoned lover, and the conclusion, with its ambiguous narrative voices, shows Ralegh not only brilliantly giving his readers the opportunity to enter into different roles in the discovery of love's disillusions in a bleak universe, but also adapting the ballad to his own personal and political agendas, in what Leonard Forster terms 'political Petrarchism'.[14] The 'holy land' becomes an idealization of the court; the 'way' to Walsingham becomes the pathway courtiers take to the Queen's presence and from which he is now, like the lover of the poem, excluded. The original Lady of Walsingham was of course the Virgin Mary. The lady of Ralegh's poem may be powerful but, unlike the Queen of Heaven, she is clearly mortal. And knowing his ambition and his view of his own merit, it would be perfectly in character for this pilgrim to blame the lady and to attribute his fall from favour as her falling away from her 'old' lover:

> I have loved her all my youth,
> But now old, as you see,
> Love likes not the falling fruit
> From the withered tree.

The angel-like figure may be, in appearance, 'by her gait, by her grace', a Queen, but she is fickle, misled, ungrateful – and yet it is vital at the same time that she is praised as remains wise, all-powerful, eternal.

---

13 *The Penguin Book of Renaissance Verse 1509–1569*, ed. David Norbrook and Henry R. Woudhuysen (Harmondsworth: Penguin, 1993), 531–2; May, *The Elizabethan Courtier Poets*, 347, 215.

14 Leonard Forster, *The Icy Fire: Studies in European Petrarchism* (Cambridge: Cambridge University Press, 1969), 122–47.

Ralegh's poem, like most versions of the ballad, uses the traditional metaphor of pilgrimage. This, too, is a curiosity that reflects the shifting and contradictory ideological struggles of the final decade of the century. Pilgrimages had been abolished for nearly sixty years. Grace Tiffany has shown how the concept of pilgrimage underwent a transformation after the Dissolution. For Catholic pilgrims, at the end of their journey had been a place made holy by its association with a desired object, the statue of Our Lady, as well as holy relics, all material embodiments and not just reminders or memorials of a profound mystery. For Protestants, by contrast, 'pilgrimage' was a metaphor justified by the fallen nature of man, not ending in a sacred place or person, but finally only, for the elect, in God: 'To the Protestant mind there are ... no sacred places, only redeemed souls'.[15] The sacred site is replaced by the interiorization of the journey itself and the pilgrimage is conceived as being in the believer's mind. So in sonnet 5 of Philip Sidney's *Astrophil and Stella*, the Protestant Petrarchan lover knows that he should not deify the beloved, since 'on earth we are but pilgrims made, / And should in soul up to our country move'.[16] But in Ralegh's poem, pilgrimage is neither a journey of dedication to a special, holy place nor even a journey undertaken for the sake of discoveries made on the way. Indeed, for Tiffany, Ralegh exemplifies a further stage of the protestantization of pilgrimage, adding commercialization and militarization to his 'religious impulses', combining Protestant zeal with terrorist pillage.[17] But while these extensions of the metaphor may indeed be present, for Ralegh pilgrimage is directly associated with the allure and power of the virgin Queen of England.

So to what extent does Ralegh's vision look back to the other Virgin, the Queen of Heaven, as opposed to the virgin Queen of England? By the seventeenth century, claims the modern Catholic theologian Tina Beattie, 'Mary had been all but eradicated from the Protestant consciousness'.[18] Her claim is an understandable overstatement though it reflects what most of the Protestant leaders themselves would have wished – and especially those for whom the transference of the Virgin's aura to the Queen of England was a powerful political tool. Interestingly, however, in Ralegh's poem, there are powerful traces of what was increasingly becoming a fragmented, even lost world. The poem contains echoes of the devotion

---

15 Grace Tiffany, *Love's Pilgrimage: The Holy Journey in English Renaissance Literature* (Newark: University of Delaware Press, 2005), 118, 28–34.
16 *The Poems of Sir Philip Sidney*, ed. William A. Ringler Jr (Oxford: Oxford University Press, 1961), 167.
17 Tiffany, *Love's Pilgrimage*, 28.
18 Tina Beattie, *Eve's Pilgrimage* (London: Burns and Oates, 2002), 138.

once accorded to the Virgin, but its tone is too nostalgic and wistful to be a simple parody of Catholic devotion. Our Lady of Walsingham has been transformed into an ageing and (as Ralegh knew all too well) unpredictable earthly goddess. The Lady for whom the bereft pilgrim yearns may well be a figure of royal power, but she is a mortal, not an eternal, Queen. While it is over-simple to say that Elizabethans transferred their feelings for the Virgin Mary to Elizabeth, there is no doubt that Elizabethan propaganda did exploit the connection. Ralegh's poems consistently invest the ageing Queen with the epithets of the Virgin. He is the worshipper; she is powerful and unapproachable (at least so it must have appeared to the bereft and egocentric Ralegh, as he languished in the Tower in the early 1590s, and during other periods of disgrace), but able, if she turns back to him, to bring solace and forgiveness. Many of Ralegh's other poems, especially those written around the time when, in the early 1590s, he was in disgrace with the Queen, are similarly self-advertising, expressing adoration of the Queen and deeply hurt by her rejection, and always with his own political agenda in mind. His long poetical fragment, 'Ocean to Scinthia' – which echoes the Walsingham poem in uncanny ways, as Latham pointed out – is the barely revised draft of a fragment of an appeal to the Queen, or perhaps evidence of an internal debate within that part of his mind he knew to be occupied by her power. In 1592, Ralegh wrote to Cecil: 'my heart was never broken till this day, that I hear the Queen goes away so far off – whom I have followed so many years with so great love and desire, in so many journeys, and am now left behind her in a great prison alone'. The sentiments are echoed in the poem:

> She hath left me here all alone,
> All alone, as unknown,
> Who sometimes did me lead with herself,
> And me loved as her own.[19]

Like the masochistic, self-deprecating medieval worshipper of the Virgin, the poet is drawn irrevocably to the poem's lady, knowing she determines his salvation, and that, even when most stern and unyielding, she must be revered and worshipped.

But when he evokes the image of the Queen into his imagination as his muse, is there, in a sense, a rival muse present? Ralegh's adaptation of the Walsingham ballad has traditionally been read as an individual cry of protest and pain. But it can be read as a cry of rejection occurring almost (at least as he feels it) at a cosmic level, reflecting an abandon-

---

19 Norman Lloyd Williams, *Sir Walter Ralegh* (London: Eyre and Spottiswoode, 1962), 112.

ment that he experiences when excluded from the royal presence. The poem evokes the collective fantasy that the Elizabethan court is immune to change – an harmonious, static world, the secular equivalent of the eternal world presided over by the Queen of Heaven – while realising that it is in fact ruled by change and unpredictability. Ralegh may assert that Elizabeth reigns over change (as Spenser so eloquently does in *The Faerie Queene*) but he knows she is all too mortal. Unlike the Virgin, the lady of this poem is not an intercessor – there is, emphatically, no higher power than hers. Any higher power – God, a Christ figure, the Virgin herself – has no place in such a world. But then, what is the alternative to the inevitable feelings of despair? When he is, like his pilgrim, abandoned, to whom can he complain except to the Queen? The world that built and nurtured Walsingham is gone, literally in ruins, and there is nowhere else to turn. So he turns to projecting his own despair upon an old ballad – which, intriguingly, carries with it a whole other area of loss and abandonment.

In Ralegh's poem, therefore, there are echoes of that earlier, gradually fading world. Writing on Petrarchan poetry generally, Dorothy Stephens comments that 'whereas a muse may either inspire or withhold inspiration, the feminine figure that resides in a male poet's head sometimes has intricate agendas of its own'.[20] It is possible that Ralegh did not know that the Walsingham ballad had Catholic associations, but two conflicting discourses centred on two Queens are present in the poem even if Ralegh acknowledges only one of them. The Walsingham poem records a moment of equivalent disillusion with the mortal, virgin Queen. But because it is derived from and carries echoes of the lost Walsingham, the poem nevertheless knows the other, even if its author does not: it carries the remnants of an earlier discourse that disrupts and fissures Ralegh's adaptation of the Ballad, most probably without his being conscious of it.

What the poem bears witness to, therefore, is a cultural phenomenon of some importance. The transformation of a Catholic society of 'image-worshippers' into a Protestant one of 'image-breakers' and 'image-haters',[21] as Margaret Aston phrases it, was never fully completed, and was accompanied by a slowly increasing nostalgia – a word, Philip Schwyzer points out, not recorded in England before 1549 and its usage closely

---

20 Dorothy Stephens, *The Limits of Eroticism in Post-Petrarchan Narrative* (Cambridge: Cambridge University Press, 1998), 9.
21 Margaret Aston, *England's Iconoclasts. Volume 1: Laws Against Images* (Oxford: Clarendon Press, 1988), 29.

tied to the huge transformation of the English countryside by the sight of ruined remnants of the Old Religion.²² Stephen Greenblatt speaks of the 'fifty-year effect' after the 'charismatical ideological struggle' of the 1530s, as the next generation increasingly 'look back with longing at the world they have lost'.²³ For some late Elizabethans the golden age proclaimed by the regime's propaganda was not their own, insecure, debt-ridden, and economically depressed, with its ageing Queen and nervous theological polarizations, but a time that lay before Henry VIII turned upon the monasteries. By the 1590s, as Schwyzer comments on the sixth book of *The Faerie Queene*, in even so patriotic a Protestant as Spenser, there appears to be a 'sudden wavering in allegiance to the historical Reformation'. His great poem records not merely his own but his generation's anxieties about what England had done fifty years earlier to its religious heritage. 'Was Spenser', asks Schwyzer, following in the long tradition of scholars who have puzzled over the ending of Book VI, 'at last giving vent, perhaps unconsciously, to long-repressed traditionalist yearnings'?²⁴ As I have argued elsewhere, an aspect of this nostalgia was centred on the transformation of the Virgin's presence in Protestant literature and popular culture. It is as if something she represented (or misrepresented) would not disappear but insisted on speaking through the emergent discursive structures of early modern England.²⁵

This near-confluence of the two virgin Queens in Ralegh's poem and in the broader ideological struggles of the age can be set alongside another more physical moment where they clash, this time in Ralegh's political career only a few years later. In 1596, he took part in the sack of Cadiz in Spain, serving under, and frequently quarrelling with, the Earl of Essex. The town, R. B. Wernham notes, was 'portioned out ... to be systematically sacked' by the invaders who, by Ralegh's own report, were 'all running headlong to the sack ... tumultuous soldiers, abandoned to spoile and rapine, without any prospect of persons'. During the raid, a statue of the Virgin Mary was seized and mutilated by the English. They took it into the marketplace, cut the figure of the infant Jesus from the Madonna, stabbed at the statue's breasts, chopped off the arms and slashed the face,

22 Philip Schwyzer, *Literature, Nationalism, and Memory in Early Modern England and Wales* (Cambridge: Cambridge University Press, 2004), 73.
23 Stephen Greenblatt, *Hamlet in Purgatory* (Princeton: Princeton University Press, 2002), 248.
24 Philip Schwyzer, *Archaeologies of English Renaissance Literature* (Oxford: Oxford University Press, 2007), 237, 246.
25 Gary Waller, *The Virgin Mary in Late Medieval and Early Modern English Literature and Popular Culture* (Cambridge: Cambridge University Press, 2011), chapter 5.

and nearly beheaded it.[26] The statue was, in effect, anthropomorphized and then mutilated because she had not delivered on what to the English Protestants would have been taught were blasphemous and false and female promises. That cultural misogyny is, as a number of commentators have argued, a distinctive feature of Reformation polemic.[27] Medieval (and later) saints' legends are full of weeping or bleeding statues, and one of the claims disputed by Catholic and Protestants was whether statues or relics might react in some way to real or threatened desecration. When the statues did not respond (and, in fairness, some Catholic propagandists publishing on the Continent or in Catholic Ireland asserted that many did, by weeping, bleeding, or miraculously disappearing), how did the iconoclasts themselves react? They jeered that the destruction of some of the more famous relics and images – that of Our Lady of Walsingham among them – did not respond, retaliate, or escape. They could be destroyed, most especially by burning, just as heretics were. But iconoclastic frenzy was often accompanied by resentment and fear. While there must have been triumph at overcoming what the reformers believed to be hundreds of years of superstition, it is likely that some reactions included a residue of almost cosmic disappointment. Part of the triumph must have been seeing that no miracle occurred, that it was possible to break free of the idol's power. But there must have been anguish that long-revered relics and images did not respond. The extremity of desecration – turning altar stones and holy water stoups into kitchen tables, stools, or toilets, for instance – showed that the iconoclasts were accepting, at least in part, the magic that they represented, as if despite their convictions, they were afraid that the magical powers of the idols might somehow be effective. In the 1520s, the German Protestant Andreas von Karlstadt observed that he had become more vehement a destroyer of idols when he noted his own fear before the images: 'I have in myself a harmful fear', he records, 'which I would fain be rid of, but cannot'.[28] In England, Diarmaid MacCulloch

---

26 R. B. Wernham, *The Return of the Armadas* (Oxford: Clarendon Press, 1994), 104, 100, 105; Penry Williams, *The Later Tudors: England, 1547–1603* (Oxford: Oxford University Press, 1998), 350–6. For a more detailed discussion of the *Vulnerata* in Cadiz, see Alison Shell, *Catholicism, Controversy and the English Literary Imagination, 1558–1660* (Cambridge: Cambridge University Press, 1999), 200–7.

27 For a variety of comments on the iconoclasts' mixture of righteousness and guilt, especially when it bordered on the psychopathic, and was directed towards the Virgin, see Diarmaid MacCulloch, 'Mary and Sixteenth-Century Protestants', in *The Church and Mary*, ed. R. N. Swanson (Rochester: Boydell Press, 2004), 204–5; Patrick Collinson, *The Birthpangs of Protestant England* (New York: St Martin's Press, 1988), 98; Aston, *Faith and Fire*, 295; Waller, *The Virgin Mary*, 42–54.

28 Margaret Ruth Miles, *Image as Insight: Visual Understanding in Western Christianity and Secular Culture* (New York: Beacon Press, 1985), 107.

has commented that Hugh Latimer's scorn of idols, especially of female saints and most especially of the Virgin, betrays a similar 'uneasy mixture' of gendered 'derision and anthropomorphism'. When the magical world dies, its death may be mourned, even by the executioners.[29] From the Catholic side, there were frequent jeers that the miracles effected by relics and images continued in Catholic lands and that the power of the newly resurgent Counter-Reformation Virgin engendered fear and madness among heretics.[30]

At the end of Ralegh's poem, with its moving evocation of loss, disillusion, and nostalgia, there is an affirmation of sorts as the lover re-dedicates himself to an ideal of love that is timeless and yet, as the poem has overwhelmingly shown, impossible. One could imagine a different move: in the hands of Catholic like Arundel or Byrd the poem might take an emphatic movement back to the Shrine of Walsingham, and end with a re-dedication to the Queen of Heaven. But not with Ralegh – nor, by the last decade of the century, with Protestant England generally. We are in a world that has abandoned Our Lady of Walsingham – but it is a world which, as it were, she herself has not quite abandoned. In Ralegh's hands the Ballad becomes a refrain of protest, certainly not for the return of Catholicism but rather for something he cannot name that is lost and irrecoverable, something indefinable (at least by Ralegh) that had gone out of Elizabethan life. Given the visibility of the ruins (not only of Wals-

---

29 MacCulloch, 'Mary and Sixteenth-Century Protestants', 204–5. Ethan Shagan likewise notes the uneasy guilt of those plundering the Abbey of Hailes: Ethan H. Shagan, *Popular Politics and the English Reformation* (Cambridge: Cambridge University Press, 2003), 162–3. At Walsingham itself, the Holy House and the vial of the Virgin's milk would have been immediately destroyed, probably with a similar mixture of glee and guilt. The site of the Holy House is visible today as a slightly raised rectangle grassed over and, eerily, according to an archeological investigation in 1961, covers with just a few inches of soil and grass the ashes of the Virgin's chapel beneath. See Gary Waller, *Walsingham and the English Imagination* (Aldershot: Ashgate, 2011), chapter 3.

30 In 1657 the German Jesuit Wilhelm Gumppenberg published the *Atlas Marianus*, a compendium of over twelve hundred Marian pilgrimage sites. He highlights the statue of Our Lady of Tewkesbury which 'survived all the fury of the heretics' during the upsurge of Protestantism, and in 1625 chose the moment to retaliate against further attempted desecration by causing an impious Protestant who tried to destroy it, to throw himself 'in a state of frenzy', into a well to his death: Edmund Waterton, *Pietas Mariana Britannica* (London: St Joseph's Catholic Library, 1879), II:147. St John Eudes, founder of the Society of the Heart of the Mother Most Admirable, in 1648 envisaged the Virgin looking down, as Queen of Heaven, at the 'numberless multitude and frightful enormity' of heretics and blasphemers who had rejected her. God, he says, 'has given her sovereign power over all created things; therefore she would not lack the power, if such were her will, to avenge most justly the many atrocious insults offered by men to their God and Savior'. See Saint John Eudes, *The Admirable Heart of Mary*, trans. Charles di Targiani and Ruth Hauser (New York: P. J. Kenedy, 1948), 140–1.

ingham but right across the landscape), 'destroyed' is perhaps too extreme a term, but the traces of Walsingham that continue had undoubtedly been transformed, and in Ralegh's hands (at least until the Queen returned him to court), into undifferentiated despair.

We can perhaps understand the pivotal position of Ralegh's Walsingham poem in the 1590s by glancing briefly at two other poetical variations of the Walsingham ballad. The first poem is by Sir Robert Sidney. The poem's situation is yet another variation of the basic starting-point of the Walsingham Ballad, a faithful woman asking whether the pilgrim has encountered her absent lover:

> Yonder comes a sad pilgrim,
>   From the east he returns,
> I will ask if he saw him
>   Who for me absent mourns.

Like Ralegh, Sidney adapts the Ballad's starting point to his own situation. The Lady is a projection of his wife, who 'doth rest / Near Medway's sandy bed' near the Sidney estate at Penshurst in Kent. Sidney's journeys away were frequent, and in his poem are contrasted with those he wishes to be making, not to a distant shrine, but to her. The poem's pilgrim has been sent, we learn, by the exiled knight of whom the lady asks for news, to affirm his devotion to her. The pilgrim, a strikingly papist-sounding aged father, in itself a nostalgic trace of an older world evoked by the Ballad no longer current in Protestant England, asks her by what tokens he might recognize her knight:

> Many one see, my lady,
>   As we come, as we go:
> By what tokens, how should I
>   Your knight from others know?

We can hear the language and rhythms of Ralegh's version in the background. But Sidney's poem moves in a different direction. The lady replies that he can be known for his steadfastly wearing 'griefs livery', and that he faithfully turns his eyes westward, back towards Kent and Penshurst itself, 'where love holds fast his heart'. The pilgrim acknowledges to the Lady that he once saw such a one, but tells her that the knight now has died 'near to the sea ... on a sandhill', looking westward towards where he knows she waits, and vows his love for her with his last breath. The Lady's response takes the poem into the conventional world of Petrarchan ideals: how could he die since she is his life? The pilgrim's philosophy is, by contrast, stark and stoical: the universe he invokes is hostile to any such idealization, nor does it seem to provide any religious consolation. It is the lonely universe of Protestant masculinity, ruled by the stern God of the Reformers, from which the original lady of Walsingham has been exorcized: 'Heav'n no more behold doth he / He lies deep in dark grave'.[31]

It is tempting, as with Ralegh, to compare Sidney's 'lady' with the Lady of the original Walsingham. 'Near unto the sea this knight / Was brought to his last will', the poem reads; to Erasmus, whose slightly fictionalized account of his visit to Walsingham remains our most detailed account of the Shrine before its dissolution, the Virgin of Walsingham is 'Parathalassiae', the 'Virgin-by-the-sea', and one of her particular cares was mariners on the seas between East Anglia and the Low Countries.[32] From the Netherlands, Robert looked, not across to the Virgin in Walsingham but – dutiful Protestant and (largely) constant husband that he was – a little further south, back towards Kent, to Penshurst Place, and his wife. Much of Robert's verse can be read as a moving expression of a frustrated male politician's escape-world, yearning for the security of his wife and family back home. As in Ralegh's Walsingham poem, what is missing is any woman figure beyond what he termed, in a letter to his wife, the 'world and the actions of it'.[33] There is certainly no alternative virgin Queen, no replacement of one heavenly Virgin Queen by another. Instead, in the poem's devotional world, it is the grieving married lady of Penshurst who replaces the Lady of Walsingham. She embodies what is good, rare and fair; her breath is 'Life-nursing'; she has a 'heav'n-opening face', epithets that recall those traditionally accorded the Queen of Heaven. Where she is not is a 'dark cave / Where her lights do not shine', and his last wish is to be buried near her.

The second comparison that is helpful to our positioning of Ralegh's poem is the version of the Walsingham ballad that Shakespeare scatters across Act 4, scene 5 of *Hamlet*, the scene in which the bereaved and distracted Ophelia sings a plaintive lament, seemingly a fragment of a song of lost love that seems not just to reflect on the loss of her father or even of Hamlet's love, but to have much broader cultural impact somewhat in the way Prospero's farewell speeches at the end of *The Tempest* do. It is yet another version of the Walsingham ballad, without the characteristic introduction but with the unmistakable melody in the background. Here are Ophelia's lines, without the interspersed dialogue with Gertrude:

---

31 *The Poems of Robert Sidney*, ed. P. J. Croft (Oxford: Oxford University Press, 1984), 185–95.
32 Erasmus, *The Pilgrimage of Pure Devotion*, 28–9.
33 *Domestic Politics and Family Absence: The Correspondence (1588–1621) of Robert Sidney, First Earl of Leicester, and Barbara Gamage Sidney*, ed. Margaret P. Hannay, Noel J. Kinnamon, and Michael G. Brennan (Aldershot: Ashgate, 2005), 36.

> How should I your true love know
> From another one?
> By his cockle hat and staff,
> And his sandal shoon ...
> He is dead and gone, lady,
> He is dead and gone;
> At his head a grass-green turf,
> At his heels a stone ...
> White his shroud as the mountain snow
> Larded with sweet flowers
> Which bewept to the grave did not go
> With true love showers.[34]

Alison Chapman shows that Ophelia's ravings are 'marked by a surge of allusions to medieval Catholic piety': throughout the play Ophelia is surrounded by the Catholic trappings that Elizabethan authorities had tried to eliminate. Yet Ophelia's orisons – her posing as a pious devotee with a prayer book – and Hamlet's quip about her getting to a nunnery still associate her with the lost Catholic world. Isolated and alienated in a society that traps and exploits her, she can be taken as representing the alienation suffered by Catholics within the new, harsh world of Protestantism, with its empty fallen, material universe and its transcendent, masculine God. Does Shakespeare invite us, Chapman asks, to censure Ophelia for 'resorting to such suspect forms of piety'? Or has she found herself in a world 'which has driven her to such extremes and in which she can only voice such forms of piety in mad isolation and at the moment of death'? Do the allusions here to Walsingham, and so to England's Catholic past, reinforce in Protestant minds suspicion of the old religion centred on Walsingham as sexually corrupt? Or does the bleak Protestant universe of (with the ambiguous exception of the Ghost) Lutheran Denmark and Protestant England bring about her madness and give her no comfort in the way traditional religion would have? When Hamlet advises her to go to a nunnery, what did that connote in Protestant England? A false hope? A deluded attempt to escape? A joke? Or a lost possibility of salvation of which her madness reminds her in vain?[35] Ophelia's lover, like the Walsingham pilgrim in Ralegh's poem, has gone, apparently never to return, and she waits for him in vain. She is frozen in her place by her role as daughter or a potential wife: 'I hop'd', confesses Gertrude, 'thou

---

34 William Shakespeare, *Hamlet*, IV.v.23–6, 36, 38–40.
35 I draw here on the stimulating analysis by Alison A. Chapman, 'Ophelia's 'Old Lauds': Madness and Hagiography in *Hamlet*', *Medieval and Renaissance Drama in England* 20 (2007), 111–35.

shouldst have been my Hamlet's wife' (V.i.245). It is a wish reflecting the pious Protestant belief that dutiful marriage is the most fulfilling role for woman's desires and aspirations, though it is not, it seems, realizable in a world in which purgatorial ghosts appear only to a faithful remnant, or one that, in multiple and contradictory ways, is out of joint. Neither virgin Queen, the all too mortal English one nor the immortal yet seemingly illusory heavenly one, is present in or evoked by the poem. 'Walsingham' has become a lonely and despairing cry in the darkness.

By the end of the century, then, Walsingham has acquired associations that confirm the fading of the magical world of the destroyed shrine. But although the specifically Catholic associations of Our Lady of Walsingham have almost entirely gone, it is as if Walsingham has come to represent something broader in the consciousness (and the unconscious) of Elizabethans that Ralegh in particular was able to respond to and memorably evoke. Something, the age seems to say, has been lost, whether that is youth or love or identity, something which we cannot perhaps identify and might be surprised to know where it came from and what its original significance was. Just as the image of Our Lady of Walsingham (and other representations of the Virgin) incorporated contradictory (especially sexual) elements that pious Christian devotees would have been surprised or shocked to know about, so earnest late Elizabethans singing, listening to, re-writing, or just making casual reference to the Walsingham ballad may not have been aware of its origins even though some (like Arundel or Byrd, one might argue) identified deeply and consciously with its original power. The surfacing of poems and lyrics associated with Walsingham gives us a specific focus for at least some of the age's unease. Ralegh and his Protestant contemporaries saw the cult of the Virgin as delusion and sinfulness, with the only ultimate reality what he was to plead for in his last poetic fragment, probably written before his execution in 1617: 'And from the earth, the grave, and dust, /The Lord shall raise me up, I trust'.[36] In such a world, there is no place for the Virgin. At least in his mind, she is not beside him, not there to appeal for intercession, and at the end, not even embodied in another human being, even an earthly Queen. Ralegh's wonderful lyric anticipates that forlorn and seemingly irredeemable end.

---

36 Rudick, *Poems*, 30.

11

Patrilineal Ralegh

Judith Owens

We are accustomed to thinking of Sir Walter Ralegh as a player in the glamorous, frequently, and ultimately for him, treacherous, world of Elizabethan and Jacobean courtiership. Stephen Greenblatt has taught us to imagine Ralegh as a man with an enormous talent for self-fashioning and self-performance, especially at the brink of death. Biographers and historians have highlighted his various roles as courtier, soldier, seafarer, explorer, poet, patron, on again-off again favourite of the Queen – very public, and publicized, roles all of them. Ralegh's supposed affiliation with a 'school of night' and his alleged atheism have likewise garnered much attention. We are used to asking how well or how ill-advisedly Ralegh played his assorted public roles. We are accustomed to sounding the depths of his scepticism.

We are even quite used to thinking of Ralegh as a husband, because his clandestine marriage to Elizabeth Throckmorton catapulted him from favour for a time. We are not as accustomed to thinking of Ralegh as a father. While we have become very conversant with how, and with what results, Ralegh performed his affection for the Queen, we do not really have a vocabulary yet for talking about the political and affective dynamics of Ralegh's fatherhood. Nor have we developed a sustained interest in how patrilineal imperatives might have shaped Ralegh's views of sovereignty or conditioned his pieties.[1] Yet Ralegh's career provides us with

1 Stephen Greenblatt, *Sir Walter Ralegh: The Renaissance Man and His Roles* (New Haven: Yale University Press, 1973), introduced the idea of Ralegh as a player of roles, an assumption that underlies many treatments of Ralegh. Important biographical studies of Ralegh include Edward Edwards, *The Life of Sir Walter Raleigh*, 2 vols (London: Macmillan, 1868); A. L. Rowse, *Ralegh and the Throckmortons* (London: Macmillan, 1962); and Robert Lacey, *Sir Walter Ralegh* (London: Weidenfeld and Nicolson, 1973). Analyses of Ralegh's poetry that emphasize his courtly poetry and courting of the Queen include Philippa Berry, *Of Chastity and Power: Elizabethan Literature and the Unmarried Queen* (London: Routledge, 1989); Robert Stillman, '"Words cannot knytt": Language and Desire in Ralegh's *The Ocean to Cynthia*', *SEL* 27 (1987), 35–51; Anna Beer, in *Sir*

a range of texts on to which we can map considerations of the actions, assumptions, and attitudes required to maintain family ties, particularly father and son bonds, paternal authority, and family estates and status. In this chapter, I will address such considerations with particular reference to the *Discoverie of Guiana*, *Instructions to a Son*, Ralegh's contribution to the flourishing minor genre of paternal advice, and 'Three things there bee', Ralegh's short poem of fatherly admonishment. I will refer as well to a portrait of Ralegh and his son Wat, arguably intended by Ralegh to commemorate the promises of patrilineage, in order to highlight certain patrilineal dynamics in Ralegh's writing.

My purpose is to show that patrilineal imperatives inform Ralegh's work in substantial and sometimes contradictory ways. Specifically, when Ralegh's own fatherly feeling is bracketed off, the idea of patrilineage smoothly underwrites his envisioning of empire and commonwealth, furnishing a model of sovereignty that complements – even rivals – Elizabethan monarchy as well as providing a position of authority that is uncompromisingly secular and staunchly independent of Crown and court. The corollary, adumbrated in *Instructions* and powerfully realized in 'Three things there be', is that fatherly feeling overwhelms Ralegh's ability either to maintain personal authority or to petition the authority of state or god. My chapter thus contributes to critical studies of Ralegh by working an under-remarked vein in his writing. Secondarily, my chapter adds both to our understanding of the tensions between family and state in early modern England and to the growing interest in the history of emotion, particularly in family life.[2]

Walter Ralegh and His Readers in the Seventeenth Century (London: Macmillan, 1997), revises many biographically-based analyses of Ralegh's writing by supplying a context that makes room for Ralegh as 'a significant political writer' (16); and in *My Just Desire: The Life of Bess Raleigh, Wife to Sir Walter* (London: Ballantine Books, 2003) introduces competing perspectives on Ralegh's life by focusing on Bess, Ralegh's wife. Fred Tromly has generously shared with me some work he has undertaken on Ralegh and his son Wat, in the context of *Shakespeare's Fathers and Sons: The Debt Never Promises* (Toronto: University of Toronto Press, 2010).

[2] Much recent interest in emotional history focuses on familial relations and childhood in the Middle Ages and early modern period, revising as it does so Philippe Ariès's increasingly challenged thesis that parent–child relationships before the Englightenment were emotionally barren. For a recent critique of Ariès's *Centuries of Childhood: A Social History of Family Life* (1960), tr. Robert Baldick (New York: Alfred Knopf, 1962), see Albrecht Classen, 'Introduction', *Childhood in the Middle Ages and the Renaissance*, ed. Albrecht Classen (New York: Walter de Gruyter, 2005).

1. Fathers and sons in *Discoverie of Guiana*

The Discoverie of Guiana, a tract that measures what Lowell Duckert in Chapter 7 above analyses as the purposefully ever-receding reach of Ralegh's vaulting ambition, also gauges just how thoroughly patrilineage informs Ralegh's imagining of empire. Offered an arena – the 'new world' – removed from the constraints of court and Queen, Ralegh, not surprisingly perhaps, extols the actions of courageous, determined, and purposeful men in securing for England this land rich in promises of gold and freedom from Spanish imposition. More surprisingly, Ralegh discovers in Guiana the rich promise of patrilineal governance. His investment in patrilineage is both considerable and largely implicit, calculable not from statements but from subtleties of language, imagery, and rhetorical patterns that permit us to reach conclusions ranging beyond the declared aims of his promotional tract. At key moments in the rhetorical invention of Guiana, patrilineal structures and authority, not Elizabethan sovereignty, form the substratum underpinning Ralegh's vision of empire.

Ralegh's dedicatory letter to Charles Howard and Robert Cecil, the accusations that swirled when he returned empty-handed from Guiana, and the editorial pressures brought to bear in the publication of the tract make clear what might be the appeal to Ralegh of patrilineage. And the appeal is insistent. Notwithstanding the declaration in the dedicatory letter that the voyage to discover Guiana is an enterprise better suited to 'boies' than to someone who is 'in the winter of his life', Ralegh's tract suggests repeatedly that Guiana *is* in fact a country for old men, and especially old men who are fathers.[3] Nearly without exception, the men whom Ralegh encounters in the New World are represented by him as knowledgeable, even wise: with their knowledge of the labyrinthine river system, they make the best pilots; with their experience with surrounding nations and political alliances, they make the best strategists; with their understanding of human nature, they make the best leaders. Such knowledge and such qualities of character, perhaps even more than quantities

---

3 Sir Walter Ralegh, *The Discoverie ... of Guiana*, ed. V. T. Harlow (1928), 3. Subsequent citations are to this edition. Harlow appears to be unique in printing 'boies less blasted by misfortune'; other editors print 'bodies'. My thanks to Fred Tromly for drawing my attention to this crux. Recent readings of *Discoverie* have tended to focus on its colonialist and gendered assumptions about empire and 'others', or on its rhetorical compensations for failures of enterprise. See, for example, Mary Fuller, 'Ralegh's Fugitive Gold: Reference and Deferral in *The Discoverie of Guiana*', *Representations* 33 (Winter 1991), 42–64 and Louis Montrose, 'The Work of Gender in the Discourse of Discovery', *Representations* 33 (Winter 1991):1–41. To my knowledge, no one has brought to Ralegh's *Discoverie* the focus on patrilineage that I am proposing.

of gold, are what will lead to the founding of a 'mighty and bewtifull' empire. Ralegh does not have the gold – hence the need for this defensive treatise; he believes he does have the knowledge and character. And the New World must have seemed to him to furnish an arena for action considerably more expansive than the world in which he often moved at home in England. There Ralegh was frequently conditioned by practice and politics to assume positions of almost adolescent subservience.

The reactions and rumours that accosted Ralegh upon his return from Guiana in 1595, accusations that he finds himself compelled to counter in the dedicatory epistle as well as in an address to the reader, surely reminded him that his schemes and ambitions were continually curtailed. In his epistle to Howard and Cecil, Ralegh expresses the hope that his journey will be recognized as having been a 'painful pilgrimage', but holds out no real expectation that such will be the case since he is so hedged about by suspicions. He is suspected of having hidden out in Cornwall for the duration of his supposed journey; he is accused of having allied himself to the King of Spain. Ralegh emerges in the prefatory matter as a man whose prospects are much diminished. This is the reason he undertook so arduous and hazardous a journey, to 'recover but the moderation of excesse, and the least taste of that greatest plentie formerly possessed' (4). But his achievements have been whittled down in the rumour mill. Further, his detractors cannot even appreciate the scope of his adventure; they imagine he would have been content to 'run from Cape to Cape, and from place to place, for the pillage of *ordinarie prizes*' (4; my emphasis). The Ralegh who can dream large in speculation of 'that mighty, rich, and beawtifull Empire of Guiana' is now forced to defend the profitableness of his journey from an unidentified Alderman in London who, having seen sample ore of poor quality, was 'pleased … therefore to scandall all the rest, and to deface the enterprize as much as in him lyeth' ('To the Reader', 8). The Ralegh who toiled so manfully and heroically in search of Guiana and the Golden Citie, 'accompanied with many sorrows, with labour, hunger, heat, sickness, and peril' must now seek from Howard and Cecil 'a double protection and defence' (4, 3), in order to pursue the Guiana project.

As Joyce Lorimer demonstrates convincingly in her recent edition of the *Discoverie of Guiana*, Ralegh's recounting of his journey was subjected to careful, calculated scrutiny by Cecil and others in an editorial process that she concludes was likely a 'bruising personal experience' for him.[4]

---

4 Joyce Lorimer, ed., *Sir Walter Ralegh's 'Discoverie of Guiana'* The Hakluyt Society (London: Ashgate, 2006), xl.

Lorimer's thorough canvassing of the differences between Ralegh's manuscript version and the printed text indicates that his patrons reined him in, making a 'concerted effort' to 'tone down his hyperbole, and to substitute sober, considered judgement for excited recollection and inflationary strategizing'.[5] We can suppose that Ralegh felt keenly the effects of such forced subservience. Extant letters written by Ralegh in the years around the Guiana expedition, especially those written from the West Country, show him to be someone accustomed to offering advice, advancing solutions, and intervening with powerful men on behalf of those with less or compromised influence.[6] In contrast to the circumscribed arena of the court and London, the New World must have promised room for the exercise of agency and initiative of the kind he enjoyed in the West Country. Echoing Anthony Pagden's conclusion that Ralegh was a 'would-be *conquistador*', who was not at all interested in establishing trade or settlement, Lorimer observes that the tone of Ralegh's unexpurgated, manuscript version was decidedly 'swashbuckling' in its promotion of empire founded on 'gold and glory'.[7]

---

5 Lorimer, ed., '*Discoverie*', xl.
6 Letters endorsed by Ralegh in the months prior to his 1595 expedition to Guiana depict him as energetic, well-informed, and competent in his advancing of business related to the Stannaries, to local (West Country) disputes, and to Ireland. In petitioning for the 'continuance of transportation of pipestaves out of Ireland to the [Canary] Islandes', for example, Ralegh 'doubts not but his lordship [Charles Howard, Lord Admiral] will farther so honest a motion' (Letter no. 63, *The Letters of Sir Walter Ralegh*, ed. Agnes Latham and Joyce Youings (Exeter: University of Exeter Press, 1999)); he intervenes briefly but confidently in a matter of wardship on behalf of someone in danger of being 'overborn by his adverse partie' (Letter no. 64); he reacts with measured requests to attempts by men seeking to circumvent the 'directions' of Ralegh and others 'concerning the right of [sic] a tynworke in Cornwall' (Letter no. 66); he writes in support of one Captain Davis, who has been arrested and 'accused of some notorious villany', advising Robert Cecil that the accuser is 'dissolute and fugitive' and has concocted the charges (Letter no. 67); he reminds Sir Thomas Egerton that Queen Elizabeth, upon complaint from Ralegh, has reiterated that matters related to tinneries must remain in the 'absolute jurisdiction of the Stannery', and that 'all abuses uppon [his, i.e., Ralegh's] information shalbe presentlie reformed' (Letter no. 71); he pleads on behalf of one Master Michell, who is owed money by the Queen (Letter no. 78); he intervenes in disputes regarding land holdings in Ireland, petitioning in support of Patrick Condon, for instance, 'that he may be restored to the possession of his lands in Ireland.... [which] he quietlie enjoyed ... untill Hide by a wrong information prevailed against him'. Ralegh counts on his own position, authority, and local knowledge to have the power to persuade, writing that 'I have knowen him a long time, his lands are adjoyning to mine.... I know him to be as well able to serve Her Majestie as any man in that parte' (Letter no. 74). See Michael Booth in Chapter 6 above on Ralegh's penchant for positions of rebellion against authority. Booth's linking of Ralegh's rebelliousness with his brilliant use of metaphor offers tangential support for my reading of Ralegh's rhetorical construction of *Discoverie* as evidence for his intellectual distance from Elizabethan sovereignty.
7 Anthony Pagden, *Lords of All the World: Ideologies of Empire in Spain, Britain, and*

In light of such pronounced tendencies to promote conquest and empire over trade and settlement, commentators have looked closely at Ralegh's representation of indigenous peoples, often characterizing Ralegh as, consciously or not, duplicitous. These readers stress that Ralegh's professions of respect for the Amerindians are undercut by the imperialist designs he is pursuing.[8] While it is beyond the scope of this chapter to enter directly into this critical debate, I would suggest that an underremarked feature of Ralegh's tract, its investment in patrilineal structures and authority, adds another layer to the representation of Amerindians, one which does permit Ralegh to stake out common ground rather than merely grounds for conquest.

The charting of patrilineal imperatives can begin with the observation that, however much Ralegh presents his voyage of discovery as an act of service and homage to Queen Elizabeth, an action respecting only 'her Majesties future Honour and riches', he is eager from start to finish to attest to the wisdom, initiative, and talents of *men*, including himself.[9] He does so in the first instance by presenting himself as an assiduous seeker after the knowledge that will be required to create in the New World an empire. Having covered in a dozen or so lines the voyage from England to

---

France, c. 1500–c.1800 (New Haven: Yale University Press, 1995), 67; Lorimer, ed., '*Discoverie*', lxiii.

8 The 'ethnographic' dimension of Ralegh's treatise has received considerable attention. Recently, for instance, Aaron Eastley, 'Exploiting El Dorado: Subalternity and the Environment', *Journal of Commonwealth and Postcolonial Studies* 13.2–14.1 (2006–7), in tracing the legacy of the early modern fantasy of rapaciousness that showed little regard for either land or people, observes that the 'historically rooted ideologies of elite privilege' that underpinned tracts such as Ralegh's 'continue to do violence to both land and people' (40). Neil Whitehead, ed., *The Discoverie of the Large, Rich and Bewtiful Empyre of Guiana* (Manchester: Manchester University Press, 1997), has insisted on the need to qualify that approach to *Discoverie* in asking 'whether its ethnological reportage offers substantive insight into past native cultural practices' (4). John Holmes, 'The Guiana Projects: Imperial and Colonial Ideologies in Ralegh and Purchas', *Literature and History* 14.2 (2005), concludes that Ralegh's 'account of his encounters with native Americans ... remains remarkable for its radical refusal to endorse a perception of racial difference or otherness' (11). From her comparison of the printed *Discoverie* to Ralegh's manuscript version, Lorimer has concluded that the expressions of benevolence toward the Amerindians that characterize the printed version (and help to distinguish English from Spanish approaches to the New World) do not accord with the licence seemingly given by Ralegh to Englishmen to carouse and ask for gold where they might (lxiii). See also Alden Vaughan, Chapter 8 above.

9 My finding that Ralegh sidelines Queen Elizabeth is directly counter to that advanced recently by William Hamlin, 'Imagined Apotheoses: Drake, Harriot, and Ralegh in the Americas', *Journal of the History of Ideas* 57.3 (1996), who contends that 'Ralegh's greatest tool for native coercion is the image and extravagant reputation of his Queen'(417). In a reading that complements mine while covering very different ground, Duckert in Chapter 7 above emphasizes Ralegh's efforts to 'showcase his own narrative superiority' (228).

Trinidad, Ralegh advises the reader of the particular pains he took once they reached the island: 'I my selfe coasted it in my barge, close abord the shore and landed in every Cove, the better to know the iland. ... I left the shippes and kept by the shore, the better to come to speach with some of the inhabitantes, and also to understand the rivers, watring places and portes of the iland' (10). Following a stop at Parico, where 'we ... sawe no people', Ralegh 'rowed to another port, called by the naturals *Piche*' (12). Although Ralegh could not have learned the local name of the port from the forays he has just described – as he has just told us, he 'sawe no people' on these sallies – he nevertheless implies, rhetorically, that he gleaned this knowledge as a result of his exploratory ventures, his leaving his ships and rowing close to shore.

Ralegh's underlying interest in showing himself to be a man fitted to assume command in the New World emerges also, in these early pages, in his aligning himself with the local leaders, and in his distinguishing of himself from Don Anthonio de Berreo, the Spanish governor of Trinidad whose own New World exploits and explorations hover continually around the borders of Ralegh's expedition. From the Indian traders who 'euery night' come aboard his ship in defiance of Berreo's orders and punishments, Ralegh hears 'the most lamentable complaints of [Berreo's] cruelty'. He learns that Berreo 'had deuided the iland and giuen to euery soldier a part, that he had made the ancient *Casiqui* which were Lordes of the country to be their slaves, that he kept them in chains, and dropped their naked bodies with burning bacon, and ... other torments' (14). When Ralegh enters the city of S. Joseph and finds these tales of torture to be true, he puts 'to the sword' the *Corp du guard*, takes Berreo captive and, 'at the instance of the Indians ... set [Berreo's] city *S. Josephs* on fire'. Historical evidence confirms that Ralegh treated his captive Berreo well, according him the courtesies due a 'well descended' gentleman (15). But in his tract, Ralegh demonstrates his own superiority to Berreo by *rhetorically* restoring to eminence and dignity the *casiqui* who had been debased by Berreo. Whereas Berreo had enslaved and tortured them, Ralegh accords them their titles and names:

> in the city ... there were 5 of the Lords or litle kings (which they cal *Casiqui* in the west Indies) in one chain almost dead of famine, and wasted with torments: these are called in their own language *Acarewana*, and now of late since English, French, and Spanish are come among them, they cal themselves *Capitaynes* because they perceive that the chiefest of euery ship is called by that name. Those fiue in the chaine were called *Wannawanare, Carroaori, Maquarima, Tarroopanama,* and *Aterima*. (14)

What might seem to be a curiously pedantic interest in the fact that the *casiqui* choose now to call themselves 'captains' after the manner of Europeans proves instead to be another effective rhetorical tack. The names of the men who are with him in his voyage are peppered through his recounting of the events in Trinidad: Captain Whiddon, Captain Calfield, Captain George Clifford, Captain Keymis. By this means, Ralegh can associate himself – he is *Captain* Ralegh, after all – and his compatriots with the lords of the island. Rhetorically, it is the gathering together of captains, the English ones and those who are lords or little kings, that enables the expedition to discover Guiana to get underway: 'We then hastened away towards our purposed discouery, and first I called all the Captaines of the iland together that were enemies to the Spaniards' (15). Ralegh's assertion of common cause among the English captains and the *casiqui* can be inferred also from his implicit conflating of injuries inflicted on both groups by Berreo, a conflation that is the more remarkable since the respective attacks by Berreo are separated in time by a year or more. In the narrative present of the tract, Ralegh's setting fire to S. Joseph's is justified as revenge for 'the former wrong', with the immediate reference being to Berreo's debasement of the *casiqui* and the implied reference being to Berreo's ambushing of Captain Whiddon's men the previous year.

The rhetorical manoeuvres I have been describing are all the more telling in that Ralegh's promotion of the acts and agency of men immediately precedes his recounting of what he told the *casiqui* about Elizabeth, and is followed immediately by what is almost a paean to the patrilineal governance that has shaped Guiana. 'I made them understand', writes Ralegh, 'that I was servant of a Queene, who was the great *Casique* of the north, and a virgin, and had more *Casiqui* under her than there were trees in their iland' (15). Ralegh thus endorses the monarchal rule of his Queen. And he represents her as a champion of freedom from Spanish oppression; he also 'made [the *casiqui*] to understand' that

> she was an enemy of the *Castellani* in respect of their tyrannie and oppression, and that she delivered all such nations about her, as were by them oppressed, and having freed all the coast of the northern world from their servitude had sent me to free them also, and withal to defend the countrey of *Guiana* from their invasion and conquest. (15)

But Ralegh has, as it were, pre-empted the Queen's position as defender by relating first his actions against Berreo in Trinidad. Moreover, his formulation – 'I made them to understand' – keeps him in the position of authority: *he* shapes the understanding of the *casiqui* with respect to Elizabeth, just as he controls their response to the image of the Queen. 'I shewed them her maiesties picture', he declares, 'which they so admired and honoured, as it had been easie to have brought them idolatrous thereof' (15). Yet he does not bring the *casiqui* to the point of such obeisance to Elizabeth.

As if he recognizes that he has been a little stingy in his extolling of Elizabeth, Ralegh begins the next paragraph by affirming that 'the like *and a more large discourse* I made to the rest of the nations ... so that in that part of the world her maiestie is very famous and admirable' (15; my emphasis). He concludes this short paragraph, though, with the reminder that he captured Berreo: 'having *Berreo* my prisonour I gathered from him as much of *Guiana* as he knew' (15). Again, it is Ralegh's very manful military action of having captured Berreo, along with his skill in gathering knowledge, that will prove to be the key to Guiana. Furthermore, as we read right after this, it was military might that established Guiana in the first place. Guiana was achieved by a younger son who fled a civil and fratricidal war in Peru, taking with him 'many thousands' of soldiers and vanquishing 'all that tract and valley of America which is situate betweene the great rivers of Amazons and Baraquona' (17). Ralegh is, one suspects, as impressed with the grandness of these imperial gestures as he is with the fabled richness of Guiana – a suspicion confirmed by comparing the rhetorical sweep of the description of Guiana's founding with the restrained and respectful accumulation of noun clauses describing Elizabeth's greatness in the passage cited above.

Although Ralegh endorses the sovereignty of Queen Elizabeth, his doing so is qualified, as we have seen, by the fact that his praise of her is wedged between passages representing the efficacy of masculine military might. It is qualified, too, by Ralegh's implicitly juxtaposing to the Queen's rule the patrilineal governance that has shaped Guiana into the 'mighty, rich, and beawtifull Empire' that it is reported to be. In answer to those who wonder how Guiana came to be 'so populous, and adorned with so manie great Cities, Townes, Temples, and threasures', Ralegh reports that 'the Emperour now raigning is discended from those magnificent Princes of Peru' (17). Patrilineage tacitly underwrites not only Guiana's incredible wealth ('it hath more abundance of Golde then any part of Peru') but also its stability: 'it is governed by the same lawes ... the same religion ... the same forme and pollicies in government' as '[were] used in Peru'. The ostensible implication of Guiana's being an extension of the Peruvian forms of governance is the encouragement such likeness gives to any English plans for invasion: if Peru was conquerable, then so is Guiana. But one also hears approbation in Ralegh's tone – approval of the extension through time and space, via patrilineage, of the judicial, religious, and governmental forms that make Guiana great.

We can gauge more precisely just how fundamental to Ralegh's envisioning of strong polities is his trust in patrilineage by following the implications and metaphoric logic of a curiously digressive passage introduced by Ralegh as a 'digression not unnecessary' (49). He speaks proudly of his having been favoured by the Guianans far more than was the Spaniard Berreo, because he, Ralegh, attained knowledge of the 'true remedies for poisoned arrows' (49). We have seen already that Ralegh has a vested interest in demonstrating his superiority to Berreo and in discovering grounds of common cause between the Amerindians and the English. English superiority to the Spanish is frequently an organizing principle in English depictions of their travels in the New World, and Ralegh throughout his political career remained staunchly anti-Spanish. But the digression about remedies reveals political conceptions that do not quite rise to the level of conscious articulation in the way that generalized English enmity toward the Spanish does. Ralegh considers this favouring of him to be all the more extraordinary because knowledge of the 'cure' is jealously guarded: not 'one among thousands' of Indians knows it, only soothsayers and priests 'who do conceal it and *only teach it but from the father to the sonne*' (49; my emphasis).

There is more to this site of privilege than Ralegh's feeling like a favoured son, more even than the insistence once again on the importance of patrilineage. Emerging from this 'digression not unnecessarie' is Ralegh's conviction that patrilineal structures are necessary to the safeguarding of the kingdom of England. 'There was nothing', Ralegh declares in his digression, 'whereof I was more curious, than to finde out the true remedies of these poisoned arrowes'. He is keen for this knowledge, not simply because of the 'mortalie of the wound' made by these arrows but because of the particular gruesomeness of the effects of the poison before death:

> the partie shot indureth the most insufferable torment in the world, and abideth a most uglie and lamentable death, sometimes dying starke mad, sometimes their bowels breaking out of their bellies, and are presently discoloured, as black as pitch, and so unsavery, as no man can endure to cure, or to attend them. (49)

What is more, 'there was never Spaniard, either by gift or torment that could attain to the true knowledge of the cure, although they have martyred and put to invented torture I know not how many of them' (49). As was the case with the events in Trinidad recounted earlier by Ralegh, the Spanish mistreatment of the Amerindians excludes them from a circle of knowledge-sharing that does embrace Ralegh. We see a similar cluster of motifs and imagery earlier in the *Discoverie*, in Ralegh's Letter to the Reader, when he urges the conquest of Guiana as a way to safeguard England from the defensive war with Spain that he believes is almost certain to happen if Spain is allowed to continue unchecked its amassing of New World fortunes. His recourse is to the frequently applied metaphor of the body politic: 'whatsoever kingdome shalbe inforced to defend it selfe, may be compared to a body daungerouslie diseased, which for a season may be preserved with vulgar medicines, but in a short time ... must fall to the ground, and be dissolved' (10). Like the bodies struck by poisoned arrows, the diseased body politic cannot be cured with 'vulgar', that is, commonly known, medicines. And, just as Ralegh has been privileged with the patrilineal knowledge of the remedy for the poisoned-arrow wounds, so too, runs the implication, is he the man for the preserving of England to be accomplished by establishing an empire in the New World and by this means thwarting the Spanish. 'I have therefore laboured all my life', he reminds his audience, 'both according to my small power, and persuasion, to advance al those attempts, that might eyther promise return of profit to our selves, or at last be a lett and impeachment to the ... Spanish nation' (10). As we have already begun to see, the establishing of empire in the New World, which will prove so salutary to the health of England, depends upon the agency of men and the observance of patrilineage.

Several aspects of Ralegh's adherence to patrilineal imperatives come together with particular force in his representation of exchanges with Topiawari, the very old king of Aromaia. Neil Whitehead contends that Ralegh's meetings with Topiawari furnished him reliable intelligence about indigenous polities, a fact that makes Ralegh's recounting of their meetings especially relevant to our consideration of Ralegh's political imagination.[10] So, too, do the facts that once again Ralegh both stresses the agencies of men and implicitly juxtaposes to Elizabethan sovereignty the form of rule that he discovers in the New World, granting more weight, rhetorically, to the latter. At the outset, Ralegh presents himself to Topiawari as 'servant' of the Queen, whose 'pleasure it was' that he 'should undertake ... to deliver [the Guianans] from the tyrannie of the Spaniards'. He continues at some length,

10 Whitehead, ed., *The Discoverie*, 67–9 and passim. Vaughan in Chapter 8 above describes *The Discoverie* as 'good amateur geopolitics' (252).

dilating at large (as I had done before to those of *Trinedado*) her Maiesties greatnes, her justice, her charitie to all oppressed nations, with as manie of the rest of her beauties and vertues, as either I coulde expresse, or they conceive, all which being with great admiration, attentively heard, and marvellously admired, I began to sound the olde man as touching *Guiana*, and the state thereof, what sort of common wealth it was, how governed, of what strength and pollicy, how farre it extended, and what nations were friends or enemies adjoining, and finally of the distance, and the way to enter the same. (51)

As presented in this dilation, Elizabeth's virtues do not precisely pale in comparison to Ralegh's own exertions; but the praising of her in such general and abstract terms seems calculated to set off the more sharply pointed instrumentality of Ralegh's questions, and so to highlight the fact of his being the commander, here on the ground, so to speak. Ralegh's extolling of the strengths of men includes Topiawari, who is known as the proudest and wisest of the men whom Ralegh encounters and who is the one most respected by Ralegh for his political judgement: 'This *Topiawari* is held for the proudest, and the wisest of al the *Orenoqueponi*, and so he behaved himselfe toward me in all his answers ... as I marvelled to find a man of that gravity and judgement, and of so good discourse that had no helpe of learning nor breed' (52).

Crucially, Topiawari is also a father, one whose understanding of empire and nation, as related by Ralegh, is fundamentally indistinguishable from his paternal affection. Describing to Ralegh the conflicts that have carved out the current political terrain of Guiana, Topiawari answers Ralegh's questions 'with a great sigh (as a man which had inward feeling of the losse of his countrey and liberty, especially for that his eldest sonne was slain in a battel on that side of the mountaines, whom he most entirely loved)' (51). National genealogies cannot be separated out from familial ones; Topiawari 'remembered in his fathers life time when he was very old, and himselfe a yoong man that there came down into that large valley of Guiana, a nation from so far off as the Sun slept ... with so great a multitude as they could not be numbered or resisted' (51). Nor can the securing of future empires be severed from family ties: when Ralegh leaves for home, forced by circumstances to postpone until the next year any 'enterprize against the Epuremei', enemies of Topiawari's nation, Topiawari 'freely' gives to Ralegh his 'onelie sone' to take with him to England, hoping 'that though he himselfe had but a short tyme to live, yet that by [the means of Ralegh and the English] his sonne should be established after his death' (63). In return, Ralegh – who on this journey has no son of his own to offer in exchange – leaves behind one Francis Sparrow, a servant of one of Ralegh's captains, and a 'boy' of his own called Hugh Goodwin' (63).

This trading of boys strikes us today as reprehensible, not much different from the kidnapping, often with removal to Europe, of Amerindians to serve as guides and intermediaries.[11] I have no wish to gloss over such ugly flexing of cultural muscle. But I do wish to suggest that, as rendered in Ralegh's treatise – that is, rather touchingly – the fatherly exchange of son and boys conducted in the interest of establishing empires confirms the impression created by *Discoverie of Guiana* that patrilineal imperatives condition Ralegh's conception of sovereignty, commonwealth, and empire in ways that cannot be explained fully by purely pragmatic considerations or ostensible political aims. Furthermore, partly because they do not rise to the level of overt representation or manipulation, these imperatives remain almost seamlessly interwoven with other strands in Ralegh's thinking about empire.

If patrilineage figures in *Discoverie of Guiana* only subterraneously, it is sharply foregrounded in a painting of Ralegh with his son Wat and provides the *raison d'être* of Ralegh's *Instructions to a Son*. In both of these works, as in *Discoverie*, the strength of patrilineal imperatives becomes a measure of Ralegh's distance from, even resistance to, court and sovereign power. One of the promises of the portrait is the assurance that the patrilineal occasion commemorated by the painting is in many ways a sufficient one – sufficient to compensate for past and perhaps pending losses at court – losses of the position, influence, remuneration, and liberty that Ralegh at times enjoyed. One of the intentions of Ralegh's Advice, a work possibly undertaken during Ralegh's imprisonment in the Tower, is, in

---

11 Alden Vaughan, 'Sir Walter Ralegh's Indian Interpreters, 1584–1618', *William and Mary Quarterly* 59.2, History Cooperative online, 1, estimates that Ralegh himself sponsored 'perhaps twenty American natives … foster[ing] the practice of transporting American natives to England, training them to speak English, introducing them to Anglican Christianity, assuring their return to America, and reaping tangible benefits from their support of England's imperial ventures'. Emphasizing that Ralegh was the first English colonizer to pointedly encourage the acquisition of English in the men he conveyed to England, and noting that he did so to furnish interpreters and guides for expeditions to Carolina and Guiana, Vaughan observes that Ralegh nevertheless inspired in these Amerindians 'lasting loyalty to Sir Walter and his nation', 2. Vaughan notes that such trans-Atlantic exchanges were not always so sanguine. Nor were 'loyalties' always secured. Stephen Greenblatt, *Marvellous Possessions: The Wonder of the New World* (Chicago: University of Chicago Press, 1991), cites, for example, Cartier's experience with kidnapped, trained 'interpreters' who did not remain 'wedded to his own interests' (108).

Anna Beer's estimation, 'to find (or to rediscover) an authoritative voice'.[12] Ralegh constructs a position of authority from which to instruct his son in the careful management of *personal* estate and reputation, matters considered almost entirely without reference to court and Crown. But *Instructions* is inflected also with tensions not represented in the painting, small crises of paternal authority that crack the cool, calculating, and, occasionally, cynical polish of Ralegh's Advice as well as subtle, but potentially seismic, misalignments of parenting and piety.

2. Father and son in painting

The portrait of Sir Walter Ralegh and his son Wat that hangs in London's National Portrait Gallery leaves no doubt that the two sitters are father and son. The costume, posture, and even facial expression of the boy mirror closely those of the adult: 'Like father, like son' reads the caption under this picture in a recent article by Robert Lawson-Peebles on influential representations of Ralegh in painting and in print.[13] Although the portrait registers the resemblance as an as-yet-unfulfilled promise by making the boy's habit blue – the Renaissance colour of hope – the extent to which the boy mimics his father encourages the foregone conclusion that Wat will grow up to become like his father. The setting for the portrait, perhaps intended to suggest Sherborne, Ralegh's West Country home, insinuates another supposition into this representation of father and son: the expectation that the boy will grow into his father's (at this moment) still considerable estate. The furnishings depicted in the portrait are not ostentatious, but the solid table with its curved and ornately carved foot and fringed tablecloth, the heavy curtain, and the parqueted or tiled floor convey the impression of substance. The space, sufficiently light-filled to produce shadows that fall behind and to the left of the sitters, and the floor, with its large tiles, hint at grandness that does not need to be displayed. The great expectations for the boy are grounded as well in his apparent acquiescence to the demands placed on him as he leaves behind his childhood. The painting is dated 1602, when Wat would have been eight years old – just about the age when a boy began to wear doublet and breeches. Wat appears unfazed by the weight of expectation – unless we begin to imagine that the bench just visible behind him is

---

12 Anna Beer, *Sir Walter Ralegh and His Readers*, 127.
13 Robert Lawson-Peebles, 'The Many Faces of Sir Walter Ralegh', *History Today* 48.3 (1998), 18. Lawson-Peebles mistakenly claims that the portrait was painted in 1588; young Walter was born in 1593.

placed there conveniently for Wat to sit on to rest from the demands of standing for the portrait.

I have suggested already that the lack of ostentation does not devalue the room, but it does gesture toward a signal quality of the setting: its isolation from the world of display that was the courtly sphere in which Ralegh spent much of his time and ambition. In her biography of Bess Throckmorton Ralegh, Anna Beer observes that Sherborne Lodge 'embodied a rejection of the court and its values', noting in particular that the 'servants' quarters were separated from the rooms of the family, further removing Sherborne from the spatially and socially enmeshed old ways of living'.[14] An inscription in the darkened top left corner of the portrait points even further away from the Elizabethan court. It reads: '1602 / Sr Walter Ralegh Knight Lord Warden of / the Stanaries [Capt] of the [Guard Gouenrr: of Virginia] & of the Isle of Yarsey & her M. Lieute / nant general of the Counties of Deuonshyre & Cornwall'.[15]

With the exception of the reference to Ralegh's post as Captain of the Guard, a position he recovered following his imprisonment in 1592, the list of Ralegh's titles and offices identifies him as a West Country man ready and able to take advantage of the opportunities represented by the new world even further to the west and by the wealth to be amassed from stannaries, that is, tin mines, in the West Country. Like the reference to Virginia, the seed-pearls on Ralegh's doublet associate him with seafaring – the movement away from England – that punctuated his career. But, just as the reference to Ralegh's being Captain of the Guard reminds us of his closeness to the Queen, so too do the pearls – which figure so frequently in depictions of Elizabeth – connect him to court and sovereign. It would be a mistake, then, to say that this portrait of Ralegh removes him entirely from the Queen's sphere of influence. Nevertheless, the strongest gestures in the painting underscore Ralegh's independence of Queen and court. Regardless of whether or not the portrait was painted at Sherborne, then, it reflects removal from the courtly world and a corresponding focus on the world of father and son. This effect is emphatically heightened by the lack of windows giving on to any prospect outside the patrilineal occasion marked by the portrait. The focus on the patrilineal space and moment is further intensified by close quarters: not much distance, seemingly a stride or two, separates viewer from father and son and, because

14 Anna Beer, *My Just Desire*, 70.
15 I am grateful to Erika Ingham, Assistant Curator, National Portrait Gallery, who provided me with the inscription, which is no longer decipherable on either reproductions or the actual portrait.

there is no window behind the subjects to draw us beyond them, we are compelled to take the measure of their relationship.

The intense focus on the father–son relationship surely reflects fatherly pride, perhaps even Ralegh's willingness to yield pride of place to his son – who is positioned ever so slightly ahead of his father, and whose costume is painted in the costly colour blue. It is Wat's face, not Ralegh's, that takes up the light shining in from the unrepresented window. So, there is pride. But there is very little, if any, affection and there is absolutely no intimacy. Father and son do not touch: each seems scarcely aware of the other's presence, or, if aware, only stiffly so; each could well be a stand-alone subject in the portrait. Precisely because the dynamics of family life, however warm or strained or messy they might have been, are not even glimpsed in this representation of Ralegh and his son, nothing distracts from the promise of patrilineage.[16]

3. Father and son in *Instructions to a Son*

At least initially, intimacy or strong fatherly feeling seems missing from Ralegh's *Instructions to a Son* as well. While impersonal, general counsel often strikes the keynote in Advices, Ralegh's tract goes further than

16 The portrait of Ralegh and Wat shares elements of composition, setting, furnishings, costuming, and poses with other paintings of the period. But in its intense focus on the father / son resemblance and its marked lack of manifest affection, the Ralegh and son portrait seems singular. Other paintings of family groupings, for example, convey a wider range of family dynamics, at least partly because the mother of the child or children is one of the sitters; those same family groupings typically register some intimacy between parent(s) and children. Children in those groupings, as well as children depicted alone and without parents present, often hold a toy, stand by a pet, or pore over their studies, to indicate their immersion in activities relevant to their age; Wat's focus, on the other hand, is on resembling his father. In this regard, the Ralegh and son portrait can be aligned with Laurel Reed's observation that portraits of children from this period are often intended 'to commemorate the child's future public role or to strengthen the public view of the family by celebrating dynastic continuity', 'Art, Life, Charm, and Titian's *Portrait of Clarissa Strozzi*', in *Childhood in the Middle Ages and the Renaissance*, ed. Albrecht Classen (Berlin and New York: De Gruyter, 2005), 357. Reed notes as well that full-length portraits are 'relatively uncommon' in the period 'for non-noble or non-royal sitters' (363). The figures in several portraits of noblemen, monarchs, and princes of the period, including one of Prince Henry, painted a decade or so after Ralegh's, share elements of stance, costuming, setting and air of command, indicating just how conventional was the depiction of men and youth who held or were expected to hold positions of power and authority. Perhaps in instructing the painter, Ralegh drew on these pervasive conventions to assert the importance of this particular patrilineage. If so, this is evidence not simply of Ralegh's famous 'damnable pride' but also of his staunch adherence to the idea of patrilineal rule. On portraits of the period, see, for example, Lorne Campbell, *Renaissance Portraits* (New Haven: Yale University Press, 1990); on portraits of children by artists in the Netherlands, see *Pride and Joy: Children's Portraits in the Netherlands 1500–1700*, ed. Jan Baptist Bedaux and Rudi Ekkart (Amsterdam: Ludion Press, 2000).

those of some of his contemporaries in depersonalizing the occasion and tenor of advice. Both William Cecil, Lord Burghley, and Henry Percy, Earl of Northumberland, for example, begin by gesturing toward private, domestic relations: Cecil by alluding to the beneficent influences of mother and tutor that his son enjoyed in childhood and youth; Percy by sounding his own death knell and offering his advice as his 'last gift' to a son who has not reached the age of majority.[17] At its start, Ralegh's Advice seems already well removed from familial scenes: 'There is nothing more becoming a wise man than to make choice of friends', Ralegh begins, 'for by them thou shalt be judged what thou are' (19). What follows is advice about preserving an estate and reputation that could be fitted to any young man of means, to any young man, moreover, who is already on the cusp of adulthood, well beyond childhood and youth. In Ralegh's Advice, the only two allusions to the infancy and childhood of the addressee are designed to teach the son that the affections of infancy, childhood, and youth are fleeting and insubstantial: friends made in young years will 'never' please the adult (19); an infant's 'love' for his nurses, wet and dry, lasts only as long as the nursing (21). The only reference to how his son Wat should conduct himself in relationship to his mother takes the very oblique form of counsel regarding how much, what kind, and with what provisos a husband should leave property to his wife: a wife should be accommodated, until she remarries; most property should be left to heirs and 'house'(22). Many householder wills of the time do set limits on what the widow can expect, but many are also generous not simply in providing material wealth but in trying to ensure that affective ties remain strong. Ralegh's own will left virtually everything to Wat, and, in recommending the course of action that he does here in his Advice, Ralegh is essentially instructing Wat to disengage his affections from his mother.[18]

The writer of the Letter to the Reader appended to a 1632 edition of *Instructions* recognizes and extols the generality and impartialness of Ralegh's tract, remarking enthusiastically that 'Here then thou hast, gentle reader, those instructions that have been so much and so long desired by many', and noting that wide circulation of the advice does no 'injury ... to him for whom alone they were at first written' because 'faithful counsel

17 William Cecil (Lord Burghley), *Certain Precepts for the Well Ordering of a Man's Life*, in *Advice to a Son*, ed. Louis Wright, Folger Shakespeare Library (Ithaca: Cornell University Press, 1962); Henry Percy (Earl of Northumberland), *Advice to His Son*, ed. G. B. Harrison (London: Ernest Benn Ltd, 1930).
18 In her discussion of Ralegh's will of 1597, Agnes Latham, 'Sir Walter Ralegh's Will', *R.E.S.* New Series, XXII.86 (1971), observes succinctly that '[a]ll is concentrated on a little boy of four' (130).

in matters general is ... the chief of those benefits named by the wise Roman which may be communicated to others without detriment either to the giver or him to whom it is particularly given' (17). The writer of the 1632 preface can be excused for detaching the advice from its primary audience. Not only do the features I have just identified encourage such detachment, so too does the fact that Ralegh does not even identify himself as the father of the addressee until half-way through the tract when he urges Wat to 'believe thy father in this' (28).

When Ralegh does at this mid-way point draw expressly on his paternal authority, it is in the context of what becomes one of the most heated passages in an otherwise decidedly cool treatise. Chapter V treats explicitly a topic that threads through virtually all the Advice, care of personal estate. He identifies three courses that must be followed, insisting at length on the third: the importance of not putting up 'surety' for another. Ralegh's wording – his son should not 'be' surety for another (27) – begins to suggest the extent to which Ralegh is teaching Wat that personhood equals material wealth. The vehemence with which Ralegh extends this point indicates not only that the question of being surety for another touches a raw nerve in Ralegh but also that Ralegh conflates worldly and spiritual, or moral, welfare to a degree not characteristic of the Advice genre. Percy, for instance, distinguishes carefully between worldly comforts and contentment of the mind in justifying his intention to teach his son the path to worldly security. Burghley's Advice is entirely more moral in tone; although he offers counsel on pragmatic matters, he clearly subordinates worldly success to the moral and virtuous life.

Ralegh, in contrast, directs the most intense moral imagining in his treatise to the consequences of posting surety for another. To do so is to 'be wounded for other men's faults and scourged for other men's offences', to 'be made an ass to carry the burden of other men'. Ralegh counsels that his son should 'from suretyship as from a manslayer or enchanter bless thyself'. What is at risk in suretyship, these similes imply, is more than just material loss, more even than loss of life and limb. In posting surety, one hazards one's will, mind, and spirit to demonic control. Poverty is 'a curse of God'; it is 'a shame amongst men, an imprisonment of the mind, a vexation of every worthy spirit'. If poor, 'thou shalt drown in thee all thy virtues, having no means to show them; thou shalt be a burden and an eyesore to thy friends'; 'thou shalt be driven basely to beg and depend on others; to flatter unworthy men; to make dishonest shifts; ... to do infamous and detested deeds' (28). Moral bankruptcy and spiritual thraldom follow so closely on the heels of financial ruin as to be indistinguishable from it. Moreover, Ralegh's related convictions that the poor man is an 'eyesore', deformed (like a leper?), and that 'virtue' can be manifested only through 'means', convey covertly the message that there can be no inward strength of character.

At this moment, then, the first time in *Instructions* that Ralegh invokes his paternal authority, he does not *instruct* his son at all, if by 'instruct' we mean the 'building in' of strengths, supports, and resources. The lack of instruction in this figurative sense is underlined by the use in this same chapter of another metaphor related to both inwardness and instruction. When Ralegh urges Wat to 'believe thy father' in this matter of posting surety, he also directs Wat to 'print it in thy thought' (28). Drawing its force from the textual practices of the humanist schoolroom, the trope of printing lessons in thought or memory is one that seems to have been considered particularly apt for moments of filial instruction. Burghley urges *his* son to 'imprint ... in [his] mind' the precepts that his father gives him.[19] Echoing Burghley, Polonius advises his son, Laertes, to 'character' in his memory the 'few precepts' that his father devises. A still more famous son, Hamlet, vows that the ghostly Hamlet's 'commandment all alone shall live / Within the book and volume of [his] brain', that 'from the table of [his] memory / [He'll] wipe away all trivial fond records, / All saws of books, all forms, all pressures past / That youth and observation copied there'.[20] For Hamlet, as for Burghley, highly charged moments of fatherly instruction are imagined to work inward reform – of memory, character, and spirit. For Polonius, on the other hand, as numerous critics have observed, fatherly advice aims to shape reputation and social relations. Like Polonius's, Ralegh's Advice pays mere lip service to the idea of inward reform.

In the case of Ralegh, this hollowness represents what I am calling an abdication of fatherly responsibility, a crisis in authority which, while it does not produce major faultlines in the grounds of paternal authority, does introduce fissures nonetheless. To trace these fractures, I would like to turn to the closing gesture of Ralegh's *Instructions*, the moment at which Ralegh offers fatherly benediction. In that final short chapter, Ralegh affirms a coincidence of aims between God's ways and his own, with respect to Wat's tutelage, implying that the two of them work in tandem: Ralegh's fatherly instruction, sinking into Wat's heart, prepares the boy to be directed by God and his heart to be filled with God's grace.

---

19 Burghley, *Certain Precepts*, 9.
20 William Shakespeare, *Hamlet*, ed. Susanne Wofford (Boston: Bedford Books, 1994), I.iii.58–59; I.v.98–103.

In so affirming, Ralegh elides the differences between his and God's ways, seeming to forget that his own advice to his son has almost always directed him to close, or to empty, his heart.

The divergence between God's ways and Ralegh's fatherly instruction can be felt in the subtle but nonetheless real contradictions that riddle Ralegh's discussion of poverty. Right after cautioning his son that posting surety might lead to what Ralegh represents as the debasement and depravity of poverty, Ralegh reminds Wat, almost in passing, that he should 'relieve the poor' (Chapter V, 28). He returns to this theme in Chapter VIII, warning that Wat should 'not take anything from the poor, for the cry and complaint thereof will pierce the heavens'. It is 'detestable before God ... to wrest anything from the needy and labouring soul'. Wat should 'Remember this precept: he that hath mercy on the poor lendeth unto the Lord, and the Lord will recompense him what he hath given' (29). Recognizing the need to distinguish between the two states of poverty he has evoked, debased and worthy, Ralegh is quick to add that he does 'not understand those for poor which are vagabonds and beggars, but those that labour to live such as are old and cannot travail ... poor widows and fatherless children ... poor tenants driven to poverty by mischance' (29–30). Ralegh's recourse here is to the common distinction between worthy poor and sturdy beggars, and his stance reflects the class assumptions of his time: it is no debasement for the worthy poor to beg; it is a social and spiritual obligation for noblemen to relieve them. Poverty in this context amounts to spiritual capital for both the worthy poor, with their 'labouring souls', and the charitable nobleman. Leaving aside the fact that the distinction between the worthy and the degraded poor derives from class biases that do not figure in godly admonitions to relieve the poor, the fact remains that Ralegh cannot imagine that his own son would number among the worthy poor, should he spiral into poverty through mismanagement of his estates or through posting surety. Ralegh does not, it seems, have much confidence in his ability – as a father – to make his son worthy of either man's charity or God's grace. Ralegh's very first chapter predicts that this will be the case. There, in advising Wat in the choice of friends and the forming of social relations, Ralegh counsels his son to keep cloaked any defects of character: 'But if thou be subject to any great vanity or ill, *from which I hope God will bless thee*, then therein trust no man, for every man's folly ought to be his greatest secret' (19 – 20; my emphasis). It is customary for parents in Ralegh's day to invoke God's help in keeping their children from going astray. In urging Wat to keep his failings secret from anyone but God, however, Ralegh seems pointedly to evade any role he might play in fostering Wat's spiritual welfare. For Ralegh in *Instructions to a Son* only the means to maintaining reputation and estate fall within the earthly father's purview; the means to virtuous and moral character fall within God's only.

4. Father and son in 'Three things there be'

While it is not quite right to say that strong fatherly feeling is what cracks the polished veneer of *Instructions*, it is the case that Ralegh's own fatherhood does, specifically his evasions of the demands of fatherhood, reiterated in sermons, homilies, and handbooks and developed from the analogy, so prevalent in the period, that fathers should be to children as God is to humankind. Far from being a loose comparison, the analogy that likened fathers to God generated very specific roles and responsibilities for fathers, prominent among them spiritual custodianship. Hence the custom of the father's blessing. Ralegh's benediction in his Advice, as I have just argued, only appears to merge seamlessly with God's giving of grace. Ralegh's astonishing poem of fatherly admonishment, 'Three things there be', pries apart even more irreparably the link between parenting and piety. Further, whereas both *Instructions* and the portrait of Ralegh and his son maintain easily and without repercussions distance from court and Crown, the poem engages troublingly with state power. Thus, while the poem is short, its implications are long in its demonstration of how and with what consequences an occasion of filial admonishment absorbs affect.

In contrast to the portrait of Ralegh and son, where the familial relationship between the two subjects is immediately evident, 'Three things there bee' renders the relationship between the speaker and auditor nearly impossible to decipher, at least initially. Until line 8, we do not even know who is speaking or to whom. Moreover, again in contrast to the portrait, with its delineation of great expectations for the boy, the poem burdens the boy with only the dimmest of hopes, indeed with the direst of predictions – however much those predictions are framed in gallows humour. Still in contrast to the portrait, with its stiffness of relations and its cool distances between father and son, the poem is freighted with strong feeling, although not, as we shall see, simple fatherly affection. For ease of reference and because I will be returning to almost each line of this poem in the analysis to follow, I will quote it here in its entirety:

> Three things there bee that prosper all apace
> And flourish while they are a sunder farre
> But on a day they meete all in a place,

> and when they meet they one an other marr
> And they bee these, the *Wood*, the *Weed*, the *Wagg*
> The *wood* is that that makes the Gallowes tree
> The *weed* is that [which] strings the hangmans bagg
> The *Wagg* my pretty knave betokens thee
> Now marke dear boy, whilst these assemble not,
> Green springs the tree, hemp growes, the wag is wilde
> But when they meet it makes the timber rot
> It fretts the halter, and it choaks the childe
> God bless the child.[21]

One of the most influential critics to discuss this poem, Agnes Latham observes that 'what begins in lightness of heart, ends in earnest'. She forecloses the reach of the poem, however, in objecting to the view that the poem is tragic or painful and contending instead that, the 'mounting seriousness' of tone notwithstanding, 'to threaten a child with the gallows' must be 'an Elizabethan nursery-joke' – albeit a 'grim one'.[22] Without denying the gallows humour in the poem, I would suggest that to read the poem as merely a joke, even a deadly serious one, is to mistake the poem: to accord far too much certainty to it and its speaker; to simplify its tone and movement; and to reduce the complexity of the relationship between father and son. The poem moves, rather, from easy, even glib, riddling to remonstrance that is deeply enigmatic with respect to both parenting and piety.[23]

The first lines are confident and categorical in their posing of the terms of the riddle, aphoristic in structure and tone, conventionalized in imagery and idea. Such tendencies in the verse are heightened, in the first two lines, by the four monosyllabic words that begin the poem, by

21 I am using the version of 'Sir *Walter Rawleigh* to his sonne, Walter' that Michael Rudick reprints in his *The Poems of Sir Walter Ralegh: A Historical Edition* (Tempe, AZ: Renaissance English Text Society, 1999) rather than the version adopted by Agnes Latham. Rudick observes that Latham's version is the 'only one of the four known texts that carries neither title nor attribution' (176). The version Latham uses ends not with a strangulated half-line, but with the comfortable piety of 'Then bless thee, and beware, and let us pray / We part not with thee at this meeting day'.
22 Agnes Latham, ed., *The Poems of Sir Walter Ralegh* (Cambridge, MA: Harvard University Press, 1951), 140.
23 In an eloquent reading that I discovered after completing my own analysis of the poem, Linda Gregerson stresses the complexity and power of the poem, noting that it 'tries to wrest an exception from the future it has summoned' and that it 'abandons the language of riddle and spell for the language of prayer, the language of wishing-against-all-odds'. She does not adduce form in tracing this complexity, as I will do, however, or single out Ralegh's own fatherly feeling as the elixir that transforms the poem from conventional, even pat, riddling to profound perplexity. 'Sir Walter Ralegh to his son', *Atlantic Unbound*, Online version, January 30, 2002.

the emphatic alliteration that informs each of the two clauses in the first line, by the sibilance that threads through the first two lines, and by the subtler patterns of alliteration, assonance, and consonance that link the first two lines through chiasmus ('*th*ree ... *th*ey;' '*th*ere ... fa*rr*e' [proximate vowel sounds in Ralegh's English]; 'thing*s* ... *s*under'; 'pro*s*per apa*c*e ... flouri*sh*'). As befits a riddle, the first categorical imperative, 'Three things there bee', quickly yields to a second, 'but on a day they meet ... and when they meet', and the search for an answer to this riddle is on, with the repeated word 'meet' adding perhaps a subtle twist. Although 'meet' as used here means primarily 'come together', its widely used adjectival sense of 'fitting' hovers over these lines, with the result that 'marre' in the line 'and when they meet they one another marre' seems somewhat *unmeet* for the context. Such jarring of expectation piques the auditor's interest in the riddle, setting up the answer which is not yet the final answer to the riddle: 'And they bee these, the *Wood*, the *Weed*, the *Wagg*'.

Careful control of intention and expectations informs the poem until this point: firm handling of tone, metre, syntax, and verbal patterns that positions the speaker as worldly, authoritative, a little wry, and not at all inclined to second-guess himself. But as the speaker moves closer to providing the answer to the riddle he has posed, his control begins to falter, the loss of control signalled initially by the slight break in parallelism when he turns to address Wat for the first time in the poem. When the speaker declares what 'wood' and 'weed' signify, he does so with noun clauses. The effect of such deliberative construction is to create distance between the speaker and his subject, as well as to attenuate the connection between the signifier and what it signifies. But, when the speaker declares what 'wag' means, he does so with a directness of address that collapses the distance between him and his subject, that is, his son Wat, as well as between the wag and Wat: 'The *Wagg* my pretty knave betokens thee'. No relative pronoun attenuates the identification of Wat with the wag, while the epithet 'my pretty knave', which applies logically to Wat, sits right next to the Wag, its position serving to elide any distance between Wat and the until-now-merely-hypothesized Wag.

The faltering of confidence and authority that I am describing is signalled also by the slowing of the narrative impulse that has prompted the poem to this point. Until now, the poem's trajectory has been unimpeded, carried along by the insistent parallelism, the repeated 'And's, the relative lack of imagery, and the near-anonymity of the speaker. But with the turn to direct addressing of the boy comes a deepening of the riddle's import that brings us, the speaker, and the poem's implied auditor, up short. Suddenly, the riddle does not reflect conventional, collective, aphoristic wisdom so much as it registers admonishment that is singular, personal, and not in the least assured – not least, as we shall see, because of the illogical associations that will gather around the idea of wildness introduced in line 10 (as well as in its unspoken opposite: civility).

In lines 8 and 9, though, the weight of personal meaning is carried by the apostrophes to the son: 'my pretty knave'; ' Now marke dear boy'. With the shift from 'pretty knave' to 'dear boy' comes not only a deepening of feeling but also a dropping of the speaker's, the father's, emotional guard. As an expression of endearment, 'pretty knave' is hedged with something that is certainly not mockery, but that is teasing in its proffering of affection nonetheless – as if the father cannot quite yet bring himself to frank expressions of love. The very voicing of these words, especially 'pretty', with its consonants clipped at the tip of the tongue, gauges a certain tightness. 'Dear boy' seems, by contrast, a more expansive expression of fondness, partly because of the fuller vowel sounds and the softened consonants – effects amplified by the round 'now' at the start of the phrase – and partly because 'dear boy' reflects closer, because less self-conscious, relational ties than does 'pretty knave'. The pun on 'dear' as both loved and costly intimates that the father is beginning to realize what would be the emotional cost to him of the loss of his son. The access of emotion is felt also in the heaviness of line 9, which begins with four emphatic monosyllables, and in the suddenly different sense of time.

In beginning with four emphatic beats, this, the third quatrain, parallels the first two. But the structural parallelism only highlights the differences from the first two quatrains. In them, in keeping with the aphoristic tendency of the opening lines, some indefinite future is posited: 'on a day they meet' and 'when they meet'. When the speaker addresses his son directly, the time is emphatically 'now'. In the first two quatrains, the speaker's language is relatively neutral and abstract; when the father speaks directly to Wat, his language becomes more charged as concrete words – 'springs', 'rot', 'fretts', 'choaks' – carry the burden of admonishment.

And this language and the closing moments of the poem carry an extraordinarily heavy burden of admonishment – for both Wat and his father. We can only surmise about the effects on Wat of his father's dire prophecy that he will one day hang. We witness the effects on the father. Once again, sentence structure cues us to some of these effects. The parallelism that has been so insistent through most of the poem and that has underwritten the speaker's distancing of himself from his subject and son now buckles under the weight of the father's deepening anxiety: 'Green springs the tree, hemp growes, the wag is wilde'. Three short clauses; three different constructions that are almost but not quite parallel, with the uneven parallelism accentuated by the variant metrical feet, the spondees.

In addition to registering an access of emotion, the disrupted construction introduces a paradox, one set in motion by the insistently green-springing tree and the thriving hemp, imagery that concretizes the flourishing mentioned in line 2. Life seemingly remains in store for the wag – for as long as he remains 'wild', beyond the pale of discipline. But it is just such discipline, presumably, such training up or 'breeding', to use a term Ralegh uses elsewhere, that would prevent Wat's becoming fit for the gallows. In the deep logic of the poem, the wildness that fits Wat to the noose is the quality that gives him life. The terrible irony of this paradox measures the speaker's sense of utter helplessness as a father. Once pushed to the brink of contemplating his son's death, Ralegh can only respond with a piety uncharacteristic of him, petitioning God to do what all the conventional parenting wisdom of the day said was the duty of the father: 'bless the child'. There is a still more withering irony in play here. 'Wildness' demarcates a condition that is not only beyond the pale of familial discipline, but that, in lying outside the civil order altogether, incurs the threat of penalties that are state-sanctioned. Again, because Wag's wildness carries the promise of life, Wat's very coming into the fold of civility – which would prevent his hanging – would paradoxically deaden him nevertheless.

I began this section of my chapter by asking how and with what consequences an occasion of filial admonishment accommodates a strongly affective response. Ralegh's poem of advice, 'Three things there be', suggests that the consequences are considerable: what is at risk of crumbling is the scaffolding which supported patriarchal authority. And it is at risk of collapsing because the implied analogy, ubiquitous in the period, that likened a father's authority both to a sovereign's authority and to God's authority, that analogy has broken apart. The fatherly feeling that makes the exercise of paternal authority purposeful and meaningful overwhelms the occasion of instruction, sets the father's authority against that of state or sovereign, and recasts the father as a helpless petitioner for God's intervention – intervention that itself carries no guarantee of success now that the triumvirate of god, sovereign, and father has been sundered. The patrilineage that seamlessly underwrites Ralegh's political imagination when Ralegh's own fatherhood is not engaged in the enterprise unravels when it is.

12

Ralegh's image in art[1]

Vivienne Westbrook

I shall call the protagonist of this story 'Ralegh'. I do not like to call him 'Sir Walter': as such he seems no more than a cliché, a posture, an adornment of English Heritage biscuit-tins and humorous No Smoking signs. He is caught in the dead space of recurrence. He is forever having to lay down his cloak in the mud, to parley with red-skinned Indians, to puff elabourately on a long clay-pipe. The pipe is his trademark, as familiar as Florence Nightingale's lamp and Nelson's empty sleeve.[2]

Introduction

In response to an internet search for 'Walter Ralegh in art', the 'Public Domain Clip Art' website retrieves two items: the first by Hilliard and the second by 'H' monogrammist. The site suggests that such images may be 'Great for cards, invitations, decorations and much more!'[3] While in the first instance Raleigh is categorized as an explorer, in the second he is categorized as a politician, but for no obvious reason. In the first portrait he wears an intricately designed lace ruff and ear pearls of a courtier. In the second portrait he wears a cape, and stands with his hand on his sword as a soldier. Both pictures are in the National Portrait Gallery collection, two of no fewer than 43 portraits, all but 16 of which are available online at the NPG's domain page. In fact, in the sixteenth century Ralegh was usually depicted as a wealthy courtier or a soldier, but through time he acquired a pipe that was to become, along with the sword and the cape, the most defining and enduring of his attributes across the whole range of representational media.

---

1 Thanks are due to Larry Tise and Mark Nichols for inviting me to present an earlier version of this paper at the Tower of London Conference, to St John's College, Cambridge, the National Science Council of Taiwan, and the North Caroliniana Society's Archie K. Davis Fellowship which facilitated the research.
2 Charles Nicholl, *The Creature in the Map: A Journey to El Dorado* (London: Cape, 1995), 3.
3 www.pdclipart.org /displayimage.php?album=88&pos=60.

Figure 12.1 Nicholas Hilliard, Miniature portrait of Sir Walter Ralegh (c. 1581–84).

Hilliard's miniature of Ralegh, earlier thought to be Henry Howard, was painted in 1585 at the height of Ralegh's influence with Elizabeth.[4] By

---

4 Roy Strong notes that 'When in the collection of the Earls of Carlisle at Castle Howard it was known as Henry Howard, Earl of Northampton. Its true identity was established by C. S. Emden in 1948 by comparison with the oil copy of this type at Vienna, part of the vast portrait collection assembled by Archduke Ferdinand of Tyrol (1529–1595). The Vienna miniature bears a contemporary inscription identifying it as Raleigh.' See Roy Strong, *Tudor and Jacobean Portraits* (London: HMSO, 1969), 255.

this time, he had been knighted, appointed vice-admiral of the west, Lord Lieutenant of Cornwall, and Lord Warden of the stannaries.[5] To the visitor of the National Portrait Gallery, an explanatory panel to this portrait defines him as a: 'Soldier, sailor, poet and writer' (NPG 4106). Clearly the man that Hilliard depicted with his delicate lacework collar is the writer /poet.[6] Hilliard's 1577 self-portrait is remarkably similar. Hilliard faces the opposite direction to Ralegh but there can be no mistaking the fact that Ralegh's 1585 portrait is painted after the fashion of Hilliard's own. Of all of the portraits that Hilliard 'executed' at Elizabeth's court no other two are so alike. When Hilliard wanted to paint a soldier, he chose Essex. 'Robert Devereux, 2nd Earl of Essex (1566–1601), Soldier; favourite of Elizabeth I' (NPG 6241) was painted in 1587 when he had just returned from his victories at Zutphen and was Ralegh's chief rival at court.

In the portrait by 'H' monogrammist, executed in 1588 (NPG 7), the NPG panel draws attention to Raleigh's pearls: 'Ralegh's dramatic costume is lavishly embellished with pearls, symbols of purity and much favoured by Elizabeth I. The pearls on his cloak form the rays of a 'sun-in-splendour', a common heraldic device that can also be seen on the sleeves of Elizabeth I's dress'. Indeed, the pearl work is intricate and detailed, but it was Hiliard who was the acknowledged master pearl painter of his generation; being first and foremost a jeweller, Hilliard tended to take more care than was usual in the depiction of jewels in his portraits. When worn by Elizabeth pearls signified purity and chastity, but when applied to Ralegh surely they signified something else? In this portrait, Ralegh wears not one but two pearls, thereby creating a startling visual, with the promise of an audible effect. In his time pearls were prized not merely for their purity but for their natural perfection and, as in this portrait, wisdom. The NPG panel points to the significance of the pearl in creating a visual relationship between Ralegh and Elizabeth. The pearly ostentation of his cloak defines him in the Armada year, not as the great explorer and defender of England but in his more sedentary role as Elizabeth's adviser. Spenser's now famous letter to 'the Right noble, and Valorous, Sir Walter Raleigh knight, Lo. Wardein of the Stanneryes, and her Majesties lieftenaunt of the county of Cornewayll', explained that the purpose of the *Faerie Queene* (1589) was 'to fashion a gentleman or noble person

---

5 Mark Nicholls and Penry Williams, 'Ralegh, Sir Walter (1554–1618)', *Oxford Dictionary of National Biography* (Oxford: Oxford University Press, 2004; online edn, May 2005), www.oxforddnb.com /view /article / 23039.
6 This is one of the most elaborate ruffs in all of the collection; only Mary Herbert, Countess of Pembroke (1590) receives such a detailed lacework treatment. See NPG 5994.

in virtuous and gentle discipline'. By this time, Ralegh had succeeded in this area of his life, at least. Stephen Greenblatt suggests something of the importance of presentation and representation to Ralegh when he notes that 'throughout his career, Ralegh sought to give his life the quality of art, to raise his actions and his sufferings from the level of the private individual to the level of the universal' (109).[7] Recent criticism has sought to match the events described in Spenser's magnum opus with the events of Ralegh's campaigns, especially those in Ireland. Thomas Herron has pointed out that Ralegh's victory in County Cork in 1581, though allegorized by Spenser in Book III, was also related in Holinshed (1586) by John Hooker, who subsequently dedicated his work to Ralegh, while Spenser made Ralegh 'look good in adverse Irish circumstances' (195).[8] In spite of his 'achievements' in Ireland, however, contemporary portraits of Ralegh more often depicted him with pearls, which he no doubt reserved for his court engagements.

In the portrait of 1602 by an unknown artist (NPG 3914), Ralegh is depicted, yet once more in his pearls, in a domestic setting with his son. Jonathan Goldberg suggests: 'It is not only their names that echo. In stance and expression, and despite differences in costume – mere variations upon a theme – this picture proclaims that sons are the images of their fathers' (91).[9] In so doing, the portrait promises continuity not merely in art but in nature /nurture, and constitutes Ralegh as both a maker of fashion and a maker of men in the promise of a dynasty that Elizabeth herself can no longer hope to provide.[10] In the explanatory panel to this portrait, which is itself a portrait, Ralegh is described as:

> A military and naval commander and writer, Ralegh first caught Queen Elizabeth's eye in 1581. He was in favour for most of the 1580s but was

---

7 Stephen Greenblatt, *Sir Walter Ralegh: The Renaissance Man* (New Haven: Yale University Press, 1973), 169.
8 Thomas Herron, *Spenser's Irish Work: Poetry, Plantation and Colonial Reformation* (Aldershot: Ashgate, 2007), 195.
9 Jonathan Goldberg, *James I and the Politics of Literature* (Baltimore and London: Johns Hopkins University Press, 1983), 91.
10 Nigel Llewellyn's study of the Royal body in the sixteenth century reminds us of the need for James to establish his succession as legitimate and continuous and his recourse to monumentalizing Elizabeth. He argues that 'In the 1590s there had been a rumour that the old Queen was to be commemorated in her father's tomb at Windsor. Others predicted that no child of Henry VIII's would ever have a monument. However, Robert Cecil, well aware of the political power of the Monumental Body, vowed: "Rather than fail in payment for Queen Elizabeth's tomb, neither the Exchequer nor London shall have a penny left"'. See Nigel Llewellyn, 'The Royal Body: Monuments to the Dead, For the Living', in *Renaissance Bodies*, ed. Lucy Gent and Nigel Llewellyn (London: Reaktion Books, 1995), 225.

imprisoned in 1592 for his part in an intrigue and subsequently forbidden to appear at court. This portrait was painted in 1602 when Ralegh was at the height of his renewed favour with the Queen. It shows him together with his son Walter who is made to mimic his father's confident pose. Both father and son are dressed in splendid costumes; Ralegh's jacket is embroidered with seed pearls and his son's blue suit is silver-braided. A contemporary of Ralegh described him as 'framed in so just a proportion and so seemly an order, as there was nothing in him that a man might well wish to have been added or altered'.

Little did Ralegh realize just how drastically his fortunes were about to change, for in the 1617 portrait by Simon de Passe (NPG D22914) Ralegh became a paratextual illustration to his voluminous *History of the World*, written during his incarceration in the Tower of London. In this engraving Ralegh, the writer, has assumed the shiny frontal lobes, globular eyes and pendulous reading bags which we associate not with portraits of Ralegh but with Martin Droeshout's 1623 folio engraving of the super-monumentalized Shakespeare. It is not the true image of Ralegh that it claims to be, but it does succeed in emphasizing his status as a man of gravitas and learning. In Robert Vaughan's engraving, after Simon de Passe, published in 1650, five character-defining items are included on a small bookshelf in the top right hand corner of the frame: Plutarch, Pliny, and Galen rest vertically on a horizontal Bible beneath which is Ralegh's own *History of the World* (NPG D28000). These items clearly reinforce key moments of Ralegh's life while, again, foregrounding his role as a learned author. The impact of such images in books are harder for a twenty-first-century computer-graphically saturated culture to comprehend, but Alberti, whose treatise *On Painting* (1435–36) was hugely influential in the sixteenth century, calls to mind Plutarch's story that 'Cassander, one of the captains of Alexander, trembled through all his body because he saw a portrait of his King' (63). Paratextual portraits, such as Vaughan's Ralegh, were certainly sites of authority that demanded admiration, but they were also intended to mentally prepare and focus the reader for the work of reading ahead.

In what might be regarded as an early attempt at a biography, Robert Naunton's *Fragmenta Regalia* (1641) described Ralegh as an autodidact: 'a handsome and well-compacted person, a strong natural wit, and a better judgement, with a cold and plausible tongue whereby he could set out his parts to the best advantage, and to these he had the adjuncts of some general learning, which by diligence he enforced to a great augmentation, and perfection; for he was an indefatigable Reader, whether by Sea or Land, and none of the least observers both of men, and the times'.[11] Although Ralegh is depicted with maps and books in seventeenth-century images of him, notably in the engraving by Simon de Passe and its subsequent numerous imitations and adaptations, it isn't till the early nineteenth century that he is depicted as a reader, in an engraving by Henry Chawnes Shenton (c. 1825–50). With his cape thrown over his chair and his long clay pipe in his hand, an unmistakable Sir Walter Ralegh is depicted avidly reading at his desk. (NPG D1209).

In 1677 John Shirley, Ralegh's first major biographer, remembered him chiefly as an industrious historian who, if for no other reason, deserved to be rescued from oblivion; but Shirley faced several challenges in attempting to represent his subject objectively. One obvious problem was the lack of complete historical records; another was the loss of context-dependant collective memory within which to read what 'fragmentia' remained. Shirley explained: 'Distance of time doth sometimes, like some mediums, make the streightest Actions seem crooked, and sometimes gives them the advantage of Landscapes, which appear taking and agreeable afar off, tho' when nearly search'd and pry'd into by a curious and intelligent Eye, they seem rude, harsh and unpleasant'. In view of the inevitable temporal and spatial shifts in interpretation, Shirley aimed to steer a course between 'those who in their Annals drive on with an implicit faith; and Those, who to get the reputation of Observers and Men of Reach, steal into the private Recesses of Princes, and disrobe Majesty itself to find some Deformities [about] their Prince, that Interest of State should cover; the best Vail for all deform'd Actions'.[12] Echoing Alberti, Shirley argued that it is possible to provide a portrait of Ralegh without including those defects that would spoil the image. Aside from conscious agendas, Earnest Strathmann noted in 1951 the temporal, spatial, and cultural transformational processes that affect representation: 'time has continued to blur our picture of Ralegh, and its ravages have been repaired only in part by our access to a greater fund of primary information, such as letters and state papers, than the early biographer knew. Some of Ralegh's straightest actions have been made crooked, and acts which were 'rude, harsh, and unpleasant' have been softened by time'(16). He complained that 'He has appeared posthumously in even more roles than those attempted in his tempestuous life-time, and his reputation has changed as near-contemporaries who

---

11 Robert Naunton, *Fragmenta Regalia* (London, 1641), Wing: N250–746. 31.
12 John Shirley, *The Life of the Valiant & Learned Sir Walter Raleigh, Knight* (London: J. D. for Benj. Shirley, 1677), A3v.

shared his intellectual background yielded to writers who judged him by different standards'.[13]

Agnes Latham was to declare in her opening remarks to her 1929 edition of Ralegh's poems that 'It is difficult to believe in Sir Walter Ralegh. There is and always has been something legendary, something fantastic and not quite credible about him. Even to his contemporaries he seemed a man of more than normal stature: so monstrously proud, so dangerously subtle, and in the end so horribly wronged'.[14] For Latham, Ralegh was someone with whom one might sympathize while resisting the temptation to defend him.

On the stage, Ralegh was similarly ambiguous. In John Banke's *The Unhappy Favourite* (1682) Ralegh is introduced by Lord Burleigh as 'the gallant Raleigh' as he delivers three bills for Elizabeth's consideration. His address begins with: 'Long live the bright Imperial Majesty / of England, Virgin Star of Christendome, / Blessing, and Guide of all your Subjects Lives, / who wish the Sun may sooner be extinguish'd / From the bright Orb he Rules in, than their Queen / Shou'd e're descend the Throne she now makes happy'. Ralegh continues in this vein, much to Elizabeth's delight, until he delivers the third bill in which it is suggested that Essex be executed. This brings about a furious response from Elizabeth, who warns them all that had she the spirit of her father 'With one short Syllable I shou'd have ram'd. / Your Impudent Petitions down your Throats, / And made four hunderd of your Factious Crew / Tremble, and grovle on the Earth for fear'. It is left to Ralegh to respond: 'Thus prostrate at your Feet we beg for Pardon. / And humbly Crave your Majesties Forgiveness [petitioners kneel]' (12). Infuriated by the way that Essex has treated the Queen, Ralegh responds with a vehemence that reveals the antagonism between the two men. Ralegh says: 'Ambitious Minds feed dayly upon Passion. And ne're can be at Rest within themselves, / Because they never meet with Slaves enough / To treat upon, Mechannicks do adore 'em / And Lords and States-men to have Cringes from; / Like some of those strange Seas that I've been on, / whose Tydes are alwayes Violent and Ruff, / Where Winds are seldom blowing to molest 'em. / Sh'had done a Nobler Justice, if instead of / That School-boyes Punishment a Blow, / Sh'had snatch'd a Holbard from her nearest Guard, / And thrust it to his Heart; for less than that / Did the bold Macedonian Monarch Kill / Clytus his Friend, and braver Souldier far'. When Elizabeth eventually

---

13 Ernest Strathmann, *Sir Walter Ralegh: A Study in Elizabethan Scepticism* (New York: Columbia University Press, 1951), 271.
14 Agnes Latham, ed., *The Poems of Sir Walter Raleigh* (London: Constable & Co., 1929), 1.

decides to set a date for Essex's execution, Lord Burleigh and Ralegh ensure that it is carried out swiftly. This dramatized rivalry between the two men has some basis in truth, as Penry Williams notes: 'Political heir to Leicester, spiritual heir to Philip Sidney, Essex seemed the epitome of the courtly hero: handsome, adventurous, ambitious, a brave soldier, and a fair poet'.[15] It is easy to imagine why Ralegh would feel threatened by Essex, yet at his own execution Ralegh particularly wanted to clear up any 'misunderstanding' that had been circulating orally about his deep satisfaction at the execution of Essex. However, as Stephen Greenblatt has pointed out, Ralegh 'swears that he wept when the earl of Essex was beheaded but omits to mention his letter to Robert Cecil urging him, in effect, to be merciless and to press for the execution of their dangerous enemy'.[16]

At the turn of the century Ralegh was being presented in a more favourable light on and off stage. George Sewell's *The Tragedy of Sir Walter Rawleigh* (1719) offered an unlikely portrayal of Ralegh as an English martyr: 'To shame the last, and warn the present age'.[17] Sewell's prefatorial address to the play assured the Right Honourable James Crags, Esq., Secretary of State, that there was personal profit to be gained by endorsing memorials to great men: 'Protect the virtuous memory of the dead, as you do the brave acts of the living, and the world will be afraid or asham'd to censure what you approve'. The play's final tribute to Ralegh is delivered by Howard, Earl of Suffolk:

> Arms are no more; the Soldier's friend is lost.
> Be idle then my sword, till happy time
> Shall bid thy Country arm; then shine again,
> Wave on the Deck, or glitter on the plain;
> Revenging Rawleigh's loss on guilty Spain.[18]

In the 1735 engraving by George Vertue (1683–1756), prepared for publication in Oldys edition of Ralegh's *History of the World*, Ralegh is similarly depicted as a soldier.[19] Here, Vertue includes the embellishments that we have come to associate with Holbein's ambassadors: Ralegh's hand

---

15 Penry Williams, *The Later Tudors England, 1547–1603* (Oxford: Clarendon Press, 1995), 326.
16 Stephen Greenblatt, *Sir Walter Ralegh: The Renaissance Man* (New Haven: Yale University Press, 1973), 19–20.
17 George Sewell, *The Tragedy of Sir Walter Raleigh* (London: for John Pemberton, 1719), JRL R66880.
18 George Sewell, *The Tragedy of Sir Walter Raleigh* (London: for John Pemberton, 1719), JRL R66880.5.3.
19 Strong, *Tudor and Jacobean Portraits*, 259.

rests on a globe, and in the foreground there are maps and a skull on which an axe is resting, a tool of Ralegh's career and the instrument of his final dispatch. Peter Scheemaker's limestone bust of Ralegh appeared in the same year as one of sixteen classically sculpted busts of British worthies at Stowe. It must have been a difficult choice, but in the current mood Ralegh was placed not amid the men of letters – Alexander Pope, Sir Thomas Gresham, Inigo Jones, John Milton, William Shakespeare, John Locke, Sir Isaac Newton, and Sir Francis Bacon – but rather with those famed for their actions in political and military service to their country: King Alfred, the Black Prince, Queen Elizabeth I, King William III, Sir Francis Drake, John Hampden, and Sir John Barnard. Ralegh was placed between King William III and Sir Francis Drake. George Lyttelton's inscription read: 'Sir Walter Raleigh a valiant soldier and an able statesman, who endeavouring to rouse the spirit of his master for the honour of his country against the ambitions of Spain, fell a sacrifice to the influence of that court, whose arms he had vanquish'd and whose designs he oppos'd.'[20] In the Scottish poet James Thomson's *Seasons* first published in 1727, Ralegh was again situated next to Drake 'who made [the Queen] mistress of the deep, / And bore thy name in thunder round the world' (ll.1494–95). Ralegh received a sustained treatment:

> ... But who can speak
> The num'rous worthies of the maiden reign?
> In RALEGH mark their ev'ry glory mix'd;
> RALEGH! The scourge of Spain! Whose breast with all
> The sage, the patriot, and the hero, burn'd.
> Nor sunk his vigour when a coward reign
> The warrior fetter'd, and at last resign'd,
> To glut the vengeance of a vanquished foe.
> Then, active still and unrestrain'd, his mind
> Explor'd the vast extent of ages past,
> And with his prison-house enrich'd the world;
> Yet found no times in all the long research,
> So glorious or so base as those he prov'd,
> In which he conquer'd, and in which he bled.
>
> (1495–1508)

This eulogy to Ralegh by Thomson, the author of *Rule Britannia* which was later set to music by Thomas Arne, appeared opposite Philip Audinet's version of Vertue's Ralegh (NPG D5586) as a preface to Volume One

---

20 Thanks are due to Michael Bevington at Stowe School, who provided the inscription upon request.

of Arthur Cayley Esq's *Life of Sir Walter Ralegh* (1805). Following this poem, Cayley's preface began dramatically with a criticism of King James: 'Nearly two centuries have elapsed since Sir Walter Ralegh resigned his neck to the block, and bequeathed to posterity a singular example, with what cruelty a weak prince can sacrifice the life of a valuable subject'.[21] He then went on to attack the representation of Ralegh by William Oldys in his 1736 edition of *The History of the World* and in Thomas Birch's 1751 edition of Ralegh's miscellaneous works. Cayley complained that they had 'both failed of success in giving the best representation which existing materials afforded of the knight's story. Oldys, though a diligent and accurate collector of facts, appears to have been deficient in taste in the arrangement and display of them; while the conciseness of plan proposed to himself by Dr Birch, did not allow him to do the knight justice, had he been so disposed' (vi). Even whilst the historians battled it out over which arrangement of the surviving materials best depicted Ralegh, in the eighteenth century Ralegh was largely represented as the valiant soldier who was sacrificed to Spain because of King James.[22] However, in *The Biographical Magazine containing Portraits and Characters of Eminent and Ingenious Persons of every age and nation* (1794), a magazine that began with William Shakespeare and ended with Lord Lyttelton, the author didn't know where to put Ralegh and in the end included him between Ariosto and Sir Christopher Wren.[23] The opening sentence revealed something of this exasperation: 'Rawleigh, alike eminent in the field, and in the closet, presents a life the most fertile of incidents, of all our illustrious men' (29). Nailing his colours firmly to the mast, the author declared that Raleigh 'was condemned to die, at the age of 60, on the 29th of October 1618, by one of the most flagrant acts of injustice which a despot ever committed'. It concluded: 'He died, as he had lived, with the wisdom of a philosopher, and the fortitude of a hero. This illustrious man was, at once, a scholar, a statesman, a navigator, and a soldier. We know not in which to admire him most – such was the felicity and rarity of his genius!'

The portrait and engraved images of Ralegh in his own time were subsequently repeated, revised, and adapted for a wide range of uses, but in the nineteenth century Ralegh became a popular subject for historical paint-

---

21 Arthur Cayley, *The Life of Sir Walter Ralegh, Knight* (London: W. Blackadder, 1805).
22 Even in the engraving supplied by B. Cole, for *The New Universal Magazine* in 1752 and which, unusually, depicted Ralegh prostrate on the block, the laurel hanging over the frame's image had a large sword cutting through it and a quill crossing over it. Ralegh holds a copy of his *The History of the World* which he displays to the world in his right hand.
23 *The Biographical Magazine* (London: for Harrison and Co., 1794).

ings. Michael Dobson and Nicola Watson cite *The gallantry of Sir Walter Raleigh* (Samuel Drummond, 1828), *Sir Walter Raleigh spreading his cloak as a carpet for Queen Elizabeth* (William Theed, 1853), and *Sir Walter Raleigh laying down his cloak for the Queen* (Andrew Sheerboom, 1875) as examples of the kinds of genre paintings that were extremely popular throughout the period. Dobson and Watson suggest that 'This heavily modernized notion of the nature of Elizabeth's power was reinforced and perhaps even necessitated by Victoria's presence on the throne'.[24] Victoria was no Virgin Queen but hers was a Golden Age and her fecundity an encouraging sign of continuity, strength, and prosperity. But these paintings are also clearly about Sir Walter's gallantry. The cape, so often used in the sixteenth century to signify dissembling, was to become enduringly synonymous with gallantry in representations of Ralegh.[25] One of the more famous paintings of him in this period was that of John Everet Millais, a depiction of *The Boyhood of Ralegh* (1870). Whilst this painting has been interpreted in numerous ways, from political allegory to yet another boys' own adventure fantasy, of which there were many published in the nineteenth century, at base it is the only depiction we have of an 'unfashioned' Ralegh in the process of being shaped by story, with a toy boat appropriately in the foreground and the yet-to-be traversed sea beyond him. In the monumentalizing nineteenth century, then, it is unsurprising to find that Ralegh was monumentalized across the range of representative media, in written and visual forms, from bibliographies to miniature sculptured chess pieces, but usually as a gentleman adventurer.[26]

Aside from statues, paintings, and memorial libraries, some nineteenth-century British monumentalizers thought that the best way of remembering Ralegh was to publish his works, biographies or bibliographies. In

---

24 Michael Dobson and Nicola Watson, *England's Elizabeth* (Oxford: Oxford University Press, 2002), 151.
25 Although it is anecdotal, Trevelyan has suggested that the cape episode might have more substance to it. 'The cloak episode, said to have happened at Greenwich and usually regarded as a fairy story, could easily have been true, being perfectly in keeping with Raleigh's character – an extravagant gamble on his part. What is more, the seals he adopted in 1584, as Captain of the Queen's Guard and Governor of the Colony of Virginia, quite clearly show a cloak enveloping his coat of arms like wings, above his new and tactfully chosen motto, *Amore et Virtute*.' Raleigh Trevelyan, *Sir Walter Raleigh* (London: Allen Lane, 2002), 47.
26 The NPG archive sitter box 2 has a rather incomplete collection of pictures of statues and monuments of Ralegh, but it does contain several pictures of nineteenth-century statues as well as a Dieppe carved ivory figure from the late nineteenth century. At 18.3 cm high it must qualify for consideration as the smallest sculpture of Ralegh extant, aside from miniature reproductions intended as children's toys. It was on sale at Christie's between 16 and 17 April 2003 for a suggested sum of £300–500.

1886 T. N. Brushfield embraced the monumental task of creating a Ralegh bibliography. Brushfield pointed out that, whilst much of Ralegh's work had remained unpublished during his lifetime, this was largely due to the fact that most of it was written during James's reign. He assured the reader that much had been preserved in manuscript, to which Oldys testified, and was in the collections of the British Museum and the Bodleian, among other libraries. Although some of the texts had been falsely attributed to Ralegh, Brushfield assured his reader: 'Of the great popularity of his works we have ample evidence in the number of editions of some of them, e.g., the *History of the World* and the *Remains*. The *Discovery of Guiana* was translated into many of the European languages'.[27] He explained that he had even collated the various editions of every work to ascertain their authenticity and register any variations. He concluded his preface to the 1886 edition by noting that 'Perhaps no celebrity has had his biography more frequently written than Sir Walter; and though the list be long, other accounts were contemplated by Gibbon, J. Payne Collier, Macvey Napier, W. Hepworth Dixon, and Martin Tupper. These biographies I have divided into two classes: – the principal ones and the short memoires; the latter very numerous, and many of them trivial in character; but in notices of these, as of the more important works, accuracy and completeness have been the great object'. It seems that interest in Ralegh was escalating at the turn of the century, for in his 1908 edition Brushfield declared that he had added almost one hundred studies. His 1908 list of biographies was sequenced chronologically, beginning with Robert Naunton's *Fragmenta Regalia* (1641) and numbered 115 items of which the first forty-one were biographies and the remainder memoirs. Items 113–15 were listed without dates but the fact that item 112 was printed in 1906 suggests that Brushfield's bibliography was the most complete up to the time of printing.

Among the treatments of Ralegh's life in Brushfield's bibliography was the now famous assessment of Ralegh's undertakings in Ireland by John Pope Hennessy (1883).[28] Pope Hennessy described Ralegh as: 'one of the most daring and active of those eminent Englishmen who have done much to render British government permanently difficult – if not more than difficult – in Ireland' (5). Relying heavily on Froude, Pope Hennessy delineated the accounts of slaughter and torture of Irish men and women, and the devastating deforestation of the country, but as Christopher

---

27 T. N. Brushfield, *A Bibliography of Sir Walter Ralegh Knt*, 1886; Second Edition with Notes Revised and Enlarged with Portraits and Facsimilies (Exeter: James G. Commin, 1908), 12.

28 John Pope Hennessy, *Sir Walter Ralegh in Ireland* (London: Kegan Paul, Trench, & Co., 1883).

Burlinson has recently pointed out, his final assessment of Ralegh was 'surprisingly forgiving'.[29] Pope Hennessy describes Ralegh at times with some distant admiration and explains that Ralegh behaved in Ireland in the tradition of English men entrusted with its governance up to that time, because of which he ultimately failed as they all had done: 'With his master, Lord Grey, and his companion Spenser, he commences full of confidence. The confidence gives place to repressive measures, suited to the fashion of the age – women hanged, children put to the sword, Irish leaders poisoned by hired assassins. Lord Grey, after governing and struggling for years writes to the Queen that he is ruined and the country is ruined, and he implores to be recalled. Ralegh sums it all up in three words, 'this loste land!' (72). Twentieth-century writers tended to be more critical of Ralegh's Irish episodes. Hugh Ross Williamson, in a 1951 hagiographical sketch of the man, suggested that the episode was best left to oblivion: 'It is horrible to remember Raleigh in Ireland; it is horrible to remember any Elizabethan in Ireland. We may leave it at that, not attempting to excuse the inexcusable. At the same time, Ralegh left also the legend of his courage, differing in this, if not in pitilessness, from his companions.'[30] Seamus Heaney in his poem 'Ocean's Love to Ireland' depicted Raleigh's engagement with Ireland as rape. But while British control in Ireland declined, Ralegh's simple and unfortified house at Youghal, Myrtle Grove, remained intact.[31]

In popular magazine and newspapers, Ralegh continued to occupy an important place. In an 1843 edition *Punch* reported an incident in which a stall-keeper, 'fired with the old chivalrous spirit of Sir Walter Raleigh' had thrown down his stock of pocket handkerchiefs for Victoria to walk over but, true to the age, had subsequently sold them at a profit.[32] An 1846 edition of *Punch* featured Ralegh in an imaginary conversation with William Cobbett. Both men are seated on a large potato; Ralegh smokes his pipe and listens patiently to Cobbett's complaint about Ralegh's introduction of the potato to Ireland and its impact on corn crops.[33] In a later edition in 1887 a headline, 'Raleigh Too Bad', it was reported that Ralegh's house at Brixton Rise was to be auctioned off. This event became symbolic of the destruction of British heritage sites to make way for

---

29 Christopher Burlinson, *Allegory, Space and the Material World in the Writings of Edmund Spenser* (Cambridge: D. S. Brewer, 2006), 168.
30 Hugh Ross Williamson, *Sir Walter Raleigh* (London: Faber and Faber, 1951), 22.
31 See Tadhg O'Keeffe, 'Plantation-era Houses in Munster: A Note on Sir Walter Raleigh's House and Its Context', in *Ireland in the Renaissance*, ed. Thomas Herron and Michael Potterton (Dublin: Four Courts Press Ltd, 2007), 274–88.
32 *Punch, or the London Charivari* (London, 5 August 1843), 61.
33 *Punch, or the London Charivari* (London, 5 December 1846), 237.

buildings that would serve the immediate needs of growing industrial communities. Ralegh's house was being 'given over', as *Punch* termed it, 'to the untender mercies of the Jerry Builder'.[34] In unmasked contempt it went on to argue that the erasure of the historic properties was also an erasure of cultural memory: 'And shall Jugson, the Jerry-builder, with his mud-bricks and slime-mortar, his warped timber and his peeling stucco, banish even the memories of the great Elizabethans from their ancient haunts? Forbid it, O Spirit of the Jubilee Year! Let the Jubilators Raleigh – we mean *rally*, round Raleigh's Old Mansion'. It ended with a rallying cry 'Let not his house who witched Old England's eyes / Before base Jugson fall on Brixton Rise'.[35] If Ralegh's house represented what was still tangible of the great British past more generally, then, as a review of Philip Edwards' biography in *The Pall Mall Gazette* observed, Ralegh represented what was greatest about the Elizabethan past in particular. The reviewer observed that 'the characteristic work of the Elizabethans was to unite that old personal prowess and individual variety of eminence with the knowledge, the speculation, the unbounded intellectual curiosity of the new era. Never did all the active powers of cultivated man work in better harmony. And what the Elizabethan age was among the ages, Ralegh was among Elizabethan men.'[36]

In 1897 John Buchan published an essay on Sir Walter Raleigh, in which he described him as one whose 'fate it has been to live as a memory in English hearts, to have his name used as a synonym for high-hearted valour, and to shine resplendent in many monographs; while in serious history he has either usurped a major place by virtue of his reputation, or suffered the neglect of one who has left few tangible results. His many biographers have almost invariably fallen into the fatal trick of eulogy, and the ordinary reader is still perplexed with a gallery of contradictory portraits'. Buchan's suggestion was that a true history of Raleigh would synthesize the archival records in a more faithful and fair representation of the man. He continued: 'This pre-eminently is the proper field for the psychologist of history, the lover of strange souls and mingled motives; for we have groaned too long under the affliction of those who would leave historical portraiture to the mere romancer or crush a manifold personality into the bounds of a narrow theory.'[37] The response in *The Pall*

---

34 *Punch, or the London Charivari* (London, 9 July 1887), 6.
35 Ibid.
36 'Sir Walter Ralegh', *The Pall Mall Gazette* (London, 3 December 1868), issue 1190, 11.
37 John Buchan, 'Sir Walter Raleigh', Stanhope essay 1897, Elibron Classics Series Replica Edition ... unabridged facsimile of the edition published in 1897 by B. H. Blackwell (Oxford: Adamant Media Corporation, 2005), A2.

Mall Gazette to Buchan's attempt to draw the 'portrait of the first Imperialist, as a man of action' was that, 'readable' aside, it 'failed to acknowledge sufficiently the status of Raleigh as a man of letters'.[38]

The *Penny Illustrated Paper* of 29 January 1910, reported that Devereaux's play of *Sir Walter Ralegh* was playing at the Lyric Theatre in the West End of London. It ran for 131 performances with Lewis Waller in the title role and Winifred Emery, a.k.a. Mrs Maude, as Elizabeth. It was subsequently reported that the play would be revived with Winifred Emery in her former role while Mr Maude would be taking upon himself the role of Sir Walter, the former Sir Walter having turned to an American play by C. M. S. McLellan entitled *The Strong People*.[39]

In the twentieth century new technologies in commercial radio, film, television, and eventually the internet, enabled wider circulation of representations of Ralegh. He was not the dominant presence in movies such as Michael Curtiz's *Private Lives of Elizabeth and Essex* (1939), Walter Forde's *Time Flies* (1944), and Henry Koster's *Virgin Queen* (1955), although Shekhar Kapur compensated for this relative lack of cinematic representation in his 2007 film *Elizabeth: The Golden Age*, where Ralegh fulfils the roles of Elizabeth's lover in all but deed, adviser, and moral guide and, in the climax of the film, protects England from Spanish invasion virtually singlehandedly. With commercial communication technologies came advertizing commercials with captivating quips and images shaped to sell mass-produced items.[40] In North Carolina, a major tobacco region, Ralegh was to become an obvious choice as an advertising icon for a range of tobacco products. In the 1930s and 1940s he appeared on tins, packets, and posters, occasionally with glamorous women. For reasons known to the censors, smoking was depicted on the big screen before, after, and always instead of sex. Smoking became sexy and Ralegh started to look like Errol Flynn.

Ralegh made appearances in pop songs, radio, and TV sketches. Bob Newhart's NBC TV comedy sketch 'The introduction of Tobacco to

---

38 'The Bran-Pie of Current Literature', *The Pall Mall Gazette* (London, Saturday, 21 August 1897), issue 10111, 2.
39 *P.I.P.: Penny Illustrated Paper and Illustrated Times* (London, 29 January 1910), 146. For the subsequent article on Mr and Mrs Maude see *P.I.P.: Penny Illustrated Paper and Illustrated Times* (London, 26 February 1910), issue 2544, 274. See the Lyric Theatre history at: www.stagebeauty.net /.
40 See www.fundinguniverse.com /company-histories /Brown-amp;-Williamson-Tobacco-Corporation-Company-History.html. Brown and Williamson's website tells us that the Sir Walter brand 'had been marketed on a regional basis by the J. G. Flynt Tobacco Company since 1884. B & W purchased it in 1925 and began distributing it nationally. Sir Walter Raleigh eventually became one of B & W's hallmark brands.'

Civilization' in which Ralegh conveys his excitement about his shipment of 80 tonnes of leaves in a telephone call to its destined English port, is still remembered with affection. In Newhart's 1961 sketch the heroic icon was rendered a misunderstood figure, though one apparently sufficiently in touch with the people to be a maker of fashion. Newhart listens incredulously as Ralegh tells him that the leaves can be chewed, put in a pipe or rolled into paper, put between the lips and set fire to. In 1984 a TV commercial for 'Hamlet Cigars, the mild cigar' in which Ralegh, prompted by the Queen, drops his cape over a puddle, only to realize as she steps on it that it is a manhole. The Queen quickly disappears into the supposed puddle to the amazement of all and, recognizing his fault, Ralegh turns to leave only to be apprehended by the guard. In the final frame of the advert Ralegh consoles himself in the Tower of London by drawing on his Hamlet! On the evening of 3 June 1984 Iain Hamilton premiered his *Raleigh's Dream, an Opera in Prologue and Eight Scenes* at Reynolds Theatre in Duke University's Bryan Centre. When a reporter from *The News and Observer* asked Hamilton what the *Dream* was about he replied: 'It's about a man who has an ideal which isn't practical, but which drives him on and destroys other people in the process. That's the real essence. You should be able to put it on a postage stamp' (8E). Indeed, as philatelists know, Sir Walter has certainly been stamped. More recently, he featured in a series of 'British Explorers' stamps issued in 1973. While David Livingstone and H. M. Stanley sold at 3p and Sir Francis Drake at 5p, Sir Walter was rated at 7½p, second only to Charles Stuart at 9p. The image was adapted from Hilliard's 1585 Raleigh with the addition of his ship in the background and, of course, the Queen's head in the top right corner in gold.

In an article entitled 'Remembering Sir Walter Raleigh' which featured in *The News and Observer*, Sunday 20 August 1972, the reporter argued: 'To most North Carolinians, Raleigh is generally known as a gentleman of great courtesy who put his coat in a mud puddle for Queen Elizabeth to step on; the founder of Roanoke Island; the discoverer of tobacco; and who for some obscure reason was beheaded'. Interestingly, the only factually accurate piece of information here is treated as anecdotal while the anecdotal and factually unreliable information is given as the reason for Raleigh's importance, the kind of misjudgement that often occurs during adaptation.

If, as Henri Lefebvre insists, a monument's power resides at least in part in its imperishability, then it is important to remember to create it in a material that will indeed stand the test of time. Robert Anthony, the Curator of the North Carolina Collection in the Wilson Library of the University of North Carolina at Chapel Hill, recently reported that 'the wooden statue of Sir Walter that stood for a number of years on Budleigh Street in Manteo is no more. For some reason, it proved especially appealing to the local woodpeckers, who eventually did poor Sir Walter in.'[41] This commissioned statue of Ralegh had a rather difficult life. In 1975 R. K. 'Tree' Harniman completed his 24ft statue of Ralegh. The sculpture was not well received and Harniman was invited to amend the grotesque representation of North Carolina's hero. In an article which appeared in the Raleigh *News and Observer* 26 July 1984: 'Artist returns to scene of crime' it was explained that Tree had 'carved the English explorer from a 507-year old cypress pulled from a nearby swamp for the American Bicentennial.... It served its purpose during the course of America's 200th birthday, as it toured up and down the east coast before it settled here' (16). According to Tree, the statue, reportedly the largest wooden statue in the world, travelled more miles (3,000) than Sir Walter had ever done. It settled in Manteo, a veritable totem to the discovery of the Americas. It remained there throughout the quatercentennial celebrations before the woodpeckers moved in. It finally had to be removed in sections and Sir Walter's head was chopped off, not for the first time. Happily, there remain four other statues of Sir Walter in Raleigh, two of which are wooden statues, believed to have functioned in the nineteenth-century as tobacco advertisements. One of these is in the City Museum and the other in The Sir Walter Raleigh Rooms, recreated partly from the oak panelling of a sixteenth-century English manor, at the University Library in Chapel Hill. Two others, by Bruno Lucchesi, are in bronze – one being a maquette. The commissioning of these sculptures stands as much as a testament to the tenacity of Raleigh's citizens as to their hero. Eighty-four years of endeavour, beginning with that of Col. J. M. Heck in 1892, and then by Gen. Carr in 1901, who raised much of the money in penny donations from schoolchildren, and subsequently by Sam Ragan, was finally rewarded in the commissioning and completion of a statue in 1976.[42] The realization of a Ralegh statue in Raleigh was the culmination of historical effort and large donations; Brown and Williamson Tobacco Corporation, who had made extensive use of Ralegh in their advertising campaigns, made the largest individual donation of $17,500. Their own Sir Walter Raleigh Aromatic tobacco,

---

41 Robert Anthony delivered the news to the Sir Walter Raleigh Research Circle, The Tower of London, 9–11 January 2009.
42 Ernie Wood, staff writer, *The News and Observer*, 21 November 1976, section IV, 8.

offers 'a rich aroma and a mellow, comfortable smoke' to this day.[43]

As the city of Raleigh prepared to celebrate its four-hundredth anniversary, 1584–1984, a committee was assembled and three years of events, replete with commemorative artefacts, were planned; at the centre of these events stood Sir Walter. Transatlantic lectures, conferences, exhibitions, statues, pageants, books, and the building of a sixteenth-century-style trimast vessel were high on the agenda. An article in *The Charlotte Observer* 24 June 1984 reported that the *Elizabeth II* was to become 'North Carolina's first travelling historic property'. As the celebrations drew nearer a wide variety of ephemera was also generated, among which were brass rubbings and colouring sheets of Sir Walter and Elizabeth I, still extant, and 1,584 commemorative silver medals that were minted and sold at $60 each. *The Current Newspaper* of 19 April 1984 suggested that the medal would be a fitting 'remembrance of your visit to the land of beginnings'. The prospect of a Royal visit created huge excitement, and predictably drew comparisons, from newspaper reporters, cartoonists, and historians, between Raleigh and Queen Elizabeth I, and the modern city and Elizabeth II. In the end it was Princess Anne who participated in the celebrations. In the 8 July 1984 edition of the *News and Observer* the Governor of North Carolina, Jim Hunt, was depicted in a cartoon laying his cloak down for Princess Anne. The paratext explained that, although Princess Anne would be spending less than twenty-four hours in North Carolina, her visit 'had lots of people scurrying to make it perfect'. This was, after all, still twenty-four hours more than Ralegh had ever actually spent in the place.

Back in England, as the new millennium approached, the momentum increased in the move to remove Sir Walter Ralegh's three-foot-high monument from Whitehall.[44] The chief problem was not Ralegh but the inappropriate size of his representation. Westminster debated for years over the matter of Sir Walter's embarrassing smallness, all only serving to prove Henri Lefebvre's theory that 'Turmoil is inevitable once a monument loses its prestige' (222). Since his destruction was clearly out of the question the question became about where to put him. Lord McIntosh suggested that St Margaret's churchyard was appropriate since Ralegh was buried there. However, that idea was not well received by St Margaret's, who already had an 1882 stained glass window and his bones. Petitions for

---

43 www.tobaccoreviews.com /blend_detail.cfm?TID=1913, accessed 24 December 2010.
44 See Vivienne Westbrook, 'What Remains of Rawleigh /Raleigh /Ralegh', *Entertext* 6.3 (2007), 867–90, for a fuller discussion of the Westminster debate over the Ralegh statue in the 1990s.

Figure 12.2 Jacobus Houbraken, engraver, Sir Walter Raleigh, 1739, from *Heads of Illustrious Persons of Great Britain*, Knapton, London, 1734–52.

the transfer of the statue to East Budleigh, his birthplace, were repeatedly refused, and in the end British American Tobacco stepped in to fund the erection of a new statue. Vivien Mallock created a portrait sculpture of Ralegh, six feet tall, with a sheathed sword on his left hip, and 'the cape', once again defining Raleigh as courtier and soldier. The 'tiny little statue' as Baroness Trumpington called it was moved to the Royal Naval Academy in Greenwich and Ralegh redefined there on a very large plinth as the 'great' Admiral. An important caveat for memorializers may be drawn from this tale: when one is turning a subject into an object, build big!

No one has yet petitioned parliament for the planting of a Sir Walter Ralegh David Austen Rose outside Westminster Palace, in his memory. Even if a whole bed of Ralegh roses 'smelling precious sweet' was to be planted, there would be little chance of it being recognized as such, even less 'When defaced by Winter's cold and sleet' ('Ocean' 21.244). How would it work as a memorial to Sir Walter, rather than as just a reminder of what rose beds looked like before people started paving them over to accommodate the third car? And so to borrow from Ralegh's own art:

> All droops, all dies, all trodden under dust,
> The person, place, and passages forgotten,
> The hardest steel eaten with softest rust,
> The firm and solid tree both rent and rotten.
> Those thoughts so full of pleasure and content,
> That in our absence were affection's food,
> Are razed out and from the fancy rent,
> In highest grace and heart's dear care that stood,
> Are cast for prey to hatred, and to scorn
> Our dearest treasures and our heart's true joys,
> The tokens hung on breast and kindly worn
> Are now elsewhere disposed or held for toys.
>
> (21.276–87)[45]

Having briefly surveyed the image of Ralegh in art through the centuries, we notice that in spite of the fact that he has been represented positively and negatively, and pushed off his plinth on more than one occasion, Ralegh continues to inspire ever more bold and interesting ways of remembering him. Clearly, there is no danger of him being disregarded, and there are certainly worse fates than to be 'held for toys'. I eagerly await the Sir Walter Ralegh Game Boy. Meanwhile, Paul Green's

---

45 Sir Walter Ralegh, 'The Ocean's Love to Cynthia' (1590s) Chadwyck-Healey English Poetry Full-Text Database.

Lost Colony continues to hold the title of the longest-running outdoor drama on the coast of North Carolina, and 'Raleigh Wide Open', an annual event held at the end of July each year in Raleigh, N.C., keeps Sir Walter in a festive context. The focus of the July 2011 RWO advertising poster was an adaptation of the Jacobus Houbraken Raleigh (1739) clutching an electric guitar.

13

Where's Walter? The screen incarnations of Sir Walter Ralegh

Susan Campbell Anderson

It is no secret that many writers, most notable among them Agnes Latham and Pierre LeFranc, have explored the rich and varied life of Sir Walter Ralegh. In their explorations, scholars have scripted a variety of personas for him, ranging from the sentimental to the pragmatic. He is the swashbuckling soldier and seaman who travelled to France to defend the Huguenots, to Spain to sack Cadiz, and to the English Channel to defeat the Armada. At the same time, he is the brutal villain who victimized the Irish, Italians, and Spanish at Smerwick. He is the starry-eyed explorer who found England a foothold in the Americas and defended its native peoples against those who would subjugate them, yet he is the self-serving imperialist who presided over a devastating final voyage to Guiana that resulted in the violent deaths of Spanish, English, and Native peoples alike, including his own son. He is the unassuming Devon youth who made his way to court to charm a Queen, and gave her favour away for the love of a good woman. And finally, he is the man who engaged in a dramatic fifteen-year-long struggle for his life, ultimately failing to win his cause.[1]

The most fully realized vision of the intricately scripted life of Ralegh is achieved by Stephen Greenblatt.[2] Working his way towards what will later

---

1 Many thanks to C. M. Armitage, Mark Ledden, and Tarshia Stanley for patient reading and criticism of this chapter. The spelling of Ralegh is regularized as such unless another author or filmmaker spells the character's name differently and must be quoted directly.
2 *Sir Walter Ralegh: The Renaissance Man and His Roles* (New Haven: Yale University Press, 1973). By this remark I do not mean that his is the most complete Ralegh biography; Greenblatt is quick to disclaim this idea himself in his book. I simply mean that Greenblatt here recognizes the potential of Ralegh as character and of literature as playscript. See also Agnes M. C. Latham, *Sir Walter Raleigh* (London: Longmans, Green, & Co., 1964); Pierre LeFranc, *Sir Walter Ralegh: écrivain, l'œuvre et les idées* (Paris: University of Laval Press, 1968); Robert Lacey *Sir Walter Ralegh* (London: Phoenix Press, 1973); and Ralegh Trevelyan, *Sir Walter Raleigh: Being a True and Vivid Account of the Life and Times of the Explorer, Soldier, Scholar, Poet, and Courtier* (New York: Henry Holt, 2004) for Ralegh biographies.

become his influential theory of self-fashioning, he asserts that Ralegh himself worked to 'fashion his own identity as a work of art'.[3] He did so, Greenblatt asserts, both through his writing and by playing a series of 'roles' as he passed through life. 'He was an actor,' Greenblatt writes, 'and at the great public moments of his career he performed unforgettably.'[4] As the first chapter of Greenblatt's *Sir Walter Ralegh: The Renaissance Man and His Roles* suggests, at no time did Ralegh perform more memorably than during the events leading up to and surrounding his death. The story is one of intrigue, suspense, pathos, and even comedy. By all accounts, Ralegh faced his actual execution with grace and courage:

> The truly memorable death scenes of the age, on the scaffold, at home, or even on the battlefield – Sir Thomas More, Mary, Queen of Scots, Sir Philip Sidney, John Donne, Ralegh, Charles I – were precisely that: *scenes*, presided over by actor-playwrights who had brilliantly conceived and thoroughly mastered their roles. Ralegh's epitaph upon himself, his memorable witticisms, his final speech to the crowd were all carefully weighed elements of such a role. His was an unforgettable performance. But then ... Ralegh had been preparing for his last scenes for a long time.[5]

In short, Ralegh's story is an actor's story, one (if Greenblatt is correct) crafted by its own maker for the world-as-stage.[6] By extension, then, it clearly should lend itself easily not just to the stage but to the screen. Indeed, the IMDb (Internet Movie Database) lists seventeen entries for 'Sir Walter Ralegh' as a film or television character.[7] Yet stunningly, *all* of them, with the exception of the children's television special *My Friend Walter* (1992) and the postwar Bette Davis vehicle *The Virgin Queen* (1955), which will emerge in later discussion as problematic with respect to its intended focus on Ralegh, feature Ralegh either as a peripheral or supporting character, not as the focal character of the film or television programme.

It would be tempting, therefore, to dismiss Ralegh altogether as a significant feature in British and American television and film about the Tudor and Stuart periods. Upon closer scrutiny, though, it becomes apparent

---

3 Greenblatt, *Sir Walter Ralegh*, ix.
4 Ibid., 1.
5 Ibid., 15.
6 For an extensive inquiry into Ralegh's understanding of the metaphor of the 'stage play world', see chapter 2 of Greenblatt's book.
7 'Sir Walter Raleigh'. *IMDb: The Internet Movie Database.* 30 April 2009. www.imdb.com /character /ch0028262. This list includes the short, silent comedy reel, *Sir Walter Raleigh*, dir. Bryan Foy (Universal, 1925), which appears elsewhere on the database. A complete filmography appears at the end of this chapter.

that Ralegh does indeed occupy a pivotal, if not central, space within that body of work. Ralegh's significance as a structural adjunct cannot best be determined by contrasting the particulars of his biography to the film portrayals of the man, however satisfying the compelling choices made by the filmmakers featured in this chapter may make that particular form of comparative analysis. Since biography itself is a literary and historical construction that must be read critically, my intention here is not to stand a putatively 'real', historical Ralegh beside his cinematic representations, but rather to follow Terry Eagleton's suggestion that we are meant to grasp 'forms, styles, and meanings as the products of a particular history'[8] by showing how each of these films must be situated in its own historical era to gain an understanding of Ralegh's import as a cultural icon. Doing so allows the critic to see that Ralegh's more general associations – with Queen Elizabeth, with complex relations to authority and to women, with naval exploits and militarism, and, above all, with the New World – allow him to serve as a perfect cipher for the rapidly transforming anxieties of modern/postmodern Anglo-American society. Because Ralegh is so fully intertwined with our narratives about the Elizabethan period, and because those narratives are in turn fundamentally linked to the narratives we choose to construct about ourselves, he continues to be a vital and productive part of our filmic past and promises distinct possibilities for its future.

Like a favourite period ornament, Sir Walter Ralegh has made numerous appearances in film and television, but nearly always as a supporting player in someone else's story. He often appears as a foil against which one of Elizabeth's other favourites – usually Essex – stands out in stark contrast. This tradition is established early in films about the Elizabethan period,[9] starting with 1939's *The Private Lives of Elizabeth and Essex*, a freehanded adaptation of Maxwell Anderson's 1930 play *Elizabeth the Queen*,[10] starring Bette Davis and Errol Flynn, with Vincent Price as Ralegh. From the beginning, Price's Ralegh is used to establish the relationship between Elizabeth and Essex and continues to do so for the rest of the film. How he figures into this relationship, and what this relationship is meant to convey, however, cannot be established without

---

8 *Marxism and Literary Criticism* (Berkeley: University of California Press, 1976), 2.
9 England in particular saw a period of nationalistic 'Tudor Film' during the early twentieth century that culminated during the Second World War; see Billie Melman, *The Culture of History: English Uses of the Past, 1800–1953* (Oxford: Oxford University Press, 2006). Tristram Hunt's review provides a provocative critique of this book: 'Tucking into History', *History Workshop Journal* 66 (2008), 237–42.
10 *Elizabeth the Queen: A Play in Three Acts* (London: Longman, 1930).

examining the forces that contribute to what Greenblatt would term the 'circulation of social energy'[11] around the film.

Elizabeth and Essex, with its lush, Technicolour beauty, its clean, elaborate sets, its extravagant costumes, its pounding score – even its modification of Anderson's original play to include a musical number, battle scenes, and a sword fight – is certainly a bid for the loyalty of Depression-Era customers in need of escape. As Richard Schickel and George Perry note,

> *The Private Lives of Elizabeth and Essex* fits into a genre of 1930's Warner Bros. films that has been defined by the critic Nick Roddick as 'Merrie England', historical pageants of medieval and Tudor times which provided opportunities for spectacle, action, and sumptuous settings to gratify audiences who at the same time may have felt that they were soaking up a little culture and educational knowledge, albeit carefully distilled by Hollywood.[12]

But in 1939, with Britain on the brink of a full-blown armed conflict with Germany, and the American government struggling to maintain neutrality, the film engages actively with the political tensions of its time, becoming a conduit for American anxieties regarding war and a means by which director Michael Curtiz, as well as the Warner brothers themselves, can engage in a dialogue regarding the threat of war.

Warner Brothers had already earned a reputation among the major studios for its 'active social conscience'[13] when, in 1939, just before releasing *Elizabeth and Essex*, it released what Colin Shindler has called 'the most impressive anti-Nazi document to be made in Hollywood before America's entry into the war', *Confessions of a Nazi Spy*.[14] Although applauded by many as a courageous argument in favour of American intervention in European affairs, the film earned the ire of much of the American public, many members of the U.S. Congress, the Hays Office (the studio censorship body), and, of course the German Consulate.[15] Although Jack and Harry Warner had wired President Roosevelt that they would 'like to do

---

11 *Shakespearean Negotiations: The Circulation of Social Energy in Renaissance England* (Berkeley: University of California Press, 1989).
12 *Bette Davis: Larger Than Life* (Philadelphia: Running Press, 2009), 136.
13 Colin Shindler, *Hollywood in Crisis: Cinema and American Society, 1929–1939* (London: Routledge, 1996), 157.
14 Ibid., 207.
15 Ibid., 205–10. For a more detailed historical account of the intersection between the Warner brothers' production choices and their political sympathies, particularly their interest in assisting Jewish victims of Nazi oppression, see ibid., chapter 11. See also Cass Warner Sperling, *The Brothers Warner* (Lexington: University Press of Kentucky, 1994), 232–5.

all in [their] power within the motion picture industry ... to show the American people the worthiness of the cause for which the free peoples of Europe are making such tremendous sacrifices',[16] they appear to have softened their approach for their next film. Using what Shindler terms 'a historical dress treatment of the contemporary world situation', *Elizabeth and Essex* pits an isolationist Elizabeth against an interventionist Essex.[17] The following year's release of the Warner Brothers' next Elizabethan swashbuckler, *The Sea Hawk*,[18] also directed by Michael Curtiz and also starring Errol Flynn and Olivia de Havilland, stands as yet another interventionist effort, substantiating what appeared to be the aims of the studio: screenwriter Howard Koch explicitly said that he saw *The Sea Hawk*'s Elizabeth abandoning a policy of appeasement in order to engage in a war with Spain.[19]

Curtiz situates *Elizabeth and Essex* from the start within a military context, opening with leisurely, wide, establishing shots in ripe Technicolour, first of a ship firing all cannons, then of Essex approaching Elizabeth's palace, followed a few paces behind by Ralegh, Howard, and a huge army. The film then cuts to a medium shot, affording us the opportunity to see Essex's opulent armour and his handsome, affable face. The extravagant score emphasizes the action; all of the elements of the *mise-en-scène* reinforce Essex's masculinity and heroism, serving to build the viewer's loyalty to Essex and establish his superiority to Ralegh before the events of the following scenes.

It is only then that director Michael Curtiz ventures to lay the foundations for the relationship between Elizabeth and Essex, and he uses Ralegh to do so. After a brief interlude in which she explains privately to Sir Francis Bacon that 'the necessities of a Queen must transcend those of a woman', Elizabeth is revealed in her state hall, a striking presence enthroned in vivid green and clad in regal purple. Her first lines to Essex establish the conflict between them that will characterize the rest of the film: 'Do you kneel in homage, my Lord Essex, or in shame?' Her assessment of Essex's conduct at Cadiz succinctly encapsulates Depression-Era arguments for resisting war; overtaxing her already starving people has failed to pay off with tangible benefits, and now she will be

16 Quoted in Shindler, *Hollywood in Crisis*, 218.
17 Ibid.
18 *Confessions of a Nazi Spy*. Dir. Anatole Litvak. Prod. Jack Warner and Robert Lord (Warner Bros, 1939). *The Sea Hawk*. Dir. Michael Curtiz. Prod. Henry Blanke and Hal B.Willis (Warner Bros, 1940).
19 Shindler, *Hollywood in Crisis*, 218.

forced to tax them again. Dismissing Essex's claims that he has acted 'for the glory of England' and that any failures on his part lie at her feet for recalling the English fleet prematurely, she asks whether her people can subsist on laurel wreaths. If the English have succeeded at all in Spain, she pronounces, it is because of the actions of Ralegh and Howard, who made war not to advance themselves like Essex, but to protect England. Elizabeth's provocative praise for Ralegh and Howard draws out a telling reaction from the fiery Essex: he angrily turns his back on Elizabeth, for which the Queen, with ever-moving hands and pursed lips, strikes him across the face, as tradition holds she once did. Significantly, a shocked-looking Ralegh steps into the frame at just this point in the action. As Essex storms from the room and the score reaches a climax, Price's proud and patrician Ralegh is waiting with an extended arm to escort Elizabeth from the presence room. Tellingly, although he has yet to utter a single line, it is Price's Ralegh who allows Curtiz to demonstrate Essex's tempestuous, impulsive, and thoroughly untamed nature, thereby delineating the relationship between the film's two protagonists and staking out the political territory that the narrative will explore.

In an ensuing scene, Ralegh is again used to triangulate the relationship between Elizabeth and Essex. The picture's *femme fatale*, Lady Penelope (Olivia de Havilland), uses Ralegh's poetry to drive a wedge between the two lovers. As the Queen, distraught over her falling out with Essex, gazes at herself in a looking glass, Penelope offers to soothe Elizabeth's frayed nerves by singing Marlowe's 'Passionate Shepherd' and Ralegh's 'Nymph's Reply'. The Queen is at first amused, observing with a robust laugh, 'So, Sir Walter has turned rhymester!' But while the historical poems carry no implication that the beloved in question is older than the Passionate Shepherd, the script rewrites Ralegh's and Marlowe's poems to fit the plot of the film, so that Lady Penelope is able to turn Ralegh's poem into a cruel joke: 'The words will fit perfectly,' she says', a woman in love with a man much younger than herself!' With flashing eyes, she sings,

> If I could be as young and fair as you
> Believe what every shepherd said was true
> These pretty speeches might me move
> To live with you and be my love.[20]

---

20 Cf. Ralegh's 'Nymph's Reply': 'If all the world and love were young / And truth in every shepherd's tongue / These pretty pleasures might me move / To love with thee and be thy love' (1–4). The entire poem appears in Sir Walter Ralegh, *The Poems of Sir Walter Raleigh: Collected and Authenticated With Those of Sir Henry Wotton and Other Courtly Poets from 1540 to 1650*, ed. J. Hannah (Fayetteville, AR: Juniper Grove, 2007), 11–12.

Curtiz here uses a series of rapid cuts, first from Elizabeth gazing at her reflection, to Penelope's satisfied strumming of a lute, to Elizabeth's stiffening expression as it dawns on her that she is being publicly ridiculed as Penelope croons:

> In lovers' vows there is but little truth
> And love cannot endure without its youth
> The flowers fade when summertime is ended
> Our love is dead, a love we thought so splendid
> But were I young and loved so well
> Then I might hold you close forever

With this pointed reworking of the actual poem, a fictional Ralegh makes his presence known by ventriloquizing through Lady Penelope. And again, though Price doesn't utter a line, his character becomes the interstitial presence through which others articulate their relationships. Refiguring the Nymph of Ralegh's poem as an older woman, Curtiz and his team are able to emphasize Elizabeth's age in comparison with Essex's, without having actually to use an older actress; in truth, Davis was only thirty-one years old when she appeared in this film compared to Flynn's thirty years. The scene culminates in Elizabeth's breaking all of the mirrors in the scene in satisfaction of another story from the Elizabethan apocrypha. As the camera peers over Elizabeth's shoulder at her fractured image in the broken shards of glass, the viewer sees that Ralegh's fictional voice has been used to lay bare Elizabeth's fractured identity. As she told Bacon earlier, she is both woman and monarch; here is confirmation that she is unable to integrate the two into an effective whole. The woman's identity as an older, insecure lover leaves the leader hobbled by hesitancy and misgiving.

The incident with Ralegh's poem might be marked as merely an isolated portrait of a woman past her prime if it did not so rapidly locate itself in the context of war, simultaneously gendering the interventionist and isolationist political positions. In another significant deviation from Anderson's play, Elizabeth finds herself alone at the end of this scene with Margaret, one of her ladies in waiting, who weeps, she says, both for her own loneliness and that of her Queen. Margaret is delighted when Elizabeth, moved by Margaret's feminine sympathy, decides to recall her lover, who is serving in Ireland. Almost immediately, Elizabeth learns that her army in Ireland has been decimated, and that Margaret's lover is among the fallen. While the human cost of war is highlighted, so is Elizabeth's indecisiveness. 'Not another man goes to Ireland,' she says, before Bacon convinces her that pulling out of Ireland leaves her vulnerable to Spain.

Reluctantly, she accepts the need to stay the course: 'My policy has always been peace and this war was forced upon me,' she objects.

Essex, too, figures his differences with Elizabeth in terms of gender. Apparently, his hawkish disposition springs from his masculine *virtú*. In answer to Bacon's remark that 'You quarrelled with her, because she wished to keep peace and you wanted war,' he responds, 'War? There is war – with Spain. But such a silly, frightened, womanish war as only a woman would wage!' Likewise, when Elizabeth accuses, 'You think you'd rule England better because you're a man,' he retorts, 'I do indeed. And that's exactly where you fail. You can't think and act like a man.' This figuration of Elizabeth's tenuous, feminine isolationist policy against Essex's confident, masculine interventionist resistance appears to advocate unequivocally for Warner Brothers' activist agenda; the doves in FDR's administration are 'silly, frightened, womanish', while the hawks are by extension manly, self-assured, heroic. Yet the film fails to sustain this imperative indefinitely. The script declines to allow either Elizabeth or Essex to occupy the moral high ground for long, and so complicates the political import of the picture. Despite Elizabeth's warnings against Essex travelling to Ireland to quell Tyrone's rebellion, Essex does so with disastrous results, ultimately setting the stage for his own execution. Tripped up by his own pride and ambition, he is arrested for his attempt on the Queen's throne. Elizabeth appears to have been right after all; although Essex claims the prerogative of gender, Elizabeth carries with her the wisdom of age.

On the morning of his execution, Elizabeth tells Essex that she has one greater love than him: 'England – that is my greatest and most enduring love. And when I think of what you would do to my country if you were king, I will see you dead, yes, and your soul condemned to eternity forever, before I'd let you do it.' Their encounter continues, explicitly locating the narrative back within the context of the approaching Second World War:

> *Essex*: Do you think I don't love England?
> *Elizabeth*: You do. But your love does not match your lust for power. For the greater glory of Essex, you would make war upon the world and drag your country down and drown her in a sea of debts and blood.

By the end of the film, Elizabeth has recognized the unpalatable necessity of violence in the face of a threat to the stability of the state. A true patriot, she must act to rein in a threat left unchecked for too long, no matter what the personal cost. The force of her convictions is enough to convince even Essex: 'Perhaps you're right, and I'd have made a sorry king. So then it's better this way.' Thus, his refusal to beg for his life is not finally because doing so is 'incompatible with his manly dignity',[21] but because the better part of himself recognizes the danger he represents to England. He advises Elizabeth, 'if I did [beg for life], I'd be your death or you'd be mine. You and England must live. Isn't that true?' Recognizing the verity of his words, Elizabeth responds, 'Yes'. By shifting the figurative paradigm, fixing Essex as militaristic aggressor and Elizabeth as the interventionist, Curtiz achieves a twofold accomplishment: first, he eventually uncouples the film's message from considerations of gender, and second, while he clearly recognizes the necessity of military intervention, he refuses to demonize those who oppose the impending war.

The tragedy of the picture, though, is that Essex's downfall comes about at all, and responsibility for this chain of events sits squarely on the shoulders of what Essex calls 'Ralegh and his clique'. Despite his boasts that he can 'outflank such numbskulls', Essex fails to recognize the threat they represent. Mocking Ralegh as he shows off his new silver armour in hopes of impressing the Queen, Essex humiliates his rival by outfitting the palace guard in identical garb. Implicit in his actions, of course, is his assumption that the stiff, spiritless Ralegh has no hope of outwitting his own lively, agile intellect. But in short order, Ralegh, Cecil, and Burleigh have manipulated Essex into demanding the unenviable assignment of Lord Protector of Ireland by first nominating Ralegh for the post. Subsequently, Ralegh and Cecil conspire to intercept Elizabeth's and Essex's letters to one another to set an enmity between them. When they are threatened with exposure upon Essex's return, Ralegh cannily encourages his co-conspirators, 'Make this a war between them – keep [Elizabeth and Essex] apart!' Clearly Essex has underestimated Ralegh, and doing so will cost him his life.

Thus, in the homecoming scene, in the musical number, and in the subsequent scenes in which Ralegh and his cohort conspire against Essex, Ralegh serves not only to articulate relationships and character but also literally to disrupt communication between the film's two main characters. This function is crucial to a fruitful reading of the picture's political significance: it suggests that alongside the possible need to intervene in European affairs sits the fundamental need in a healthy society for an open communication between opposing sides. This communication is too often obstructed by bloodless bureaucrats (like Ralegh, Cecil, and Burleigh) working for their own interests. Ralegh and his clique call to mind the faceless functionaries and obfuscating politicians who stand in

---

21 Michael Dobson and Nicola J. Watson, *England's Elizabeth: An Afterlife in Fame and Fantasy* (Oxford: Oxford University Press, 2002), 277.

the way of responsible civic action. If there is an identifiable villain in Jack Warner's or Michael Curtiz's society, it is they. Essex shouts when he understands he has been outmanoeuvred by his rivals: 'I see what Cecil and his friends are plainly enough: yellow rats who only show their teeth when cornered, who bow and smile and scrape and spend their nights gnawing the chairs and floors out from under us all.' The audience stands on notice that insidious, obsequious pencil pushers threaten to undermine the foundations of society. 'This is your day, Cecil,' Elizabeth accuses on the morning of Essex's execution, 'The snake in the grass endures ... the snakes and the rats they shall flourish, and those who are noble and free of soul shall go down'.

By 1942, the United States had already joined the war when Warner Brothers released its iconic *Casablanca*, also directed by Michael Curtiz.[22] Of course, this time, the film's plot explicitly centres on the early days of the Second World War, telling the story of a man who must choose whether to take action in the face of injustice or to do nothing. Like Elizabeth, he chooses the former at great personal cost. His dilemma calls to mind Belial's advice to Satan in Book 1 of *Paradise Lost*. Faced with eternal damnation, Belial suggests doing nothing in hopes that things may eventually improve: 'Thus Belial, with words clothed in reason's garb, / Counseled ignoble ease and peaceful sloth, / Not peace' (1.226–8)[23]. Milton reminds us that peace achieved by indolence and ignorance is not true peace; only a peace achieved through knowledge and free will will last. Similarly, the greatest danger alluded to by *Casablanca*, *Confessions of a Nazi Spy*, *The Sea Hawk*, and, of course, *The Private Lives of Elizabeth and Essex*, would be for the United States to remain neutral as a means of avoiding a choice at all. In that context, Ralegh's most important function in *The Private Lives of Elizabeth and Essex* is to caution the audience to make informed and active political choices, lest the freedom to choose be taken away.

The Virgin Queen (1955) did indeed seek to allow Ralegh to tell his own story, but did not altogether succeed, not only because of the relative prominence of its chosen stars but also because of its situation within the particular historical circumstances surrounding the aftermath of the Second World War. While exceptional circumstances had enabled thousands of women to experience unprecedented autonomy in the workplace during the war, now they were expected to return to the domestic sphere to resume their duties. The question is, would they? And what about the

---

22 *Casablanca*. Dir. Michael Curtiz, Prod. Hal Wallis and Jack Warner (Warner Bros, 1942).
23 John Milton, *Paradise Lost*, ed. David Scott Kastan (Indianapolis, IN: Hackett, 2005).

men who had returned from the war to find that women had moved into their sphere of influence? Would they find a place in a new order, or find a way to reestablish the old one? Jackie Byars notes that during the decade of the 1950s,

> the social fabric of America had begun to weaken. The interconnected social institutions composing its warp and woof had never before been called into question as they were in the 1950's. As women of all ages, races, marital and maternal statuses, and socioeconomic classes flooded out of their homes and into the workplaces of America, the family structure began to change, previously sacrosanct gender roles began to alter, and struggles over the meaning of *female* and *male* became particularly evident in the cultural atmosphere. Change was imminent but not yet explicitly acknowledged.[24]

Her study on Hollywood melodrama of this period asserts that 'a family-centred culture became America's bulwark against fears of another economic depression, against the insecurity caused by the discovery of atomic energy, and against communism'.[25] Because Americans responded to the trauma of the times by retrenchment into traditional institutions, they saw working women as a direct threat to those institutions.[26] Sophisticated filmmakers exploited the potential of the medium and the genre to suggest the complexity of the issues embodied in this conflict.[27]

For Byars, central to the functioning of gender roles in melodrama is Marjorie Rosen's analysis of stereotypes. Common to melodramas from the 1930s, 1940s, and 1950s is the stereotype of the 'Woman Alone'. Whereas in the earlier decades, she appears as warm, loving, productive, and focused on noble sacrifice – 'The Woman Alone suffers, but she does it with dignity' – in the 1950s, she becomes a desperate outcast (74–6).[28] Concludes Byars:

> in the Hollywood genre most directly concerned with the issues of gender construction and family structure – the melodrama – working outside the home became tantamount to prostitution for female characters. The Woman Alone came to embody the threat of female emancipation; the Woman Alone became suspect. The Wife, the Mother, and the Daughter

---

24 Jackie Byars, *All That Hollywood Allows: Re-Reading Gender in 1950's Melodrama* (Chapel Hill: University of North Carolina Press, 1991), 8.
25 Ibid., 79.
26 Ibid., 86.
27 Ibid., 19.
28 Ibid., 74–6. We can see this contrast clearly by looking at *Elizabeth and Essex*. While the Elizabeth of *The Virgin Queen* is petty, desperate, and grasping, the Elizabeth of the former film is protective, loving, and, in the end, nobly sacrifices her happiness for the good of the nation.

– in their many manifestations – became the only truly viable female alternatives in the film melodramas of the 1950's.[29]

Byars's analysis, when extended to *The Virgin Queen*, allows us to see that the film is less a swashbuckling historical costume piece than a domestic drama in which Richard Todd's Husband must choose between Bette Davis's Woman Alone /Career Woman[30] and Joan Collins's Ideal Bride.

Indeed, the production team, headed by director Henry Koster, effectively roots *The Virgin Queen* in the film language of postwar Hollywood. The result responds more to the poetics of middle-class 1950s America than to that of aristocratic 1590s England. Shot entirely in southern California, it is one of Twentieth Century Fox's earlier releases recorded with the new widescreen Cinemascope film process. Thus its attractive, head-on establishing shots depend less on conveying historical accuracy than on taking advantage of this new technology to appeal to a newly affluent audience: we first meet Ralegh in a clean, bright, tavern populated by colourfully costumed extras. Significantly, he is placed in the foreground at left, so that when the Earl of Leicester enters at the rear right, the audience can appreciate just how wide a shot can be achieved before Ralegh literally leaps across the tavern to join Leicester. Reiterating the idea that this is just postwar America in disguise, the women's costumes in particular are more a 1950s idea of what a sixteenth-century woman ought to be wearing;[31] one critic bemoans that the ladies in waiting are 'young, glamorous, and Max-Factorized to an absurd degree',[32] and the viewer cannot help but notice the satin high heels peeking out from under Beth Throgmorton's dress when one is not distracted by her flashy diamond earrings.

The film goes to great lengths to establish itself in this historical moment both from within the narrative of the film and with the resonant casting choice of Richard Todd as Sir Walter Ralegh. As a paratrooper during The Second World War, Todd had been one of the first British officers to land in Normandy on D-Day. He was known particularly in Britain for his roles in war stories and swashbuckling romances, having been nominated for an Academy Award and won a Golden Globe for

---

29 Ibid., 77.
30 Interestingly, Dobson and Watson, though not necessarily referring to Byars's work, terms Bette Davis's character in *Elizabeth and Essex* a 'Career Woman' (*England's Elizabeth*, 282).
31 See Deborah Harkness's remarks in 'Virgin Territory', *The Virgin Queen*, dir. Henry Koster (1955, Twentieth Century Fox, DVD, 2008).
32 Schickel and Perry, *Bette Davis*, 219. See *The Hasty Heart*, dir. Vincent Sherman, prod. Robert Clark. (Warner Bros, 1949).

one war film, *The Hasty Heart*, in 1949.[33] Remarks film historian John Cork, 'Todd himself was considered very much of a man's man. You can see this in the swashbuckling sword-fighting scene early on.'[34] Deborah Harkness agrees: 'I think that Richard Todd's experiences in The Second World War living in a country that was really hard hit by war but also playing war heroes on film, really helps him to bring that element into his portrayal of Ralegh. Ralegh was a military hero.'[35] Todd seems to have enjoyed continued success with this persona; he went on to work with *Virgin Queen* director Henry Koster on the well-received *D-Day: The Sixth of June* the following year.[36]

From the beginning, the script seeks similarities between Elizabethan England and 1950s America by figuring the former as a postwar society: in the first scene a man with an eye patch tells Leicester (when asked to free his coach from a ditch), 'the last time I went out on the Queen's business was to the Irish Wars I went. Here's all I got for that; to free your coach might cost me the other one!' Likewise, the film capitalizes on Todd's postwar persona by emphasizing Ralegh's identity as a doughty former soldier: 'Now my friend,' says Ralegh, 'I too am late come from the Irish wars and am as poor as you, but I have spent nights in the Irish bogs that make this seem like July sunshine.' Later, invited by Elizabeth to evaluate a piece of armour emblazoned with the love of Mars and Venus, his thoughts are only for the practical; armour 'has saved my life on occasion', Ralegh observes. Accused by Elizabeth of flattery, Ralegh answers, 'Flattery is something the soldier never learns.'

In this postwar moment, Walter, like many former soldiers, must decide what to do with the remainder of his life. The film finds its answer by equating Elizabethan New World imperialism with American Manifest Destiny: 'I've done with wars,' Ralegh tells Leicester, 'I've long had a dream to sail to the New World in ships of my own design. I feel the Queen would share that dream.' To achieve his plan, he must, in his own words, 'conquer' the Queen. Here is the central conflict of the film, for he returns to a society changed by war in which women have moved into

---

33 Geoff Mayer, *Guide to British Cinema* (Westport, CT: Greenwood Press, 2003), 366–8.
34 In 'Virgin Territory', *The Virgin Queen* (2008).
35 Ibid.
36 Jay Matthews terms *D-Day: The Sixth of June* one of the three best films about D-Day. See 'Battle to Buy D-Day Movie', *Washington Post*, 3 June 1994, N63. Further, Melanie Williams notes that Todd's war films were seen as a 'mainstay of British national cinema'. See 'The Most Explosive Object to Hit Britain Since the V2!' *Cinema Journal* 46 (2006), 85–107. See *D-Day: The Sixth of June*. Dir. Henry Koster. Prod. Charles Bracket (Twentieth Century Fox, 1956).

positions of autonomy and authority. Elizabeth instead proves herself the conqueror, and much of the film is a process of domesticating Ralegh, by degrees, through a series of indignities, and Ralegh fighting to free himself from that domestication.

It is important that the narrative should establish Ralegh as a worthy opponent for the Queen, and it does so in a series of scenes establishing his character. Ralegh first gains the ear of the Earl of Leicester to win an audience with Elizabeth, then bests a tailor in a match of wits that yields him the cloak of the French ambassador. When we finally see him (as expected) laying out his cloak for the Queen to tread on, we know him as a risk taker (he can never recover his cloak). His gamble is rewarded, for the Queen is unsure whether to be amused or annoyed. 'You're clever, Walter,' Leicester remarks. 'No sir, but sometimes a man must catch the nearest wave,' replies Ralegh.

The domestication process begins when Elizabeth throws wine on his doublet, finishing with, 'It is winter weather, and no time to talk of voyaging. Fill my goblet, Walter.' As he does so, his first capitulation to her, she gives a knowing smile. He soon finds himself arranging picnics on Her Majesty's hunting outings. His complete submission is established when, despite having repeatedly refused to do so ('I am not a lapdog!'), he sits obediently on a striped cushion at the Queen's feet. Thus, Ralegh, like the returned soldier of the 1950s, appears in danger of finding himself subjugated and emasculated by the unruly postwar Woman Alone.

Acting as Ralegh's conscience during this process is Elizabeth (Beth) Throgmorton.[37] Commenting on what she sees as Ralegh's compromising his manhood for advancement, she mocks, 'I had no right to think you the man I thought you were.' Explicitly revealing his new status as a domestic pet, she says, 'I pity you: you have no ships and the Queen has a new lapdog.' When Ralegh retorts that 'Dogs bark: and if they bark long enough and loud enough, they're listened to. I shall have my ships.' She reminds him that in his current state he will never realize his dreams: 'Nay. But a well-fed lapdog barks but gently. And you shall feed well, captain.' The message is clear: if Ralegh remains subject to the whims of a woman, he will never move forward with his plans.

Ralegh begins the process of reclaiming his manhood and rejecting the world of Elizabeth's court when his honour is called into question in the Privy Council. Shouting at the Queen, 'It is no honour for a man to humble himself,' he continues:

37 Beth Throgmorton is called Bess Throckmorton in Shekar Kapur's *Elizabeth: The Golden Age*, the final film discussed in this chapter.

I wish to serve not you, but England! And I find myself in an aviary full of tame birds! All England's not confined in the walls of this court but rides proud and free on the ocean boarded only by her destiny and hope. Yet while every other nation in Europe is pointing the bows of its ships towards the Indies and beyond, we English stand idly by counting our pence. But some Englishmen watch the sun and the waves and dream of a future that will shine with the brightness of a hundred suns. Thank God I'm of their company!

Here, the court represents an inverted power relation in which woman is on top and man, whose proper identity should exist independent of the home, can find no proper place within its walls. This Woman Alone wishes to trap a potential Husband into a sterile, unproductive and ultimately false domesticity, when he could be freely and truly serving his country. Ralegh's recognition of the court's degrading inversions and dogged commitment to writing himself into a narrative of ascendant and autonomous masculinity allows him to win the heart of Beth, the Ideal Bride, who offers a fertile, true domesticity in which home and career are safely separated. Their secret marriage and her pregnancy follow hard upon. When Elizabeth takes Ralegh back under her protection, Ralegh must choose between his ambitions and his new bride.

One scene in particular reveals the domestic politics involved in the figuration of the relationships among Ralegh, Beth, and Elizabeth, and suggests the growing instability of the ideology of the family in the postwar United States. After the exposure of their marriage, Beth steals into the Queen's bedchamber to plead for her husband's life: 'If you kill Walter Ralegh, you rob an English subject of a father. And why do you do this wrong to a child? From jealousy! Is that worthy of the Queen's Majesty?' Here the most powerful moment of the film occurs. Elizabeth, clothed in white, in stark contrast to the deep claret curtains that surround her bed, pulls off her sleeping cap to reveal a chalky face and balding head:

> *Queen*: Twenty years since a fever took my hair. Do you think I've ever put myself on the lists against pretty faces and empty heads? I am Elizabeth Tudor. Men have loved me. Not with a dandling love you toss a white kitten, but men have loved me because I struck sparks from their minds. I matched spirit with spirit. Walter Ralegh was one.
> *Beth*: But it is I who carries his child.
> *Queen*: [Sarcastically] Be very proud. When I was eighteen, my physicians told me I could never bear a child. I am glad. England was child enough for me!
> Take this strumpet away! Take her away!

We are presented with two women and two images of power: one old, politically potent, and intellectually stimulating but ultimately sterile, the other young, full of domestic promise, courage, and fruitfulness. Thus, the film figures Ralegh's choice between two power relations: a new one in which working woman – Woman Alone – rules supreme and domesticated man attends to her needs, and the other in which things are as they were, where domesticated woman – the Ideal Bride – supports her husband's dreams and leaves him free to range.

The next scene reveals his choice. Elizabeth visits Ralegh minutes before his execution. The latter, manly, unrepentant, cleaves to his dream of sailing to the New World and makes it clear that the Queen no longer has a place in his life:

Ralegh: You have often bad me leave your presence; I bid you now to leave mine!
Queen: On what authority?
Ralegh: Dead men have authority! And I am one.
Queen: Walter, Walter, I needed you and you betrayed me!
Ralegh: I loved you Madam, I loved you as a man loves a great Queen, it's that love you betrayed.
Queen: But I'm also a woman, a woman not too young.

Elizabeth may be a woman, but she is no woman for him, and he has banished her from his life, asserting his rightful, manly authority.[38] The Queen's response to Ralegh reveals his final triumph:

I won't be served by underlings. You shall sail the ship yourself. This does not mean I forgive you nor the slut you married. I want the world you promised me. And I don't want to dream of a brat crying as I dreamt last night. I was once a brat crying because of the headsman's axe. Those cargoes you bring back had best be rich and rich and rich!

Threading through Elizabeth's words (as in the bedroom scene with Elizabeth and Beth) is contemporary anxiety over the dissolution of the family unit: children must not be left without parents, especially fathers as breadwinners. Ralegh must not just leave Elizabeth's court, he must banish it, for to stay would be a dead end. Choosing Beth means not only a continuation of the prewar way of life but also a continuation of life itself. The last scene of the film, after seeing Ralegh sailing off to the

---

38 There is an echo here with what Dobson and Watson find to be a conflict between New World and Old World values in *Elizabeth and Essex*: Davis represents the 'stiflingly maternal' Old World, while Flynn 'points towards a visionary future in a New World, where a proper manliness will be rewarded and women will know their place' (*England's Elizabeth*, 276–9).

New World in the arms of his pregnant wife, reveals, as others have noted, Elizabeth at her desk, isolated, the lonely career girl left with nothing but work to do.[39] The Woman Alone is pushed out of society, leaving the Husband and his Ideal Bride to seek out a productive world.[40] Thus, *The Virgin Queen* leaves the audience with the message that conventional, prewar domesticity can and must be reestablished.

Whether the film succeeds in driving its message home is another story altogether. For all the triumph implied by Ralegh's culminating voyage into the west, viewers of the film, like scholars of the actual history, must be struck by the extent to which this particular Sir Walter Ralegh, like the historical Ralegh before him, suffers at the hands of a remarkable Queen and at the hands of remarkable historical circumstance. The film's original working title, *Sir Walter Raleigh* (*sic*, after the short story on which it was based), was eventually abandoned in favour of *The Virgin Queen* after extended debate over the pronunciation of Ralegh's name.[41] It is hard to believe that the great stature of star Bette Davis and the prior success of *The Private Lives of Elizabeth and Essex* had no influence on their decision as well. Either way, the change in title succeeded in bringing Elizabeth I and Bette Davis into focus over the film's intended title character, Sir Walter Ralegh, and star, Richard Todd.[42] Film historian John Cork reminds us that, though the film was intended to be a story about Sir Walter Ralegh, it is Bette Davis's performance that 'captures the viewer' and that, although Todd was being groomed as a young leading man for Fox, he never really regained his star stature after being overshadowed by Davis in this picture.[43] Indeed, Davis's performance is courageous and utterly without vanity; she even had her head shaved for the role. With Davis-As-Star commanding the imaginative space of the film, her own

---

39 Cf. Deborah Harkness: 'The picture gives you the sense of Ralegh's life coming to a complete and fulfilling end the moment he is granted his ships and can go to the New World. In reality, Ralegh has a very difficult time under Elizabeth I and her successor, James I'. and John Cork: 'It appears as though Sir Walter Ralegh has achieved a grand victory by being allowed to have ships from Queen Elizabeth to sail on his grand adventure' ('Virgin Territory').

40 In an interesting innovation on historical record, Ralegh's ship becomes the home that encloses the married couple. The double bed he has built on board becomes a plot point earlier in the film. Of course, in *The Discovery of Guiana*, Ralegh describes leaving his wife at home on his departure, which occurs long after his rapprochement with the Queen. See Sir Walter Ralegh, *The Discoverie of the Large, Rich, and Beautiful Empire of Guiana*, ed. Robert H. Schomburgk (London: Hakluyt Society, 1848).

41 'Virgin Territory'.

42 See Deborah Harkness's remarks, ibid.

43 Ibid. According to Geoff Mayer, Todd nevertheless remained extremely popular in Britain into the next decade, starring in several influential films (*Guide to British Cinema*, 368).

self-fashioning contributes to the unstable ideology contained therein. While by all accounts trapped in an unhappy, alcohol-plagued marriage in which both partners used their adopted children as weapons against one another, she and her current husband, Gary Merrill, presented a united front to the public.[44] That Davis publicly performed the accepted norms of femininity (as a happy, productive wife and mother) while at the same time embarking on a successful career defied the stereotype of the Woman Alone. In doing so, she created a space in which she might through her acting in the film explore far more transgressive formulations of power. Ralegh may get a New World, but it might not be the one he expects; the family will never be as it was before the war. It is a testament to the power of Davis' charismatic performance that despite her physical appearance in the bedroom scene, when she so searingly advises Joan Collins, 'Be very proud', we are apt to question Ralegh's final choice of companion.

If Bette Davis and Richard Todd are perhaps unevenly matched, the stars of Shekhar Kapur's *The Golden Age* (2007) hold their own a bit more comfortably. *The Golden Age*, a sequel to 1998's Oscar-nominated *Elizabeth*,[45] is in many ways less successful than Kapur's much admired earlier picture; as such it debuted to less-than-glowing reviews.[46] Yet to dismiss the film out of hand is to overlook at least two striking accomplishments. First, *The Golden Age* departs inventively from the narrative form of its predecessor. Second, like *The Virgin Queen* before it, *The Golden Age* instantiates the concerns of its immediate historical context, in this case the 9/11 terrorist attacks on New York and Washington DC, with clarity and force. Those events, as well as the subsequent wars in Iraq and Afghanistan, increased the threat of terrorism worldwide and magnified

---

[44] For a recent account of Bette Davis's life and a guide to her films, see Schickel and Perry, *Bette Davis*. Despite his parents' acrimonious marriage, Davis's son apparently grew up to live a relatively happy, normal life, proving a comfort to his mother in her old age, further giving the lie to ideology supported by the films of the 1950s (205).

[45] *Elizabeth*. Dir. Shekar Kapur. Prod. Tim Bevan and Eric Fellner (Polygram, 1998).

[46] See Arthur J. Pais, 'King of Queens', *India Abroad* (New York) 21 September 2007, M5. Further, Carina Chocano writes, '*Elizabeth: The Golden Age* gives new meaning to "costume drama" in that it is a drama primarily about costumes', in 'How the Strong Survive', *Los Angeles Times*, 12 October 2007, home ed., E1. Lisa Schwarzbaum similarly says, 'Too bad Kapur's new glittering sequel also shows up feeling prematurely old, square, and cautious', in 'Throne off Course', *Entertainment Weekly*, 19 October 2007, 102. Karl French feels that, unlike *Elizabeth*, *The Golden Age* 'lacks the dramatic conceit and narrative thrust that made the original so riveting'. See 'From Virgin Queen to Tudor Woes', *Financial Times* (London) 1 November 2007, 17. Desson Thomson calls the film a 'bloated costume opera' in 'Full Court Dress: *The Golden Age* Is a Costume Drama That Omits the Latter', *Washington Post*, 12 October 2007, C1.

fixation on both the rising tide of international violence, including the 3/11 Madrid rail bombings and 7/7 London Underground bombings, and the subsequent wave of government reactions in Europe and America, including the restriction of personal liberties in the form of warrantless wiretappings, extraordinary rendition of suspected terrorists, abuse of prisoners in detention facilities such as Abu Ghraib, and the holding of prisoners without writ of *habeas corpus* at Guantanamo Bay.[47] Kapur's plot may become a bit crowded,[48] but his desire to reflect his audience's powerful engagement with terror and control necessitated the inclusion of the Babington Conspiracy and the trial and execution of Mary Stuart, as well as the existentially threatening invasion of the Spanish Armada. As producer Tim Bevan says in the bonus material to the film, the team fully intended to 'make a film that spoke to a contemporary audience' by coming up with a 'religious fanatic [i.e., Philip II] who will stop at nothing basically to have their [sic] message shot through'.

Needless to say, Clive Owen's Sir Walter Ralegh sits at the centre of this film. He serves not only as a mechanism to define themes and characters for the audience, he is also clearly the means by which Cate Blanchett's Elizabeth is meant to understand herself as a woman and a monarch. He serves as the fulcrum on which she learns to balance her personal and her political lives. Elizabeth, constrained by her position, must put her country's needs before her own personal desires. She relies on a Dick Cheney-esqe Francis Walsingham (Geoffrey Rush), who uses torture and subterfuge to recover the intelligence that allows her to maintain and consolidate power. Thus channelling modern anxieties over shrinking personal freedoms, terrorism, and religious conflict, as well as the questionable methods of leaders like George Bush and Tony Blair, Elizabeth looks to Ralegh to help her evade those fears. Instead, Ralegh provides Elizabeth with a means of facing them. By doing so, he speaks to the audience about the nature of terror.

Courtney Lehmann maintains that *Elizabeth* is an anti-feminist 'erotic biography' that conflates sexual politics with *Realpolitik*.[49] Elizabeth's

[47] For a useful exploration of some of the legal and ethical complexities surrounding world reaction to 9/11 and the reaction of Anglo-American leaders, see *The Polarized Presidency of George W. Bush*, ed. George C. Edwards and Desmond S. King (Oxford: Oxford University Press, 2007), as well as *Global Responses to Terrorism: 9/11, Afghanistan, and Beyond*, ed. Mary Buckley and Rick Fawn (London: Routledge, 2003).

[48] Cf. French: 'The plan was apparently to present a more complex story, but things just get muddled and even - in the climactic defeat of the Armada - very nearly risible' (*From Virgin Queen*, 17).

[49] 'Crouching Tiger, Hidden Agenda: How Shakespeare and the Renaissance Are Taking the Rage out of Feminism', *Shakespeare Quarterly* 53 (2002), 264.

sexual relationship with Robert Dudley guides her most crucial political decisions, and 'most disturbing is that even as Elizabeth's 'body natural' belongs less and less to Lord Robert, her 'body politic' increasingly belongs to Walsingham'.[50] Thus, at the end of the film, when Elizabeth appears to her people, newly invented as a Protestant Virgin married to her nation, it is at the behest of her handlers, and not, as scholars of the period have affirmed, a result of her own political caginess;[51] Kapur has cheated Elizabeth of her own agency and shown that 'career success means nothing without a man'.[52] Certainly *The Golden Age* retains to a certain degree this sense of erotic biography. At first glance, the film seems to follow a similar trajectory; writers Michael Hirst and William Nicholson have simply replaced Dudley with Ralegh, who similarly betrays Elizabeth, who in turn must find a way to weather the political crisis at hand (this time the Babington Plot and invasion of the Spanish Armada instead of the Norfolk Rebellion) on her own.

But upon closer inspection, Ralegh's role is richer and more complex than is Dudley's in *Elizabeth*. Certainly Ralegh remains a supporting character; Kapur makes little effort to give him much interiority or exceptional dimension. However, he does build on Ralegh's romantic historical associations – his reputation as a seafarer, explorer, privateer, colonizer, trader, and lover – to build dimension to Elizabeth's character, and Ralegh is allowed to articulate explicitly some of the most important themes of the film. The New World is the imaginative ground across which Ralegh and Elizabeth play out their courtship. Having earlier told her lady, Bess Throckmorton (Abbie Cornish), 'There must be any amount of princes in the undiscovered land across the sea – find me an honest one of those', the two find themselves contemplating a procession of prospective royal suitors for Elizabeth when Ralegh arrives. A long shot reveals him following the same protracted path towards Elizabeth's throne that the portraits of her supplicants have just followed. The camera cuts to a low angle closeup of Ralegh, playing up his stature as he explains: 'I have just returned from the New World, Majesty. I have claimed the fertile coast in your name and called it *Virginia* in honour of our Virgin Queen'. Elizabeth quips back: 'Virginia? And when I marry, will you change the name to Conjugia?' Two shots of Elizabeth and Walsingham at one end of what is actually Winchester Cathedral and Ralegh and the Spanish Ambassador at the other suggest that Ralegh and Elizabeth can hold their

---

50 Ibid.
51 Ibid., 265.
52 Ibid., 262.

own against each other in this huge space, as they establish a sense of equality and attraction. They are a match; here is her prince from across the sea. When he presents Native Americans to her, she asks, fascinated, 'Have they no ruler of their own?' Ralegh's answer, 'None to match England's Queen', is the first hint that the New World might be a *tabula rasa* on which the two might enact their fantasies (he will later tell Bess Throckmorton: 'It is something, after all, to take a blank on the map and build a shining city').[53] His gifts to her: potatoes, 'very nourishing' and tobacco, 'very stimulating'. The final gift, gold, which draws ire from the Spanish ambassador, brings the Queen back to reality:

> *Elizabeth*: I cannot accept the fruits of piracy, Mr. Ralegh.
> *Ralegh*: Philip of Spain is no friend of England, Majesty. The more gold I take from him, the safer you will be.
> *Elizabeth*: Well, well. A political pirate.

With Ralegh's imprecation that she (and perhaps we) cannot shy from confrontation with those who mean her harm, Elizabeth and the audience are reminded that, though she may long for a life free of the constraints of her office, she will never extricate political interests from her personal relationships. Apparently disappointed, she dismisses Ralegh with a 'Welcome home', and turns to Howard. But as he retreats down the long aisle, her eyes stray from Howard to follow him away.

Kapur continues to develop a relationship between Elizabeth and Ralegh in which Ralegh represents her potential freedom, not a huge departure from the Elizabeth-Dudley relationship, but here, he pushes it further and in different directions. He associates Ralegh metonymically with the New World to the point that Ralegh represents Elizabeth's desire not simply for erotic freedom (in fact, their relationship is quite chaste compared to that of Dudley and Elizabeth) but physical and ideological freedom as well. One scene in particular drives home this fact. It is mostly a monologue by Ralegh in which he recounts quietly the thrill of first sighting land on a sea voyage. But it is made dynamic by Kapur's camerawork, which amplifies the sense of Elizabeth's engagement with his words:

> Can you imagine what it is to cross an ocean? For weeks you see nothing but the horizon, perfect and empty. You live in the grip of fear. Fear of

---

53 Interestingly enough, the historical Ralegh doesn't seem to have figured the New World in this way. Though admittedly he held the ambition of establishing a colony in what would become North Carolina, in *The Discovery of Guiana* he describes in detail the numerous 'cities' and complex nation-states already in existence in the Americas.

storms. Fear of sickness on board. Fear of the immensity. So you must drive that fear down deep into your belly. Study your charts. Watch your compass. Pray for a fair wind. And hope: pure, naked, fragile, hope.

Kapur includes ample but leisurely cuts through a series of painterly shots, his camera always moving, pushed along by A. R. Rahman's here understated score: a tableau of Elizabeth's rapt ladies, Ralegh standing in front of a seated Elizabeth, her dress a deep blue to match the ocean of his tale, her eyes fixed in a slight frown of concentration, a closeup of Ralegh enjoying the telling of his own tale, a closeup of Elizabeth, still focused intently on Ralegh. In this moment, he becomes the literary Ralegh's Poet of the Ocean, without any of the accompanying bitterness or disappointment. Kapur and his writers heighten this sense of engagement and the impression that Ralegh is serving as Elizabeth's prince from the sea by having Hatton interrupt with news of negotiations with Elizabeth's latest suitor. 'Let them wait,' she answers. 'Go on, Mr. Ralegh.' He continues:

> At first it is no more than a haze on the horizon. So you watch. You watch. Then it's a smudge, a shadow on the far water. For a day. Another day. The stain slowly spreads along the horizon, taking form, until on the third day, you let yourself believe. You dare to whisper the word. Land – Land, Life, Resurrection. The true adventure, coming out of the vast unknown, out of the immensity, into new life. That, Your Majesty, is the New World.

The scene ends with a closeup of Elizabeth breathing slightly harder as joy, regret, and envy seem to play across her face. At the end of the scene, then, we see that what Ralegh has to offer Elizabeth is an escape from a constrained life, from political obligation, from enforced marriage, to new life and a grand adventure. What Ralegh has to offer the viewer, and what Elizabeth does not yet see, is that he also offers the way out of a life of enslavement to fear and uncertainty. In a life dominated by war, terrorism, and political and religious fanaticism, we must force our fears down, trust our compass, and hope against hope. We should not fear the unknown, but embrace it.

But, as in the previous sequence, Elizabeth apparently fears that Ralegh's promise is only illusory. In the next scene in this sequence, Elizabeth remarks to Ralegh: 'I like your immensities. Your ocean is an image of eternity, I think. Such great spaces make us small. Do we discover the New World, Mr. Ralegh, or does the New World discover us?' Ralegh answers that 'You speak like a true explorer.' Perhaps, then, Elizabeth's subjectivity and identity, if they are not entirely in her own control, are not in the control of lovers and political handlers, either, or at least this seems to be the hope that Elizabeth is nursing.[54] But when Ralegh then requests a Royal Warrant and asks her to 'reward my mission, not me … then you leave me free to like you in return.' She replies cautiously, suspiciously, as the score shifts to a minor key, 'Go on.' He tells her: 'I think it must be hard for so great a Queen to know the simple pleasure of being liked for herself.' As in the scene when she ignores him in favour of Howard, Elizabeth replies dismissively, 'Now you grow dull.' Ralegh, who has earlier agreed to Bess Throckmorton's admonishment to 'Pay [Elizabeth] the compliment of truth', has indeed been truthful with Elizabeth about his ambitions, but, in doing so, he has exposed Elizabeth's deepest fear: that his affection might not be genuine. She may have dismissed him from her presence, but the next scene finds Elizabeth and Bess trying a pipe of tobacco, clearly revealing that Ralegh still remains with her.

As Elizabeth's personal fears increase, the fears of the nation begin to come to a climax. As it becomes increasingly apparent that England is under threat of invasion by the Spanish under the leadership of a fanatical Phillip II and that Mary Stuart poses a more immediate threat to the stability of the throne, so too it becomes apparent to Elizabeth that a future with Ralegh in the New World is clearly a fantasy. She forcefully expels the Spanish ambassador from the court, but not before he lays bare the connections among Ralegh, her personal desires, and her present troubles with Spain: 'Your so-called *piratas*, your pirates attack our merchant ships daily. And you … you think we don't know where the orders come from? The whole world knows these pirates sail up the Thames, all the way to your royal bed.' There is a kernel of truth in his insult; clearly, try as she might, Elizabeth will never be able to separate her conceit of Ralegh from his political reality. In the world of the film, she has tolerated his piracy at least in part because of her affection for him and because of the promise he holds for her dreams of personal freedom.

It is at this point that their relationship undergoes a fundamental change, for Elizabeth makes it unequivocal to Ralegh that the two have no future. Leaving her encounter with the ambassador, she confronts a waiting Ralegh: 'What are you staring at? Lower your eyes. I am the Queen! You are not my equal, sir, and you never will be.' Only after Elizabeth's scorching reprimand does Ralegh begin the affair with Bess

---

54 The image of Elizabeth stepping across the puddle under Ralegh's cape seems emblematic of Elizabeth's limited travel experience in this film, as images of water abound. Interestingly, Cate Blanchett has said that, one of the appeals of playing this character was that, as cultured as she was, she had never left the shores of England; hence, she is easily moved by Ralegh as a hero. See 'The Reign Continues', *Elizabeth: The Golden Age*, dir. Shekhar Kapur (2007, Universal, DVD, 2008).

Throckmorton that will culminate in their marriage. Hence, Ralegh's shift in affections can hardly be termed a betrayal. Indeed, Ralegh cannot really be said to have chosen another woman at all, for Kapur makes clear that Bess is simply an extension of Elizabeth herself. Ralegh calls Bess 'a second Elizabeth' when he first meets her, while the costumers usually choose to clothe Bess in a paler shade of the same colour as the Queen. Despite her expression of injury at their marriage, it is Elizabeth who orchestrates Ralegh's and Bess's relationship, living vicariously through her lady in waiting, echoing the language Ralegh has used about her: 'I envy you Bess. You are free to have what I cannot have. You are my adventurer.' Forcing them to dance an intimate *volta* together, Elizabeth dismisses Walsingham with 'Leave us. I want both of them left alone.' Kapur then cuts to a montage in which shots of a young, dancing Elizabeth from the previous film are intercut with those with an elder Elizabeth dancing with Ralegh herself. The scene ends with Elizabeth looking on, clearly lost in a reverie in which Bess acts as her *doppelgänger*. This doubling continues as Bess and Ralegh consummate their relationship, slowly undressing one another while Elizabeth disrobes herself in front of a mirror in her candle-filled chamber.

In the meantime, Elizabeth becomes increasingly gripped by a fear that threatens to paralyse her. While consulting with John Dee, Elizabeth asks about her 'private life'. 'These are affairs of State,' he tells her, emphasizing what Elizabeth has been rebelling against for the entire film, that her private life and her political life cannot be separated. As he studies her face in closeup, he observes:

> *Dee*: Wonderful. Such strength. You will need all your strength in the days to come. But you doubt yourself, my child. I have not seen fear in your face for such a long time.
> *Elizabeth*: Have I reason to fear?
> *Dee*: Something has weakened you. There are hard days coming.

After the attempt on her life and Mary's complicity in the plot is revealed, Ralegh asks her, 'Since when were you so afraid?' Elizabeth's reply is revealing: 'I'm always afraid'. In the face of this fear, Elizabeth risks being unable to take the necessary action to govern: she can barely bring herself to sign Mary Stuart's execution order. In the execution sequence, Kapur cuts alternatively from the scene in which Mary faces the axe in a crowded room, serene and sure of herself, to Elizabeth, pacing the massive stone passageways of her palace, accompanied only by her ladies, weeping, crying out, 'it must be stopped!' and, finally, throwing herself on the floor to be caught up in Ralegh's embrace. The portrait is of two rulers, the one apotheosized, the other vulnerable and earthbound. The difference between the two is their fear; Mary lacks it because of the strength of her convictions. Following hard upon comes the revelation that all of Walsingham's spying has been for naught: the Spanish have deliberately manipulated the English into war though false intelligence. While Elizabeth learns that her political foundation is utterly flawed, the audience comes to learn a lesson for their own times: that governments cannot be made secure through intimidation, torture, and the restriction of personal liberties.

As it becomes progressively clear, then, that this is a film about fear – about a woman's personal phobias, about a leader's apprehensions over her own ability effectively to lead, and about a nation gripped by terror – Sir Walter's role also becomes clear, both to Elizabeth, and to the audience. If he is not there to act as Elizabeth's partner, he is there to teach Elizabeth how to live life without fear. Here, his words to Elizabeth about the New World bear repeating: 'you must drive that fear down deep into your belly. Study your charts. Watch your compass. Pray for a fair wind. And hope: pure, naked, fragile, hope.' Elizabeth can only defeat her fears by facing them and maintaining a steadfast optimism in the face of adversity. Of Mary's execution, he tells Elizabeth: 'Kill a queen and all queens are mortal. We mortals have many weaknesses. We feel too much. Hurt too much. All too soon we die. But we do have the chance of love.' Elizabeth must embrace her mortality and all the curses and blessings that go along with it if she is to drive her fear down. Yet she must fight for life with all her being. 'What do you do in a storm when you're facing your death?' she asks Ralegh. He tells her, 'The closer I come to death, the more I want to live.' To do so, she must understand what Kapur has said is one of the central themes in the film: the importance of 'love in the context of power and betrayal'.[55]

A few scenes later, having arrested both Ralegh and Bess for treason, Elizabeth goes to see Dee again. Elizabeth pounds on his desk, demanding that Dee give her some kind of hope. When he refuses to promise her a favourable outcome in the war with Spain, she slumps into a chair, her face drawn in disconsolation. But Dee's next words echo those of Ralegh throughout the film: 'This much I know: when the storm breaks, each man acts in accordance with his own nature: some are dumb with terror; some flee, some hide, and some spread their wings like eagles, and soar on the

---

55 Ibid.

wind'. As Elizabeth listens, the camera zooms slowly in from medium shot to closeup; she grows suddenly still as her face reveals dawning comprehension and wonder: 'You are a wise man, Dr Dee.' Finally, Elizabeth sees that she is not unique in lacking control over her future, but she does have control over her actions; she can hide in fear or use adversity to lift herself higher. Ralegh is a man who has ignored his fears and spread his wings on the storm. Through him, Elizabeth does not find the freedom of escape to the New World, but rather freedom of spirit. She will not repeat Walsingham's errors. The consubstantial nature of her freedom, the freedom of the nation, and Ralegh's freedom is revealed immediately after, as Elizabeth explains to her council:

> My lords: I can offer you no words of comfort. This Armada that sails against us carries in its bowels the Inquisition. God forbid it succeeds, for there will be no more liberty in England, of conscience or of thought. We cannot be defeated. ... Release Ralegh. He is forgiven, as I too long to be forgiven.

Having learned to live a life free of fear and embraced the grace of forgiveness and love, Elizabeth is now able to rule decisively and actively; her speech at Tilbury becomes emblematic of her ability to live and lead without fear. The victory over the Armada and the forces of religious intolerance are a foregone conclusion. The film, then, is not a statement condemning the present wars in Iraq and Afghanistan, but rather an admonition against those forces that Kapur feels threaten to defeat from within: cowardice and the resulting infringement of personal liberties.

The penultimate scene of the picture leaves us with an encounter among Elizabeth, Bess, and Ralegh. Elizabeth stands in Ralegh's sunny home, and says, 'So Elizabeth has a son.' Hence, the doubling between Elizabeth and Bess is continued yet again; we have a sense that this child belongs to all three of them. When Elizabeth offers to bless the baby, Bess readily places the child in her arms. A golden light gradually highlights her loving, maternal expression as she says in voiceover, changing the historical Elizabeth's original words from 'burden' to 'freedom': 'I am called the Virgin Queen. Unmarried, I have no master. Childless, I am mother to my people, God give me strength to bear this mighty freedom. I am your Queen. I am myself.' Here is Kapur's Elizabeth for a post-9/11 age. If she ended the last film as Virgin, she is now a Madonna. Unlike in Kapur's first film, she rules alone; she has no handlers to control her or to torture those who challenge state policy (Walsingham has died, saying, 'you won't need me any more'). She loves freely and unconditionally. And

Ralegh has pointed the way to this New World, though she has had to find it on her own.

Kapur cautions his audience that, in his own democratic society, leadership is a choice, not a burden, and as such it carries with it the responsibility of protecting the personal freedoms of others, notwithstanding our desire to prevent another 9/11. However, in the end, we have very little control over whether others choose to act out violently against us. Kapur's Ralegh offers his audience the ability to face its fears with love, courage, and hope.

What kind of Ralegh might speak to the current historical moment? One that speaks to the challenges of globalization and multiculturalism? One that encodes the growing loss of confidence in government both in England and America? One that resonates significantly with the world financial crisis? One that responds sensitively to concerns about what some see as American imperialism? Or one that considers the ongoing wars in Afghanistan and Iraq? Of course, if a film is a result of the productive forces that lie beneath it, one can never predict exactly what this Ralegh will look like. However, a film treatment that reflects any of these concerns might do well to imagine a Ralegh who stands aside from the story of Elizabeth. A reimagining of his relationship with another monarch, James I, and an inclusion of his arrest, imprisonment, deliverance, and eventual rearrest and execution could be the stuff that movies are made on. One can imagine a heroic Ralegh, like many in recent years, handicapped by penury, forced to seek favour from a weak-minded, autocratic ruler. Given his one chance at redemption, he embarks on a disastrous mission to Guiana, losing his son and closest friend because of a failure (of his men, of course) to read unfamiliar cultural cues. Perhaps this Ralegh actually finds El Dorado, but chooses not to reveal its whereabouts after gaining a newfound appreciation of Native American culture. He bravely returns home for execution, knowing that, at least for a time, he has protected his friends from invasion.

It remains to be seen whether a potential conjunction between current concerns and facets of the personal narrative Ralegh so meticulously crafted for himself will lead to a filmic representation like the one imagined above. It seems clear, though, that the early modern period remains a potent mirror through which to inspect our own changing historical context, and that Ralegh, whether he stands in the wings or at last at stage centre, will continue to signify.

Sir Walter Ralegh: A Filmography

Film

Elizabeth: The Golden Age. Dir. Shekhar Kapur. Prod. Tim Bevan, Eric Fellner, and Jonathan Cavendish. Perf. Cate Blanchett, Clive Owen, and Geoffrey Rush. Universal, 2007. DVD. 2008.

Roanoke: The Lost Colony. Dir. Bertie Stephens. Prod. Bertie Stephens. Perf. Charlotte Hunter, Ivor Potter, Andy Courtney, Brogan West, and James Alexander. BSDS Productions, 2007.

The Story of Mankind. Dir. Irwin Allen. Prod. Irwin Allen. Perf. Ronald Colman, Hedy Lamarr, Vincent Prince, and Edward Everett Horton. Warner Bros, 1957. DVD. 2009.

The Virgin Queen. Dir. Henry Koster. Prod. Charles Brackett. Perf. Bette Davis, Richard Todd, and Joan Collins. Twentieth Century Fox, 1955. DVD. 2008.

Time Flies. Dir. Walter Forde. Prod. Edward Black and Maurice Ostrer. Perf. Tommy Handley, Evelyn Dall, and Leslie Bradley. General Film Distributors, 1944.

The Private Lives of Elizabeth and Essex. Dir. Michael Curtiz. Perf. Bette Davis, Errol Flynn, Olivia de Havilland, and Vincent Price. Warner Bros., 1939. DVD. 2005.

Sir Walter Raleigh (Silent). Dir. Bryan Foy. Universal Pictures, 1925.

Television

'Elizabeth I: The Virgin Queen'. *Masterpiece Theatre.* Writ. Paula Milne. Dir. Coky Giedroyc. Perf. Anne-Marie Duff, Tom Hardy, and Derek Riddell. 13 Nov. 2005. BBC1 and WGBH Boston. DVD. 2005.

'Elizabeth I'. Writ. Nigel Williams. Dir. Tom Hooper. Perf. Helen Mirren, Jeremy Irons, Hugh Dancy, and Ben Pullen. Channel 4. 29 Sep. 2005. DVD. 2005.

'Gloriana'. Writ. Lytton Strachey and William Plomer. Dir. Phyllidia Lloyd. Perf. Josephine Barstow, Tom Randle, and Clive Bayley. BBC. 23 Apr. 2000. DVD. 2006.

'The Nearly Complete and Utter History of Everything'. Writ. Mark Burton and Ben Caudell. Dir. Dewi Humpreys and Paul Jackson. Perf. Brian Blessed and Angus Deayton. BBC1. 2 Jan. 2000.

'My Friend Walter'. Writ. Gavin Millar and Michael Morpurgo. Dir. Gavin Millar. Perf. Ronald Pickup, Prunella Scales, and Polly Grant. ITV. 24 Apr 1992. VHS. 1992.

'Potato'. *Blackadder II.* Writ. Richard Curtis and Ben Elton. Dir. Mandie

Fletcher. Perf. Rowan Atkinson, Tim McInerny, Miranda Richardson, and Simon Jones. BBC1. 23 January 1986. DVD. 2006.

'Orgy and Bess'. *Carry on Laughing*. Writ. Barry Cryer and Dick Vosburgh. Dir. Alan Tarrant. Perf. Sidney James, Barbara Windsor, Hattie Jacques, and John Carlin. ITV. 25 Jan. 1975. DVD. 2004.

'Roberto Devereux'. *Video Artists International: Telecast from Wolf Trap Farm Park*. Writ. Salvatore Cammarano. Dir. Kirk Browning. Perf. Beverly Sills, John Alexander, Richard Fredricks, and David Rae Smith. 27 Jul. 1975. DVD. 2001.

'Sweet England's Pride'. *Elizabeth R: BBC Video*. Writ. Ian Rodger. Dir. Roderick Graham. Perf. Glenda Jackson, Robin Ellis, Ronald Hines, and Nicholas Selby. BBC2. 24 Mar. 1971. DVD. 2001.

'The Merry Wives of Windsor'. *The Plays of William Shakespeare: Vol. 5*. Writ. William Shakespeare. Dir. Jack Manning. Perf. Gloria Grahame, Leon Charles, Valerie Seelie-Snyder, and Jeffrey G. Forward. Kultur Video. 1971. DVD. 2001.

'Elizabeth the Queen'. *Hallmark Hall of Fame*. Writ. Maxwell Anderson and John Edward Friend. Dir. George Schaefer. Perf. Judith Anderson, Charlton Heston, and Michael Allinson. NBC. 31 Jan. 1968.

Sir Walter Ralegh bibliography (1986–2010)

Christopher Mead Armitage

This Bibliography lists items published in various media since 1986, the publication year of Jerry Leath Mills's *Sir Walter Ralegh: A Reference Guide* to items published 1901 to 1984, with detailed annotations; and Christopher M. Armitage's *Sir Walter Ralegh, An Annotated Bibliography [1576–1986]*, listing almost two thousand items from Ralegh's time to 1986.

Adams, Simon Lester. 'Favourites and Factions at the Elizabethan Court.' *Leicester and the Court: Essays on Elizabethan Politics (Politics, Culture, and Society in Early Modern Britain)*, edited by Simon Lester Adams. Manchester: Manchester University Press, 2002. 46–67.

Aragona, Jared Lane. 'Utopian Canvas: Visionary Aspects of Early English-American Literature, 1497–1705.' Ph.D. diss., The University of Arizona, 2005.

Armitage, Christopher M. *Sir Walter Ralegh, An Annotated Bibliography*. Chapel Hill; London: North Carolina University Press for America's Four Hundredth Anniversary Committee, 1987. 236pp.

Atkin, Graham. 'Raleigh, Spenser, and Elizabeth: Acts of Friendship in *The Faerie Queene* Book IV.' In *Edmund Spenser: New and Renewed Directions*, edited by J. B. Lethbridge. Madison, NJ: Fairleigh Dickinson University Press, 2006. 195–213.

Awad, Joseph. 'Sir Walter Ralegh, On the Eve of His Execution, To Dr Tounson.' *The Sewanee Review* 119.2 (Spring 2011), 196–7

Bajetta, Carlo M. 'Ralegh's Early Poetry and Its Metrical Context.' *Studies in Philology* 93.4 (1996): 390–411.

Bajetta, Carlo M. 'Sir Walter Ralegh and the Goddess-Queen.' In *The Goddess Awakened: Partnership Studies in Literatures, Language and Education*, edited by Antonella Riem Natale, Luisa Conti Camaiora, and Maria Renata Dolce. Udine: Forum, 2007. 223–40.

Bajetta, Carlo M. 'Unrecorded Extracts by Sir Walter Ralegh.' *Notes and Queries* 43.2 (1996): 138–40.

Bates, Catherine. *Masculinity, Gender and Identity in the English Renaissance Lyric*. Cambridge, New York: Cambridge University Press, 2007, 263pp.

Bednarz, James P. 'The Collaborator as Thief: Ralegh's (Re)Vision of *The Faerie Queene*.' *English Literary History* 63.2 (1996): 279–307.

Bednarz, James P. 'Marlowe and the English Literary Scene.' In *The Cambridge Companion to Christopher Marlowe*, edited by Patrick Cheney. Cambridge: Cambridge University Press, 2004. 90–105.

Beer, Anna R. *Bess: The Life of Lady Ralegh, Wife to Sir Walter*. London: Constable, 2004. 320pp.

Beer, Anna R. '"Left to the World without a Maister": Sir Walter Ralegh's *The History of the World* as a Public Text.' *Studies in Philology* 91.4 (1994): 432–63.

Beer, Anna R. *Sir Walter Ralegh and His Readers in the Seventeenth Century: Speaking to the People*. Basingstoke, New York: Macmillan; St. Martin's, 1997. 208pp.

Beer, Anna R. 'Sir Walter Ralegh's *Dialogue betweene a Counsellor of State and a Justice of Peace*.' In *The Crisis of 1614 and the Addled Parliament: Literary and Historical Perspectives*, edited by Stephen Clucas and Rosalind Davies. Aldershot, Burlington, VT: Ashgate, 2002. 127–41.

Beer, Anna. 'Textual Politics: The Execution of Sir Walter Ralegh.' *Modern Philology: A Journal Devoted to Research in Medieval and Modern Literature* 94.1 (1996): 19–38.

Betteridge, Thomas, ed. *Borders and Travellers in Early Modern Europe*. Aldershot, Burlington, VT: Ashgate, 2007.

Borchard, Kimberly. 'The Science of History: Empiricism and Historiography in the First Century of Spanish Colonialism in the New World.' Ph.D. diss., The University of Chicago, 2009.

Bourke, Roger. '"The Moon's My Constant Mistress": Robert Graves and the Elizabethans.' *Gravesiana* 3.1 (2007): 75–85.

Britton, Dennis Austin. 'Allegory and Difference in Ralegh and DeBry: Reading and Seeing the *Discoverie*.' *The Journal of Medieval and Modern Studies* 41.1 (Winter 2011), 117–36.

Brooks-Davies, Douglas; Brooks-Davies, Mary. 'The Numbering of Sir Walter Ralegh's *Ocean to Cynthia*: A Problem Solved.' *Notes and Queries* 38 (236).1 (1996): 31–4.

Buckman, Ty. 'Forcing the Poet into Prose: "Gealous Opinions and Misconstructions" and Spenser's Letter to Ralegh.' *Studies in the Literary*

Imagination 38.2 (2005): 17–34.

Burgess, Helen J. '"Nature Without Labour": Virgin Queen and Virgin Land in Sir Walter Ralegh's *The Discoverie of the Large, Rich and Bewtiful Empyre of Guiana*.' In *Goddesses and Queens: The Iconography of Elizabeth I*, edited by Annaliese F. Connolly and Lisa Hopkins. Manchester: Manchester University Press, 2007. 101–14.

Campbell, Marion. 'Inscribing Imperfection: Sir Walter Ralegh and the Elizabethan Court.' *English Literary Renaissance* 20.2 (1990): 233–53.

Canny, Nicholas P. 'Raleigh's Ireland.' In *Raleigh and Quinn: The Explorer and His Boswell (Papers Presented at the International Sir Walter Raleigh Conference, Chapel Hill, North Carolina, 27-28 March 1987)*, edited by H. G. Jones. Chapel Hill, NC, 1987. 87–101.

Centrewall, Brandon S. 'A Reconsideration of Ben Jonson's Contribution to Sir Walter Ralegh's *The History of the World*.' *Ben Jonson Journal: Literary Contexts in the Age of Elizabeth, James and Charles I* (2000): 539–54.

Chandran, K. Narayana. 'Ezra Pound and Sir Walter Raleigh: Allusions to "The Lie" in Some Lustra-Blast Poems.' *Neophilologus* 78.3 (1994): 497–503.

Chandran, K. Narayana. 'Sir Walter Ralegh's "Three Things There Be" and T. S. Eliot's *Little Gidding III*.' *Notes and Queries* 55.4 (2008): 506–7.

Cheney, Patrick. 'The Laureate Choir: The Dove as a Vocational Sign in Spenser's Allegory of Ralegh and Elizabeth.' *Huntington Library Quarterly: A Journal for the History and Interpretation of English and American Civilization* 53.4 (1990): 257–80.

Coates, Corey Harper. 'Empires of the Historical Imagination.' Ph.D. diss., University of Toronto, 1999.

Coote, Stephen. *Play of Passion: Life of Sir Walter Raleigh*. Basingstoke: Macmillan, 1993. 256pp.

Cottegnies, Line. 'Le Récit d'exploration à la Renaissance: The Discovery of Guiana de Sir Walter Ralegh (1596), entre anthropologie implicite et récit colonial.' In *De Drake à Chatwin: Rhetoriques de la découverte*, edited by Frédéric Regard. Lyon: ENS, 2007. 53–82.

Cottegnies, Line. 'Waterali Goes Native: Describing First Encounters in Sir Walter Ralegh's *The Discovery of Guiana* (1596).' In *British Narratives of Exploration: Case Studies of the Self and Other (Empires in Perspective)*, edited by Frédéric Regard. London: Pickering and Chatto, 2009. 51–62.

Craig, Martha J. 'The Protocol of Submission: Ralegh as Timias.' *Genre: Forms of Discourse and Culture* 29.3 (1996): 325–39.

Crowley, Lara M. 'Manuscript Context and Literary Interpretation: John Donne's Poetry in Seventeenth-Century England.' Ph.D. diss., University of Maryland, College Park, 2007.

Culhane, Peter. 'Philemon Holland's Livy: Peritexts and Contexts.' *Translation and Literature* 13.2 (2004): 268–86.

Cunningham, Karen. '"Spanish Heart in an English Body": The Ralegh Treason Trial and the Poetics of Proof.' *Journal of Medieval and Renaissance Studies* 22.3 (1992): 327–51.

Davies, Rosalind. '"The Great Day of Mart": Returning to Texts at the Trial of Sir Walter Ralegh in 1603.' *Renaissance Forum: An Electronic Journal of Early Modern Literary and Historical Studies* 4.1 (1999): 22 paragraphs. Electronic publication.

Dees, Jerome S. 'Colin Clout and the Shepherd of the Ocean.' *Spenser Studies: A Renaissance Poetry Annual* XV (2001): 185–96.

Demaray, John G. *From Pilgrimage to History: The Renaissance and Global Historicism.* New York: AMS Press, 2006. 250pp.

Dillard, R. H. W. 'The Elizabethan Novels: Death of the Fox.' In *George Garrett: The Elizabethan Trilogy*, edited by Brooke Horvath, Irving Malin, and Fred Chappell. Huntsville, TX: Texas Review, 1998. 22–33.

Dolle, Raymond F. 'Captain John Smith's Satire of Sir Walter Raleigh.' In *Early American Literature and Culture: Essays Honouring Harrison T. Meserole*, edited by Kathryn Zabelle Derounian-Stodola. Newark: University of Delaware Press, 1992. 73–83.

Drummond, C. Q. 'Style in Ralegh's Short Poems.' *South Central Review* 3.1 (1986): 23–36.

Eastley, Aaron. 'Exploiting El Dorado: Subalternity and the Environment.' *Journal of Commonwealth and Postcolonial Studies* 13.2–14.1 (2006–7): 38–58.

Edwards, Philip. 'Tragic Form and the Voyagers.' In *Travel and Drama in Shakespeare's Time*, edited by Jean-Pierre Maquerlot and Michele Willems. Cambridge: Cambridge University Press, 1996. 75–86.

Erickson, Wayne. 'Spenser Reads Ralegh's Poetry in(to) the 1590 *Faerie Queene*.' *Spenser Studies: A Renaissance Poetry Annual* XV (2001): 175–84.

Erickson, Wayne. 'Spenser's Letter to Ralegh and the Literary Politics of *The Faerie Queene*'s 1590 Publication.' *Spenser Studies: A Renaissance Poetry Annual* X (1992): 139–74.

Everton, Michael. 'Critical Thumbprints in Arcadia: Renaissance Pastoral and the Process of Critique.' *Style* 35.1 (2001): 1–17.

Farley, Kevin Dean. '"Consum'd in Going": Recitation and Revocation in

Elizabethan Endings.' PhD diss., University of North Carolina, Chapel Hill, 1998.

Frei, Joyce Carluccio. 'The Cinematic History and Elizabeth: Issues in Queen Elizabeth Films of the Twentieth Century.' D.Litt. diss., Drew University, 2005.

Fuller, Mary C. 'Ralegh's Fugitive Gold: Reference and Deferral in *The Discoverie of Guiana.*' In *New World Encounters*, edited by Stephen Greenblatt. Berkeley: University of California Press, 1993. 218–40.

Gaudio, Michael. 'America in the Making: John White and the Ethnographic Image, 1585–1890.' Ph.D. diss., Stanford University, 2001.

Gibson, Jonathan. 'French and Italian Sources for Ralegh's "Farewell False Love."' *Review of English Studies: A Quarterly Journal of English Literature and the English Language* 50.198 (1999): 155–65.

Gossett, Suzanne. 'A New History for Ralegh's Notes on the on the Navy.' *Modern Philology: A Journal Devoted to Research in Medieval and Modern Literature* 85.1 (1987): 12–26.

Graves, Roy Neil. 'Raleigh's *Moral Advice.*' *Explicator* 63.4 (2005): 204–8.

Gray, Vera. 'A Leat on Roborough Down and an Early Seventeenth-Century Tinners' Dispute.' *Devonshire Association Report and Transactions* 122 (1990): 71–82.

Greene, Roland. 'Petrarchism Among the Discourses of Imperialism.' In *America in European Consciousness, 1493–1750*, edited by Karen Ordahl Kupperman. Chapel Hill, NC: University of North Carolina Press for the Institute of Early American History and Culture, Williamsburg, 1995. 130–65.

Griffiths, Robert Gordon. 'Expedient Truths: Aspects of Narrative Representation in Elizabethan Voyage Literature.' PhD diss., University of Victoria, 2001.

Hamana, Emi. 'The Wonder of the Virgin Queen: Through Early Colonial Discourse on Virginia.' In *Hot Questrists after the English Renaissance: Essays on Shakespeare and His Contemporaries*, edited by Yasunari Takahashi and Yasuo Tamaizumi. New York: AMS, 2000. 37–52.

Hamilton, Lynn. 'Donne's "The Bait".' *Explicator* 46.3 (1988): 11–13.

Hamlin, William M. 'Imagined Apotheoses: Drake, Harriot, and Ralegh in the Americas.' *Journal of the History of Ideas* 57.3 (1996): 405–28.

Hamlin, William M., ed. 'A Lost Translation Found? An Edition of *The Sceptick* (c. 1590) Based on Extant Manuscripts [with Text].' *English Literary Renaissance* 31.1 (2001): 34–51.

Hammer, Paul E. J. '"Absolute and sovereign mistress of her grace"? Queen Elizabeth I and Her Favourites, 1581–1592.' In *The World of* the Favourite, edited by John Huxtable Elliott and Laurence W. B. Brockliss. New Haven, CT, London: Yale University Press, 1999. 38–53.

Hawkes, Terence. *That Shakespeherian Rag: Essays on a Critical Process*. London: Methuen, 1986. 131pp.

Hedley, Jane. 'Motives for Metaphor in Gascoigne's and Ralegh's Poems.' In *Approaches to Teaching Shorter Elizabethan Poetry*, edited by Patrick Cheney and Anne Lake Prescott. New York: Modern Language Association of America, 2000. 184–9.

Herbertson, Jonathan Wayne. 'Sir Walter Raleigh and the Quest for El Dorado.' Ph.D. diss., Arizona State University, 1993.

Heron, Maureen Michelle. '(In)vested Interests: The Economy of Authorship in Columbus' "Diario" and Ralegh's "Discoverie".' PhD diss., Yale University, 1996.

Herron, Thomas. 'Ralegh's Gold: Placing Spenser's Dedicatory Sonnets.' *Studies in the Literary Imagination* 38.2 (2005): 133–47.

Herron, Thomas. *Spenser's Irish Work: Poetry, Plantation and Colonial Reformation*. Aldershot: Ashgate, 2007. 268pp.

Herron, Thomas (ed. and intro.). *Sir Walter Ralegh in Ireland*. Sir John Pope Hennessy. Dublin: University College Dublin Press, 2009. 153pp.

Hila, Marina. 'Dishonourable Peace: Fletcher and Massinger's *The False One* and Jacobean Foreign Policy.' *Cahiers Elisabéthains: A Biannual Journal of English Renaissance Studies* 72 (2007): 21–30.

Hill, Christopher. *Intellectual Origins of the English Revolution Revisited*. Oxford: Oxford University Press, 1997. 424pp.

Hiscock, Andrew. 'Barking Dogs and Christian Men: Ralegh and Barbarism.' In *Writing the Other: Humanism versus Barbarism in Tudor England*, edited by Zsolt Almasi and Mike Pincombe. Newcastle upon Tyne: Cambridge Scholars, 2008. 196–215.

Hiscock, Andrew. '"Provide for the Future, and Times Succeeding": Walter Ralegh and the Progress of Time.' In *The Uses of the Future in Early Modern Europe*, edited by Andrea Brady and Emily Butterworth. New York: Routledge, 2010. 90–109.

Hiscock, Andrew. 'Walter Ralegh and the Arts of Memory.' *Literature Compass* 4.4 (2007): 1030–58.

Holmes, John. 'The Guiana Projects: Imperial and Colonial Ideologies in Ralegh and Purchas.' *Literature and History* 14.2 (2005): 1–13.

Hyland, Paul. *Ralegh's Last Journey: A Tale of Madness, Vanity and Treachery*. London: HarperCollins, 2003. 242pp.

Jowitt, Claire. 'Scaffold Performances: The Politics of Pirate Execution.' In *Pirates?: The Politics of Plunder, 1550–1650 (Early Modern Literature in History)*, edited by Claire Jowitt. Basingstoke: Palgrave Macmillan, 2006. 151–68.

Kelsey, Lin. 'Spenser, Ralegh, and the Language of Allegory.' *Spenser Studies: A Renaissance Poetry Annual* XVII (2003): 183–213.

Kim, Hwa-Seon. 'The Female Body on the Margin of Colonialism: Diario, *The Discovery of Guiana*, and *The Tempest*.' *Journal of English Language and Literature / Yongo Yongmunhak* 46.4 (2000): 965–87.

Kinney, Arther F. 'Reading Marlowe's Lyric.' In *Approaches to Teaching Shorter Elizabethan Poetry*, edited by Patrick Cheney and Anne Lake Prescott. New York: Modern Language Association of America, 2000. 220–5.

Klingelhofer, Eric C. *Castles and Colonists: An Archaeology of Elizabethan Ireland*. The Manchester Spenser, Manchester University Press, 2010. 192pp.

Knight, Ronald D. *T. E. Lawrence's Irish Ancestry and Relationship to Sir Walter Raleigh*. Weymouth: R. D. Knight, 2000. 153pp.

Kono, Barbara S. 'Defining the British National Character: Narrations in British Culture of the Last Two Centuries.' Ph.D. diss., University of Massachusetts Amherst, 1999.

Kunze, B. Y. and D. D. Brautigam. 'Introduction.' In *Court, Country and Culture: Essays on Early Modern British History in Honour of Perez Zagorin*, edited by B. Y. Kunze and D. D. Brautigam. Rochester, NY: University of Rochester Press, 1992. xi–xvii.

Lacey, Robert. *Sir Walter Raleigh*. London: Phoenix, 2000. 415pp.

Lacy, Mark Swanson. 'Neither Joshua nor Cincinnatus: The Intellectual Origins of the Anglo-American Martial Synthesis, c. 1530–c. 1700.' Ph.D. diss., The University of Wisconsin, Madison, 2005.

Latham, Agnes Mary Christabel and Joyce Alice Youings, ed. *The Letters of Sir Walter Ralegh*. Exeter: University of Exeter Press, 1999. 403pp.

Lawson-Peebles, Robert. 'The Many Faces of Sir Walter Ralegh.' *History Today* 48.3 (1998): 17–24.

Lethbridge, J. B. 'Ralegh in *The Faerie Queene* III and IV: The Primacy of the Moral Allegory.' *Studia Neophilologica* 64 (1992), 55–66.

Lethbridge, J. B. 'Spenser's Last Days: Ireland, Career, Mutability, Allegory.' In *Edmund Spenser: New and Renewed Directions*, edited by J. B. Lethbridge. Teaneck / Maidson, NJ: Fairleigh-Dickinson University Press, 2006. 302–36.

Litt, Dorothy E. 'The Poetics and Politics of Naming: The Case of Sir Walter Ralegh and His Queen.' *Names: A Journal of Onomastics* 39.4 (1991): 319–24.

Lockey, Brian C. "'A Language All Nations Understand": Portraiture and the Politics of Anglo-Spanish Identity in Aphra Behn's *The Rover*.' *Journal of Medieval and Early Modern Studies* 39.1 (2009): 161–81.

Lorimer, Joyce, ed. *Sir Walter Ralegh's Discoverie of Guiana*. London: Ashgate, 2006. 360pp.

Lorimer, Joyce. *Untruth and Consequences: Ralegh's Discoverie of Guiana and the 'Salting' of the Gold Mine*. London: Hakluyt Society, 2007. 22pp.

Makurenkova, Svetlana. 'Intertextual Correspondences: The Pastoral in Marlowe, Raleigh, Shakespeare, and Donne.' In *Russian Essays on Shakespeare and His Contemporaries*, edited by Alexandr Parfenov and Joseph G. Price. Newark, DE: University of Delaware Press, 1998. 185–200.

Mancall, Peter C., ed. *The Atlantic World and Virginia, 1550–1624*. Chapel Hill, London: North Carolina University Press, 2007.

Marotti, Arther F. 'A Response to Michael Rudick.' In *New Ways of Looking at Old Texts, III*, edited by W. Speed Hill. Tempe, AZ: Renaissance English Text Society, with Arizona Centre for Medieval and Renaissance Studies, 2004. 143–6.

Martin Arista, Javier. 'On the Fragmented Character of Sir Walter Raleigh's *The Eleventh and Last Booke of the Ocean to Scinthia*: A Sentential Analysis.' *Studium: Filologia* 8 (1992): 197–209.

May, Steven W. 'How Ralegh Became a Courtier.' *John Donne Journal* 27 (2008): 131–40.

May, Steven W. *Sir Walter Ralegh*. Boston: Twayne, 1989. 164pp.

McCabe, Richard A. '"Thine owne nations frend /And Patrone": The Rhetoric of Petition in Harvey and Spenser.' *Spenser Studies* XXII (2007): 47–72.

McCrea, Adriana Alice Norma. *Constant Minds: Political Virtue and the Lipsian Paradigm in England, 1584–1650*. Toronto and London: University of Toronto Press, 1997. 342pp.

McInnes, David. 'The Golden Man and the Golden Age: The Relationship of English Poets and the New World Reconsidered.' *Early Modern Literary Studies: A Journal of Sixteenth- and Seventeenth-Century English Literature* 13.1 (2007): 19 paragraphs. Electronic publication.

Miller, Shannon Michelle. 'The Raleigh Enterprise and the New World.' PhD diss., University of California, Santa Barbara, 1992.

Mills, Jerry Leath. 'Sir Walter Ralegh (1554? – 29 October 1618).' In *Sixteenth-Century British Nondramatic Writers: Fourth Series*. Detroit, MI: Gale, 1996. 200–16.

Mills, Jerry Leath. *Sir Walter Ralegh: A Reference Guide*. Boston: Hall, 1986. 116pp.

Modarelli, Michael. 'A Golden World for "Ocean": Spenser and Ralegh Revisited in *Colin Clouts Come Home Againe* (1595).' *Bulletin of the Society for Renaissance Studies* 24.1 (2006): 1–10.

Montrose, Louis. 'The Work of Gender in the Discourse of Discovery.' *Representations* 33 (1991): 1–41.

Montrose, Louis. 'The World of Gender in the Discourse of Discovery.' In *New World Encounters*, edited by Stephen Greenblatt. Berkeley: University of California Press, 1993. 177–217.

Moore, Peter R. 'Did Ralegh Try to Kill Essex?' *Notes and Queries* 41.4 (1994): 463–67.

Moran, Michael G. *Inventing Virginia: Sir Walter Raleigh and the Rhetoric of Colonization, 1584–1590*. New York; Frankfurt: Lang, 2007. 261pp.

Morris, Jeffrey B. 'Poetic Counsels: the Poet–Patron Relationship of Spenser and Ralegh.' PhD diss., Pennsylvania State University, 1994.

Morris, Jeffrey B. 'To (Re)Fashion a Gentleman: Ralegh's Disgrace in Spenser's Legend of Courtesy.' *Studies in Philology* 94.1 (1997): 38–58.

Nicholls, Mark. 'Sir Walter Ralegh's Treason: A Prosecution Document.' *English Historical Review* 110 (1995): 902–24.

Nicholls, Mark and Penry Williams. *Sir Walter Raleigh: In Life and Legend*. London: Continuum Publishing Corporation, 2011. 378pp.

Nohrnberg, James. 'Britomart's Gone Abroad to Brute-land, Colin Clout's Come Courting from the Salvage Ire-land: Exile and the Kingdom in Some of Spenser's Fictions for "Crossing Over".' In *Edmund Spenser: New and Renewed Directions*, edited by J. B. Lethbridge. Teaneck / Maidson, NJ: Fairleigh-Dickinson University Press: 2006. 214–91.

Nohrnberg, James. 'Supplementing Spenser's Supplement, a Masque in Several Scenes: Eight Literary-Critical Meditations on a Renaissance Numen Called *Mutabilitie*.' In *Celebrating 'Mutabilitie'*, edited by Jane Grogan. Manchester: Manchester University Press, 2010. 85–135.

Oberg, Michael Leroy. 'Between 'savage man' and 'most faithful Englishman': Manteo and the Early Anglo-Indian Exchange 1584–1590.' *Itinerario* 24.2 (2000): 146–69.

Oberg, Michael Leroy. 'Gods and Men: The Meeting of Indian and White Worlds on the Carolina Outer Banks, 1584–1586.' *North Carolina Historical Review* 76.4 (1999): 367–90.

O'Keefe, Tadhg. 'Plantation-era Great Houses in Munster: A Note on Sir Walter Raleigh's House and Its Context.' In *Ireland in the Renaissance, c. 1540–1660*, edited by Thomas Herron and Michael Potterton.

Dublin: Four Courts, 2007. 275–88.

Oram, William A. 'Raleigh, the Queen, and Elizabethan Court Poetry.' In *Early Modern English Poetry: A Critical Companion*, edited by Patrick Cheney, Andrew Hadfield, and Garrett A. Sullivan, Jr. New York: Oxford University Press, 2007. 113–24.

Oram, William A. 'Spenser's Raleghs.' *Studies in Philology* 87.3 (1990): 85–98.

Oram, William A. 'What Did Spenser Really Think of Sir Walter Ralegh When He Published the First Instalment of *The Faerie Queene*?' *Spenser Studies: A Renaissance Poetry Annual* XV (2001): 165–74.

Padel, Ruth. *Sir Walter Ralegh: Poems Selected by Ruth Padel*. London: Faber and Faber, 2010. e-book.

Pedersen, Tara Elizabeth. 'Confounding Categories of Knowledge: Mermaids in Early Modern English Theatrical Culture.' Ph.D. diss., University of California, Davis, 2009.

Ramirez, Luz Elena. *British Representations of Latin America*. Gainesville, FL: University Press of Florida, 2007. 212pp.

Ramirez, Luz Elena. 'Empire and Americanism: British Representations of Latin America.' Ph.D. diss., The University of Texas at Austin, 1998.

Read, David. 'Ralegh's *Discoverie of Guiana* and the Elizabethan Model of Empire.' In *The Work of Dissimilitude: Essays from the Sixth Citadel Conference on Medieval and Renaissance Literature*, edited by David G. Allen and Robert A. White. Newark; London: University of Delaware Press; Associated University Press, 1992. 166–76.

Rose, McKenna Suzanne. 'Caliban's Robes: Transformative Domestic Spaces within Early Modern Utopias.' MA thesis, University of Nevada, Reno, 2006.

Rudick, Michael. 'Editing Ralegh's Poems Historically.' In *New Ways of Looking at Old Texts, III*. Tempe, AZ: Renaissance English Text Society, with Arizona Centre for Medieval and Renaissance Studies, 2004. 133–42.

Rudick, Michael, ed. *The Poems of Sir Walter Ralegh: A Historical Edition*. Tempe, AZ: Arizona Centre for Medieval and Renaissance Studies, 1999. 239pp.

Rudick, Michael. 'The Text of Ralegh's Lyric, "What Is Our Life?"' *Studies in Philology* 83.1 (1986): 76–87.

Rudick, Michael. 'Three Views on Ralegh and Spenser: A Comment.' *Spenser Studies: A Renaissance Poetry Annual* XV (2001): 197–203.

Salas, Charles G. 'Ralegh and the Punic Wars.' *Journal of the History of the Ideas* 57.2 (1996): 195–215.

Sanders, Laura Emily. 'Between Quest and Conquest: Elizabethan Romances of Ireland and the New World.' Ph.D. diss., University of Southern California, 1998.

Santowski, Britta. 'Transgressing Terms of Gender in "The Faerie Queene": Britomart, Radigund and Artegall.' MA thesis, Memorial University of Newfoundland (Canada), 1995.

Schmidt, Benjamin. 'Reading Ralegh's America: Texts, Books, and Readers in the Early Modern Atlantic World.' In *The Atlantic World and Virginia, 1550-1624*, edited by Peter C. Mancall. Chapel Hill, NC: Published for the Omohundro Institute of Early American History and Culture, Williamsburg, Virginia, by the University of North Carolina Press, 2007. 454-88.

Schmidt, Benjamin, editor. *The Discovery of Guiana*. Boston: Bedford / St. Martins, 2008. 173pp.

Schulting, Sabine. 'Travellers' Tales: Narrativity in Early Modern Travelogues.' In *Anglistentag 1999 Mainz: Proceedings*, edited by Bernhard Reitz and Sigrid Rieuwertz. Trier: Wissenschaftlicher Verlag, 2000. 429-38.

Shawcross, John T. 'A Contemporary View of Sir Walter Ralegh.' *ANQ: A Quarterly Journal of Short Articles, Notes, and Reviews* 5.2 3 (1992): 131-3.

Simons, John. 'The Times Broadsheets: A Canon for the Front.' *Literature and History* 11.2 (2002): 39-51.

Sisk, John P. 'The Guiana Connection.' *Hudson Review* 43.1 (1990): 85-98.

Smith, D. K. *The Cartographic Imagination in Early Modern England: Re-Writing the World in Marlowe, Spenser, Raleigh and Marvell*. Aldershot, Burlington, VT: Ashgate, 2008.

Smith, Lacey Baldwin. *Treason in Tudor England: Politics and Paranoia*. London: Cape, 1986. 320pp.

Song, Eric Byung Chan. 'Dominion Undeserved: The Critique of Nation and Empire in Milton's Later Work.' Ph.D. diss., University of Virginia, 2007.

Speed, Stephen. 'Cartographic Arrest: Harvey, Raleigh, Drayton and the Mapping of the Sense.' In *At the Borders of the Human: Beasts, Bodies and Natural Philosophy in the Early Modern Period*, edited by Erica Fudge, Ruth Gilbert, and Susan Wiseman. New York: Palgrave, 2002. 110-27.

Stevens, Paul. 'Milton's "Renunciation" of Cromwell: The Problem of Raleigh's Cabinet-Council.' *Modern Philology: A Journal Devoted to Research in Medieval and Modern Literature* 98.3 (2001): 363-92.

Stillman, Robert E. '"Words Cannot Knytt": Language and Desire in Ralegh's *The Ocean to Cynthia*.' *SEL: Studies in English Literature, 1500-1900* 27.1 (1987): 35-51.

Suárez, Socorro and Tazon, Juan E. 'Dialectical Tension in Sir Walter Ralegh's Life and Work.' In *Actas del I congresso nacional de la Sociedad Española de Estudios Renacentistas Ingleses (SEDERI) / Proceedings of the National Conference of the Spanish Society for English Renaissance Studies*, edited by Javier Sánchez. Saragossa: Sociedad Española de Estudios Renacentistas Ingleses (SEDERI), 1990. 45-53.

Tashma-Baum, Miri. 'A Shroud for the Mind: Ralegh's Poetic Rewriting of the Self.' *Early Modern Literary Studies: A Journal of Sixteenth- and Seventeenth-Century English Literature* 10.1 (2004): 34 paragraphs. Electronic publication.

Teague, Frances. 'Jonson's Drunken Escapade.' *Medieval & Renaissance Drama in England: An Annual Gathering of Research, Criticism and Reviews* 6 (1993): 129-37.

Trevelyan, Raleigh. *Sir Walter Raleigh*. London: Allen Lane, 2002. 621pp.

Vaughan, Alden T. 'Sir Walter Ralegh's Indian Interpreters, 1584-1618.' *William and Mary Quarterly* 59.2 (2002): 341-76.

Vaughan, Alden T. *Transatlantic Encounters: American Indians in Britain, 1500-1776*. Cambridge, New York: Cambridge University Press, 2006. 337pp.

Wagner, John Albert. 'Sir Peter Carew of Mohun's Ottery: A Biography.' Ph.D. diss., Arizona State University, 1995.

Walton. Steven Ashton. 'The Art of Gunnery in Renaissance England.' Ph.D. diss., University of Toronto (Canada), 1999.

West, William N. 'Gold on Credit: Martin Frobisher's and Walter Ralegh's Economies of Evidence.' *Criticism: A Quarterly for Literature and the Arts* 39.3 (1997): 315-36.

Whitehead, Neil L. 'The Historical Anthropology of Text: The Interpretation of Raleigh's *Discoverie of Guiana*.' *Current Anthropology: A World Journal of the Human Sciences* 36.1 (1995): 53-74.

Whitehead, Neil L. 'Monstrosity and Marvel: Symbolic Convergence and Mimetic Elaboration in Trans-Cultural Representation: An Anthropological Reading of Ralegh's Discoverie ...' *Studies in Travel Writing* 1 (1997): 72-95.

Whitehead, Neil L. transcriber, annotater and introducer. *The discoverie of the large, rich, and bewtiful empire of Guiana*, Manchester: Manchester University Press, Normal, OK: University of Oklahoma Press 1997. 232pp.

Whitehead, Neil L. 'Sacred Cannibals and Golden Kings: Travelling the Borders of the New World with Hans Staden and Walter Ralegh.' In *Borders and Travellers in Early Modern Europe*, edited by Thomas Betteridge. Aldershot: Ashgate, 2007. 169–85.

Wilson, Jenny. 'Sir Walter Ralegh's History of the World: Its Purpose and Political Significance.' *The Historian* 59 (1998): 10–15.

Withers, Charles W. J. 'Geography, Enlightenment, and the Paradise Question.' In *Geography and Enlightenment*, edited by David N. Livingstone and Charles W. J. Withers. Chicago, IL, and London: Chicago University Press, 1999. 67–92.

Wood, Tanya Caroline. 'Borrowing Ralegh's Mantle: William Cavendish's Address "To the Lady Newcastle, on Her Booke of Poems".' *Notes and Queries* 47.2 (2000): 183–8.

Yemendzi-Malathouni, Smatie. 'The Poet as Historian: A Critical Edition of Anne Bradstreet's "Grecian Monarchy".' Ph.D. diss., Aristoteleio Panepistimio Thessalonikis (Greece), 1991.

Zim, Rivkah. 'Writing Behind Bars: Literary Contexts and the Authority of Carceral Experience.' *Huntington Library Quarterly* 72.2 (2009): 291–311.

Zurcher, Andrew. 'Getting it Back to Front in 1590: Spenser's Dedications, Nashe's Insinuations, and Ralegh's Equivocations.' *Studies in the Literary Imagination* 38.2 (2005): 173–240.

Index

Note: 'n.' after a page reference indicates the number of a note on that page.

Abbott, George 269
Ackrill, John L. 149n.24
Adams, Simon 8n.26
Adamson, J.H. 92n.12
Alberti, Leon Battista 331–332
Anderson, Maxwell 350–351, 354
Anderson, Susan 25
Andrews, Kenneth R. 58n.50, 270n.20
Anthony, Robert 342
Aplers, Paul 171, 172n.14, 199n.100
Ariès, Philippe 303n.2
Ariosto, Ludovico 76–77, 157–158
Aristotle 149–150, 202, 268n.34, 269
Armitage, Christopher M. 25
Aryanpur-Kashani, Manoochehr 4n.10
Aston, Margaret 294, 296n.27
Aubrey, John 33n.9, 105, 203, 209, 215–216, 234

Baker, David J. 270n.20
Baker, Herschel 4n.10
Bakhtin, Mikhael 179n.39
Banke, John 333
Barclay, Alexander 262
Barfield, Owen 202, 207
Beattie, Tina 292
Bedaux, Jan Baptist 317n.16
Bednarz, James P. 96, 113n.36, 133, 144n.11, 160n.50, 162

Beer, Anna 10n.35, 23, 127n.72, 141n.3, 147n.19, 302n.1, 315–316
Berger Jr., Harry 142n.6
Berry, Philippa 162, 302n.1
Best, George 243–244
Birch, Thomas 5n.11, 15, 336
Bishop, Carolyn J. 109n.23
Blanchett, Cate 366
Bloom, Harold 178n.33, 179n.35
Boccaccio, Giovanni 76–78
Bonta, Mark 222n.12
Booth, Michael 23, 127n.72, 306n.6
Bradbrook, M.C. 169, 170n.9
Brady, Ciaran 21n.44
Braudel, Fernand 59
Breen, Colin 121n.57
Brink, Jean R. 94–95, 114n.37, 160n.51
Brookshire, Bradley 286n.6, 287, 289
Brown, Mary Ellen 288
Brushfield, T. N. 25, 338
Bryson, Anna 146n.17
Buchan, Alexander M. 32n.5, 38n.16
Buchan, John 340–341
Bucher, Bernadette 250n.22
Bull, John 286–287
Burchmore, David W. 121n.59
Burke, Kenneth 171
Burlinson, Christopher 118n.50
Burrow, Colin 156, 158, 158n.48

Index

Byars, Jackie 358–359
Byrd, William 286, 297, 301

Caesar, Julius 263
Campbell, Lily B. 4n.10
Campbell, Lorne 317n.16
Campbell, Mary B. 223n.13, 278
Canny, Nicholas P. 121n.57, 134n.94, 135n.95, 136n.102, 139, 270n.20
Carew, George 75
Cayley, Arthur 336
Cecil, Robert 3, 7, 8n.25, 8n.27, 11–12, 21–22, 74–75, 85–86, 102, 108–110, 116n.44, 118, 131, 141, 224, 253, 271, 293, 304–305
Cecil, William 108, 110, 116n.44, 318–320
Chamberlain, John 200
Champernowne, Arthur 259
Champernowne, Henry 258–259
Chapman, Alison 286, 289, 300, 300n.35
Chapman, George 219
Chaucer, Geoffrey 76, 235
Cheney, Patrick 34n.10, 95, 102n.7, 163, 163n.58, 171n.11, 178
Cheshire, Neil M. 267n.28
Chocano, Carina 365n.46
Christopher Burlinson 338–339
Churchyard, Thomas 244n.6, 258
Cicero 263, 268n.34
Clanton, Stacy M. 38n.16, 101n.5
Classen, Albrecht 303n.2
Clifford, George 59
Cobbett, William 339
Collins, Joan 359, 365
Collinson, Patrick 296n.27
Conti, Natale 35, 48n.31, 50, 79n.80
Cope, Anthony 262
Cork, John 360, 364, 364n.39
Coutts, Eleanor 115n.42
Craig, Alexander 176
Craik, Katherine 156
Creighton, Louise 15n.40

Croft, Pauline 103, 134
Cromwell, Oliver 6n.17
Curr, Matthew 145n.15
Curtiz, Michael 351–354, 356–357

Davis, Bette 349–350, 354, 363n.38, 364–365
De Bry, Theodor 242, 249–251, 254–255
De Gómara, Francisco López 243n.3
De Havilland, Olivia 352–353
De las Casas, Bartolomé 245
De Montaigne, Michel 86–88
De Passe, Simon 331–332
Dean, Leonard F. 4n.10
Dees, Jerome S. 106n.16, 111n.28, 122n.59, 123n.66, 136n.101, 147, 154
Deleuze, Gilles 222
DeNeef, A. Leigh 10n.35, 133n.90
Dobrzycik, Jerzy 83n.87
Dobson, Michael 337, 356n.21, 359n.30, 363n.38
Doherty, Kieran 57n.48
Donne, John 181–182, 191
Drake, Francis 59, 62–63, 249, 272
Drayton, Michael 177–179
Du Bellay, Joachim 41–44, 83n.87
DuBartast, Sallust 83
Duckert, Lowell 23, 304, 307n.9
Duncan-Jones, Katherine 284

Eagleton, Terry 350
Eastley, Aaron 307n.8
Edmondes, Clement 263
Edwards, David 8n.26, 272
Edwards, Edward 91n.9, 93n.20, 302n.1
Edwards, Philip 340
Eggert, Katherine 234n.26
Ekkart, Rudi 317n.16
Elliott, J. H. 258
Ellis, Thomas 244n.6
Erasmus, Desiderius 285, 299

Erickson, Wayne 10n.34, 10n.35, 23, 89n.3, 96n.33, 111n.28, 111, 114n.39
Everton, Michael 142n.6, 144

Fauconnier, Gilles 203, 208, 209n.17, 213n.30
Ficino, Marsilio 151
Fitzwilliam, William 109, 118
Flannagan, Roy 179
Fleck, Andrew 11n.36
Fletcher, Giles 266
Fletcher, John 156n.39
Flynn, Errol 350, 352, 354, 363n.38
Folland, H.F. 92n.12
Forker, Charles R. 260n.12
Forster, Leonard 291
Forsythe, R.S. 173n.18
Fowler, Alastair 154n.35
Foxe, John 260, 273–274
Frede, Dorothea 150
French, Karl 365n.46
Frobisher, Martin 243–244
Frohock, Richard 100, 101n.3
Fuller, Mary C. 100, 101n.3, 225–226, 234, 240, 304n.3

Gallagher, Lowell 79n.80
Garner, Richard 177n.31
Gascoigne, George 10, 90, 282
Gassendi, Pierre 83n.87
Gibbon, Edward 4, 17
Gilbert, Humphrey 59, 263, 266, 272
Gill, Roma 61
Goldberg, Jonathan 330
Gorges, Arthur 75, 90, 165n.62, 262
Gosse, Edmund 129n.79
Goux, Jean-Joseph 226n.15
Gray, M.M. 118n.48
Greenblatt, Stephen 5, 101n.4, 106, 106n.16, 107n.18, 108n.19, 109n.22, 126n.70, 141n.5, 214, 220n.6, 295, 302, 314n.11, 330, 334, 348–349, 351
Greene, Roland 128, 232

Greene, Thomas M. 175n.25, 184
Greenlaw, Edwin A. 91n.10
Greg, W.W. 94, 94n.25
Gregerson, Linda 323n.23
Grogan, Jane 104n.11
Grotius, Hugo 265
Guattari, Félix 222
Guicciardini, Francesco 265
Guy-Bray, Stephen 145n.14, 145n.15, 147n.18

Haber, Judith 145
Hadfield, Andrew 111n.29, 270n.20
Hair, P. E. H. 270n.20
Hakluyt, Richard 61–62, 243, 249–250, 255, 270
Hamlin, Hannibal 13, 24
Hamlin, William 307n.9
Hannibal 264–265
Harkness, Deborah 234n.26, 359n.31, 360, 364n.39
Harlow, Vincent T. 231n.21
Harriot, Thomas 84, 230n.20, 231n.21, 234, 268
Hatton, Christopher 69, 109n.23, 220
Hawkins, John 59
Hayman, S. 93n.20, 94n.22
Heaney, Seamus 7n.23, 103–104, 104n.11, 105, 339
Heffner, Ray 95n.27
Heninger Jr., S.K. 185n.57
Hennessy, John Pope 31n.1, 338–339
Herodotus 266, 269
Herrick, Robert 177, 181
Herron, Thomas 3, 7n.23, 10n.35, 22–23, 111n.29, 114n.39, 116n.44, 117n.47, 118n.48, 118n.50, 126n.69, 271, 330
Hersey, Frank Wilson Cheney 1n.1, 7n.23
Hill, Christopher 4n.10
Hilliard, Nicholas 327–329, 342
Hiscock, Andrew 9n.31, 24, 264n.20, 266n.26

Hobbes, Thomas 266n.26
Holland, Philemon 148n.23
Hollander, John 174, 178n.33, 184, 189n.70
Holmes, John 307n.8
Homer 67, 126
Hooker, John 113, 116, 271, 330
Horace 263
Horner, Joyce 123n.65, 124n.68, 126n.69, 127n.71, 129n.78, 130, 130n.83, 135n.98
Houbraken, Jacobus 345, 347
Howard, Charles 304–305
Howard, Philip 72, 290, 297, 301
Hulton, Paul 250n.22
Hume, David 219
Hunt, Tristram 350n.9

Irwin, Margaret 6n.17
Irwin, William 177n.29

Jacan, Micaela 147n.18
Jenkins, Raymond 94, 94n.21
Jenkinson, Anthony 60–62
Johnson-Haddad, Miranda 75n.77
Jorgensen, Paul A. 9n.31
Judson, Alexander C. 91n.9, 94n.21

Kaplan, M. Lindsay 160n.50
Kapur, Shekhar 365–369, 371–374
Keats, John 185–187
Kelsey, Lin 92, 111n.28, 123n.66, 127n.72, 127, 148n.22, 163n.58
Kempe, William 263
Kerman, Joseph 287
Keymis, Lawrence 253, 276
Klingelhofer 21n.44, 83n.87, 121n.56, 137n.107
Knapp, Jeffrey 52n.44
Koch, Howard 352
Koller, Katherine 10n.35, 89n.3, 111n.28
Koster, Henry 359–360
Kraynak, Robert P. 266n.26

Kristeva, Julia 179n.39
Kupperman, Karen Ordahl 255

Lacey, Robert 45n.25, 69n.64, 75n.77, 91–92, 103n.10, 105n.13, 119n.51, 134n.95, 302n.1, 348n.2
Latham, Agnes 1n.2, 2, 3n.8, 32n.5, 38n.16, 90n.5, 101n.5, 105n.15, 107n.18, 116n.44, 117n.47, 284, 293, 318n.18, 323, 333, 348, 348n.2
Lawson-Peebles, Robert 315
Leddy, Michael 177n.29
Lefebvre, Henri 342, 344
LeFranc, Pierre 106, 107n.18, 116n.44, 122n.62, 348, 348n.2
Lehmann, Courtney 366
Lenihan, Pádraig 272
Lethbridge, J. B. 99n.36, 115n.39, 159–160, 162
Levy, F. J. 4n.10, 99
Lim, Walter S. 48n.32, 100, 119n.53
Livy 263
Llewellyn, Nigel 330n.10
Lodge, Thomas 173–174, 184
Lorimer, Joyce 5n.13, 227n.18, 305–306, 307n.8
Lucan 90, 165n.62
Lucchesi, Bruno 343
Luciani, Vincent 4n.10, 9n.31
Lucretius 86
Lyttleton, James 83n.87, 100n.1

McCabe, Richard 111n.29, 137n.105
McCarthy, Conor 117n.46, 117n.47
MacCarthy, Florence 22
MacCarthy-Morrogh, Michael 21n.43, 115n.42, 116n.44
MacCulloch, Diarmaid 296–297, 297n.29
McKeown, Adam 9n.31
Machacek, Gregory 177n.31
Machiavelli, Niccolò 265
Maginn, Christopher 22n.47
Maley, Willy 94n.21, 111n.29, 270n.20

Mallock, Vivien 346
Mancall, Peter C., 62n.56
Mandeville, John 219, 236–240
Marlowe, Christopher 6, 52n.44, 60, 104n.12, 133, 143, 260
Martin, Catherine Gimelli 151
Martin, Rodger 6n.17
Marvell, Andrew 182–183
Matthews, Jay 360n.36
May, Steven W. 93, 95, 100n.1, 101n.6, 105n.15, 108n.21, 115n.40, 130n.82, 134n.92, 284
Mellers, Wilfrid 287n.9
Melman, Billie 350n.9
Meyer, Sam 91n.8, 92, 99n.36, 112n.32
Meyers, Benjamin 129n.78
Mill, John Stuart 31–33
Millais, John Everet 337
Miller, David Lee 140, 151, 157n.43, 158, 164
Miller, Shannon 227, 270n.20
Mills, Jerry Leath 1n.1, 3n.8, 4n.10, 5n.11, 10n.35, 11n.37, 25, 38n.16, 89, 92, 100, 100n.1, 101n.3, 101n.5, 111n.28, 117n.47, 123n.63, 141n.4, 152n.32, 154n.35
Milton, John 1, 6n.17, 145, 177–180, 179n.35, 357
Moloney, Karen M. 105n.14
Montrose, Louis 80n.82, 304n.3
Morris, Jeffrey B. 95, 114n.39
Murrin, Michael 61–62

Nashe, Thomas 289
Naunton, Robert 331, 338
Nelson, William 233n.24
Nicholl, Charles 234n.26
Nicholls, Kenneth 136n.103
Nicholls, Mark 2n.7, 5, 6n.17, 8n.25, 9n.31, 170n.9, 329n.5
Nohrnberg, James 3, 10n.35, 23, 31n.1, 35n.12, 46n.27, 48n.32, 64n.58, 71n.68, 76n.78, 79n.80, 98, 99n.36, 114n.39, 127n.72

Norris, John 272
North, Thomas 262

O'Callaghan, Michelle 144n.10
O'Keeffe, Tadhg 339n.31
Oakeshott, Walter 114n.37, 137n.106, 234n.26
O'Connell, Michael 91n.10
O'Driscoll, Dennis 104n.11
Oldys, William 5n.11, 15, 336, 338
Oram, William A. 9n.29, 10n.35, 89n.3, 91n.10, 92, 95, 96n.31, 99, 103n.9, 109n.25, 111n.28, 114
Ovid 262–263
Owen, Clive 366
Owens, Judith 24, 114n.39, 118n.48, 160n.50, 162

Padel, Ruth 102, 129n.78
Pagden, Anthony 243n.3, 306
Pais, Arthur J. 365n.46
Parmenius, Stephen 266–267
Patrides, C. A. 15
Patterson, Lee 235
Peckham, George 244
Percy, Henry 318–319
Peri, Carmella 184n.52
Perry, George 351, 359n.32
Petrarch 43
Plato 148n.23
Pliny 266
Plutarch 263
Popper, Nicholas 19
Price, Vincent 350, 353–354
Protagoras 208
Protevi, John 222n.12
Purcell, Henry 33n.9
Puttenham, George 39n.17, 48, 155

Quinn, David Beers 91n.9, 93, 93n.20, 118, 119n.51, 134n.95, 136n.102, 137n.105, 219, 243n.2, 246n.12, 249, 250n.22, 267n.28

Ramachandran, Ayesha 88n.96
Rapple, Rory 259, 268, 270
Redford, Peter 21n.46
Reed, Laurel 317n.16
Richmond, H.M. 172n.14
Ricks, Christopher 199
Riggs, David 170n.9, 172
Rollins, Hyder 166n.2
Rosen, Marjorie 358
Rosenmeyer, Thomas G. 142n.7, 143n.9, 168n.7
Ross, William David 149n.24
Rowse, A. L. 1n.2, 34, 75n.77, 302n.1
Rudick, Michael 2n.3, 2, 9, 19–20, 111n.28, 140–141, 162, 165n.62, 165n.63, 166n.2, 284
Rynne, Colin 100n.1, 134n.95, 137n.105, 137n.107

Sallust 262–263
Salmon, Vivian 247n.14
Savile, Henry 262
Scheemaker, Peter 335
Schickel, Richard 351, 359n.32
Schmidt, Benjamin 5n.13, 219n.5, 226, 240n.35, 259
Schofield, Malcolm 149n.24
Schomburgk, Richard 219n.5, 240–241
Schomburgk, Robert Hermann 129n.80
Schwarzbaum, Lisa 365n.46
Schwyzer, Philip 294–295
Settle, Dionyse 244n.6
Sewell, George 334
Shagan, Ethan 297n.29
Shakespeare, William 69, 131, 173–175, 178–180, 179n.35, 193, 289, 299–300
Shannon, Laurie 146n.17, 148n.21
Shapiro, James 184n.53
Shell, Alison 290, 296n.26
Shenton, Henry Chawnes 332
Shepard, Alexandra 146n.17

Shindler, Colin 351–352
Shirley, John W. 243n.2, 247n.14, 332
Sidney, Philip 49n.37, 116, 142n.6, 144, 269, 292
Sidney, Robert 298–299
Siewers, Alfred K. 222n.11
Smith, Jeremy 286
Smith, John 254–256
Smith, Roland 117n.46
Speller, Jules 83n.87
Stallybrass, Peter 255
Stebbing, William 91n.9, 93n.20
Stephens, Dorothy 294
Stibbs, John H. 4n.10
Stillman, Robert 106, 141n.5, 142n.6, 302n.1
Strabo 263, 266
Strachey, William 254–255
Strathmann, Ernest A. 4n.10, 332
Strong, Roy 328n.4

Tacitus 262–263
Tait, Clodagh 272
Tashma-Baum, Miri 106, 147n.19
Tennenhouse, Leonard 100n.1, 101n.4, 121n.56
Tennyson, Alfred 7n.22, 145, 187–188
Terence 263
Thevet, André 243n.3
Thomas, Nigel J.T. 150n.26
Thompson, Edward 91n.9, 96, 170n.9
Thomson, Desson 365n.46
Thomson, James 335
Thoreau, Henry David 7
Tiffany, Grace 292
Todd, Richard 359–360, 364–365
Trevelyan, Raleigh 1n.2, 117n.47, 337n.25, 348n.2
Trim, David J. B. 258
Tromly, Fred 303n.1
Turner, Frederick 83n.87
Turner, Mark 203, 208, 209n.17, 213n.30

Van Es, Bart 153
Vaughan, Alden T. 5n.13, 24, 230n.20, 251n.25, 254n.31, 268, 307n.8, 312n.10, 314n.11
Vaughan, Robert 331
Vertue, George 334
Virgil 54, 80n.82, 263

Wallace, Willard M. 1, 91n.9, 93n.20, 95n.28
Waller, Gary 297n.29
Walton, Izaak 143n.8, 166–168, 171, 174, 181, 190–191
Warner, J. Christopher 114n.39, 122n.59
Watson, Nicola J. 337, 356n.21, 359n.30, 363n.38
Webster, John 260, 271
Wernham, R. B. 295
West, William 226n.15
Westbrook, Vivienne 8n.24, 25, 344n.44
White, John 242n.1, 247–251
Whitehead, Neil 237n.31, 307n.8, 312
Williams, Franklin B. 90n.6
Williams, Lloyd 49n.37
Williams, Melanie 360n.36
Williams, Norman Lloyd 45n.25, 69n.64, 109n.23
Williams, Penry 2n.7, 5, 6n.17, 8n.25, 9n.31, 170n.9, 329n.5, 334
Williamson, Hugh Ross 339
Wilson, Richard 61n.53
Wilson-Okamura, David Scott 80n.82
Woods, Susanne 166n.2, 284
Wordsworth, William 183–185, 188
Wyatt, Thomas 43, 193

Yates, Frances 131n.88
Youings, Joyce 3n.8, 90n.5, 116n.44, 117n.47, 137n.105

Zurcher, Andrew 90n.7, 112n.61, 164

EU authorised representative for GPSR:
Easy Access System Europe, Mustamäe tee 50,
10621 Tallinn, Estonia
gpsr.requests@easproject.com

www.ingramcontent.com/pod-product-compliance
Lightning Source LLC
Chambersburg PA
CBHW020258240426
43673CB00039B/632